UNDERSTANDING THE CENSUS

A Guide for Marketers, Planners, Grant Writers and Other Data Users

Library Edition

Michael R. Lavin

Epoch Books, Inc.
Library Edition distributed by the Oryx Press

Copyright © 1996, by Epoch Books, Inc.

All rights reserved, including the right of any reproduction
in whole or in part in any form.

Design and typography by:

shuffaloff press

260 Plymouth
Buffalo NY 14213 USA

653 Euclid Ave.
Toronto ON M6G 2T6 CAN

ISBN 0-89774-995-2 (cloth)
ISBN 0-9629586-1-1 (paper)

Cloth edition distributed by the Oryx Press

Epoch Books, Inc.
22 Byron Avenue
Kenmore, New York 14223

Understanding the Census

CONTENTS

List of Figures

Preface

"NOBODY IS AN EXPERT on the decennial Census, not even those of us who work for the Census Bureau. The data collection effort is too massive, the methodology too complex, and the publication output too voluminous for any individual to understand every aspect."

This statement, which I heard many years ago at the first Census Bureau training workshop I ever attended, made an understandably vivid impression in my mind. At the time, as a new librarian largely unfamiliar with the complexities of Census data, I found the sentiment simultaneously intimidating and reassuring. At the very least, it was comforting to know that others were overwhelmed by the same material as myself. Over the years, as I have worked with Census publications on a regular basis, the truth of that statement has been reinforced time and again. After nearly 20 years of using Census resources, not a week goes by that I don't learn something new about this amazing body of statistics. The need for a guide which explains the intricacies of the decennial Census seemed clear. It is this need which spurred the creation of *Understanding the Census*.

The Importance of Using Census Data Properly

The decennial Census of Population and Housing is the most extensive demographic survey in the United States. No other resource provides such a comprehensive picture of America's people, households, and housing stock. It is a vital source of information for decision-makers and researchers in business, government, the media, academia, and the nonprofit sector.

The 1990 Census is the first in history to be published on compact disc (CD-ROM) and the first to be widely disseminated via the Internet. This means that more decennial Census data has been published than ever before. Better yet, new technology makes this prodigious output more accessible to the general public. Also for the first time, the entire nation has been divided into "Census Blocks," so information can be retrieved for areas as small as a city block.

The decennial Census is such an enormous undertaking that it takes the government several years to tabulate and publish the results. 1990 data will be used for marketing, planning, and demographic analysis for the remainder of the decade. Now more than ever, Census users need a down-to-earth guide to help them effectively utilize this massive storehouse of information.

How difficult can it be to locate and understand needed Census data? Even experienced users, alert to the many pitfalls and idiosyncrasies associated with Census publications, fall victim to occasional mistakes. A single example may illustrate the profound importance of this point. Recently, while introducing a class of graduate students to the basics of Census resources, I was surprised to discover two different figures reported for the number of non-English speakers who feel they do not speak English well. According to a print publication entitled *Detailed Population Characteristics: United States* (*CP-2*), in 1990 the number of adult U.S. residents who spoke a language other than English in the home and who also felt they did not speak English well was 11,594,259. According to a similar table in a CD-ROM product called *Summary Tape File 3C*, the number was 5,764,638. Nothing in the accompanying documentation offered any explanation for this enormous discrepancy. The answer became clear only after comparing various numbers on the two tables. The 1990 Questionnaire Item dealing with this topic asks foreign-language speakers to describe their ability to speak English according to one of the following categories: "Very well," "Well," "Not well," or "Not at all." When tabulating data for persons who don't speak English well, *STF 3C* summed the responses to the latter two categories, while *CP-2* included all categories except, "Very well."

The ramifications of choosing one number or the other are fairly significant. The 1990 Census identifies 25.5 million persons age 18 or older who speak a language other than English in the home. *CP-2* indicates 45% percent of these individuals believe they do not speak English well. According to *STF 3*, the number is actually 23%. The difference lies in the definition of the phrase, "speaks well." The important point is that many casual Census users would not recognize that alternate definitions exist. This illustrates one of the cardinal rules of Census use: never take any numbers at face value.

Purpose

The purpose of this book is threefold: to explain Census concepts, methods, terminology, and data sources in an understandable manner; to assist Census users in locating needed Census data; and to impress upon readers how easy it is use inappropriate figures, or to interpret appropriate numbers incorrectly. The book is designed as a working handbook for Census users, but it can also be used as a textbook. The chapters are written so they can be read from start to finish, but because of the sheer amount of detail presented, it is unlikely that anyone will come away with a firm grasp of the material in a single reading. It is hoped that Census users will also treat this work as a reference book, consulting it to answer specific questions as the need arises.

Understanding the Census assumes no prior knowledge on the part of its readers. Each chapter introduces basic concepts before investigating more advanced topics. Sufficient detail is provided so that even experienced Census users can learn new information.

It is also important to stress what this book is not intended to accomplish. Although planning for the 2000 Census is well underway, this is a guide to the 1990 Census, so no discussion of future events will be found. Second, *Understanding the Census* is not a scholarly treatise, nor is it a critical evaluation of Census methods and procedures. Although the book describes some of the limitations inherent in the Census-taking process, it is beyond the scope of *Understanding the Census* to assess how the Census might be conducted more efficiently or accurately. Similarly, it is beyond the book's scope to

explore the many political controversies surrounding the 1990 Census, from the readjustment debate to the decision to count overseas military personnel in the Apportionment Population. Readers interested in learning more about such topics will find a selection of resources listed in Appendix E, "For Further Reading."

By the same token, this book is not meant as a blind apology for the Census Bureau and its methods. Although the United States Census of Population and Housing is widely regarded as the very best census in the world, it is not without its problems, as any Census Bureau official would readily admit. Wherever appropriate, *Understanding the Census* points out limitations in the resulting Census data, or in the Bureau's publications and software.

Organization

Understanding the Census is presented in five sections. Part One (Chapters 1-4) begins by providing an overview of the Census and describing some of the many uses of decennial Census data. It concludes with a two-chapter exploration of how the 1990 Census was conducted, from planning and preparation, to enumeration, processing, and tabulation. Part Two (Chapters 5-7) explains important Census terminology: geographic definitions as well as subject-oriented concepts. To enhance the reader's understanding, Chapter 7 provides an Item-by-Item discussion of the 1990 Questionnaire.

Part Three (Chapters 8-10) builds upon the two prior sections by describing all of the 1990 Census publications (in print form and CD-ROM) and explaining how to use them. Chapter 10 explores many of the limitations of Census data, discusses some of the common pitfalls in Census use, and suggests ways to find needed data quickly and effectively.

Part Four presents a variety of special topics which readers may wish to investigate. Chapter 11 expands on some of the geographic concepts introduced in Chapter 6. Chapter 12 offers a brief, step-by-step explanation of how Census data are used to apportion seats in the U.S. House of Representatives. Chapter 13 provides a detailed look at the Bureau's EXTRACT software program, which was introduced briefly in Chapter 8. The final chapter examines other electronic Census products, including magnetic tape files and the *CENDATA* database. A discussion of Internet resources appears in Chapter 14 because the Bureau's Web site, which is now a very popular and useful dissemination medium, did not exist at the time the main chapters were written.

The final section contains supplemental information for reference purposes. Appendix A is a brief list of the acronyms and initialisms used in the text. Appendix B presents a list of all Metropolitan Areas and their component parts, based on definitions in effect for the 1990 Census. Appendix C reproduces the Long Form version of the 1990 Census Questionnaire, minus the accompanying instructions to respondents. Appendix D is a complete list of all data tables appearing in the Bureau's most heavily used CD-ROM products: *STF 1* and *STF 3*. Appendix E offers a short, selective guide to other publications relating to the 1990 Census.

Special Features

Understanding the Census includes 160 Figures, more than half of which were created specifically for this book. Some Figures reproduce sample tables or menus from major Census publications. Others summarize important concepts, chronicle the sequence of events in the Census-taking process, or compare important characteristics of Census products.

Another important feature is the series of sidebars appearing throughout every chapter--more than 350 in all. Three types of sidebars are presented. **New in '90** identifies important changes which took place between the 1980 and 1990 Censuses. These include changes in methodology, definitions, technology, and publication formats. The **Census Tips** feature points out important guidelines for finding and using Census data, as well as identifying common misconceptions about the Census. **Q&A** explores frequently asked questions. This feature is intended to explain why certain aspects of the Census behave as they do, especially those which appear to make little sense when first encountered. Throughout the book, numerous examples are provided to clarify the discussion, including several step-by-step case studies.

To enhance the value of *Understanding the Census* as a reference tool, an especially detailed index, beginning on page 518, has been included. Here users will find topics grouped together by category as well as listed alphabetically.

A word or two should also be said about certain conventions adopted by the book. Because the Census Bureau typically uses common terminology in very uncommon ways, words which have special meaning in the Census are capitalized throughout the text. For example, when the Bureau's concept of Family is discussed, the term is capitalized, but if the word is used in the generic sense, it appears in lower case. Throughout the book, the word "Census" refers to the 1990 Census of Population and Housing. The term "Bureau" refers to the United States Bureau of the Census.

Late Changes

One might think that writing about an event which takes place once every ten years would afford an author the luxury of aiming at a fixed target, but such is not the case. Many of the plans announced by the Bureau for 1990 were changed along the way, in some cases more than once. As *Understanding the Census* went to press, the Census Bureau was engaged in a major reorganization of the agency, including the dismantling of the Data User Services Division. The Bureau is also reevaluating its various online dissemination mechanisms, including the *CENDATA* system, the *Census/BEA Electronic Forum*, and the Internet Web site itself.

A related problem is the length of time required to release the many data products generated from the decennial Census. Most major publications had appeared by the late summer of 1994, but some still await publication. For example, six new *Subject Summary Tape Files* were issued on CD-ROM in October of 1995. Every effort was made to incorporate late-breaking changes into the text, right up to press time.

Buffalo, New York
December, 1995

Acknowledgements

WRITING THIS BOOK has been a tremendous learning experience. Many individuals have provided assistance and encouragement at various times during the four years of its creation. I have always found employees of the Census Bureau to be courteous, competent, highly dedicated, and extremely willing to help. I am deeply indebted to many individuals at the Bureau who provided forthright, detailed, and knowledgeable answers to the many questions which I posed while researching *Understanding the Census*. The list is far to long to repeat, but I will mention those current and former employees who were especially generous with their time: Frederick G. Bohme, Peter Bounpane, James Fitzsimmons, Richard Forstall, John Rowe, Marshall L. Turner, Jr., Tom Walsh, Karen Wheeless, Jane Woods, and Paul Zeisset. Special thanks go to Fred Gatlin of the Bureau's Public Information Office, who provided an outstanding selection of publicity photos and figures for possible inclusion in the book. Gregg Abbott and Tim Jones, of State and Regional Programs, deserve special mention; they have always handled my information requests promptly and efficiently. The staff of the Boston Regional Office has also been extremely helpful, including former employee Christine Payne.

Many colleagues have read drafts of various chapters and offered important corrections. Among them are Cynthia Cornelius, Joyce Davoli, George Emery, Marcia Nigro, Judith Robinson, Jane Rosenfeld, Jane Weintrop, and Bruce Weymouth. Bob Scardamalia, Director of the New York State Data Center, offered extensive, extremely detailed suggestions for many of the chapters, and the book is far better as a result. I deeply value Bob's support during the project, and his friendship over the years.

Mary Bauer and Charlotte Hedgebeth proofread portions of the final manuscript. Don Arndt and Pam Cjaza assisted with bibliographic research and document retrieval.

Don Hartman and Susan McCartney helped keep the project on track during its more difficult moments. Additional support was provided by Judy Adams and Karen Smith of Lockwood Library, who enabled me to adjust my work schedule to accomplish this arduous task. Thanks are also due to my colleagues in Lockwood's Business and Government Documents Center for their many acts of kindness and inspiration. I have learned a great deal from these talented and dedicated individuals.

A very special acknowledgement goes out to Michael Boughn of Shuffaloff Press. Michael conceived the book's design and painstakingly laid out each complicated page. He often worked under frustrating conditions and grueling deadlines, voicing nary a complaint. *Understanding the Census* would not exist without his outstanding efforts and I cannot thank him enough.

Cover art was designed by Tim Eng and modified by James Dougher.

As always, this book is dedicated with great love to Irene and Andrew, for their abiding patience, understanding, and support.

Understanding the Census

Chapter 1

Census Fundamentals

Census Fundamentals

NO OTHER country collects and publishes as much statistical information as the United States. Data are gathered and released by government agencies, market research firms, opinion pollsters, universities, trade and professional associations, newspapers and magazines, and many other organizations. Every conceivable aspect of our society is measured and analyzed, but one of the most frequently examined is demographic information—statistics on the number, distribution, and characteristics of people.

The unquestioned mother lode of United States demographic data is the decennial Census, known officially as the Census of Population and Housing. The reason for this is simple: no one except the federal government could attempt to collect information about every man, woman, and child in the country on a systematic basis. A quick fact will drive this point home in dramatic fashion: the 1990 Census cost the government approximately $2.6 billion to collect and produce. Distributed over the entire decade, this amounts to one dollar per person per year.

Methods of Population Measurement

There are three basic ways to collect information on the number and characteristics of people in the nation: maintain a population register; mount a census; or conduct sample surveys. Before beginning our exploration of the United States Census, a brief comparison of the three methods is in order.

Population Registration

One method a government can use to count their population is to create a file on every person when they are born. For the rest of each person's life, important personal developments would be added to the file as changes occurred. Every time a person moved, for example, the government would be notified. When the person died, his or her name would be removed from the register. The

Q&A

Is a census really necessary in the U.S.? Couldn't the government determine population totals based on existing records?

Population can indeed be estimated by cumulatively adding all new arrivals (births and new immigrants), then subtracting all "departures" (deaths and emigrants). But such a method is limited in several ways. First, although the arrival and departure of foreigners is carefully recorded, statistics on foreign travel by U.S. citizens are less precise. Second, no central records are kept for internal migration—the movement of residents within the country, from one municipality, county, or state to another. Without a mandatory registration system for all movers, population estimates below the national level are subject to significant error. Third, vital records only capture basic demographic data (age, race, sex), ignoring social and economic characteristics of the population.

In fact, the government does calculate population estimates between Census years based on data from vital events registration and other administrative records. However, these inter-censal estimates depend on detailed and accurate decennial counts to serve as benchmarks.

The primary purpose of a population register is to enable a government to keep track of individual citizens.

system would be permanent, compulsory, and continuously updated. In order to measure the size of the population at a given time, the government could simply count the number of current registrants. Such systems are not widely used throughout the world; they are currently utilized by about a dozen nations. Traditionally, population registers were used in the far east, Scandinavia, and the former Communist-bloc nations.

The primary purpose of a population register is to enable a government to keep track of individual citizens. Under an authoritarian regime, such registration helps maintain political control. Under more benign governments, civil registration is useful for law enforcement and the administration of public welfare programs. A good example of a current system of population registers can be found in Taiwan, where every resident is provided an identity card and has an individual census registration record. Until recently, the Taiwanese system was administered by its police force. A 1992 amendment to the census law changed this to dispel the image of a police state.

The ability to compile population statistics is a by-product of the civil registration process; the system's main purpose is administrative. To a certain degree, compiling data from the register disrupts the day-to-day work of record keeping. In fact, most countries with population registers also conduct a regular census. The duplicated effort serves as a periodic check on the accuracy of the register, and provides the government with additional population characteristics not captured through registration.

While few modern nations maintain universal population registers, most others have specialized registers and systems for recording "vital events" (births, deaths, fetal deaths, marriages, divorces, adoptions). Vital statistics registers are necessary for establishing legal records (to prove date and place of birth, for example). They are also important for monitoring infant mortality and other health statistics. Here again, statistical compilations are a by-product of the registration process. In the United States, vital events are reported by hospitals, funeral directors, clergy, and the courts, as well as by individuals applying for marriage licenses or other official permits. Events are recorded by county or municipal clerks, who in turn submit totals to state health departments. The states supply data to the National Center for Health Statistics, which publishes national summaries.

The idea of civil registration may sound foreign to most Americans, but a variety of specialized registers are maintained in the United States. Citizens registering to vote, motorists renewing their driver's licenses, and retirees applying for Social Security benefits all trigger the creation of registered data. The difference between the United States and Taiwan is we have no composite centralized files, despite any impressions to the contrary. Each addition or change to a specialized register is not forwarded to a central agency which maintains a master file on each individual. Data collection of this type would clearly be anathema to Americans, who would view it as an encroachment upon their freedom and privacy. If nothing else, such a system would be cumbersome and ineffective in a country whose population is so large, diverse, geographically dispersed, independent, and mobile as that of the United States.

Enumeration and Sampling

An alternative to maintaining a universal population register is to conduct a census—a systematic enumeration, or head-count, of every resident of the country. Governments have taken censuses since ancient times, and several are mentioned in the Bible. The Gospel of Luke recounts the most famous census of all, though its actual occurrence is subject to considerable debate. According to Luke, Caesar Augustus ordered a census of the empire at the time of Jesus's birth; Mary and Joseph thus traveled from Nazareth to Bethlehem to be counted at Joseph's ancestral home. Censuses such as this were conducted for purposes of military conscription or taxation. The term itself comes from the Latin "censure," which means "to tax" or "to value." Early censuses usually counted males of military age, heads of households, landholders, or similar selective groups; women and children were seldom counted. Early

censuses were also important for measuring a country's resources. For example, England's Domesday Inquest of 1086 was ordered by William I to assess the wealth of his newly conquered realm.

 ### Census Tip

A census can count any type of entity so designated by the census takers. A census of business would be a systematic enumeration of every business establishment, a census of agriculture would count farms and farm products, and so on. A population census counts the number of people and their characteristics.

Because population figures could reveal a nation's military strength, results of early censuses were carefully guarded, but in modern times, public access to census data is largely taken for granted. To illustrate the importance of a census in free societies, consider the case of Joseph Stalin's Soviet Union. During the 1930s, that nation's population was virtually decimated by the effects of a terrible famine and of Stalin's Great Purge. Although the exact number of deaths is still unknown, millions of Soviet citizens starved, were executed, or perished in forced labor camps. Because population totals from the Soviet Union's 1937 census would chillingly document the effects of this crushing oppression, Stalin suppressed the results and ordered census workers shot. Another census, containing significantly doctored data, was published in 1939.

Various nations lay claim to conducting the first modern census. Sweden's census of 1749 is frequently cited in this regard. England's Board of Trade conducted numerous censuses of the American colonies, beginning with a Virginia census in 1624. The United States Census, which began in 1790, is the world's longest-running continuous national census. England and France fol-

Early censuses usually counted males of military age, heads of households, landholders, or similar selective groups; women and children were seldom counted.

Because population figures could reveal a nation's military strength, results of early censuses were carefully guarded, but in modern times, public access to census data is largely taken for granted.

lowed in 1801. By the middle of the 19th century, 24 nations were conducting regular censuses. Today, nearly every country in the world conducts them.

Unlike civil registers, the sole purpose of a modern census is to compile statistical information. According to United Nations guidelines, a population census must have six key features, as described below.

1. **National Sponsorship.**
   Only a government has the resources to conduct a thorough census, and only a government has the power to compel citizens to participate in the process.
2. **Defined Territory.**
   The geographic coverage must be defined precisely, and boundary changes from one census to the next must be clearly identified.
3. **Universality.**
   All persons residing within the defined territory must be counted, with no omissions or duplication.
4. **Simultaneity.**
   The census must take place on a fixed date. As nearly as possible, persons should be counted at the same, well-defined point in time. Individuals born after the reference date, or who die before that date, are excluded from the count.
5. **Individual enumeration.**
   Data should be collected separately for each individual. Tabulations may summarize data for households, families, or other aggregations, but the individual person remains the basic unit of enumeration.
6. **Publication.**
   A census is not complete until results have been compiled and published.

Censuses should take place on a recurring basis, to enable a nation to measure its progress over fixed time intervals. Some countries conduct censuses every ten years (decennially), and a few mount them every five years (quinquennially); however, most national censuses occur with irregular frequency, as they are needed. Censuses generally capture more than a total population count. The opportunity is usually taken to measure personal, social, and economic characteristics of the inhabitants.

Census data can be gathered through direct enumeration or self-enumeration. Direct enumeration involves government employees, called enumerators, who collect information by questioning each individual or household. In some cases, the country is immobilized on census day and residents are forbidden to leave their homes until they have been counted. In other countries, individuals must report to a central location to be counted. However, most nations utilizing the direct method send enumerators door-to-door to conduct the census. Under self- enumeration, questionnaires are provided to individuals to fill out on their own. Completed forms are either picked up by enumerators later, or mailed back to the government.

A third method of counting a nation's population is to conduct a sample survey. Instead of enumerating every individual, a representative sample is queried. Selected persons are surveyed according to a specified sampling rate (one person out of every twenty, one out of six, etc.). If the sampling methodology is statistically valid, conclusions can be drawn about the entire population based on answers provided by the sampled respondents. The higher the sampling rate, the more reliable the results will be. When conducting a nationwide survey, the sample size is usually insufficient to draw conclusions about small areas such as individual cities, towns, or counties. (More will be said in Chapter 10 about sampling methods and their limitations.)

Governments generally do not employ sample surveys to determine official population counts. Instead, sampling is used to obtain estimates of specific population characteristics. Many nations conduct sample surveys as part of the actual census to collect more detailed data on education, income, labor force, and housing stock. Sampling lowers the cost of the entire census and reduces the burden on individuals, who would

Census data can be gathered through direct enumeration or self-enumeration.

A third method of counting a nation's population is to conduct a sample survey. Instead of enumerating every individual, a representative sample is queried.

Characteristics of Three Population Measurement Methods			
Criterion	Registration	Census	Sample
Accuracy	Strong	Moderate	Moderate
Precision (freedom from sampling error)	Strong	Strong	Weak
Subject Detail	Weak	Moderate	Strong
Geographic Detail	Strong	Strong	Weak
Timeliness	Strong	Weak	Strong
Affordability	Moderate	Weak	Strong
Ease of Implementation	Moderate	Weak	Strong
Individual Privacy	Weak	Moderate	Strong

Figure 1-1

Comparing the Methods

No method of population measurement is ideal. Figure 1-1 summarizes key advantages and disadvantages of the three major techniques. A compulsory population register can provide accurate, timely data for the nation and for small geographic areas. It is relatively affordable and easy to administer, but does not provide much subject detail beyond basic demographic characteristics. Perhaps the greatest weakness of a registration system is the potential for official abuse. In a democratic society with strong concerns for privacy and individual rights, not to mention a long tradition of "rugged individualism," compulsory, centralized registration is not politically viable.

Sample surveys can be extremely timely, affordable and easy to conduct. Unlike other methods, sampling can provide detailed data on population characteristics. Sampling can also be used to estimate population characteristics between census years, and to evaluate the accuracy of a census after it has been conducted.

Sample surveys can be extremely timely, affordable and easy to conduct. Unlike other methods, sampling can provide detailed data on population characteristics.

on population characteristics. The primary weaknesses of sampling are its inability to provide data for small geographic levels, and its lack of precision, largely due to sampling error.

A population census also has significant limitations. It is less accurate than a universal register due to coverage errors; no matter how well the census is conducted, some people will be missed and others will be double-counted. Another drawback is its cost and magnitude. For nations with large, diverse populations and extensive land areas, conducting a census is a daunting task of mind-boggling complexity and expense. Because it can only be mounted every five to ten years, the resulting data are not very timely. Moreover, although individual privacy can be protected if proper safeguards are implemented, public perception of confidentiality can be a problem; a successful census is generally based on individuals' willingness to respond. The overwhelming advantage of this method is its ability to provide data for extremely small levels of geography.

Overview of the United States Census

The United States Census has been conducted decennially since 1790, in years ending with zero. It is mandated by the Constitution, for the purpose of determining political representation in the House of Representatives. The Constitution stipulates that Congress must determine the method of conducting the Census, "...in such Manner as they shall by Law direct." For many years, Congress enacted a new Census law for every decade, though such laws often entailed only slight amendments to the existing legislation. In 1954, all Census laws currently in force were consolidated as Title 13 of the

Q&A

Why is the Census conducted only every ten years?

The cost and effort of mounting a decennial Census make it difficult to attempt such a comprehensive undertaking more frequently. In its present state, the Census requires virtually every day of the ten-year cycle to plan, prepare, conduct, and publish.

In a 1976 Amendment to the Census law, Congress authorized a mid-decade Census to commence in 1985. Such an effort was envisioned to be much less detailed than the decennial version, and the law explicitly exempted the results from use for Congressional apportionment. However, Congress has never appropriated funds for a mid-decade Census, and none was taken in 1985. Although the law remains on the books, no Census will take place in 1995 for the same reason.

The goal of every Census is to produce as complete and accurate a count as possible, in as timely a manner as possible, and with the lowest cost and response burden as practical.

United States Code. Title 13 specifies the powers and duties of the Census Bureau, the types of data it can collect, and the basic procedures for conducting the decennial Census. Under this law, all U.S. residents are required to provide complete and truthful responses to Census inquiries, and the confidentiality of all responses is guaranteed.

The goal of every Census is to produce as complete and accurate a count as possible, in as timely a manner as possible, and with the lowest cost and response burden as practical. The Census Bureau readily admits that locating and counting 100% of the people is an impossible job. Distrust of the government, changing lifestyles, mobility of population, people with something to hide, those living outside the bounds of normal social habitation, and general apathy present significant obstacles to a complete count. The best hope is to miss as few people as possible—a goal the Bureau has had two hundred years of experience to achieve.

As its name suggests, the Census of Population and Housing is actually two censuses conducted concurrently. The Census of Population counts the nation's inhabitants and their personal, social, and economic charac-teristics. The Census of Housing, which was first taken in 1940, counts the number of residential dwellings and their physical and financial characteristics. The following discussion summarizes some of the key concepts and procedures relating to the Census. Each will be covered in greater detail later in the book.

Basic Principles

Conducting a house-by-house enumeration in a country as large as our own presents an incredible challenge. Francis Asa Walker, Superintendent of the 1870 and 1880 Censuses, had this to say about the task:

> The labor of organizing and energizing a census is such that no man can conceive who has not himself undertaken it, or at least stood close by and watched the machine in full operation.

What was true over 100 years ago is even more so today. The Census "machine" will be described in Chapters 3 and 4; in the meantime, the brief facts shown in Figure 1-2 indicate the magnitude of the 1990 Census.

To minimize costs and ensure privacy, recent Censuses have been self-enumeration instruments. Questionnaires are designed to be completed by most households without the assistance of enumerators. The 1960 Census was the first to use the mails to deliver Questionnaires, and 1970 was the first to use the mails for return of completed forms. By 1990, 84% were delivered by mail and 94% were designed for mail return.

While Mailout/Mailback reduces costs, it by no means makes the job simple. Addresses must be identified and comprehensive mailing lists must be generated. Then, millions of households must be visited in person, including those in remote areas, those with poor mailing addresses, those which fail to return a Questionnaire, and those which return incomplete or inconsistent forms.

Another important means of reducing costs

Size and Scope of the 1990 Census

▶ 10 years to plan, execute, tabulate, and publish.

▶ $2.6 billion total cost over 10 years.

▶ $1.4 billion of that spent during Census year alone.

▶ 1.6 million potential employees recruited and tested.

▶ 551,000 temporary workers hired.

▶ 300,000 workers employed from April through June, 1990.

▶ 484 temporary field offices opened.

▶ Network of 6,900 terminals linked to 530 VAX minicomputers.

▶ 7 million Census Blocks mapped, covering entire nation.

▶ 250,000 base maps produced for enumerators.

▶ Census Questionnaire translated into 32 languages.

▶ 274 million Questionnaires printed.

▶ 5,000 tons of paper used in printing.

▶ Over 50 million Housing Units visited by enumerators.

▶ 102 million completed Questionnaires received and processed.

▶ 63 million of these received within 3 weeks of Census Day.

▶ High-speed cameras filmed 90 pages of Questionnaires per minute.

▶ Computer scanners read 900 pages of film per minute.

▶ 90% of processing completed by August 1990.

▶ 253.5 million people counted, including residents of U.S. Outlying Areas and certain U.S. citizens stationed abroad.

Figure 1-2

for every household member.

1990 Questionnaires were mailed in late March, and respondents were asked to answer based on conditions in the household as of April 1, 1990. As completed Questionnaires flowed in, they were checked against a master address list to identify households which did not respond. Nonrespondents were then visited by an enumerator. In fact, the Bureau conducted many different follow-up activities to ensure as accurate and complete coverage as possible. All field work had to be completed prior to the end of 1990. By law, a final population count must be submitted to the President by December 31 of the Census year.

The Census covers the entire United States, including its foreign territories. These territories are known collectively as the Outlying Areas, and are comprised of Puerto Rico, the U.S. Virgin Islands, Guam, American Samoa, the Northern Mariana Islands, and Palau. Data for the Outlying Areas are reported separately from the rest of the United States.

The Census counts residents of the United States, regardless of their citizenship status.

NEW in '90

In 1980, Outlying Areas covered by the Census included the Trust Territory of the Pacific Islands, which has since been broken up. Two of its former components are still counted by the Census: the commonwealth territory of the Northern Marianas, and the unincorporated territory of Palau (also called the Republic of Palau). Two remaining components of the former Trust Territory now have looser ties to the United States, and neither is included in the 1990 Census. The excluded areas are the Marshall Islands and the Federated States of Micronesia.

Another important means of reducing costs is the use of a sample survey.

is the use of a sample survey. Every household in the United States must answer a short list of essential questions, but approximately 17% of the population must answer additional questions about their social, economic, and housing characteristics. The sampled households receive the Long Form version of the Questionnaire, while all others receive the Short Form. A question-by-question explanation of both forms will be found in Chapter 7. A facsimile of the Long Form is shown in Appendix C. One Questionnaire is provided for each household, with separate columns

Q&A

Why is April First chosen for Census Day?

Despite any temptation to think otherwise, the choice for Census Day has nothing to do with April Fools' celebrations. The reference date for conducting the Census was chosen to maximize the chance of reaching people at home. On April 1, school is in session and fewer people are on vacation. Also, the most severe winter weather is over by this time, making it easier for enumerators to cover their routes.

Census Day was not always in April. The reference date for the first four Censuses was August 1. From 1830 through 1900, the date was moved to June 1. Census Day for 1910 was April 15, then changed the following decade to January 1. The reference date was reset at April 1 for the 1930 Census, where it has remained ever since.

One of the most important features of the decennial Census is its ability to report data for very small levels of geography.

Short-term visitors are excluded from the Census, as are foreigners stationed at embassies and other diplomatic postings, but foreign citizens otherwise working or living in the U.S. are counted. Conversely, most Americans living or working abroad are excluded as nonresidents, but short-term foreign travelers are counted at their usual place of residence.

One of the most important features of the decennial Census is its ability to report data for very small levels of geography. To accomplish this, the Bureau uses a computer database, called TIGER, to divide the entire country into small areas known as Census Blocks. Approximately seven million Blocks were created for the 1990 Census. More will be said about TIGER and Census Blocks in Chapter 6.

A last important concept to introduce at this point is confidentiality of Census data. The Bureau's sole mission is to collect statistics, not to supply information on individual people or businesses. Title 13 of the *United States Code* ensures the confidentiality of Census records, and establishes penalties for violating the law. All Census records are sealed from public view for 72 years, after which time they may be used by the general public for historical and genealogical research. The following procedures and legal provisions ensure that individual privacy is maintained.

▶ Census Questionnaires do not ask for individuals' Social Security numbers.

▶ Computer tapes of Census statistics do not contain personal names.

▶ No one except authorized employees of the Census Bureau may examine completed Census forms.

▶ Bureau employees may not reveal information about individuals to anyone, under penalty of fine, imprisonment, or both.

▶ Individual Census records may not be turned over to any other government agency under any circumstances, even under subpoena.

▶ Census records are kept in specially designed storage facilities under strict security.

▶ The Freedom of Information Act does not apply to individual Census records.

▶ Published Census reports cannot reveal

NEW IN '90

The 1990 Census totals include certain United States citizens living abroad: federal government employees working overseas, military personnel stationed on foreign bases, and the dependents of both groups. These groups were not counted in the 1980 Census, though they were in 1970. For 1990, foreign military and government personnel are included in the official population count for Congressional apportionment, but are excluded from totals of the resident population. A more detailed discussion of Census residency requirements can be found in Chapter 5.

statistics which could be used to identify characteristics of any individual person, household, or business.

Diligent concern for Census confidentiality has not always been the case. From 1790 through 1830 the Census law required completed forms to be posted in two of the most public places in every Enumeration District. This enabled residents to make sure they were counted and to correct any erroneous information. From 1840 through 1870, Census takers were instructed to keep records confidential, but no legal restrictions were imposed. Beginning in 1880, and continuing to this day, all Census employees have taken an oath of confidentiality, and since 1890, penalties have been established for breaking that oath.

In 1910, William Howard Taft issued the first Presidential Proclamation on Census confidentiality, a tradition which has been followed in every subsequent Census. Although Taft's Proclamation stated that the Census was used for statistical purposes only, no law prevented the government from using Census records in other ways. In fact, records from the 1910 Census were used during World War I to verify young men's ages and prosecute draft evaders. This loophole was closed in 1929 by a more comprehensive confidentiality law. The principle of confidentiality lies at the heart of the Census process; without a guarantee of privacy, individuals would be much less willing to respond to the Census.

Types of Data Collected

The format and information available in the Census has varied over the decades. The first Census asked only six questions of each family: name of head of the family; the number of free White males age 16 and above; the number of free White males under age 16; the number of free White females; the number of slaves; and all other persons, regardless of gender or race. The age breakdown for males was used to gauge the number of individuals available for military service. James Madison and other statesmen recognized the Census's potential for identifying important characteristics of the young nation, but early Censuses were limited to basic questions.

Aside from counting the total population, the first Censuses focused on assessing the country's military and industrial potential. The 1810 Census included a largely unsuccessful attempt to measure the output of the nation's manufacturing establishments. The 1820 Census was the first to capture occupational information; respondents were asked their employment according to broad industry classification—agriculture, commerce, or manufacturing. With each successive Census, the range of questions gradually increased, beginning with more detailed age breakdowns. As Figure 1-3 shows, some of the longer-standing questions dealt with such matters as citizenship, literacy, physical and mental disability, marital status, and place of birth.

The Census also measured topics other than population, including agriculture, business, schools, government, and more. By 1880, 233 separate schedules were used to ask more than 13,000 questions, most of which did not relate to population issues. Beginning in 1900, the Census again focused on population, and other questions gradually dropped off. A separate Census of

The format and information available in the Census has varied over the decades.

Q&A

Can the government force people to answer the Census?

Under Title 13, all residents are obligated to answer Census questions completely and truthfully. This has been a feature of the Census law since 1790. Failure to comply can result in fines and/or imprisonment. In practice, however, few people have been prosecuted for refusing to answer the Census. The success of each decennial census depends largely on public cooperation.

Manufactures was taken in 1905, and marked the first Census taken independently of the decennial effort. Today, nine separate non-population Censuses are conducted at five-year intervals, in years when the population Census is not taken. Since 1940, the decennial Census has been limited to population and housing.

The Census of Population counts the number of people in the United States, identifies where they live, and describes their characteristics. The Census of Housing measures the availability, location, and condition of our housing stock. To understand more about Census content, one must become familiar with the Questionnaire itself. A list of the major topics covered by the 1990 Short and Long Forms can be seen in Figure 1-4. The Questionnaire for 1980 was quite similar, although there are key differences which will be discussed in Chapter 7.

Questions on the number of people residing in each geographic area, the number of households and families, and general population characteristics are asked of 100% of the households. General characteristics include sex, age, race, Hispanic Origin, marital status and the familial relationships of household members. Detailed questions regarding social and economic characteristics appear on the Long Form, and are asked of the sample population only. Among the categories in this group are education (years of school completed, degrees earned, and current enrollment status), nativity (place of birth, citizenship, and year of immigration), ancestry (nationality and language spoken at home), labor force (employment status, place of work, and occupation), and income. Questions are also asked on veteran status, disabilities, travel to work, the total number of children born to adult female respondents, and the address where each person lived and worked five years previously.

Housing questions follow a similar pattern, with basic questions asked of 100% of the population and detailed ones asked of the sample. The 100% questions provide data on the number of Housing Units, the size and

Chronology of Selected Census Questions Asked

Topic	Decades Covered
Age	1790 + [1]
Sex	1790 + [1]
Color or race	1790 +
Slave status	1790 - 1860
Citizenship	1820 - 1830, 1870, 1890 +
Industry employed	1820, 1840, 1910 +
Disability	1830 - 1930, 1970 +
Education or literacy	1840 +
Place of birth	1850 +
Occupation	1850 +
Pauperism	1850 - 1910
Criminals	1850 - 1910
Married in previous year	1850 - 1890
Mortality	1850 - 1890
Wage rates	1850 - 1890
Parents' birthplace	1870 - 1970
Births	1870 - 1880
Marital status	1880 +
Employment status	1880 - 1910, 1930 +
Prisoners	1880 - 1910
Institutionalized	1880 - 1890, 1910
Housing	1890 +
Year of immigration	1890 - 1930, 1970 +
Number of children ever born	1890 - 1910, 1940 +
Language spoken	1890 - 1940, 1960 +
Parents' language	1910 - 1920
Income	1940 +
Spanish Origin	1970 +

[1] Free Whites only until 1820

Figure 1-3

type of building, whether the occupant owns or rents, and the amount of rent paid or the dollar value of the home. Census enumerators collect data on all vacant Housing Units; this information is included in the 100% tabulations.

Sample questions are more numerous and include information on the source of water and of sewage disposal, whether the Unit is a condominium, the year the structure was built, the year the present occupant moved in, the heating facilities and fuel used, the cost of utilities, the number of bedrooms, and the presence of telephone, kitchen, and plumbing facilities. The sample housing questions also ask about the number of cars, trucks and vans owned by each household.

From this reasonably small number of questions, and the ability to cross-tabulate

From a reasonably small number of questions, and the ability to cross-tabulate responses, many important public policy facts can be derived.

1990 Census Questionnaire
Complete Count versus Sample Questions

COMPLETE COUNT ITEMS

POPULATION

Relationship to householder
Sex
Race
Age
Marital status
Hispanic Origin
Family size (D)
Household size (D)
Family type (D)
Household type (D)
Persons in Unit (D)

HOUSING

Type/size of building
Number of rooms in Unit
Large acreage or commercial use
Tenure (rented or owned)
Presence of mortgage
Value of property if owned
Monthly rent if not owned
Meals included in rent
Vacancy status and reason vacant
Duration of vacancy
Persons per room (D)

SAMPLE ITEMS

POPULATION

School enrollment
Educational attainment
State or country of birth
Citizenship & year immigrated
Language spoken at home
Ability to speak English
Ancestry/ethnic origin
Where resided 5 years ago
Veteran status/period served
Disability
Children ever born
Current employment status
Hours worked per week
Place of employment
Travel time to work
Means of travel to work
Persons in car pool
Year last worked
Industry/employer type
Occupation/class of worker
Self-employed
Weeks worked last year
Total income by source
Poverty status (D)
Type of group quarters (D)

HOUSING

Type of structure
Complete plumbing facilities
Use of property as farm
Source of water
Method of sewage disposal
Year structure built
Year householder moved into unit
Type of heat and heating fuel
Cost of utilities and fuel
Complete kitchen facilities
Number of bedrooms
Number of bathrooms
Presence of telephone
Number of cars, vans, & trucks
Amount of real property taxes
Property insurance costs
Monthly mortgage payment
Taxes/insurance in mortgage
Second mortgage payment
Condominium status
Condominium fee
Mobile home shelter costs
Total housing costs (D)

(D) indicates information not asked on form but derived from available data.

Figure 1-4

responses, many important public policy facts can be derived. For example, how many people live below the poverty level? How many people change jobs? How many women are single heads of households? How many people travel to work in car pools? How many have moved in the past five years? An important point to remember is that much of this information does not come from explicitly asked questions, but is derived from the raw data. Household and family characteristics, for example, are derived from the data describing each individual on a Questionnaire and the relationship of those individuals to the "head of household."

Valuable information on the housing conditions of the country are also derived in this manner. The quality of housing in a neighborhood can be assessed by factors such as the age of the dwellings, the absence of plumbing or heating facilities, and the number of vacant and boarded-up units. Overcrowding can be determined by comparing the size of the household to the number of rooms. The ability to derive information explains why certain questions are included in the Census. For example, the 1990 Questionnaire asks property owners if their homes are located on more than ten acres, or on land which includes commercial buildings. The purpose of this question is to calculate median home values more accurately. Inclusion of commercial and farm property would distort the average value of residential real estate.

Census publications are issued in a variety of formats, including paperbound books, maps, news releases, microfiche, computer tapes, CD-ROMs, and an online database. Most reports are geographically oriented, with separate volumes for individual states or groups of states. These publications, referred to as Census products, present aggregate data for specific levels of geography: states, counties, Metropolitan Areas, Census Blocks, etc. Broad subject categories are often broken down to show frequency distributions, such as age by single year or income by $10,000 increments. Summary data are often presented as percentages, medians, and means. A typical example of a summary table appears in Figure 1-5. Looking at the statistics for the city of Rockford, Illinois, for example, the reader can quickly determine that 31.6% of the city's 1990 population fell within the ages of 25 and 44, and its median age was 32.9 years. The table also indicates 80.1% of the population lived with their families,

Table 1. Summary of General Characteristics of Persons: 1990—Con.

[For definitions of terms and meanings of symbols, see text]

State Urban and Rural and Size of Place Inside and Outside Metropolitan Area County Place and [In Selected States] County Subdivision [1,000 or More Persons]	All persons	Percent of all persons							Median age	Persons 18 years and over— Males per 100 females	Percent of all persons		In group quarters	Persons in group quarters	
		Under 5 years	Under 18 years	18 to 24 years	25 to 44 years	45 to 64 years	65 years and over	80 years and over			In households			Total	Percent institutionalized
											In families	Non-family householders and non-relatives of householder			
PLACE AND COUNTY SUBDIVISION— Con.															
Rockdale village	1 709	7.3	23.2	10.1	30.5	19.3	16.9	2.6	34.0	96.4	81.7	18.3	–	–	–
Rock Falls city	9 654	8.1	27.5	10.3	28.7	18.2	15.3	3.8	33.2	83.5	83.9	14.9	1.1	107	86.0
Rockford city	139 426	8.1	26.0	10.0	31.6	17.7	14.7	3.8	32.9	86.0	80.1	17.1	2.8	3 971	65.5
Rock Island city	40 552	7.1	24.7	12.5	27.2	18.3	17.3	4.6	34.3	83.0	75.3	19.4	5.3	2 138	34.0
Rockton village	2 928	7.0	26.0	7.8	33.5	19.3	13.4	2.5	34.7	90.1	86.4	13.6	–	–	–
Rolling Meadows city	22 591	7.2	23.0	11.7	37.2	20.0	8.1	1.5	32.1	101.3	82.1	16.5	1.4	323	62.2
Rome CDP	1 902	6.4	25.6	7.6	33.7	24.3	8.8	1.5	35.2	101.3	89.2	10.8	–	–	–
Romeoville village	14 074	7.9	30.2	14.8	32.9	18.4	3.8	.4	27.6	105.9	89.2	6.1	4.7	668	15.4
Roodhouse city	2 139	7.8	27.2	9.2	26.4	19.0	18.1	4.2	35.0	86.2	84.2	15.8	–	–	–
Roscoe village	2 079	7.3	29.3	7.3	38.2	17.7	7.6	1.3	31.3	96.0	91.8	8.2	–	–	–
Roselle village	20 819	8.4	28.9	7.8	40.4	16.1	6.7	1.1	31.6	92.8	89.7	9.9	.5	101	77.2
Rosemont village	3 995	8.0	21.2	14.3	38.3	15.4	10.8	1.6	29.8	106.7	74.0	26.0	–	–	–
Roseville village	1 151	5.5	22.1	6.6	22.8	19.1	29.5	11.8	43.4	73.2	79.0	13.1	7.9	91	100.0
Rosewood Heights CDP	4 821	6.2	24.6	7.9	29.0	25.2	13.2	1.9	37.1	93.4	90.5	9.5	–	–	–
Rosiclare city	1 378	5.2	22.7	8.7	24.9	20.8	22.9	6.7	39.8	75.7	79.1	16.6	4.3	59	100.0
Rossville village	1 334	6.1	25.6	6.9	26.6	20.8	20.1	4.9	37.6	86.5	84.7	15.3	–	–	–
Round Lake village	3 550	9.8	27.7	14.1	34.1	15.9	8.2	1.5	29.0	94.8	84.9	14.8	.3	9	–
Round Lake Beach village	16 434	10.3	35.6	10.6	36.4	12.0	5.4	1.0	27.0	95.0	90.1	9.3	.7	111	89.2
Round Lake Heights village	1 251	11.7	35.5	11.2	34.2	13.5	5.6	.6	27.1	102.8	92.8	7.2	–	–	–
Round Lake Park village	4 045	8.9	33.4	10.0	36.7	13.9	6.0	1.0	28.4	101.6	88.9	10.9	.2	10	–
Roxana village	1 562	6.3	22.3	9.2	28.1	22.7	17.7	4.2	37.1	86.0	86.5	13.5	–	–	–
Royalton village	1 191	5.7	21.4	10.2	26.0	21.7	20.7	4.5	39.7	81.7	82.4	17.6	–	–	–
Rushville city	3 229	6.1	22.4	8.0	25.4	19.4	24.9	8.3	39.9	74.5	79.2	17.3	3.5	112	100.0
St. Anne village	1 153	8.3	30.5	8.8	27.2	19.4	14.1	2.3	32.5	92.5	88.7	11.3	–	–	–
St. Charles city	22 501	7.6	28.4	8.2	35.7	18.3	9.4	2.2	33.3	92.5	87.2	12.0	.8	178	75.3
St. Elmo city	1 473	6.3	25.0	8.1	27.0	18.8	21.1	7.5	36.3	79.4	81.7	14.5	3.8	56	100.0
St. Joseph village	2 052	6.5	27.8	7.1	33.6	19.6	11.8	2.4	34.5	88.7	88.4	10.9	.7	14	–
Salem city	7 470	6.6	25.6	8.0	27.9	19.1	19.4	6.1	36.2	81.0	80.4	15.6	3.9	294	100.0
Sandoval village	1 535	8.9	31.4	9.1	28.4	16.2	15.0	4.2	30.8	84.4	85.9	14.1	–	–	–
Sandwich city	5 567	7.0	26.6	8.2	29.8	18.7	16.7	5.7	34.3	87.0	82.2	14.0	3.7	207	90.3
Sauk Village village	9 926	8.2	34.7	11.1	33.3	17.0	3.8	.4	27.4	96.5	92.3	7.4	.3	30	100.0
Savanna city	3 819	6.4	23.1	8.7	26.2	19.8	22.2	5.8	38.2	84.2	78.1	19.2	2.7	103	100.0
Savoy village	2 674	8.9	23.1	8.2	37.6	14.7	16.5	7.4	32.6	80.0	74.7	16.6	8.7	232	100.0
Schaumburg village	68 586	6.5	23.6	10.5	41.0	17.6	7.3	1.8	31.8	92.3	80.8	18.8	.3	223	97.8
Schiller Park village	11 189	7.6	22.7	12.6	35.4	20.1	9.2	1.0	31.6	103.7	84.4	15.6	–	–	–
Scott AFB CDP	7 245	14.8	41.7	13.5	41.7	2.9	.2	.1	22.8	113.6	91.8	.9	7.3	529	3.0
Seneca village	1 878	8.5	30.6	9.2	28.7	19.5	12.0	2.3	32.4	90.5	90.8	9.2	–	–	–
Sesser city	2 087	6.2	25.3	7.6	26.1	18.5	22.6	5.1	37.9	82.3	85.1	14.9	–	–	–
Shawneetown village	1 575	6.2	21.8	9.0	23.1	22.1	23.9	6.8	42.0	76.4	77.8	16.2	6.0	95	100.0
Shelbyville city	4 943	6.2	22.7	7.8	26.6	19.6	23.3	7.7	38.9	83.9	79.3	17.1	3.6	180	91.7
Sheldon village	1 109	6.0	25.5	8.1	28.1	19.9	18.3	4.8	35.5	80.7	83.2	13.7	3.1	34	91.2
Sheridan village	1 288	4.7	18.2	40.4	22.1	11.0	8.2	1.0	22.3	291.4	51.2	6.1	42.7	550	100.0
Sherman village	2 080	7.3	30.5	5.4	35.6	16.9	11.6	3.7	35.2	86.1	88.1	8.2	3.7	77	100.0
Shiloh village	2 655	8.7	26.9	10.0	40.7	16.2	6.2	.8	30.9	100.4	87.4	12.6	–	–	–
Shorewood village	6 264	8.3	32.0	8.5	35.7	19.1	4.8	.6	32.0	97.2	94.5	5.5	–	–	–
Sidney village	1 027	9.0	26.2	8.2	35.5	17.1	13.0	2.6	32.8	87.6	89.5	10.5	–	–	–
Silvis city	6 926	7.8	28.5	9.5	29.7	18.5	13.7	3.0	32.7	83.4	83.9	15.2	.9	59	94.9
Skokie village	59 432	5.4	20.3	7.1	27.9	23.9	20.7	4.1	41.4	84.0	87.4	11.3	1.3	774	86.0
Sleepy Hollow village	3 241	8.9	30.3	7.5	36.3	21.3	4.7	.7	33.7	97.9	95.0	5.0	–	–	–
Smithton village	1 587	7.5	28.0	7.4	32.9	16.9	14.8	2.8	34.0	86.5	85.9	8.1	5.9	94	–
Somonauk village	1 263	7.2	27.9	8.7	31.8	17.7	13.9	3.6	33.3	87.1	89.2	10.8	–	–	–
South Barrington village	2 937	7.7	33.1	8.3	30.9	24.5	3.2	.7	35.2	98.3	98.1	1.9	–	–	–
South Beloit city	4 072	6.5	23.1	11.3	31.3	20.1	14.3	3.2	33.4	92.8	80.1	19.4	.5	22	100.0
South Chicago Heights village	3 597	5.6	20.1	10.1	29.0	23.0	17.8	3.0	37.1	96.6	84.5	15.5	–	–	–
South Elgin village	7 474	7.8	27.9	9.1	36.1	17.5	9.4	3.2	31.3	89.7	86.9	9.6	3.5	259	100.0
Southern View village	1 906	5.7	18.0	7.0	30.0	17.8	27.2	8.7	40.3	72.9	77.5	16.5	5.9	113	100.0
South Holland village	22 105	5.5	21.8	8.8	25.4	26.8	17.2	3.9	40.3	90.3	90.8	6.0	3.2	706	96.2
South Jacksonville village	3 187	5.1	22.4	6.8	28.0	21.6	21.1	4.4	40.3	76.3	83.1	16.9	–	–	–
South Pekin village	1 184	8.3	34.2	8.5	32.3	17.1	7.9	1.7	28.8	90.5	91.5	8.5	–	–	–
South Roxana village	1 961	8.0	29.4	10.2	32.3	20.1	8.0	.7	31.2	92.0	89.9	10.1	–	–	–
Sparta city	4 853	7.0	28.4	8.3	27.7	18.2	17.4	5.9	34.4	80.1	82.5	13.5	4.0	193	100.0
Springfield city	105 227	7.4	24.3	9.4	33.5	18.0	14.9	4.0	34.0	80.2	76.2	21.8	1.9	2 036	70.0
Spring Grove village	1 066	8.9	33.7	6.6	36.8	17.2	5.8	1.2	31.2	100.3	94.5	5.5	–	–	–
Spring Valley city	5 246	6.6	26.0	8.2	27.9	18.3	19.5	5.0	35.9	86.5	84.1	15.3	.6	32	100.0
Staunton city	4 806	6.4	25.1	8.2	27.6	17.5	21.7	6.4	37.0	79.7	84.0	14.1	1.9	89	100.0
Steeleville village	2 059	5.5	23.4	7.8	26.6	21.1	21.0	4.7	39.1	89.5	85.5	14.5	–	–	–
Steger village	8 584	7.5	25.4	10.9	34.5	18.7	10.6	1.7	31.3	97.4	85.1	14.9	–	–	–
Sterling city	15 132	7.0	25.9	8.7	30.3	18.6	16.5	4.2	34.2	84.0	81.0	16.9	2.0	307	87.9
Stickney village	5 678	6.0	19.2	9.4	29.4	21.6	20.3	3.2	38.5	92.7	81.9	13.4	4.7	266	13.9
Stockton village	1 871	6.2	23.0	8.1	25.3	21.3	22.3	6.2	38.9	83.1	82.3	15.8	2.0	37	100.0
Stone Park village	4 383	9.2	31.0	12.0	32.1	17.8	7.0	1.2	28.5	108.8	91.3	8.7	–	–	–
Stonington village	1 006	6.3	27.4	7.2	26.1	19.9	19.4	3.9	36.1	83.9	88.7	11.3	–	–	–
Streamwood village	30 987	10.1	30.0	9.7	41.7	15.2	3.4	.5	29.2	98.3	91.8	8.2	–	–	–
Streator city	14 121	7.2	25.7	7.7	26.9	19.7	20.0	5.2	36.1	82.8	82.5	15.9	1.5	218	90.8
Sugar Grove village	2 005	8.6	30.0	8.2	34.6	21.6	5.6	.6	32.2	93.5	92.8	7.2	–	–	–
Sullivan city	4 354	6.4	23.9	6.9	28.0	18.7	22.5	6.6	38.1	75.9	81.5	14.6	3.9	170	91.2
Summit village	9 971	8.4	28.0	12.3	31.4	16.7	11.6	2.0	30.2	104.4	86.0	13.9	.2	16	–
Sumner city	1 083	5.6	19.9	8.5	24.9	20.2	26.4	10.1	42.0	78.4	66.9	14.7	18.5	200	92.5
Sunnyside village	1 529	9.0	37.2	6.7	37.1	15.4	3.5	.7	30.4	98.3	94.9	5.1	–	–	–
Swansea village	8 201	7.2	23.9	7.9	35.0	17.4	15.9	4.5	34.5	84.7	80.7	14.5	4.8	395	100.0

GENERAL POPULATION CHARACTERISTICS   **ILLINOIS 9**

Figure 1-5

17.1% lived in nonfamily households or with someone else's family, and the remaining 2.8% lived in Group Quarters. Major Census products will be introduced in Chapters 8 and 9. Help with understanding and interpreting data tables can be found in Chapter 10.

 Census Tip

Census data are presented for all levels of geography, starting with the nation as a whole and ending with individual Census Blocks. Sample data (information gathered from the Long-Form Questionnaires) are available down to a level of aggregation known as the Block Group. Reports for individual Census Blocks show 100% counts only. This is because sampling rates are not inclusive enough to provide accurate estimates for such small geographic areas.

Cost of the Census

At a cost of nearly $2.6 billion over the ten- year cycle, the 1990 Census was the most expensive in history.

At a cost of nearly $2.6 billion over the ten-year cycle, the 1990 Census was the most expensive in history, more than double 1980's total of $1.1 billion. To make a more meaningful cost comparison, however, amounts should be recast as per capita figures. The 1990 Census cost about $10.40 per person, or $25 per household. After adjusting for inflation, the 1980 cost was about $20 per household, an increase of 25%.

Where did all that money go? Figure 1-6 lists annual expenditures which the Bureau allocated to decennial Census activities. (At the time of this writing, the full budget cycle had not been completed, so FY 1992 and 1993 figures are estimates.) Slightly more than 50% of the total allocation went toward actual data collection—printing and mailing Questionnaires, hiring and training enumerators, etc. The broad category of operations accounted for another 26%. The third-

costliest function was product development and publication, an activity which has continued well into FY 1993. Each of the remaining activities represented less than 5% of the decennial budget, but a small percentage of $2.6 billion is still a lot of money. For example, the Bureau spent $86.7 million on computer equipment and other data processing costs associated with the Census, and $113 million on statistical research and evaluation.

As might be expected, the timing of expenditures paralleled the amount of activity devoted to decennial planning and operations each year. Spending increased gradually as Census Day approached, then tapered off after data collection was completed. Approximately 54% of the total outlay occurred in FY 1990, which ran from October 1989 through September 1990.

The U.S. Bureau of the Census

An introduction to the Census should include a description of the agency responsible for the effort: the U.S. Bureau of the Census (referred to throughout this book as the Bureau). The following sections will touch on the nature of our federal statistical system, the organization and structure of the Bureau, and the Bureau's responsibilities in addition to the decennial Census.

The Federal Statistical System

While most countries have central statistical offices, this has never been the case in the United States. The remarkable range and extent of our government's statistical efforts grew piecemeal, according to the dictates of legislation and in response to emerging needs. It evolved into a far-flung, highly decentralized system.

Most government agencies produce statistics as a by-product of their administrative

Department of Commerce
Bureau of the Census
10 Year Budget Cycle Table
(Dollar amounts in thousands

										Estimated	Obligations
										1992	1993	Total
Activity	FY84	FY85	FY86	FY87	FY88	FY89	FY90	FY91	Subtotal	Estimate	Estimate	Estimate
Planning, Direction and Management	$5,538	$5,168	$7,144	$7,890	$10,601	$12,736	$13,438	$13,946	$76,461	$11,489	$11,032	$98,982
Test Censuses and Dress Rehearsals	3,456	11,707	17,878	16,691	19,406	1,802	442	0	71,382	0	0	71,382
Data Collection	994	405	995	7,593	36,326	75,880	1,115,292	52,020	1,289,505	15,573	4,429	1,309,507
Operations	1,169	3,371	11,135	25,070	106,735	191,211	188,618	119,874	647,183	12,127	15,158	674,468
Product Development and Data Dissemination	1,431	3,688	3,841	5,223	5,096	55,912	10,413	19,668	105,272	27,809	22,908	155,989
Promotion and Outreach	400	1,021	1,872	4,263	8,953	27,183	23,053	7,366	74,111	27	0	74,138
Statistical Research and Evaluation	557	2,518	3,547	4,951	6,715	8,406	30,842	35,654	93,190	13,213	6,977	113,380
Other Activities	0	0	0	0	0	1,013	1,153	3,688	5,854	0	820	6,674
Data Processing Systems- Decennial Data Capture	0	629	583	14,068	27,552	18,977	19,051	3,862	84,722	1,941	0	86,663
Prior Adjustments										(5,882)	(2,383)	(8,265)
Total 1990 Decennial Census	13,545	28,507	46,995	85,749	221,384	393,120	1,402,302	256,078	2,447,680	82,179	61,324	2,591,183

Note: FY84 through FY91 are actual obligations adjusted for prior year recoveries.
  FY93 President's budget
Source: Unpublished data supplied by the U. S. Bureau of the Census, Decennial Managment Division.

Figure 1-6

and regulatory duties. Some, such as the Council of Economic Advisors, the Congressional Budget Office, and the Bureau of Economic Analysis, analyze existing data produced by other organizations. Few federal agencies exist solely to collect and disseminate statistics. Among the prominent organizations of this type are the Bureau of the Census, the Bureau of Labor Statistics, the National Center for Health Statistics, the National Center for Education Statistics, the Department of Agriculture's Statistical Reporting Service, and the Energy Information Administration.

Many problems are associated with such a diverse, decentralized statistical system. Among the most serious is the paperwork burden imposed on citizens and businesses. A second concern is the overlapping of existing statistical programs. This occurs when different agencies study the same topic from varying perspectives, or when they are required by law to monitor program compli-

ance or to allocate funds according to a predetermined formula. A third problem is the high cost of collecting, tabulating, and publishing data.

The decentralized activities of federal statistical agencies have been supervised by the U.S. Office of Management and Budget (OMB) since 1942. The Federal Reports Act requires the government to collect only the information it needs to perform its regular functions. This basic philosophy was strengthened by the Paperwork Reduction Act of 1980 and its subsequent amendments. Under these laws, OMB has the authority to approve or disapprove any statistical programs or publications agencies wish to initiate. OMB monitors duplication and waste, evaluates effectiveness of statistical programs, and develops standards and policies agencies must follow. OMB also creates and defines such federal statistical standards as Metropolitan Statistical Areas and the Standard Industrial Classification System.

The decentralized activities of federal statistical agencies have been supervised by the U.S. Office of Management and Budget (OMB) since 1942.

Census Bureau Organization and Structure

The Census Bureau did not exist as a permanent agency until 1902. The first nine Censuses were conducted by Federal Marshals, who interrupted their normal duties to count the population. During this period, Marshals reported to various agencies: directly to the President (1790); to the State Department (1800 through 1840); and to the newly-formed Department of the Interior (1850 through 1870). The 1880 Census was the first not conducted by the Marshal Service. The Census law for 1880 empowered the Superintendent of the Census to recruit and hire enumerators, clerks, and "special agents" to conduct decennial operations. The new Census Office, situated within the Department of the Interior, was strictly a temporary agency, disbanded upon completion of the decennial Census. This pattern of temporary mobilization continued through the 1900 Census, but by that time, operations had become too complex to be organized from scratch each decade. Because an accurate and timely enumeration could no longer be taken without the benefit of continuity, planning, experienced employees, and professional management, Congress created a permanent Census Office in 1902. The Office remained part of Interior until the following year, when it was transferred to the Department of Labor and Commerce. When that Department was split in 1913, the Census Bureau was assigned to the Commerce Department, where it has remained ever since.

Today, the Bureau of the Census is a major government agency with several thousand permanent employees. The Bureau relies on computer specialists, programmers, statisticians, demographers, geographers, economists, and other professionals to conduct its ongoing operations. Figure 1-7 shows a general picture of the Bureau's organizational structure. The Director of the Bureau, who is appointed by the President and confirmed by the Senate, reports to the Under Secretary for Economic Affairs of the Commerce Department. Next comes the Deputy Director, followed by seven Associate Directors, each responsible for one of the following major functional areas: the Decennial Census; Demographic Programs; Economic Programs; Field Operations; Statistical Design, Methodology, and Standards; Information Technology; and Administration. Under each of these areas is a variety of Divisions. For example, the Associate Director for the Decennial Census and his Assistant Director are responsible for the Decennial Management Division, the Decennial Statistical Studies Division, and the Geography Division. As the next decennial Census approaches, this area will expand to include planning, promotion, field operations, and other activities. For now, planning for the 2000 Census is coordinated by a special project staff which reports to the Associate Director for Statistical Design.

In 1942, the Bureau's headquarters moved from Washington to the near-by suburb of Suitland, Maryland. The drab, imposing exterior of the Suitland facility looks much like a large prison, but it houses a sophisticated complex of offices. The main structure, called Federal Office Building Number 3, was constructed with large bays and covered catwalks, so it could be converted to wartime purposes if necessary. Federal Office Building Number 4 was built in 1946. The Bureau leases additional office space in a variety of buildings located within a six-mile radius of the Suitland complex. A shuttle bus service links the Suitland offices with one another and with the Commerce Department headquarters in Washington.

An auxiliary Census facility was established in 1958. The Bureau's data preparation Division is located in Jeffersonville, Indiana, across the Ohio River from Louisville, Kentucky. "J- ville," as it is called by Bureau employees, is the permanent site for the Bureau's microfilming and mapmaking operations, the secure storage of prior Census records, and many clerical functions. The

When the Department of Labor and Commerce was split in 1913, the Census Bureau was assigned to the Commerce Department, where it has remained ever since.

Today, the Bureau of the Census is a major government agency with several thousand permanent employees.

main facility is housed in a large brick building originally constructed as a hospital for Union soldiers during the Civil War. A third Census site, located in Pittsburg, Kansas, was home to the Bureau's Personal Census Service Branch. This site was closed in 1991 and its operations were transferred to Jeffersonville.

The Bureau maintains 12 Regional Offices throughout the country to coordinate local field activities and to assist the public in using Census data. Two other sources of assistance are worth noting. One is the Bureau's Data User Services Division (DUSD) in Suitland. DUSD maintains a Customer Services hot line, publishes a variety of Census guides, catalogs, and newsletters, and coordinates several Census outreach networks. One of these networks, is the State Data Center (SDC) program, comprised of state and local organizations which provide assistance to Census users in their areas. More will be said about DUSD and the State Data Center program in Chapter 10. A list of telephone contacts for the Bureau, its Regional Offices, and the SDC program can be found in the annual *Census Catalog and Guide* and the Bureau's Internet server.

The Bureau also maintains 12 Regional Offices throughout the country to coordinate local field activities and to assist the public in using Census data.

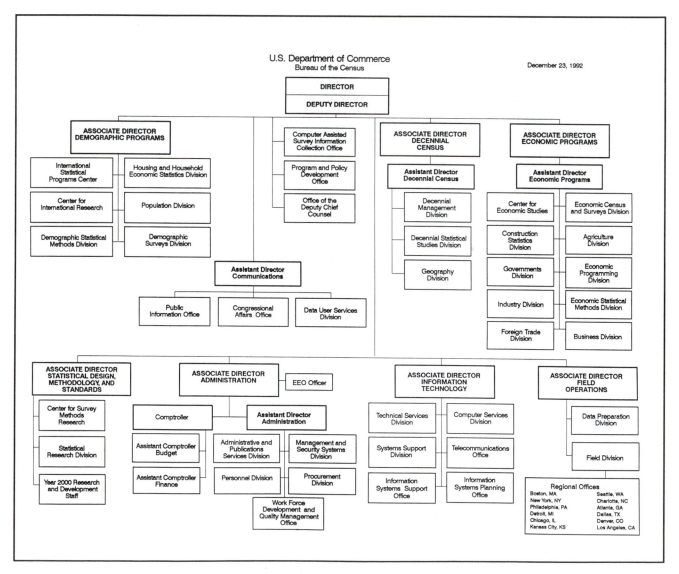

Figure 1-7

The Other Nine Years

What does the Bureau do between decennial enumerations? The enormous publicity surrounding each decade's Census Day tends to overshadow the work which takes place during the other nine years. From a certain point of view there is no "in between;" the decennial Census requires a ten-year cycle from start to finish. It takes several years after each Census to publish the results, evaluate the quality of the data, and review the effectiveness of decennial operations. Planning for the next Census begins literally before the current one has been completed.

The Bureau, however, does much more than conduct the decennial Census. It mounts numerous economic censuses and surveys, conducts ongoing demographic surveys, calculates population estimates and projections, supports research on statistical methods, studies international population trends (employing demographers who specialize in particular areas of the world), and provides a variety of training and user assistance services. For example, the Bureau trains personnel from the statistical agencies of other countries, and provides technical assistance to developing nations. Although the United States does not have a central statistical office as most countries do, the Bureau of the Census comes closer to playing such a role than any other agency.

The Bureau conducts ten additional Censuses covering government, agriculture, manufactures, mineral industries, retail trade, wholesale trade, finance, service industries, transportation, and construction industries. Each of these occurs once every five years, for years ending in two and seven. Most of the quinquennial Censuses are updated by annual sample surveys. Another major economic survey is the annual *County Business Patterns* series. In addition, the Bureau collects, tabulates, and publishes monthly foreign trade statistics. This extensive series provides detailed data on U.S. imports and exports by specific commodity and country of origin or destination.

Another major function of the Bureau is to conduct surveys for other agencies on a cost-recovery basis. The oldest and most extensive of these is the Current Population Survey (CPS), which is conducted monthly for the Bureau of Labor Statistics. The CPS program, which measures characteristics of the employed and unemployed, began in 1940 as a Works Progress Administration survey called the *Monthly Report on the Labor Force*. When the WPA was disbanded in 1942, the Census Bureau continued the survey. Today, the CPS interviews more than 60,000 households per month. In addition to monthly labor force data, the CPS is also used as a vehicle to collect statistics for other agencies.

Numerous additional surveys are conducted for agencies as diverse as the National Endowment for the Arts and the National Institute on Aging. Topics range from teenage attitudes toward smoking to the characteristics of adults serving a sentence of probation. Some surveys are conducted on a recurring basis, others are one-time studies. A brief guide to some of the largest on-going surveys can be found in Figure 1-8.

History of the Census

Like the nation it chronicles, the Census has grown in complexity with each succeeding decade. While it is beyond the scope of this book to offer a detailed history of the Census, a few key developments will be discussed. Figure 1-9 highlights significant events in Census history.

Early Censuses

The first census took place in 1790, little more than a year after the Constitution was at last ratified. Congress passed the first Census legislation in March, and Secretary of State Thomas Jefferson arrived in New York City (the first capital) barely in time to issue

---

From a certain point of view there is no "in between;" the decennial Census requires a ten-year cycle from start to finish.

The Bureau conducts ten additional Censuses covering government, agriculture, manufactures, mineral industries, retail trade, wholesale trade, finance, service industries, transportation, and construction industries.

Major Ongoing Surveys Conducted by the Bureau of the Census

Title: **American Housing Survey.**
Purpose: Current data on housing conditions.
Sample Size: 60,000 Housing Units (National Sample). 4,700 Housing Units (each Metropolitan sample).
Sponsor: U.S. Department of Housing and Urban Development.
Frequency: Biennial.

Title: **Consumer Expenditure Surveys.**
Purpose: Measures household expenditures on consumer goods.
Sample Size: 9,000 households (Quarterly Interview Survey). 8,200 households (Diary Survey).
Sponsor: U.S. Bureau of Labor Statistics.
Frequency: Continuous throughout every month.

Title: **Current Population Survey.**
Purpose: Labor force and other population characteristics.
Sample Size: 71,000 households.
Sponsor: U.S. Bureau of Labor Statistics and others.
Frequency: Monthly, with various annual supplements.

Title: **Household Food Consumption Survey.**
Purpose: Dietary data.
Sample Size: 15,000 households.
Sponsor: U.S. Department of Agriculture.
Frequency: Decennial.

Title: **National Crime Victimization Survey.**
Purpose: Effects of crimes on their victims.
Sample Size: 60,000 households per cycle.
Sponsor: U.S. Bureau of Justice Statistics.
Frequency: Continuous, with monthly interviews.

Title: **National Health Interview Survey.**
Purpose: Amount and distribution of illness and disability.
Sample Size: 50,000 households annually.
Sponsor: National Center for Health Statistics.
Frequency: Weekly.

Title: **National Prisoner Statistics Program.**
Purpose: Characteristics of incarcerated adults.
Sample Size: Complete count data from administrative records.
Sponsor: U.S. Bureau of Justice Statistics.
Frequency: Annual, on a flow basis.

Title: **National Survey of College Graduates.**
Purpose: Estimates the size and characteristics of population with science and engineering education.
Sample Size: 216,000 persons.
Sponsor: National Science Foundation.
Frequency: Biennial.

Title: **National Survey of Fishing, Hunting, and Wildlife-Associated Recreation.**
Purpose: Data on wildlife-related recreational activities.
Sample Size: 68,000 persons.
Sponsor: U.S. Fish and Wildlife Service.
Frequency: Quinquennial.

Title: **Private School Survey.**
Purpose: Characteristics of private and parochial schools.
Sample Size: Complete count (approximately 25,000 schools).
Sponsor: National Center for Education Statistics.
Frequency: Annual.

Title: **Schools and Staffing Surveys.**
Purpose: Staffing patterns in public and private schools.
Sample Size: 68,000 teachers and 13,200 principals.
Sponsor: National Center for Education Statistics.
Frequency: Every three years.

Title: **Survey of Income and Program Participation.**
Purpose: Measures eligibility and participation in federal assistance programs and characteristics of participants and nonparticipants.
Sample Size: 14,000 to 20,000 households.
Sponsor: U.S. Bureau of the Census.
Frequency: Continuous, with monthly interviews.

Figure 1-8

instructions to the federal Marshals. Seventeen Marshals represented the thirteen states plus the territories of Kentucky, Tennessee, Vermont, and Maine. Each was empowered to divide his District into smaller areas and hire as many assistants as deemed necessary. Marshals were paid a flat fee, ranging from $100 to $500, depending on the size of their District. Assistants were paid one dollar for every 150 rural residents counted, plus one dollar for every 300 urban residents. An additional two dollars was paid for every completed Census schedule posted in a prominent public place. Hefty penalties were imposed for failing to complete the enumeration on time: assistants would forfeit $200; Marshals would forfeit $800. The format of the tally was specified by the Census law, but no standard forms were provided. In fact, Marshals had to supply their own materials, and completed schedules were submitted on various types and sizes of paper.

As enumerators traveled throughout the nation on horseback and foot, they were met with occasional suspicion and resistance. Failure to respond to Census questions could result in a $20 fine, to be shared between the government and the Marshal's assistant. Enumerators began working on August 2, 1790. Despite the extensive territory covered and the difficult travel conditions, schedules were completed by October, 1791 for every District but South Carolina. Special legislation extended the deadline for this state, which submitted its final schedules in March, 1792. The total cost was $45,000 (roughly $300,000 in 1990 dollars).

Succeeding Censuses were similar to the first in most respects. The Censuses of 1810 and 1820 attempted to gather statistics on the number of manufacturing establishments and their output, but results were haphazard. The 1830 census marked the first use of uniform printed schedules, but major changes did not take place until 1840. The 1840 legislation called for creation of a temporary Census Office to centralize decennial operations. It was also the first to ask additional demographic questions, including school attendance, literacy, occupation, and mental disability. Unfortunately, it was also the most bungled Census to date. Not only did it take 18 months to complete, but the American Statistical Association challenged the accuracy of its results, based on numerous "discrepancies, contradictions, and improbabilities."

The 1850 Census is considered the first to follow modern enumeration principles because it was the first to capture the characteristics of individuals rather than entire families. Prior Census schedules listed each family on a single horizontal line, with family characteristics (number of adult males, etc.) shown in vertical columns. The 1850 schedule listed each person's name on a separate line, with vertical columns showing characteristics for that person. Because of the problems encountered in 1840, Congress appointed a Census Board to determine the content of the 1850 Questionnaire, and professional statisticians were consulted for advice. Marshals were charged with making a careful examination of all Census returns and instructing their assistants to conduct any necessary recounts. Responsibility for the Census was transferred from the State Department to the newly formed Department of the Interior. 1850 also marked the first appointment of an outside individual to serve as Superintendent of the Census.

The Census in Transition

From 1850 through 1890 the Census Questionnaire grew to gargantuan proportions, overwhelming the ability of the Federal Marshals to collect it or the government to tally it. Questions on libraries, newspapers, crime, government, and a host of other areas were introduced. By 1890 a total of over 13,000 possible questions could be asked by the Census takers, using 233 different forms to do so. Not only did it take years to tabulate the results, but the increased complexity of

As enumerators traveled throughout the nation on horseback and foot, they were met with occasional suspicion and resistance.

The 1850 Census is considered the first to follow modern enumeration principles because it was the first to capture the characteristics of individuals rather than entire families.

questions made errors inevitable. One step toward solving the problem was the gradual professionalization of the enumeration process. Beginning with 1880, Federal Marshals no longer conducted the Census. Instead, 30,000 temporary enumerators were hired after passing an open, non-competitive exam. While enumerators collected basic population data, engineers and other skilled professionals were hired as "special agents" to collect the technical data asked of manufacturing establishments. Still, a combination of budget shortfalls and sheer volume of data caused delays in tabulation; the last report for 1880 was published in 1888, three years after the temporary Census Office had been closed.

The solution to tabulation problems would come from automation. Until 1870, results were tabulated with paper and pen, on long tally sheets. A rudimentary mechanical tallying machine, called the Seaton Device, was employed in 1870 and 1880. It was a wooden box with a series of rollers, through which long rolls of Census schedules were threaded. The machine didn't record results, but made hand tabulation simpler by aligning columns from multiple Questionnaires. The first true automatic tabulating machine was invented by Census employee Herman Hollerith, just in time for the 1890 Census.

Hollerith, an 1879 graduate of Columbia's engineering school, worked as a special agent on the 1880 Census. While there, he met Dr. John Shaw Billings, head of the Census's vital statistics operation. Billings suggested that punched cards, like those controlling the Jacquard carpet loom, could be used for automatic tabulating. Throughout the following decade, Hollerith experimented with various designs, ultimately obtaining three key patents in the late 1880s. His tabulating system won an open competition sponsored by the government, and was promptly employed in the 1890 Census.

The system had three components. A "pantograph punch" mechanically transcribed responses from Questionnaires onto individual punch cards. Each card represented one person, and each hole corresponded to a particular characteristic; a hole in column seven, row nine, indicated a literate citizen, for example. (An earlier version of Hollerith's system employed a railroad conductor's hand punch. After punching 12,000 holes during a test for the Baltimore Department of Health, Hollerith experienced what was probably the modern era's first case of carpal tunnel syndrome.)

The second component was the tabulator itself. The operator would place a punch card in the "press box" and depress a lever to close the box. Forty pins in the box's upper jaw would then attempt to connect with forty mercury-filled cups in the lower jaw. Wherever a hole in the punch card permitted the connection to be made, an electric circuit was completed, causing a hand on the face of one of the forty corresponding dials to advance one unit. At the end of the day, the dials' totals would be recorded and reset for the next day's tally. Because each card represented one person's responses, cards could be rearranged and retabulated to create such cross-tabulations as sex by age group.

The third component was the sorter, a wooden box with 26 compartments. Notches punched in the edge of the card would trigger one of the 26 compartment doors to pop open. The operator would then remove the tabulated punch card from the press box and place it in the proper compartment for additional tabulation. Using Hollerith's system, Census clerks processed data four times faster than the previous decade.

In 1896, Hollerith organized the Tabulating Machine Company to manufacture the machines and punch cards. At first, Hollerith leased or sold his machines to the government, but after the Census Bureau became a permanent agency in 1902, it established its own engineering department and machine shop, and enhanced Hollerith's basic designs for its own use. Meanwhile, Hollerith's company was destined to play a central role in modern business history. In 1910, the firm combined with two others to

The solution to tabulation problems would come from automation.

The first true automatic tabulating machine was invented by Census employee Herman Hollerith, just in time for the 1890 Census.

form the Calculating-Tabulating-Recording Co., which changed its name in 1924 to International Business Machines (IBM).

Beginning in 1845, consistent requests were made to establish a permanent agency to conduct the Census. A variety of reports were presented to Congress in the 1890s, and several bills were introduced, but none passed. The topic arose again when legislation for the 1900 census was debated. Although a permanent agency was still not approved, the 1900 legislation included several improvements, including the appointment of a Census geographer and several chief statisticians, and limiting the decennial Census to four topics: population, mortality, agriculture, and manufactures. As mentioned earlier, a permanent agency was finally established in 1902.

Modern Censuses

Since 1890, the burden of Census questions has been reduced significantly. Many have been eliminated as being nonessential, or because data are available through other sources. Questions not related to the population have been gradually removed from the decennial Census and incorporated into other censuses conducted at other times. The first Census of Housing took place in 1940, but by this time questions on agriculture, manufacturing, and other business activities were no longer asked as part of the Population Census.

The 1940 Census was notable for another reason, namely the first use of sample surveys. Probability sampling had been tried during agricultural surveys in the 1920s, and in an experimental census of unemployment conducted by the Civil Works Administration in 1933. The 1940 Census employed a 5% sample to reduce processing costs, expedite tabulation, and reduce the reporting burden. In this first effort, specified individuals in a household were sampled. For example, the third person in a household would answer the sample questions, while other members would answer the 100%

questions only. A similar technique was used in 1950, but individuals answered a single sample question only. The first person would answer sample question one, the second would answer sample question two, and so on. Beginning in 1960, entire households were sampled. If the Housing Unit was designated for sampling, everyone in the household responded to all sample questions. Sampling rates have varied over the decades. In 1970, for example, some questions were asked of 5% of the population, some of a second 15% sample, and others of both (a 20% sample).

The 1950 census saw the introduction of computer technology, though on a limited basis. Two University of Pennsylvania engineers, John Mauchly and J. Presper Eckert, created the world's first electronic computer, which was used for ballistic calculations during World War II. The device, dubbed ENIAC for Electronic Numerical Integrator and Calculator, was the prototype for the Bureau's computer. Morris Hansen, the Census Bureau's chief statistician at the time, was a major catalyst in the development of modern computing. Hansen had met Mauchley by chance, and quickly saw the potential offered by ENIAC. He lobbied Congress for funds to develop a computer for large-scale statistical tabulations, and in 1946 a joint project between the Census Bureau and the National Bureau of Standards was approved. Mauchly and Eckert's UNIVAC I, the Universal Automatic Computer, became the first computer designed for commercial applications. UNIVAC still required labor intensive data coding and card punching, but it accelerated Census processing enormously. It was used to handle about 20% of the 1950 Census returns.

The next major breakthrough in census processing was the invention of FOSDIC (Film Optical Scanning Device for Input to Computers) in the mid-1950s. FOSDIC enabled Bureau employees to convert Questionnaires onto microfilm and scan the filmed responses directly into the computer. FOSDIC and UNIVAC were employed ex-

Since 1890, the burden of Census questions has been reduced significantly.

The 1950 census saw the introduction of computer technology, though on a limited basis.

tensively in the 1960 Census, and most data were tabulated electronically. This Census also saw the introduction of mail-out Questionnaires. In large urban areas, Questionnaires were delivered by the Postal Service. Households were instructed to keep the completed forms until they were picked up by an enumerator. The 1970 Census carried self-enumeration one step further; 60% of all households were instructed to return their completed forms by mail. These changes in Census methodology and technology show how the Bureau has grown to meet the challenges of a complex society, as Figure 1-9 illustrates.

Major Census Developments

YEAR	DEVELOPMENT
1787	First nation in history to mandate a census in its constitution.
1790	U.S. Marshals conduct first Census.
1830	First use of uniform Questionnaires.
1849	Responsibility for Census transferred to U.S. Department of the Interior.
1850	Uniform geographic boundaries employed.
	First Census to measure characteristics of individuals rather than families only.
1870	Rudimentary mechanical tabulator used.
	Census results displayed in map formats.
1878	First *Statistical Abstract of the United States*.
1880	Specially trained enumerators replace U.S. Marshals.
	Enumerators required to take confidentiality oath.
1890	Hollerith electric tabulating machines introduced.
1902	Census Bureau becomes a permanent agency.
1903	Census Bureau transferred to U.S. Department of Commerce and Labor.
1910	First Census Tracts.
1913	Census Bureau moves to Commerce Department when existing agency splits.
1940	Statistical sampling techniques introduced.
	First Census of Housing.
	First Census Blocks.
1942	Bureau takes over Current Population Survey.
	Bureau moves to current headquarters in Suitland, Maryland.
1947	U.S. Bureau of the Budget establishes standard definitions for Metropolitan Areas.
1950	UNIVAC computer first used.
1953	FOSDIC optical scanning device introduced.
1958	Additional Bureau facilities opened in Jeffersonville, Indiana and Pittsburg, Kansas.
1960	First use of mailed Questionnaires.
	Entire Census tabulated electronically.
1967	GBF/DIME computerized geographic system developed.
1970	First computerized address coding guide.
1978	State Data Center program begins.
1980	Over 90% of Census Questionnaires delivered by mail.
1984	CENDATA online system unveiled.
	Work begins on TIGER database.
1987	First CD-ROM product released.
1988	Planning begins for 2000 Census.
1990	Entire nation Blocked for 1990 Census.
	Bicentennial Census takes place.
	Advances in computer technology allow more Census processing to take place in District Offices.

Figure 1-9

Summary

The Bicentennial Census paints a vivid picture of our nation's changing demographic patterns. Its final tally reveals a resident population of 248,709,873. The increase over 1980 is a mere 9.8%, representing the second-lowest decade of growth in the nation's history (the lowest was during the decade of the Great Depression). Perhaps more stunning is the fact that over one-quarter of this increase results from immigration alone. More than 85% of these new arrivals came here from Central America, Mexico, South America, and Asia. Cultural diversity isn't simply a slogan, it's a fact of modern life.

The country's largest minority group continues to be African Americans, making up 12.1% of the total population. Hispanics constitute 9% of the population, Asians 2.9% and Native Americans only 0.8%. Hispanics represent the fastest-growing minority group in raw numbers, but a quick look at percentage change shows the Asian-American population growing more rapidly. The Hispanic segment increased 53% over 1980, while the Asian segment grew by 107.8%.

America now boasts 39 Metropolitan Areas with populations of one million or more. A more telling fact is that fully one-half of all the nation's inhabitants lives in these 39 population centers. At the same time, our rural population continues to decline, as it has done for the past 200 years. Only 24.8% of the nation's inhabitants now live in rural areas.

We are also an aging population. The median age has increased to 32.8 years nationwide, up from 29.6 years in 1980. While the population at large has grown only slightly, the elderly segment has increased by 22%. One out of every eight residents is now age 65 or older.

Average household size in the United States also continues its decline. In 1980 it was 2.75 persons per household; now the figure is down to 2.63. Nearly 11 million families are headed by women with no husband present, an increase since 1980 of slightly over 25%.

At the same time, women continue to enter the labor market in increasing numbers. Nearly 57% of all adult women are now part of the civilian labor force.

These are just a few of the major demographic trends identified by the 1990 Census. Similar statistics are available for every geographic area and every population group which it covers. The remainder of this book will help the reader to locate, understand, and interpret these numbers. It begins with a discussion of how Census data are used, then continues with explanations of how the Census is taken, the terminology and concepts employed, the types of Census products available and how to use them properly, and the limitations inherent in the numbers. The book concludes with an examination of more specialized topics: rules affecting certain geographic constructs, an explanation of the Congressional apportionment process, a detailed look at a 1990 software product known as EXTRACT, and an introduction to the Bureau's Internet, online, and magnetic tape products.

Statistics are available for every geographic area and every population group which it covers. The remainder of this book will help the reader to locate, understand, and interpret these numbers.

Chapter 2

Uses of Census Data

I. Reapportionment and Redistricting
    A. Congressional Reapportionment
    B. Federal, State, and Local Redistricting
    C. State Censuses
II. Other Mandated Uses
    A. Funding Allocations
    B. Grant Applications
    C. Regulatory Compliance
III. Strategic Planning
    A. Community Planning
    B. Marketing and Site Selection
    C. Other Planning Applications
IV. Research Applications
    A. Demographic Benchmarking
    B. Academic Research
V. Personal Uses
    A. Genealogical Research
    B. Verifying Age and Identity
VI. Matching Census Data to Research Needs
VII. Summary

Chapter 2

Uses of Census Data

THE FUNDAMENTAL purpose of the Census, as mandated by the Constitution, is to reapportion seats in the U.S. House of Representatives. But from the beginning, George Washington, James Madison, and other like-minded framers of the Constitution realized the decennial Census could serve many other needs. It could provide a national inventory of human capital and help gauge the country's potential for growth. It could measure the nation's economic well-being, celebrate the vast diversity of its people, or identify areas of social distress. Over time, a continuing Census could become a barometer of national progress. And for 200 years, it has done all of that. But the Census does far more than paint a portrait of who we are as a nation, where we are going, and where we have been. It is used for a wide variety of specific purposes, by people from all walks of life. The value of the Census is limited only by the imaginations of those seeking to use it.

Questions asked by the decennial Census are designed primarily to meet the needs of the federal government. In fact, many applications of Census data are mandated by federal and state law. Principal mandated uses include Congressional reapportionment, legislative redistricting at all levels of government, the allocation of billions of dollars of federal and state aid, and numerous types of regulatory compliance. The federal government also employs Census figures in program planning and evaluation, budgeting, survey design, and research.

Census data are vital to many users outside the federal government as well, including marketers, entrepreneurs, human resource managers, lawyers, journalists, grant-writers, community planners, political activists, academic researchers, and genealogists. A 1987 report from the Congressional Research Service suggested that Census use by the business community alone far outweighs usage by the government. This chapter introduces some of the many ways in which Census information is put to use, beginning with Congressional reapportionment and other mandated functions, and ending with several examples of personal uses by individuals.

Q&A

With so many other sources of current data available, what makes the Census so special?

Three key features make the decennial Census unmatched by any other demographic, social, or economic survey. First is its universal coverage. The federal government is the only organization with the means to mount such a massive and costly undertaking, and the only one with the legal authority to compel everyone to participate. Second, because the Census utilizes standard methodologies, definitions, and geographic units, the resulting data are comparable everywhere in the country. Third, and most important, the Census is the *only* nationwide source of data for very small geographic areas. With information reported for Blocks, Block Groups, small towns, and remote rural areas, the Census is a vital resource for localized planning and analysis. Though it is only produced once every ten years, the Census is a unique and indispensable research tool.

Reapportionment and Redistricting

Census data are used to redistribute Congressional representation based on the population of the states, and indirectly, to allocate state representation in the Electoral College. Gaining or losing a Congressional seat is a momentous political event. For a state, it means an increase or decrease of power. For an individual Congressperson, it can mean political survival or death; if the state loses a seat, then someone will no longer have a District to represent.

Once the number of seats has been reapportioned among the states, the next step is to redraw Congressional District boundaries, an activity which also requires the use of Census data. The Constitution addresses reapportionment (and by implication, redistricting) only for the House of Representatives. Subsequent federal and state laws, together with state constitutions and a series of court cases, have extended this usage to include state and local legislatures as well. Thus every ten years, Census results have a profound impact on all levels of America's political landscape.

Congressional Reapportionment

The United States Constitution was the first in the world to mandate a recurring census of population. The delegates to the Federal Constitutional Convention were faced with determining a means of political representation that would be fair to small and large states alike. Small states favored equal representation, while large states endorsed proportional representation. The impasse was broken by the Great Compromise, which called for a House of Representatives, with membership allocated among the states according to population size, and an upper chamber with two Senators per state. Another controversy relating to the Census was the manner by which states would contribute payments to reduce the war debt. Delegates suggested that direct taxes also be imposed proportionally. In a census, each state would strive for a large population count to increase its political representation, but would prefer a lower count to reduce its share of the tax burden. The countervailing forces would help ensure an accurate Census count. However, direct taxation based on the Census turned out to

The United States Constitution was the first in the world to mandate a recurring census of population.

Thus every ten years, Census results have a profound impact on all levels of America's political landscape.

be impractical and was never implemented.

The relevant portion of the Constitution can be found as part of Article I, Section 2, which reads:

> Representatives and direct taxes shall be apportioned among the several States which may be included in this Union, according to their respective Numbers, which shall be determined by adding the whole Number of free Persons, including those bound to Service for a Term of Years, and excluding Indians not taxed, three-fifths of all other Persons. The actual Enumeration shall be made within three Years after the first Meeting of the Congress of the United States, and within every subsequent term of ten Years, in such Manner as they shall by Law direct.

"All other Persons" referred to the slave population. Southern states wanted to count slaves as persons for the purpose of apportionment; northern states wanted to exclude slaves from the count. The New Jersey Compromise resulted in the three-fifths rule, with every five slaves to count as three persons. Although slavery was abolished by the Thir-

---

Results of Congressional Reapportionment for 103rd Congress

Number of U.S. Representatives Gained or Lost by State Based on 1990 Census Results

Gainers		Losers	
California	+7	New York	-3
Florida	+4	Illinois	-2
Texas	+3	Michigan	-2
Arizona	+1	Ohio	-2
Georgia	+1	Pennsylvania	-2
North Carolina	+1	Iowa	-1
Virginia	+1	Kansas	-1
Washington	+1	Kentucky	-1
		Louisiana	-1
		Massachusetts	-1
		Montana	-1
		New Jersey	-1
		West Virginia	-1
Total Seats Gained	19	Total Seats Lost	19
Number of States	8	Number of States	13

Figure 2-1

NEW IN '90

New Congressional boundaries based on 1990 apportionment data took effect for the 103rd Congress, which convened in January, 1993. As shown in Figures 2-1 and 2-2, 19 seats shifted in the House of Representatives. Thirteen states, primarily in the northeast and midwest, lost one or more seats. Of the eight states which gained seats, all but one were located in the south or west. These changes illustrate a continuing shift in population, illustrated by the 1970/1990 comparison in Figure 2-3. The south and west accounted for 89% of the population growth in the 1980s and 90% in the 1970s.

---

teenth Amendment in 1865, the three-fifths rule was not explicitly revoked until ratification of the Fourteenth Amendment in 1868. Indentured servants were bound to their employers for "a Term of Years" (usually three to seven) only, and were otherwise considered free. Servitude of the colonial variety died out by the early 1800s, making the Constitution's phrasing largely irrelevant. Although contract labor remained legal throughout most of the 19th century, the "bound in Service" terminology was removed from the Fourteenth Amendment. (Later, the Foran Act of 1885 prohibited most employers from prepaying an immigrant's passage in return for contract labor.) "Indians not taxed" referred to those living on Reservations or in the Indian Territories. The Fourteenth Amendment retained the original language in this regard, and most Indians were excluded from the apportionment count until the 1940 Census.

The Constitution specifies a size range within which each state's representation must fall. Every state must have at least one Representative, but no more than one per 30,000 inhabitants. This means the smallest possible

"Indians not taxed" referred to those living on Reservations or in the Indian Territories. The Fourteenth Amendment retained the original language in this regard, and most aboriginal peoples were excluded from the apportionment count until the 1940 Census.

Changes in Congressional Delegations, 1980-1990

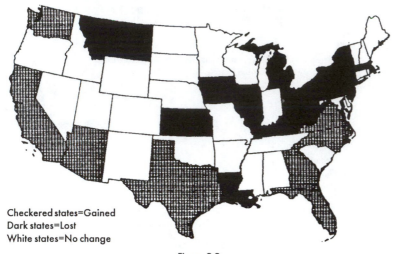

Checkered states=Gained
Dark states=Lost
White states=No change

Figure 2-2

1991.

Reapportionment affects not only Congressional representation, but allocation of electors in the Electoral College, the mechanism by which the President and Vice President are actually chosen following the popular vote. Article 2, Section I of the Constitution provides that each state shall appoint as many electors as it has members of Congress. The minimum number of electors per state is three, since every state is entitled to two Senators and at least one Representative.

Federal, State, and Local Redistricting

Congressional reapportionment triggers a second process called redistricting, which a cynic once defined as political homicide through cartography. If a state's Congressional allotment is reduced from four seats to three, boundaries must be redrawn to incorporate the change. But redistricting occurs even in states experiencing no apportionment changes. A series of U.S. Supreme Court decisions in the 1960s established the doctrine of "one person, one vote." Fair representation means one person's vote must carry the same weight as any other's, so each

> **Reapportionment affects not only Congressional representation, but allocation of electors in the Electoral College, the mechanism by which the President and Vice President are actually chosen following the popular vote.**

number of United States Representatives would be 50. The largest number, based on the 1990 Apportionment Population, would be 8,301 Representatives (249,022,783 divided by 30,000). For many years, however, the size of the House has remained fixed at 435 Representatives, and this is the number allocated among the states. Census law requires the Bureau to provide reapportionment statistics to the President within nine months of the Census date. The deadline for 1990 state apportionment totals was January 1,

Q&A

How are Census data used to reapportion Congressional Districts?

The Census Bureau plays a dual role in the apportionment process: first, by conducting the Census; and second, by calculating the number of Representatives to which each state is entitled. The Constitution does not specify how Districts are to be allocated, so Congress itself determines the method the Bureau must follow for redistributing Congressional seats.

The Bureau follows guidelines outlined in the Apportionment Act of 1941. Seats are allocated in such a way that each District contains approximately the same number of inhabitants, which is more difficult than it sounds. For many decades, the size of the Congressional delega-

tion increased to keep pace with a growing population, but the size of the House has been fixed at 435 since 1912. Because Districts cannot cross state lines, it is mathematically impossible to create equal representation across the country. The number of persons per Representative necessarily varies from one state to another, but the Supreme Court has ruled that every District must be "substantially equal." To minimize size differences, the Bureau utilizes a statistical technique called the Method of Equal Proportions to allocate seats among the states. Details of the process are described in Chapter 12.

member of Congress must represent the same approximate number of people. Although it is impossible to create Congressional Districts of equal population from one state to the next, equality can and must be achieved within a given state. Once the Bureau determines the number of Congressional seats for each state, it is up to the state legislatures or governors to redraw boundaries for their Congressional Districts.

"One person, one vote" also applies to state and local representation. By the 1960s, many states had not redrawn legislative boundaries for many decades, resulting in greater political power for rural areas. A more serious concern involved certain southern states, where gerrymandering intentionally disenfranchised black voters. (Gerrymandering is the redrawing of legislative districts to minimize the political power of an opposition group. It is named after an incident in 1812, when Massachusetts governor Elbridge Gerry's Jeffersonian Party rearranged election districts in the elongated shape of a salamander.) The political gerrymander remains a time-honored tradition, but redistricting along racial boundaries was struck down by a series of Supreme Court decisions, culminating in 1969 with Allen v. the State Board of Elections. Under the Voting Rights Act of 1965 and its amendments, the U.S. Justice Department is charged with monitoring and enforcing equal representation by race.

A 1975 amendment to the Census law established basic procedures for state redistricting. The governor of every state must

NEW IN '90

For 1990, 46 states participated in the Bureau's voluntary program for matching Voting District boundaries to Census Blocks; Kentucky, Mississippi, Montana, and Oregon were the only states which declined. In the previous decade, only 23 states were involved in the program.

Three additional innovations contributed to much more sophisticated analysis of 1990 redistricting data: the availability of PL 94-171 reports on CD-ROM; the Bureau's powerful TIGER geographic database, also on CD-ROM; and commercially produced desktop mapping software.

draft a plan describing how bipartisan redistricting will be accomplished. The plan must be submitted at least three years prior to the Census date, for approval by the U.S. Secretary of Commerce. The law also requires the Bureau to provide redistricting statistics to the governors within one year of the Census date (i.e., by April 1 of the following year). These figures are called PL 94-171 data, after the Public Law number of the 1975 Amendment. The law specifies only that total population counts be provided; any additional data are negotiated by the Census Bureau and the states.

A 1975 amendment to the Census law established basic procedures for state redistricting.

 Census Tip

The *Public Law 94-171 Data* series was published primarily for redistricting purposes. Because it was the first major 1990 Census product to be released, *Public Law 94-171 Data* was also used as an early source of basic population statistics for local areas. Once 1990 redistricting operations were completed, much of the data contained in these products became obsolete. Users should now consult other Census publications to obtain official 1990 statistics.

Net Gain or Loss by Region: Comparison of Apportionment Results from the Most Recent Two Censuses		
Region	1970/1980	1980/1990
Northeast	-9	-7
Midwest	-8	-8
South	+8	+7
West	+9	+8

Figure 2-3

Redistricting numbers are issued in the form of printouts, computer tapes, and CD-ROM disks entitled _Public Law 94-171 Data._ In addition to state population totals, 1990 tabulations are shown for every political geography within the state, as well as for Tracts, Block Groups, and Census Blocks. Data tables list total population and voting-age population; all totals are further divided by race and Hispanic Origin.

Under a voluntary program with the states, the Bureau supplies Block maps to the appropriate redistricting agency in every state prior to the Census date. For the 1990 Census, maps were provided in 1989. The state agencies then superimpose existing Voting District boundaries, and return the maps to the Bureau. As a result, the Bureau can tabulate PL 94-171 data for statewide Voting Districts, though these boundaries do not always conform exactly to Block groupings. When PL 94-171 tabulations are presented to the states, they are accompanied by computer-drawn maps of Census Blocks and Voting Districts. A designated state agency then coordinates redistricting for the state legislature. A similar process takes place for counties, cities, and other local jurisdictions.

Census data are used to create legislative districts of equal population and to ensure racially balanced representation, but the Census Bureau's responsibility ends when PL 94-171 reports are supplied. The manner by which state and local districts are redrawn is governed by the Voting Rights Act, as well as by state constitutions, municipal charters, and state and local laws. In most cases, a special task force, a local planning agency, or legislative staff members analyze the Census data and recommend new boundaries for the proposed districts. The final boundaries are determined through the political process, often by the legislative bodies themselves. The ability to provide Census data for existing Voting Districts is crucial because politicians need to assess the impact of changing boundaries on party affiliation. PL 94-171 data allow those involved in redistricting to compare 1990 population to local voter registration patterns and voter behavior data.

State Censuses

For many years, individual states conducted their own mid-decade censuses upon which apportionment decisions for state legislatures were based. New York State, for example, conducted a decennial census from 1795 to 1925. Wisconsin conducted five censuses between 1836 and 1847, followed by a decennial census from 1855 to 1905. Many territories sponsored one or more censuses in preparation for their admission to the Union as states (e.g., Kansas in 1855 and 1859; Montana census in 1885). Only 17 states have never conducted their own census. State enumerations were usually less detailed and less accurate than corresponding federal Censuses. Due to the complexity and expense of these endeavors, state census-taking gradually disappeared, and any legal requirements specified by state constitutions were amended. At the height of state census- taking in the mid-19th century, 24 states or territories were involved. In 1905, 15 states conducted their own censuses; by 1945, the number had dwindled to four. After 1955, only two states continued to take a census: Kansas and Massachusetts.

 Census Tip

State censuses can be an excellent source for historical and genealogical research. A complete listing of state censuses was compiled by Henry J. Dubester and published by the Library of Congress in 1948. A microfilm compilation of state census publications, based on Dubester's bibliography, has been issued by Kraus International Publications (formerly KTO Microform) of Millwood, New York.

Under the Kansas state constitution, legislative reapportionment occurred in the ninth year of every decade, making it impractical to utilize federal Census data. A decennial census, conducted for more than 100 years by the Kansas Department of Agriculture, was abolished in 1979. Because the constitutional requirement for a ninth-year reapportionment remained, a special law was passed authorizing a 1988 census. This headcount emulated federal Census procedures, employed 1,500 temporary enumerators, another 3,000 clerical workers, and cost approximately $3 million. In November, 1988, a constitutional amendment was ratified which mandated state apportionment in the third year of each decade, effectively tying the process to release of federal Census data.

The Massachusetts census was also based on a provision of its state constitution, but it did not involve a traditional enumeration. Instead, the Secretary of State would instruct city and town clerks to count the number of residents through use of administrative records. To encourage cooperation, municipalities were paid one dollar for every inhabitant counted. This imprecise process took place every ten years, in years ending in five. The 1985 census cost $5.7 million in payments to municipalities plus $800,000 in administrative expenses. Following Kansas's lead, Massachusetts approved a constitutional amendment abolishing its state census in November, 1990. Thus Massachusetts has the distinction of being the last state to abolish its requirement for a state census (in 1990), while Kansas was the last state to actually conduct one (in 1988).

Other Mandated Uses

The government relies on Census data for many other purposes besides Congressional reapportionment and redistricting. In fact, federal and state laws specify that Census statistics must be used for government funding allocations, grant applications, and regulatory compliance. One of the Bureau's 1990 *Content Determination Reports*, entitled *Federal Uses of Decennial Census Data*, cited several hundred federal laws mandating more than 500 specific uses of the decennial Census.

Funding Allocations

Billions of dollars of federal aid are distributed to states and local communities according to formulas based on decennial Census figures. For example, the allocation formula for the Adult Education Act includes a variable for the number of people over age 18 with fewer than five years of school. Among other major programs incorporating Census figures in their formula grants are highway planning and construction; airport improvements; job training for the disadvantaged; medical facilities for inner cities and rural areas; the Head Start Program; minority business development; Community Development Block Grants; the school breakfast program; low income rental assistance; bilingual education; the supplemental food program for Women, Infants, and Children (WIC); Medicaid; rehabilitation of public housing; alcohol, drug abuse, and mental health services; and transportation services for the elderly and disabled. A wide array of federal agencies are involved in these programs, including the Federal Highway Administration, the Farmers Home Administration, the Economic Development Administration, and the Departments of Agriculture, Education, Health and Human Services, Housing and Urban Development, Transportation, and Labor. Most funds are allocated to the states, which in turn distribute them to local areas, but some programs provide grants directly to counties or other sub-state jurisdictions.

Some allocation formulas specify the use of decennial data even when more current sources are available. Other formulas request data which are only found in the Census. For example, the Census is the only official government source which distinguishes popula-

The government relies on Census data for many other purposes besides Congressional reapportionment and redistricting.

Billions of dollars of federal aid are distributed to states and local communities according to formulas based on decennial Census figures.

Q&A

Exactly how much federal money is allocated based on decennial Census data?

A definitive amount is difficult to determine. One reason is variance from year to year: for each fiscal year, total appropriations change, as do the number and type of grant programs, and the allocation formulas themselves. More important, every grant program utilizes a different formula, many of which are only partly based on decennial Census data. Some formulas tie a percentage of total outlays to the amount received the year before. Others distribute some money to the states on an equal basis, and the rest according to population or housing variables. Certain outlays are dependent on matching grants from state or local governments. Some programs include non-Census data in their formulas, including such measures as miles of highway or number of beneficiaries currently receiving the service. Programs may also use data sources more current than the decennial Census, including inter-censal estimates of population and per capita income, local unemployment rates, or school enrollment figures.

A 1991 study from the General Accounting Office identified 100 federal programs which included population data in their allocation formulas in FY 1991, with total outlays of $116 billion. Of these, only 30 programs used population data from the decennial Census alone, with outlays of $33.4 billion. The amount of federal money tied in some way to Census data is probably somewhat higher than this, but it serves as a good ballpark figure. In recent years, articles in the popular press have tended to cite numbers ranging from $25 to $40 billion in yearly federal aid.

The Department of Housing and Urban Development's (HUD) Community Development Block Grant Program is a typical example of a federal formula grant which incorporates Census data.

tion information for urban and rural areas. Census data are also used to establish eligibility thresholds. For example, only Urbanized Areas are eligible for certain health care and transportation funds, and Urbanized Areas are designated by the decennial Census.

The Department of Housing and Urban Development's (HUD) Community Development Block Grant Program is a typical example of a federal formula grant which incorporates Census data. The program actually comprises several specific grants covering the following political units: states; American Indian tribes and Alaska Native Villages; and large metropolitan cities and counties. Grants are used for neighborhood revitalization, economic development, and improvement of community facilities and services. Emphasis must be placed on projects which improve conditions for low- and moderate-income persons, eliminate slums or areas of urban blight, or improve conditions which pose a serious threat to the community's health and welfare. Grant money can be used for a wide range of activities, including rehabilitation of buildings, acquisition of real property, and improvement of public facilities such as water and sewer systems. Political entities may only receive funding under one of the grant components; metropolitan cities may not receive additional federal funds from their county, and urban counties may not receive additional funds from their state. Two formulas are used to calculate disbursements, with each political entity receiving the higher amount of the two. The decennial Census variables employed are total resident population, number of persons with income below the poverty level, number of Housing Units with 1.01 persons or more per room, number of Housing Units built in 1939 or earlier, and lag in population growth from 1960 to the present.

State governments utilize Census data in ways similar to their federal counterparts. It is estimated that an additional $40 billion per year in state funding allocations are based on Census data.

Census Tip

Summary information about the statistical variables incorporated in federal formula grants can be found in the U.S. General Service Administration's *Catalog of Federal Domestic Assistance*, published annually with mid-year updates.

Grant Applications

The other side of the funding issue involves grant applications. Under government allocation formulas, states or local governments often obtain funds without specifying projects in advance. To receive annual disbursements, governments simply submit paperwork indicating their desire to participate in the program, verifying their eligibility, and providing the necessary statistics utilized by the allocation formula. At the end of each year, the government submits a report describing how the funds were used.

In contrast, many grant programs require detailed applications, accompanied by explanations of the planned project and how the money will be spent. Applications may be made at the federal, state, or even local level, depending on the program. As described above, portions of HUD's Community Development Block Grant monies are allocated by formula to county governments. Individual communities may then apply to the county for funds to be used for specific improvement projects, from renovating a senior citizen center to providing handicapped access to public buildings.

Grant-writers use Census data to justify need and identify the size and characteristics of the population to be served. The following examples illustrate ways in which government agencies have utilized the Census to obtain funding for specific projects:

- A school district identified Block Groups with high concentrations of

Hispanic households, low median rents, and large numbers of single-parent households. A grant was obtained for a special pre-school program for Hispanic children.

- To qualify for additional federal assistance, a state emergency services agency used Census data to show that a community hit by tornado had large percentages of elderly, unemployed, and low-income persons.

Similarly, nonprofit organizations submit statistics on their service population when applying for funding, whether from government agencies, private foundations, or other sources. For example, United Way agencies must submit annual service profiles before receiving funds from this charitable organization. Some information can be obtained from an organization's internal records, but Census data are indispensable for identifying the number of potential clients not being reached. Because community-based groups need to describe the characteristics of their neighborhoods, Census Tract and Block Group data are especially useful.

Regulatory Compliance

Federal and state agencies rely on Census data to monitor compliance with numerous laws and regulations. Under the U.S. Jury Act, the Department of Justice looks at population characteristics to ensure that juries represent a cross-section of their communities. The Justice Department also utilizes Census data to enforce the Voting Rights Act. School districts whose desegregation plans are subject to continuing supervision by federal courts must use the Census to help track their progress. Other agencies which utilize Census data in this way include the Labor department's Office of Federal Contract Compliance, the Equal Employment Opportunity Commission, and the Environmental Protection Agency.

The other side of the funding issue involves grant applications. Under government allocation formulas, states or local governments often obtain funds without specifying projects in advance.

Federal and state agencies rely on Census data to monitor compliance with numerous laws and regulations.

To conduct business in a lawful manner, companies also must submit Census data to various regulatory agencies. Under the Home Mortgage Disclosure Act, banks must compare characteristics of recent mortgage recipients to racial data at the Census Tract level; bank regulators use these reports to ensure that lenders do not engage in discriminatory practices. Utility companies compare their customer records to Census data to show they are reaching households in rural areas. Project planners in all industries incorporate Census figures when drafting mandatory Environmental Impact Statements. Before approving new commercial development—a new shopping mall, a waste disposal facility, a natural gas pipeline—state and local governments require companies to assess the impact of the project on its surrounding communities. Environmental Impact Statements typically include population, housing, and commuting statistics in their analysis.

Census Tip

The Bureau produces a special database, called the *Equal Employment Opportunity File*, which is available on computer tape or CD-ROM. This product provides age, race, sex, and Hispanic Origin breakdowns for six broad employment categories, for the unemployed with work experience, and for several hundred individual occupations. Data are presented for the United States, states, Metropolitan Areas, counties, and Places and Minor Civil Divisions with populations of 50,000 or more.

The Civil Rights Act of 1964 and other federal and state laws prohibit discrimination in the work place. Establishments employing 100 or more workers, together with federal contractors receiving more than $50,000 in government revenues and em-ploying 50 or more workers, must submit annual reports on their labor force composition to the Equal Employment Opportunity Commission. Employers' occupational data by race, sex, and Hispanic Origin are compared with labor force characteristics for the surrounding geographic area from which they recruit applicants. Comparisons are made for broad job groups or for individual occupations, then labor utilization rates are calculated. If the resulting rate for women or minority members is too low, the employer should consider affirmative action to correct the imbalance. For example, if 9% of an employer's machine operators are Black, but 18% of all machine operators in the surrounding community are Black, that employer's utilization rate for machine operators is only 50%. Many employers exempt from EEO guidelines also utilize Census data on labor force composition, recognizing the value of maintaining a diverse work force, and the importance of guarding against potential lawsuits.

Another mandated application of Census data involves the established authority of local governments under state law. The powers of a particular political entity, including the ability to levy certain taxes, are determined by its population size as well as its incorporation status. Cities in New York State, for example, must have a minimum population of 5,000 to qualify for an independent police force.

Strategic Planning

The Census is an important source of information for long- and short-term planning decisions. Here again, federal agencies are the primary intended users, but the Census is also vital to state and local governments, businesses, and nonprofit organizations. The government uses Census data to identify program needs, study historical trends, and measure the effectiveness of existing programs. For example, the National Endowment for the Arts uses Census figures to

To conduct business in a lawful manner, companies also must submit Census data to various regulatory agencies.

The Census is an important source of information for long- and short-term planning decisions.

study the employment status of artists. The National Science Foundation looks at Census data to monitor the status of women and minorities in science and engineering. The Bureau of Labor Statistics incorporates Census data into its projections of future occupational supply and demand. VISTA, ACTION, and the Foster Grandparent Program depend on the Census to target geographic areas in need of their services. Among the many other federal agencies which use the Census for planning purposes are the Small Business Administration, the Department of Agriculture, the National Council on the Handicapped, and the National Center for Health Statistics.

The following sections describe some of the many applications of Census data for community planning, marketing, site selection, capital budgeting, and other planning purposes.

Community Planning

For local governments, the Census is an essential resource for comprehensive planning. To promote livable communities, agencies at the municipal, county, and regional levels must develop long-range plans to determine the best uses of land and other public resources. Land use planning leads to changes in zoning ordinances, which regulate the types and intensity of use which a given parcel of land may have. Among the Census variables important to land use planning are population density, population growth, distribution of Housing Units, and commuting patterns. Communities experiencing intensive population build-up must engage in growth management: controlling the impact of rapid growth by limiting commercial and industrial development, over-building, and destruction of natural resources. Housing data are especially important for community planning, to assess the quality of the housing stock, study residential stability, establish minimum housing standards, and determine the availability of affordable housing.

School Districts are heavy users of Census data. The figures are used to redraw school district boundaries, assess the need for expanded facilities, anticipate demand for special education programs, and implement new services. Planning for new school buildings must begin years in advance of the actual need, so school officials must keep abreast of changing population patterns. Many Districts which sold buildings due to declining enrollments in the early 1980s were caught unawares by a new baby boomlet, as large numbers of working women opted to have children at a later age.

One of the most interesting uses of Census data is for disaster preparedness. Civil defense agencies, fire departments, and other groups providing emergency services depend upon local Census numbers to develop evacuation and assistance plans. When Springfield, Massachusetts experienced a large leak of deadly chlorine gas in the summer of 1988, emergency workers moved quickly into areas with special evacuation needs, including those with large concentrations of elderly residents and foreign-language speakers. Targeted neighborhoods had been identified in advance through the use of Census reports. Similarly, when St. Louis, Missouri suffered an unprecedented heat wave, Census data helped identify neighborhoods with older residents living alone; a door-to-door campaign was then mounted to assist those whose health was endangered by the heat.

Census reports on small areas are especially useful for identifying pockets of need in the community. Census figures at the Tract or Block Group level can help pinpoint areas of poverty, high unemployment, substandard housing, or large concentrations of non-English speakers. Public services, such as housing rehabilitation, subsidized rent or utility programs, health clinics, bilingual education classes, vocational training, or Meals on Wheels programs can then be targeted where they are needed most. Planning for services can focus on areas as small as a city block. While sample data such as income and educational attainment are not available at the Census Block level, 100%

One of the most interesting uses of Census data is for disaster preparedness.

Census reports on small areas are especially useful for identifying pockets of need in the community.

characteristics, such as age, race, household composition, housing value, and rental payments, are important indicators of economic and social conditions within Census Blocks. Communities can also use Blocks as the basis for reconfiguring their service boundaries—police precincts, sewer districts, and the like—or for establishing neighborhood planning areas. Without small-area data from the Census, a tremendous burden would be placed on local governments to collect and tabulate their own statistics, an effort which many communities have neither the money nor expertise to handle.

Marketing and Site Selection

Business firms of every type and size utilize Census data to target their marketing areas, assess the potential for new products or services, select locations for retail or service sites, and design advertising, direct mail, or promotional campaigns. Large corporations can usually afford to pay for commercially-produced demographic information, but they too turn to the Census for its wealth of data.

In an age of increasingly specialized niche marketing, mail order companies use demographic characteristics of ZIP Code Areas to target direct mail campaigns. Major food manufacturers examine Census data when trying to determine the amount of shelf space their products should have in particular supermarket locations. Media buyers look to Census products when designing advertising campaigns. Given the proliferation of extremely targeted cable TV networks, such as the Nostalgia Channel, Telemundo, or MTV, the Census can provide objective data to help determine which audience has the most buying power. Magazine publishers, television networks, and radio stations also use Census figures to attract advertisers, bolstering claims that their audience has more desirable characteristics. Sales managers find the Census helpful in setting boundaries for sales territories and establishing sales quotas.

Manufacturers utilize the information to forecast sales, design new products, and change their product mix.

Analysis of demographic data can help marketers anticipate changing trends in consumer attitudes, behaviors, and lifestyles. Age, race, sex, household composition, education, and income all relate in some way to demand for consumer goods. Marketers were quick to exploit changes shown by the 1980 Census. Growth in single-person households, for example, prompted companies to introduce single-serving portions of packaged foods, while an increase in dual-career couples was accompanied by the advent of all-night supermarkets, gourmet microwavable dinners, and nationwide chains of day-care centers.

Baby boomers have had a remarkable impact on marketing trends throughout the past several decades by virtue of the group's sheer size. Demographers and other social scientists are quick to point out that the baby boom extended over many years, making it difficult to generalize about a single population cohort. Nevertheless, marketers remain attuned to the changing interests of boomers and their families. (Evidence of this continuing love affair can be found in a successful marketing newsletter called the *Boomer Report*). As this influential generation ages, implications for consumer products and services are manifold. Boomers' new-found preoccupation with health concerns has prompted a proliferation of such new products as plaque-fighting mouthwash, toothpaste for sensitive gums, turkey bacon, and low-salt snack foods. Restaurants are offering more vegetarian fare and health clubs are gearing advertising to more sedentary married couples rather than svelte, fashion-conscious singles. Less strenuous hobbies and sports are gaining in popularity. Alcohol consumption continues to fall. Cosmetic surgery is on the increase, as are sales of hair-loss and skin-care products. Predicting consumer trends based on demographic projections is always a haphazard enterprise, but marketers ignore Census data

Business firms of every type and size utilize Census data to target their marketing areas, assess the potential for new products or services, select locations for retail or service sites, and design advertising, direct mail, or promotional campaigns.

Boomers' new-found preoccupation with health concerns has prompted a proliferation of such new products as plaque-fighting mouthwash, toothpaste for sensitive gums, turkey bacon, and low-salt snack foods.

Predicting consumer trends based on demographic projections is always a haphazard enterprise, but marketers ignore Census data at their peril.

at their peril.

Real estate developers, franchisors, and new business owners rely on the Census when selecting sites for specialty stores, banks, restaurants, fast food outlets, and other retail or service locations. Because Census data are presented for numerous levels of geography, site analysis can be done whether the appropriate market area is a local neighborhood or a metropolitan area. The Census is especially useful because business people can look beyond standard geographies such as cities or townships, and incorporate information about surrounding areas in their analysis. To illustrate the diversity of ways the Census can be used in site-selection decisions, consider the following examples. An orthodontist, seeking to relocate his practice, sought communities with large numbers of teenagers and above-average median household income. A new business owner, looking for a suitable location for her hardware store, combined Census data on age of structure and year-moved-in to identify Census Tracts with large numbers of new homeowners living in older houses.

Real estate brokers rely on small-area data to compare monthly rent, market value, age of the housing stock, and other neighborhood statistics. (In 1987, when it looked as though many of the traditional housing questions would be deleted from the 1990 Questionnaire due to budget pressures, the National Association of Realtors volunteered its membership to help conduct the Census. Happily, such drastic measures were not required.)

Governments and

Because Census data are presented for numerous levels of geography, site analysis can be done whether the appropriate market area is a local neighborhood or a metropolitan area.

nonprofit organizations also engage in marketing. The Defense Department uses the Census to help set military recruitment quotas, to locate recruiting offices, and to target direct mail campaigns. Charitable groups set fund-raising goals by geographic area. Service organizations such as Big Brothers of America use data on family composition, poverty rates, and other Census information to estimate the number of volunteers needed per area. Churches, museums, cultural organizations, libraries, hospitals, and community-based human service agencies use Census information to choose locations for service outlets and plan new programs. Data from the Census help these organizations to know more about the people they serve, and to target groups with special needs such as the poor, the aged, handicapped, working mothers, veterans, those who don't speak English, and adults with no high school diploma. Because Census publications are inexpensive and readily available, they are one of the main research tools used by nonprofit agencies.

NEW IN '90

The desktop computing revolution of the 1980s has created what one veteran observer of market demographics termed "the liberation of Census data." In order to manipulate 1980 Census figures or create customized reports, users needed mainframe computers or large minicomputers, plus trained programmers. Now that virtually all major 1990 Census reports are available on CD-ROM, users can extract data, perform complex analyses, and print the results in myriad formats, all on a personal computer. Identifying counties with the highest percentage of college graduates, for example, is a reasonably simple task. By purchasing commercially-produced mapping software, together with the Bureau's *TIGER Line Files* on CD-ROM, marketers can also generate customized maps of Census data, juxtapose their own customer data with Census characteristics, and create arresting visual displays unthought of in previous decades.

Other Planning Applications

Governments, large corporations, and small businesses alike employ Census statistics when drafting budgets, making capital expenditure decisions, assessing human resource needs, and planning transportation routes. The federal government includes demographic data in its annual budget analysis, especially to help project the number of people or households which will qualify for particular social programs.

Local governments use the Census when planning such capital improvements as extending water and sewer lines, widening highways, building libraries or community centers, and so on. Private industry turns to Census numbers for similar capital investment decisions. For example, public utility companies use data on the number of households, fuel type, and related facts to help forecast energy demand; plan investments in plants and equipment; close down, retool, or relocate existing facilities; and anticipate revenues.

Many factors determine where a company will locate a new manufacturing plant, warehouse, or administrative facility, but a major concern is an adequate supply of skilled workers. Planners look at numbers of workers in particular occupational groups, levels of educational attainment in the community, commuting patterns, numbers of people ready to enter the labor force, and overall population growth. Or they may look for more specific labor needs. When locating a major operator assistance center, one major phone company seeks areas with sufficient numbers of housewives without college educations.

Labor force data are important for other types of planning activities as well. Personnel officers in all types of organizations use the Census to forecast labor supply, assess future training needs, and plan recruitment activities. Detailed and affordable information is critical to entrepreneurs planning a small business venture. For start-up companies which provide consumer products or services, Census publications can help business owners estimate market potential. Such estimates are major components of a business plan, a pro forma cash flow statement, or a loan application.

Census reports are useful for a variety of transportation management decisions. Local governments consult the Census when locating bus stops or traffic signals, building parking lots, and setting speed limits. Trucking companies, package delivery firms, and other businesses involved in the movement of goods or people utilize TIGER, the Census Bureau's geographic database, to improve their routes. One analysis of the $600 billion transportation services industry estimated that computerized route planning could cut delivery costs by 5-15%.

Research Applications

Census data are vital components of numerous research activities, from academic studies to government surveys. Researchers use the Census to study characteristics of specific population groups or geographic areas, to track changes over time, to estimate population size and characteristics between Census years, and to forecast demographic trends.

Demographic Benchmarking

One of the most prevalent applications of the decennial Census is as a benchmark for other demographic research. Although it is only conducted every ten years, the Census's comprehensive scope, wide-ranging subject coverage, and unparalleled geographic detail make it the definitive starting point for all other demographic analysis. Three major benchmarking applications are worth discussing: designing sample surveys, calculating demographic estimates and projections,

Personnel officers in all types of organizations use the Census to forecast labor supply, assess future training needs, and plan recruitment activities.

Census data are vital components of numerous research activities, from academic studies to government surveys.

One of the most prevalent applications of the decennial Census is as a benchmark for other demographic research.

and developing consumer databases.

Survey research is an increasingly important source of information in our society, including public opinion polls, market research reports, and government surveys of all types. A valid sample must closely resemble the population universe it attempts to approximate. This means that survey takers must have concrete data with which to compare. Survey benchmarking involves two steps: designing the sampling method prior to the survey, and following the survey, properly weighting the results to make estimates about the entire population. Without a detailed, comprehensive, and accurate Census, sample surveys would not be possible.

Many important government surveys utilize Census data in sample design.

Many important government surveys utilize Census data in sample design. Among those which utilize Census data to create sampling frames are HUD's survey of metropolitan housing quality, and unemployment estimates from the BLS. Census data are also used in constructing complex economic indicators such as the Consumer Price Index and the Gross Domestic Product.

Census benchmarking is vital to certain types of demographic analysis which do not involve sample surveys.

Census benchmarking is vital to certain types of demographic analysis which do not involve sample surveys. The most notable of these is the calculation of inter-censal population estimates and the forecasting of long-term population projections. The detailed picture provided by the Census every ten years enables researchers to estimate conditions between decades and to forecast future population, especially at the local level. For both types of analysis, the starting point is the most recent decennial Census.

Techniques of population estimates and projections are beyond the scope of this book, but a brief discussion of commercial providers of demographic data is appropriate. Such major companies as National Demographics & Lifestyles, CACI Marketing, Claritas/NPDC, and Donnelley Demographics combine population statistics with consumer information from a variety of sources to create profiles which enable marketers to target their advertising, direct mail, distribution, and promotional efforts more efficiently. These data providers offer a variety of services, including population estimates and projections for local areas, customized market reports for specified geographies, and the ability to match the characteristics of clients' existing customer lists with those of potential target markets.

One such approach is geodemographic clustering, a technique pioneered by Jonathan Robbin, founder of Claritas, in the early 1970s. This methodology employs market surveys of consumer behavior and expenditure patterns to generate demographic profiles of households exhibiting particular lifestyles. Census data can then be used to identify ZIP Code Areas with the heaviest concentrations of households meeting those demographic and housing characteristics. Erik Larson, author of the 1992 book *The Naked Consumer,* refers to marketing tools using geodemographic clustering and similar methodologies as "recombinant data products" because they merge Census statistics with information from other sources to create detailed profiles of different market segments.

American Demographics magazine, which has tracked the burgeoning demographic data industry since 1979, now identifies more than 350 companies which specialize in providing information on consumer demographics. In the 1970s, Census figures were a major component of these statistical products. Commercial data companies now have access to many other information sources, including household mailing lists, massive consumer surveys, manufacturers' warranty cards, and supermarket scanner data. Today, leading private data companies downplay the value of Census data in their overall product mix, but at the very least, the Census is a primary means of benchmarking and evaluating the accuracy of their market estimates.

Academic Research

The academic community also uses Census information extensively. Social scientists obtain data to study quality of life, composition of households and families, occupational patterns, and a host of other concerns. Sociologists, political scientists, economists, demographers, and geographers are particularly heavy users of the Census. Demographic data are sure to be a component used to study problems as varied as the effect of unemployment on crime or the relationship between family size and income. Sociologists incorporate Census results when analyzing changing social trends, such as women marrying at a later age, or grown children returning to live with their parents. Examples of similar uses include:

- the relationship of earnings to educational attainment
- earnings differentials by age, race, or sex
- social mobility from one generation to the next
- the role of gender in occupational choice
- living arrangements of the elderly
- patterns of housing segregation
- the assimilation of recent immigrant groups

Medical researchers also rely on Census data to study rates of illness or disease among different segments of the population. In order to compare their own data on the incidence of disease, researchers need to know the total size and characteristics of the various population groups in the study.

The field of history provides an excellent example of the richness of Census data for academic research. The abundant detail provided by the Census is an endless laboratory for social and economic historians, whether tracing changes from one decade to the next, or analyzing demographic patterns during a particular point in time. In some cases, historians pour over the actual Census returns of individuals, much as they would study old diaries, letters, or other primary documents. In other cases, they turn to aggregated statistical reports. The University of Illinois's Supercomputer History Project, for example, analyzes dozens of statistical variables across hundreds of individual counties, seeking demographic patterns which can help explain historical developments.

The abundant detail provided by the Census is an endless laboratory for social and economic historians, whether tracing changes from one decade to the next, or analyzing demographic patterns during a particular point in time.

Census Tip

In addition to standard Census products, social scientists can use a set of special computer files called the *Public Use Microdata Sample (PUMS)*. Unlike other Census information, *PUMS* allows researchers to study characteristics of individual people or households, rather than aggregate statistics. *PUMS* provides a sampling of individual Census returns, stripped of all identifying information so individual privacy is assured. Because individual responses are shown, *PUMS* allows researchers to retabulate Census information as though they had conducted the survey themselves.

Census Tip

To graphically illustrate the movement of population over time, the Census Bureau has developed a concept known as the geographic center of population. The center of population is that point at which an imaginary flat, weightless, and rigid map of the United States would balance if every person in the country weighed the same. Figure 2-4 depicts the westward (and more recently, the southwestward) movement of the population center, from 1790 to 1990.

Census data enables historians to examine changing trends in family structure, occupations, or literacy, and to compare characteristics across population groups—property ownership, income distribution, or duration of residence, to cite a few examples. They can study overarching topics such as urban growth or the progression of westward migration. Perhaps more important, Census data allows historians to examine small populations, such as self-employed women or individuals institutionalized in mental hospitals, or specific geographic areas, such as a single frontier town. One of the most fertile areas of Census-based research is the study of Black American history. Historians have used Census data to contrast the characteristics of large and small slaveholders, study the role of Freedmen during Reconstruction, and trace the migration of southern Blacks to the north in the early 20th century.

Comparing two successive Censuses can be helpful in measuring significant changes in American life. As an example, the decade between 1910 and 1920 saw massive waves of European immigration, the monumental devastation wrought by World War I, and a deadly influenza pandemic. Similar comparisons are valuable at the regional or local levels as well. The 1920 Census, for example, offers a last look at Florida before its first great population and investment boom.

The most famous use of Census data by a historian was Frederick Jackson Turner's "The Significance of the Frontier in American History," a paper he first delivered at the 1893 meeting of the American Historical Association. This brief essay, which profoundly influenced several generations of future historians, attributed the development of the American character to the abundance of unsettled land and the ability of the nation to continually expand westward. Turner, then a young historian at the University of Wisconsin, was inspired by the 1890 Census

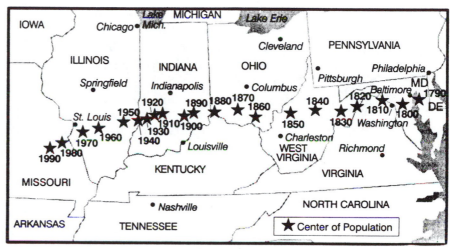

No. 3. Center of Population: 1790 to 1990

["Center of population" is that point at which an imaginary flat, weightless, and rigid map of the United States would balance if weights of identical value were placed on it so that each weight represented the location of one person on the date of the census]

YEAR	North latitude			West longitude			Approximate location
	°	′	″	°	′	″	
1790 (August 2)	39	16	30	76	11	12	23 miles east of Baltimore, MD
1850 (June 1)	38	59	0	81	19	0	23 miles southeast of Parkersburg, WV
1900 (June 1)	39	9	36	85	48	54	6 miles southeast of Columbus, IN
1950 (April 1)	38	50	21	88	9	33	8 miles north–northwest of Olney, Richland County, IL
1960 (April 1)	38	35	58	89	12	35	In Clinton Co. about 6 1/2 miles northwest of Centralia, IL
1970 (April 1)	38	27	47	89	42	22	5.3 miles east–southeast of the Mascoutah City Hall in St. Clair County, IL
1980 (April 1)	38	8	13	90	34	26	1/4 mile west of De Soto in Jefferson County, MO
1990 (April 1)	37	52	20	91	12	55	9.7 miles southeast of Steelville, MO

Figure 2-4   Source: Statistical Abstract of the United States

to pen his influential essay. Robert B. Porter, the Superintendent of the 1890 Census, had recently written:

> Up to and including 1880 the country had a frontier of settlement, but at present the unsettled area has been so broken into by isolated bodies of settlement that there can hardly be said to be a frontier line.

This obituary for the western frontier was itself prompted by the observation that nowhere in 1890 was there a territory with fewer than two persons per square mile.

Personal Uses

Individuals can turn to Census products to meet certain needs in their everyday lives. One such need relates to community involvement. Parents seeking funding for a new playground or an after-school program,

The most famous use of Census data by a historian was Frederick Jackson Turner's "The Significance of the Frontier in American History."

homeowners fighting a planned hazardous waste site in their neighborhood, a community group opposing excessive development in their town—all benefit from using Census data to support their positions. Two uniquely personal applications also come to mind: age verification and genealogical research.

Genealogical Research

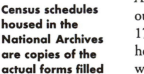

As of this writing, microfilm copies of all existing records from 1790 through 1920 are available to the public.

Although Title 13 of the *U.S. Code* protects the confidentiality of Census records for living persons, Title 44 specifies that older Census schedules must be made public after 72 years. As of this writing, microfilm copies of all existing records from 1790 through 1920 are available to the public. Genealogists and historians eagerly await each decade's release of previously confidential information. Microfilm records of the 1920 Census, consisting of 2,076 reels of population schedules and 8,500 index reels, were opened to the public in March, 1992. In the initial months following the data's release, 350 researchers per day flocked to the National Archives's Washington facility alone.

Census schedules housed in the National Archives are copies of the actual forms filled out for every family or household. From 1790 through 1840, only the head of household's name was recorded. Beginning with 1850, names of all household members are shown. Records from two Censuses have been destroyed by fire. 1790 schedules from six states or territories were burned by the British during the War of 1812; schedules from the remaining eleven states and territories remain intact. Virtually all 1890 Census records were destroyed in a 1921 fire. A few fragments were salvaged, representing a handful of local areas and covering a meager 6,000 family names.

Census reels are arranged by decade, then by state and county. A single reel may contain schedules for one or more counties. For the most recent available decades, schedules are listed within county by Enumeration

District—the boundaries established by the Bureau for conducting that decade's Census. To locate information on a particular family, researchers must have a fairly good idea where the family lived at the time of the Census, then identify the appropriate Enumeration District for that street. Many commercially-produced finding aids have been created to assist genealogists in their research, including surname indexes to the Census reels of many states. The National Archives maintains street-name indexes to Enumeration Districts for some Censuses. Soundex indexes of surnames for the Censuses of 1880, 1900, and 1920, and for 21 states of 1910 are also available. The Soundex files are microfilm reproductions of 3x5" cards, arranged according to the phonetic spelling of each family name. For example, the names Magee, McGee, MacKee, and similar variations would all be filed under the Soundex code M 200, while variations of Burke are filed under B 620. Soundex records list the name, age, and birth place of every household member, including cross-references from persons whose names differ from those of their household heads.

 Census Tip

Microfilm reels can be viewed at the National Archives headquarters or any of its 11 Regional Archives. Copies of individual reels can also be purchased or rented from the National Archives. Many public and academic libraries, state archives, and historical societies maintain collections of Census microfilm for their state or local area, as do genealogical libraries maintained by the Church of Jesus Christ of Latter Day Saints.

Census schedules on microfilm are also valuable for other types of historical research. Biographers and local historians trying to verify information about a town inhabitant will find this resource especially helpful, as

Census schedules housed in the National Archives are copies of the actual forms filled out for every family or household.

will those seeking more personal details about the characteristics of a particular street or neighborhood. As an example, Census records can be used to research Laura Ingalls Wilder, author of the *Little House on the Prairie* series. The 1880 Census reel for Kingsburg County, Dakota Territory provides facts about Laura Ingalls as a child, together with information on her family and neighbors. A 1900 Census reel for Wright County, Missouri, shows Laura as a young married woman.

Verifying Age and Identity

Those Census records more current than 72 years are completely confidential, but individuals can request official transcripts of their own Census responses. Why would anyone want or need to make such a request? To verify their age, place of birth, citizenship, or relation to parents. The transcript is recognized as a legal document by all federal and state agencies and by private employers, and can provide documentation to obtain a passport, driver's license, delayed birth certificate, voter registration, or marriage license. It can also prove eligibility for Social Security or Medicare benefits, an inheritance, or death benefits from life insurance policies. (In many cases, the applicant must also show an affidavit from the appropriate State Bureau of Vital Records, verifying that no birth certificate is available.) For a fee, the Bureau will search through Census returns from past decades to locate information about an individual applicant. The Bureau presently maintains copies of all Census returns from 1910 through 1990. This amounts to more than one billion records on approximately 50,000 reels of microfilm.

The Age Search service began in 1902, when the Bureau was established as a permanent agency. At that time, many veterans of the Civil War (or their widows or heirs) required documentation to receive pension benefits, but had no birth certificates. A similar wave of interest was created in 1936 with the passage of the Social Security Act, and a third in 1965 with the enactment of the Medicare program. At one time, few states had comprehensive, mandatory birth registration systems, so Census records were among the only official records of a person's birth date. Demand for the service has dwindled with each passing year; by the early 1930s, all states had instituted birth registration systems, largely at the Bureau's behest. However, many persons are still alive who were born prior to the existence of such systems, and others require Census records for specialized circumstances. Heirs can request transcripts for a deceased parent, for example, and the service can also be used for genealogical research. The Bureau receives approximately 30,000 requests for age/identity verification per year, compared to a peak demand of 700,000 per year during the early 1940s.

The Bureau scrupulously guards the confidentiality of personal information, as mandated by Census law. Individuals can request data only about themselves, about someone for whom they are a guardian or legal representative, or about a deceased spouse or blood relative. Data will not be released if it violates a living person's privacy. For example, a police officer, private investigator, or attorney cannot use Census records to help locate missing persons, even in compassionate situations, nor can estranged family members utilize the service to track down birth-parents or natural children given up for adoption. If records are requested for an entire household, everyone involved must sign the authorization form. If information about a deceased person is needed, the applicant must supply proof of the person's death and verify blood relationship or legal responsibility. In fact, individuals seeking official transcripts from the 1910 or 1920 Censuses must still sign an authorization form, even though data from these decades are now publicly available to anyone. Census

Those Census records more current than 72 years are completely confidential, but individuals can request official transcripts of their own Census responses.

The Bureau scrupulously guards the confidentiality of personal information, as mandated by Census law.

How can I obtain a personal Census transcript?

Application forms can be obtained at most Social Security offices, those post offices which handle passport applications, field offices of the Census Bureau or the National Archives and Records Service, or by contacting the Bureau at this address:

Census Bureau Data Preparation Division
Personal Census Search Branch
P.O. Box 1545
Jeffersonville IN 47131-0001
(812) 288-3300

You must specify the decade you want searched, and identify the address where you lived at the time of the Census in question. Because microfilmed records are arranged geographically, an accurate address is vital. For age verification, you should request a tran-

script from the first Census which took place after your birth. Searches may take up to two months to complete, depending on current caseloads; passport requests are given priority, and are usually processed within seven working days.

As of this writing, the fee for a single search and basic transcript is $40.00; a typed facsimile of the actual Census return costs an additional $6.00. Information on other household members is available for an additional $10.00 per name if the request accompanies the original application (and if the other individuals provide authorization). Fee increases are announced periodically in the *Federal Register*.

rolls accessible to the general public are maintained by the National Archives, not the Census Bureau. These precautions are taken to prevent the slightest possibility of a mix-up in answering an applicant's confidential request.

By law, the Bureau's Age Search service must be operated on a cost-recovery basis. The basic fee entitles the applicant to a single name search in one decade's Census, plus an official transcript. The transcript provides the applicant's name, age at time of Census, state and county of residence, state or country of birth, relationship to household head, and name of household head. Parents names will be shown only if they lived in the same household as the search subject. Information varies slightly for each decade, depending on the questions asked during that Census. Where available, the applicant can request transcript information on citizenship, race, sex, and occupation. For an additional fee, a typed facsimile of the complete Census return can be provided. This "full Census schedule" shows only that portion pertain-

ing to the applicant. To obtain the responses for other household members, an additional fee must be paid for each name, and written permission must be obtained from each person.

Matching Census Data to Research Needs

Certain applications of Census data are fairly obvious. Social agencies contemplating programs on English as a Second Language will quickly turn to Census questions on language spoken at home. But additional data to support the need for ESL programs can be obtained from questions on country of residence five years ago, educational attainment, and employment status. Information about local housing conditions can be gathered from Census data on age of housing, persons per room, vacancy rates, availability of plumb-

By law, the Bureau's Age Search service must be operated on a cost-recovery basis.

Users should be creative when using the Census.

ing and heating facilities, and several other variables. Users should be creative when using the Census. For example, personal income is not reported at the Census Block level, but median rent and median housing value are, and both figures can serve as surrogates for household income. Other appropriate applications are limited only by the ingenuity and imagination of the user.

 Census Tip

Before beginning any project involving Census data, take the time to match Census questions to your research needs. Are you overlooking information which could be potentially useful? A brief review of the Census Questionnaire, in light of your present needs, will likely suggest additional applications of the available data.

Census users can analyze data in a more meaningful way by making appropriate comparisons among different geographic areas, against state or national averages, or across decades.

Census users can analyze data in a more meaningful way by making appropriate comparisons among different geographic areas, against state or national averages, or across decades. Recasting figures as medians, means, percentages, or rates of change can be especially helpful. Consider the general population and housing characteristics listed in Figure 2-5. The table compares three communities in the Buffalo, New York PMSA. The town of Amherst is a largely upper-middle class suburb with a predominantly White population. The city of Buffalo can be characterized as a blue-collar area with large numbers of minority residents. Like many large cities in the northeast, Buffalo continues to experience a declining population and a stagnant economy. Census Tract 069, located on Buffalo's lower west side, is one of the poorer neighborhoods in the city.

In almost every category of economic and social well-being represented in Figure 2-5, Buffalo shows more dismal results than its suburban neighbor, while Tract 069 is poorer than the city at large. Amherst enjoys rela-

tively high housing values for upstate New York, as well as low unemployment, high levels of education, and median household income well above the national average. Nearly three-quarters of all Housing Units are owned by their occupants and almost every household has at least one vehicle. In contrast, Buffalo experienced high unemployment in 1990, its median household income was less than half of Amherst's, and like many older cities, it continued to grapple with an aging housing stock. Perhaps the most telling indicator is the high percentage of population living below the poverty level. On a positive note, Buffalo's vacancy rates remained fairly low, despite the large amount of rental housing available (less than half the city's Housing Units are owner-occupied).

Overall, Buffalo has a fairly small Hispanic population, but at more than 25%, Tract 069 has one of the highest concentrations of Hispanics in the city. This neighborhood's poverty rate is staggering, the number of female householders with no husband present is quite high, the population is younger, 15% of all households have no telephone, and nearly half do not own a vehicle. Quality of life trails that of the city in virtually every category except vacancy rates.

In order to make the comparisons discussed above, data had to be chosen from among all the other numbers found in the appropriate Census publications. Once selected, the figures were presented in a manner that would facilitate analysis. Other data could have been used, and some of the numbers shown could have been compared to state or national averages as well, but Figure 2-5 provides a fairly clear comparison of the three communities. Depending on the user's purpose, all manner of additional Census data could be helpful.

It is also important to have at least a basic familiarity with the geographic areas under examination, especially to help explain apparent discrepancies in the data. For example, despite its otherwise lackluster standing, Tract 069 exhibits an unexpectedly high median housing value. This anomaly is due largely to the presence of a fairly new subdivision built by the city as part of a substantial revitalization effort. Similarly, what accounts for the relatively high percentage of children attending Buffalo's private schools? The answer lies partly in the high percentage of Catholic families who send their children to parochial schools, and partly in the long-standing problems of the public school system. As a final example, what explains the larger percentage of foreign-born residents in the town of Amherst? Amherst is the home of the largest university in the SUNY system; most of the foreign students live on or around the Amherst campus, and many of the University's foreign-born professors and physicians live in the surrounding town. In all three examples, none of the explanatory information can be found in the Census itself, so it is usually a good idea to supplement Census figures with local knowledge

Summary

If the Census were only used for legislative apportionment, a simple postcard Census, consisting of three or four basic questions, would suffice. Considering the enormous variety of uses to which Census data are applied, the actual number of questions asked is really quite reasonable. And because the Census can be used for limitless purposes, the enormous cost of producing it is generally considered a worthwhile investment.

As this chapter has shown, the Census can be a gold mine of information for research, planning, and decision-making purposes. But failure to consult Census publications can have disastrous results, even for major corporations with access to other data sources. One of the nation's largest waste disposal companies recently sought to locate a new landfill in what it believed to be a largely rural town on the outskirts of a Metropolitan Area in upstate New York. Corporate planners failed to notice the town had experienced tremendous population growth since 1980,

As this chapter has shown, the Census can be a gold mine of information for research, planning, and decision-making purposes.

and that the area in question was near several new, fairly high- priced subdivisions. The well-educated, upper-income residents mounted an overwhelmingly effective campaign to block the move. The company could have avoided this setback by checking newly released 1990 Census reports before selecting their site. But by the time the firm encountered this unexpected resistence from the community, it had already invested in soil surveys, test drilling, and other preliminary expenditures.

A final point about the value of the Census is that decennial data are rarely used in isolation. Researchers should combine appropriate Census information with statistics from other available sources, including the Bureau's current population surveys, economic Census reports, and myriad publications from other federal, state, and local agencies, associations, and commercial data producers. Most important, as each decade's Census data grows older, decennial statistics should be compared to more current estimates to gain a sense of changing conditions. Keeping these caveats in mind, decennial Census products can provide a wealth of useful information for innumerable research situations.

Comparing Three Communities
in the Buffalo, NY Metropolitan Area

Characteristic (1990 Census)	Amherst town	Buffalo city	Tract 069 (Buffalo)
Total population	111,711	328,123	10,254
Pop. change, 1980-90	+2.8%	-8.3%	+1.5%
Total households	41,320	136,436	4,001
White population	92.9%	64.8%	68.7%
Black population	2.8%	30.7%	11.1%
Hispanic population	1.1%	4.9%	25.6%
Pop. under 18 yrs. old	22.0%	24.0%	29.1%
Pop. 65 yrs. or older	15.1%	14.8%	12.7%
Median age	36.2 yrs.	32 yrs.	28.8 yrs.
Female householder, no husband present	8.1%	20.2%	24.7%
Foreign born	8.1%	4.5%	6.3%
High school graduates	89.3%	67.3%	63.0%
College graduates	41.1%	16.0%	11.9%
Children attending private school	14.2%	16.0%	4.5%
Unemployment rate	4.1%	11.6%	15.4%
Median household income	$41,466	$18,482	$12,525
Persons living below poverty level	5.4%	25.6%	37.9%
Median value, owner-occupied housing	$139,300	$46,700	$38,300
Median monthly rent	$436	$255	$248
Housing Units built before 1939	10.1%	68.1%	74.3%
Owner-occupied Units	74.8%	43.1%	29.0%
Rental vacancy rates	7.2%	7.8%	6.2%
Units lacking complete plumbing facilities	0.1%	0.5%	1.2%
Units with no telephone	0.04%	9.1%	15.4%
Units with more than one person per room	0.07%	2.1%	4.9%
Households with no vehicles	5.7%	34.0%	47.9%

Exhibit 2-5

Chapter 3

Planning the Census

Planning the Census

CONSIDER THIS often-told (though probably apocryphal) story from the 1970 Census. An enumerator was trying to persuade an elderly householder to answer the decennial Questionnaire by explaining the many important uses of Census data. After listening patiently, the old woman answered, "That's very nice, young man, but if I need to know the population of the United States, I'll look it up in the *World Almanac.*" While the story might seem far-fetched, most users of federal statistics tend to take data for granted. Such people never doubt that needed figures will be available, nor do they question where the numbers come from. Unlike Athena, Census data do not spring full-grown from Zeus's forehead.

Census Day was April 1, 1990, but the decennial Census required ten years of solid effort, from 1983 through 1993. The operation was divided into five broad stages, each overlapping the next, as the following rough timetable shows:

Planning   1983-1988
Preparation   1985-1990
Enumeration   March-December, 1990
Publication   1991-1994
Evaluation   1991-1993

With a budget of $2.6 billion over the ten-year cycle, the cost of the 1990 Census was more than double that of the 1980 effort. Although the lion's share of that budget was devoted to the actual collection and processing of Census data, more than seven years of planning and preparation came before a single Census form was mailed.

Early Planning Activities

The goal of each Census is to count as many people as possible, as accurately as possible. Careful planning helps accomplish this goal in a cost-effective, efficient, and timely manner. Preliminary planning for 1990 started even before results from the 1980 Census were published, but major efforts began in 1983. The planning process lasted well into

1988 and involved intensive research both inside and outside the Bureau. After important issues were identified and various options were delineated, the Bureau presented its ideas for public comment, conducted field tests of new equipment and methods, and staged full-scale Dress Rehearsals. Figure 3-1 shows a timetable of major planning activities for 1990.

Seeking Outside Advice and Comment

The first phase of planning, as in every decade, was an evaluation of the successes and failures of the previous Census. Bureau staff spent several years studying every aspect of 1980 Census operations, looking for areas of potential improvement. Comments and criticism from external sources were also studied carefully, including Congressional oversight hearings, reports from the U.S. General Accounting Office (GAO), and testimony from the many lawsuits filed by individual cities and states protesting 1980 Census undercounts. The research process continued with internal study groups, outside advisory committees, consultants, and public hearings.

NEW IN '90

Planning efforts for the 1990 Census began a year sooner than those of the previous decade.

Numerous in-house committees were established to investigate specific issues. Topics included field operations, enumeration of special groups, mail delivery, community outreach, geography, coverage improvement, and quality control. External advisory committees were also formed. In January 1984, the Bureau asked the National Academy of Sciences to create a Panel on Decennial Census Methodology. This expert panel examined the Bureau's sampling methods, its evalua-

Chronology: 1990 Census Planning

1983	1980 Evaluation Studies Completed
Jan. 1984	Panel on Decennial Census Methodology Appointed
Jan. 1984	Federal Agency Council Established
April 1984-Oct. 1985	Local Public Meetings Program
March - Nov. 1984	Address List Compilation Test
Jan. - Sept. 1985	New Jersey and Florida Test Censuses
Jan. - Sept. 1986	California and Mississippi Test Censuses
March - Sept. 1986	National Content Survey
Aug. 1986	Minority Advisory Committees Established
Fall 1986	Prototype CD-ROM Product Tested
Dec. 1986	MPO Cooperative Program Announced
Jan. - Sept. 1987	North Dakota Test Census
Fall 1987	OMB Objects to Questionnaire Content/Sampling Rate
Jan. - Sept. 1988	Dress Rehearsals
March 20, 1988	Dress Rehearsal Census Day
March 1988	OMB and Census Bureau Agree on Questionnaire
March 1988	CD-ROM "Test Disk 1" Released
April 1, 1988	Congressional Deadline for Questionnaire Content
Dec. 1989	Barbara Bryant Named Bureau's Interim Director

Figure 3-1

tion of Census undercount, and the value of administrative records for address list compilation. In August, 1986, four Census Advisory Committees were formed to provide recommendations on minority issues. The four Committees—representing Blacks; Hispanics; American Indians and Alaska Natives; and Asians and Pacific Islanders—discussed such issues as recruiting temporary Census employees, improving Questionnaire content, and increasing public awareness. Consultants were hired in 1984 to recommend automation solutions to meet the Bureau's exacting requirements.

Numerous in-house committees were established to investigate specific issues.

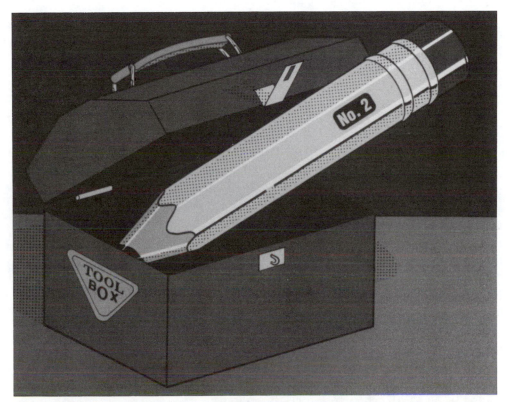

THE ONLY TOOL YOU NEED TO ANSWER THE CENSUS.

A simple pencil, a little time. That's all it takes to fill out your census form. So when it arrives, just reach for your pencil, mark your answers, and send it back to us. What's the census? It's the count of America's population—where we live and how we're doing. Your answers, of course, are strictly confidential.

ANSWER THE CENSUS BY APRIL 1, 1990

It counts for more than you think!

CENSUS '90

U.S. Department of Commerce
BUREAU OF THE CENSUS

Example of promotional material for 1990 Census public awareness campaign.
(Bureau of the Census photo)

The U.S. Office of Management and Budget (OMB) played a critical role in Census planning. Since 1947, the OMB has been charged with overseeing and coordinating federal statistical programs; these duties were expanded by the Paperwork Reduction Act of 1980. The OMB must approve all federal data collection instruments and statistical publications, including those relating to the decennial Census. The agency determines whether data-gathering activities are needed for the functioning of government, and whether resulting data could be obtained from other sources. The OMB also examines the cost of the activity and the burden it places on respondents. Costs and burdens are weighed against public benefits—the needs of data users and the constitutional and legal requirements for specific statistical information. This watchdog role often places the OMB in an adversarial relationship with the Bureau. Nevertheless, the Office of Management and Budget was an important participant in the 1990 planning process. Early in the decade, the OMB established the Federal Agency Council on the 1990 Census. The Council was chaired by an OMB representative and was comprised of high-ranking officials from federal agencies which used Census data and could comment on government data needs. The Bureau itself formed ten Interagency Working Groups (IWGs) to solicit federal expertise in such areas as poverty, Native Americans, and the labor force. The IWGs submitted recommendations to the Bureau and the Federal Agency Council.

Recommendations were also provided through the Congressional oversight process. The House Committee on the Post Office and Civil Service, and its Subcommittee on Census and Population, held hearings throughout the planning and preparation stages. In the years preceding the 1990 Census, the GAO conducted numerous investigations of decennial preparations, usually at the request of the House Subcommittee. GAO recommendations, in the form of briefing and audit reports, were submitted to

Congress, the OMB, and the Bureau. Topics of GAO investigations ranged from the content of the 1990 Questionnaire to the Bureau's employee recruiting methods.

Beginning in 1983, Bureau planners met with legislators, state and local officials, minority and ethnic groups, academic and professional associations, statisticians, and data users from the business community. Among the many organizations consulted were the Population Association of America, the National Urban League, the U.S. Conference of Mayors, and the American Statistical Association. A variety of major conferences were convened during the planning phase. In January, 1984, a national conference on minority concerns was held. In 1986, mayors and other representatives from the nation's cities were invited to one of two conferences to discuss local government involvement, from employee recruitment to verification of geographic boundaries. Less elaborate meetings were also arranged. In 1985 and 1986, Bureau employees traveled around the country to hold twelve regional meetings with Native American organizations, for example.

The most extensive series of meetings was the Local Public Meetings (LPM) program, sponsored in conjunction with State Data Centers. From April, 1984 through October, 1985, Bureau representatives staged 65 public hearings, with at least one held in every state, Puerto Rico, and the U.S. Virgin Islands. Here the Bureau presented preliminary Census plans, introduced topics under consideration, answered questions, and recorded comments and suggestions from the audience. More than 5,000 people participated in the Local Public Meetings, representing all types of data-user organizations: small businesses, professional associations, universities, community service groups, libraries, and state and local governments. Four issue papers were prepared for LPM attendees, covering population concerns, housing, geography, and data products.

Another aspect of planning was coordina-

The U.S. Office of Management and Budget (OMB) played a critical role in Census planning.

More than 5,000 people participated in the Local Public Meetings, representing all types of data-user organizations.

tion with the various organizations helping with the decennial Census, including the United States Postal Service, the Government Printing Office, and the State Data Center network. An excellent example of such efforts was a joint program with the Federal Highway Administration, called the Metropolitan Planning Organization (MPO) Cooperative Program. MPOs are federally funded transportation planning agencies established in every Metropolitan Area of the country. Because the decennial Census contains questions on travel to work to help transportation planners, the Bureau requested help from the MPOs to develop a nationwide list of major employers. Respondents write-in the location of their place of work on the Census forms, but in 1980, only half of the respondents listed an actual street address. By developing an employer database for 1990, the Bureau could create a computer program to assign addresses to write-in responses. With the promise of federal funds to conduct the work, 92% of all MPOs participated in the program, which began in 1987.

Comments and advice were solicited and received from many other sources, including correspondence from the public; requests for comment were a common feature of the Bureau's *Data User News* bulletin in the years prior to 1990. Input was helpful for establishing the Census budget, planning automation requirements, and determining objectives for upcoming field tests.

Questionnaire Design

As in 1980, the 1990 Census employed two separate Questionnaires: a Short Form and a Long Form. The Short Form consisted of basic questions asked of 100% of the population. The Long Form contained the same questions as the Short Form, plus additional, more detailed questions. The Long Form was sent to a representative sample of House holds.

Questionnaire design captured more public attention than other aspects of planning

Data users, local officials, and legislators may have paid little attention to technical issues of methodology, but they were acutely sensitive to Questionnaire design.

The Bureau was deluged with requests from all types of special interest groups seeking inclusion of additional questions.

because it was the most visible. It was also among the most important concerns: if a question did not appear on the Census form, no data could be collected on that topic. Data users, local officials, and legislators may have paid little attention to technical issues of methodology, but they were acutely sensitive to Questionnaire design. Determining which questions to ask and how to ask them was serious business. Figure 3-2 summarizes the many steps taken during the long process of content planning.

Planning Questionnaire Content

The Bureau did not select questions for its own purposes, or because the information was needed by the business community. Questions were included because data were needed by federal, state and local governments to establish public policies and programs. The Bureau was deluged with requests from all types of special interest groups seeking inclusion of additional questions. Questions such as "How many pets do you have?" "Do you use vitamin supplements?" and "Do you own a VCR?" were rejected out of hand. The burden of paperwork on the respondent and the cost of Census processing made the addition of each new question a major decision.

 Census Tip

Sample questions have been asked by the Census since 1940, but in 1940 and 1950, specified individuals in every Household were sampled. Beginning in 1960, the current method of sampling all members within designated Households was begun.

A variety of major issues was addressed by Census planners. Which questions from 1980 should no longer be asked and what new questions should be added? Which questions should appear on the Short Form and which

Content Planning Path for the 1990 Census

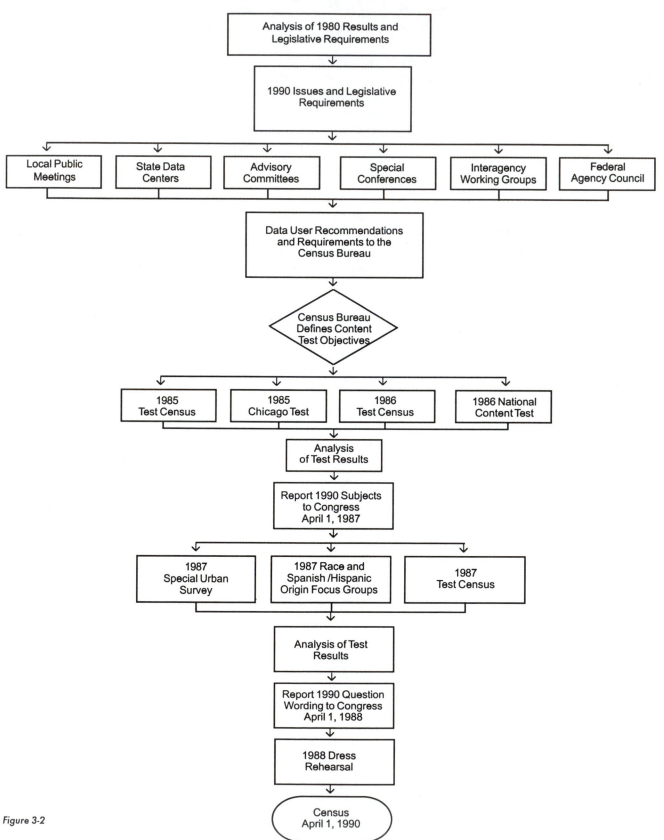

Figure 3-2

on the Long Form? What was the most appropriate sampling rate and sampling methodology? How could questions allow comparability to data from previous Censuses, yet still reflect contemporary concerns?

The format and wording of questions was also examined. How detailed should individual questions be? Which should involve multiple-choice responses and which have write-in answers? Could questions be made more understandable through better phrasing? At what point would the Questionnaire become too long, inhibiting response rate and accuracy of responses? These issues were critical because the majority of Census operations are conducted by mail; the Questionnaire was designed to be understood without enumerator assistance.

The starting point for Questionnaire analysis was the 1980 form; in order to measure how the country had changed over time, planners sought a reasonable similarity to the previous decade's questions. However, certain questions were no longer useful or appropriate, and new questions were needed to capture current or emerging trends. The history of the Census reflects the nation's changing concerns and interests. At the turn of the century, ancestry and immigration were important to Census-takers; in 1930, employment status was stressed; in 1940, questions on housing finances were introduced. Specific topics relating to 1990 Questionnaire content included data on the handicapped, the homeless, educational attainment, housing arrangements of the elderly, language spoken at home, and racial breakdown.

The Local Public Meetings, Interagency Working Groups, and other planning vehicles described above were major sources of input on Questionnaire content. One of the most important sources was the Federal Agency Council, which helped identify administrative data needs. For example, existing legislation and regulations were examined to identify statistical information mandated by law.

Once major content areas were identified,

wording and format were rigorously tested to ensure the final Questionnaire would yield useful, reliable results. Specific questions were tested in the 1985 Pre-Tests and in focus groups conducted as part of the Tampa (1985), Los Angeles (1986), and Mississippi (1986) Pre-Tests. The major test, called the National Content Survey (NCS), was a nationwide sampling of 48,000 Households. Seven different Questionnaire versions (three Short, four Long) were distributed in March, 1986. Two types of envelope design were also tested. In June, 40% of the original NCS respondents participated in follow-up interviews to determine how well the questions were understood. Many of the questions tested in the National Content Survey never made it to the 1990 Questionnaire. Among them were questions seeking data on dual job-holders (i.e., moonlighting), presence of smoke detectors, total number of miles driven the previous year, and detailed listings of specific disabilities. In 1987, focus groups were convened to further test clarity of Questionnaire language.

Obtaining Questionnaire Approval

Planning for Questionnaire content and design follows a strict timetable. First, the forms must be approved by the Office of Management and Budget, as must the sampling rates to be employed. By law (Title 13 of the U.S. Code), the Bureau must report to Congress on the Questionnaire's general content by April 1, 1987. The list of questions to be asked must be submitted to Congress by April 1, 1988. Because of the massive printing job, the final Questionnaire had to be ready in early 1989.

The integrity of the 1990 Questionnaire content was severely jeopardized throughout the approval process. A GAO report issued in May, 1986 voiced serious concerns about most housing questions, concerns which were later echoed by the OMB. In their study, GAO investigators found several federal agencies used sample Census data even when

Many of the questions tested in the National Content Survey never made it to the 1990 Questionnaire.

The integrity of the 1990 Questionnaire content was severely jeopardized throughout the approval process.

Postal carrier sorts mail prior to 1990 Questionnaire delivery.
(Bureau of the Census photo)

complete count data were available. Although these agencies strongly indicated their need for 100% housing data, in practice, they were not using it. Other concerns mentioned in the report focused on the quality of Questionnaire responses and the response rate. The longer and more complex the Short

Q&A

All things considered, how well did the 1990 Questionnaire turn out?

The answer to that question awaits further post-Census analysis by the Bureau. However, there is no question that Questionnaire language continues to baffle respondents. Even William Safire, the New York Times's language maven, criticized the Question-naire's clarity, style, and grammar. Though many of Safire's remarks were humorous or pedantic, others were right on target. Despite rigorous testing, review, and oversight, many questions were undoubtedly misinterpreted by respondents. Although the Bureau has extensive experience in designing questionnaires, the perfect instrument is an unattainable goal.

Form, the less likely Households would respond completely, or at all. Questions with write-in responses were challenged because the Bureau did not tabulate all write-in responses from 1980. The Bureau was also criticized for not adequately testing the literacy skills required to answer the Questionnaire or the amount of time required to complete it. In Pre-Tests, lower-income Households experienced greater difficulties understanding the forms, but all groups had problems. The GAO report urged the Bureau to test an abbreviated, more user-friendly version of the Short Form. It specifically recommended moving eight housing questions from the Short Form to the Long. The report concluded the Short Form should be limited to the most basic population and housing questions needed to obtain an accurate population count.

In July, 1987, the OMB provided the Bureau with a list of the proposed 1990 questions requiring further justification. The OMB, as always, was concerned about respondent burden, cost of administering and processing the data, response rate and quality, and the ability of the Bureau to collect and tabulate data in a timely fashion. Thirty questions (nearly one-third of the proposed total) were challenged, including all housing questions on the Long Form. The Bureau assumed these 30 would be dropped

from the 1988 Dress Rehearsals, and therefore would not likely appear on the 1990 Questionnaire. Faced with a deadline to respond to the OMB by September 14, the Bureau issued a memo publicizing the challenged questions. Senator Paul Sarbanes (D-MD), chairman of the Joint Economic Committee, quickly requested hearings on the issue.

An underlying theme of OMB objections was the proper role of government in data collection. Should government support market research for the private sector at taxpayer expense? Do business people really use Census data, or do they turn to more timely sources from commercial data providers? Hundreds of letters from data users poured in; most supported the challenged questions. Speakers from such organizations as the National Association of Homebuilders and the National League of Cities testified on the Bureau's behalf. During the hearings, OMB representatives indicated the 30 questions were not slated for deletion, but were flagged for further study. The agency's stance was curious, given the lateness of their objections. Most of the targeted questions had appeared in the Census for decades and had been thoroughly tested during the 1990 planning process. Furthermore, the OMB's own Federal Agency Council had approved them earlier. The Joint Committee was unanimous in expressing support for the questions.

An underlying theme of OMB objections was the proper role of government in data collection.

The OMB also recommended a reduction of the 1990 sampling rate, from 19 million Households to 10 million.

The OMB also recommended a reduction of the 1990 sampling rate, from 19 million Households to 10 million. By mid-September, the agency had dropped most of its objections to the Questionnaire, but remained steadfast on sampling rates. All but three of the Long Form questions were approved, and the OMB recommended moving seven housing questions from the Short Form to the Long. The Dress Rehearsals, which began in March, 1988, utilized the Questionnaire agreed to in September. Meanwhile, another deadline neared: Congressional approval of the 1990 Questionnaire by April 1. On March 22, 1988, a bipartisan group of congressmen, led by Senator Sarbanes, signed a letter urging the President to defer to the Census Bureau's professional judgment. Agreement between the two agencies was announced on March 29. The three endangered Long Form housing questions were retained. Three of the challenged Short Form questions remained on the Short Form, and the remaining four were transferred to the Long Form. Of greater importance, the OMB agreed to a sampling rate of 17.7 million Households, about 1.6 million fewer than if the 1980 rate had been used.

Other Questionnaire controversies arose during the planning process. Political discussion arose early regarding whether legal status of noncitizens should be asked (the result was a resounding, "No."). In January, 1988, an OMB notice appeared in the *Federal Register* asking for public comment on the Bureau's racial categories. Numerous responses urged a new question for multi-racial or mixed-race individuals, but the suggestion was not incorporated. Even after the April, 1988 deadline, additional challenges were raised by Congress itself. In May, Representative Robert Matsui (D-CA) introduced a bill requiring specific listings for 11 racial subcategories for the Asian/Pacific Islander population. This issue was deemed important due to the large influx of Asian immigrants during the 1980s. The Bureau's proposed Questionnaire called for a single category for Asian/Pacific Islander, followed by a line for write-in answers for specific type. Variations of this question had been tested in the National Content Survey, the Los Angeles Pre-Test, the Dress Rehearsal, and a special Urban Survey conducted in 1987. In all cases, the Bureau believed better answers were received through write-in responses. To provide specific choices on the Questionnaire would require listing 25 major racial groups, not 11.

Geographic Preparations

Another key area of Census planning was the creation of accurate geographic boundaries.

Another key area of Census planning was the creation of accurate geographic boundaries. More will be said about geographic concepts and definitions in Chapter 6; for now, some of the basic steps in creating and updating geographic boundaries will be described. A major development for 1990 was the decision to divide the entire nation into small quadrangles called Census Blocks and to report data down to the Block level. In prior Censuses, Blocks existed primarily in Metropolitan Areas, and most were actual city blocks. But what was the best way to create a continuous grid of Blocks from coast to coast? How many should there be and how large should each one be? Ultimately, more

NEW IN '90

Fourteen questions appearing on the 1980 Questionnaire were dropped from the 1990 forms. Many of these were dropped at the Bureau's own recommendations, and most others were of lesser importance than the ten saved in March of 1988. It can be said that the Census Bureau (and data users) won this battle, in large part due to public and Congressional support. 1990 Questionnaire content will be discussed in detail in Chapter 7.

than seven million Blocks were created. In urban areas, city blocks continued to be used; in rural areas, Census Blocks constituted larger territories of varying land area, but with populations of approximately 70 Households each. To prepare for nationwide Blocking, Block boundaries needed to be clearly marked, whether they were city streets or dry riverbeds. Census geographers also needed to place Blocks within their surrounding political boundaries, such as cities, townships, and counties.

Boundaries for the 1990 Census were established in three phases.

Boundaries for the 1990 Census were established in three phases. Phase one was the creation and numbering of Census Blocks. This operation came first because Blocks were necessary for accurate geocoding and enumeration. Block boundaries were drawn by Census geographers using TIGER, the Bureau's newly-created computerized mapping system. TIGER maps were based on satellite photos, USGS maps, and the Bureau's own maps (more will be said about this amazing system in Chapter 6). Once entered into TIGER, every Block was automatically numbered by computer. To ensure accuracy and comprehensive coverage, the resulting Block maps were checked in two ways. As part of the Pre-Census Local Review process,

the Bureau sent maps to planning officials in all local governments, asking them to verify Block boundaries and street names. Maps were also corrected and updated by Census field workers in the course of conducting their regular work. Such updating took place before Census Day, during the Address Pre-List and Precanvass operations, and during the Census enumeration itself. Pre-List, Precanvass, and Local Review will be discussed in greater detail later in the chapter.

At the same time, aggregations of Blocks—called Block Groups, Tracts, and Block Numbering Areas—were also created. Block

NEW IN '90

All maps used in 1990 Census operations, including those for Precanvassing, Pre-Census Local Review, enumeration, and follow-up, were generated by TIGER.

Groups were created by the Bureau, while Block Numbering Areas were established at the state level by the State Data Centers. Tract boundaries were determined by local

Q&A

Why is geographic planning so vital to the success of a decennial Census?

The Census Bureau doesn't just count people, it locates them. Each person (and his or her accompanying characteristics) must be allocated to an appropriate state, county, and so on, down to the Block level. If the underlying geography is flawed, the corresponding data will be flawed as well.

Early creation of an accurate geographic database is essential for two major reasons. First, in order to count people, the Bureau must first find them. Without accurate Block maps, entire streets could be missed. Street location is especially impor-

tant for door-to-door enumeration; Census takers carry the Bureau's Block maps with them as they conduct the Census.

Second, each address must be linked to the appropriate geography in order to count it properly. This operation is known as geocoding. For example, how can the population of a county be determined without knowing which addresses fall within the boundaries of that county? Any Census statistic is meaningless without a geographic reference.

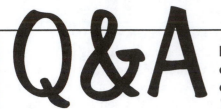

How were Block Numbers assigned to streets which came into existence between the beginning of 1988 and Census Day?

Nationwide Block numbering had to be in place by the end of 1987 in order to proceed with subsequent Census operations. New streets constructed after 1987 were included on Block maps as they were identified; however, they were included within the boundaries of existing Blocks.

advisory groups called Census Statistical Area Committees (CSACs). The CSACs were created in the spring of 1985 and their recommendations were submitted no later than June 30, 1986. All phase one boundaries were created and numbered by the end of 1987.

The second phase involved verification of political boundaries, done in conjunction with state and local authorities. Once again, coordinates for these entities were entered into the TIGER system. Political borders recognized by the 1990 Census are those which were in place on January 1, 1990. Thousands of municipalities change their boundaries between Censuses, and the Bureau's Geography Division must ensure that maps used by enumerators are current and accurate. Several mechanisms were established to track changes in political boundaries. Between Censuses, the Bureau conducts an ongoing Boundary and Annexation Survey, usually on an annual basis. This voluntary survey is sent to state and local governments, asking them to note any recent changes in their territorial limits. The Boundary and Annexation Survey assumed added importance as the decennial Census approached. For the 1988 Survey, detailed TIGER maps were sent to local officials in the summer and fall of 1988. No official Survey was conducted in 1989, though local planners were asked to submit boundary changes as part of the Local Review process. A final Boundary and Annexation Survey

Thousands of municipalities change their boundaries between Censuses, and the Bureau's Geography Division must ensure that maps used by enumerators are current and accurate.

was conducted in December, 1989.

The third phase of boundary determination could be implemented only after the Census had been conducted. For every Census, the Bureau employs a variety of fictitious geographic entities solely for statistical reporting purposes. Several types of these so-called Statistical Units are defined according to population criteria. Boundaries for two of these Units—Urbanized Areas and Census Designated Places—could only be determined once the Census counts had been tabulated. Creation of these Statistical Units took place after initial 1990 tabulations became available, but before publication of Census results. Boundaries of all Urbanized Areas are determined by the Census Bureau, based on population density. Census Designated Places are created at the request of local officials, based on population-size criteria established by the Bureau.

Other Planning Issues

Among the other issues explored by Census

 Census Tip

Metropolitan Areas (MAs) are another type of Statistical Unit dependent on population criteria. However, because MAs are defined based on commuting patterns, which take several years to tabulate, the 1990 Census used the MA boundaries and definitions in place at the time of the decennial Census. New MA boundaries, based on 1990 commuting patterns, were not issued until December, 1992, and therefore were not used in 1990 Census publications.

planners were methodology, automation, concepts and definitions, and the format and content of Census publications. Methodological concerns were among the most important: improving cooperation with local governments and community groups, reducing enumeration and processing errors, obtaining better response rates, and counting individuals most likely to be missed. Increased automation was likely to play a key role in improving Census operations. In 1984, a full-time manager was hired to investigate new technologies, plan automation strategy, and oversee the acquisition of equipment, from letting contracts to deploying machines.

Even the Census' underlying concepts and definitions were reexamined, from who should be counted to how Race should be defined. Shifts in family structure, living arrangements, the labor force, and other fundamental elements of society suggested possible changes in basic Census concepts. For example, were better distinctions between urban and suburban areas needed? Was the standard definition of a Housing Unit no longer meaningful? Do we need a better measure of urban population? Should illegal aliens be counted? After examining these issues, and others like them, few changes were made. However, the fact they were questioned at all helps illustrate that little was taken for granted in planning the 1990 Census.

A final group of issues involved the form which published Census results would take. At what geographic levels should data be reported? Should the Bureau produce ZIP Code reports? How much detail should appear in published form? How should tables be arranged: using a traditional subject approach, or profiles of geographic areas? What types of hierarchical arrangements should be used? What about historical data? Could the publication process be speeded-up so crucial reports are released sooner? And finally, what publication media should be used: paper, microfilm, or electronic?

Electronic dissemination was a major plan-

ning issue. Data from the 1970 and 1980 Censuses had been published on magnetic tape, but use was limited to organizations having mainframe computers and programming staff. Floppy diskettes afforded little storage capability to accommodate the enormous size of decennial Census. *CENDATA*, the Bureau's online database system, was initiated in 1984, but to date hadn't been utilized to present large decennial files. Early in the planning process, the Bureau began exploring a then-novel publication medium called Compact Disc-Read Only Memory (CD-ROM). A prototype Census CD-ROM was produced in 1986 and tested at various sites. The possibility of CD-ROM publishing brought another question: was it the Bureau's responsibility to develop user-friendly software, or was this better left to the private sector? An overview of the Bureau's CD-ROM development program can be found in Chapter 8.

Product questions were a large part of the Local Public Meetings Program, but the Bureau also convened ten regional Census Product Meetings in 1986, to obtain specific input on the format and content of proposed 1990 publications. These were followed by a National Conference on Data Products. In the summer of 1988, the Bureau asked the Association of Public Data Users (APDU) to form a working group on Census Products. Based on this input, detailed proposals for 1990 data products were drafted by late 1988. More will be said about Census publications in Chapters 8 and 9.

Field Testing

Though Census planning was thorough and detailed, many aspects required testing under field conditions. What looked good on paper might not work well in practice. Field testing had three components: tests or surveys relating to specific operations; small-scale Censuses, called Pre-Tests, exploring alternate methods; and finally, full-scale Dress Rehearsals to test all aspects of the final opera-

Early in the planning process, the Bureau began exploring a then-novel publication medium called Compact Disc-Read Only Memory (CD-ROM).

Even the Census' underlying concepts and definitions were reexamined, from who should be counted to how Race should be defined.

Promotional material targeting Alaska Native and American Indian Areas.
(Bureau of the Census photo)

tion. Figure 3-3 shows the dates and locations of the Bureau's major field tests.

One specialized test has already been mentioned: the National Content Survey (March, 1986) tested wording and format for various Questionnaire prototypes. Beginning in 1985, specific automated processes were rigorously tested. Another early test involved address compilations. The 1990 Census was primarily a mail-out operation, making mailing list preparation one of the most important aspects of decennial planning. But what was the best method of developing a nationwide mailing list? For example, could existing administrative records from federal, state, and local governments be used to develop comprehensive lists? To answer such questions, the Bureau launched a large-scale Address List Compilation Test in 1984. Locations were sought which simulated realistic workloads, exhibited significant population growth since 1980, possessed a suitable mixture of institutions and other Special Places, and contained significant minority populations. Planners chose two urban sites in Connecticut and three rural sites in Texas and Georgia. Three methods were tested: using the Bureau's 1980 address list, purchasing commercial mailing lists, and ordering specially created computer lists from the Postal Service. Each of these methods was then updated by either a postal carrier recheck or a street canvass by Census workers. No single method proved best; each produced some addresses the others did not, and all required significant updating. As a result, a combination of methods would be used to conduct the Census.

The next phase involved large-scale field tests of enumeration and processing procedures, which the Bureau called Pre-Tests. A variety of locations were chosen, exhibiting different combinations of population density, housing stock, racial characteristics, and so on. Pre-Tests were conducted in Jersey City and Tampa in 1985, in portions of Los Angeles County and rural Mississippi in 1986, and in North Dakota in 1987. Indian

Census Field Tests

Year	Location	Type
1984	Hartford, CT Bridgeport, CT Hardin County, TX Gordon County, GA Murray County, GA	Address List Compilation Test
1985	Jersey City, NJ Tampa, FL	Test Census
1986	Nationwide	National Content Survey
1986	Los Angeles County, CA (20 communities) east-central Mississippi (8 counties, 1 Reservation)	Test Census
1987	North Dakota (10 counties, 2 Reservations)	Test Census
1988	St. Louis, MO east-central Missouri (14 counties) eastern Washington (8 counties, 1 Reservation)	Dress Rehearsal

Figure 3-3

Reservations were included within the latter two territories. Questionnaires were sent to every Household in each area, simulating an actual Census.

Pre-Tests were designed to evaluate particular operations. The Jersey City test explored a two-stage Census, with a 100% Questionnaire distributed to every address, followed by a 20% sample survey mailed in a second phase. In Tampa, automation of various clerical processing was tested. The 1986 tests were designed to study methods of speeding up the timetable, cutting costs, and improving

NEW IN '90

Field testing for 1990 began two years earlier than for the previous Census. The first tests for 1980 took place in 1976.

accuracy. They included new Questionnaire wording and design, further tests of automated procedures, use of computerized maps, and centralized processing of forms. The later tests implemented various methods of improving the count: Post-Census Local Review, assistance for foreign language speakers, reminder cards, and telephone follow-up instead of door-to-door enumeration. Post-Census adjustment of counts was also tested. The Mississippi Pre-Test examined rural address listing and Questionnaire delivery to remote areas. The North Dakota test was designed to refine rural operations tested in Mississippi the year before.

Once individual procedures were tested and established, the entire operation was tried out. These "mini-Censuses," called Dress Rehearsals, tested the full array of procedures, work flows, promotional activities, equipment, and follow-up operations, including a Post-Enumeration Survey. The three Dress Rehearsals were held in St. Louis (a hard to enumerate urban area), suburban Missouri (with a mixture of cities of varying size, plus rural areas), and rural Washington (with sparsely populated areas and Indian Reservations). The Dress Rehearsals were the first full test of all automated processes. Such special operations as counting the homeless population were also tested. Census Day for the Dress Rehearsals was March 20, 1988.

Facilities and Staffing

Five years of planning and field testing were followed by intensive preparation efforts: producing Block-level maps for the entire country, hiring and training staff, opening field offices and Processing Centers, developing comprehensive mailing lists, publicizing the Census, designing outreach programs, working with local governments, and finally, printing and distributing more than 200 million Questionnaires. Figure 3-4 is a timetable of major pre-Census activities.

Opening Temporary Offices

Constructing the infrastructure for a decennial Census is much like creating a World's Fair: virtually overnight, an enormous edifice is constructed and thousands of workers are employed; then, when its purpose has been fulfilled, buildings are quickly dismantled or abandoned and employees are laid off. To conduct the decennial Census, the Bureau needed to open temporary facilities all over the country, as shown in Figure

Constructing the infrastructure for a decennial Census is much like creating a World's Fair

Chronology: 1990 Census Preparation	
1984	Funds Appropriated by Congress
Spring 1985	Census Statistical Area Committees Contacted
June 30, 1985	Deadline for CSAC Participation Requests
June 30, 1986	Deadline for CSAC Boundary Proposals
Nov. 1986	Elected Officials Contacted for Local Review
July 1987	Local Review Guidebook Sent to Local Officials
Aug. 1987 - 1989	Local Review Workshops Offered
1988	Processing Centers Opened
Jan. 1988 - March 1989	TAR Creation
Spring 1989	Questionnaires Sent to Printers
Summer 1989	Block Maps Sent for Local Review
July 1988 - Jan. 1989	1988 Prelist
Summer - Fall 1988	1988 Boundary and Annexation Survey
Sept. 1988 - May 1989	APOC (3 phases)
March 1989 - Jan. 1990	District Offices Opened
April - July 1989	Precanvass
June - Aug. 1989	APOC Reconciliation
June - Sept. 1989	1989 Prelist
Oct. - Nov. 1989	Pre-Census Local Review
April 1989 - April 1990	Updating TIGER
Dec. 1989	1990 Annexation and Boundary Survey
Jan. 1, 1990	Reference Date for Political Boundaries
Jan. - March 1990	Local Review Recanvass
Jan. - Feb. 1990	Special Place Prelist
Feb. 1990	Questionnaire Printing Completed
Feb. - May 1990	Public Service Announcements
March 1990	USPS Casing Check
March 5, 1990	Questionnaires delivered to USPS
March 1990	Multilingual "Early Alerts" Mailed

Figure 3-4

3-5. Preparing for the Census included selecting sites for local offices, renting space, purchasing or leasing computers, furniture, and other equipment, establishing telecommunications links, and similar mundane but necessary tasks.

 Census Tip

Tabulations from the Dress Rehearsals and Test Censuses were published as individual Census reports. Combined data from the Dress Rehearsals were even issued in CD-ROM format. For the areas covered--Tampa, Jersey City, St. Louis, etc.--these publications provide detailed intercensal population and housing data.

The Census Bureau's major permanent locations are its headquarters in Suitland, Maryland, a Processing Center in Jeffersonville, Indiana, and 12 Regional Offices (ROs). The primary work of the Regional Offices in non-Census years is to assist the public in locating and using Census data, to coordinate field work for the Bureau's ongoing surveys, and to provide support for other non-decennial activities. To accommodate the increased demands of the 1990 Census, each RO established a temporary Regional Census Center (RCC). In some cases, the RCC was located in the same building as the RO; in others, the facilities were separate. A thirteenth RCC was opened in San Francisco to assist with West Coast operations. The Regional Census Centers coordinated recruitment, hiring, and community outreach in their regions, and supervised the activities of the local District Offices. Directors of the Regional Offices also served as Directors of the RCCs.

The Bureau also established 484 temporary District Offices (DOs): 449 devoted to the full range of field operations and local processing activities; 35 limited to promotion and recruitment functions. Another nine

DOs were opened in Puerto Rico. About one-fourth (109) of the District Offices were opened in early 1989 to conduct pre-Census tasks; the remainder were opened several months before actual Census operations began. Each District Office reported to the Regional Census Center in its area.

Most of the automated data processing activities were conducted at one of seven regional Processing Centers. In addition to the permanent Center in Jeffersonville, six temporary Processing Centers were established. Locations were chosen based on the geographic distribution of District Offices and availability of local labor. Each Processing Center serviced an average of 40 DOs. The Baltimore and Kansas City Processing Centers opened in 1987 because of their role in Pre-Census operations. The Baltimore Office also served as the test site for all computer software used in the Census.

To reduce costs at its many temporary facilities, the Bureau purchased cardboard office furniture, including desks, tables, room dividers, and file boxes. For example, 68,000 woodgrain cardboard desks were utilized by employees at all levels. As one Census worker said, "The only equipment that

Most of the automated data processing activities were conducted at one of seven regional Processing Centers.

Decennial Census Facilities, 1990

Census Bureau Headquarters
   Suitland, MD

Regional Offices (ROs)

Atlanta, GA	Detroit, MI
Boston, MA	Kansas City, MO
Charlotte, NC	Los Angeles, CA
Chicago, IL	New York, NY
Dallas, TX	Philadelphia, PA
Denver, CO	Seattle, WA

Regional Census Centers (RCCs)

Atlanta, GA	Detroit, MI
Boston, MA	Kansas City, MO
Charlotte, NC	Los Angeles, CA
Chicago, IL	New York, NY
Dallas, TX	Philadelphia, PA
Denver, CO	Seattle, WA
San Francisco, CA	

Processing Center

   Jeffersonville, IN

Decennial Processing Centers

Albany, NY	Jacksonville, FL
Austin, TX	Kansas City, MO
Baltimore, MD	San Diego, CA

Local District Offices (DOs)

   484 District Offices
      449 field offices
      35 promotional offices

Figure 3-5

wasn't biodegradable was the computers." Most of the computer equipment was purchased, but about one-fourth of the local DOs utilized leased computers and peripheral equipment. Installing hundreds of sophisticated computer networks in local offices across the country was a particular challenge. Up to six months was required to establish and test the telecommunication links between each DO and its RCC, between RCCs and the Processing Centers, and between the Processing Centers and Bureau Headquarters.

Recruiting the Work Force

The two sections of the Bureau which focus on decennial activities—the Decennial Planning Division and the Decennial Operations Division—have relatively small permanent staffs. As Census Day approached, employees from other Divisions were temporarily transferred to help with the Census and assume key management positions. At the regional level, employees from the Regional Offices were often promoted temporarily to manage operations of the Regional Census Centers. For the most part, however, the Bureau hired temporary employees to work in the RCCs, Processing Centers, and local District Offices.

Recruiting a temporary work force of more than half a million employees was a daunting task. During the peak months of April to June, 1990, over 300,000 workers were employed. This peak work force consisted of 200,000 field workers, 2,700 field supervisors, 7,000 computer specialists, and more than 100,000 clerical workers, including data entry clerks and phone operators. Although most employment needs were for unskilled workers, skilled and semi-skilled workers were also needed, including systems managers, computer technicians, and camera operators. Each District Office employed a District Manager and five full-time assistant managers responsible for recruiting, field operations, electronic data processing, office operations, and general administration. These managers were themselves temporary employees hired specifically for the Census. Employment at District Offices varied from 600 to 900 field workers and 175 to 450 clerical workers. Some jobs at the Processing Centers were open for the duration of the Census, but District-level jobs were filled as work flow dictated. Most employees worked forty-hour weeks for three to eight weeks.

To obtain such a work force, 2.2 million people were interviewed and 1.6 million of these were tested. The Bureau sought workers who could follow directions, work accurately, and complete their assignments effectively. Possession of a high school diploma or equivalency degree was a minimum requirement. Special requirements were sought for "field enumerators," the actual Census takers. In order to dispel public mistrust of the Census, field workers needed to be friendly, outgoing, empathetic, and understanding of other cultures. An effort was made to hire individuals from the neighborhoods where they would be working, which improved an enumerator's familiarity with the territory and increased acceptance by the public. Minorities and bilingual enumerators particularly were sought. Enumerators were also required to have a home phone and their own transportation, which in some areas meant a boat or an all-terrain vehicle. As in prior Censuses, an Executive Order from the President waived civil service requirements for temporary workers.

Recruitment was coordinated by the 13

Recruiting a temporary work force of more than half a million employees was a daunting task.

Q&A

Why were recruiting goals so important?

The major reason was the potentially high turnover rates among temporary workers, especially in urban areas. Many people accepted the work, then quit after several days. In the 1988 Dress Rehearsals, the Bureau saw 80% employee turnover from initial hiring to completion of operations. The smaller applicant pool presented a Catch-22 for the Bureau: the best possible workers were needed, but as recruiting goals went unmet, less desirable applicants were hired, including those who didn't perform as well on the employment test. A smaller applicant pool also meant that training often was hurried, or workers from outside areas were brought in. District managers had less flexibility to fire workers with poor work habits or job performance. Finally, with fewer workers, operations could fall behind schedule, increasing costs and delaying other work.

During the 1980 Census, 30% of the temporary jobs went unfilled, so 1990 planners saw potential recruiting shortages as a major problem.

Regional Census Centers, each of which had a recruitment director. The regional recruiters were hired two years prior to the Census. Public Service Announcements, paid advertisements, local news stories, and other methods were used to publicize the Bureau's employment needs. At the District Offices, local recruiters were themselves temporary workers who received the standard one-week of management training, plus an additional week of on-the-job training. These local recruiters would then contact likely organizations in the community—religious and ethnic groups, senior citizen centers, etc.—touting the Census not only as a temporary job opportunity, but an interesting experience. Arrangements were made with community centers, libraries, state employment agencies, and other public facilities to host "open houses" and screening sessions. The recruiters would then travel to these locations, describe the work of the Census, provide job applications, and administer an employment test.

During the 1980 Census, 30% of the temporary jobs went unfilled, so 1990 planners saw potential recruiting shortages as a major problem. Fears were borne out by experiences during 1989 Prelist operations, when most communities fell short of their recruiting goals. The Bureau's recruiting goal for Prelist was four applicants for every worker hired. For the Census itself, needs were much greater because of the more difficult nature of enumeration; depending on the geographic area, anywhere from six to ten recruits were sought for every employee hired. Such large worker pools were necessary because high turnover rates were anticipated. Based on the more modest four-to-one ratio, the Bureau hoped to recruit two million qualified applicants by March 1990; the actual number who had passed the test by the end of March was one million. Fully 85% of the District Offices did not meet their recruiting goals. However, success varied widely by area, with one District having sufficient recruits, while a neighboring District experienced shortages.

The sheer number of workers needed and short duration of the work were main reasons for the poor recruiting performance. Low pay, lack of benefits, and concerns for personal safety were others. The job itself presented frustrations, mainly from interaction with a suspicious and uncooperative public. During prior Censuses, approximately 90% of field workers were housewives; with more women in the work force in 1990, fewer traditional homemakers were available. The economy also played a role; the more affluent the area, the more difficult it was to recruit. The situation might have been worse except for several changes enacted to help. Based on GAO recommendations, a variable pay scale was adopted, with rates varying by geographic area. The U.S. Department of Health and Human Services permitted states to allow welfare recipients to work on the Census temporarily without losing their AFDC benefits. A similar waiver from the U.S. Department of Housing and Urban Development allowed tenants of public housing projects to maintain their housing subsidies while working on the Census. A law was also passed in August, 1989, allowing federal and military retirees to work on the Census without losing pension benefits. Despite recruiting shortages, most District Offices hired sufficient numbers. In other cases, workers were shifted to other locations after their initial work was completed.

Hiring and Training Staff

The Bureau's employment test consisted of 28 multiple-choice questions designed to measure clerical, organizational, numerical, and evaluative skills. In part, the test was an aptitude instrument, designed to determine the type of Census work best suited to the applicants abilities. However, it was also a screening instrument, testing basic reading and arithmetic skills. The test was available in both English and Spanish. In addition to taking the test, applicants had to pass an FBI background check, basically to determine whether they had been convicted of any felonies. Those who passed the screening stages were placed in a computerized job pool maintained by the RCCs, and were hired as needed. Once hired, workers swore an oath of confidentiality and began training.

Training such a rapidly assembled, short-term work force was a formidable challenge, especially considering the more than 150 job titles involved. Training was typically conducted in a cascading fashion: DO managers and assistant managers were trained at Bureau headquarters. They returned to District Offices to train supervisors, who trained crew chiefs, who trained enumerators. More than 500,000 workers were trained in the field offices. A variety of methods were employed, including classroom lectures, videos, verbatim scripts, and On-the-Job Training. District Managers received one week of general management training in addition to instruction on specific Census operations. For example, data processing managers took a computer operator's course offered by Digital Equipment Corporation, the Bureau's primary computer supplier. Field enumerators received up to five days of local training. Throughout training, workers were tested to make sure they understood the material. Training addressed turnover problems by focusing on morale issues and cross-training.

> Training such a rapidly assembled, short-term work force was a formidable challenge, especially considering the more than 150 job titles involved.

Q&A

Why was so much effort devoted to Address List Compilation?

The Bureau strove to create the most complete and accurate address list possible, *before* Census Day. Any Households not shown on the list ran the risk of not receiving a Questionnaire. Most Households missed in the initial mailing would be identified through follow-up activities, but sending enumerators door-to-door was enormously expensive. The more Households missed in the mail-out, the more labor intensive the Census became. Incomplete mailing lists also diluted the effectiveness of door-to-door operations where they were truly needed. The more time enumerators spent on routine follow-up, the less time could be spent on hard-to-enumerate areas.

Address List Compilation

Because most decennial Census operations were conducted through the mail, the Bureau created a comprehensive mailing list of residential addresses. For the 1990 Census, the agency sought to create the most extensive mailing list in history. Unfortunately, no single source of addresses was sufficient for the Bureau's needs. During the Address List Compilation Test of 1984 and other Pre-Tests, various combinations were tried. Findings from these studies showed that no single method of address compilation was sufficient for developing an up-to-date, comprehensive list. Two methods were ruled out entirely: using existing administrative records from federal, state, or local governments; and purchasing specially-created lists from the United States Postal Service (USPS). For 1990, the Bureau settled on a combination of methods, including field canvassing, purchase of commercial mailing lists, and follow-up checking from the USPS.

Address compilation for 1990 involved a variety of activities designed to create comprehensive mailing lists, and to check, update, and correct them as the Census approached. Figure 3-6 shows the various steps taken to create and revise the lists.

For the 1990 Census, the agency sought to create the most extensive mailing list in history.

List Creation

Two operations focused on creation of the address lists: purchasing commercial lists to create a computerized Tape Address Register (TAR); and canvassing neighborhoods on foot to create manual Address Registers (the Prelist operation). As the various Address Registers were developed, they were merged to form a master computer file called the Address Control File (ACF). In remote areas of the country, a third method was employed; here, the Address Registers were compiled at the time of the Census, as enumerators went door-to-door collecting the forms.

Two critical issues affected mailing list creation. First, mailing addresses had to be detailed enough to allow the Postal Service to deliver them. Second, addresses had to be linked to their corresponding Census geography, an operation known as geocoding.

The Tape Address Register (TAR) was a computerized list of

Two critical issues affected mailing list creation. First, mailing addresses had to be detailed enough to allow the Postal Service to deliver them. Second, addresses had to be linked to their corresponding Census geography, an operation known as geocoding.

Address Compilation Procedures

Tape Address Register (TAR)
<commercial mailing lists>

Address Prelist, Phase 1
<urban and suburban canvassing>

Address Prelist, Phase 2
<rural canvassing>

Address Control File (ACF) Creation
<merging the lists>

Special Place Prelist
<identifying Group Quarters>

Advance Post Office Check (APOC) Phase 1
<postal check of TAR list>

Advance Post Office Check (APOC) Phase 2 and 3
<postal check of Phase 1 Prelist>

APOC Reconciliation
<field work to correct APOC problems>

Precanvass
<Census spot check of TAR list>

Pre-Census Local Review Recanvass
<field work to reconcile Local Review challenges>

Casing Check

List/Enumerate
<list compilation for remote areas>

Figure 3-6

addresses in heavily populated urban and suburban areas. TAR was developed by purchasing a variety of commercial mailing lists, merging the lists, eliminating duplication, and automatically geocoding the lists using address-range data from the TIGER computer files. Using this method, the Bureau was able to identify 56 million Households which could be linked to Census geography. The Tape Address Register was compiled in 1988.

Commercial mailing lists were inadequate for many areas of the country for two reasons. First, the Bureau's computerized geographic database (TIGER) contained address ranges only for streets in large Metropolitan Areas. This meant that commercial mailing lists for addresses outside Metropolitan Areas could not be geocoded for Census use. Second, addresses in rural areas were often inadequate for postal deliver purposes. To capture addresses in these areas, a different method, called Address Prelist, was conducted. During Prelist operations, 35,000 temporary Census workers created manual Address Registers which were then converted to machine-readable form in the District Offices and uploaded to the Address Control File at Bureau headquarters.

Armed with computer-generated street maps, field workers literally walked or drove up and down streets and identified individual addresses. This operation required workers to list the mailing address of every

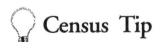 **Census Tip**

Strictly speaking, the decennial Census does not attempt to locate people, but residences. In the process of answering the Questionnaire, the people who happen to live at each address are counted. The Address Control File contains no personal names; it is a list of residential addresses only.

residence, assign a Census Block to the address, and mark its location on their maps. In the process, the maps were also updated, with new streets added and appropriate corrections made.

Prelist was conducted in two stages. The first phase, which took place in 1988, covered urban and suburban territories lying outside Metropolitan Areas. When completed, phase one identified approximately 27 million addresses. The second phase, conducted in 1989, covered closely settled rural areas and seasonal housing areas, and identified 11 million addresses. Half of the nation's counties were included in Prelist operations. Two of the Bureau's temporary Processing Centers coordinated these activities, dividing the nation into two parts. The Baltimore Center covered the eastern portion, the Kansas City Center the western portion.

A final Prelist operation, called the Special Place Prelist, began in January of 1990. The purpose here was to identify all special-purpose dwellings and group residences, called Special Places. Special Places included rooming and boarding houses, residential motels and hotels, marinas, college dormitories, military barracks, nursing homes, and similar facilities. Preliminary lists were developed based on input from local planning agencies, the 1988 and 1989 Prelist operations, and other prior Census operations. During the Special Place Prelist, these addresses were visited by enumerators to verify their status. A resulting list of "Group Quarters" was then developed by the Baltimore Processing Center.

List Checking

The TAR and Prelist operations resulted in a master list of residential addresses, called the Address Control File. Subsequent address activities were designed to update and correct the ACF. The first component of checking operations was called the Advance Post Office Check (APOC), which took place in three stages. A private contractor was

Commercial mailing lists were inadequate for many areas of the country.

Armed with computer-generated street maps, field workers literally walked or drove up and down streets and identified individual addresses.

hired to convert data from the ACF into millions of index cards containing single addresses. The cards were then sent to local post offices, where postal workers sorted them by category: deliverable, undeliverable, and duplicates. Where possible, postal workers corrected addresses, and filled out blue "add cards" for Units on their route which were not listed on the ACF. The first APOC, conducted in the fall of 1988, was based on the original TAR list. The second and third

NEW IN '90

1980 Precanvass lists for apartment buildings showed only a building's street address; for 1990, Precanvass printouts showed individual apartments in multi-Unit buildings.

APOCs, conducted from February to May of 1989, checked the 1988 Prelist. The 1989 Prelist was excluded from APOC operations because these rural addresses would not receive Census Questionnaires in the mail.

Another phase was APOC Reconciliation, where Census enumerators checked problems identified during APOC. Using the Post Office lists of added addresses, undeliverables, and duplicates, enumerators hit the streets to verify addresses, geocode them, and add them to the Census maps. Duplicate addresses were verified and deleted from the lists.

The next major follow-up operation was known as Precanvass, and involved only the TAR portion of the Address Control File. Precanvass took place in May and June of 1989, after the TAR phase of APOC was completed. In this operation, 20,000 enumerators once again set forth to verify the accuracy and completeness of the address lists. This step was necessary because of problems unique to Metropolitan Areas, such as multiple addresses in the same building. For

apartment buildings, an attempt was made to verify the number of Housing Units in the building. For single-Unit neighborhoods, a spot check of every third address was made. Once again, missed addresses were added to the lists, geocoded, and marked on the maps.

A final inspection, called the Casing Check, was conducted by the Postal Service in March, immediately before the Census. Once again, post offices were provided with mailing addresses on individual index cards. All postal carriers have mail sorting areas for their routes, and every address on the route has its own slot. During the Casing Check, postal carriers placed the index cards in their appropriate sorting slots, enabling them to identify missing addresses, duplicates, and undeliverables. Once again, cards were filled out for new addresses. The new cards were send to the Bureau's District Offices for additional field checking and geocoding, then returned to a regional Processing Center to be added to the Address Control File. Before the Census Questionnaires were finally mailed, the ACF had been checked many times.

Census Tip

In addition to the Address List Compilation and follow-up activities which took place prior to Census Day, field workers continued to make additions and corrections to the ACF as the Census was conducted.

Pre-Census Local Review

An important component of Census preparation was the input and involvement of local governments, Indian Reservations, and Alaska Native Villages. All 39,000 government jurisdictions were invited by the Bureau to participate in the Local Review process. Of these, 25,000 governments agreed to partici-

A final inspection, called the Casing Check, was conducted by the Postal Service in March, immediately before the Census.

An important component of Census preparation was the input and involvement of local governments, Indian Reservations, and Alaska Native Villages.

pate. In November, 1986, the Director of the Bureau sent a letter to the highest elected official in every local government. Officials were asked to appoint a liaison for Local Review activities, preferably a planning official familiar with local housing counts. In July, 1987, participants received a Local Review guidebook. Beginning in August, more than 400 workshops were offered around the country, conducted by State Data Centers or state agencies responsible for the Bureau's Federal-State Cooperative Program for Population Estimates. At these workshops, local officials were instructed how to use local maps and administrative records to identify discrepancies in Census maps and address counts, and how to document those discrepancies so the Bureau could investigate and possibly correct them.

> ## NEW IN '90
>
> For 1980, no Pre-Census Local Review took place, though a Post-Census Local Review program was initiated.

and technical guidelines for checking boundaries using local tax and zoning maps. In the fall of 1989, each participating government was sent a computer printout with Block-by-Block counts showing the number of Housing Units and the number of Special Places identified by the Bureau. These counts were based on the TAR and Prelist activities conducted by the Bureau. Local governments then utilized administrative records--lists of building and demolition permits, property tax payments, water bill receipts, and similar files--to identify Blocks where addresses might have been missed. Throughout the process, technical assistance was available from the State Data Center network. If discrepancies were de-

> ## NEW IN '90
>
> Continuous updating of the Address Control File was a major enhancement for 1990. In the past, changes to address lists were done by hand. For 1990, the master ACF was updated throughout every stage of Address List Compilation, Enumeration, and Census follow-up. After field workers noted changes on their Address Registers, local databases were corrected in the District Office and uploaded to the ACF.

Local Review operations had both Pre-Census and Post-Census phases. Pre-Census Review was conducted only in those areas where the Mail Out/Mail Back enumeration method would be used. In contrast, all governments were eligible to participate in the Post-Census Review. Post-Census operations will be discussed in Chapter 4.

Pre-Census Local Review was designed to help identify incorrect geographic boundaries, missed addresses, and addresses assigned to the wrong Census Block. In the summer of 1989, local officials were supplied with computer-generated Census Block maps

tected, local officials sent documentation to the Bureau. Census Blocks with identified discrepancies were then recanvassed by enumerators prior to the Census.

Final Stages of Preparation

As Census Day neared, the final stages of preparation involved publicity and other promotional activities, community outreach programs, and printing and delivering the Census Questionnaire.

Pre-Census Local Review was designed to help identify incorrect geographic boundaries, missed addresses, and addresses assigned to the wrong Census Block.

Q&A

Why provide local officials with Housing Unit totals only? Why not provide them with the actual address lists to be used in the Census?

The Census Bureau interprets its confidentiality limitations very strictly. Even though the Address Control File contains no personal names, the Bureau considers the provision of individual addresses as a violation of the law.

Promotion and Outreach

Without public cooperation, a complete and accurate Census count is impossible. Publicity, promotion, and community outreach were vital components of Census preparation. Promotional activities were designed to accomplish various goals, listed below:

- generate public awareness of the coming Census
- describe the importance of accurate Census data to individual communities
- motivate individuals to complete and return their Questionnaires
- instruct people how to fill-out the forms
- build public support
- stress the confidentiality of Census records
- allay public fears that personal information would be used by other government agencies.

For 1990, $73 million was budgeted for promotional activities, but millions of dollars more were donated through in-kind services. For example, an estimated $68 million in Public Service Announcements (PSAs) aired on local television and radio stations, cable systems, and appeared in local newspapers, transit ads, and billboards. The PSA campaign, which ran from February through May of 1990, was coordinated by the nonprofit Advertising Council. Promotional spots were taped using a variety of notable figures, from President Bush to L.A. Dodger Fernando Valenzuela. The Bureau itself produced flyers, posters, bumper stickers, and buttons for mass distribution. Many of these explained that Census information would not be used for income tax, selective service, immigration, or law enforcement purposes. Others stressed the importance of Census data to the community. Slogans included "Answer the Census: It Counts for More than You Think," and "Any Way We Add It—It Makes Good Sense to Answer the Census."

Much of the effort to promote the Census was voluntary. In addition to the PSA campaign, businesses, local governments, and nonprofit organizations devoted staff time, facilities, and equipment to the promotional effort. At the local level, corporate sponsors donated art work, printing, supplies, and refreshments. Approximately 300 major corporations launched national activities, among them J.C. Penney, Safeway, CVS, and General Mills. Corporate campaigns included Census announcements on customer mailings, utility bills, shopping bags, and employee newsletters.

Census inserts were included with public assistance checks and with paychecks for public employees. Flyers were sent home with children enrolled in the Head Start program. Schools participated in an extensive Census Education Project. The Census Bureau sent curriculum packages for grades K-12 to every school district in the nation. The package included lessons, activities, and

Without public cooperation, a complete and accurate Census count is impossible. Publicity, promotion, and community outreach were vital components of Census preparation.

For 1990, $73 million was budgeted for promotional activities, but millions of dollars more were donated through in-kind services.

instructional guides. Through the Bureau's National Services Program, more than 100 national organizations endorsed the Census, including civil rights groups, religious organizations, and professional associations. In some areas, state or local governments budgeted money for Census promotion. New York City spent $1.5 million alone, excluding money spent by the nonprofit "New York Counts" organization.

In the years leading up to the Census, the Bureau established a variety of mechanisms to solicit community involvement. The mayors of 350 major cities were asked to establish Complete Count Committees comprised of influential members of the community. These committees were charged with planning and implementing local promotion initiatives. The Complete Count Committees served as vehicles to discuss local concerns, promote the Census at the neighborhood level, and help recruit Census enumerators. Promotional activities were coordinated by the 13 Regional Census Centers.

> At a cost of $18 million, printing the Short Form was the largest single print contract ever let by the Government Printing Office.

Printing the Questionnaire

Printing the 1990 Questionnaire was a massive job taking 13 months to complete. 274 million Questionnaires were printed, plus mailing envelopes, first-class return envelopes, instructions, and promotional inserts. In addition to the standard Short and Long Forms, special Questionnaires were printed for such special populations as members of the armed forces, shipboard merchant seamen, institutional residents, and the homeless. Some 5,000 tons of custom-milled paper were used, enough to wrap around the earth twice. Because of the Bureau's exacting technical standards, machine-readable requirements, and massive job size, few commercial printers were capable of handling the task. At a cost of $18 million, printing the Short Form was the largest single print contract ever let by the Government Printing Office. The Short Form was printed by Moore Business Forms at its Thurmont, Maryland and Logan, Utah facilities. The Long Form, at a cost of $8 million, was printed under joint contract by Editors Press (Hyattsville, Maryland) and Webcraft Technologies (Washington, D.C.). All printing was completed by February, 1990.

The entire job involved coordination among the Bureau, the Postal Service, the Government Printing Office, and the contractors. Each Questionnaire displayed an individual mailing address generated by the ACF, and a computer-readable bar code identifying the Census Block of that address. From the three print sites, a complex timetable specified distribution to the nation's post offices.

Forms were boxed sequentially by destination and shipped in 500 of the Postal Service's largest tractor-trailers. Delivered to local post offices in early March, the Questionnaire packages were mailed out during the week of March 23. Total postage costs were $25 million.

NEW IN '90

Greater emphasis on outreach to minority populations was a hallmark of planning for 1990. In many cities, Local Census Steering Committees were established to conduct outreach activities with minority organizations. The Bureau also initiated a Census Awareness and Products Program (CAPP). CAPP specialists, working out of the 13 RCCs and selected field offices, focused on outreach to minority groups in urban areas.

General advertising copy for the Census was created by the Ogilvy and Mather agency, but three minority-owned agencies created campaigns aimed at the Black, Hispanic, and Asian communities. Numerous promotional activities also targeted specific ethnic or racial groups. For example, Coca-Cola sponsored a series of Latino music concerts entitled "Concierto Censo '90."

Summary

Years of planning, public input, field testing, and preparation led up to Census Day, 1990. The process was not without problems, from the struggle over the 1990 Questionnaire and sampling rate, to difficulties in recruiting. The Pre-Tests, Dress Rehearsals, and Address Compilation activities indicated what would work and what would not. They also served as tests of the cost and timetable for the actual Census. During the Jersey City test, only 38% of all Households mailed back Questionnaires. This was largely due to the mayoral election taking place during the test period. With official and public attention focused on the election, the Census test received little publicity. The Los Angeles test also encountered difficulties, with a 27% return rate overall. The poorest returns came from southern Los Angeles County. Rather than hire additional employees to conduct follow-up activities, it was decided to simply eliminate ten communities from the test. Other operations went better. During 1989 Precanvassing, in which 20,000 field workers canvassed 56 million Households, 86% of the District Offices completed work on time or within one week of deadline. The remaining DOs completed work within two weeks of deadline, and the entire operation was conducted within budget. Despite all the planning, testing, and preparation, nothing could predict the actual outcome. Would Households mail back their Questionnaires in sufficient numbers? Would field work proceed on schedule? Would the new technologies perform without breaking down? Answers to these and similar questions would come only after the Census had been conducted.

Despite all the planning, testing, and preparation, nothing could predict the actual outcome.

Chapter 4

Conducting the Census

I. Counting the Population
    A. Principal Collection Methods
    B. Special Population Counts
    C. The Human Face of the Census
II. Improving the Count
    A. Public Awareness Campaigns
    B. Post-Census Local Review
    C. Follow-Up Activities
    D. Post-Enumeration Survey
III. Processing Census Data
    A. Overview
    B. Step by Step through the Process
        1. Preliminary Operations
        2. Filming and Digitizing
        3. Editing and Follow-Up
    C. Census Technology
IV. Problems Conducting the 1990 Census
    A. Low Response Rate
    B. Fabrication of Census Data
    C. Other Problems
V. Tabulation and Publication
    A. Tabulating the Results
    B. The Publication Process
        1. Product Mix
        2. Publication Timetable
VI. Summary

Chapter 4

Conducting the Census

THE UNITED STATES CENSUS is the most extensive statistical operation in the world, involving the largest mobilization of civilian personnel and resources in the United States. Every ten years, thousands of temporary employees fan out across the country to help count every man, woman, and child in the nation. Although recent Censuses have been designed primarily as mail operations, millions of Households must be visited by Census employees, either in initial enumeration or follow-up activities. For 1990, the labors of more than half a million workers were required, with some 300,000 employed during the peak months of April to June, 1990.

One of the best ways to understand the meaning and limitations of 1990 Census data is to examine how the Census was conducted. This chapter focuses on data collection and processing operations. Data collection involved three phases: initial enumeration; contacting Households which did not respond; and a variety of post-Census checking and follow-up operations. Processing operations took place in the temporary District Offices and Processing Centers, following a carefully orchestrated timetable. Once Questionnaires were filled-out and collected, the completed forms were checked-in, processed, edited, and tabulated.

Counting the Population

By Census Day (April 1, 1990) most United States Households had received a Questionnaire, either in the mail or by hand-delivery. The majority of Households (83%) received the Short Form, which asked 14 basic population and housing questions; the remaining 17% received the Long Form, containing the basic 14 questions plus an additional 59 questions. A variable sampling rate, described in Chapter 10, ensured that approximately one out of six Households answered the Long Form.

The Bureau employed a variety of methods to distribute and collect Questionnaires, plus numerous follow-up procedures to ensure a complete Census count. Figure 4-1 shows

Chronology: 1990 Census Enumeration and Follow-Up

Feb. 1990	Enumerate Remote Areas of Alaska
March - April 1990	Update/Leave Operation
March - May 1990	List/Enumerate Operation
March 20-21, 1990	Shelter and Street Nights
March 23, 1990	Questionnaires Delivered to Households
March 23 - April 26, 1990	Questionnaire Assistance
March 30, 1990	Reminder Cards Mailed
March - May 1990	"Didn't receive Questionnaire" calls
March 31, 1990	Transient Night
March - Dec. 1990	Data Processing
April 1, 1990	Census Day
April 1990	Special Places Enumeration
April 1990	Undeliverable Questionnaires Collected from USPS
April - June 1990	Telephone Follow-Up
April 23, 1990	Approximately 65% of Mailback Forms Returned
April 26 - July 1990	Non-Response Follow-Up
April 26 - May 30, 1990	Random check interviews
June - July 1990	Vacant Unit Check
June - Aug. 1990	Field Follow-Up
June - Sept. 1990	"Were You Counted?" Campaign
July 1990	99% of Addresses in ACF Enumerated
July - Dec. 1990	Post-Enumeration Survey
Aug. 1990	90% of Data Processing Completed
Aug. - Sept. 1990	Post-Census Local Review
Sept. 24, 1990	Deadline for Local Review Replies
Aug. - Nov. 1990	Local Census Offices Closed
Sept. - Oct. 1990	Local Review Recanvass
Dec. 31, 1990	Deadline for State Population Counts
April 1, 1991	Deadline for Sub-State Counts
June 1991	Revised PES data released

Figure 4-1

the timetable for these operations.

 Census Tip

Under Census guidelines, people are counted at their "usual place of residence," meaning the address where they live most of the year.

Three main data collection methods were employed in the 1990 Census.

Principal Collection Methods

Three main data collection methods were employed in the 1990 Census. Approximately 84% of U.S. Households received Questionnaires in the mail and were instructed to return them by mail, in a method called Mailout/Mailback (MO/MB). Another 10% of Households had forms delivered by enumerators and were instructed to return them by mail (the Update/Leave method). The remaining 6% received unaddressed Questionnaires in the mail and were instructed to hold them for enumerators to pick up (the List/Enumerate method). The three methods reflected the Bureau's ability to create accurate address lists and the Postal Service's ability to deliver the forms. Figure 4-2 compares principal features of the three methods.

Mailout/Mailback was the most cost-effective method, and the Bureau attempted to use it wherever possible. However, it could be used only in areas where geocoded address lists could be developed and where addresses accurately reflected the exact physical location of each Housing Unit. As described in Chapter 3, address list compilation had been accomplished in two ways: through the Tape Address Register (and revisions of TAR during Precanvass operations); and through phase one of Prelist. By using Mailout/Mailback for the "easy to find" addresses, personnel and resources were freed to concentrate on harder-to-locate Housing Units. In many large, urban areas, the Bureau removed particular Census Blocks from the MO/MB lists and enumerated them via traditional door-to-door methods. These included Blocks with heavy concentrations of vacant buildings and those with public housing projects.

The remaining two methods were used in areas where the Bureau had not compiled address lists in earlier operations, or where

---

NEW IN '90

1990 Census packets were mailed out five to nine days earlier than in 1980, allowing respondents more time to complete the forms. Questionnaires were mailed out on or about March 23.

Characteristics of Principal Data Collection Methods

Feature	Collection Method Mailout/Mailback	Collection Method Update/Leave	Collection Method List/Enumerate
Percentage of Households	84%	10%	6%
Area Type	Most areas	Rural areas with poor mail address	Remote, sparsely populated areas
Delivery Method	Mailout (addressed)	Enumerator delivered	Mailout (unaddressed)
Collection Method	Mailback	Mailback	Enumerator pick-up
Address Compilation Method	TAR, with Precanvass follow-up; Prelist phase I for smaller areas.	Prelist phase II, with enumerator follow-up during Census.	No pre-Census compilation. List developed at time of enumeration.
District Office Type	Type 1 or 2	Type 2	Type 3
Initial Processing	Processing Centers for Type 1 areas; District Offices for Type 2.	District Offices	District Offices

Figure 4-2

addresses were insufficient to allow Postal Service delivery. The Update/Leave method was employed primarily in the South and Midwest. Enumerators used the Address Registers compiled in 1989 during phase two of Prelist. Shortly before April 1, 1990, they recanvassed the areas, updated Address Registers, and at the same time, left Questionnaires at each Household. Respondents were instructed to return completed forms by mail.

Update/Leave was also utilized for public housing projects in large urban areas.

The third method, List/Enumerate, was used in extremely remote, sparsely populated areas, where it was simply too costly or difficult to develop an Address Register prior to the Census. This method was also utilized on many American Indian Reservations and areas with high concentrations of seasonal housing. Although only 6% of all House-

Q&A

Why couldn't Questionnaires be mailed out in the Update/Leave areas?

Ideally, every dwelling in Mailout/Mailback areas would have a unique number and every street would have a name (e.g., 8651 Main Street.) Unfortunately, much of the country uses rural route numbers and/or box numbers for postal delivery. Such route numbers are literally postal routes, not highway or road names. Box numbers on these routes change as new structures are built. Even route numbers change in high growth areas; to balance the work load among rural carriers, the post office renumbers the routes. And many Households don't use the rural box number

in their address, relying on the postal carrier to know the route.

Using such addresses is fine for postal delivery, but not for Census geocoding, where every structure must be uniquely identified and placed in its appropriate Census Block. For enumerators to identify each structure properly, 1990 Address Registers and Census maps were extremely specific. A typical rural address would be "Route 2, Box 14: blue house on left side of Highway 11, three miles north of Cox Road."

---

holds were located in these areas, they encompassed fully 50% of the nation's land area, mainly in the northern and western United States.

In List/Enumerate areas, local post offices were given unaddressed Questionnaire packets for delivery to every Household on their carriers' routes. Short Forms only were delivered. Enumerators, supplied with extra Questionnaires, blank Address Registers, and Block maps, were assigned specific territories. Beginning March 30, these enumerators identified and visited every Household in their territories and collected filled-out forms. If the Questionnaire was not already completed, as was often the case, the enumerator conducted an interview to complete it. At every other Household, enumerators used the Long Form to collect additional data. The Address Register was thus compiled at the time of enumeration. Each Housing Unit was added to the Register, geocoded, and marked on the Census map as enumerators covered their territories.

A variation of List/Enumerate was used in remote areas of Alaska. Although Alaska's population is concentrated in its larger cities, 20% of the inhabitants are spread over 80% of the state's land area. For 1990 operations,

aerial photographs and "fly overs" identified remote Native Villages and other settlements. Snowmobiles, planes, and even dogsleds were used to reach these remote areas beginning in mid-February, 1990. The Census had to be taken in winter, because travel was more hazardous during the spring thaw, and afterward, villagers dispersed to trap, hunt, or fish. Therefore, enumerators counted the population while inhabitants were still socked in for the winter. A Census liaison recruited enumerators from the settlements, then local team leaders were selected to train and supervise workers. During a first visit, forms were distributed to the local enumerators. During a second visit, completed Questionnaires were collected and follow-up activities conducted.

Snowmobiles, planes, and even dogsleds were used to reach these remote areas beginning in mid-February, 1990.

NEW IN '90

Only two enumeration methods were used in 1980: 90% of all Households were covered by Mailout/Mailback; 10% were covered by List/Enumerate (which in 1980 was called the Conventional method). The Update/Leave method was completely new for 1990.

As in other remotely-settled areas, one out of two Households received the Long Form.

Special Population Counts

Special procedures were developed to count individuals not living in Households. The Bureau's complex definitions of Households and Group Quarters are described in Chapter 5. For the present discussion, however, think of the Group Quarters population as those persons not living in a typical house or apartment.

Special Counts were conducted for transients, individuals living in shelters or on the street, military personnel, crews of merchant vessels, occupants of other Group Quarters, and certain citizens living abroad. During these operations, data were recorded on special Census forms called Individual Census Reports (ICRs), Shipboard Census Reports (SCRs), and Military Census Reports (MCRs). These forms were similar to regular Questionnaires, and both Long and Short Forms were used. The major differences were the absence of housing questions, and the fact that each form counted an individual rather than an entire Household.

Locations of such Group Quarters as col-

Special Counts were conducted for transients, individuals living in shelters or on the street, military personnel, crews of merchant vessels, occupants of other Group Quarters, and certain citizens living abroad.

lege dormitories and nursing homes were identified by the Special Place Prelist. During the Census, enumerators visited these locations, obtained lists of residents, and delivered ICR forms. Most residents were given the Short Form, though a sample received the Long Form. Enumerators returned in a few days to collect the forms and conduct follow-up activities. Where direct follow-up wasn't possible, as when a resident was too ill to respond, data were obtained from the staff or from institutional records.

Military personnel and their dependents, including the crews of military vessels and service persons stationed abroad, were counted with the assistance of the Department of Defense and the Coast Guard. On each ship or military installation, a project officer was designated to coordinate the Census. All personnel filled out an MCR or SCR. Personnel living off-base normally received two forms: an MCR from the project officer; and a regular Questionnaire mailed to their home address. Duplication was coordinated by the project officer. For shipboard crews, individuals could designate whether their regular address was on ship or shore. Personnel stationed abroad and their dependents listed their "home of record" as their stateside address.

How did the Census count individuals and families who were away from home on Census day?

Individuals staying at a second home, mobile home park, or campgrounds on Census Day received a Census form at their temporary address during regular Census operations. The first question asked whether the address on the Census form was their usual place of residence; if not, they were instructed to include the complete address of their usual residence. Forms for these individuals were carefully checked under both addresses to ensure no one was missed or double counted.

Individuals traveling on vacation or brief business

trips (whether in the U.S. or abroad) would find a Questionnaire when they returned home, or would be counted in Census follow-up operations. Enumeration and follow-up continued through the summer and fall of 1990.

What about individuals living outside the country for longer durations? The decennial Census counts U.S. residents only. For the most part, American citizens living abroad are not counted in the Census. Exceptions to the Bureau's residency guidelines are described in Chapter 5.

Crews of merchant vessels were counted with the assistance of the U.S. Maritime Administration. Lists were obtained of all vessels under U.S. flag, and SCRs were sent to each, regardless of location. As with military personnel, merchant marines could claim their usual residence on ship or shore, but not both.

The so-called "Homeless Census" attracted a great deal of media attention and public criticism, which will be discussed in Chapter 10. At this point, a quick description of the methodology will suffice. The Bureau has attempted to count America's street and shelter population for many decades. For 1990, these efforts were bolstered, but the Bureau made no claim to conduct a comprehensive count of the homeless, nor did it even define the term "homeless" for Census purposes. Two "S-Nights" were designated for the 1990 census: Shelter Night, on March 20; and Street Night, on March 21. More than 15,000 enumerators participated in these operations, at a cost of $2.7 million. The homeless themselves were recruited and paid to help enumerate. Prior to the Census, requests were sent to the highest elected official of every major city, requesting lists of shelters; hotels and motels charging less than $12 per night; and street locations where the homeless were known to congregate. Approximately 90% of the cities supplied such lists. Locations were also identified through Prelist operations and through the cooperation of local community groups and human service organizations.

Shelter Night was conducted from 6:00 PM to midnight on March 20, though in some areas, operations continued the following night. A total of 11,000 shelters were enumerated, including those providing assistance to families. A small percentage of shelter operators did not cooperate; in these cases, enumerators stood outside the structure and counted people as they left. Both Short and Long Forms were used.

Street Night took place on March 21, in two stages. The first phase, from 2:00-4:00 AM, targeted such previously identified lo-

cations as alleys, streets, bus terminals, and parks. All visible persons were counted unless they wore a uniform or otherwise appeared to be working. The second phase, from 4:00-8:00 AM, focused on abandoned and boarded-up buildings. Here enumerators watched and counted any individuals leaving the building. Some 24,000 street locations were observed during Street Night. Short Forms only were used and enumerators tallied age, Race, and sex characteristics by observation.

A related operation, called Transient Night, targeted locations with identifiable transient populations, from migrant labor camps to circuses and carnivals. Transient Night occurred on March 31.

The Human Face of the Census

An army of temporary field workers was employed to prepare for and conduct the 1990 Census. Many stages of the Census involved field operations, including the three Prelists; Precanvassing; the List/Enumerate and Update/Leave operations; Group Quarters enumerations; Street, Shelter, and Transient Nights; and numerous follow-up activities. Whether traveling on foot, or by car, boat, or dogsled, these workers were truly the foot soldiers of the Census. Among them were homemakers, students, retirees, and the unemployed. Some enumerators worked full-time elsewhere during the day, working for the Bureau on evenings and weekends. Armed with maps, address lists, an official portfolio, and a red, white, and blue Census badge, these workers traveled the city streets and country roads of America. In their quest to count the population, enumerators ventured into every conceivable habitat, from tenement buildings to remote swamps. One journalistic account aptly described this effort as "the largest posse ever assembled on the North American continent."

Hourly wages for field work varied by geographic area, but ranged from $5 to $8 per hour. Workers provided their own trans-

---

The so-called "Homeless Census" attracted a great deal of media attention and public criticism.

In their quest to count the population, enumerators ventured into every conceivable habitat, from tenement buildings to remote swamps. One journalistic account aptly described this effort as "the largest posse ever assembled on the North American continent."

A 1990 Census enumerator visited all those housing units which did not respond to the Census Questionnaire. As do all Bureau employees, enumerators take an oath to protect the confidentiality of individual Census responses.
(Bureau of the Census photo)

The FACT system (Film and Automated Camera Technology) sped 1990 Census processing. The FACT system photographed each Census Questionnaire onto microfilm. The microfilm was then scanned and the data transferred into computer files. (Bureau of the Census photo)

portation but were reimbursed for mileage, usually from $.21 to $.24 per mile. Travel time was included in the hourly pay. No production quotas were imposed, but performance norms were established by geographic location and type of work. Workers who exceeded productivity and quality standards received a one-time bonus after six weeks of work, ranging from $75 to $325.

NEW IN '90

During the 1980 Census, workers were paid piece-rate wages (by the number of Households visited, Questionnaires completed, and so on) a practice which may have encouraged overcounting. The hourly rates used in 1990, combined with bonus incentives, were seen as a more effective compensation package.

Different environments presented different challenges for field workers. In many urban apartment buildings, enumerators struggled to identify unmarked apartments. In rural areas, houses often had no distinct address. In many areas of Florida, mobile homes were hidden off the road or tucked into woods. In northeast Washington state, workers had to comb thousands of acres of forest to locate the cabins of hardy souls seeking solitude or an alternative lifestyle. Enumerators also faced unexpected peril, from dog bites to the more unusual examples listed in Figure 4-3.

Most problems facing enumerators were far more mundane: trying to reach people in a society which spends less and less time at home; dealing with respondents tired of answering surveys; coping with foreign languages and cultures; and most of all, interviewing people who viewed the Census as rude or downright threatening. Whether respondents resented the Census as an invasion

Tales from the Census Front: The 1990 Campaigns

Monticello, MI
An elderly homeowner, plagued by teenage vandals, mistakenly shot a Census enumerator. The enumerator not only recovered, but went back to Census-taking. "We were impressed," coworkers stated. The homeowner apologized and all charges were dropped.

Cedar Rapids, IA
An enumerator was suspended by the Bureau for violating his confidentiality oath after informing local police that a resident he interviewed appeared to be smoking marijuana. Police took no action against the alleged offender.

Fort Lauderdale, FL
While conducting S-Night operations, two female enumerators were robbed at knife-point of jewelry and cash. After reporting the incident to police, the women resumed their work shift.

Compton, CA
A female enumerator was greeted by the sight of a nude man answering his door. When she asked him to put some clothes on, the man responded, "No. If you count me, you have to count me as I am." The enumerator's answer: "No problem."

Black Rock Desert, NV
After crashing in the desert while conducting field work, an enumerator spent a frigid night in her car. She was rescued by a search party the following day.

San Juan, PR
Two Census workers found a baby who had been kidnapped and left in a shopping bag near a garbage dumpster.

Michigan's Upper Peninsula
Enumerators variously reported being sprayed by a skunk, chased by a bear, and encountering a moose.

Brooklyn, NY
Three Census workers were shot at as they approached an abandoned building to count the homeless. The enumerators fled the scene, assuming the shots were intended to scare them off. They resumed their work at another location ten minutes later.

Alton, IL
A 32-year old woman was charged with battery after grabbing an enumerator by the neck and biting her shoulder. When a neighbor rushed to the worker's aide, she too was attacked. The woman apparently thought the enumerator was a fundraiser. Said a Bureau spokesman, "To be attacked and bitten is unusual. Usually our biggest problem is people not being home."

Figure 4-3 .

of privacy, or feared the government would use resulting data against them, many did not welcome enumerators with open arms. On the other hand, many respondents were more than happy to speak with enumerators, and in some cases, Census workers profoundly touched the lives of lonely or housebound individuals, if only for a moment.

Improving the Count

Many activities—before, during, and after the initial count—were designed to make the 1990 Census as complete and accurate as possible. The major methods involved public awareness campaigns, the Post-Census Local Review program, and numerous follow-up operations.

Public Awareness Campaigns

Despite diverse promotional activities, widespread use of Public Service Announcements, and extensive community involvement prior to Census Day, many Americans were simply unaware of the 1990 Census. Research con-

ducted by the Bureau following the 1980 Census indicated that for many, receiving a Questionnaire in the mail was their first indication a Census was underway. For this reason, the 1990 Questionnaire packet included a colorful, "Count Yourself in on the Census" brochure, explaining the purpose and value of the Census. Enclosed instructions were printed in English and Spanish. The envelope itself, variations of which had been tried in several field tests, was a large green and white envelope marked "Official 1990 U.S. Census Form." From Census Day through April 25, the Bureau ran a publicity campaign with the message, "There's still time to answer the Census." A week after Questionnaires were delivered, all addresses in the Mailout/Mailback and Update/Leave areas received a reminder card in the mail.

As mentioned in Chapter 3, much of the Bureau's promotion, advertising, and outreach efforts focused on various minority populations. Explaining the Census to non-English speakers was a special concern for 1990. In addition to hiring bilingual enumerators and phone operators in targeted neighborhoods, the Bureau utilized a variety of programs. A week prior to mailing the Questionnaire, a multilingual "Early Alert"

Many activities— before, during, and after the initial count—were designed to make the 1990 Census as complete and accurate as possible.

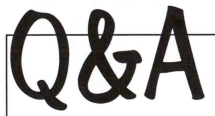

The pay was low, benefits were nonexistent, the work was often stressful, and the job was temporary. So why become a Census enumerator?

Answers given by enumerators ranged from the practical to the romantic. The unemployed were hungry for a paycheck. Students were looking for a summer job. Retirees sought an opportunity to keep busy. Some needed a second job with flexible hours. Others hired on for patriotic or charitable reasons. Some saw it as a civic duty or a chance to do something for the community. In several areas, members of the League of Women Voters volunteered to work on the Census, then donated earnings to their local chapter. Many workers simply thought it would be an interesting experience. But as one put it, "It's gotta be more than money. Nobody takes this abuse just for the pay." To some it was just a job, but many took great pride in their work, from the Texas enumerator who used a rowboat to cross the rising tide of spring-time flood waters, to the South Bronx Census-taker who worked from his wheelchair.

brochure was mailed to all Households in designated areas. With text in English, Spanish, and six Asian languages, the brochure announced the coming Census, described its importance to the community, explained how to obtain assistance, and listed toll-free help lines. Separate numbers were given for each of the eight languages. In many cities, the Bureau staffed local assistance centers to provide help in completing the Questionnaire or provide forms to those who never received them. In other areas, assistance centers were staffed by volunteers or sponsored by local governments. The Bureau also designed Language Assistance Guides in 32 languages, from French to Tagalog. These guides contained translations of Census questions and instructions, for use by enumerators and assistance centers.

The Bureau also designed Language Assistance Guides in 32 languages, from French to Tagalog.

A final public awareness activity, called the "Were You Counted?" campaign, took place in the summer. Request forms were reproduced in local newspapers and through other sources, and toll-free numbers were publicized, providing another chance for the uncounted to reply.

NEW IN '90

Compared to the previous Census, twice as many governments were involved in 1990 Post-Census Local Review. In 1980, 12,400 governments agreed to participate; the number for 1990 was 25,000.

The program was not only greatly expanded for 1990, but data were also more detailed: for 1990, Housing Unit counts were provided at the Block level; for 1980, counts were provided only for aggregations of Blocks, called Enumeration Districts.

Post-Census Local Review

After primary enumeration activities concluded, local governments again were invited to review the results of Census operations. In May and June, all 39,000 governments were sent new Census maps showing Block boundaries corrected during field work. Beginning in August, all governments received a computer printout with preliminary counts of Housing Units and Special Places for every Census Block in their area. The Post-Census Review differed from its Pre-Census counterpart in two respects. First, it was sent to all 39,000 governments, not just those in large Urbanized Areas. Second, the Special Place count showed the actual Group Quarters population, not simply the number of Group Quarters. As with the Pre-Census Review, Housing Unit counts listed only the number of Units, not the population living in them.

The Bureau sent Local Review tabulations to local governments via certified mail. Officials were given 15 days to challenge the preliminary counts, with a final deadline of September 24. Once again, discrepancies had to be Block-specific and sufficiently documented. Concrete examples might include overlooking a new housing subdivision, missing a hospital or prison, or working with incorrect geographic boundaries. Approximately 7,000 governments submitted documented challenges, representing 166,000 Census Blocks.

 Census Tip

Population and Housing Unit counts submitted to governments under the Local Review program were intended for internal use only. Final counts would not be tabulated and published until all Census operations were completed. In many areas, preliminary Local Review Figure s were leaked to the press, causing some data users to make decisions based on incomplete and incorrect numbers.

Follow-Up Activities

Throughout April, Census District Offices made periodic sweeps of the local Post Offices to collect undeliverable Questionnaires.

Q&A

What if no one at a given address could be reached during the NRFU phase?

After repeated tries, enumerators turned to the Last Resort method. A building manager, postal carrier, or neighbor was contacted to help determine whether the address was Vacant, or if the residents were away for an extended time. Last Resort was also a source of information about the inhabitants. If neighbors had sufficient knowledge, their responses were used to identify the basic characteristics of the non-responding Household.

And what if the Last Resort method yielded no additional information? When enumerators could not verify whether an address was occupied, or when they couldn't determine the number of occupants, the address was marked Vacant. All Questionnaires for Vacant Units, whether verified or not, were placed in the "Vacancy Check" category, triggering one more round of checking at a later date.

in the ACF had been counted.

Field workers accomplished several tasks during NRFU visits: first, to verify that each missing Questionnaire represented a valid residential address; second, to determine whether the Housing Unit was Vacant or Occupied; and third, to obtain a completed Questionnaire from occupied Units. A resident of each non-respondent Household was interviewed, even if they indicated a form already had been returned by mail. As with the "Were You Counted?" campaign, duplication was caught by the ACF. Responses were accepted from any occupant 15 years or older. If no one was home, an official notification was left to alert the Household of the visit. Enumerators were required to make two additional visits and three phone calls on different days and at different times. Also during NRFU, enumerators checked their Address Registers one more time in pursuit of missing addresses.

By April 23, only 65% of all Questionnaires had been returned.

Census workers then tried to correct addresses and redeliver the forms. Requests for Questionnaires also came from other sources, including the "Were You Counted?" campaign, and calls received by the Bureau's toll-free numbers, the District Offices, local government hot lines, and legislators' offices. Missed addresses were checked against the Address Control File and added to the database if necessary. In many cases, replacement forms were then hand-delivered and picked up by field workers. Numerous other follow-up activities were mounted to improve the Census count, but they basically fell into two categories: Non-Response Follow-Up (NRFU) and Recanvassing.

By April 23, only 65% of all Questionnaires had been returned. The next phase of Census operations, Non-Response Follow-Up, took place from the end of April through July. As completed forms flowed in, their bar codes were scanned and checked against the Address Control File at Census headquarters, which served as a central inventory. In this way, workers could determine which Households had not responded. Enumerators then took to the streets in all Mailout/Mailback and Update/Leave areas. During this short period, enumerators visited 34 million Households. By the end of July, 99% of all addresses

💡 Census Tip

Throughout every phase of Census operations, field workers attempted to locate Housing Units not listed on their Address Registers. Interviews and direct observation were helpful in identifying "hidden" apartments located in attics, garages, or basements.

A second type of follow-up involved Edit Checks. As returned Questionnaires were processed, they were edited, both manually and by computer. Forms with incomplete or

NEW IN '90

A special follow-up program, called Parolee/Probationer Coverage Improvement, was introduced for 1990. In April, government employees in every state but Maine agreed to send Questionnaires directly to individuals on parole or probation. Although 2.6 million individuals fit that description, the initial response was low. During follow-up, enumerators used administrative records to obtain basic address and demographic information on parolees and probationers. The ACF was then searched for duplication, and missing Questionnaires were added if the address could be geocoded.

Because each Questionnaire contained a space for the respondent's phone number, most follow-up work was conducted by phone.

internally inconsistent responses were separated for checking. For example, if the answers for a five-year-old child indicated he was married or had completed college, the discrepancies would be caught in the computer edit. Because each Questionnaire contained a space for the respondent's phone number, most follow-up work was conducted by phone. If a respondent could not be reached after repeated calls, a field worker would visit the address.

Another phase of field follow-up was the Vacancy Check. Throughout June and July, enumerators revisited every address marked "Vacant" or "Delete." During previous op-

erations, an address was deleted if the field worker found it was a commercial establishment, a condemned building, an empty lot, or otherwise not a valid Housing Unit. By rechecking these addresses, field workers could locate Households which were incorrectly identified as Vacant or nonresidential the first time around. The Vacancy Check was especially important in light of the Bureau's policy of marking an address Vacant if its true status could not be determined during the initial enumeration. Vacancy was determined by the Unit's status as of April 1; therefore, a new tenant contacted in June could verify the apartment indeed had been Vacant in April.

The final field operation was Recanvassing, an activity triggered by Local Review challenges. Recanvassing took place only in Blocks where reported discrepancies exceeded a range specified by the Bureau: an undercount of one Housing Unit or more, or an overcount of at least five Units. Where local evidence suggested Housing Units or Group Quarters had been missed, field workers revisited those Blocks. Approximately 6% of the nation's Housing Units were rechecked during this phase, which lasted from August through October. In many cases, local government records were outdated, or the municipality's interpretation of a Housing Unit did not

Q&A

Why didn't the Bureau simply compare Census returns to existing administrative records (state motor vehicle registrations, etc.) to determine discrepancies and undercount?

The Bureau believed the minimal benefits did not justify the high cost of record checking. During the 1980 Census, list-matching was used to check seven million names against administrative records. Fewer than 2% were added to the final count; the rest were duplicates. When New York City provided the Bureau with a list of 16,500 names thought to be missing from the 1980 Census, 1,155 were verified, at a cost of $250 per name. In a 1986 Pre-Test, improved matching techniques were employed. Once again, about 2% of the names were not duplicates, but the cost of checking was $70 per name. While a nationwide list-matching effort could possibly improve the count by 2%, the cost of checking millions of names would have been prohibitive.

Why was the Post-Enumeration Survey an effective means of documenting the Census undercount?

PES results were themselves only estimates, subject to sampling error and other statistical errors. As one demographer phrased it, the PES is like a capture/recapture study in wildlife biology; the subjects are tagged, then captured and examined at a later date. The difference is humans can be better at avoiding detection. Even so, the PES remains the best means of measuring undercount.

More than 20% of the nation's Housing Units were visited during such follow-up operations as Local Review Recanvassing, Vacancy Check, and the "Were You Counted?" campaign.

conform to Census definitions. In these situations, the challenges were not substantiated. In other cases, geocoding errors were discovered, resulting in Households being assigned to the wrong Block, but no net gain in population for the community. Local governments were notified of Local Review corrections in November.

More than 20% of the nation's Housing Units were visited during such follow-up operations as Local Review Recanvassing, Vacancy Check, and the "Were You Counted?" campaign. Adding the Non-Response Follow-Up activities, approximately half of all addresses were visited or revisited as part of the Bureau's normal checking routines.

As follow-up activities wound down, Census workers operated under a rapidly approaching deadline. By federal law, final Census tabulations had to be submitted to the President by December 31, 1990, which meant that field work could not drag on through the fall. The 484 temporary Census offices could not be closed until all field operations were completed, but one by one, the District Offices did close.

Post-Enumeration Survey

Even with such elaborate follow-up procedures, the decennial Census could not count every resident of the United States. But how many people were actually missed? The Bureau estimated the Census undercount in two ways: demographic analysis and the Post-Enumeration Survey.

Demographic analysis compares the final counts from the decennial Census to total population estimates derived through other means. The Bureau routinely estimates the national population using birth and death records and migration data. These national estimates are published monthly, year-in and year-out. Comparing the April 1990 estimate to the decennial enumeration was one way to investigate undercount. However, the monthly estimates were themselves imprecise and insufficiently detailed.

A second method was to conduct a sample survey to find out if people were counted in the Census. The Post-Enumeration Survey (PES) designated a nationwide sample of Census Blocks, then interviewed every Household on each of the sampled Blocks. In 1990, 2,000 Bureau interviewers visited approximately 165,000 Households. During the 15 minute interview, the respondent was asked to identify the name, age, Race, sex, and birth date for every member of the Household, and where they were living on April 1. Addresses were then matched against decennial Census responses. Some people surveyed in the PES were uncounted by the Census; conversely, some people counted at a given address in the Census did not show up in the PES. The PES methodology thus identified people who were missed, counted at the wrong address, or double counted. In this way, the Bureau estimated the degree of undercount or overcount by age, Race, or sex, then compared undercount by geographic area.

Processing Census Data

Processing of Census data began even as Questionnaires continued to flow in. Figure 4-2, shown earlier, illustrates the relationship between collection method and processing location. Processing took place at either a District Office or a regional Processing Center, depending on the area. Residents in Type 1 areas, comprised of Urbanized Areas (densely settled areas with population greater than 50,000), mailed Questionnaires directly to one of the seven Processing Centers. Because large cities presented the greatest enumeration problems, this method freed District Offices in densely populated areas to concentrate on such activities as Non-Response Follow-Up and Vacancy Checks. It also relieved those offices of additional recruiting burdens, since fewer employees were needed. Approximately 20% of all forms came from Type 1 areas. Type 2 areas covered most non-Urbanized locations, except for the most remote rural territories, which were Type 3 areas. Questionnaires from Type 2 and 3 areas were received at the local District Offices. The DOs processed Mailback Questionnaires from smaller cities, suburbs, and rural areas, as well as all enumerator-collected Questionnaires.

Overview

As Questionnaires were received by District Offices, the bar code on each form was scanned into a computer using a hand-held

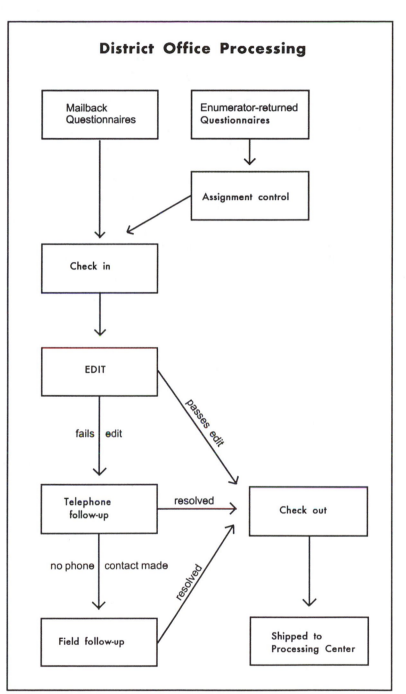

Figure 4-4

NEW IN '90

In 1980, all Mailback Questionnaires were sent to the District Offices, where check-in and editing were handled manually. No initial processing took place at the Processing Centers.

laser wand. Once scanned, bar codes were matched against the Address Control File at Bureau headquarters to determine which addresses had not returned a form. Next, envelopes were opened and sorted, then edited by clerical staff. Editors checked each Questionnaire to ensure it was completed properly; the editors' work was double-

The Processing Centers housed sophisticated equipment for converting Census Questionnaires into machine-readable form.

checked by other employees called verifiers. Questionnaires which passed the editing phase were then boxed and shipped to the nearest Processing Center for further work. A Questionnaire failed the edit stage if answers were incomplete. These were sent to Telephone Follow-up, where the Household was contacted to complete the form. If the no contact was made after five phone calls, the Questionnaire was referred to Field Follow-Up. Once problems were resolved, these forms were also sent to the regional Processing Center. Figure 4-4 summarizes District Office workflow.

For those forms mailed directly from Households to a Processing Center, initial workflow was essentially the same. One difference involved bar code scanning; because Processing Centers received 170,000 Questionnaires per day during the weeks following Census Day, high-speed scanners were used rather than hand-held wands. The other difference involved Questionnaires failing the manual edit; those requiring Field Follow-up were returned to a District Office for enumerator action.

Operations at the Processing Centers were distinguished by the work which took place after initial editing. The Processing Centers housed sophisticated equipment for converting Census Questionnaires into machine-

readable form. Whether received from District Offices or direct from Households, forms which passed the initial edit stage were sent to Camera Preparation, where they were readied for microfilming. The Questionnaires were then filmed by high-speed automated cameras, and converted into digitized form by specially designed machines called FOSDIC. Computers next edited each Questionnaire, looking for internal inconsistencies. Once again, those failing the edit check were separated for follow-up. Powerful minicomputers transmitted the resulting data to Census headquarters via dedicated, secure telecommunications links. To control this complex workflow, every Questionnaire was monitored through each stage of the process by a computerized Control and Tracking System. Workflow at Processing Centers is summarized in Figure 4-5.

Step by Step Through the Process

Each Processing Center employed some 1,500 temporary workers during peak processing months, running two shifts 16 hours per day. To convey a better sense of processing operations, let's follow the progress of a Questionnaire received from a Type 1 area, mailed directly to a Processing Center.

Preliminary Operations

Incoming mail from the Postal Service was handled completely by machine, including recording (Check-In), sorting, and opening. High-speed lasers scanned the bar codes, recorded their receipt, and sorted the forms by location and type. Each bar code was a unique 11-digit number identifying the District Office and the individual address. In addition to the bar code, every Question

Census Tip

Computerized Census files do not contain personal identification information such as names or Social Security numbers. The automated process which converts Questionnaires into computer files cannot "read" name information. During Surname Capture, names at selected addresses are keyed-in by data clerks, but are used only for quality control purposes. These files are kept separate from the database containing the demographic information on each Household. The keyed-in names do not appear in the Bureau's final data files.

naire had a sorting code attached to its address. Two-digit codes were used to identify the following four categories: Short Form, single-Unit; Long Form, single-Unit; Short Form, multi-Unit; and Long Form, multi-Unit. Questionnaires were sorted first by District Office, then by type. Each of the

four categories was processed separately. The two types of multi-Unit forms (those coming from apartment buildings) went through an added step called Surname Capture, where a personal name was entered into the Census database for each address. This was also done for rural addresses without distinct house

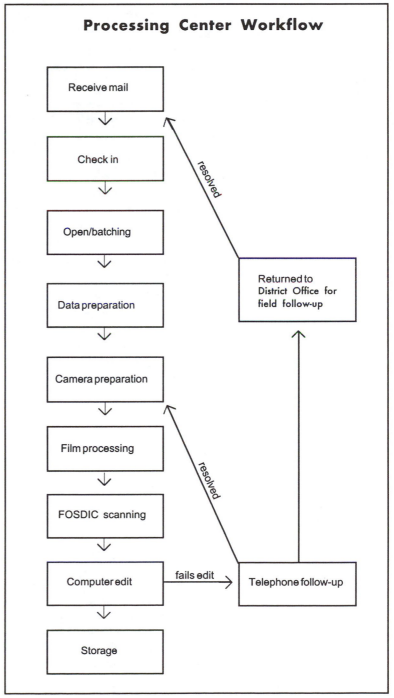

Figure 4-5

numbers. In situations where Field Follow-Up was required, Surname Capture helped avoid potential mistakes or confusion due to imprecise apartment numbers or street addresses, and prevented duplication of Census returns.

Step two was known as Open and Batching. Envelopes were opened by machine, then clerks unfolded, creased, and laid each form out straight. The machine-sorted forms were then sent to data preparation clerks, who "bubbled-in" the portion of each Questionnaire marked, "For Census Use." This information was used during the computer-edit phase. Smudged or incomplete bubbling was also corrected during this operation. Questionnaires with missing answers were sent to the Telephone Follow-Up Unit, where workers contacted Households by phone. Finally, a piece of special tape was affixed to the last question for the last individual on each Questionnaire, which instructed the automatic camera when to stop filming. From here, forms went to the Camera Preparation Unit, where they were batched and boxed for filming. A single box (also called a Batch) consisted of 450 Short Forms or 100 Long Forms. A Camera Unit (the quantity contained on a single reel of microfilm) consisted of four Batches. Each Camera Unit was numbered for monitoring by the computerized Control and Tracking System.

The system worked flawlessly; throughout the 120 days of filming, no backlogs or down-time were experienced.

Filming and Digitizing

The microfilming process utilized the Bureau's FACT-90 (Film and Automated Camera Technology) system. High-speed cameras with strobe lights and automatic page-turners filmed one Camera Unit at a time. FACT-90 cameras were capable of filming 130 Short Form pages per minute, or 90 Long Form pages. The system worked flawlessly; throughout the 120 days of filming, no backlogs or down-time were experienced. Completed rolls were then sent through automated developing machines containing tanks of developing solution. Quality control clerks inspected every roll, looking for scratches, water spots, or stray marks that might interfere with data conversion.

Developed film was sent to FOSDIC (Film Optical Sensing Device for Input to Computers), the Bureau's customized data scanners. The seven Processing Centers employed three FOSDIC scanners apiece, with each machine capable of scanning 1,000 pages per minute. The Questionnaires had been designed specifically for the FOSDIC system. On negative microfilm, each filled-in bubble appeared as a white circle read by the scanner. Light passed through the circle and the resulting pattern of dots was translated into digital information. A simple microcomputer attached to each scanner recorded the data in

Q&A   How were write-in answers processed?

Both the Short and Long Forms contained write-in responses which could not be read by FOSDIC. Several of these responses were used for editing purposes only, but others, such as name of American Indian tribe, or previous place of residence, were used for data tabulation. Data entry clerks keyed these responses into computers by hand. Software designed by the Bureau then automatically coded each answer into a numbered response for tabulation. In the case of numeric responses (monthly mortgage payment, rent paid, etc.), the coding process was fairly straightforward. For other responses, coding was more complex. For example, the computer would check the keyed-in response for occupation against a lengthy list of standard Census codes for occupational names, including synonymous terms.

Q&A

What happened to individual Questionnaires once the Census was completed?

The actual Questionnaires were shredded. Microfilmed copies were shipped to the Bureau's storage facility in Jeffersonville, Indiana. Individuals can request a copy of their own Questionnaire, but the forms are otherwise confidential. Microfilm reels of older Censuses are kept in the National Archives, where they are also confidential. After 72 years, the National Archives opens its Census files to the public for genealogical and historical research. The Census rolls for 1920 were made public in March, 1992.

Blocks was chosen for the PES, and every Questionnaire from within those Blocks was separated for later work on the Survey. Questionnaires which failed due to machine error were sent to the Repair Unit, where an employee fixed the problem. Questionnaires failing due to content error were sent to the Markup Unit, where problems were circled. In some cases, the error could be corrected here, based on other information contained on the form. In other cases, the form was forwarded to the Processing Center's own Telephone Follow-Up Unit.

digitized (machine-readable) form. Digitized files were then uploaded to the Processing Center's minicomputer.

Editing and Follow-Up

The digitized Questionnaires next underwent computer editing. A computer program examined each form for multiple answers to the same question, and such inconsistencies as conflicting marital status (e.g., husband married, wife divorced). Computer editing also caught missing answers resulting from FOSDIC's inability to read a response. Questionnaires were categorized into four types: acceptable, standard form; acceptable, Post-Enumeration Survey; fail, machine error; and fail, content or coverage error. The computer also produced an Edit Diary, a printout indicating the specific questions causing problems on each form. The printouts were sent to the Diary Split Unit, where staff sorted Questionnaires and sent them to other processing departments. Other types of computer editing, known as Allocation, Substitution, and Confidentiality Edits, will be discussed in Chapter 10.

Processing of standard "acceptable" forms was essentially finished, and these were stored temporarily by Camera Unit number. Acceptable forms slated for the Bureau's Post-Enumeration Survey were stored separately. A stratified, random sampling of Census

During Telephone Follow-Up, operators attempted to reach Households to obtain missing information or clarify inconsistent answers. (The Questionnaire asked respondents to supply a phone number for either daytime or evening calling.) Questionnaires without phone numbers were sent back to District Offices for Field Follow-Up, as were those from Households which could not be reached after five calls. District Offices were also notified of addresses not matched against the Address Control File, which triggered a Non-Response Follow-Up visit.

Completed or corrected forms reentered the workflow, where the steps were repeated until the process was complete. As mentioned earlier, initial processing for Types 2 and 3 District Offices was performed at the local level, then sent to a Processing Center for further work. Once received, these Questionnaires also went to camera preparation, filming, FOSDIC, computer edit, and so on. Finally, digitized data from the Processing Center's super-minicomputer were transmitted over secure lines to the mainframe computer at Census headquarters.

During Telephone Follow-Up, operators attempted to reach Households to obtain missing information or clarify inconsistent answers.

NEW IN '90

The 1980 Census was primarily a manual operation, slow, labor intensive, error prone, and difficult to monitor. Most functions were performed by hand, including mapmaking, Address List updating, Questionnaire check-in, Non-Response monitoring, and basic editing. For example, 37,000 clerks were required to place templates over each Questionnaire to verify that only one response was given for each question. Because District Offices had no computer facilities, many operations were handwritten, then keyed-in later at another location.

For 1990, all the above-mentioned activities were automated. Some technological advances involved complete changes in procedures, such as the "smart programs" which automatically coded write-in responses. Others simply improved existing operations, such as fine-tuning FOSDIC for enhanced pattern recognition, enabling machines to scan faster and deal more easily with smudges and erasures.

Census Technology

The 1990 Census was the most automated in history. Many of the 1990 improvements in accuracy, timeliness, and cost-effectiveness were directly attributable to technological advancements.

1990 operations were billed by Bureau publicists as the first completely automated Census. Given the amount of human intervention required, this was an exaggeration, but boasting was understandable. The 1990 Census was the most automated in history. Many of the 1990 improvements in accuracy, timeliness, and cost-effectiveness were directly attributable to technological advancements.

A General Accounting Office report issued in 1983 urged the Bureau to explore greater use of new technology and earlier planning for automated activities, recommendations the Bureau pursued. Various options were explored throughout the remainder of the decade, then tested in the Bureau's Pre-Tests and Dress Rehearsals. The Baltimore Processing Center was the beta test site for all computer equipment and software used in 1990. The Bureau was quick to investigate emerging technologies such as CD-ROM, but a later GAO report criticized the use of older FOSDIC technology instead of Optical Mark Recognition (OMR) equipment. OMR scans Questionnaires directly into machine-readable form, bypassing the microfilm stage. Actually, OMR was tested in the 1988 Tampa Pre-Test, but did not work well at that time. However, OMR probably will be used in the next Census.

Much of the equipment was designed by the Bureau for its exclusive use, including FOSDIC, the FACT-90 system, and the microfilm processors. FOSDIC was invented by a Bureau engineer in 1952, and page-turning cameras were developed in the early 1960s; both have been improved for every Census since that time. The laser sorters employed in the Processing Centers were heavily modified versions of an existing commercial product. Figure 4-6 suggests the extent to which technology was utilized in 1990. Total automation costs approached $125 million, including such major expenditures as 21 FOSDIC scanners at $100,000 apiece, and fourteen super-minicomputers, each at $250,000 or more.

The Bureau's computing needs were prodigious, even at the local level. Instead of employing microcomputers at local offices, the Bureau sought more powerful minicomputers which could be networked for multiple users. A Request for Proposals was published in September, 1986, specifying a need for up to 600 minicomputers of various types. The contract, ultimately worth some $80 million, was awarded to Digital Equipment Corporation (DEC) the following spring. It called for 450 MicroVAX II minicomputers for the DOs, plus more than 100 larger minicomputers and super-minis for Bureau Headquarters, the RCCs, and Processing Centers. Later, based on computer performance during the 1988 Dress Rehearsals, it was discovered that greater computing speed and memory were required at the District Office level. The Bureau sought to upgrade their MicroVAX IIs to more powerful MicroVAX 3500s. To keep the upgrade within budget, 105 were purchased and the

Major Census Equipment Used

The 1990 Census required the use of 4 mainframe computers, 581 networked minicomputers, 6,900 computer terminals, and a variety of specially designed equipment, with a total cost of $125 million.

BUREAU HEADQUARTERS

4 Mainframe Computers
1 Unisys 1100/74
2 Unisys 1100/84s
1 Unisys 1100/94

30 Minicomputers
4 VAX 8700s
4 VAX 8810s
2 VAX 8530s
20 smaller VAX models

PROCESSING CENTERS

12 High-speed Laser Sorters
21 FOSDIC Scanners
72 FACT-90 Cameras
18 Custom Microfilm Processors

35 Minicomputers
6 VAX 8810s
23 VAX 8530s
6 smaller VAX models

REGIONAL CENSUS CENTERS

36 Minicomputers
12 VAX 8530s
24 smaller VAX models

DISTRICT OFFICES

467 MicroVAX 3500 Minicomputers
105 purchased
362 leased

Figure 4-6

Q&A

What happened to all the computers after Census operations were completed?

Most equipment at the temporary Processing Centers, including the super-minicomputers, were transferred to the Suitland computer complex. All equipment from the RCCs was redeployed to permanent locations. Of the 467 MicroVAX 3500s in District Offices, 362 were leased. The remainder, after being offered to other agencies within the Department of Commerce, were resold under the U.S. General Service Administration's surplus equipment program.

remainder were leased.

In addition to an array of super-minicomputers, Bureau Headquarters employed four Unisys 1100 mainframes of varying size. Headquarters computing operations involved the TIGER geographic system, the master Address Control File, and ultimately, the tabulation and publication of Census data. At the Processing Centers, computers were needed for Questionnaire check-in, data entry for written responses, FOSDIC scanning, data uploads, and edit checks. The Baltimore Processing Center housed a National Support Center to assist field offices with software problem. Also housed here was a "SWAT Team" of technical experts who could fly out to other Processing Centers to repair vital equipment. The RCCs used computers to keep regional files of job applicants, handle payroll, and create management reports. For example, such reports analyzed recruitment activity to determine the most successful methods for every District Office. At the DOs, computers were used for office administration, Questionnaire check-in, and follow-up activities.

Telecommunications connections among the various offices was a major concern for Census planners. Never before had the Bureau linked so many locations or transferred so much data electronically. Data connections were based on workflow: District Offices were linked to their Regional Census Centers; RCCs were linked to their Processing Centers; and Processing Centers were linked to Bureau Headquarters. Connections for RCCs, Processing Centers, and Headquarters utilized high-speed, dedicated Ethernet lines. These lines were highly secure, ensuring the confidentiality of transferred records. DOs were connected to RCCs via slower, 2400-baud modems, which were used to transfer administrative data, such as payroll records and progress reports. No confidential information was ever transmitted over unsecure lines. For example, District Offices submitted updates to the ACF by mailing revised computer tapes.

NEW IN '90

A sophisticated Management Information System (MIS), running on a Suitland minicomputer, allowed Bureau managers to monitor Census operations and make quick decisions, such as reallocating resources where they were needed most. A scheduling module tracked the progress of 40,000 different Census activities, each with assigned starting and ending dates. The MIS also enabled the Bureau to track costs through every stage of operations and better manage its budget. The system was capable of providing daily reports down to the District Office level.

Problems Conducting the 1990 Census

From start to finish, the 1990 Census was dogged by criticism from the press and local politicians. If these accounts were to be believed, Census operations were flawed, bungled, and behind schedule from the outset. Despite such public impressions, the 1990 Census proceeded fairly well, though the operation encountered its share of problems. A task as costly, complex, and extensive as the Census—not to mention one with so many political and economic consequences—would naturally experience snafus under the best of circumstances. Problems relating to planning and preparation were discussed in the previous chapter. Controversies with wider political ramifications, such as the differential undercount, the homeless issue, and count

adjustment, will be discussed briefly in Chapter 10. Here we will focus on decennial field operations, where two of the largest problems involved a low response rate and intentional falsification of Questionnaires.

Low Response Rate

The most serious problem plaguing the 1990 Census was the poor response rate for Mailback Questionnaires. Initial response to the 1980 Census was 75%. Based on indications seen during Pre-Tests and the Dress Rehearsal, the Bureau anticipated a lower response in 1990, and budgeted for a 70% return. By the end of April, however, the results were a dismal 63%. The low return rate meant more resources were required for Non-Response Follow-Up. For each percentage point below the budgeted target, follow-up would cost an additional $10 million.

The poor response rate stigmatized the entire Census operation. Many headlines gave the impression that only 63% of the nation's population *would* be counted, playing down the Bureau's extensive follow-up activities. When Representative Charles Schumer (D-NY) stated, "We are currently on track for the least accurate count in U.S. history," he was voicing a common public sentiment. Because of widespread reports that many Households had not received Questionnaires, several independent polling organizations surveyed the public on this issue. Selected results from four separate polls are summarized in Figure 4-7. Despite the low response rate actually experienced, each of the surveys found at least 88% of their respondents said they had returned the form. Similarly high percentages said they had

The most serious problem plaguing the 1990 Census was the poor response rate for Mailback Questionnaires.

For each percentage point below the budgeted target, follow-up would cost an additional $10 million.

Low response was a nationwide problem, but return rates followed certain geographic patterns. Ironically, areas with the highest population gains—notably the south and west—exhibited the poorest response. California, Texas, and Florida all showed state-wide rates below 60%. Such southern cities as Austin, Nashville, and New Orleans had rates of 50% or lower. Returns were highest in the midwest, with Wisconsin showing 75%. Another clear patten was lower response in urban areas. For example, the rate in Chicago was 52%, while in the surrounding suburbs it was 70%. Similar discrepancies were seen in low- versus high-income areas.

Fabrication of Census Data

A second problem was intentional falsification of Questionnaires by Census workers. In every Census, temporary workers have been caught "curb stoning," filling out fictitious responses from the street rather than conducting Household interviews. Door-to-door enumeration was difficult work, especially when Households failed to respond in the first place. During 1990 field operations, however, several cases were reported of fabrication by crew chiefs and district managers. News stories reported widespread irregularities at District Offices in New York City, Chicago, and New Jersey. During the hectic final weeks of local operations in June and July, 1990, DOs were under pressure from their Regional Census Centers to complete follow-up procedures. In Hackensack, approximately 10% of NRFU work had not been completed as deadlines approached, possibly prompting the district manager to organize mass falsifications. Workers were allegedly instructed to create fictitious residents at missing addresses, alternating one, two, and three-person Households. If actual forms were later received in the mail, they were supposedly destroyed because the computer would reject them as duplicates. In a

---

Questionnaire Response: Results of Public Opinion Polls

The results of four independent surveys taken at the time of the 1990 Census are compared below. All four surveys asked whether the household received a Questionnaire and whether the form had been completed and returned. Three asked whether it was difficult to understand or complicated to fill out. All four were conducted by telephone of a nationwide sample of the adult population.

A. ABC News/Washington Post
   1,004 participants
   conducted April 20-24, 1990

B. Washington Post
   1,004 participants
   conducted April 20-24, 1990

C. Gallup Poll
   1,239 participants
   conducted April 19-22, 1990

D. New York Times
   1,462 participants
   conducted April 18-22, 1990

Response	Results by Polling Organization			
	A.	B.	C.	D.
Yes, form received	88%	90%	89%	84%
No, form not received	9%	8%	9%	14%
Don't know	3%	2%	2%	—
Yes, form returned	88%	89%	90%	90%
No, form not yet returned	9%	9%	10%	10%
Don't know	3%	2%	—	—
Very easy to complete	62%	67%	67%	NA
Somewhat easy	35%	31%	19%	NA
Somewhat difficult	2%	2%	6%	NA
Very difficult	1%	—	4%	NA
Don't know	1%	—	4%	NA

NA = question not asked in this poll

Source of data: Public Opinion Online (POLL database)
                      Roper Center for Public Opinion Research
                      University of Connecticut; Storrs, CT

Figure 4-7

received the form and that it was very easy or somewhat easy to complete. Of course, what people say to a pollster and what they actually do are not always the same.

Q&A

Why were 1990 return rates so unexpectedly low?

Research conducted following the 1980 Census found two factors contributing to low response: failure to receive the form, and never *starting* to fill it out. These reasons continued to hold true for 1990. Despite the distinctive, clearly labeled envelope, many Questionnaires undoubtedly fell victim to the junk mail syndrome. Failure to begin the form resulted from many forces. In retrospect, the Bureau probably emphasized the April first target date too heavily. Many people who failed to complete the form by Census Day assumed it was too late to do so. Some found the forms confusing and complex. Others feared such consequences as deportation or loss of government benefits.

Socioeconomic changes also played a part in the lower 1990 response. By 1990, people were spending less time at home, were increasingly skeptical of government, and were barraged by surveys of every type. In past decades, civic duty had been a strong motivating force; in 1990, the poor Census response often paralleled low voter participation rates. As the results of several independent public opinion polls (summarized in Figure 4-8) indicated, failure to return the Questionnaire was not due to a philosophical objection to the Census, but simply that people were too busy to do so.

Chicago District Office, workers were allegedly ordered to fabricate anywhere from 90 to 350 forms per day in late June. Where occupancy could not be established for an address, workers created a fictitious single-person Household. Again, valid Questionnaires were allegedly destroyed if received after phony forms were submitted. In Manhattan's southern District Office, responses were also allegedly faked. If incomplete responses were obtained during NRFU, workers were supposedly instructed to count the address as Vacant.

Much of the problem could be blamed on lack of managerial experience at the local level. In central New Jersey, three of the four DO managers resigned at the height of field operations. In Hackensack, the sixth-ranking supervisor was promoted to district manager. A potential misunderstanding of Census procedures may have also contributed to the problem. Under Bureau guidelines, if enumerators were unable to determine whether an address was occupied after repeated attempts, the location was marked Vacant. In this way, the address would be visited again during the Vacancy Check phase.

This procedure was also used in cases where the number of occupants was unknown, usually in instances of Last Resort responses. This procedure may have led to the type of abuses allegedly seen in Chicago and New Jersey.

Responding to media accounts of fabrication, the Bureau examined returns from every District Office, looking for large-scale irregularities. Out of 447 offices, 24 were deemed suspicious, including one or more DOs in Chicago, Washington, D.C., and New York City, and in seven New Jersey counties. Offices were reopened, experienced enumerators were rehired, and from late October through November, 1990, these areas were recanvassed. In Chicago, every address enumerated during the last week of

Responding to media accounts of fabrication, the Bureau examined returns from every District Office, looking for large-scale irregularities.

NEW IN '90

Forms used by 1980 enumerators provided a space for "unknown" for occupancy status. This category was omitted from 1990 forms because the Bureau wanted field workers to make a "best faith determination" for each address. Lack of the unknown category caused confusion in the latter weeks of NRFU operations; after receiving complaints from many DOs across the nation, the rule was changed, allowing field workers to designate unknown status.

Reasons for Low Return Rate: Results of Public Opinion Polls

Three of the four polls described in Figure 4-X asked those respodents who had not yet returned a Questionnaire why they had not done so. Responses in the New York Times poll were coded differently than those of the ABC/Washington Post and the Washington Post polls.

Reason for not returning Census Questionnaire	Response by Poll A.	B.	D.
Forgot about it	4%	7%	*
Haven't gotten to it	20%	17%	
Haven't had time	12%	16%	*
Think it's supposed to be picked up by Bureau	17%	13%	
Lost or misplaced it	12%	12%	
Against idea of a Census	2%	1%	
Questions too personal/ invasion of privacy	4%	2%	2%
Don't like it	2%	1%	
Just received it	5%	4%	
Too complicated	–	1%	8%
Other reasons	9%	13%	27%
Unsure/don't know	16%	16%	4%
Not important			6%
Too busy/forgot			51%
Thought it was junk mail			2%

* Responses combined in NYT poll.

Source of data: *Public Opinion Online* (*POLL* database)
Roper Center for Public Opinion Research
University of Connecticut; Storrs, CT

Figure 4-8

Other Problems

Other problems receiving media attention included non-delivery of forms in certain localities, continuing recruitment shortages, disputes over Local Review, and abuses of the Last Resort method. Non-delivery of Questionnaires was not a significant problem in 1990, but it was a potentially embarrassing one. The residents of entire apartment buildings or subdivision failed to receive forms, and in a few cases, whole towns were missed. In New York City, forms for one building were left in the foyer and children used them for paper airplanes. In a Los Angeles poll, 19% didn't recall receiving a Questionnaire. In all, five million forms were undeliverable, due to faulty addresses, incorrect ZIP Codes, or other postal problems. Such results, representing about 5% of the total, were low compared to typical commercial mailing campaigns. Returning to the national poll results shown in Figure 4-7, between 84% and 90% of survey respondents recalled receiving a Census Questionnaire. In the two Washington Post polls, however, large percentages of those who had not received a form reported difficulties trying to obtain one from the Bureau. Negative publicity of this type did not help the Bureau's image. Political press conferences held in front of missed buildings, and broadcast interviews with prominent citizens who did not receive Questionnaires did little to bolster confidence in the Census. In reality, undeliverable mail was anticipated, and follow-up activities had been designed to ameliorate the problem. Field workers picked up undelivered mail from Post Offices, then attempted to correct addresses and deliver forms by hand. Approximately 1.8 million of these were subsequently delivered.

Another reason for non-delivery was Housing Units which did not appear on Address Registers. Despite the thoroughness of list compilation and checking operations, some addresses were missed. Telephone hot lines, the "Were You Counted?" campaign, and

NRFU was revisited. In New Jersey, 18,000 addresses were contacted. The Inspector General's Office of the Commerce Department also initiated an investigation into alleged wrongdoing.

Q&A

How did the Bureau guard against falsified data?

Numerous quality control features were built into normal Census operations. Local supervisors conducted spot checks of enumerators' work by re-interviewing a small sample of addresses. Field workers were also required to report to crew chiefs daily. Although work quotas were never imposed, supervisors judged enumerators' work against average productivity rates in their areas. Clerical workers were closely supervised, and many of the data entry and editing operations were automatically checked by other workers or "verifiers." Although Census workers could be fined and/or jailed for falsifying data, those caught were typically dismissed.

Widespread fabrication was often detectable by the pattern of responses, especially in Questionnaires completed during the final weeks of operations. For example, inspectors watched for unusually high numbers of single-person Households, such tidy repetitions as Hackensack's 1-2-3 pattern, or large numbers of Questionnaires with skimpy information but not listed as Last Resort responses.

And what of fabrication at higher levels in the organization? The honesty and dedication of front-line employees proved an excellent safeguard against supervisory abuses; the cases in Chicago, New Jersey, and other areas were brought to light when other workers went to the press. In the words of one Hackensack crew chief, "I was livid. I had just spent three months doing quality control and here they were falsifying data."

Nationwide, approximately 3% of all Questionnaires were based on Last Resort data.

other follow-up operations attempted to correct these omissions.

Initial recruiting shortages were described in Chapter 3, but recruiting remained a problem throughout Census operations. The lower-than expected Mailback response placed further stress on the system. In many areas, the Bureau implemented pay raises to attract additional workers during the later stages of Non-Response Follow-Up. Field work for the Census has been likened to recruiting soldiers during the Civil War; raw recruits were given a few days of training, then thrust into battle. However, overall quality of the temporary work force was good and most operations were completed on schedule.

The Last Resort method, where enumerators obtained data from neighbors, postal carriers, or other knowledgeable individuals, was another source of potential problems. Last Resort data were often supplied by building superintendents, public housing managers, or in affluent areas, even door-men. Unfortunately, these individuals often had little knowledge of residents. Heavy reliance on this method would be cause for concern. Nationwide, approximately 3% of all Questionnaires were based on Last Resort data. In New York City, the figure approached 7%. The largest trouble spot was the District of Columbia, where the two DOs submitted Last Resort forms for 40% and 23% of their respective totals. Here the District Offices were reopened and the suspect addresses were recanvassed.

Complaints resulting from Post-Census Local Review also received media coverage, with politicians taking the opportunity to label the 1990 Census the most inaccurate ever. After Recanvassing the Census Blocks having documented discrepancies, the Bureau found many challenges to be groundless, based on outdated or incorrect municipal records. Where local records might show apartment buildings, Recanvassing found commercial structures or undeveloped land.

For example, New York City claimed 414 dwellings were missed in the Gateway National Recreation Area; Recanvassing discovered three lifeguard stands.

Tabulation and Publication

Collecting and processing Census Forms is not an end in itself. The resulting data must be tabulated, organized, and released to the public. Data tabulation and publication are long-term operations. Efforts began almost as soon as the processed Forms were received, and continued for several years thereafter. The following sections offer a brief introduction to the tabulation process, the major forms of Census products, and the publication timetable.

Tabulating the Results

After all Questionnaires had been digitized and transferred to mainframe computers at Bureau headquarters, the files were edited to create Basic Record Tapes (BRTs). These tapes contained the individual responses from each Questionnaire, minus any personal identification. Street addresses did not appear on BRTs, but Census Block geocodes for every address did. In this way, data could be summarized for every geographic level tabulated by the Census.

Once the processed Census Questionnaires had been converted into Basic Record Tapes, the final stage of processing was data tabulation. Computer programs summed individual responses to obtain totals for different geographic entities—cities, townships, counties, and so forth. Depending on the variable, data were tabulated in several forms, including total counts, frequency distributions, medians, and mean values. The results represent an amazing array of characteristics of persons, Families, Households, and Housing Units, and for various subgroups of each. The programs also cross-tabulated selected responses by age, Race, sex, or other charac-

teristics. Bureau statisticians supervised the tabulation of response categories from the individual records on the BRTs, including the creation of such derived measures as Family composition. Results were reviewed and edited by the Bureau's professional staff, then converted into a variety of internal summary tapes. From these internal files, the Bureau generated the actual Census publications—both print and electronic. As their name suggests, the summary tapes contained statistical summaries only. Tabulation was conducted state-by-state, with results produced on a flow basis.

At this point it is appropriate to remember a particular aspect of prior processing: Short and Long Forms were sorted and processed separately. This resulted in two types of summary tapes. Some contained complete-count data taken from the Short Forms and the 100% portion of the Long Forms; others contained sample data from the Long Forms only. Sample data were then weighted and statistically "inflated" to create estimates for the entire population.

Short and Long Forms were sorted and processed separately.

 **Census Tip**

P.L. 94-171 tabulations were the first 1990 Census results to be released to the public.

Complete-count data took precedence and were tabulated first. This enabled the Bureau to focus on the primary purpose of the Census—Congressional reapportionment, and state and local political redistricting. By law (Public Law 94-171), December 31, 1990 was the deadline for submitting state-level population totals to the President. The deadline for sub-state totals was April 1, 1991. These so-called P.L. 94-171 tabulations were then used for reapportionment and redistricting. Considering that several Census follow-up operations continued well into the

Complete-count data took precedence and were tabulated first. This enabled the Bureau to focus on the primary purpose of the Census—Congressional reapportionment, and state and local political redistricting.

autumn of 1990, these deadlines left the Bureau very little time to finish preliminary tabulations.

The Publication Process

The results of the publication process, whether issued in paper or electronic form, are called Census products. earlier in the product planning stages, the Bureau had determined the basic appearance and content of the individual products. The publication staff wrestled with myriad issues: which summary statistics would be presented, what types of cross-tabulations would be calculated, what levels of geography would be shown, which physical formats would be utilized, and how their content would vary from one format to another. Decisions were based on a variety of factors, including experience from prior Censuses, the legislative requirements of federal programs, and input from data users. Early decisions were refined and revised as the actual data tables were designed, created, and edited.

Product Mix

Given the enormous size and complexity of the decennial Census effort, it should be no surprise that the resulting products are voluminous and varied. The 1990 product mix encompasses dozens of titles in several formats, including paper (print) Reports, CD-ROM Files, magnetic tapes, and online databases. Individual products are described elsewhere in the book: print Reports in Chapter 9, CD-ROM Files in Chapter 8, and other electronic formats in Chapter 14.

The major electronic products are called *Summary Tape Files* (*STFs*), so named because they contain summarized data only; responses from individual Households do not appear on the tapes in any form. For smaller levels of geography, such as Census Blocks, certain data fields were further camouflaged to preserve the confidentiality of individual respondents. (The Confidentiality Edit process is described in Chapter 10.)

The various *Summary Tape Files* are sold to data users on magnetic tape (reel or cartridge) and on CD-ROM. The same internal source files were used to produce most 1990 Census Reports published in paper format, with a direct correspondence between *STF* Files and printed Reports.

Figure 4-9 compares noteworthy characteristics of tape, CD-ROM, online, and print as publishing formats. The primary advantages of magnetic tape are that it is published sooner than the other formats, and that it offers certain types of detailed data not found in other formats. The major disadvantage is

> The 1990 product mix encompasses dozens of titles in several formats, including paper (print) Reports, CD-ROM Files, magnetic tapes, and online databases.

Comparison of Publication Formats
(Rankings by characteristic)

FORMAT	Popularity among Users	Speed of Release	Amount of Data Detail	Ease of Use	Affordability (1)
		CHARACTERISTICS			
CD-ROM	1	3	2	3	3
Paper	2	4	4	1	2
Magnetic Tape	3	1	1	5	4
Microfiche	4	5	3	2	1
CENDATA	5	2	5	4	5

(1) Affordability is based on the cost of obtaining an equal amount of data from each source. CENDATA is not appropriate for retrieving massive amounts of data.

Figure 4-9

that it is difficult to use, requiring large computer systems and the necessary expertise to deal with them. The advantage of paper products are their familiarity, their affordability, and the fact that no special equipment is needed to use them. However, a surprising number of disadvantages are associated with this traditional medium. A complete collection of Reports takes up a great deal of space, and even then, not all subjects and geographic levels are covered in the print products. Locating the necessary tables can also be difficult and time-consuming. But the primary disadvantage is that print Reports are the last to be issued during each phase of the publishing process.

CD-ROM is a new publishing medium for 1990. As described in Chapter 8, the Bureau embraced this useful technology quite early in the planning process. Despite the Bureau's initial enthusiasm for CD-ROM products, no one in the agency imagined that the new medium would ever supplant traditional paper products. However, the value and popularity of CD-ROM products has exceeded all of the Bureau's expectations, in part because of the user-friendly software included on every disc product. It is now the most heavily-used format for retrieving 1990 Census data.

The two remaining formats shown on Figure 4-9 are a bit more specialized. CENDATA, the Bureau's online database product, is designed to provide rapid dissemination and quick retrieval for frequently requested Census data. It provides only a fraction of the tables found in other formats, and is intended to address specific ready-reference needs rather than in-depth ma-

Q&A

Why doesn't the Bureau issue 1990 Census files on floppy diskette?

Diskettes can hold comparatively little data, which makes them an inappropriate medium for such large files. The Bureau publishes some of its smaller, nondecennial files on diskette, including intercensal population estimates for states and local areas. For 1990, the only Census products to appear on diskette are subfiles of *Public Law 94-171 Data* and certain titles in the *Selected Population and Housing Data Paper Listings* (CPH-L) series.

nipulation. The system, which is surprisingly easy to use, is described in Chapter 14.

The Bureau originally intended to produce a diversity of microfiche products for 1990, as it had for the previous Census. However, the unexpected popularity of CD-ROM products made the older technology all but obsolete, causing the agency to cancel virtually all 1990 microfiche publications.

Publication Timetable

Census publications are issued according to a detailed timetable. As required by law, the first to be released were the *Public Law 94-171 Data* files, used for state and local redistricting. These appeared in numerous formats, including tape, CD-ROM, diskette, and computer printout. Once the redistricting files were distributed, release dates for the remaining publications followed a title-by-title sequence. Complete-count files appeared before sample files were issued. Within each of the two categories, the most detailed subject breakdowns appeared last. For complete-count publications, for example, *STF 1* arrived before *STF 2*. Within the sample publications, *STF 3* was released before *STF 4*. Specialized files, such as the *Subject Summary Tape File* series, appeared much later. Each title was produced for one state at a time, on a flow basis. The Bureau generally handled smaller states first. Larger states and those

The value and popularity of CD-ROM products has exceeded all of the Bureau's expectations, in part because of the user-friendly software included on every disc product. It is now the most heavily-used format for retrieving 1990 Census data.

with more complex geographies tended to be issued last. The *STF 1A* timetable, for example, saw Arkansas and Vermont processed before California and Texas. After all states had been issued within a particular series, a United States Summary File was released. Finally, after all the geographic areas were covered, publication would begin on the next product Title.

Within each product Title, the processing order for the various formats also appeared in sequence, as follows:

▸ Magnetic tape
▸ CENDATA (where applicable)
▸ CD-ROM
▸ Paper

Those Files intended for inclusion on *CENDATA* were often loaded within hours of the magnetic tape version's completion. Where applicable, *CENDATA* was usually the fastest source of new releases.

When the Bureau first planned the timetable for 1990 release dates, agency officials hoped to issue CD-ROM products within weeks of the magnetic tape version's release. However, the original plan did not incorporate the more sophisticated end-user software which was subsequently included on every CD-ROM disc. The software is custom-designed for every product, which slows the release of each new CD-ROM series. As a result, the various CD-ROM titles appeared anywhere from two months to nine months after the release of their tape counterparts.

Print Reports are the last to appear in the publishing sequence. For example, although the last of the tapes for *STF 3A* was released in September, 1992, the print counterparts were issued much later. *CPH 5*, containing abbreviated data from *STF 3*, appeared in the late Spring of 1993. CP 2 and *CH 2*, the detailed paper counterparts to the tape Files, did not arrive until the summer of 1994.

Official schedules of release dates were revised throughout the process. Certain publications slated for release were later canceled due to unanticipated budget shortfalls.

NEW IN '90

Despite delays and setbacks in the 1990 product release schedule, many of the major data Files and print Reports appeared sooner than their 1980 counterparts. A variety of product-design decisions played a role in the earlier release. For example, *STF 1A* contains no data for Metropolitan Areas (MAs) or Urbanized Areas (UAs) because it takes longer for the Bureau to tabulate information for these specialized geographic levels. Similarly, state-specific products, whether on tape, CD-ROM, or print, contain no information for portions of geographic entities which lie outside their state boundaries. Examples of such cross-state geographies include Metropolitan Areas and federal Indian Reservations. Data users looking for 1990 tabulations on MAs, UAs, and Indian Areas had to wait for national-level products (such as *STF 1C* and *STF 3C* on CD-ROM, or the various national summary print Reports) or had to sum the component parts on a state-by-state basis. Although these 1990 changes created an inconvenience for some data users, the state-specific reports were issued more rapidly than in the past.

This was especially true for *Subject Summary Tape Files* (*SSTFs*) and their print counterparts (called *Subject Reports*). These reports address more specialized topics and were thus assigned lower priority than other, more basic publications. The Bureau originally hoped to issue 40 titles in the *SSTF* series. The series was later reduced to 22 titles, and finally, cut to 20.

Conversely, previously unplanned products were announced later in the process, often due to popular demand. For example, *STF 1D* and *STF 3D*, containing Congressional District data for the 103rd Congress, was originally scheduled to appear in print and on tape only. However, a CD-ROM disc combining data from both files was released unexpectedly in early 1994. Another surprise addition was the *TIGER/Census Tract Street Index*, released on CD-ROM in early 1995. The Bureau has also made unexpected product enhancements, most notably the inclusion of user-friendly software on the revised *TIGER/Line Files*.

Q&A

Why do the Bureau's announced timetables for product release dates seem so unreliable?

1990 product release dates for magnetic tape products have been on schedule, for the most part. CD-ROM and print releases were less predictable. Sometimes variations were due to production problems encountered after the files left the Bureau's control. In other cases, erroneous data on the tape Files themselves necessitated the release of revised CD-ROMs. The latter situation occurred most dramatically with the *STF 3A* discs.

In some cases, previously announced timetables were altered due to changes in usage patterns or product design. Because most 1990 CD-ROM products include more sophisticated software than originally planned, the discs took longer to create.

Similarly, the unanticipated popularity of the entire CD-ROM line prompted the cancellation of most microfiche titles.

The major reason for the variance from target dates relates to available resources. As with other aspects of budgeting for the decennial Census, the Bureau estimated the total cost of the publishing effort over the life of the decade; amounts were allocated annually to cover those costs. Remember also, the Bureau must continue to conduct, tabulate, and publish the results of its other ongoing statistical programs, including the Economic Census and the Current Population Survey.

 Census Tip

The Bureau issues revised calendars of release dates as conditions change, and newly-released products are listed in the Bureau's *Monthly Product Announcement* newsletter. Another way to check on new products and anticipated release dates is to consult *CENDATA*, the Bureau's online database, or the agency's Internet server.

The entire publishing process takes several years. The first *Summary Tape Files* for 1990 began appearing in April, 1991.

The entire publishing process takes several years. The first *Summary Tape Files* for 1990 began appearing in April, 1991. The last of the major print Reports was published in September, 1994. More specialized Reports continued to be released after the major series were completed. The first *Subject Summary Tape Files* were issued in April, 1994, and the remaining five titles in the series are scheduled to appear in 1995. In fact, if additional money becomes available, Reports that were previously canceled due to budget cuts may

be reinstated before the end of the decade. The final *Subject Report* from the 1980 Census, entitled *Characteristics of American Indians for Tribes and Selected Areas: 1980*, was published in March, 1990.

Summary

Despite the enormity of the task and the variety of problems encountered, the 1990 Census was completed on time and P.L. 94-171 deadlines were met. Contrary to impressions portrayed by the press, most operations proceeded according to plan. New technologies and procedures met or exceeded expectations, and operations were often completed ahead of schedule. The 1990 Census represented the Bureau's greatest effort to date to minimize undercount and improve accuracy. Address lists and Census counts underwent extensive checking through the use of independent procedures and follow-up operations. Data processing was also subject to numerous quality control mechanisms. The Bureau's Management Information System meant better control of budgeting, personnel, and workflow, which in turn meant that problems could be identified and corrected more rapidly. Operational changes designed to improve coverage and accuracy included the following:

- earlier planning
- more targeted promotional activities
- increased outreach to minorities and non-English speakers
- an expanded Local Review program
- revised procedures for address compilation and data gathering
- increased use of automation
- improved processing methods
- a larger Post-Enumeration Survey.

Much of the operation's success can be attributed to nearly a decade of planning and preparation, and the cooperation of numerous organizations, including the United States Postal Service, the State Data Center network, and local governments.

Still, the 1990 Census was not without disappointments. Keeping the logistics of such a complex enterprise on track was a constant challenge. Total costs exceeded the original budget, largely due to the low response rate and unanticipated federal salary increases. (The low response rate alone added $70 million of additional expenses.) The Census undercount, which will be discussed in Chapter 10, was also larger than anticipated. However, many observers believe the undercount would have been far worse without the extraordinary preparation and effort which was undertaken to minimize it. As an example, fully 90% of the Bureau's promotional budget was directed at that 10% of the population hardest to count.

Evaluating the Bureau's success on publication release dates is more complicated. Census planners had ambitious goals to publish all 1990 products far sooner than had been done in the previous decade. In the end, some titles were completed slightly ahead of schedule, some appeared a bit behind schedule, and others were woefully late. Compared with 1980, however, 1990 product release dates either matched or exceeded prior results. By mid-1994, most of the major 1990 products had been published, a pattern similar to the previous decade.

It is easy to criticize the Bureau's publishing performance, but in reality, their 1990 timetable was far too optimistic, given the scope and complexity of the eventual output. The Bureau actually acquitted itself fairly well, when one considers that a brand new electronic medium was successfully launched, complete with customized, user-friendly software. Add to this the fact that 1990 products offered more subject detail and far more geographic detail than ever before, and the publishing program should be judged a success by any standard.

Could the 1990 Census have been handled better? In retrospect, Bureau officials feel that not much could have been done differently. Public Service Announcements tended to air late at night, when few viewers were watching. Planning for certain operations could have begun sooner, and the Bureau could have been less rigid in adhering to field guidelines. Given the difficulty some Households had in obtaining a Questionnaire, for example, District Offices should have been authorized to conduct interviews by telephone where warranted. Negative publicity and political opposition also should have been handled better. New York City Mayor Dinkins's pronouncement that preliminary Census results were "unadulterated nonsense," for example, did little to instill confidence in the Census process. Instead of publicly criticizing low response rates and related issues, politicians would have served the public interest far better by encouraging people to complete and return the forms. On the other hand, Bureau officials chose not to debate their critics publicly, which in retrospect was probably an unwise decision. Planning for the 2000 Census has been underway for several years, but the complexities of that

Compared with 1980, however, 1990 product release dates either matched or exceeded prior results.

Could the 1990 Census have been handled better? In retrospect, Bureau officials feel that not much could have been done differently.

topic fall outside the scope of *Understanding the Census.* The major question following 1990 is whether the traditional "head count" method has outlived its usefulness. Escalating costs, societal changes, and increased public apathy may be pointing in that direction.

Chapter 5

Subject Terminology and Concepts

I. Rules and Procedures Affecting Census Concepts
    A. Residency Guidelines
        1. Place of Usual Residence
        2. Overseas Population
        3. Resident Population
    B. Methodological Guidelines
        1. Reference Dates
        2. Self-Identification
        3. Write-In Responses
        4. Data Imputation
II. Housing Concepts
    A. Living Quarters
        1. Housing Units
        2. Group Quarters
    B. Occupancy Characteristics
        1. Vacancy Status
        2. Housing Tenure
        3. Farm Residence
    C. Structural and Financial Characteristics
III. Population Concepts
    A. Households and Families
        1. The Role of Householders
        2. Households
        3. Families and Subfamilies
    B. Race and Hispanic Origin
        1. Spanish/Hispanic Origin
        2. Race
    C. Nativity, Language, and Ancestry
    D. Income and Poverty Status
    E. Employment and Labor Force Status
IV. Summary

Subject Terminology and Concepts

It is impossible to correctly interpret Census data, and in some cases even impossible to find data, without a grounding in basic concepts, geographic units, and definitions. Many of these concepts are not only unique to the Census, they are quite bewildering when first encountered. The Bureau is notorious for using commonly understood terms in specially defined ways. Many definitions are counter-intuitive, as in the case of Vacant Housing Units, which can actually be inhabited at the time of the Census. The Bureau also employs subtle distinctions to differentiate related concepts. For example, Metropolitan, Urban, and Urbanized are *not* synonymous terms and treating them as such will result in enormous errors. Sometimes it seems as though the Bureau goes overboard with the complexity and detail of its rules and guidelines. Virtually every major definition contains significant exceptions that are difficult to remember and confusing to interpret.

The following chapters focus on the most important Census concepts and terms, alerting the reader to key areas of concern. Chapter 5 begins with fundamental methodological concepts, then introduces definitions relating to population and housing subjects. Wherever possible, distinctions between similar terms are explained. Chapter 6 introduces geographic concepts and definitions. Chapter 7 describes every Item on the 1990 Questionnaire, explaining additional terminology as needed. Taken together, these three chapters will help users understand what is being measured by the Census, and perhaps more important, what is not measured.

Rules and Procedures Affecting Census Concepts

Some of the most fundamental Census guidelines tend to be taken for granted by data users. Who is excluded from the total population? How are people counted if they are away from home, or if they maintain two

Why do Census definitions contain so many confusing exceptions?

When struggling with the frustrations of Bureau terminology, it helps to remember the decennial Census counts and describes the characteristics of everyone in the United States. Few statistical agencies, here or abroad, must cope with such a large, diverse, and complex population. For example, the Bureau must account for every variation in people's Living Quarters, from houseboats to communes. Fitting endless variations into standard categories is seldom simple, and exceptions are bound to creep in. Detailed definitions are necessary to maintain consistency in data collection and tabulation, as well as to help users apply and interpret the numbers correctly.

residences? How does the Bureau classify and count the many write-in responses appearing on Questionnaires? How do Census tabulations account for missing forms or blank responses? The answers to these and other basic questions have enormous impact on the meaning of Census numbers.

 Census Tip

Every data product published by the Census Bureau includes a set of definitions for the terms used in that product. For print Reports, definitions are found in an appendix. For CD-ROM products, the definitions are listed as auxiliary files. The Bureau also publishes a complete dictionary of decennial terminology, called the *1990 Census of Population and Housing Guide: Part B. Glossary.* Researchers new to the Census should consult these sources frequently.

The decennial Census counts residents of the United States, regardless of their citizenship status.

Residency Guidelines

The decennial Census counts residents of the United States, regardless of their citizenship status. This concept seems readily understandable, but specific guidelines are not always clear-cut or obvious. Rules governing who is counted and to what location they are assigned contain numerous exceptions, some of which invite misinterpretation by Census users.

The Bureau attempts to collect statistics on every person living in the United States and its territories. General residency guidelines were described in Chapter 1, but the complexity of this topic warrants further discussion. In most cases, foreign nationals staying in the United States temporarily at the time of the Census are excluded from the count because they have not established U.S. residence. Among these exclusions are foreign tourists, business travellers, and those visiting family or friends. However, foreign students enrolled in U.S. colleges and universities are counted as residents, as are foreigners with work visas. Foreign personnel assigned to diplomatic missions are excluded because embassies and consulates are considered foreign soil. This exclusion is based on practical and legal considerations: Census enumerators cannot set foot on diplomatic property without that government's permission.

Place of Usual Residence

For residency guidelines, the question of *where* is every bit as important as *who*. Following a practice dating back to the first Census, the Bureau counts people at their Place of Usual

Residence. This is defined as the place where the person lives and sleeps most of the time. Individuals with no Place of Usual Residence (transients, the homeless, etc.) are counted where they are found at the time of enumeration.

Once again, these guidelines are not always straightforward. College students are counted at the place they are living while attending school, but children attending boarding school are counted at their home address. Military personnel stationed in the United States are counted at their duty station (on base or off, depending on where they maintain a residence). Shipboard personnel can choose either their ship's address or their current on-shore residence. For apportionment purposes only, military personnel stationed abroad are counted at their "home of record," the address given at the time of their enlistment. Inmates of Institutions are counted at the Institution, but hospital patients undergoing short-term treatment list their home address. Vacationers, business travelers, and others away from home temporarily on Census Day are counted at their usual address.

The Place of Usual Residence is not necessarily where a person happens to be on Census Day. It can also differ from the person's mailing address, voting residence, or legal residence. Nor is it always the place a person feels is home. A prisoner serving a five-year sentence might not view the prison as his usual residence, but the Census Bureau does. A young Marine stationed at Camp Lejeune for two years might think of Brooklyn as "home," but to the Bureau, her Place of Usual Residence is in North Carolina.

To avoid double-counting, each person must designate a single address for Census purposes. "Snow birds" and others maintaining more than one residence are instructed to list the address where they live most often. Individuals who spend equal amounts of time at each of two addresses may designate either location, but not both. As more people maintain dual addresses, guidelines for determining Place of Usual Residence become increasingly difficult to apply. Employees who commute between cities (including members of Congress and state legislators), married couples who live apart from one another for employment reasons, and children alternating between two Households exemplify the impact of changing lifestyles on Census methodology.

Overseas Population

Guidelines governing the treatment of United States citizens living abroad are equally com-

> **To avoid double-counting, each person must designate a single address for Census purposes. "Snow birds" and others maintaining more than one residence are instructed to list the address where they live most often.**

Q&A

Are illegal aliens counted by the Census?

Although the Census asks questions on citizenship and country of birth, respondents' legal status is not counted. Illegal aliens (undocumented immigrants) who respond to the Census are counted along with everyone else. However, foreign citizens residing in the United States without government consent are less likely to return a Census form or answer an enumerator's questions. Many of these individuals live with another Household or have no permanent address, so they are easily missed by the Census. Pre-Census publicity and outreach programs emphasize the confidentiality of Census records and stress that data will not be shared with the Immigration and Naturalization Service, but aliens living in fear of deportation may find such assurances difficult to believe.

Q&A

To what geographic location are shipboard residents allocated?

Personnel of military and merchant vessels can claim their Usual Residence on ship or shore, but not both places. Those who claim shipboard residence are allocated to various locations depending on the whereabouts of the ship on Census Day. If the ship is docked in the United States, its shipboard residents are allocated to that port. If at sea, with a U.S. port of departure, that port is designated. If at sea with a foreign port of departure but U.S. destination, the port of destination is used. If at sea between foreign ports, or docked at a foreign port, those claiming shipboard residence are considered overseas residents. In all cases, crew members choosing an address on shore are counted there, regardless of the ship's location or registry.

plex, once again depending on each person's circumstances. Americans on vacation or brief business trips abroad are counted, but American citizens living, working, or attending school in a foreign country generally are excluded from the Census. Crew members of merchant ships registered under U.S. flag may be counted, depending on the ship's location on Census Day and the type of residence claimed by the crew member.

To make matters more confusing, certain nonresidents who are excluded from basic Census totals are counted for purposes of Congressional apportionment only. The following categories of citizens stationed abroad are enumerated as part of the 1990 Apportionment Population:

- military personnel
- the crews of U.S. military vessels on foreign seas or in foreign ports
- civilian employees of the federal government, such as State Department employees in foreign service posts
- dependents of the above-mentioned groups, if also living abroad.

The Bureau has collected data on overseas personnel since 1900, but has never included these numbers in the official count of Resident Population. However, 1990 marks the second time overseas military and government personnel have been included in the

To make matters more confusing, certain nonresidents who are excluded from basic Census totals are counted for purposes of Congressional apportionment only.

Apportionment Population. The other instance occurred in 1970, when an exception was made to count the large numbers of Americans serving in the Vietnam War.

Overseas personnel were added to the 1990 Apportionment Population at the behest of Congress. Congressional members showed significant bipartisan support for this inclusion, and various bills were introduced in both Houses during the 100th and 101st Congresses. In August, 1989, the Bureau announced that the Apportionment Population would include military and civilian employees stationed abroad, making it unnecessary for Congress to pass a law on the matter.

The Bureau obtained data on these employees primarily through administrative records. The U.S. Office of Personnel Management provided the Bureau with a list of federal agencies with employees abroad, including the Department of Defense (DOD). Of these, 32 agencies were found to employ U.S. citizens, but only 30 could provide data on their employees' stateside homes. (The Peace Corps was the only major overseas employer which did not participate in the enumeration.) Twenty of the agencies provided counts for both employees and their dependents abroad; ten agencies provided counts for employees only. The DOD also conducted a mail survey of its civilian employees abroad, because the Department's existing records did not contain information about the stateside homes of its civilian workers. Unfortunately, only 20% of the DOD's civilian employees responded to the questionnaire.

The DOD accounted for 98% of the population abroad, while the State Department accounted for 1.5%. The remaining 0.5% was distributed among the other 28 agencies. The Bureau counted 919,810 employees and dependents living abroad and eligible for inclusion in the Apportionment Population. The figure was determined in the manner shown in Figure 5-1.

A controversial issue relating to the overseas military population was exactly how to allocate each person to a "home state." One method would be to use the individual's

The Bureau counted 919,810 employees and dependents living abroad and eligible for inclusion in the Apportionment Population.

most recent domestic duty station, defined as the last military assignment before going abroad. Using this method would unfairly benefit states with large military bases. A second approach would be to allocate everyone based on their legal residence—the state which they designate for income tax purposes. However, many persons stationed abroad choose a state with no income tax as their legal residence, which would unfairly benefit those states. The method which was finally used for 1990 was the person's home of record, meaning the location indicated when the person first enlisted or re-enlisted. A Congressional Research Service report issued in June, 1990, later confirmed that this was in fact the most equitable means of distribution. Nevertheless, when Massachusetts lost a Congressional seat to the state of Washington as a result of allocating the overseas population, the entire process was challenged in the courts. The U.S. Supreme Court ultimately upheld the Bureau's methods and Massachusetts lost a Congressional District.

COMPONENTS OF THE 1990 OVERSEAS POPULATION

Persons counted [1]	942,844
Less: persons whose "home state" was a U.S. territory or commonwealth. [2]	16,999
Total overseas population	925,845
Less: crews of U.S. merchant ships between foreign ports or docked at foreign port.	3,026
Overseas federal employees and dependents	922,819
Less: persons whose "home state" was the District of Columbia. [3]	3,009
Overseas component of Apportionment Population	919,810

[1] The Bureau did not count U.S. citizens living abroad unless they were federal employees, dependents of those employees, or crew members of U.S. merchant vessels.

[2] The resident population of the Outlying Territories (3,862,238 persons) is excluded from the definition of Americans overseas.

[3] Residents of the District of Columbia are excluded from the Apportionment Population.

Figure 5-1

Census Tip

The overseas population is included in the figures used to allocate the number of Congressional seats per state, but not to redraw Congressional District boundaries or to make redistricting decisions for political subdivisions at the state or local levels. The reason is simple: administrative records used to tabulate the overseas population provide information at the state level only; employees' former street addresses are not reported.

Resident Population

Users of national-level Census data must remember the distinction between the Apportionment Population and the Resident Population. The Apportionment Population includes residents of the 50 states together with federal employees stationed abroad, but excludes residents of the District of Columbia. The resulting figures are used only to determine the number of Congressional seats allocated to each state. Once the Bureau has calculated the allocations, and the U.S. Supreme Court has settled the inevitable lawsuits challenging those calculations, the numbers are soon forgotten. (The mechanics of the apportionment process, together with the state-by-state results for 1990, are discussed in Chapter 12.)

The Resident Population includes inhabitants of the 50 states and the District of Columbia, but excludes federal civilian and military personnel stationed abroad. The Resident Population—248,709,873 persons in 1990—is the number typically cited as the "official" decennial population of the United States.

Note that residents of Puerto Rico and the other Outlying Territories are excluded from both the Apportionment Population and the Resident Population of the United States. Results of the decennial Census of Outlying Areas are published separately.

To make data comparable, the Bureau must describe people's characteristics at a particular point in time. For most questions asked in the 1990 Census, the appropriate Reference Date is April 1, 1990.

Methodological Guidelines

Chapters 3 and 4 describe the process of planning and conducting the decennial Census and provide readers with an understanding of the methods used by the Bureau to collect, process, and tabulate data. The following sections explore those aspects of Census methodology which relate directly to subject content.

Reference Dates

Simultaneity is a key requirement of any enumeration. To make data comparable, the Bureau must describe people's characteristics at a particular point in time. For most questions asked in the 1990 Census, the appropriate Reference Date is April 1, 1990. Among the topics relating to this date are place of residence, Vacancy status, age, marital status, presence of children, and educational attainment. If a respondent's birthday falls on April 5, he must cite his age as of April 1, regardless of when the Questionnaire is filled out. Since many Households answer the Census several weeks, or even several

Q&A

As long as each person chooses a single location, why not allow Census respondents to determine their Place of Residence?

The need for consistency and comparability of Census data makes residency guidelines too important to leave to individual choice. Without standard rules, making sense of the numbers would be nearly impossible. Consider the case of a small town with a large college population. If each student were free to choose whether they were counted at home or school, demographic data for the town would be extremely difficult to interpret.

Money and power represent more compelling reasons. Because Census figures are used for legislative apportionment, redistricting, and the distribution of government funds, decisions affecting Place of Residence have far-reaching consequences. The Congressional debate over counting overseas military personnel illustrates the high stakes of the Bureau's residency rules, and the ramifications of different guidelines. Following traditional Census methodology, the Place of Usual Residence for overseas military personnel is overseas, but Congress wanted them to be counted in their home states. Once the Bureau agreed to include overseas personnel in the 1990 Apportionment Population, the question of how to define "home" became a hotly contested issue.

months, after Census Day, paying attention to the Reference Date is no trivial matter.

Certain Census questions refer to an interval of time rather than a specific date. All Income data relate to a Reference Year, which for the 1990 Census is 1989. In other words, respondents are asked to specify their total money Income for the previous year.

Questions on Employment Status, Hours Worked, and Journey to Work pertain to a Reference Week. The 1990 Census Reference Day and Reference Year are the same for all respondents, but the Reference Week varies. Respondents are instructed to base answers to employment questions on the calendar week immediately preceding the date they complete the Questionnaire or answer the enumerator.

Self-Identification

Because the Census Questionnaire is designed to be a self-administered instrument, answers to many questions are based upon respondents' perceptions of themselves and their Households. This principle of self-identification is fairly new to Census methodology. Up to and including the 1970 Census, enumerators designated certain population and housing characteristics based on direct observation. For example, a person's Race was determined according to his or her appearance. Now, people choose their own answers, whether they complete the Questionnaire themselves or they are interviewed by an enumerator. When an enumerator visits a Household to complete a Questionnaire, respondents are asked to identify their Race, even if the answer seems obvious.

The Bureau provides guidelines to help respondents complete the Questionnaire accurately, but individuals are free to answer as they see fit. The application of this principle can be illustrated by the following example. The Census asks several questions about physical or mental conditions which limit respondents' ability to work or to care for themselves in the home. Under these guidelines, a blind person may not think of blindness as a disabling condition, while persons with minor infirmities might consider themselves disabled. Other characteristics directly affected by self-identification are Ancestry, Race, Hispanic Origin, and Housing Value.

Self-identification poses problems when respondents don't know the answer to a particular question. Except for one Item dealing with the year a structure was built, the 1990 Questionnaire provides no opportunity to answer, "I don't know." Persons unsure of an answer are asked to make an educated guess. For example, homeowners are asked to specify the market value of their property as if it were being offered for sale at that moment. Since few individuals are knowledgeable about current housing values in their neighborhood, responses are based on personal opinion. Each person's home is valued at whatever amount he or she believes it to be worth.

> **Self-identification poses problems when respondents don't know the answer to a particular question.**

NEW IN '90

During prior Censuses, many respondents found it difficult to answer the housing question which asked the year a structure was built. Without consulting a Title Abstract or other legal documentation, the answer was often based on faulty recollection or pure guesswork. Renters in particular had no idea of the age of a building in which they lived. The 1990 Questionnaire resolved this problem by adding a new category for "Don't know."

Write-In Responses

Most Items on the Census Questionnaires utilize a multiple-choice format: a list of specified responses is provided and individuals mark the answer which best fits their situation. Characteristics such as Ancestry, tribal affiliation, place of work, occupation, mortgage payment, and utility costs are not suited to a multiple-choice format, so they require write-in responses. Answers to these questions are typed into Census databases by data-entry clerks. Computer programs then

> **Most Items on the Census Questionnaires utilize a multiple-choice format: a list of specified responses is provided and individuals mark the answer which best fits their situation.**

match responses to standard codes created by the Bureau.

Numeric responses are handled easily by the Bureau's coding programs. A write-in response indicating a monthly mortgage payment of $550 would be coded for tabulation in the $500 to $699 category, for

example. Verbal (non-numeric) responses require more sophisticated programming. To correctly tabulate words in a written response, Bureau computers must link numerous synonyms to the proper Census code. For example, the 1990 Census uses 236 Industry Codes, arranged into 13 major groups. Each Industry is represented by a three-digit code. If a person indicates she works in a yogurt factory, her response will be linked by the computer to Industry Code 101, "Manufactured Dairy Products." Similar three-digit codes have been established for occupational titles. The Bureau's occupational classification system recognizes 501 categories. The codes are arranged into summary levels and major groups, which are shown in Figure 5-2. Occupational Codes are linked to 30,000

1990 CENSUS OCCUPATIONAL CLASSIFICATION SYSTEM

(Figures in parentheses represent the number of occupations classified within each group.)

Managerial and Professional Specialty Occupations

003 - 037	Executive, Administrative, and Managerial Occupations (29 codes)
043 - 199	Professional Specialty Occupations (106 codes)

Technical, Sales, and Administrative Support Occupations

203 - 235	Technicians and Related Support Occupations (22 codes)
245 - 285	Sales Occupations (24 codes)
303 - 389	Administrative Support Occupations, Including Clerical (55 codes)

Service Occupations

403 - 407	Private Household Occupations (5 codes)
413 - 427	Protective Service Occupations (11 codes)
433 - 469	Other Service Occupations (29 codes)

Farming, Forestry, and Fishing Occupations

473 - 499	[No Major Group breakdowns] (19 codes)

Precision Production, Craft, and Repair Occupations

503 - 699	[No Major Group breakdowns] (102 codes)

Operators, Fabricators, and Laborers

703 - 799	Machine Operators, Assemblers, and Inspectors (66 codes)
803 - 859	Transportation and material Moving Occupations (24 codes)
864 - 889	Handlers, Equipment Cleaners, Helpers, and Laborers (20 codes)

Military Occupations

903 - 905	[No Major Group breakdowns]

Experienced Unemployed Not Classified by Occupation

909	Unemployed, last worked 1984 or earlier

Figure 5-2

NEW IN '90

Automated coding of write-in responses is a new feature of 1990 Census procedures. "Smart programs" not only streamline the coding process, but reduce potential error associated with manual coding and review. Following the 1980 Census, several questions requiring write-in responses were never tabulated due to the high cost of the manual operation.

---

individual job titles derived from the Labor Department's *Dictionary of Occupational Titles*, the Defense Department's *Military Occupation Index*, and the Bureau's own experience with prior Census returns and survey responses. As shown in Figure 5-3, Occupational Code 348, "Telephone Operators," is linked to 56 job titles, from P.B.X. Operator to Jackboard Operator. The coding software also looks for appropriate responses from related questions, such as Educational Attainment and Industry. For example, an occupational response of "Interceptor" will be coded "Telephone Operator" whenever the Industry response is coded 441, Telephone Communications Industry.

ADMINISTRATIVE SUPPORT OCCUPATIONS, INCLUDING CLERICAL

344 BILLING, POSTING, AND CALCULATING MACHINE OPERATORS —Con.

Proof clerk—*700*
Proof-machine operator—700
Proof operator—700
Reconciliation-machine operator—700
Transit-proof-machine operator—700
Tray checker—641

345 DUPLICATING MACHINE OPERATORS

Braille coder
Compotype operator
Copy machine operator
Copy room technician
Dexigraph operator

Ditto-machine operator
Duplicating-machine operator
Duplicator—Exc. tool machine shop 320
Dupligraph operator
Graphotype operator

I.B.M. operator, copying, duplicating, etc.
Micro-photographer
Mimeograph operator
Mimeographer
Multigraph operator

Multigrapher
Multilith operator
Offset-duplicating-machine operator, clerical
Offsetting-machine hand
Photocopying-machine operator

Photographic-machine operator
Xerox-machine operator
Xerox operator

346 MAIL PREPARING AND PAPER HANDLING MACHINE OPERATORS

Addressing-machine operator
Addressograph operator
Advertising inserter
Canceling-machine operator
Envelope-sealer operator

Folding-machine operator—Any not listed above
Inserting-machine operator—Exc. 100- 392
Mailing-machine operator
Sealing-and-canceling-machine operator
Wing-mailer-machine operator—171,172

347 OFFICE MACHINE OPERATORS, N.E.C.

Bursting-machine operator
Business-machine operator
Camera operator, microfilm or microfiche
Check embosser
Check-sorter operator—700

Check-writing-machine operator
Checking-machine operator
Coin-machine operator—700,701
Coin-rolling-machine operator
Coin wrapper

Coin-wrapping-machine operator
Collator operator—Exc. 171,172
Currency sorter—700-702
Document photographer
Embossing machine operator—Any not listed above

Embossograph operator, office machines
Equipment operator, n. s.—700-712, 831,842,862
Letter-opener operator
Line-o-scribe operator
Listing-machine operator

Machine operator, n. s.—700-712,831, 842,862
Microfilm cameraman
Microfilm-machine operator
Microfilm mounter
Microfilm operator

347 OFFICE MACHINE OPERATORS, N.E.C.—Con.

Microfilmer
Office-machine operator
Recordak operator
Set-o-type operator
Sign-machine operator, printing

Ticket-machine operator
Transit clerk
Transit-department clerk—700

348 TELEPHONE OPERATORS

A operator—441
Branch-exchange operator
Call girl—402
Central-office operator—441
Change-number operator—441

Charge operator—441
Clerk, route—441
Combination operator—441
Command and control specialist—FGOV 932
Communication-center operator—421

Complaint operator—441
Desk operator—441
Directory-assistance operator—441
Directory operator—441
Emergency operator—441

Exchange operator—441
Information operator—(441)
Intercept operator—441
Interceptor—441
Interceptor operator—741

Inward-toll operator—441
Jackboard operator—442
L.D. operator—441
Local operator—441
Long-distance operator—441

Long-lines operator—441
Monitor, n. s.—441
Multiple-marking operator—441
Observer—441

Operator
  With class of worker exc. OWN—441

P.B.X. operator
Position observer—441
Private-branch-exchange service adviser—441
Rate-quoting operator—441
Recording operator—441
Routing operator—441

Service observer—441
Student operator—441
Switchboard operator—Exc. 180-192, 450,452
Switching clerk—442
Tandem operator—441

Teachers, exc. elementary & secondary
  Operator's—441
  P.B.X.—441
  N. s.—441

Telephone clerk, telegraph office— 442
Telephone-exchange operator
Telephone girl
Telephone operator, n. s
Telephone-switchboard operator
Test operator—441

Through operator—441
Time operator—441
Toll operator—441
Toll-relief operator—441
Toll-service observer—441

Traffic observer—441,442
Traffic operator—441,442
Trouble operator—441

353 COMMUNICATIONS EQUIPMENT OPERATORS, N.E.C.

Alarm operator—Fire department 910
Dispatcher, oil—422
Dispatcher, relay—422
Equipment operator, n. s.—442
Facsimile machine operator

Fax machine operator
Machine operator, n. s.—442
Morse operator—442

Operator
  With class of worker exc. OWN—442
  With class of worker exc. OWN— News syndicate 741
  With class of worker exc. OWN— Railroad station 400

Protective-signal operator
Receiver, n. s.—442
Relay telegrapher—442
Service observer—442
Telautograph operator
Telegraph dispatcher—(442)

Telegraph operator—(442)
Telegrapher
Telegrapher agent—400
Telegraphic-typewriter operator— (442)
Telephone-answering-service operator- -741

Ticker operator—(741)
Train operator, exc. engineer—400
Wire-photo operator, news—171,172
Wires-transfer clerk—700-702

354 POSTAL CLERKS, EXCEPT MAIL CARRIERS

Assistant
  N. s.—412

Assorter—412
City clerk—412
Clerk, n. s.—412
Counter clerk, n. s.—412
Dead-mail checker—412
Delivery clerk—412

Distribution clerk—412
Distributor—412
Equipment operator, n. s.—412
L.S.M. operator—412
Machine operator, n. s.—412

Mail agent—412
Mail assorter—412
Mail boy—412
Mail caller—412
Mail clerk—412

Mail-distribution-scheme examiner— 412
Mail distributor—412
Mail girl—412
Mail handler, sorting mail—412
Mail opener—412

Mail-order clerk—412
Mail rider—412
Mail sorter—412
Mail weigher—412
Mailing clerk—412

Mailing-section clerk—412
Mailroom clerk—412
Money-order clerk—412
Parcel-post clerk—412
Post office clerk—412

Postal clerk—412
Postal transportation clerk—412
Sorter—412
Sorting-machine operator—412
Special-delivery clerk—412

Stamp clerk—412
Window clerk—412
Z.M.T. Operator—412

Census Tip

The numbering systems used for Industry and Occupational Codes in the decennial Census differ from the more familiar Dictionary of Occupational Title (DOT) and Standard Industrial Classification (SIC) numbers used in other government publications. The Bureau publishes a two-volume guide to 1990 Census codes: the *Classified Index of Industries and Occupations,* and the *Alphabetical Index of Industries and Occupations.*

The Bureau consults with many experts to devise codes for such characteristics as country of birth and Language Spoken at Home. Nearly 1,000 separate codes were developed for Ancestry groups alone. Census Bureau specialists are responsible for editing the coded responses. This includes looking for inconsistent answers and resolving problems not handled by the coding programs. For example, write-in responses to questions on Language Spoken at Home are edited by workers trained to recognize variations in names of the world's languages.

Data Imputation

Except for two Items dealing with Ancestry and Year Structure Built, the 1990 Census contains no tabulation categories for "don't know" or "not reported." Data subcategories in Census publications always total to an appropriate 100%. Does this mean the Bureau obtains responses from all persons for all questions? Unfortunately not. Despite painstaking follow-up efforts during the enumeration and processing stages, some Households are never heard from, and many of the Questionnaires mailed back to Processing Centers contain blank or incomplete answers. The Census Bureau handles these omissions using a procedure known as data

Imputation. During the editing process, Census Bureau computers supply fictitious responses programmed to approximate the missing information. Incomplete information about a person or Housing Unit is supplied through a computer editing technique known as Allocation. The computer fills in missing responses by assigning the same response given by a similar individual. In cases where no information is available for any members of a Household (i.e., no Questionnaire was returned), the computer editing procedure is called Substitution. Here, a full set of responses is assigned, taken from another completed Questionnaire. Allocation and Substitution involve the wholesale creation of imaginary Census responses, but research has shown these methods actually improve the overall quality of Census data. More important, the Bureau publishes statistics on the percentage of Imputation for every variable and every level of geography, enabling Census users to properly evaluate data. As discussed in Chapter 10, these tables are indispensable for identifying data items with exceptionally high Imputation rates within a particular geographic area.

Census Tip

All blank responses are subject to data Allocation except one: missing responses on Ancestry are assigned to an "Ancestry not given" category in Census publications.

A third type of Imputation is the Confidentiality Edit. For smaller levels of geography, data on certain individuals and Housing Units cannot be divulged because they would reveal personal information about that person or Household. To circumvent this problem, the Confidentiality Edit swaps data for one Household with that of a similar Household located in a different geographic area. Imputation methods and their effect on

During the editing process, Census Bureau computers supply fictitious responses programmed to approximate the missing information.

For smaller levels of geography, data on certain individuals and Housing Units cannot be divulged because they would reveal personal information about that person or Household.

the accuracy of Census data are discussed in greater detail in Chapter 10.

Housing Concepts

A solid grounding in basic housing concepts is vital for all Census users, even those with no interest in studying housing characteristics. Why? Because many key population definitions are tied to housing concepts. For this reason, major housing terms will be defined first. The following sections introduce one of the most fundamental distinctions in Census methodology: the difference between Housing Units and Group Quarters. Among the other housing concepts discussed below are Vacancy Status, home ownership, rental costs, and Housing Value.

Living Quarters

The type of dwelling in which a person lives helps determine how he or she is counted in the Census. The Bureau defines Living Quarters as any space intended or used for human habitation. Living Quarters are nor-

The Bureau utilizes two broad categories of Living Quarters: Housing Units and Group Quarters (GQs).

mally found in structures built for residential use, such as houses, apartment buildings, mobile homes, dormitories, or nursing homes.

 Census Tip

Technically speaking, the concept of Group Quarters is not a housing topic, since GQs are excluded from the Bureau's definition of housing stock. However, since GQs are defined in relation to Housing Units, it makes sense to discuss them together.

Examples of atypical Living Quarters include prisons, tents, vans, a room in a warehouse or garage, and shelters for the homeless. The Bureau utilizes two broad categories of Living Quarters: Housing Units and Group Quarters (GQs). Housing Units constitute the basic inventory of our nation's housing stock, while Group Quarters represent communal living arrangements designed to meet specific needs. As described in Chapters 3 and 4, the Group Quarters population is identified and counted using specialized enumeration techniques. According to the

---

TYPES OF LIVING QUARTERS

GROUP QUARTERS

Institutions	Noninstitutions
Correctional Facility	Military Quarters
Hospital	Rooming House
Mental Hospital	College Dormitory
Nursing Home	Group Home
Juvenile Institution	Maritime Vessel
Other Institution	Homeless Shelter
	Street Location
	Other Noninstitutional

HOUSING UNITS

Vacant	Occupied
For Sale	Owner-Occupied
For Rent	Renter-Occupied
Awaiting Occupancy	
For Migrant Workers	
Seasonal, Recreational, or Occasional Use	
Other Vacant	

Figure 5-4

1990 Census, more than 242 million people, constituting 97.3% of the total population, live in Housing Units. The remaining 2.7% reside in Group Quarters. Figure 5-4 illustrates the relationships among categories of Living Quarters.

Housing Units

Most people live in Housing Units, which the Bureau defines as dwellings occupied as separate Living Quarters, or if Vacant, intended for separate occupancy. A Housing Unit can be a single room, a group of rooms, or an entire structure. One building may contain many Housing Units, as in the case of an apartment building. The occupants of a Housing Unit may be a single Family, a Family plus one or more Nonrelatives, several "families" living together, a lone individual, or any group of nine or fewer unrelated persons.

The Bureau employs three criteria for determining whether a dwelling is a Housing Unit:

- the occupants must live and take meals separately from other people in the structure
- the Unit must provide direct access from outside the structure or through a common hall
- occupants must be related to one another, or if unrelated, the Unit must consist of fewer than 10 unrelated people.

The best way to clarify the Housing Unit concept is to provide examples. A single-family house is clearly a Housing Unit, while a two-family house (a duplex, a double, etc.) is comprised of two Housing Units. An apartment building, a row of townhouses, or a group of condominiums each consists of multiple Housing Units, because every apartment or home has a separate entrance and is designed for separate occupancy. Most rooming houses are not Housing Units, because occupants do not have separate access from the outside, or in the case of common hallways, because the boarders take their meals

together. Similarly, if a homeowner takes in a boarder, the boarder's room would not be considered a separate Housing Unit in most cases. But if the boarder's room has a separate outside entrance, and the boarder does not take meals with the homeowner, the room is considered a Housing Unit, regardless of its size. The key to understanding this criterion is that the occupants must be able to enter their room(s) without walking through someone else's Living Quarters.

Availability of separate cooking facilities is another important criterion for Housing Units, but certain dwellings pose a challenge for this classification guideline. A nursing home or a residential facility for the care of well-aged persons would generally not be counted as a Housing Unit because its residents take meals together. But what about apartment buildings for the elderly? In many buildings of this type, residents occupy independent apartments containing kitchen facilities, but may eat some meals in a common dining room. The Bureau calls such dwellings congregate housing, and classifies them as Housing Units.

Can a tent, boat, or recreational vehicle be a Housing Unit? Yes, if it is occupied as someone's Place of Usual Residence. A new home under construction is considered a Housing Unit only if all exterior doors and windows are in place and all interior floors have been installed. Otherwise, the dwelling is not yet part of the housing stock. Similarly, a newly built mobile home is a Housing Unit only if has been moved to the site of its intended occupancy; those located on dealers' lots are not counted. Rooms in hotels, motels, and similar lodging facilities are Housing Units only if 75% or more of the establishment's existing accommodations are occupied by long-term residents. Buildings which are being demolished, have been condemned, or lack a roof or exterior walls are excluded from the pool of Housing Units. If a residential building is boarded-up for protective purposes but is not condemned, it is counted as a Housing Unit. Nonresidential structures—stores, office buildings, factories, and the like—are not Living Quarters, and therefore not Housing Units. However, if a room or group of rooms within such a building is used as the Usual Residence of the owner; a custodian, night watchman, or other employee; or a tenant, those rooms count as a Housing Unit.

NEW IN '90

The Census Bureau recognizes congregate housing as a distinct category for the first time in 1990. Such Units are identified by asking renters whether the cost of some or all meals are included in their monthly rent.

Group Quarters

By definition, any Living Quarters not counted as Housing Units are categorized as Group Quarters. Most GQs are comprised of ten or more unrelated people living together, but certain facilities are counted as Group Quarters regardless of the number of inhabitants. Persons living in GQs typically have no individual address. Figure 5-4 shows some of the principal types of Group Quarters.

Group Quarters are divided into two major categories: Institutions and Noninstitutional Group Quarters. Institutions are characterized by the level of supervision or control they exercise over their patients, residents, or inmates. An Institution is authorized to administer care to its charges, or to exercise custody over them. Institutionalized persons generally have limited contact with their surrounding communities. Their mobility is restricted to the grounds of the Institution; to leave the grounds, they must obtain a pass or be accompanied by an escort. Institutional status does not necessarily relate to the size of a facility, the level of medical care provided, or the length of stay of its inhabitants. Examples of Institutions are correctional facilities (prisons, jails, detention centers,

work farms, correctional halfway houses, and similar entities), nursing homes, mental hospitals, hospitals for the chronically ill, schools and hospitals for the mentally or physically handicapped, and juvenile care facilities (orphanages, schools for juvenile delinquents, homes for abused or neglected children).

All other GQs are counted as Noninstitutional Group Quarters. Certain facilities fall into this category by definition, including college dormitories, fraternity and sorority houses, military barracks and dormitories, workers' dormitories (migratory farm camps, bunkhouses for ranch hands, logging camps, etc.), military and maritime vessels, hospital dormitories for nurses and interns, and shelters for abused women.

Other types of facilities are classed as Noninstitutional Group Quarters only if ten or more unrelated persons live in the facility; otherwise they are counted as Housing Units. Among this category are rooming and boarding houses, community-based homes and halfway-houses (including those for the mentally ill, mentally retarded, physically handicapped, unwed mothers, alcoholics, or substance abusers), religious quarters (convents, monasteries, etc.), and off-campus college housing. It should be stressed that Group Quarters status for these facilities depends solely upon the number of inhabitants. An off-campus apartment rented by five unrelated roommates is a Housing Unit, but an apartment shared by ten roommates is a GQ.

Two types of Noninstitutional Group Quarters bear special mention: emergency shelters for homeless persons, and Visible Street Locations. Individuals falling under these categories were counted during the Bureau's S-Night activities, described in Chapter 4. All homeless shelters are classified as Noninstitutional Group Quarters and all residents are counted in the Group Quarters population. Homeless shelters include missions, emergency shelters with overnight sleeping facilities, Salvation Army shelters, hotels and motels used entirely for the home-

Nonresidential structures—stores, office buildings, factories, and the like—are not Living Quarters, and therefore not Housing Units.

By definition, any Living Quarters not counted as Housing Units are categorized as Group Quarters.

less, and "flophouses" (hotels and motels charging $12 or less per night, excluding taxes). Youth hostels, YMCA and YWCA hotels, commercial campgrounds, and other facilities for travelers or transients are excluded from the homeless shelter category. Any persons counted in Visible Locations (parks, bridges, doorways, alleys, bus stations, all-night movie theaters) or seen emerging from boarded-up buildings are also included in the Group Quarters population.

 Census Tip

The Census Bureau does not define "homeless." Data on homeless persons can be found in Census publications by summing various categories of the Group Quarters population, depending upon how users wish to define the concept.

Distinctions between Group Quarters and Housing Units can be confusing. Even more confusing are certain distinctions between Institutions and Noninstitutional GQs. Two facilities serving similar functions could be grouped in different categories, depending on the type of facility. For example, a community-based home for the mentally retarded is Noninstitutional, while a school or hospital for the mentally retarded is an Institution. A home for abused children is an Institution if it provides long-term care (usually lasting more than 30 days), while a shelter providing short-term care for runaway children is Noninstitutional. When in doubt, consult Census documentation.

Occupancy Characteristics

The Census measures housing occupancy from two points of view. First, all Housing Units are classified as either Occupied or Vacant. Occupied Housing Units then are divided into Owner-Occupied and Renter-Occupied Units. In Census parlance, the owner/renter classification is called Housing Tenure.

Vacancy Status

The Bureau considers a Housing Unit Occupied if it is the Place of Usual Residence of the people living there at the time of enumeration, or if the occupants are temporarily absent (on vacation, etc.). A Unit is Vacant if, at the time of enumeration, it is not listed as anyone's Place of Usual Residence. Vacant Units are classified into several categories, as shown in Figure 5-5. Note that Units intended for seasonal, recreational, or occasional use are counted as Vacant, even if they are inhabited at the time of the Census. These include summer homes, hunting cabins, and time-sharing condominiums. Facilities for migrant farm workers are only counted as Housing Units if they are independent dwellings. By definition, all facilities located within an employer-owned migrant farm camp are classed as Group Quarters, regardless of the number of inhabitants.

The "Other Vacant" grouping encompasses Vacant Units which are not for sale or rent, not awaiting occupancy, and not held for

The Bureau considers a Housing Unit Occupied if it is the Place of Usual Residence of the people living there at the time of enumeration, or if the occupants are temporarily absent (on vacation, etc.).

NEW IN '90

In 1980, all Vacant Housing Units were divided into two broad categories: Seasonal, and For Year-Round Use. Seasonal totals were further divided into three groups covering occasional use, recreational use, and use by migrant workers. For 1990, the Year-Round category was dropped because it implied all Year-Round housing had similar structural characteristics. (In practice, the Year-Round determination was based on the use to which the Unit's owners employed it, not the inherent nature of the structure.) The 1990 Questionnaire also collapsed the three 1980 subcategories of Seasonal housing into two: migrant; and seasonal, recreational, or occasional use. The second change was made because the older categories overlapped and caused confusion for respondents and data users.

occasional use. This category includes Housing Units used for storage purposes, estates undergoing probate, boarded-up properties, houses taken off the market because they didn't sell, and structures which are simply not being used by their owners.

As shown in Figure 5-5, the 1990 Census counted 102.3 million Housing Units in the United States, of which 92.0 million are Occupied and 10.3 million are Vacant. Adding together the first three categories of Vacant Units indicates roughly 50% of them are for sale, for rent, or awaiting occupancy. Approximately 30% are seasonal, recreational, or occasional-use Units, while the remaining 20% are some form of "Other Vacant." The table format used by the Bureau in Figure 5-5 is misleading because it implies all boarded-up structures fall under the category of Other Vacant. Actually, any type of Vacant Unit can be boarded-up (e.g., a boarded-up summer cottage). Most boarded-up Units can be characterized as "Other," however, so very few Census publications provide data on boarded-up Units within the remaining categories. Also remember that many boarded-up buildings are not residential structures at all, and are not counted in the decennial Census.

Census Tip

The concept of Usual Residence Elsewhere presents a peculiar paradox: if everyone in a Household is away from home (their Place of Usual Residence) at the time of enumeration, the Census counts the Unit as Occupied, even though it is temporarily uninhabited. Conversely, if everyone staying in a Housing Unit indicates their Usual Residence is elsewhere, that Unit is counted Vacant, even though it is temporarily inhabited. This makes sense if you remember every person must claim only one residence, or they will be double-counted.

United States Inside and Outside Metropolitan Area

	United States
All housing units	**102 263 678**
POPULATION	
All persons	**248 709 873**
Persons in occupied housing units	242 012 129
Per occupied housing unit	2.63
Owner-occupied housing units	162 303 028
Per owner-occupied housing unit	2.75
Renter-occupied housing units	79 709 101
Per renter-occupied housing unit	2.42
TENURE BY RACE AND HISPANIC ORIGIN OF HOUSEHOLDER	
Occupied housing units	**91 947 410**
Owner-occupied housing units	59 024 811
Percent of occupied housing units	64.2
White	52 432 648
Black	4 327 265
American Indian, Eskimo, or Aleut	318 001
Asian or Pacific Islander	1 050 182
Other race	896 715
Hispanic origin (of any race)	2 545 584
White, not of Hispanic origin	50 860 725
Renter-occupied housing units	32 922 599
White	24 447 457
Black	5 648 896
American Indian, Eskimo, or Aleut	273 371
Asian or Pacific Islander	963 553
Other race	1 589 322
Hispanic origin (of any race)	3 456 134
White, not of Hispanic origin	22 773 024
VACANCY STATUS	
Vacant housing units	**10 316 268**
For sale only	1 260 233
For rent	3 046 638
Rented or sold, not occupied	807 631
For seasonal, recreational, or occasional use	3 081 923
For migrant workers	34 944
Other vacant	2 084 899
Boarded up	207 626

Figure 5-5

Vacancy Status may appear to be a straight-forward concept, but one anomaly is frequently misunderstood. If all occupants of a Housing Unit indicate their Usual Residence is elsewhere, then the Unit is classified as Vacant. Consider the case of an out-of-town manager who is living in a company-owned apartment for a few weeks while she works on a project at corporate headquarters. Because the apartment is not her Usual Residence, the Bureau counts it as a Vacant Unit, even though she is living there temporarily. Situations such as this may seem uncommon, but the same rule applies to most seasonal and recreational Units inhabited at the time of enumeration.

Housing Tenure

Any Occupied Housing Unit which is used by its owner or co-owner as the Place of Usual Residence is defined as Owner-Occupied.

Any Occupied Housing Unit which is used by its owner or co-owner as the Place of Usual Residence is defined as Owner-Occupied. The category is further divided by those owned with a mortgage and those owned free and clear.

All Occupied Housing Units not inhabited by their owners or co-owners are counted as Renter-Occupied. This definition includes those Units whose residents pay cash rent, and those where no rent is paid. The latter

category includes Housing Units on military bases, Units provided free by friends or relatives, and Units occupied by caretakers, managers, clergy, or others as part of their terms of employment.

NEW IN '90

For 1990, the Bureau distinguishes between homes owned free-and-clear and those owned with a mortgage. In prior Censuses, the meaning of ownership was not clearly understood by everyone. If the home were still mortgaged, many respondents felt they did not really own the property.

Farm Residence

Housing Units situated on farm property are counted in the totals for all Housing Units, but the Bureau also provides separate tabulations on certain types of farm housing.

The Farm Residence category is limited to single-Unit houses (including mobile homes) which are located on an active farm. To distinguish between working farms and homes where the owner operates a small truck garden, the Bureau counts any single-Unit

Q&A

Why doesn't the Census Bureau simply ask people whether they reside in two homes?

The 1970 Census was the only one which asked a question about dual residence. For 1990, the Bureau tested several methods of identifying multiple homes. One version of the test Questionnaire asked each person in the Household whether they lived in more than one dwelling. Another version asked the same question of the Household as a whole. Specific wording in both versions asked whether respondents maintained a second residence where they lived for 30 days or more during the previous year. Both versions required re-

spondents to turn to a separate section of the Questionnaire to provide data on the second dwelling. For a variety of reasons, neither version was incorporated into the final Questionnaire. First, the question was too lengthy and complex. Second, regardless of wording and format, the test question tended to confuse respondents. Finally, the responses were highly inconsistent, producing unreliable results. For example, many residents who answered "yes" on the test Questionnaire, said "no" during follow-up interviews.

dwelling located on one acre or more and selling at least $1,000 of agricultural products during the Reference Year.

Most persons living in Farm Residences are counted in a category known as the Farm Population. As used in the decennial Census, Farm Population is a misleading term because it excludes certain people who might reasonably be considered part of this category. The following groups are not part of the Farm Population, even if they are farm workers:

- ▸ persons living in Group Quarters on Farm property
- ▸ persons living in multi-Unit buildings on farm property
- ▸ persons living in a Farm Residence in an Urban area
- ▸ persons living in Rural areas, but not in a Farm Residence.

The definitions of Urban and Rural land areas are discussed in Chapter 6.

 Census Tip

The decennial Census tabulates demographic, social, and economic characteristics of persons who live on farms, as well as characteristics of Farm Households and single-Unit farm houses. Relevant population and housing data are typically reported for the "Rural Farm" portions of states and counties.

Structural and Financial Characteristics

Several housing concepts pertain to the physical characteristics of the Unit. The 1990 Questionnaire carries questions on the number of Rooms in the Unit, the number of Bedrooms, the availability of complete kitchen and bathroom facilities, the number of Units in the structure, and whether the structure is attached or detached from neighboring buildings. Even these seemingly basic concepts require exacting definitions. Rooms, for example, are counted as whole rooms used for living purposes. This definition excludes bathrooms, "pullman kitchens," open porches, hallways, foyers, utility rooms, attics and basements (unless finished for living purposes), and unfinished storage space. The definition of Bedroom is equally specific. Questionnaire guidelines instruct respondents to count any Room which would be listed as a bedroom if the house or apartment were placed on the market for sale or rent.

The Census collects data on various housing costs for both Tenure categories. Financial characteristics range from second (subordinate) mortgages, condominium fees, and mobile home fees, to more basic matters such as utility costs and mortgage payments. Two of the most frequently used characteristics for marketing and economic analysis are rental costs and Housing Value.

The Bureau employs two different measures of rental costs: Contract Rent and Gross Rent. Contract Rent is the monthly cash payment agreed to by landlord and tenant, regardless of furnishings, utilities, meals, or other services which may be included. If a Unit is Vacant and For Rent, an amount is reported for "Rent Asked." Gross Rent is a more inclusive measure, covering Contract Rent plus the cost of any additional utilities or fuels paid directly by the tenant. Utility costs are defined as payments made to private or municipal utility companies for electricity, gas, and water. Fuel costs include

> ### NEW IN '90
>
> The Bureau's definition of Bedroom changed radically for 1990. In prior Censuses, Bedrooms were self-identified as any Room used mainly for sleeping, regardless of its intended purpose. An enclosed porch used as a bedroom was counted as a Bedroom in 1980, but not in 1990. Conversely, a Room designed as a bedroom but being used as a den, office, sewing room, or the like, would not count as a Bedroom in 1980, but would in 1990.

The Bureau employs two different measures of rental costs: Contract Rent and Gross Rent.

the purchase price of oil, kerosene, wood, or similar heating fuels.

Housing Value is asked of all Owner-Occupied Units, including condominiums and mobile homes, plus all Units being bought or for sale. For Occupied Units, Value is the owner's estimate of how much the property would sell for if it were placed on the market. If a Unit is Vacant and For Sale, an amount is reported for "Price Asked." Housing Value reflects the total price of the home, the lot, and any other buildings situated on the lot.

Housing Value is not reported for business residences nor for homes situated on extensive acreage. If a person owns and lives in an apartment located above a store, operates a medical office out of the home, or lives on property used for other business activities, the Value of the overall property would distort those of regular residential Units. Therefore, the Questionnaire asks whether the property is used as a business or medical office. To be counted as a business property, the establishment should be recognizable from the street and have a separate outside entrance. The business may be attached to the residence, or located elsewhere on the property. Single-Unit homes situated on ten or more acres of land are excluded for similar reasons.

Population Concepts

Most data users are familiar with basic demographic concepts such as household, family, race, and ethnic origin. Unfortunately, the decennial Census uses these and other terms in very precise ways, which creates a continual problem for researchers who assume they understand the language. Nearly every major population definition utilized by the Bureau contains exceptions which are neither obvious or predictable.

The following section focuses on the population concepts most likely to cause confu-

sion: Household and Family Relationships; Race and Hispanic Origin; Ancestry and National Origin; Income and Poverty Status; and Employment Status.

 Census Tip

Never take Census terminology for granted, no matter how basic. Even when you have previous experience with a particular concept, it doesn't hurt to refresh your understanding with a quick check of definitions.

Housing Value is not reported for business residences nor for homes situated on extensive acreage.

Households and Families

Households are not the same as Families. Census definitions of both are quite specific and vary from common usage. To be counted as a member of a Household or Family, a person must live in a Housing Unit. Persons living in Group Quarters are not counted as part of any Household or Family, because Group Quarters are not Housing Units.

Households and Families come in all sizes and combinations, which makes classifying them a challenge. The following sections discuss various types of living arrangements and how they are treated in the Census. A variety of important Census terms are also introduced, including Householder, Nonrelative, Subfamily, and Own Child.

To be counted as a member of a Household or Family, a person must live in a Housing Unit. Persons living in Group Quarters are not counted as part of any Household or Family, because Group Quarters are not Housing Units.

The Role of Householders

The starting point for understanding Households and Families is the Census Bureau concept of Householder. By definition, a Householder is simply the person listed in Column 1 of each Household's Census Questionnaire. Any adult member of the Household can be listed as the Householder, but the Bureau recommends choosing the person in whose name the Unit is owned or rented, whether male or female. What about

Q&A

If the wife in a married-couple Family is listed in Column 1 of the Questionnaire, is the Unit counted as having a female Head of Household?

No, because the Bureau doesn't utilize that terminology, and because the word Householder is not meant to imply leadership, authority, or wage-earning ability in the Household. The concept is used solely as a means of defining familial relationships among Household members and for classifying Households by type. However, the Bureau does employ a category for "Female Householder, No Husband Present."

---

homes that are owned or leased jointly? Because the Census is a self-enumerated instrument, either party can choose to be Householder. In most married-couple Families, however, the husband is listed first. (Perhaps for the same reasons that husbands get to drive the car on family outings.) In older Censuses, the person listed in Column 1 was known as the Head of Household, but this archaic and value-laden terminology was dropped in 1980.

 Census Tip

Any person who lives alone (in a Single-Person Household) is also counted as a Householder.

The Census Bureau divides Householders into two categories: Family Householders, who live with their Family; and Nonfamily Householders, who live alone or with Nonrelatives. The Householder plays a unique role in the Census because all Household and Family relationships are linked to that individual, and because every Household is classified according to the characteristics of its Householder. Family size, for example, is determined by each Household member's relationship to the Householder, not to others in the Unit. The importance of this concept will become clearer later in the chapter, when different types of Households and Families are described.

The Householder plays a unique role in the Census because all Household and Family relationships are linked to that individual, and because every Household is classified according to the characteristics of its Householder.

Households

A Household consists of all persons living together within an Occupied Housing Unit. Household members do not need to be related to one another, as long as they share living arrangements within a Housing Unit. A Household can consist of a lone person, an unmarried couple, two to nine unrelated roommates, a Family (with or without children), or Nonrelatives living with a Family. Every Household has one Householder, the person listed in Column 1 of the Questionnaire.

 Census Tip

By definition, the number of total Households in any geographic area equals the number of Householders, which equals the number of Occupied Housing Units. This three-way equality holds true only for complete-count characteristics, however. Values for sample data may not match due to sampling error.

Households are divided into two categories, as shown in Figure 5-6. A Nonfamily Household consists of one or more individuals living in a Housing Unit where none of the Household members are related to the Householder. A person living alone constitutes a Single-Person Household, which is a

HOUSEHOLD TYPES

A Household is comprised of all members of an Occupied Housing Unit.
Residents of Group Quarters are not considered Household members.

Family Households

Married Couple Household
    with children present
    with no children present

Male Householder, No Wife Present
    with children
    without children

Female Householder, No Husband Present
    with children
    without children

Other Family Households
    (e.g., siblings)

Nonfamily Households

Single-Person Household

Unmarried Partner Household
    unmarried couple household
    both male partners
    both female partners

Roommates

Figure 5-6

type of Nonfamily Household. Family Households will be described later in the chapter.

Two unrelated adults who live together and share an intimate relationship are defined as Unmarried Partners. The Bureau uses this terminology to distinguish cohabiting couples from other types of roommates. Unmarried Partners may be members of the opposite sex or two members of the same sex, and they may live with or without children. An Unmarried Partner Household includes Unmarried Partners, one of whom is the Householder. A subset of this category is the Unmaried Couple Household, where the partners are of the opposite sex.

An Unmarried Partner Household includes Unmarried Partners, one of whom is the Householder. A subset of this category is the Unmaried Couple Household, where the partners are of the opposite sex.

NEW IN '90

The designation for Unmarried Partners appears for the first time in the 1990 Census.

The number, composition, and characteristics of Households are among the most widely used Census statistics. Households are viewed by marketers and social scientists as a fundamental social and economic unit.

For many products and services, particularly the more expensive ones, purchasing decisions are made by the entire Household, not by an individual member. The 1990 Census counted nearly 92 million Households in the United States. Approximately 25% of these were Single-Person Households, while an additional 5% represented other types of Nonfamily Households. Considering the popularity of various nonfamily living arrangements in our society, Households are an increasingly important demographic construct.

Families and Subfamilies

In the world of the Census, a Family is defined as a Householder living together with one or more persons who are related to the Householder by marriage, birth, or adoption. Families are not defined by love and affection, but by a combination of living arrangements and legal relationships. Family members *must* live together. Furthermore, a specified relationship must exist between the Householder and each additional member of the Family, through birth marriage, or adoption. Unmarried couples do not constitute a Family, but the parent-child *portion* of an Unmarried Couple Household can be a Family if the parent is the Householder. Households consisting solely of unrelated roommates, boarders, Unmarried Couples, or Unmarried Partners are counted as Nonfamily Households.

Every Family constitutes either a Household in its own right, or part of a Household, but not all Households include Families. Because Families are defined by their relationship to the Householder, and because each Household has only one Householder, each Household can have a maximum of one Family. This is true even where several "families" live in the same Household, or where a Family and Subfamily live together. Examples of this fundamental Census paradox will be provided momentarily.

Census Tip

By definition, the total number of Families in a geographic area equals the number of Family Households, which equals the number of Family Householders.

Relatives of the Householder can include a spouse, natural-born children, adopted children, stepchildren, parents, siblings, grandchildren, in-laws, aunts, cousins, and so on, as long as they occupy the same Housing Unit as the Householder. Foster children are not counted as Family members. In most cases, relatives living apart from the Household are also excluded. For example, a son or daughter away at college is not counted in the Family or the Family Household.

Foster children are not counted as Family members.

Families fall into two categories: Married Couple Families and Other Families. Census tables frequently present separate tabulations for two specific types of Other Families: those with a Male Householder, No Wife Present; and those with a Female Householder, No Husband Present. Remember, however, that the Other Families category incorporates a myriad of familial relationships not shown separately in standard data tables, including a single grandparent living with one or more grandchildren, and two or more siblings living together.

People living in a Family Household who are not related to the Householder are categorized as Nonrelatives.

People living in a Family Household who are not related to the Householder are categorized as Nonrelatives. A boarder living with a Family is a member of the Family Household, but is not a member of the Family.

Census Tip

Tabulations for Nonrelatives also include unrelated persons living together in a Nonfamily Household.

The concept of Nonrelative becomes more confusing due to the following two complications: Unmarried Couples with children, and Subfamilies. Figure 5-7 presents several Household configurations which illustrate the relationships of Subfamilies and Nonrelatives living in Family Households. If a Householder lives with one or more of his or her children, that Household is a Family, regardless of the Householder's marital status. But what if the child's parent is not listed as the Householder? Consider the first example shown in Figure 5-7. Because the man and woman are not married to one another, they are not part of the same Family, even though they live together. The Householder and his daughter constitute a Family. The woman and her children are counted as Nonrelatives, even though they are related to *one another*. Remember, Families are defined solely on the basis of relationship to Householder. The roles are reversed in the second example because the woman is Householder. Regardless of which adult is listed as Householder, the Housing Unit is counted as an Unmarried Couple Household.

Census Tip

Families with no spouse present don't necessarily mean a second parent is absent.

The second complicating factor is the presence of Subfamilies. A Subfamily is a group of people who would constitute a Family if they lived in their own Housing Unit, but they live with another Family to which they are also related. More specifically, the Subfamily members must be related to the Family Householder with whom they live. The 1990 Census counted 64.5 million Families and 2.6 million Subfamilies.

A Subfamily can consist of a husband and wife (with or without children) or a lone parent with one or more children. Example

NEW IN '90

Two new Family relationships are listed on the 1990 Questionnaire: stepchildren and grandchildren. For 1980, grandchildren were tabulated from write-in responses; stepchildren were included in totals for all children.

The Subfamily is not counted as a Family in its own right because a Household can have only one Family. However, members of a Subfamily are always counted as part of the larger Family.

Modern social scientists view the concept of race as a sociological phenomenon rather than a biological condition.

3 in Figure 5-7 represents a typical Subfamily. The young mother and her two children are a Subfamily because they are related to the Householder. Notice the Subfamily is not counted as a Family in its own right because a Household can have only one Family. However, members of a Subfamily are always counted as part of the larger Family (i.e., they are subsumed under the Householder's Family).

What if a second "family" is unrelated to the Householder? In this case, not only is the smaller group not a Family, they are not a Subfamily either. Subfamilies are defined strictly by their relationship to the Householder. In Figure 5-7, the subgroups in examples 1, 2, 5, and 6 are not Subfamilies, even though the members are related to one another.

Before leaving the confusing realm of Family relationships several other specialized terms should be introduced. The Bureau uses various terms to describe children, depending on the child's age and marital status. In Census publications, a Child is a son or daughter (by birth, adoption, or marriage), regardless of the son or daughter's age or marital status. A 45 year-old son is a Child of his parents. The Bureau uses the phrase Related Child to indicate any Child under the age of 18, regardless of the Child's marital status. A subcategory of Related Child is Own Child, defined as a never married Child under 18. The Bureau's choice of terminology regarding children is extremely confusing, to say the least.

Race and Hispanic Origin

Every schoolchild learns that groups of people living in certain parts of the world look different from those living in other parts.

Such differences result from many factors, including thousands of years of climatic adaptation. Dividing the world's population into racial categories is based largely on peoples' appearance: skin color, the color and texture of hair, facial features, and physical stature. Of these characteristics, skin color is usually considered the most prominent determinant of race.

Over the years, physical anthropologists have devised various racial typologies. An early model classified human beings into three races: Caucasoid, Negroid, and Mongoloid. A later method was based on nine geographical races, including Polynesian, American Indian, European, and African. However, many people do not fit well into any standard racial group. Social scientists have never agreed on a common set of racial categories, nor on which individuals belong in each class. Many anthropologists now believe that all attempts to group people according to biological characteristics are both unscientific and arbitrary. Scientists in the field of human biology track the geographic distribution of individual genetic traits, but such studies don't constitute racial analysis in the traditional sense.

Why are human races so difficult to classify? Because individuals assigned to the same racial category can possess widely different physical characteristics. Individuals within one race may have more in common with someone from another race than with others from their own group. These blurred distinctions result from the continuous blending of populations over the course of human history. Interbreeding has occurred as a result of migration, trade, military conquest, enslavement, exploration, colonization, and similar factors. As modes of transportation have improved, the world has become smaller, and intermingling of populations has become easier and more common. Few cultures can remain socially isolated indefinitely.

Modern social scientists view the concept of race as a sociological phenomenon rather than a biological condition. Certain people look similar to oneself, while others appear

Subfamilies and Nonrelatives within Family Households

1. An unmarried couple live with three children from their previous relationships. A son and daughter are children of the woman. The third child is the daughter of the man. If the man is listed as Householder, the Family consists of the man and his daughter. They will be tabulated as an "Other Family–Male Householder, No Wife Present." The woman and her two children are counted as Nonrelatives because they are not part of a Family or a Subfamily.

      Number of Families: one.
      Family size: two (one adult, one child).
      Subfamily size: none.
      Nonrelatives: three (one adult, two children).
      Household size: five.

2. The same situation as #1 above, except the woman is the Householder. In this case, the Family consists of the woman and her two children. They will be tabulated as an "Other Family–Female Householder, No Husband Present." The man and his daughter are now Nonrelatives.

      Number of Families: one.
      Family size: three (one adult, two children).
      Subfamily size: none.
      Nonrelatives: two (one adult, one child).
      Household size: five.

3. A divorced woman and her two children move in with the woman's parents. Assuming the woman's father is the Householder, the woman and her children are included in the father's family. They also comprise a mother-children Subfamily.

      Number of Families: one.
      Family size: five (three adults, two children).
      Subfamily size: three (one adult, two children).
      Nonrelatives: none.
      Household size: five.

4. A young husband and wife live with the wife's father, who is the Householder. The Householder also has guardianship of a foster child who lives with them. The young couple are a Subfamily, but are counted as part of the Householder's Family. The foster child is a Nonrelative.

      Number of Families: one.
      Family size: three (three adults, no children).
      Subfamily size: two (two adults, no children).
      Nonrelatives: one.
      Household size: four.

5. Two families become close friends and decide to move in together, sharing the same single-Unit house. The first family consists of a husband, wife, and one son. The second family consists of another husband and wife and their two sons. The two families are not related to one another. If the husband from the second family is listed as Householder, the Census will count his family as a Family. Their friends do not constitute a Family or Subfamily. They are counted as Nonrelatives.

      Number of Families: one.
      Family size: four (two adults, two children).
      Subfamily size: none.
      Nonrelatives: three (two adults, one child).
      Household size: seven.

6. A retired married couple takes in boarders. Their current boarders are a husband and wife from China who plan to stay for a year while the husband completes his graduate studies.

      Number of Families: one.
      Family size: two (two adults, no children).
      Subfamily size: none.
      Nonrelatives: two (two adults, no children).
      Household size: four.

Figure 5-7

Race and Hispanic Origin are among the most basic demographic characteristics measured by the Census, but the concepts are frequently misunderstood.

different. Racial labels play an important part in how Americans think about one another. Such a perspective is less prevalent in nations with more homogeneous populations, or whose racial minorities constitute a very small percentage of the total population. In many countries, differences in language, nationality, or religion form a more common basis of social stereotyping than race.

The following example illustrates the way in which Census-taking reflects social concerns. The Census of Canada asks no questions about race or Hispanic Origin. Instead, a single question covers what Canada's central statistical agency calls "ethno-cultural affiliation." Black, Inuit, and North American Indian are included among the possible choices, as are English, French, Italian, and other ethnic groups.

Most people in the United States have their own concept of racial categories, usually based on a combination of physical appearance and ethnic background (ancestry, culture, language, and/or religion). The Census Bureau employs a similar approach. The Bureau's admixture of racial classifications is

further complicated by a separate typology for Hispanic/Non-Hispanic populations. Race and Hispanic Origin are among the most basic demographic characteristics measured by the Census, but the concepts are frequently misunderstood. The following two sections explore these important Census concepts, beginning with Hispanic Origin.

Spanish/Hispanic Origin

According to Census guidelines, "Hispanic" is not a racial category. The Census Bureau classifies the following individuals as Hispanic:

- persons born in Puerto Rico, Cuba, Mexico, or other Spanish-speaking countries
- persons whose ancestors came from a Spanish-speaking country
- persons who identify themselves as Spanish-speaking or Spanish-surnamed.

The latter criterion involves the principle of self-identification. People who believe they are Hispanic are counted in that category, regardless of their actual heritage. Conversely, if an Argentinean does not feel he is Hispanic, then he is not counted as such.

Hispanic Origin is not based strictly on geographic ties—a Hispanic person can be from Spain, the Philippines, or Paraguay. On the other hand, persons from Suriname or Brazil are not Hispanic, because these are not Spanish-speaking countries.

Hispanic persons may be of any Race. A Filipino of Spanish Origin is an Asian. A Cuban descendent of African slaves is Black. A Kekshi Indian from Guatemala is Indian. A Castilian from Spain is White. All are Hispanic.

Figure 5-8 cross-tabulates the 1990 Hispanic population by Race. The grouping for "Other Race" represents persons of mixed Race or those who failed to specify a standard Census category. Actually, these data are misleading. Most Hispanic Americans are of mixed Races, the result of Spain's conquest of various indigenous peoples of Mexico,

---

RACE BY HISPANIC ORIGIN: UNITED STATES

All Persons	248,709,873
Of Hispanic Origin	22,354,059
White	11,557,774
Black	769,767
American Indian, Eskimo, or Aleut	165,461
Asian or Pacific Islander	305,303
Other Race	9,555,754
Not of Hispanic Origin	226,355,814
White	188,128,296
Black	29,216,293
American Indian, Eskimo, or Aleut	1,793,773
Asian or Pacific Islander	6,968,359
Other Race	249,093

Source: 1990 Census Of Population And Housing
Summary Tape File 1C

Figure 5-8

**PERSONS OF HISPANIC ORIGIN:
UNITED STATES**

Persons of Hispanic Origin	22,354,059
Mexican	13,495,938
Puerto Rican	2,727,754
Cuban	1,043,932
Other Hispanic	5,086,435

Source: 1990 Census Of Population And Housing
Summary Tape File 1C

Figure 5-9

Spanish/Hispanic Origin is distinct from Race.

Central America, South America, and the Caribbean, as well as its use of slave labor from Africa. In nearly every Spanish-speaking country of the Western Hemisphere, the majority of people are *mestizos*, a mixture of European and Indian ancestry. More will be said later about how the Census categorizes multi-racial individuals. For the moment, the important point is Spanish/Hispanic Origin is distinct from Race. Although Cubans, Puerto Ricans, and other Hispanic groups may exhibit different values, attitudes, and social behaviors from one another, Hispanics share certain cultural similarities. The Census counts persons of Hispanic Origin separately because they constitute a large and growing minority population in the United States. Hispanics were first counted in the 1970 Census, but only as part of the five-percent sample. Spanish/Hispanic

Origin became a complete-count question for 1980. The 1990 Census identified 22,354,059 Hispanic residents, representing 6.4% of the U.S. population. Mexican-Americans comprise the largest segment, as shown by Figure 5-9. With a 53% increase in population from 1980 to 1990, Hispanics represent one of the fastest-growing minority groups in the nation. Recent Census Bureau projections indicate Hispanics may constitute 20% of the U.S. population by the year 2050.

 **Census Tip**

In Census tabulations, all persons are counted as Hispanic or Non-Hispanic. The two categories are mutually exclusive, and no other option is available.

Race

Content design for the Race question entailed more effort than any other Item on the 1990 Questionnaire. Fully seven years of planning and field testing were involved, including numerous test Questionnaires and focus groups devoted entirely to the topic of Race. Wording of this Item was debated until the time the Questionnaire went to press.

The decennial Census recognizes five broad racial groups: White; Black or Negro; American Indian, Eskimo, or Aleut; Asian or Pa-

If the Bureau doesn't consider Hispanic Origin a racial or ethnic characteristic, exactly what is it?

Hispanic is a separate, unique category. Language is the one characteristic Hispanics share--not Race, nationality, or religion. All Hispanics either speak Spanish or are descended from people who spoke it. Note, too, that Portu-

guese-speaking persons are not classed as Hispanic unless they mistakenly identify themselves as such. In a sense, Hispanic Origin is the only strictly cultural variable measured by the Census.

UNITED STATES POPULATION BY RACE

All Persons   248,709,873

White 199,686,070	
Black 29,986,060	
American Indian, Eskimo, or Aleut	1,959,234
American Indian	1,878,285
Eskimo	57,152
Aleut	23,797
Asian or Pacific Islander	7,273,662
Asian	6,908,638
Chinese	1,645,427
Filipino	1,406,770
Japanese	847,562
Asian Indian	815,447
Korean	798,849
Vietnamese	614,547
Other Asian	779,991
Pacific Islander	365,024
Polynesian	296,145
Hawaiian	211,014
Samoan	62,964
Other Polynesian	22,167
Micronesian	56,153
Guamanian	49,345
Other Micronesian	6,808
Melanesian	7,195
Pacific Islander, not specified	5,531
Other Race	9,804,847

Source: 1990 Census Of Population And Housing
Summary Tape File 1C

Figure 5-10

cific Islander (API); and Other Race. Most people of Middle-Eastern ancestry are counted as White, while persons from the Indian subcontinent are categorized as Asian.

Two of these major racial categories are further divided into subgroups. The American Indian, Eskimo, or Aleut category is divided into its three components. The Asian category is divided into 15 subgroups, including Chinese, Japanese, Filipino, Asian Indian, Hawaiian, Samoan, Korean, Guamanian, Vietnamese, and Other API.

The amazing diversity and extent of America's minority population makes this degree of specificity necessary. The non-White population, taken together with that of Hispanics who are White, constitutes 25% of the total U.S. population, double the percentage measured in 1970. Figure 5-10 summarizes the nation's racial composition by major subcategory.

 Census Tip

The American Indian classification includes the indian tribes of Mexico, Central America, and South America.

Self-identification is the key to proper understanding of racial breakdowns in the Census. Guidelines accompanying the Questionnaire instruct respondents to indicate the Race each person feels himself/herself to be. "White" simply means anyone who indicated "White" on the Census Questionnaire.

Census questions pertaining to Race include three write-in responses. Respondents indicating American Indian are instructed to report their tribal affiliation, which might be a Reservation, a nation, a tribe, or a clan. Respondents designating Other Asian/Pacific Islander are instructed to report a specific nationality such as Sri Lankan, Pakistani, or Indonesian. Figure 5-11 lists the standard subgroups reported for Asian and Pacific Islanders. The third write-in response, "Other Race," includes all persons who cannot be classified under one of the four basic racial groups.

Questionnaires containing responses of American Indian, Other API, or Other Race are reviewed by subject specialists. Where appropriate, written answers are re-coded under a standard racial category. An individual who reports Race as Arab or Lebanese will be re-coded White, while someone reporting Jamaican or Haitian will be coded Black.

The most significant drawback to the Bureau's racial classifications is the omission of a category (or categories) for mixed Races. Census instructions provide no guidance for respondents of mixed heritage. The Bureau assigns racial codes in one of three ways,

The most significant drawback to the Bureau's racial classifications is the omission of a category (or categories) for mixed Races.

depending on how a respondent completes the Questionnaire.

1. All persons of mixed heritage who designate specific racial names are assigned to the first Race specified. Someone indicating "Black-Vietnamese" will be coded Black, while another person writing "Vietnamese-Black" will be coded Vietnamese. Certain exceptions are made to this rule: respondents indicating Eurasian or Amerasian are reported as Other Asians, while French-American Indians and Spanish-American Indians are counted as American Indians.

2. A Child of mixed heritage is assigned to the mother's Race wherever possible.

3. Persons who indicate an unspecified mixed Race, such as "interracial," "biracial," or "mixed," will be coded as Other Race.

Census guidelines on mixed Race cause another complication: for certain regulatory and grant-writing situations, the U.S. Office of Management and Budget (and any state or local agency which complies with its Directives) does not recognize "Other Race" as a valid reporting category. To comply with this OMB Directive, the Bureau produces a special Imputation file which assigns a Race to each person who reported "Other Race." *MARS*, the *Modified Age/Race/Sex and Hispanic Origin* file, substitutes an Other Race response with the Race specified by another person of the same Hispanic Origin located in the same geographic area. However, standard Census products do not incorporate this methodology. Printed Census publications, CD-ROMs, and *Summary Tape Files* on computer tape all utilize the Other Race designation. *MARS* data are available only as a special computer tape file.

While on the topic of mixed racial background, a few comments regarding Hispanic Origin are in order. Although most Hispanic Americans are of mixed Race, the Bureau encourages the selection of a single Race. Unless a Hispanic individual identifies strongly with Black, Indian, or Asian origins, Census guidelines instruct the person to choose the White category. It is doubtful, however, whether many Hispanic Americans see themselves as White. Lacking a more obvious racial category to select, many His-

---

Asian or Pacific Islander Groups Reported in the 1990 Census

Asian

Chinese
Filipino
Japanese
Asian Indian
Korean
Vietnamese
Cambodian
Hmong
Laotian
Thai

Other Asian[1]
 Bangladeshi
 Bhutanese
 Borneo
 Burmese
 Celebesian
 Ceram
 Indochinese
 Indonesian
 Iwo-Jiman
 Javanese
 Malayan
 Maldivian
 Nepali
 Okinawan
 Pakistani
 Sikkim
 Singaporean
 Sri Lankan
 Sumatran
 Asian, not specified[2]

Pacific Islander

Hawaiian
Samoan
Guamanian

Other Pacific Islander[1]
 Carolinian
 Fijian
 Kosraean
 Melanesian[3]
 Micronesian[3]
 Northern Mariana Islander
 Palauan
 Papua New Guinean
 Ponapean (Pohnpeian)
 Polynesian[3]
 Solomon Islander
 Tahitian
 Tarawa Islander
 Tokelauan
 Tongan
 Trukese (Chuukese)
 Yapese
 Pacific Islander, not specified

[1] In some data products, specific groups listed under "Other Asian" or "Other Pacific Islander" are shown separately. Groups not shown are tabulated as "All other Asian" or "All other Pacific Islander," respectively.

[2] Includes entries such as Asian American, Asian, Asiatic, Amerasian, and Eurasian.

[3] Polynesian, Micronesian, and Melanesian are Pacific Islander cultural groups.

Figure 5-11

Q&A

Why doesn't the Census recognize categories for mixed Race?

Failure to account for persons of mixed Race was not an oversight by the Bureau, but a conscious decision. Much of the civil rights legislation currently in force, from the Equal Employment Opportunity Act to the Voting Rights Act, requires governments, employers, and other organizations to compile certain statistics by Race. The decennial Census remains either the primary source of such statistics, or the benchmark against which other racial data are compared. Provision for one or more multiracial categories would make tabulation more complex and the resulting data more difficult to analyze.

Considering the prevalence of mixed racial backgrounds in the United States, the Bureau's guidelines are controversial, to say the least. During the content planning process, the Bureau received extensive public comment on the issue of mixed Race, largely in favor of using multiracial categories. Because the Census compels people to choose a single Race, many individuals with mixed backgrounds feel they are implicitly forced to reject half of their heritage. Some say that being counted as "Other" is tantamount to being labelled a nonentity.

---

panics chose Other Race, and wrote "Latino," "Puerto Rican," "brown," "La Raza," or similar responses. As seen previously in Figure 5-8, 42.8% of the Hispanic population was counted in the Other Race category, compared with 51.7% who selected White.

Census Tip

The Other Race category covers write-in responses which could not be assigned to a specific Race. More than 97% of the persons counted under Other Race are Hispanics who did not select one of the standard racial responses. Much of the remaining 2.5% consists of Non-Hispanics who designated an unspecified mixed Race.

Many Census concepts are surprisingly controversial, but few elicit more heated debate than the Bureau's handling of Race. Some critics feel that grouping people by Race perpetuates racism and legitimizes stereotyping. Others find existing racial catego-

ries meaningless, given the impossibility of measuring a person's actual racial composition. Several scholars, for example, have estimated that nearly 80% of African-Americans are of mixed Race. Defenders of the Race concept see it as a means to promote multiculturalism and celebrate racial pride. At the very least, it helps the government to measure racial inequality and document cases of discrimination. Regardless of racial data's true value, the Bureau will continue to collect it as long as legislative mandates require the agency to do so.

Nativity, Language, and Ancestry

Three related Census concepts help define a person's nationality and ethnic background: Place of Birth (Nativity), Language Spoken at Home, and Ancestry. Of the three, Ancestry is the most complicated.

Nativity measures whether a person is native-born (in the United States or a U.S. territory) or foreign-born. Natives are asked to indicate a state or territory of birth, while foreign-born residents indicate a country of

Regardless of racial data's true value, the Bureau will continue to collect it as long as legislative mandates require the agency to do so.

birth. The Questionnaire instructs respondents to use 1990 national boundaries and country names, not those at time of birth. For foreign-born residents, the Census also reports data on year of entry into the United States.

Language Spoken at Home indicates whether a person speaks a language other than English in the home, either sometimes or always. Persons who speak more than one non-English language are instructed to designate the language first learned. Those living in a Household where everyone over 14 years of age speaks a language other than English, and where no one speaks English "Very Well," are designated Linguistically Isolated.

Instructions accompanying the 1990 Questionnaire describe Ancestry as a person's ethnic heritage or "roots," which can reflect the place of birth of the person, the person's parents, or ancestors.

The Census utilizes Ancestry as the term to encompass ethnic origin or national background. Instructions accompanying the 1990 Questionnaire describe Ancestry as a person's ethnic heritage or "roots," which can reflect the place of birth of the person, the person's parents, or ancestors. Ancestry is a fairly new Census concept, first appearing in 1980. Under current guidelines, people can be many generations removed from their ancestral home. Ancestry is not limited to first- or second-generation immigrants. Prior to 1980, the opposite was true. Pre-1980 Censuses asked respondents to identify Place of Birth for themselves and for both parents.

Religious affiliation is not considered an Ancestry group. Someone reporting "Shiite" or "Sephardic" is counted as "Ancestry not known." (Some exceptions are made to this rule. Responses of "Hindu" or "Sikh" are coded under Asian Indian.)

The Bureau employs approximately 1,000 codes for Ancestry groups, from Alsatian to Zimbabwean. Italian alone is divided into 23 subcategories, including Calabrian and Venetian. Codes are arranged geographically by continent, then by country or region. Numerous cross-references are also utilized. Someone indicating "Southerner," for example, will be coded under United States Ancestry.

Census Tip

Standard Census products report 38 of the most common Ancestry categories only. Detailed data can be found in a computer tape product entitled *Summary Tape File 4* or in a Subject Report (in paper and CD-ROM) entitled *Ancestry of the Population.*

Ancestry groups do not necessarily reflect modern political boundaries. Most Ancestry categories relate to locations outside the United States. Of these, some are tied to a particular country (German, Haitian), while others are associated with regional areas which cross national borders (Basque, Slovene). Certain ethnic groups which evolved within the United States are also recognized, including Pennsylvania Dutch and Cajun.

Nor does Ancestry imply strong involvement or affinity with the designated ethnic group, its language, organizations, or local communities. Someone who indicates Irish Ancestry needn't belong to the Ancient Order of Hibernians or march in a St. Patrick's Day parade. As with Race and Hispanic Origin, Ancestry is based on self-identification. Respondents choose the group or groups with which they most closely identify. A person who is one-quarter Swedish is free to select that Ancestry, if he feels Swedish is the designation which best describes him.

NEW IN '90

Standard tabulations for 1990 include several new ethnic categories: Arab, West Indian, and American. The West Indian category excludes Puerto Rican and Cuban, both of which are counted under Hispanic Origin. For the first time, respondents who did not identify with any ethnic group could be counted as Americans. In prior Censuses, individuals who designated "American" as their ethnic origin were tabulated under "Ancestry Not Specified."

PERSONS OF POLISH ANCESTRY: UNITED STATES

Polish Ancestry by Reporting Category	Number of Persons
Single Ancestry	3,834,659
Multiple Ancestry	
Polish reported first	2,708,185
Polish reported second	2,823,262
Subtotal	5,531,447
Total Polish Ancestry	9,366,106

Source: U.S. Census of Population and Housing
Summary Tape File 1C

Figure 5-12

Distinctions among Race, Hispanic Origin, and Ancestry can cause confusion. Because Ancestry codes are based on geography, African Ancestry differs from African-American.

Unlike racial categories, persons can report mixed ethnic origins, but only the first two Ancestry groups are counted. An individual writing "German-Irish," will be tabulated under multiple Ancestry, with German as the first reported group and Irish as the second. Another person writing "Irish-German" will be recorded in the reverse. Certain multiple Ancestry groups are counted as single categories because of their distinctive characteristics. Examples include Scotch-Irish, Greek Cypriot, and French Canadian.

Approximately 60% of 1990 Census re-

spondents indicated a single Ancestry group, while 30% reported multiple Ancestry. The remaining 10% either failed to report their ethnic origin or wrote an uncodable response. (As mentioned earlier, Ancestry is the only Census Item which includes a tabulation category for unreported responses.)

Figure 5-12, which reproduces 1990 data for U.S. residents of Polish descent, illustrates how the Census counts persons of multiple Ancestry. Persons indicating multiple Ancestry are counted twice: once under their first reported choice, and again under the second choice. Each of the 5.5 million people of mixed Polish Ancestry is counted again under another category, such as German or Russian.

Distinctions among Race, Hispanic Origin, and Ancestry can cause confusion. Because Ancestry codes are based on geography, African Ancestry differs from African-American. The former is counted under Africa, the latter under United States. Depending on how a Black person chooses to respond, he or she could be counted either way. A Black person can also indicate ethnic roots in the West Indies, Brazil, or other areas of the world. Similarly, persons of African Ancestry can also be White.

A second source of confusion is that Ancestry groups for Asians and Pacific Islanders

Q&A

Why does the Census continue to ask question about Ancestry?

For many people, the concept of Ancestry seems irrelevant, especially since the Census already asks questions on Language and Place of Birth. Marketers seeking to identify geographic concentrations of a particular ethnic group may find Ancestry data useful, but does this Census Item serve any legislative requirements or public policy needs? Equal opportunity laws forbid discrimination on the basis of national origin. Ancestry statistics enable members of different ethnic groups to show evidence of their minority

status, particularly at smaller levels of Census geography.

Should the Bureau focus on more recent Ancestry relationships? Censuses from 1880 to 1970 asked questions about parents' Place of Birth, and content tests for the 1990 Questionnaire explored the possibility of restoring this Census Item. Although the question received strong support from data users, lack of room on the Questionnaire prevented the Bureau from adding this Item.

No. 47. Population, by Selected Ancestry Group: 1980 and 1990

[As of **April** 1. Covers persons who reported single and multiple ancestry groups. Persons who reported a multiple ancestry group may be included in more than one category. Major classifications of ancestry groups do not represent strict geographic or cultural definitions. Ancestry data for 1980 are not entirely comparable with 1990 data. Based on a sample and subject to sampling variability; see text, section 1]

ANCESTRY GROUP	1980 (1,000)	1990 Number (1,000)	1990 Percent	ANCESTRY GROUP	1980 (1,000)	1990 Number (1,000)	1990 Percent
European: [1]				Slovene	126	124	0.1
Austrian	949	871	0.4	Swedish	4,345	4,681	1.9
Belgian	360	395	0.2	Swiss	982	1,045	0.4
British	(X)	1,119	0.4	Ukrainian	730	741	0.3
Croatian	253	544	0.2	Welsh	1,665	2,034	0.8
Czech	1,892	1,300	0.5	Yugoslavian	360	258	0.1
Czechoslovakian	(X)	315	0.1				
Danish	1,518	1,635	0.7	West Indian: [1]			
Dutch	6,304	6,227	2.5	Haitian	90	290	0.1
English	49,598	32,656	13.1	Jamaican	253	435	0.2
European	175	467	0.2	West Indian	(X)	159	0.1
Finnish	616	659	0.3				
French	12,892	10,321	4.1	North Africa and Southwest Asia:			
German	49,224	57,986	23.3	Arab	93	127	0.1
Greek	960	1,110	0.4	Armenian	213	308	0.1
Hungarian	1,777	1,582	0.6	Iranian	123	236	0.1
Irish	40,166	38,740	15.6	Lebanese	295	394	0.2
Italian	12,184	14,715	5.9	Syrian	107	130	0.1
Latvian	92	100	(Z)				
Lithuanian	743	812	0.3	Subsaharan Africa:			
Norwegian	3,454	3,869	1.6	African	204	246	0.1
Polish	8,228	9,366	3.8				
Portuguese	1,024	1,153	0.5	North America:			
Romanian	315	366	0.1	Acadian	(X)	668	0.3
Russian	2,781	2,953	1.2	American	13,299	12,396	5.0
Scandinavian	475	679	0.3	Canadian	456	561	0.2
Scotch-Irish	(X)	5,618	2.3	French Canadian	780	2,167	0.9
Scottish	10,049	5,394	2.2	Pennsylvania German	(X)	306	0.1
Serbian	101	117	(Z)	United States	(X)	644	0.3
Slovak	777	1,883	0.8				

X Not applicable.   Z Less than .05 percent.   [1] Excludes Hispanic groups.

Source: U.S. Bureau of the Census, *1980 Census of Population, Supplementary Report,* series PC80-S1-10 and *1990 Census of Population and Housing Data Paper Listing* (CPH-L-89).

Figure 5-13

are also represented by country-specific racial categories, as shown earlier in Figure 5-11. A person of Japanese descent will mark "Japanese" as a Race and as an Ancestry Group. A similar situation exists for Hispanic Origin, which also utilizes country-specific categories. Anyone of Mexican heritage is counted as "Mexican" under Hispanic Origin as well as Ancestry. Because country-specific data for Asian and Hispanic Americans are reported separately under Race and Hispanic Origin, they are not repeated under Ancestry tables. Figure 5-13, taken from the *Statistical Abstract of the United States,* shows a typical presentation of Ancestry statistics.

Notice the listings under European and West Indian exclude any Spanish-speaking countries. Also missing are any categories for Asian, Central American, or South American countries. Census codes for Ancestry groups are more detailed than the codes for corresponding Race or Hispanic Origin categories. For example, 21 separate Ancestry codes are used to describe Asian Indians, compared with only one racial code. As explained earlier, however, this level of detail does not appear in most Census products. Also remember that Race and Hispanic Origin are complete-count questions, while Ancestry is a sample characteristic.

Census codes for Ancestry groups are more detailed than the codes for corresponding Race or Hispanic Origin categories.

Income and Poverty Status

The Census measures income received by individuals, Households, and Families, but the Bureau's definition differs from that used by the Internal Revenue Service or other government agencies. The Census collects data on Money Income, which means that noncash benefits, such as food stamps, school lunches, public housing assistance, and medical care, are excluded. Also excluded are money received as capital gains (from the sale of real estate, securities, or other property), lump-sum payments (gifts, inheritance, insurance settlements), employer contributions toward health care, retirement, or other benefit funds, employer-paid business expenses, borrowed money, and withdrawals from personal savings.

Income is divided into Earnings and Other Income. Earnings are defined as wage or salary Income, or self-employment Income

The Census collects data on Money Income, which means that noncash benefits, such as food stamps, school lunches, public housing assistance, and medical care, are excluded.

(farm and nonfarm). Nonearnings include interest, dividends, net rental proceeds, social security, money payments from public assistance programs (AFDC, SSI, etc), retirement or disability programs, unemployment compensation, net gambling winnings, alimony, and child support. Income is tabulated for all persons 15 years of age or older, and covers money received during the Reference Year.

Poverty Status is designated according to thresholds originally established by federal interagency committees and prescribed by an Office of Management and Budget Directive. The method of determining Poverty Status is based upon an "economy food plan" first devised by the Department of Agriculture in 1964. The plan measures the cost of the least expensive food budget which meets minimum nutritional requirements. This "economy" food budget varies according to total Family size and number of children in the Family. Poverty thresholds are developed

Poverty Thresholds in 1989 by Size of Family and Number of Related Children Under 18 Years

Size of Family Unit	Related children under 18 years								
	None	One	Two	Three	Four	Five	Six	Seven	Eight or more
One person									
< 65 yrs.	$6,451								
65 yrs. and over	5,947								
Two persons[1]									
< 65 yrs.	8,303	$8,547							
65 yrs. and over	7,495	8,515							
Three persons	9,699	9,981	$9,990						
Four persons	12,790	12,999	12,575	$12,619					
Five persons	15,424	15,648	15,169	14,798	$14,572				
Six persons	17,740	17,811	17,444	17,092	16,569	$16,259			
Seven persons	20,412	20,540	20,101	19,794	19,224	18,558	$17,828		
Eight persons	22,830	23,031	22,617	22,253	21,738	21,084	20,403	$20,230	
Nine or more persons	27,463	27,596	27,229	26,921	26,415	25,719	25,089	24,933	$23,973

[1] Thresholds based on age of Householder

Figure 5-14

Q&A

What is the difference between a Nonrelative and an Unrelated Individual?

Nonrelatives are Household members. They can be persons in a Family Household who are not related to the Householder, or they can be unrelated persons living together in a Nonfamily Household.

Unrelated Individual is a more encompassing term, combining certain Household members and Group Quarters members. The classification for Unrelated Individuals consists of Nonrelatives, persons in Noninstitutional Group Quarters, and persons living alone. Therefore, Nonrelatives are always Unrelated Individuals, but not vice versa.

Why the additional nomenclature? Unrelated Individual is used primarily to provide broader measures of Income and Poverty Status outside the Family.

by multiplying the appropriate food budget by standard ratios of food expenditures to total expenditures, again based on Family size. No adjustments are made for regional differences in either the cost of living or consumer expenditure patterns; Poverty thresholds provide a single, nationwide set of benchmarks. However, thresholds are adjusted annually for inflation, as measured by the Consumer Price Index.

Figure 5-14 represents the 1989 Poverty thresholds used in the 1990 Census. Based on these numbers, if an unmarried Householder with two children earned less than $9,990 in 1989, her Family would fall below the Poverty threshold, and she and her children would each be counted as persons living below the Poverty Level. It should be stressed that Poverty thresholds pertain to Family Income or individual Income, *not* Household Income. If a Nonrelative (a boarder, an unrelated roommate, an Unmarried Partner, a foster child, etc.) lived in this Family Household, that person's Poverty Status would be determined independently from that of the Family members. Based on the 1989 thresholds shown in Figure 5-14, he or she would not be counted as living in Poverty unless that unrelated person were age 15 or older and had individual income under $6,451. Persons living in Nonfamily Households are counted in the same manner. The

Poverty Status of two or more Nonrelatives living together would be determined separately, based on each adult's 1989 Income, regardless of the combined Household Income.

The Bureau provides Poverty Status tabulations for Persons, Families, and Unrelated Individuals, and for various segments of each category, including children; the elderly; and Families with Female Householders, No Husband Present. At this point, a slight detour is necessary to define terminology. The Census concept of Unrelated Individual is important to the measurement of Poverty Status, but is frequently misunderstood because the Bureau's definition differs from the obvious and ordinary usage of the term. An Unrelated Individual is any person who is not part of a Family and is not an inmate of an Institution. The following types of people are counted as Unrelated Individuals:

- a Householder living alone
- a Householder living with Nonrelatives only
- a Household member who is not related to the Householder
- a person living in Noninstitutional Group Quarters.

According to this definition, an unmarried couple living together is counted as two

It should be stressed that Poverty thresholds pertain to Family Income or individual Income, *not* Household Income.

Unrelated Individuals (unless, through self-identification, they describe themselves as married). A Nonrelative boarding with another Family is also an Unrelated Individual. Five friends sharing an apartment are counted in the same manner. All residents of a college dormitory are Unrelated Individuals, but patients in an Institution are not.

The universe of Persons for Whom Poverty Status is Determined consists of all persons in Families, plus most Unrelated Individuals age 15 and older. Institutionalized persons and Unrelated Individuals under the age of 15 are excluded. Persons living in military Group Quarters or college dormitories, though defined as Unrelated Individuals, are also excluded from measurements of Poverty Status.

Figure 5-15 shows some of the common breakdowns of Poverty data reported in Census publications. The total population (not shown here) of Aurora County, South Dakota is 3,135 persons. Only 2,896 of these residents are included in the universe of Persons for Whom Poverty Status is Determined. Within that universe, 433 persons fall below the Poverty Level, representing a Poverty Rate of 15%. Data are also shown for a higher Poverty-related threshold. Persons falling below 125% of the Poverty Level represent the combination of those living in Poverty and those in near-Poverty.

Employment and Labor Force Status

The Census measures a variety of employment-related characteristics, including industry, occupation, hours worked, class of worker (private worker, government worker, self-employed, etc.), and travel-time to work. The concept which causes the greatest confusion is Employment Status: whether a person is Employed or Unemployed. Current Census definitions coincide with those used by the U.S. Labor Department, but are nonetheless complex.

The Census defines Employed persons as any civilian 16 years or older who, during the

The Census defines Employed persons as any civilian 16 years or older who, during the Reference Week, worked at a job, or who held a job but was absent from work.

Reference Week, worked at a job, or who held a job but was absent from work. The "at work" component encompasses three main categories: paid employees; the self-employed; and unpaid Family members who worked at a family business or farm for 15 hours or more during the week. The "absent" component covers those temporarily away from their job due to illness, vacation, bad weather, or work stoppage (strike or lockout). By definition, members of the Armed Forces, volunteers, and those performing unpaid work around the house are excluded from the ranks of the Employed.

Persons who work at more than one job are counted only once, at the job worked most. For 1990, the Bureau tested several questions designed to measure the characteristics of persons holding more than one job. Questions included the presence of a second job and the hours worked on that job. Because the characteristics of second jobs usually differ from those of a primary job, test questions also attempted to gather data on the industry, occupation, and class of worker. Results indicated that such questions were unduly lengthy for a self-enumerated instrument. In order to include an Item about multiple employment, the Bureau would have had to delete other questions with greater legislative or programmatic need.

People are counted as Unemployed if they meet the following four criteria: they must be civilians who are 16 years or older; they must have had no job during the Reference Week; they must be looking for work at the time of the Census; and they must be available to accept a job if one is offered. This definition includes persons laid off and waiting to be recalled. A subcategory of the Unemployed is the Experienced Unemployed: those who have worked in the past, but hold no present job.

A final concept related to Employment Status is the notion of the Labor Force. As shown below, the total Labor Force is comprised of all Employed persons, all Unemployed persons, and all members of the Armed Forces.

Table 3. Household, Family, and Group Quarters Characteristics: 1990

[For definitions of terms and meanings of symbols, see text]

United States / Region and Division / State / Metropolitan Area / Urbanized Area	Persons in households	All households
United States	242 012 129	91 947 410
REGION AND DIVISION		
Northeast	49 299 141	18 872 713
New England	12 761 912	4 942 714
Middle Atlantic	36 537 229	13 929 999
Midwest	58 070 012	22 316 975
East North Central	40 953 253	15 596 590
West North Central	17 116 759	6 720 385
South	83 131 510	31 822 254
South Atlantic	42 322 891	16 503 063
East South Central	14 783 860	5 651 671
West South Central	26 044 759	9 667 520
West	51 491 466	18 935 468
Mountain	13 361 089	5 033 336
Pacific	38 130 377	13 902 132
STATE		
New England		
Maine	1 190 759	465 312
New Hampshire	1 077 101	411 186
Vermont	541 116	210 650
Massachusetts	5 802 118	2 247 110
Rhode Island	964 869	377 977
Connecticut	3 185 949	1 230 479
Middle Atlantic		
New York	17 445 190	6 639 322
New Jersey	7 558 820	2 794 711
Pennsylvania	11 533 219	4 495 966
East North Central		
Ohio	10 585 664	4 087 546
Indiana	5 382 167	2 065 355
Illinois	11 143 646	4 202 240
Michigan	9 083 605	3 419 331
Wisconsin	4 758 171	1 822 118
West North Central		
Minnesota	4 257 478	1 647 853
Iowa	2 971 435	1 064 325
Missouri	4 971 676	1 961 206
North Dakota	614 566	240 878
South Dakota	670 163	259 034
Nebraska	1 530 832	602 363
Kansas	2 394 809	944 726
South Atlantic		
Delaware	646 097	247 497
Maryland	4 667 612	1 748 991
District of Columbia	565 183	249 634
Virginia	5 978 058	2 291 830
West Virginia	1 756 566	688 557
North Carolina	6 404 167	2 517 026
South Carolina	3 370 160	1 258 044
Georgia	6 304 583	2 366 615
Florida	12 630 465	5 134 869
East South Central		
Kentucky	3 584 170	1 379 782
Tennessee	4 748 056	1 853 725
Alabama	3 948 185	1 506 790
Mississippi	2 503 499	911 374
West South Central		
Arkansas	2 292 393	891 179
Louisiana	4 107 395	1 499 269
Oklahoma	3 051 908	1 206 135
Texas	16 593 063	6 070 937

Figure 5-15

Q&A

Who is *not* in the Labor Force?

Anyone not working and unavailable for work is excluded from the Labor Force. Institutionalized persons, children under the age of 16, full-time students, homemakers, retired persons, and persons with work disabilities are all excluded. Seasonal workers are excluded if the Census Reference Week occurs during their off-season. "Discouraged workers" who have given up their job search are also excluded. The latter two cases hinge on the same requirement. Since seasonal and discouraged workers are not looking for employment, they cannot be counted as Unemployed. Because they are not Employed, Unemployed, or in the Armed Forces, they are not Labor Force members.

▸ Civilian Labor Force = The Employed + The Unemployed
▸ Labor Force = Civilian Labor Force + Members of Armed Forces

In essence, the Labor Force concept measures the number of persons currently working or available to work.

 ## Census Tip

Certain employment-related tabulations appearing in Census publications may include or exclude particular categories of workers. For example, although the Labor Force covers only those persons age 16 or older, the Census reports income for all persons 15 and older. Conversely, certain employment tabulations may exclude the self-employed and/or unpaid Family workers.

Summary

In the topsy-turvy world of Census definitions, paradoxes abound. A Vacant Housing Unit isn't always vacant. A Bedroom isn't necessarily a bedroom. A Family may not include the entire family. People living on a farm may not be counted in the Farm Population. A Child can be an adult. Nonrelatives may actually be related to one another. Contradictions such as these present a treacherous minefield for the unwary Census user.

Much of the Census's bewildering complexity stems from the increasing diversity of America's population. Such concepts as Place of Usual Residence, Household Composition, Subfamily, and Ancestry are complicated by the Bureau's need to count and categorize every conceivable variation of demographic characteristics and living arrangements.

It is difficult to grasp complex Census concepts in a single reading, and equally difficult to remember every detail of important definitions. Serious users of Census data should consult the detailed definitions found in the Bureau's *1990 Census of Population and Housing Guide: Part B. Glossary,* or in "Appendix B of every print Report and CD-ROM File.

Researchers will also find the following guidelines helpful for coping with Census subject matter.

1. Treat every term employed by the Bureau as though it were part of a new and exotic language. Never assume its meaning is obvious or familiar.

2. Refer to Census documentation frequently.

In the topsy-turvy world of Census definitions, paradoxes abound. A Vacant Housing Unit isn't always vacant. A Bedroom isn't necessarily a bedroom.

3. Don't expect to master subtle distinctions instantly. Reinforce your understanding by comparing related concepts.

In some cases, even the published definitions are insufficient to help users understand complex terminology. Two additional techniques can further clarify confusing concepts. First, consult the Bureau's lists of subject codes to determine how a specific demographic variable is tabulated. These Code Lists are found as an appendix to every volume in the *Technical Documentation* series. One volume of *Technical Documentation* is published for each of the four Summary Tape Files. As an example, the Code List for Group Quarters provides detailed descriptions of every type of GQ, from commercial campgrounds to fire-house dormitories, and shows how each one is categorized.

A second technique is to use the data tables themselves to verify Census relationships. By adding related categories together, then checking the sums against appropriate totals shown on the same table or different tables, users can determine component parts of the whole.

This technique is especially useful for identifying potential misunderstandings. Whenever components do not add up or expected equalities do not tally, the discrepancy may indicate a more complex relationship than the user supposed. For example, the number of Married Couple Families does not equal the number of married couples because not all married couples are part of a Family, and because some couples constitute a Subfamily.

A thorough understanding of basic definitions and key concepts is a minimum prerequisite for the proper use of the decennial Census. Lack of knowledge is the root cause of many of the most serious mistakes made by Census users. Although this chapter could not introduce every population and housing subject, at the very least it has demonstrated that Census terminology should not be taken lightly.

A thorough understanding of basic definitions and key concepts is a minimum prerequisite for the proper use of the decennial Census. Lack of knowledge is the root cause of many of the most serious mistakes made by Census users.

Chapter 6

Census Geography

I. Basic Concepts of Census Geography
    A. Governmental Versus Statistical Units
        1. Governmental Units
        2. Statistical Units
    B. Statistical Equivalents
    C. Completeness of Map Grid
    D. Geographic Hierarchy
    E. Split Geographies
II. Geographic Units
    A. Metropolitan Areas
    B. Urbanized Areas
    C. County Subdivisions
        1. Minor Civil Divisions
        2. Census County Divisions
    D. Places
        1. Incorporated Places
        2. Census Designated Places
        3. Consolidated Cities and Independent Cities
    E. Smaller Statistical Units
        1. Tracts and Block Numbering Areas
        2. Blocks and Block Groups
    F. Specialized Summary Levels
        1. American Indian and Alaska Native Areas
        2. Congressional Districts and Voting Districts
        3. School Districts
        4. ZIP Code Areas
    G. Urban/Rural Classifications
        1. Urban versus Urbanized
        2. Extended Cities
III. Technical Aspects of Census Geography
    A. The TIGER System
    B. Area Measurements
    C. Geographic Boundaries
    D. Geographic Codes
IV. Summary

Census Geography

GEOGRAPHIC CONCEPTS are undoubtedly the most confusing aspect of the decennial Census. Using Census data correctly and effectively requires a clear understanding of the Bureau's geographic terminology. Why? Because all Census tables are presented according to geographic level. In order to locate data, users must first specify the type of geographic entity required—state, county, Tract, etc. Those unfamiliar with Census geography are likely to make erroneous assumptions which will result in incorrect use of data. So how difficult could it be to select appropriate geography? Statistics are needed for a particular city, so you simply look up its name, right? Not usually. For example, figures for the New York City area are presented separately for the city of New York, New York County (Manhattan), the New York Urbanized Area, the CMSA, the PMSA, combinations of PMSAs, and that portion of the New York Metropolitan Area within the state boundary. To the uninitiated, differences among choices will be unclear; to the inattentive, the possibility that such choices even exist might go completely unnoticed. The decennial Census tabulates statistics for more geographic entities than any other data source, making complete familiarity all the more difficult.

Even experienced Census users encounter frustrations with Census geography. The proliferation of terminology, rules, and exceptions to those rules can be maddening. Trying to understand (or explain) these concepts and terms is a daunting challenge.

Basic Concepts of Census Geography

This section will introduce several basic concepts important to understanding Census geography: Governmental versus Statistical Units, statistical equivalents, completeness of map grids, split geographies, and geographical hierarchy. A major problem in explaining Census geography is what to introduce first. Basic concepts are necessary to explain why certain entities are treated a particular way, but definitions of each geographic unit are necessary in order to illustrate the concepts. Because both cannot be explained well simultaneously, we'll start with concepts and follow with definitions of each major unit of geography. After finishing both sections, the reader may wish to go back and review the most important concepts to place them in proper perspective.

Before starting, two general terms must be defined: Summary Levels and entities. In Census parlance, a Summary Level represents a category of geographic jurisdiction—a particular level within the hierarchy of geographic relationships. For example, the county Summary Level consists of all counties (and county-equivalents) in the nation. A geographic entity is a specific parcel of territory within a Summary Level category. San Francisco is an entity within the Summary Level for cities; Tract 103 is an entity within the Summary Level for Census Tracts, and so on.

Governmental Versus Statistical Units

Two broad categories of Summary Levels are used in the Census: Governmental Units (GUs) and Statistical Units (SUs). Governmental Units are political entities with legally defined boundaries. Examples are states, counties, cities, towns, and villages. Statistical Units are geographical areas created by the Bureau (or by the U.S. Office of Management and Budget) for the purpose of statistical reporting. These include Blocks, Block Groups, Tracts, Block Numbering Areas, Census Designated Places, Urbanized Areas, and Metropolitan Areas. Figure 6-1 lists the most significant types of Governmental and Statistical Units.

Governmental Units

On the surface, Governmental Units seem straightforward enough; everyone is familiar with cities, villages, and other political entities. Nevertheless, the Bureau divides GUs into two additional categories: Legal Units and Administrative Units. From the stand-

In Census parlance, a Summary Level represents a category of geographic jurisdiction—a particular level within the hierarchy of geographic relationships.

Why is Census Geography so complicated?

Three main reasons come to mind. First is the sheer diversity of political units among the 50 states. In our federal system of government, each state is largely autonomous in its political structure. For example, towns are incorporated entities in most states, but are unincorporated in eight states. In some states, cities are subsumed by their surrounding townships; in others, cities can cross township or even county boundaries. It is difficult to grasp certain political relationships if they are alien to your state or if the rules governing them are contrary to local experience.

Second, to make geographic areas comparable from one part of the country to another, the Bureau must impose uniformity by creating nomenclature and definitions unique to the Census. In essence, the Bureau has manufactured a self-contained geographic universe. The resulting terminology is unfamiliar to Census newcomers.

Third, the Census reports data for very small levels of geography, down to the size of a city block. The hierarchical relationships of smaller units to successively larger ones is a common source of confusion.

Governmental and Statistical Units

GOVERNMENTAL UNITS

States	Outlying Areas
Counties	Minor Civil Divisions
Incorporated Places	Consolidated Cities
American Indian Reservations	Trust Lands
Alaska Native Regional Corporations	Congressional Districts
Voting Districts	ZIP Code Areas

STATISTICAL UNITS

Census Regions	Census Divisions
Metropolitan Areas	Urbanized Areas
Census County Divisions	Unorganized Territories
Census Areas (Alaska)	Census Subareas (Alaska)
Tribal Jurisdiction Statistical Areas	Tribal Designated Statistical Areas
Alaska Native Village Statistical Areas	Census Designated Places
Census Tracts	Block Numbering Areas
Block Groups	Blocks

Figure 6-1

Another distinction affecting Census publications is the concept of a "general-purpose government." These are entities to whom the state has granted the fullest range of legal powers, and which perform a broad range of government functions.

point of data users, the differences between the two are minor. In fact, the Bureau often refers to GUs collectively as Legal/Administrative Units. However, because the terminology appears in Census publications, each should be defined.

Legal Units are political entities which exercise jurisdiction over a specified territory whose boundaries are determined by law, treaty, or charter. Depending on the entity and the state, they may be legally incorporated or not. (More will be said about incorporated jurisdictions later in the chapter.) Examples of Legal Units shown in Census publications include counties, cities, villages, towns, American Indian Reservations, and Alaska Native Villages.

Administrative Units have boundaries established by law or regulation, and are

created to implement a specific government program or function. Sewer districts and police precincts are examples of Administrative Units, though neither one is reported in standard Census publications. Two Administrative Units which are shown in specialized Census Reports are ZIP Code Areas and Voting Districts.

Certain Governmental Units, such as school districts and Congressional Districts, are not easily classified as either Legal or Administrative entities, because they exhibit characteristics of both. The situation is further complicated by political and legal differences among the states, as well as differences within individual states. In some parts of the country, a particular type of GU serves as a "functioning government," performing some or all of the duties one typically associates with local municipalities. In other states, the same Units are actually "nonfunctioning governments." They may appear to be regular governmental bodies in name, but they exist for minor administrative purposes only, with no powers to raise revenues or provide general services. Twenty-eight states contain Governmental Units which the Bureau calls Minor Civil Divisions (MCDs). These GUs go by various names, but are usually called townships or districts. However, MCDs serve as functioning governments in part or all of 20 states only. For example, most MCDs in New York State are fully-functioning government bodies, except for the five boroughs of New York City, which are nonfunctioning (administrative) entities. In contrast, all MCDs in Mississippi (called supervisors' districts) are nonfunctioning governments. In fact, nearly half of all MCDs in the United States are nonfunctioning entities.

Another distinction affecting Census publications is the concept of a "general-purpose government." These are entities to whom the state has granted the fullest range of legal powers, and which perform a broad range of government functions. Cities and towns are general-purpose governments; townships and election districts are not.

Is it really necessary to remember these confusing nuances among types of Governmental Units?

So far we have seen a bewildering flurry of terminology relating to the seemingly simple concept of Governmental Units. A GU can be a Legal Unit or an Administrative Unit. A Legal Unit can be a functioning or nonfunctioning government. And a functioning entity may be a general-purpose government or not. How important are

these distinctions for Census users? Not terribly so, in most cases. The difference between a Governmental Unit and a Statistical Unit is far more critical to proper understanding of Census geography than grappling with all the confusing variations in types of GUs.

 Census Tip

Towns and townships are different types of governmental bodies and should not be treated synonymously. Towns, whether incorporated or not, always act as general-purpose governments. Townships are never incorporated. They may or may not serve as functioning governments, but they are never general-purpose entities.

Why introduce them here at all? In part because the terminology does appear in Census publications, so it becomes worthwhile to explain these subtle relationships. The discussion also serves as an important reminder not to take Governmental Units for granted, and to remain alert to inconsistencies in treatment across states or even within a single state.

Two points are worth remembering, however. First, purely Administrative Units are seldom tabulated in Census products, with the exceptions of ZIP Code Areas and Voting Districts, both of which appear only in specialized publications. Second, the concept of general-purpose governments is important to understanding how the Bureau treats County Subdivisions, a category of GU which is introduced later in the chapter.

A variety of important issues affect Governmental Units as they relate to the Census. Are Units legally incorporated or not? Are they subordinate to the larger Governmental Unit which surrounds them? Do their boundaries cross those of other political entities? Does the sum of land area for all entities within a particular Summary Level account for all the territory within the next higher level? Answers to these questions can vary from one state to another, and from one Summary Level to the next.

Statistical Units

Statistical Units (SUs) are fabrications of the Census Bureau or the OMB, and are therefore more difficult concepts to grasp. Because SUs were invented for purposes of data collection and reporting, they have no legal or governmental function, though in some cases they are utilized for purposes beyond the Census. Historically, the Bureau devised Statistical Units to define the territory covered by each Census enumerator. An important reason for their current existence has already been mentioned: the need to impose uniformity across an otherwise diverse geographic system. Another reason is Governmental Units do not meet the needs of all Census users. In order to report data for very small geographic areas, the Bureau must create standard boundaries for fictitious units such as Blocks, Block Groups, and Tracts.

Statistical Units (SUs) are fabrications of the Census Bureau or the OMB, and are therefore more difficult concepts to grasp.

The United states is divided into four Regions, each of which is further divided into two or three Divisions.

Larger aggregations are also necessary, so the Bureau groups states together to form Census Regions and Divisions. The United states is divided into four Regions, each of which is further divided into two or three Divisions, as shown on the map in Figure 6-2. These groupings, though modified over the years, were devised by the Bureau in 1910.

does not coincide with coverage of administrative Regions. The Boston Regional Office, for example, has jurisdiction over the New England states plus upstate New York, while the Northeast reporting Region covers New England and all Middle-Atlantic states.

 Census Tip:

Don't confuse Census Regions with the Bureau's Regional Offices described in Chapters 1 and 3. For data reporting purposes, the Bureau divides the nation into four Regions and nine Districts. For administrative purposes, the Bureau maintains 12 Regional Offices, each responsible for field activities in selected states. The shared terminology is unfortunate, because geographic coverage of Census reporting Regions

NEW IN '90

Prior to 1984, the Midwest Region was named the North Central Region.

Definitions of Statistical Units are somewhat arbitrary, but they do follow logical guidelines. Several principles govern the Bureau's thinking in establishing rules for Statistical Units. The homogeneity principle states that the boundaries of a Statistical Unit must encompass an area with similar social, economic, and housing characteris-

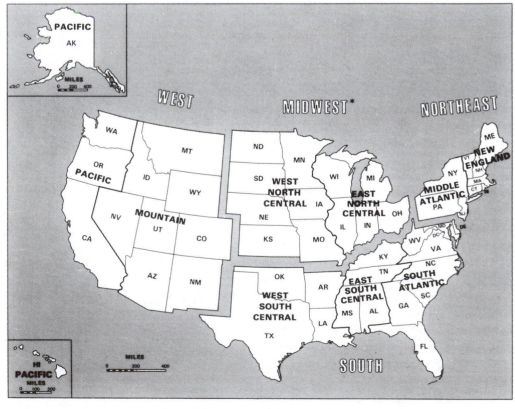

Figure 6-2

tics. For example, states within the Mountain Division are more similar to one another than to states in the West South Central Division. Another important principle deals with dominant influence; certain Statistical Units include a major city or population center and the surrounding territory which has close economic ties to the center. A third principle relates to population density. The Bureau's geographers keep careful track of every entity's land area in square miles and square kilometers. Density is computed by dividing the total number of people or Housing Units within a territory (e.g., the United States, a state, a county) by its land area. Density can be expressed as "persons per square mile" or "persons per square kilometer", as shown in Figure 6-3. Other density measurements are "Households per square mile" and "Housing Units per square mile." These densities are calculated for all Governmental and Statistical Units except ZIP Code Areas. Density actually determines the boundaries of certain Statistical Units, with the most densely settled areas included within a boundary.

Statistical Equivalents

Given the lack of standardization concerning Governmental Units across the 50 states, how does the Bureau create comparable levels of geography? One method is to make similar types of Governmental Units equivalent by definition. Another is to create Statistical Units to serve as counterparts of Governmental Units in states where a particular political entity is unknown. The importance of the latter technique will become clearer later in the chapter, but for now a single example may suffice. In 28 states, so-called Minor Civil Divisions (MCDs) are the major political subdivision of counties. In the remaining 22 states, the Bureau has created fictitious Census County Divisions (CCDs) to serve as statistical equivalents of MCDs.

A statistical equivalent need not always be a Statistical Unit of geography. Where slight

State County County Subdivision Place	All persons	Land area		Persons per—	
		Square kilometers	Square miles	Square kilometer	Square mile
Marion County—Con.					
Woodburn division	18 474	132.3	51.1	139.6	361.5
Gervais city	992	1.0	.4	992.0	2 480.0
Woodburn city	13 404	10.9	4.2	1 229.7	3 191.4
Morrow County	7 625	5 265.1	2 032.8	1.4	3.8
Boardman division	4 444	900.3	347.6	4.9	12.8
Boardman city	1 387	7.0	2.7	198.1	513.7
Irrigon city	737	2.7	1.0	273.0	737.0
Heppner division	2 127	3 047.7	1 176.7	.7	1.8
Heppner city	1 412	3.1	1.2	455.5	1 176.7
Ione-Lexington division	1 054	1 317.1	508.5	.8	2.1
Ione city	255	1.2	.5	212.5	510.0
Lexington town	286	1.1	.4	260.0	715.0
Multnomah County	583 887	1 127.3	435.3	518.0	1 341.3
Corbett division	3 732	473.3	182.8	7.9	20.4
Troutdale city (pt.)	82	.5	.2	164.0	410.0
Portland division	577 571	520.6	201.0	1 109.4	2 873.5
Fairview city	2 391	8.2	3.2	291.6	747.2
Gresham city	68 235	57.1	22.1	1 195.0	3 087.6
Hazelwood CDP	11 480	5.4	2.1	2 125.9	5 466.7
Lake Oswego city (pt.)	2 253	1.3	.5	1 733.1	4 506.0
Maywood Park city	781	.4	.2	1 952.5	3 905.0
Milwaukie city (pt.)	–	–	–	–	–
Portland city (pt.)	435 385	320.9	123.9	1 356.8	3 514.0
Powellhurst-Centennial CDP	28 756	14.0	5.4	2 054.0	5 325.2
Troutdale city (pt.)	7 770	12.3	4.8	631.7	1 618.8
Wood Village city	2 814	2.1	.8	1 340.0	3 517.5
Skyline division	2 584	133.4	51.5	19.4	50.2
Portland city (pt.)	30	.2	.1	150.0	300.0
Polk County	49 541	1 919.4	741.1	25.8	66.8
Dallas division	14 253	356.1	137.5	40.0	103.7
Dallas city	9 422	11.1	4.3	848.8	2 191.2
Falls City division	2 532	854.9	330.1	3.0	7.7
Falls City city	818	3.2	1.2	255.6	681.7
Monmouth-Independence division	13 066	281.4	108.6	46.4	120.3
Independence city	4 425	5.5	2.1	804.5	2 107.1
Monmouth city	6 288	4.2	1.6	1 497.1	3 930.0
Salem division	17 353	192.3	74.3	90.2	233.6
Salem city (pt.)	12 803	12.1	4.7	1 058.1	2 724.0
Willamina division	2 337	234.7	90.6	10.0	25.8
Willamina city (pt.)	523	.6	.2	871.7	2 615.0
Sherman County	1 918	2 132.3	823.3	.9	2.3
Moro division	866	1 364.8	527.0	.6	1.6
Grass Valley city	160	1.4	.5	114.3	320.0
Moro city	292	1.3	.5	224.6	584.0
Wasco division	1 052	767.5	296.3	1.4	3.6
Rufus city	295	3.1	1.2	95.2	245.8
Wasco city	374	2.5	1.0	149.6	374.0
Tillamook County	21 570	2 854.7	1 102.2	7.6	19.6
Bay City division	4 076	442.1	170.7	9.2	23.9
Bay City city	1 027	3.3	1.3	311.2	790.0
Garibaldi city	877	2.5	1.0	350.8	877.0
Rockaway Beach city	970	3.5	1.4	277.1	692.9
Beaver division	2 224	655.4	253.0	3.4	8.8
Nehalem division	2 801	549.9	212.3	5.1	13.2
Manzanita city	513	1.7	.7	301.8	732.9
Nehalem city	232	.8	.3	290.0	773.3
Wheeler city	335	1.6	.6	209.4	558.3
Neskowin division	2 160	353.0	136.3	6.1	15.8
Tillamook division	10 309	854.4	329.9	12.1	31.2
Tillamook city	4 001	3.9	1.5	1 025.9	2 667.3
Umatilla County	59 249	8 327.7	3 215.3	7.1	18.4
Athena division	1 662	446.1	172.3	3.7	9.6
Adams city	223	.9	.3	247.8	743.3
Athena city	997	1.4	.5	712.1	1 994.0
Northeast Umatilla division	8 923	671.7	259.4	13.3	34.4
Milton-Freewater city	5 533	4.5	1.7	1 229.6	3 254.7
Northwest Umatilla division	23 673	507.9	196.1	46.6	120.7
Echo city	499	1.5	.6	332.7	831.7
Hermiston city	10 040	14.6	5.6	687.7	1 792.9

Figure 6-3

INDEPENDENT CITIES

MARYLAND
   Baltimore

MISSOURI
   St. Louis

NEVADA
   Carson City

VIRGINIA

Alexandria	Manassas
Bedford	Manassas Park
Bristol	Martinsville
Buena Vista	Newport News
Charlottesville	Norfolk
Chesapeake	Norton
Clifton Forge	Petersburg
Colonial Heights	Poquoson
Covington	Portsmouth
Danville	Radford
Emporia	Richmond
Fairfax	Roanoke
Falls Church	Salem
Franklin	South Boston
Fredericksburg	Staunton
Galax	Suffolk
Hampton	Virginia Beach
Harrisonburg	Waynesboro
Hopewell	Williamsburg
Lexington	Winchester
Lynchburg	

All 44 independent cities are autonomous of their surrounding counties and are considered county-equivalents by the Bureau.

In the four states where independent cities exist, they are listed and shown in the county boundary maps which appear in the appendices of printed reports. In hierarchical presentations of data, independent cities appear at the end of all county listings for that state.

Figure 6-4

Statistical equivalents become blurred when a single unit of geography is assigned multiple roles by the Census Bureau.

and Palau. In Census parlance, the six territories are known collectively as the Outlying Areas. Another term seen in Census publications is the Outlying Areas of the Pacific—the territories minus the Virgin Islands and Puerto Rico.

Few concepts better illustrate the complexity of Census geography than the notion of "county-equivalents." Counties are the major political subdivision of most states. Some states have no counties, so the Bureau has designated county-equivalents. In Louisiana, counties are known as parishes. Alaska also has no counties. It has boroughs, which are treated as county-equivalents, but these do not cover the entire state. For areas of Alaska outside boroughs, the Bureau (in conjunction with the state) has created Census Areas to serve as county-equivalents. In Puerto Rico, municipios are county-equivalents. Because of its unique status, the District of Columbia is a county-equivalent as well as a state-equivalent. Four states (Maryland, Missouri, Nevada, and Virginia) have one or more cities which are autonomous from their surrounding counties; these "Independent Cities" are also considered county-equivalents. Figure 6-4 lists the Independent Cities recognized in the 1990 Census.

While we're on the topic of counties, one more point should be emphasized. Counties are important units of government everywhere they exist except in the New England states. Although counties are valid Governmental Units in New England, they are not seats of government and many residents are blissfully unaware of the county in which they live. Aside from the court system, few functions or services are organized at the county level in New England states. For this reason, towns and cities are the major state subdivisions in New England.

Statistical equivalents become blurred when a single unit of geography is assigned multiple roles by the Census Bureau. For example, the District of Columbia is a state-equivalent, but is also treated as the statistical equivalent of a county and as a Minor Civil Division. If multiple equivalencies seems

differences in terminology or political structure exist across the nation, one type of Governmental Unit can serve as the statistical equivalent of another. Even an entity as basic as a state is affected by such equivalencies. The Census Bureau defines the United States as the 50 states plus seven state-equivalents. The equivalent entities are the District of Columbia and six foreign territories under United States protection in 1990: Puerto Rico, the U.S. Virgin Islands, Guam, American Samoa, the Northern Mariana Islands, confusing, think of every District of Columbia "version" as a separate entity, each of which happens to have coextensive territory with the others (i.e., identical land areas superimposed on one another).

Completeness of Map Grid

For certain Summary Levels, the sum of the land areas of its component entities equals the land area of the next highest geographic level. In this manner, the total of all territory

in the 50 states and seven state-equivalents comprises the United States in its entirety. Within a state, the sum of all counties and county-equivalents comprises the land area of the entire state. When component parts of subordinate entities "fill up" all the space in a larger entity in this manner, it is called "completing the map grid." Most geographic Summary Levels appearing in the Census do not provide complete grid coverage. For example, city boundaries are not contiguous within a county, nor do they account for all land area within the county. Similarly, all Metropolitan Areas within a state do not complete that state's map grid. However, certain Governmental and Statistical Units do provide complete grid coverage: Blocks; Block Groups; Tracts or Block Numbering Areas; Minor Civil Divisions or Census County Divisions; counties or county-equivalents; and states and state-equivalents. This may not seem like an important concept, but it is central to explaining the behavior of Census geography. First, such Statistical Units as Census County Divisions, Unorganized Territories, and Census Areas exist primarily to fill gaps in the map grid. Second, completeness of grid is strongly tied to geographic hierarchy and the manner in which Summary Levels relate to one another. Third, if a geographic level satisfies completeness of map grid, each entity is mutually exclusive from all others of its type, meaning their boundaries do not overlap. Without map grid completion, the sum of a territory's parts would not equal the whole.

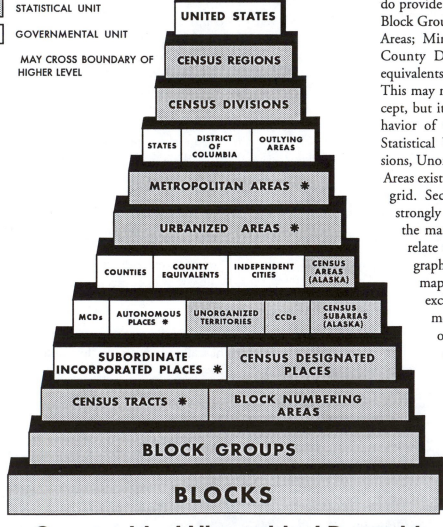

Legend:
- ▒ STATISTICAL UNIT
- ☐ GOVERNMENTAL UNIT
- * MAY CROSS BOUNDARY OF HIGHER LEVEL

UNITED STATES

CENSUS REGIONS

CENSUS DIVISIONS

STATES | DISTRICT OF COLUMBIA | OUTLYING AREAS

METROPOLITAN AREAS *

URBANIZED AREAS *

COUNTIES | COUNTY EQUIVALENTS | INDEPENDENT CITIES | CENSUS AREAS (ALASKA)

MCDs | AUTONOMOUS PLACES * | UNORGANIZED TERRITORIES | CCDs | CENSUS SUBAREAS (ALASKA)

SUBORDINATE INCORPORATED PLACES * | CENSUS DESIGNATED PLACES

CENSUS TRACTS * | BLOCK NUMBERING AREAS

BLOCK GROUPS

BLOCKS

Geographical Hierarchical Pyramid

Figure 6-5

Geographic Hierarchy

Geographic hierarchy defines the relationships among geographic Summary Levels, including both Governmental and

Statistical Units. As Figure 6-5 shows, lower levels in the hierarchy are subordinate to those above them, and each level represents a successively smaller territory. Hierarchy often ignores the difference between Statistical and Governmental Units. (In Figure 6-5, Statistical Units are shaded, Governmental Units are not.) In many cases, an equivalent Summary Level will be a Statistical Unit in one state and a Governmental Unit in another.

 ## Census Tip

Statistical and Governmental Units are intermingled within Census hierarchy. Counties (a Governmental Unit) are the basic component of Metropolitan Areas (a Statistical Unit), for example. In many situations, Census users need not remember whether a particular entity is Governmental or Statistical. Bureau publications and guides tend to overemphasize the difference, thus confusing the more important concept of superior/subordinate relationships in the hierarchy.

Hierarchy involves more than simple size relationships. Is one entity legally and/or statistically part of a larger surrounding territory, or are the two autonomous from one another? Is the population of a smaller level included in the total for a larger one? Do boundaries of one entity cross the boundaries of others? The answers differ from state to state, and often can be answered only after carefully studying the data tables and supporting documentation.

Hierarchical relationships are fundamental to accurate tabulation of the Census. Data for lower Summary Levels are summed to form totals for larger levels, so an individual Census Questionnaire must be linked to all appropriate levels of geography. A specific address exists within a Block, Tract, County Subdivision, County, and state.

Hierarchy is also important because many Census products present data in a hierarchical array—hierarchical tables display villages within townships, townships within counties, counties within states, and so on. Superior/subordinate relationships are designated in printed Census Reports by indenting the subordinate entities. Returning to Figure 6-3, the city of Rufus, Oregon falls within the Wasco Census County Division, which falls within Sherman County.

Split Geographies

When one geographic entity crosses the boundaries of another, it is called a split geography. A Census Tract which crosses a city line is thus a Split Tract.

Statistical Units frequently cross boundaries of Governmental Units: Metropolitan Areas can cross state lines, Urbanized Areas cross city boundaries, and Block Groups can cross village and town lines, for example. Similarly, Governmental Units can cross one another's boundaries: some cities cross county lines, federal Indian Reservations cross state lines, and so on. Such splits can occur whether a geographic entity is autonomous from a higher level in the hierarchy or is subordinate to it. Rules governing the splitting of Governmental Units vary from state to state. In Missouri, cities can cross the boundaries of their surrounding townships; in New Jersey, they cannot.

 ## Census Tip

Whenever the name of a geographic entity is followed by the designation "(pt.)," the accompanying data represent only one part of a split geography. A different table must be consulted to locate totals for the whole entity.

Census publications usually present statistics for a split geography in two ways—for its component parts, and for the total entity—

though not always in the same table. When a particular Summary Level is listed alphabetically, each entity is shown in its entirety; when listings appear in a hierarchical array, the split portions are shown as parts of a larger geographic level. A common mistake made by Census users is to sum component parts, assuming that all parts are being shown. In Figure 6-3, the city of Portland, Oregon appears to be split between the Portland and Skyline Divisions of Multnomah County; the sum of the populations for the two parts is 435,415. Now look at the population for Portland cited in Figure 6-6; the correct 1990 population is 437,319. Not only is Portland split by Census County Divisions within a county, but also by the boundaries of other counties. Portland actually covers portions of Clackamas and Washington Counties in addition to Multnomah.

Geographic Units

Now that the conceptual foundation has been introduced, specific types of geographic units can be discussed. The following sections are arranged by Summary Level, beginning with Metropolitan Areas, then continuing with County Subdivisions, Places, smaller Statistical Units, and specialized types of geography.

Urban growth in the 20th century has expanded far beyond city limits, making it necessary to establish a more meaningful measurement of urban geography.

Metropolitan Areas

Urban growth in the 20th century has expanded far beyond city limits, making it necessary to establish a more meaningful measurement of urban geography. The federal government met this problem in 1949 by creating the concept of standardized "metro areas." Each Metropolitan Area (MA) consists of a large population nucleus (a Central City), together with the surrounding county or counties which have a high degree of economic and social integration with that nucleus. MAs are utilized for many purposes besides the decennial Census. They serve as a key geographical construct for distributing federal funding to local areas. States and local governments use MAs for planning and statistical reporting. Marketers and others in the private sector also find the concept con-

NEW IN '90

Twelve new Metropolitan Areas were created between the 1980 and 1990 Censuses. Figure 6-7 lists MSAs designated after the 1980 Census, plus major changes in previously existing Metropolitan Areas.

PLACE AND COUNTY SUBDIVISION—Con.	
McMinnville city, Yamhill County	17 894
Madras city, Jefferson County	3 443
Malin city, Klamath County	725
Manzanita city, Tillamook County	513
Maupin city, Wasco County	456
Maywood Park city, Multnomah County	781
Medford city, Jackson County	46 951
Merrill city, Klamath County	837
Metolius city, Jefferson County	450
Metzger CDP, Washington County	3 149
Mill City city	1 555
Linn County	1 247
Marion County	308
Millersburg city, Linn County	715
Milton-Freewater city, Umatilla County	5 533
Milwaukie city	18 692
Clackamas County	18 692
Multnomah County	–
Mission CDP, Umatilla County	664
Mitchell city, Wheeler County	163
Molalla city, Clackamas County	3 651
Monmouth city, Polk County	6 288
Monroe city, Benton County	448
Monument city, Grant County	162
Moro city, Sherman County	292
Mosier city, Wasco County	244
Mount Angel city, Marion County	2 778
Mount Hood Village CDP, Clackamas County	2 234
Mount Vernon city, Grant County	538
Myrtle Creek city, Douglas County	3 063
Myrtle Point city, Coos County	2 712
Nehalem city, Tillamook County	232
Newberg city, Yamhill County	13 086
Newport city, Lincoln County	8 437
North Albany CDP, Benton County	4 325
North Bend city, Coos County	9 614
North Plains city, Washington County	972
North Powder city, Union County	448
North Springfield CDP, Lane County	5 451
Nyssa city, Malheur County	2 629
Oak Grove CDP, Clackamas County	12 576
Oak Hills CDP, Washington County	6 450
Oakland city, Douglas County	844
Oakridge city, Lane County	3 063
Oatfield CDP, Clackamas County	15 348
Ontario city, Malheur County	9 392
Oregon City city, Clackamas County	14 698
Paisley city, Lake County	350
Pendleton city, Umatilla County	15 126
Philomath city, Benton County	2 983
Phoenix city, Jackson County	3 239
Pilot Rock city, Umatilla County	1 478
Portland city	437 319
Clackamas County	707
Multnomah County	435 415
Washington County	1 197
Port Orford city, Curry County	1 025
Powellhurst-Centennial CDP, Multnomah County	28 756
Powers city, Coos County	682
Prairie City city, Grant County	1 117
Prescott city, Columbia County	63
Prineville city, Crook County	5 355
Rainier city, Columbia County	1 674
Raleigh Hills CDP, Washington County	6 066
Redmond city, Deschutes County	7 163
Redwood CDP, Josephine County	3 702
Reedsport city, Douglas County	4 796

Figure 6-6

venient for identifying large population centers. Because Metropolitan Areas enjoy widespread use beyond the Census, their boundaries are designated and defined by the U.S. Office of Management and Budget (OMB), in its role as the government's statistical policy maker.

Regulations governing the definition of Metropolitan Areas are extremely complex.

Regulations governing the definition of Metropolitan Areas are extremely complex. The following discussion focuses on basic

concepts only. Readers interested in learning more about Metropolitan Areas should consult Chapter 11.

A Metropolitan Area consists of the county in which the Central City is located, plus any adjacent counties with close ties to the core county. Such ties are determined by the commuting patterns of the working population. MAs can cross state boundaries if the combined multi-state area meets the definition of economic integration. Metropolitan Areas such as New York City, St. Louis, and Minneapolis are examples of the many MAs which are made up of counties in two or more states. To qualify as an MA, the area must contain either:

1. a city with a minimum population of 50,000, or;

2. a Census Bureau-defined Urbanized Area and a total MA population of at least 100,000 (75,000 in New England). Urbanized Areas will be defined later in the chapter.

All territory, population, and Housing Units within MAs are referred to as "Metropolitan." Though MAs account for only 20% of the land area in the United States, more than 80% of the nation's population live in a Metropolitan Area.

Census Tip

The minimum boundary of an MA is one county or county-equivalent; it can be comprised of more than one county, but never less than a single county, and never combined fragments of counties. One important exception exists to this rule: in New England, MAs are composed of cities and towns rather than whole counties, because of the relative unimportance of county governments in New England.

For the 1990 Census, Metropolitan Areas are categorized into three types, based on

---

Changes in Metropolitan Areas, 1980-1990
(Excluding Puerto Rico)

Many changes affect MAs between Censuses, including component counties, boundaries, and number of Central Cities. The following list identifies only newly-created MAs and significant changes in MA names. Changes in MA status *not* indicated here involve existing MAs which added another county since 1980, or whose name changed slightly due to additional Central City.

New MSAs

New Area	Year Established
Cheyenne, WY MSA	1985
Decatur, AL MSA	1988
Dothan, AL MSA	1983
Fort Pierce, FL MSA	1983
Houma-Thibodaux, LA MSA	1983
Jackson, TN MSA	1985
Jamestown-Dunkirk, NY MSA	1989
Merced, CA MSA	1986
Naples, FL MSA	1984
Rapid City, SD MSA	1985
Santa Fe, NM MSA	1984
Yuma, AZ MSA	1990

PMSAs Split from 1980 SMSAs in 1983

Newly-split	Formerly part of
Aurora-Elgin, IL PMSA	Chicago, IL SMSA
Beaver County, PMSA	Pittsburgh, PA SMSA
Boulder-Longmont, CO PMSA	Denver-Boulder, CO SMSA
Brazoria, TX PMSA	Houston, TX SMSA
Fort Worth-Arlington, TX PMSA	Dallas-Fort Worth, TX SMSA
Joliet, IL PMSA	Chicago, IL SMSA
Lake County, IL PMSA	Chicago, IL SMSA
Middletown, CT PMSA	Hartford, CT SMSA
Niagara Falls, NY PMSA	Buffalo, NY SMSA
Oakland CA, PMSA	San Francisco-Oakland, CA SMSA
Pawtucket-Woonsocket-Attleboro, RI-MA PMSA	Providence-Warwick-Pawtucket, RI-MA SMSA
Salem-Gloucester, MA PMSA	Boston, MA SMSA
Vancouver, WA PMSA	Portland, OR-WA SMSA

Figure 6-7 (Continued on next page)

Changes in Metropolitan Areas, 1980-1990
(Excluding Puerto Rico)
(Continued from previous page)

MAs WHICH MERGED WITH ANOTHER IN 1983

Newly-merged MA	Old MA
New Haven-Meriden, CT MSA	Meriden, CT SMSA
Columbus, OH MSA	Newark OH, SMSA
Norfolk-Virginia Beach- Newport News, VA MSA	Newport News-Hampton, VA SMSA
Richmond-Petersburg, VA MSA	Petersburg-Colonial Heights-Hopewell, VA SMSA
Charlotte-Gastonia-Rock Hill, NC-SC MSA	Rock Hill, SC SMSA
Charlotte-Gastonia-Rock Hill, NC-SC MSA	Salisbury-Concord, NC SMSA
Dayton-Springfield, OH MSA	Springfield, OH SMSA

NAME CHANGES IN 1983

New Name	Former Name
Bergen-Passaic, NJ PMSA[1,3]	Patterson-Clifton-Passaic, NJ SMSA
Middlesex-Somerset- Hunterdon, NJ PMSA[2]	New Brunswick-Perth Amboy-Sayreville, NJ SMSA
Monmouth-Ocean, NJ PMSA[1]	Long Branch-Asbury Park, NJ SMSA
Orange County, NY PMSA	Newburgh-Middletown, NY SMSA
Saginaw-Bay City-Midland, MI MSA	Bay City, MI SMSA
Scranton—Wilkes-Barre, PA MSA[2]	Northeast PA SMSA

1 One additional county added to the new MA.
2 Two additional counties added to the new MA.
3 Bergen County was part of New York, NY SMSA in 1980; Passaic County was Patterson, NJ
  SMSA in 1980.

Figure 6-7

MAs with fewer than one million persons are designated MSAs, regardless of how many counties are contained therein.

population size. The two major categories are Metropolitan Statistical Areas (MSAs) and Consolidated Metropolitan Statistical Areas (CMSAs). CMSAs are then subdivided into a third category, called Primary Metropolitan Statistical Areas (PMSAs). This proliferation of terminology tends to cause confusion. The following graphic representation may help clarify the relationships among the different types of Metropolitan Areas.

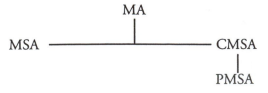

In other words, "MA" is a generic term referring to all types of Metropolitan Areas.

MAs with fewer than one million persons are designated MSAs, regardless of how many counties are contained therein. MSAs are not closely associated with other MAs in their vicinity because they are usually surrounded by Nonmetropolitan counties. Metropolitan Areas with one million persons or more may be designated CMSAs, with component parts called PMSAs. PMSAs are Metropolitan Areas in their own right, but have close economic ties to adjacent PMSAs that make up the total CMSA. For example, the Denver-Boulder, CO CMSA has a 1990 population of 1,848,319; it consists of the Denver PMSA (Denver, Adams, Arapahoe, Douglas, and Jefferson counties) and the Boulder-Longmont PMSA (Boulder County). Figure 6-8 is a list of 1990 CMSAs, with descriptions of changes which have taken place between 1980 and 1990. A complete alphabetical list of all Metropolitan Areas (MSAs, PMSAs, and CMSAs), as they existed at the time of the 1990 Census, is provided in Appendix C.

Census Tip

Until the reader becomes comfortable with various designations for Metropolitan Areas, the differences can be confusing. In a certain sense it is not essential to understand distinctions in nomenclature, but it is vitally important to remember that more than one definition of a Metropolitan Area can apply. When a Report refers to the Chicago "metro area", make sure the actual boundaries are specified and understood.

The Census Bureau creates Urbanized Areas to provide a better separation of Urban and Rural territory in the vicinity of large population centers.

The roster of Metropolitan Areas changes from year to year. The OMB establishes new MSAs when Nonmetropolitan counties gain sufficient population. Outlying counties are appended to existing Metropolitan Areas when commuting patterns change. The most extensive changes take effect following each decennial Census, based on new population totals and on the analysis of "Journey to Work" data. As discussed in Chapter 11, the OMB issued its major post-1990 revisions in December, 1992.

Census Tip

Metropolitan Areas recognized in the 1990 Census are those which existed as of June, 1990. The OMB's 1992 list of revised MAs has no effect on the major data products of the 1990 Census.

Urbanized Areas

The idea behind Metropolitan Areas is fairly easy to understand, but the related concept of Urbanized Areas (UAs) is more confusing. The Census Bureau creates Urbanized Areas to provide a better separation of Urban and Rural territory in the vicinity of large population centers. Most densely populated counties in the United States contain some territory that is rural in character. Because counties are the building blocks of all MAs outside New England, an apparent paradox is created—Metropolitan Areas with rural components.

An Urbanized Area comprises one or more Central Places (usually a large city or cities) and the surrounding, densely settled land area called the Urban Fringe. The minimum population of an Urbanized Area is 50,000 persons. To differentiate

NEW IN '90

During the 1980s, the OMB changed the regulations and terminology relating to Metropolitan Areas. Prior to July 1983, MSAs were called Standard Metropolitan Statistical Areas (SMSAs) and CMSAs were known as Standard Consolidated Statistical Areas (SCSAs). Criteria for an SMSA were similar to those of a current MSA. An SMSA had to include either: (a) a Central City of 50,000 (the same as 1990), or; (b) an Urbanized Area with a total county population of 75,000 and a Central City of 25,000.

On the surface, the latter criterion might appear less restrictive than the 1990 requirement specifying a minimum county population of 100,000. However, the 1990 criteria do not include the minimum size requirement for smaller Central Cities.

The 1990 Census recognizes 268 MSAs and 21 CMSAs (consisting of 73 PMSAs) in the United States and Puerto Rico, making a total of 362 MAs. The 1980 Census recognized 323 SMSAs and 13 SCSAs.

Consolidated Metropolitan Statistical Areas
1990 Census

Boston-Lawrence-Salem, MA-NH CMSA
　　Boston, MA PMSA
　　Brockton, MA PMSA
　　Lawrence-Haverhill, MA-NH PMSA
　　Lowell, MA-NH PMSA
　　Nashua, NH PMSA
　　Salem-Gloucester, MA PMSA

Buffalo-Niagara Falls, NY CMSA*
　　Buffalo, NY PMSA
　　Niagara Falls, NY PMSA

Chicago-Gary-Lake County, IL-IN-WI CMSA
　　Aurora-Elgin, IL PMSA
　　Chicago, IL PMSA
　　Gary-Hammond, IN PMSA
　　Joliet, IL PMSA
　　Kenosha, WI PMSA
　　Lake County, IL PMSA

Cincinnati-Hamilton, OH-KY-IN CMSA
　　Cincinnati, OH-KY-IN PMSA
　　Hamilton-Middletown, OH PMSA

Cleveland-Akron-Lorain, OH CMSA
　　Akron, OH PMSA
　　Cleveland, OH PMSA
　　Lorain-Elyria, OH PMSA

Dallas-Fort Worth, TX CMSA*
　　Dallas, TX PMSA
　　Fort Worth-Arlington, TX PMSA

Denver-Boulder, CO CMSA*
　　Boulder-Longmont, CO PMSA
　　Denver, CO PMSA

Detroit-Ann Arbor, MI CMSA
　　Ann Arbor, MI PMSA
　　Detroit, MI PMSA

Hartford-New Britain-Middletown, CT CMSA*
　　Bristol, CT PMSA
　　Hartford, CT PMSA
　　Middletown, CT PMSA
　　New Britain, CT PMSA

Houston-Galveston-Brazoria, TX CMSA
　　Brazoria, TX PMSA
　　Galveston-Texas City, TX PMSA
　　Houston, TX PMSA

Los Angeles-Anaheim-Riverside, CA CMSA
　　Anaheim-Santa Ana, CA PMSA
　　Los Angeles-Long Beach, CA PMSA
　　Oxnard-Ventura, CA PMSA
　　Riverside-San Bernardino, CA PMSA

Miami-Fort Lauderdale, FL CMSA
　　Fort Lauderdale-Hollywood-Pompano Beach, FL
PMSA
　　Miami-Hialeah, FL PMSA

Milwaukee-Racine, WI CMSA
　　Milwaukee, WI PMSA
　　Racine, WI PMSA

New York-Northern New Jersey-Long Island, NY-NJ-CT CMSA
　　Bergen-Passaic, NJ PMSA
　　Bridgeport-Milford, CT PMSA
　　Danbury, CT PMSA
　　Jersey City, NJ PMSA
　　Middlesex-Somerset-Hunterdon, NJ PMSA
　　Monmouth-Ocean, NJ PMSA
　　Nassau-Suffolk, NY PMSA
　　New York, NY PMSA
　　Newark, NJ PMSA
　　Norwalk, CT PMSA
　　Orange County, NY PMSA
　　Stamford, CT PMSA

Philadelphia-Wilmington-Trenton, PA-NJ-DE-MD CMSA
　　Philadelphia, PA-NJ PMSA
　　Trenton, NJ PMSA
　　Vineland-Millville-Bridgeton, NJ PMSA
　　Wilmington, DE-NJ-MD PMSA

Pittsburgh-Beaver Valley, PA CMSA*
　　Beaver County, PA PMSA
　　Pittsburgh, PA PMSA

Portland-Vancouver, OR-WA CMSA*
　　Portland, OR PMSA
　　Vancouver, WA PMSA

Providence-Pawtucket-Fall River, RI-MA CMSA
　　Fall River, MA-RI PMSA
　　Pawtucket-Woonsocket-Attleboro, RI-MA PMSA
　　Providence, RI PMSA

San Francisco-Oakland-San Jose, CA CMSA
　　Oakland, CA PMSA
　　San Francisco, CA PMSA
　　San Jose, CA PMSA
　　Santa Cruz, CA PMSA
　　Santa Rosa-Petaluma, CA PMSA
　　Vallejo-Fairfield-Napa, CA PMSA

Seattle-Tacoma, WA CMSA
　　Seattle, WA PMSA
　　Tacoma, WA PMSA

San Juan-Caguas, PR CMSA
　　Caguas, PR PMSA
　　San Juan, PR PMSA

*Added in 1983

Former Consolidated Areas:

Dayton-Springfield OH, SCSA
abolished in 1983; 2 SMSAs became 1 MSA.

Indianapolis-Anderson, IN SCSA
abolished in 1983; 2 SMSAs became 2 MSAs.

Kansas City, MO-Kansas City, KS CMSA
abolished in 1984; 2 PMSAs became 1 MSA.

St. Louis-East St. Louis-Alton, MO-IL CMSA
abolished in 1984; 3 PMSAs became 1 MSA.

Figure 6-8

between a Central City in a Metropolitan Area and the core of an Urbanized Area, the latter is termed a "Central Place," though in many UAs, a Central Place also serves as the Central City of the MA.

Guidelines for UAs are complex, but the Urban Fringe portion generally consists of contiguous territory having a density of least 1,000 persons per square mile. The boundaries of the Urban Fringe are based on the sum of individual Census Blocks which satisfy the Bureau's density guidelines. Shifting patterns of population density cause UA boundaries to change significantly from one decade to the next. The 1990 Census recognizes 405 Urbanized Areas (including nine in Puerto Rico); UAs encompass approximately 63% of America's population.

The key to understanding Urbanized Areas is the notion of population density surrounding large cities or Central Places.

UAs do not conform to the boundaries of any Governmental or Statistical Units except for those of their Central Places and the surrounding Blocks which make up the Urban Fringe. UAs can cross the boundaries of states, counties, MCDs, and even Metropolitan Areas. Their land area can be extensive. For example, the New York, NY-Northeastern New Jersey Urbanized Area comprises portions of 22 counties in two states. The relationships between a Metropolitan Area and an Urbanized Area are complicated and subject to exceptions. Readers interested in learning more about these relationships are directed to Chapter 11, where a more detailed comparison is presented.

The key to understanding Urbanized Areas is the notion of population density surrounding large cities or Central Places.

NEW IN '90

37 new Urbanized Areas appear in the 1990 Census, including two in Puerto Rico. All but five are located in the South or West Census Regions. Two previously-recognized UAs did not qualify in 1990 because their populations dropped below 50,000. Three existing UAs merged with neighboring UAs, making a net change of 32 between 1980 and 1990. See Figure 6-9 for a list of new UAs.

New Urbanized Areas for 1990

Brunswick, GA
Cayey, PR
Crystal Lake, IL
Davis, CA
Deltona, FL
Denton, TX
Dover, DE
Frederick, MD
Fredericksburg, VA
Greenville, NC
Hesperia-Apple Valley-Victorville, CA
Holland, MI
Humacao, PR
Hyannis, MA
Idaho Falls, ID
Indio-Coachella, CA
Ithaca, NY
Kissimmee, FL
Lewisville, TX
Lodi, CA
Logan, UT
Lompoc, CA
Longmont, CO
Merced, CA
Myrtle Beach, SC
Pottstown, PA
Punta Gorda, FL
Rocky Mount, NC
San Luis Obispo, CA
Slidell, LA
Spring Hill, FL
Stuart, FL
Sumter, SC
Titusville, FL
Vacaville, CA
Vero Beach, FL
Watsonville, CA

No longer UA (previously recognized, no longer qualify)
Danville, IN-IL
Enid, OK

Merged
Meriden, CT with New Haven CT to form New Haven-Meriden, CT
Newport News-Hampton VA with Norfolk, VA to form Norfolk-Virginia Beach-Newport News, VA
St. Petersburg, FL with Tampa, FL to form Tampa-St. Petersburg-Clearwater, FL

Figure 6-9

The concept of Urbanized Areas can be difficult to visualize. Because UA boundaries transcend political entities, data users need to consult Census maps to determine the territory covered by any UA. In fact, UA boundaries have unusual shapes, with long tendrils or blunt peninsulas of territory extending in every direction. Users also tend to confuse "Urbanized" with "Urban." The Bureau's definition of Urban (introduced later in this chapter) includes much more than the territory of Urbanized Areas and the two terms should never be used interchangeably. For these reasons, the usefulness of the UA construct is not always obvious. The truth of the matter is many Census users ignore Urbanized Areas in their analysis of Census data.

 Census Tip

Urbanized Areas are smaller in population and land area than their corresponding Metropolitan Areas. MAs include Rural territory, UAs do not. MAs conform to county boundaries, UAs do not. Think of Urbanized Areas as the most populated portions of Metropolitan Areas, even though this statement is somewhat oversimplified.

County Subdivisions

Just as states must be completely divided into counties or county-equivalents to form a complete map grid, so must counties be subdivided. Depending on the state, these subdivisions are known either as Minor Civil Divisions (MCDs) or Census County Divisions (CCDs). Two variations on this pattern—Census Subareas and Unorganized Territories—also will be discussed in this section. MCDs are Governmental Units existing in 28 states. CCDs are Statistical Units existing in the remaining states excepting Alaska. Figure 6-10 lists every state and indicates whether it utilizes MCDs or CCDs.

Minor Civil Divisions

In the states where they exist, Minor Civil Divisions consist of political entities which serve as County Subdivisions. MCDs are legally defined, unincorporated bodies. (More will be said later about governmental incorporation.) In most states, MCDs are called townships, but in New York, Wisconsin, and the six New England states they are towns. This is because towns are unincorporated in the latter eight states. Five states call MCDs by such other designations as election districts, magisterial districts, or supervisors' districts. In several other states, townships are the prevalent MCD names, but are used in conjunction with such other terms

Boundaries have unusual shapes, with long tendrils or blunt peninsulas of territory extending in every direction.

Q&A

Why did the Census Bureau create Urbanized Areas?

If few people use them, why did the Bureau go to the trouble of inventing UAs? Because without them, it would be much more difficult to distinguish between Urban and Rural land areas. (More will be said about Urban/Rural distinctions later in the chapter.) As with most statistical entities created by the Bureau, UAs enable standardized definitions to be applied consistently across a diversity of situations.

Do UAs serve other functions? A variety of federal aid programs specify UAs in their eligibility requirements, including funding for transportation planning, mass transit, and hospitals. In fact, certain areas that do not qualify as MAs meet the requirements for Urbanized Areas, and are thus eligible to receive additional federal funds.

Do Urbanized Areas have value for analytical purposes? Yes, because population density is important for studying settlement patterns, the territorial growth of Urban centers, housing development, traffic flow, and related issues.

NUMBER OF GOVERNMENTAL AND STATISTICAL UNITS BY TYPE

State	County Subdivisions Type	County Subdivisions Number	Counties	Incorporated Places	CDPs	Complete Tracting	Indpndt. Cities[3]
Alabama	CCD	390	67	439	34		
Alaska	CCD[1]	40	25	152	165		
Arizona	CCD	78	15	86	93		
Arkansas	MCD	1335	75	487	14		
California	CCD	386	58	456	420	yes	
Colorado	CCD	208	63	267	42		
Connecticut	MCD	169	8	31	86	yes	
Delaware	CCD	27	3	57	15	yes	
Florida	CCD	293	67	390	365		
Georgia	CCD	581	159	535	64		
Hawaii	CCD	44	5	–	125	yes	
Idaho	CCD	170	44	200	3		
Illinois	MCD	1679	102	1279	29		
Indiana	MCD	1008	92	566	24		
Iowa	MCD	1656	99	953	2		
Kansas	MCD	1543	105	627	4		
Kentucky	CCD	475	120	438	33		
Louisiana	MCD	627	64	301	90		
Maine	MCD	530	18	22	84		
Maryland	MCD	298	24	155	174		1
Massachusetts	MCD	351	14	39	192		
Michigan	MCD	1525	83	534	86		
Minnesota	MCD	2742	87	854	9		
Mississippi	MCD	410	82	295	29		1
Missouri	MCD	1368	115	942	19		
Montana	CCD	193	57	128	34		
Nebraska	MCD	1255	93	535	4		
Nevada	CCD[2]	67	17	18	38		1
New Hampshire	MCD	259	10	13	47		
New Jersey	MCD	567	21	320	179	yes	
New Mexico	CCD	131	33	98	76		
New York	MCD	1013	62	619	350		
North Carolina	MCD	1040	100	511	100		
North Dakota	MCD	1806	53	366	10		
Ohio	MCD	1553	88	941	111		
Oklahoma	CCD	302	77	592	6		
Oregon	CCD	211	36	241	43		
Pennsylvania	MCD	2584	67	1022	275		
Rhode Island	MCD	39	5	8	19	yes	
South Carolina	CCD	294	46	270	72		
South Dakota	MCD	1389	66	310	24		
Tennessee	CCD	462	95	336	37		
Texas	CCD	863	254	1171	105		
Utah	CCD	90	29	228	27		
Vermont	MCD	255	14	51	18		
Virginia	MCD	500	134	229	116		41
Washington	CCD	245	39	266	160		
West Virginia	MCD	277	55	230	47		
Wisconsin	MCD	1894	72	583	35		
Wyoming	CCD	71	23	97	12		
TOTAL		35,297	3,141	19,288	4,146		44

1 Alaska County Subdivisions are known as "Census Areas."
2 For 1980 Census, Nevada County Subdivisions (townships) were recognized as MCDs.
3 Independent cities are autonomous from their surrounding counties.

Figure 6-10

Q&A

How do cities fit into the MCD structure?

Cities are incorporated political entities, while MCDs are unincorporated. In eight MCD-states, cities are actually subordinate to the MCD which surrounds them. In the remaining 20 states containing Minor Civil Divisions, cities are either autonomous from their adjacent MCDs or the pattern is mixed, with some cities autonomous and some subordinate. (To see how a particular state treats its MCDs, consult Figure 6-11.) Cities may also cross MCD boundaries.

Why does the Census Bureau consider MCDs the major political subdivision of counties, instead of cities? Because cities are intermittent "islands" amid vast seas of surrounding territory. They don't fill the map grid within counties, so they cannot serve as County Subdivisions. What about completing the map grid in the 20 states where some or all cities maintain autonomy from their surrounding MCDs? Left "unattended," such cities would cause holes in the map

grid. In these states, the Bureau treats autonomous cities as statistical equivalents of MCDs, which then completes the grid. Cities serving this function are called false MCDs or pseudo-MCDs. A similar situation occurs with American Indian Reservations in Maine and New York. As a result of legislation unique to those two states, their Indian Reservations are autonomous from all other Governmental Units. To complete the map grid in Maine and New York, the Bureau counts that portion of an Indian Reservation within a county's boundaries as an MCD-equivalent in that county.

Why do false MCDs matter to Census users? Many Census Reports and data files present information according to geographic hierarchy, so MCD designations determine how and where an entity is listed in the statistical tables.

as parish, borough, gore, grant, plantation, precinct, or purchase. In Puerto Rico, MCDs are called barios. Figure 6-11 lists the names and characteristics of Minor Civil Divisions for every "MCD-state."

MCDs serve various governmental functions from state to state. Twelve states treat MCDs as general-purpose governments, granting them powers similar to those of cities or villages. In these states, most MCDs levy taxes, hold general elections, and provide a broad range of public services. Figure 6-11 lists the 12 general-purpose MCD-states. In New York, Wisconsin, and the six New England States, these general-purpose entities are called towns. The remaining four states (Michigan, Minnesota, New Jersey, and Pennsylvania) use the term township.

In the remaining 16 states where MCDs exist, their role is more limited. As shown in Figure 6-11, the state may treat these MCDs as limited-purpose functioning governments,

MCDs serve various governmental functions from state to state.

nonfunctioning administrative bodies, or a mixture of the two. In all cases, their powers are limited to those necessary for performing specific tasks, such as highway maintenance, administration of the public welfare system, or the election of county legislators. Some states don't even assign distinct names to MCDs; they are simply numbered. Figure 6-12 shows selected Minor Civil Divisions in Mississippi, where they are designated as numbered supervisors' districts.

In nine MCD states, some of the counties contain territory not included in any MCD. To complete the map grid of County Subdivisions, the Bureau has created a Statistical Unit called an Unorganized Territory (UT). UTs are MCD-equivalents, and Figure 6-11 indicates the states where they can be found. Figure 6-13 illustrates how UTs are depicted in Census publications. It shows several Unorganized Territories in Oxford County, Maine, including North

CHARACTERISTICS OF MINOR CIVIL DIVISIONS BY STATE

State	MCD Name(s)	Place/MCD Relationship	General Purpose Gov't	Function-ing/Non-functioning	Other Features
Arkansas	Township	subordinate	no	nf	2 UTs
Connecticut	Town[1]	subordinate[2]	yes	f	
Illinois	Township; Precinct	mixed[3]	no	mixed[5]	
Indiana	Township	subordinate	no	f	
Iowa	Township	subordinate[2]	no	nf	1 UT
Kansas	Township	mixed	no	mixed[5]	2 UTs
Louisiana	Parish District	mixed[3]	no	nf	1 UT
Maine	Town[1]; Plantation; Gore	autonomous	yes	f[7]	35 UTs
Maryland	Election District	mixed[3]	no	nf f	1 Independent city
Massachusetts	Town1	autonomous	yes	f	
Michigan	Township	mixed[4]	yes	f	
Minnesota	Township	autonomous	yes	f	59 UTs
Mississippi	Supervisors' District	subordinate	no	nf	
Missouri	Township	mixed[3]	no	mixed[6]	1 Independent city
Nebraska	Township; Precinct	mixed	no	mixed[5]	
New Hampshire	Town[1]; Grant; Location; Township; Purchase	autonomous	yes	mixed[5]	
New Jersey	Township	autonomous	yes	f	
New York	Town[1]; Borough	mixed[4]	yes	mixed[5]	
North Carolina	Township	subordinate	no	nf	3 UTs
North Dakota	Township	autonomous	no	f[7]	81 UTs
Ohio	Township	mixed	no	f	
Pennsylvania	Township; District	autonomous	yes	f[7]	
Rhode Island	Town[1]	autonomous	yes	f	
South Dakota	Township	autonomous	no	f	98 UTs
Vermont	Town[1]; Gore; Grant	mixed[4]	yes	mixed[5]	
Virginia	Magisterial District	mixed[4]	no	nf	41 Independent cities
West Virginia	Magisterial District	subordinate	no	nf	
Wisconsin	Town[1]	autonomous	yes	f[7]	

1 In this state, towns are unincorporated MCDs.
2 Some Incorporated Places share coextensive boundaries with an MCD.
3 All Incorporated Places are subordinate except for the largest city in the state.
4 Cities autonomous; towns or villages subordinate.
5 Most MCDs are functioning governments.
6 Majority of MCDs are nonfunctioning governments.
7 All MCDs but one are functioning governments.

Figure 6-11

SUMMARY POPULATION AND HOUSING CHARACTERISTICS

Table 1. **Age: 1990**

[For definitions of terms and meanings of symbols, see text]

State County County Subdivision Place	All persons
The State	2 573 216
Adams County	35 356
District 1	7 695
Natchez city (pt)	4 915
District 2	6 035
Natchez city (pt)	4 428
District 3	7 128
Natchez city (pt)	5 529
District 4	7 000
Natchez city (pt)	3 794
District 5	7 498
Natchez city (pt)	794
Alcorn County	31 722
District 1	6 698
Corinth city (pt.)	1 931
District 2	7 265
Corinth city (pt.)	1 817
District 3	5 601
Corinth city (pt.)	2 102
Rienzi town	339
District 4	6 000
Corinth city (pt.)	2 072
Kossuth village	245
District 5	6 158
Corinth city (pt.)	3 898
Amite County	13 328
District 1	2 409
Liberty town (pt.)	277
District 2	2 931
Centreville town (pt.)	281
Gloster town (pt.)	558
District 3	2 400
Crosby town (pt.)	166
Gloster town (pt.)	765
District 4	2 937
Liberty town (pt.)	341
District 5	2 651
Liberty town (pt.)	6
Attala County	18 481
District 1	3 988
Kosciusko city (pt.)	1 878
District 2	3 857
Ethel town	454
Kosciusko city (pt.)	1 469
McCool town	169
District 3	3 687
Kosciusko city (pt.)	1 441
District 4	3 494
Sallis town	139
District 5	3 455
Kosciusko city (pt.)	2 198
Benton County	8 046
District 1	1 597
Ashland town (pt.)	13
District 2	1 834
District 3	1 899
Ashland town (pt.)	477
District 4	1 304
Ashland town (pt.)	–
District 5	1 412
Hickory Flat town	535
Bolivar County	41 875
District 1	7 490
Benoit town	641
Beulah town	460
Gunnison town	611
Pace town (pt.)	354
Rosedale city	2 595
District 2	9 138
Cleveland city (pt.)	8 101
Pace town (pt.)	–

MISSISSIPPI 1

Figure 6-12

Oxford and South Oxford. Each UT is given a descriptive name, followed by the designation "unorg."

Census County Divisions

Census County Divisions are created by the Bureau, in cooperation with state officials and local committees. The sole purpose of CCDs is to complete the map grid at the subcounty level, providing a statistical equivalent to the MCD. They serve as County Subdivisions for states where legally established MCDs either don't exist or are not usable for that purpose. The Bureau considers existing MCDs unusable in states where they serve a specialized administrative function only, and where their boundaries are ill-defined, where the boundaries change frequently, or where the Bureau would need to use an assortment of different administrative Units to fill the map grid. For example, in Arizona, prior to the 1960 Census the Bureau used a combination of supervisory districts, election precincts, justice precincts, school districts, land-survey boundaries (called townships), and Indian Reservations as County Subdivisions. Considering this patchwork of Governmental and non-Governmental entities, the need to impose some statistical consistency becomes clear.

Boundaries of CCDs are drawn to follow visible features, and usually coincide with Census Tract or Block Numbering Area boundaries. The name of each CCD is based on a well-known local name by which it can be identified, followed by the term "division". The example in Figure 6-3 (shown earlier) lists some of the CCDs in Oregon. Multnomah County is divided into three CCDs: Corbett division, Portland division, and Skyline division.

Because CCDs are Statistical Units devised by the Bureau, the states with CCDs show no politically derived "holes" in their map grid. There is no need to create additional false entities to fill in gaps caused by autonomous cities or American Indian Reservations, as there might be in an

The sole purpose of CCDs is to complete the map grid at the subcounty level, providing a statistical equivalent to the MCD.

NEW IN '90

For Census reporting purposes, County Subdivisions in Nevada are now CCDs; in 1980, MCDs were the appropriate Subdivision in Nevada.

Table 1. **Age: 1990**—Con.

[For definitions of terms and meanings of symbols see text]

State County County Subdivision Place	All persons
Lincoln County — Con	
Waldoboro town — Con	
Waldoboro CDP	1 420
Westport town	663
Whitefield town	1 931
Wiscasset town	3 339
Wiscasset CDP	1 233
Oxford County	52 602
Andover town	953
Bethel town	2 329
Brownfield town	1 034
Buckfield town	1 566
Byron town	111
Canton town	951
Denmark town	855
Dixfield town	2 574
Dixfield CDP	1 300
Fryeburg town	2 968
Fryeburg CDP	1 580
Gilead town	204
Greenwood town	689
Hanover town	272
Hartford town	722
Hebron town	878
Hiram town	1 260
Lincoln plantation	38
Lovell town	888
Magalloway plantation	45
Mexico town	3 344
Mexico CDP	2 302
Rumford CDP (pt.)	–
Milton unorg	128
Newry town	316
North Oxford unorg	11
Norway town	4 754
Norway CDP	3 023
Otisfield town	1 136
Oxford town	3 705
Oxford CDP	1 284
Paris town	4 492
South Paris CDP	2 320
Peru town	1 541
Porter town	1 301
Roxbury town	437
Rumford town	7 078
Rumford CDP (pt.)	5 419
South Oxford unorg	455
Stoneham town	224
Stow town	283
Sumner town	761
Sweden town	222
Upton town	70
Waterford town	1 299
West Paris town	1 514
Woodstock town	1 194
Penobscot County	146 601
Alton town	771
Argyle unorg	202
Bangor city	33 181
Bradford town	1 103
Bradley town	1 136
Brewer city	9 021
Burlington town	360
Carmel town	1 906
Carroll plantation	185
Charleston town	1 187
Chester town	442
Clifton town	607
Corinna town	2 196
Corinth town	2 177
Dexter town	4 419
Dexter CDP	2 650
Dixmont town	1 007
Drew plantation	43
East Central Penobscot unorg	12

Figure 6-13

MCD state. In other words, CCDs are independent from existing Governmental Units.

In Alaska, CCDs are known as Census Subareas. Why introduce additional terminology into an already cluttered geographic

glossary? Remember certain areas of Alaska have no politically created county-equivalents, so the Bureau established fictitious Census Areas. For consistency within the state, all Alaskan county subdivisions are called Subareas, whether they fall within Census Areas (Statistical Units) or boroughs (Governmental Units).

Census Tip

Occasional users of the Census need not memorize the differences among MCDs, CCDs, UTs, and Census Subareas. It is probably sufficient to remember that County Subdivisions are statistically equivalent to one another regardless of the nomenclature employed, and that they play an essential role in data tabulation. More important is the distinction between County Subdivisions and Places, a topic which is discussed in the section below.

Places

"Place" has a very specific meaning in Census terminology, but is difficult to define except by example. The two types of Places are Incorporated Places (Governmental Units) and Census Designated Places (Statistical Units).

Incorporated Places

An Incorporated Place is a general-purpose government incorporated under the laws of its state. Incorporation bestows certain legal rights and political powers not enjoyed by unincorporated entities. Incorporated Places exist in all states except Hawaii. As with MCDs, Place designations vary by state. Cities are Incorporated Places in all states except Hawaii. Villages are less common, but are incorporated in all states where they exist. Towns are Incorporated Places everywhere

"Place" has a very specific meaning in Census terminology, but is difficult to define except by example. The two types of Places are Incorporated Places (Governmental Units) and Census Designated Places (Statistical Units).

Q&A

Exactly how do CCDs differ from MCDs?

The difference may seem somewhat arbitrary, or even illogical, but it is quite clear: MCDs are Governmental Units, while CCDs are Statistical Units. To put it another way, MCDs are political jurisdictions, whether they serve as functioning governments or not. In contrast, CCDs are purely the creation of the Bureau, serving no purpose other than Census tabulations.

But doesn't the distinction between a CCD and a nonfunctioning MCD seem pretty slim? Yes, from the point of view of governmental services. Consider the difference between Maryland and Delaware. Maryland is an MCD-state, with 297 MCDs called election districts or assessment districts. Delaware is a CCD-state, with 27 Census-defined Divisions. In both cases, the primary local government for state residents is the Incorporated Place (city, town, or village), or the county. Most residents of these states don't even know the name of their MCD or CCD. The only significant difference between County Subdivisions in these two states is that in one they are created by the state government for local administrative purposes, while in the other they are created by the Bureau to facilitate Census reporting.

Towns are Incorporated Places everywhere they exist except in New York, Wisconsin, and the six New England states, where they are unincorporated MCDs.

they exist except in New York, Wisconsin, and the six New England states, where they are unincorporated MCDs. Boroughs are incorporated except in Alaska (where they are county-equivalents) and New York (where they are MCDs).

Now for a final wrinkle in an already complex tapestry: an Incorporated Place may be a legal part of the MCD which surrounds it or it may be autonomous from any MCD. The relationship between Incorporated Places and MCDs varies from state to state. Figure 6-11 lists the Place/MCD relationships for the 28 states with MCDs. In seven states, every city, village, or other Incorporated Place is legally part of the township or other MCD that surrounds it. These are indicated as "subordinate" relationships in Figure 6-11. In ten states, Incorporated Places are always autonomous from adjacent MCDs. (Among these ten, New Jersey is unique as the only state where an incorporated village or borough can be completely surrounded by a larger MCD (township), yet remain autonomous from the entity which encompasses it.) In the remaining eleven MCD-states, the pattern is mixed, with some Incorporated Places subordinate to surrounding MCDs and other Places autonomous.

As mentioned earlier, superior/subordinate relationships are shown in printed Census Reports by indenting the subordinate entities. Figure 6-14 is an example of the now-familiar hierarchical presentation for County Subdivisions, in this case for New York State. New York has mixed Place/MCD relationships: villages are subordinate to MCDs, but cities are autonomous. For example, the village of Kenmore is part of the town of Tonawanda, but the city of Tonawanda is autonomous from all other subcounty entities. In contrast, look at the selected County Subdivisions for the state of Maine, shown in Figure 6-13. All Incorporated Places in Maine are autonomous. The only indented entities in Figure 6-13 are CDPs, which will be discussed momentarily. (Don't become confused by the MCD nomenclature in the examples above; remember, both Maine and New York are states where MCDs are called towns, not townships.)

To further complicate matters, when a subordinate Incorporated Place is split by the boundaries of two or more MCDs which surround it, political jurisdiction for that Place will also be split. Remember, however, that MCDs in most states are not general-

<table>

State County County Subdivision Place	All persons
Erie County—Con.	
Lancaster town	32 181
Depew village (pt.)	6 605
Lancaster village	11 940
Town Line CDP (pt.)	184
Marilla town	5 250
Newstead town	7 440
Akron village	2 906
North Collins town	3 502
North Collins village	1 335
Orchard Park town	24 632
Orchard Park village	3 280
West Seneca CDP (pt.)	36
Sardinia town	2 667
Tonawanda city	17 284
Tonawanda Reservation	10
Tonawanda town	82 464
Kenmore village	17 180
Tonawanda CDP	65 284
Wales town	2 917
West Seneca town	47 830
West Seneca CDP (pt.)	47 830
Essex County	37 152
Chesterfield town	2 267
Keeseville village (pt.)	882
Crown Point town	1 963
Elizabethtown town	1 314
Essex town	687
Jay town	2 244
Keene town	908
Lewis town	1 057
Minerva town	758
Moriah town	4 884
Mineville-Witherbee CDP	1 740
Port Henry village	1 263
Newcomb town	544
North Elba town	7 870
Lake Placid village	2 485
Saranac Lake village (pt.)	1 204
North Hudson town	266
St. Armand town	1 318
Saranac Lake village (pt.)	161
Schroon town	1 721
Ticonderoga town	5 149
Ticonderoga village	2 770
Westport town	1 446
Westport village	539
Willsboro town	1 736
Wilmington town	1 020
Franklin County	46 540
Altamont town	6 199
Tupper Lake village	4 087
Bangor town	2 080
Bellmont town	1 246
Bombay town	1 158
Brandon town	394
Brighton town	1 511
Burke town	1 231
Burke village	209
Chateaugay town	1 659
Chateaugay village	845
Constable town	1 203
Dickinson town	751
Duane town	152
Fort Covington town	1 676
Franklin town	1 016
Harrietstown town	5 621
Saranac Lake village (pt.)	4 012
Malone town	12 982
Malone village	6 777
Moira town	2 684
Brushton village	522
St. Regis Reservation	1 978
Santa Clara town	311
Waverly town	1 068

</table>

Table 1. **Age: 1990**—Con.

[For definitions of terms and meanings of symbols, see text]

8 NEW YORK

SUMMARY POPULATION AND HOUSING CHARACTERISTICS

Figure 6-14

purpose governments, so the actual jurisdiction may be limited. Nevertheless, the corresponding territory and population of split Places are allocated to the appropriate MCD.

This practice is illustrated by Figure 6-12. Mississippi is a state where all Incorporated Places (cities and towns) are subordinate to nonfunctioning MCDs (supervisors' districts). Notice in the Figure that most Places are split by District boundaries. Natchez city crosses the bounds of all five Districts in Adams County, for example, and each portion of the city falls under the jurisdiction of its respective District.

What about states without MCDs? Census County Divisions are creations of the Census Bureau, so political jurisdiction doesn't apply. For Census reporting purposes, however, Incorporated Places are always subordinate to CCDs.

Census Designated Places

Census Designated Places (CDPs) are Statistical Units serving as counterparts of Incorporated Places. A Census Designated Place is an unincorporated area defined as a Place by the Bureau at the request of a local government. CDPs are densely settled com-

A Census Designated Place is an unincorporated area defined as a Place by the Bureau at the request of a local government.

What's the difference between an MCD and an Incorporated Place?

The most obvious distinction is that MCDs are not incorporated. But why does the Bureau attach such significance to corporate status? Unincorporated entities usually perform fewer governmental tasks, but different legal status hardly seems sufficient reason to warrant the creation of additional, potentially confusing Census terminology. The more important difference is that the sum of all MCDs must completely fill the territory within a county. In contrast, Incorporated Places are sporadic islands of territory within a county. In many states, cities and other Incorporated Places even cross county boundaries.

munities which are locally identifiable by name. A CDP may be a township or other unincorporated political entity, or even part of such an area. CDPs often have no legal or political status but typically have well known local names. An excellent example is the Hyannis CDP in Massachusetts. Hyannis is a well-known community on Cape Cod, but it is neither a town nor a city, merely a heavily populated area within the town of Barnstable. CDP origins are frequently rooted in local history; they may reflect an early area of settlement, a township center, a major real estate subdivision, or even a postal area. Military bases typically are defined as CDPs to separate their characteristics from those of the surrounding communities.

 ## Census Tip

In the 21 states where some or all Incorporated Places are autonomous, the autonomous entities serve a dual role; the Bureau treats them as Places and as false MCDs. Data about them appear twice: as an MCD (in County Subdivision tables), and again as an Incorporated Place (in the Place tables). These dual-role entities are not double-counted when data are aggregated at the county or state level. The information is merely presented in two different formats. To avoid confusion, use County Subdivision tables when seeking data on MCDs or component parts of counties; use Place tables when seeking data on cities and other Incorporated Places.

To qualify as a CDP for the 1990 Census, an unincorporated community must meet a minimum population size established by the Bureau. The basic size criteria are 2,500 people if the community is within the territory of an Urbanized Area or 1,000 people if outside a UA. The criteria are less restrictive for CDPs within American Indian Reservations, and for Alaska, Hawaii, and Puerto

Rico. (Since Incorporated Places do not exist in Hawaii, CDPs are the only Places in that state.) Approximately 4,400 CDPs were identified for the 1990 Census. As Figure 6-10 demonstrates, CDPs are commonplace in some states, yet hardly seen in others. The reason for their scarcity in such states as Iowa and Kansas is that the most heavily populated areas are already Incorporated Places, or that rapidly growing unincorporated areas tend to be annexed by the adjoined Incorporated Place.

In Census publications, CDPs are always shown as subordinate to their surrounding MCDs or CCDs, as Figures 6-3, 6-13, and 6-14 illustrate. CDPs, like Incorporated Places, can cross the boundaries of County Subdivisions, as the "pt." designations in Figure 6-14 indicate. In some cases, an entire township or other MCD may request designation as a CDP in order to gain "Place" status in the decennial Census. However, if Incorporated Places exist within the MCD, only the portion of the MCD's territory outside the Incorporated Places can be granted CDP status. Take another look at the component parts of the town of Tonawanda in Figure 6-14. The population of the Tonawanda CDP (65,284) equals the difference between the MCD total for the town (82,464) and the village of Kenmore (17,180). This is because an Incorporated Place can never be part of a CDP, nor can a CDP be part of an Incorporated Place.

Consolidated Cities and Independent Cities

Two special categories of Incorporated Place should be mentioned, although neither is commonplace. Independent Cities, discussed earlier, are autonomous from any surrounding or adjacent counties and are thus treated

---

NEW IN '90

Criteria for CDPs were more restrictive for 1980: a minimum of 5,000 inhabitants in Urbanized Areas with a Central City of 50,000 or more people; 1,000 inhabitants for UAs with smaller Central Cities and for territory outside of UAs.

---

as county- equivalents. Independent cities exist only in four states, as shown earlier in Figure 6-4.

 Census Tip

In Census tables providing county data, Independent Cities are always shown at the end of the list, following the actual counties. For the states where they exist, Independent Cities are also listed separately on the Bureau's county-outline map for that state.

A Consolidated City is an Incorporated Place which has merged its government functions with those of its surrounding county or MCD.

A Consolidated City is an Incorporated Place which has merged its government functions with those of its surrounding county or MCD. After the merger, both the city and the county (or MCD) may continue to exist as legal entities, even though the county or MCD performs few or no governmental functions and has few or no elected officials. In most cases, smaller Incorporated Places within the merged county or MCD continue to function as separate governments, even though

they are subordinate to the consolidated government. Only six Consolidated Cities were identified for the 1990 Census: Milford, CT; Jacksonville, FL; Columbus, GA; Indianapolis, IN; Butte-Silver Bow, MT; and Nashville-Davidson, TN.

For example, the city of Jacksonville consolidated its functions with those of surrounding Duval County, making the boundaries of the two entities identical. Duval County includes four other Incorporated Places within its boundaries: the cities of Atlantic Beach, Jacksonville Beach, and Neptune Beach, and the town of Baldwin. This means the consolidated city of Jacksonville has other Incorporated Places within its borders and under its jurisdiction.

NEW IN '90

1990 is the first Census to present data for Consolidated Cities and their component parts.

Q&A
Why are Places important in Census Geography?

In the case of Census Designated Places, the answer is fairly clear: if the Bureau hadn't created the CDP as a distinct geographic entity, many communities would not exist in Census Reports; instead, they would be subsumed under larger Summary Levels. The reasons why Incorporated Places receive special Census treatment may seem less obvious. First, Incorporated Places are general-purpose governments which play a noticeable role in the lives of their inhabitants. Second, they tend to be more densely settled areas than most County Subdivisions. Over 70% of United States residents live in Incorporated Places or CDPs.

Places, whether they are CDPs or Incorporated entities, serve as the nuclei for Urbanized Areas. By definition, an Urbanized Area cannot exist without at least one Place at its core. Places also play a key role in defining Rural

territory, a concept which is introduced later in the chapter.

Another important reason pertains to the Bureau's data reporting methods. Most print Census Reports present detailed statistics for states, counties, and Places only; tables for MCDs and CCDs merely show summary data. An exception is made for the 12 states (listed in Figure 6-11) where MCDs serve the same general-purpose governmental functions as cities or other Incorporated Places. For these 12 states, printed Census products publish detailed data for MCDs as well as Places. The distinction between Places and County Subdivisions is less important in CD-ROM databases and other electronic products, where detailed data appear for both Summary Levels.

Smaller Statistical Units

One of the key advantages of the decennial Census is the availability of data for small geographic areas. All Summary Levels described below—Tracts, Block Numbering Areas, Block Groups, and Blocks—are Statistical Units created by the Bureau. Because none of these small areas have locally recognized names, they are identified through a numbering system devised by the Bureau.

Tracts and Block Numbering Areas

A key unit of Census geography is the Census Tract. Every Metropolitan Area or Urbanized Area in the United States is completely divided into Tracts. A Tract is a small subcounty area with relatively homogeneous demographic, economic, and housing characteristics. A typical Tract contains between 2,500 and 8,000 inhabitants, although a small percentage of Tracts have populations above or below that targeted range. For example, some densely settled Tracts in such large cities as New York or Chicago have populations in the 12,000 to 15,000 range. The land areas of Census Tracts vary widely, depending on population density. The more populous the MA or UA, the larger the number of Tracts it will have. Tract boundaries are determined by local committees, following Census Bureau guidelines.

Tracts are identified by four-digit numbers unique within a county, but not unique nationwide. In other words, Tract 0405 may exist in many different MAs or even adjacent counties of the same MA. Some Tracts are further identified by a two-digit "suffix" separated from the four-digit number by a decimal (e.g., 0710.02). Suffixes are designed to indicate changes which have occurred to Tract boundaries over time, or to identify a particular type of Tract. For example, a .99 suffix indicates crews aboard maritime vessels, whether military or civilian. A .99 Tract represents an actual group of ships, not a

geographic entity. These Tracts share the same four-digit Tract number as the nearest on-shore Tract, but are distinguished by their .99 suffix.

In printed Reports, maps, and the GO software used with CD- ROM products, leading zeros are dropped from Tract numbering; thus, Tract 0710.02 becomes 710.02. (More advanced users of the Bureau's computerized products should note that the Census codes for Tracts found on CD-ROMs and magnetic tape files retain the leading zeros but omit the decimals; Tract 0710.02 becomes 071002. EXTRACT users must select the "Area Name" field in order to retrieve the more recognizable form of the Tract number.)

💡 Census Tip

Although Tract boundaries remain relatively stable, they can change slightly from one decade to the next if a street or other visible boundary moves as a result of construction. Changes also occur when a county's political boundaries shift. In these instances, the Bureau creates a new Tract representing the annexed territory which was formerly part of another county. All Tracts affected by such boundary changes are identified with a two digit suffix ranging from .80 to .98. In this way, users can still compare territory to previous Censuses by adding or subtracting the separate parts. Since most of these boundary changes involve small parcels of land, Tracts identified by suffixes ranging from .80 to .98 generally contain few or no inhabitants. Most Census users incorporate data from these small parcels into the totals for the larger adjoining Tract (i.e., the Tract with the same four-digit base number.)

Aside from smallness of size, Census Tracts are important because their boundaries remain fairly stable from one decade to the

Every Metropolitan Area or Urbanized Area in the United States is completely divided into Tracts.

next, making them the only level of statistical geography which is comparable across Censuses. Users should remember that Tract boundaries are based on demographic homogeneity at the time they are established; because these boundaries remain fairly stable from one decade to the next, the characteristics of a Tract's population and housing stock may become more diverse over time.

In some cases, the population of a Tract becomes too large and must be divided into smaller parts. When this occurs, their combined boundaries remain comparable to those of past Censuses. For example, if Tract 0142 of an MSA were to become too populous, it would be divided into Tracts 0142.01 and 0142.02. The resulting entities are called Divided Tracts. Over time, two Tracts may also be combined due to significant population decline.

Tracts do not cross the borders of a Metropolitan Area, nor do they cross county or state lines, but they may extend beyond other political boundaries, especially those of Incorporated Places. However, Tracts generally follow MCD boundaries. A Tract which lies in two separate Governmental Units is called a Split Tract.

The Bureau utilizes different terminology to denote the concept of a Tract in less populated areas. Here the nomenclature is

Tracts do not cross the borders of a Metropolitan Area, nor do they cross county or state lines, but they may extend beyond other political boundaries, especially those of Incorporated Places

Census Tip

Divided Tracts should not be confused with Split Tracts. In hierarchical presentations, data on Split Tracts are reported separately for each Governmental Unit of which they are a part. For example, if one portion of Tract 101 lies within a village and the remainder falls outside the village boundary, both would be listed with the designation "101 (pt.)" to indicate the complete Tract is not represented.

Block Numbering Area (BNA). A BNA is statistically equivalent to a Tract, but it lies outside an MA or UA. BNA boundaries are determined by the Bureau rather than local committees. BNA numbers range from 9501 through 9989.99, while Tracts are assigned numbers from 0001 through 9499.99. Like Tract numbers, BNA numbers are unique within a single county only. The 1990 Census provides complete nationwide coverage for Tracts and Block Numbering Areas. Every county and county- equivalent in the United States is dividing into Tracts or BNAs.

The Census Bureau allows state and local governments to pay a fee to have their BNAs treated as Tracts. For 1990, six states (Cali-

Q&A

The distinction between Tracts and BNAs seems quite minor. Is it really necessary?

In 1990 Census printed Reports and databases, the same amount of data is published for BNAs as for Tracts. However, the differences between the two geographic units are not trivial. One reason for creating separate terminology is to emphasize the fact that BNAs lie outside Metropolitan and Urbanized Areas. As an example, New York is a highly Metropolitan state, but has extensive Nonmetropolitan and Nonurbanized territory. Of its 62 counties, 40 have Tracts and 22 have BNAs. A

second reason for the additional nomenclature is that BNAs are less densely populated than Tracts, so their land areas are usually much larger. Third, because Tract boundaries are drawn to reflect similarities in social, economic, and housing characteristics, Tracts can serve as statistical surrogates for neighborhoods. BNAs do not necessarily reflect homogeneous characteristics, so they are not as useful for analytical purposes.

NEW IN '90

Prior to the 1990 Census, much of the United States was not covered by either Tracts or BNAs. In 1990, only those counties in Metropolitan Areas received Tract numbers, plus additional counties whose state or local governments contracted with the Bureau for Tract coverage. (Five of the six states mentioned above were completely tracted for 1980; only California is newly tracted for 1990.) Block Numbering Areas for 1980 were assigned only to Nonmetropolitan Places with population greater than 10,000, and to selected areas which contracted for additional Block numbering.

In 1980, the Bureau tabulated data for 42,835 Tracts and approximately 3,600 BNAs. For 1990, the Bureau created 49,961 Tracts and 11,270 BNAs.

Census information for BNAs is now much more accessible than in the past. Maps of all Block Numbering Areas are issued as standard 1990 Census products, and population and housing data for BNAs can be found in print Reports and CD-ROM Files.

fornia, Connecticut, Delaware, Hawaii, New Jersey, and Rhode Island) contracted with the Bureau for complete Tract coverage. Approximately 200 counties outside these states also requested Tract status for their BNAs.

NEW IN '90

One of the biggest changes in the 1990 Census is that the entire nation has been blocked from shore to shore. This has created more than 7 million Census Blocks, compared with approximately 2.5 million in 1980. Prior to 1990, Block coverage was limited to the Urbanized portions of Metropolitan Areas, Places with population greater than 10,000 inhabitants, and selected states and counties which contracted with the Bureau for complete blocking. (In 1980, five states paid for complete Block numbering: Georgia, Mississippi, New York, Rhode Island, and Virginia. Note that for 1980 five states were completely tracted and five were completely blocked, but only Rhode Island was both.)

Blocks and Block Groups

The smallest area of Census geography is the Census Block. In Urbanized Areas and other densely populated areas, a Block is usually a quadrangle bounded by four streets (i.e., a city block). In sparsely populated areas, a Block has a population of approximately 70 people and is bounded by visible features (roads, streams, railroad tracks), and by such invisible boundaries as city or county limits. Census Blocks do not cross Tract or BNA boundaries. In Rural areas, a Block may encompass many square miles.

Blocks are numbered uniquely only within each Census Tract or BNA (i.e., the numbering sequence is repeated in every Tract). A Block is identified by a three-digit number, sometimes with a single alphabetical suffix. Block numbers with suffixes generally represent Blocks split by other geographic boundaries. For example, when a city limit runs through Block 101, data for the portion inside the city are tabulated in Block 101A and the section outside the city is shown in Block 101B. A Block number with the suffix Z represents a "crews-of-vessels" entity, usually a single ship. Figure 6-15 shows a portion of a Block map from a typical Metropolitan county.

 Census Tip

Blocks are the Bureau's fundamental unit of data aggregation. Every Census Questionnaire contains a numeric code identifying the Block in which that Household is located. To obtain population and housing totals for a particular geographic entity, Census computers add the relevant figures for all Blocks contained within that entity. For this reason, split Blocks are especially important. Wherever a Census Block crosses a political boundary, the computer counts only that portion within the boundary to obtain that entity's total population.

County Block Maps Sample

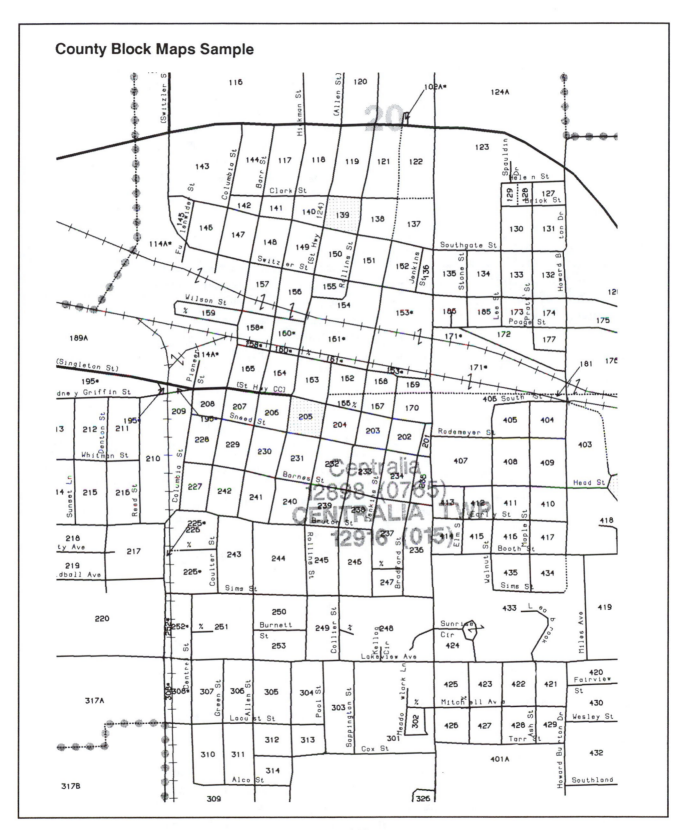

Figure 6-15

Only the responses from Short Form Questionnaires are tabulated at the Block level, which means no sample data are available for Census Blocks. Even so, the decennial Census is the only source of nationwide, non-estimated demographic information at such small levels of geography.

 Census Tip

Census Blocks in densely settled areas should not be equated with the commonplace "neighborhood" notion of a street block. The street itself is the dividing line for Census Blocks, so each side of the street will appear in a different Block. Think of the street itself as a river separating residents on one side from their neighbors "across the way." To put it another way, these Urban Census Blocks are territories including back-to-back houses rather than houses facing one another.

An intervening level of Census geography, called the Block Group (BG), appears between Blocks and Tracts. As the name indicates, Block Groups are created by combining Blocks to form larger units. Every Tract or BNA is divided into a maximum of nine Block Groups. Therefore, a BG number always consists of a single digit from 1 to 9. Block Groups generally contain between 250 and 550 Housing Units, with an ideal size of 400 Housing Units. The average population of a BG is between 1,000 and 1,200 people.

Block Groups are not shown explicitly on Census maps, but their outlines can be easily determined by circumscribing the boundaries of their component Blocks. All Census Blocks within a Block Group have the same first digit. For example, all of the "400 Blocks" shown in the lower right corner of Figure 6-15 combine to form Block Group 4 in that Census Tract. Numbering for Block Groups is unique only within each Tract or BNA; in other words, every Tract will have a BG 1.

NEW IN '90

As a consequence of the 100% blocking of the United States, the country is now completely covered by Block Groups. Prior to 1990, the Bureau used a Statistical Unit called the Enumeration District (ED) to collect and tabulate data in areas without Block Groups. However, no data were published at the ED level. Because Block Groups have been assigned everywhere in the nation for 1990, EDs are no longer used by the Bureau.

Since Block numbers are assigned by computer, a Block Group's territory is somewhat arbitrary. BGs never cross boundaries of Metropolitan Areas, Tracts, or BNAs, but may cross Urbanized Areas. Block Groups never cross state or county lines, but may cross other political boundaries. As with Tracts and Blocks, when a BG is split by political boundaries, separate tabulations will be presented for each portion that is split.

 Census Tip

Block Groups are the smallest level of geography for which the Bureau tabulates sample data. Population and housing statistics for Block Groups cannot be found in printed Census Reports, but they are provided on certain CD-ROM and magnetic tape products. Complete count data for Block Groups appear in STF 1A; sample data are found in STF 3A.

Specialized Summary Levels

Counties, Places, County Subdivisions, Metropolitan Areas, Tracts—these are the geographic Summary Levels encountered most frequently in Census products. A variety of more specialized entities are also used,

Block Groups are created by combining Blocks to form larger units. Every Tract or BNA is divided into a maximum of nine Block Groups.

including American Indian and Alaska Native Areas, Congressional Districts, Voting Districts, and ZIP Codes Areas. The following sections describe the most frequently encountered specialized Levels.

Several less common Summary Levels will be introduced elsewhere in the book because they are used in conjunction with very specialized Census products. Planning and Service Areas (PSAs), used with a CD-ROM product entitled the Special Tabulation on Aging, are described briefly in Chapter 8. Chapter 8 also introduces Public Use Microdata Areas (PUMAs), a unique geographic construct created for use with the Bureau's PUMS Files. The Census Bureau creates customized "neighborhood" boundaries as part of a special product offering called the User- Defined Area Program (UDAP). The latter construct will be discussed in Chapter 10.

American Indian and Alaska Native Areas

Native American territories appear in various forms in the 1990 Census. Indian Reservations, Trust Lands, and Alaska Native Regional Corporations are Governmental Units. Tribal Designated Statistical Areas, Tribal Jurisdiction Statistical Areas, and Alaska Native Village Statistical Areas are Statistical Units .

The 1990 Census recognizes 311 federal and state Indian Reservations whose boundaries are established by treaty, statute, and/or executive or court order. Reservations are governed by their respective American Indian tribes. State Reservations are lands held in trust by state governments for the use and benefit of a given tribe. Federal Reservations are recognized by the United States government and may cross state boundaries. Certain federal Reservations may also

go by other names, such as Pueblos, Rancherias, Communities, etc. Both federal and state Reservations may cross county, County Subdivision, and Place boundaries.

Trust Lands are territories located outside an Indian Reservation, held in trust by the federal government for either a tribe or an individual member of a tribe. Fifty Trust Lands are identified in the 1990 Census. Like federal Reservations, Trust Lands can be located in more than a single state.

Certain American Indian tribes have no Reservations or Trust Lands, yet hold jurisdiction over their tribal members. To identify such territories, the Census Bureau has created two specialized Statistical Units: Tribal Jurisdiction Statistical Areas (TJSAs) and Tribal Designated Statistical Areas (TDSAs). Both exist outside the boundaries of Reservations or Trust Lands, and both are determined in conjunction with local tribes. TJSAs are unique to Oklahoma; they generally existed as Reservations at one time, but were dissolved prior to Oklahoma's statehood in 1907. TDSAs are similar to TJSAs, but exist outside Oklahoma. The 1990 Census reports data for 17 TJSAs and 19 TDSAs.

💡 Census Tip

State Indian Reservations are distinguished from their federal counterparts in Census publications by the designation "(State)" following their names.

Alaska Native Regional Corporations (ANRCs) are Governmental Units established by the Alaska Native Claims Settlement Act of 1972 to conduct the business and legal affairs of Alaska Natives. Alaska is divided into 13 ANRCs that cover the entire state. However, only 12 ANRCs have specific boundaries; the 13th covers the various remaining land areas, and is not tabulated in the Census. Each ANRC encompasses groupings of Alaska Natives with a common heritage and common interests. The legally es-

> **The 1990 Census recognizes 311 federal and state Indian Reservations whose boundaries are established by treaty, statute, and/or executive or court order.**

NEW IN '90

TJSAs replace a single 1980 Census entity, collectively known as the "Historic Areas of Oklahoma." TDSAs, however, are completely new to the 1990 Census.

NEW IN '90

Data for ANVs are no longer tabulated in the Census. Newly created Alaska Native Village Statistical Areas replace the ANVs that the Census Bureau had formerly recognized for the 1980 Census.

tablished boundaries of an ANRC may change over time.

Alaska Native Villages (ANVs) constitute tribes, clans, groups, villages, communities, or other groups recognized pursuant to the Alaska Native Claims Settlement Act of 1972. Because ANVs do not have legally designated boundaries, the Census Bureau, in conjunction with tribal officials, established Alaska Native Village Statistical Areas (ANVSAs) for tabulation purposes. ANVSAs are located within ANRCs and do not cross ANRC boundaries. They represent the settled portions of ANVs. The 1990 Census identifies 217 ANVSAs.

Congressional Districts and Voting Districts

Congressional Districts (CDs) are the areas from which persons are elected to the U.S. House of Representatives. There are 435 CDs, apportioned among the states based on decennial Census population counts. As described in Chapter 2, each state is responsible for establishing the boundaries of its Congressional Districts, but within a state the population of CDs must be approximately equal. Congressional Districts in effect on January 1, 1990 were those of the 101st Congress, based on boundaries established after the 1980 Census. Congressional redistricting based on 1990 Census counts went into effect for the 103rd Congress, which began in January of 1993. Various 1990 Census products provide tabulations for Congressional Districts; early products utilize the 101st Congress boundaries, while later products use boundaries for the 103rd or 104th Congress.

A Voting District (VTD) is an area established by state or local governments for elec-

 Census Tip

Boundary maps for every CD in the nation are found in the Bureau's two-volume Congressional District Atlas: 103rd Congress of the United States, published in 1993. The Atlas also contains detailed alphabetical tables listing the Congressional District numbers for all counties, Places, and general-purpose Minor Civil Divisions within each state.

tion purposes. VTDs are known under various names among the various political jurisdictions within a state, including election districts, precincts, wards, and legislative districts. Voting Districts do not conform to Statistical Units used by the Census, but many states adjusted existing VTD boundaries to match Census Block outlines to facilitate data tabulation for redistricting purposes. As a result, many VTD boundaries used in the Census do not reflect legally established boundaries existing at the time of the 1990 Census. More important, statistics for VTDs do not appear in any standard Census products, with the exception of the Public Law 94-171 Data files used for redistricting.

NEW IN '90

For the 1980 Census, VTDs were referred to as Election Precincts.

School Districts

Another Governmental Unit unrecognized by the Bureau's standard statistical products is the school district. The Census Bureau has, however, created computerized school district boundary files as part of the TIGER system. TIGER creates these boundary specifications based on maps provided by state education agencies.

School districts are created by state governments. They may represent a particular segment of the school-age population (elementary, intermediate, or secondary), or they may be unified Districts representing all grade levels. Boundaries of elementary, intermediate, and secondary districts may overlap, and some territory may not be covered by any district. In some states (or parts of states), school district boundaries coincide with those of counties, MCDs, or Incorporated Places. In other states, school district boundaries have no relationship to any other Governmental or Statistical Units, and may even split Census Blocks.

Aside from the TIGER/Line Files themselves, the Bureau issues no publications containing data at the school district level. As in past Censuses, state agencies can contract with the Bureau to create Special Tabulations for school districts.

ZIP Code Areas

ZIP Codes are established by the United States Postal Service for efficient mail delivery. (ZIP is a coined acronym which stands for Zone Improvement Plan.) Because ZIP Code boundaries follow the routes of mail carriers, they do not conform to the boundaries of Governmental Units, nor to those of the Bureau's Statistical Units. In fact, ZIP Code Areas usually do not have clearly identifiable boundaries. They change periodically to meet postal requirements and they do not cover the total land area of the United States. For these reasons, Census Bureau geographers would prefer to ignore ZIP Code Areas, despite their popularity among direct mail marketers and other data users. For the 1990 Census, data are tabulated for five-digit ZIP Codes and appear in magnetic tape and CD-ROM formats.

Some ZIP Code Areas are excluded from the 1990 Census. The two major categories omitted are nonresidential ZIP Codes (commercial areas containing no Occupied Housing Units) and ZIP Codes representing rural Post Office Boxes.

NEW IN '90

The U.S. Department of Education's National Center for Education Statistics (NCES) contracted with the Bureau of the Census to conduct a Special Tabulation of key variables from the 1990 Census for every school district in the United States. The resulting data are not available as a 1990 Census publication, but were issued as part of a 43-disc CD-ROM product from NCES itself. The discs also contain financial data on school districts from the Census of Governments. The product, called the School District Data Book, was released in late 1994.

 Census Tip

1990 population and housing data for ZIP Code Areas can be found on Summary Tape File 3B, available in CD-ROM and magnetic tape format. The TIGER/Line Files contain boundary coordinates for ZIP Code Areas.

Because ZIP Code boundaries follow the routes of mail carriers, they do not conform to the boundaries of Governmental Units, nor to those of the Bureau's Statistical Units.

Urban/Rural Classifications

Before leaving the topic of geographic Units, a classification which cuts across all Census hierarchies must be discussed—Urban territory.

NEW IN '90

Following the 1980 Census, a consortium of ten private companies contracted with the Bureau to produce a special nationwide ZIP Code tabulation, which was ultimately made available to the public as a magnetic tape file. However, the 1990 Census is the first to provide ZIP Code data in a more readily accessible format.

Urban versus Urbanized

Earlier in the chapter, an Urbanized Area was described as a contiguous, densely populated territory with one or more large Central Places at its core. The people, Households, and structures within the bounds of a UA are thus characterized as "Urbanized." But how does the Bureau describe a community of reasonable population size lying outside an Urbanized Area? Is it reasonable to label a town of 15,000 people as "rural" because it's nowhere near a UA? Even if the town is surrounded by farm country, its inhabitants might not consider themselves rural. And what about the ring of smaller towns immediately beyond a UA boundary? Insufficient population density excludes them from the Urbanized umbrella, yet many observers would view them as distant suburbs of their Central City. So how does the Bureau distinguish between Urban and Rural?

The Census Bureau definition of Urban comprises all territory, population, and Housing Units in Urbanized Areas, plus those in Places of 2,500 or more persons outside UAs. In other words, the following territories are encompassed by the Urban definition:

1. Cities, villages, and other Incorporated Places of 2,500 or more persons.

The Census Bureau definition of Urban comprises all territory, population, and Housing Units in Urbanized Areas, plus those in Places of 2,500 or more persons outside UAs.

2. Census Designated Places of 2,500 or more persons.
3. All territory, incorporated or unincorporated, within Urbanized Areas.

Notice that MCDs outside Urbanized Areas are excluded from the Urban definition regardless of their size, because they are not Places.

Census Tip

Urban and Rural are mutually exclusive terms and all territory in the United States is one or the other. By definition, all Urbanized Areas are Urban, but not all Urban territory is Urbanized. Approximately 63% of the U.S. population live in Urbanized Areas, but 75% live in an Urban environment.

Rural is then defined as all territory, population, and Housing Units not classified as Urban. This includes Incorporated Places and CDPs with fewer than 2,500 people, as long as they lie outside a UA. The Bureau's definition of Rural also encompasses all Non-Urbanized Minor Civil Divisions, regardless of size, because MCDs are not incorporated.

Q&A

How does the Bureau define suburban areas?

It doesn't. The word "suburban" does not appear in Census publications, and Census geography includes no standard measure of suburban population. Many Census users define a suburb as all territory within a Metropolitan Area which lies beyond the limits of the Central City. (Census publications often divide an MA into two components: the portion within the Central City, and the remainder, usually designated "outside Central City.") This approach presents two problems.

It includes Rural territory within the MA and it includes Urban territory which is geographically remote from the Central City. An alternative is to focus on the "Urban Fringe" portion of an Urbanized Area, but this construct crosses all manner of political boundaries, so may be equally unsatisfactory. Depending on the purpose for which data are used, a variety of aggregations can be created. In practice, a suburb is whatever the user defines it to be.

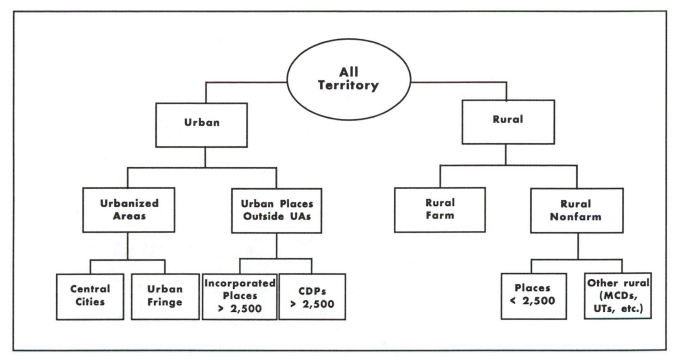

Figure 6-16

Rural territory is not synonymous with farm country. Although 24.8% of all Americans live within Rural areas, only 6% actually live on farms.

Remember, Rural territory can be located within a Metropolitan Area (an MSA, CMSA, or PMSA), but it must lie outside the Urbanized portion of the MA. Metropolitan Areas are made up of entire counties, and many counties contain both Urban and Rural components.

The Census Bureau's adjectives for population size and density have precise meanings. "Metropolitan" refers to the territory, population, and Housing Units located within Metropolitan Areas. "Nonmetropolitan" describes areas outside MA bounds. "Urbanized" refers to territory within a UA. The concepts focus on different characteristics. "Metropolitan" measures concentrated centers of economic activity, while "Urbanized" measures areas of high population density. "Urban" and "Rural" also characterize the nature of a territory or population, but cut across the boundaries of other areas. Figure 6-16 shows the relationships among Urban, Rural, Metropolitan, and Urbanized territories. Figure 6-17, though oversimplified, shows Urban and Rural territories as they might exist in and around a Metropolitan Area.

Extended Cities

Certain cities throughout the United States have extended their boundaries to include territory that is essentially rural in character. Because the extended portions cover large areas with low population density and small total populations, such cities aren't entirely urban, even though they fit the Bureau's definition. In an attempt to describe these entities more accurately, the Bureau has created a designation for Extended Cities and divided each of them into two parts. Census publications count both segments when providing data for Places, but in summary presentations of Urban/Rural population, the "rural" portion of an Extended City is excluded from the Urban definition. Extended Cities primarily affect the statistics on Urban and Rural land area, but have little effect on Urban/Rural population and housing counts, especially at the national and state levels.

 Census Tip

1990 statistics for the Urban and Rural components of every Extended City in the United States can be found in a special Census publication entitled Urbanized Areas Supplementary Report (CPH-S-1-2).

Throughout the chapter, several special designations for cities have been introduced, so this might be a good time to review them. Independent Cities are those which do not fall under the jurisdiction of a county; they are treated as county- equivalents. Consolidated Cities are those which have merged

**Geographical Relationships
Metropolitan/Urbanized/Urban**

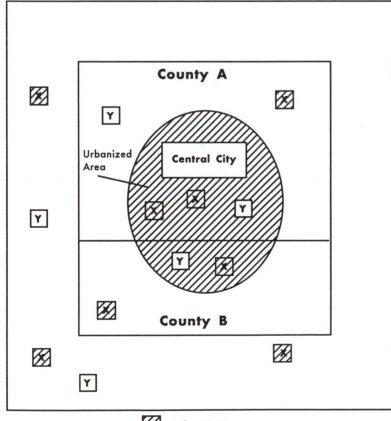

X=Place > 2,500
Y=Place < 2,500

▧ = Urban Territory
▢ = Rural Territory

Figure 6-17

their jurisdictions with a surrounding MCD or county, with both continuing to exist as coextensive entities. Extended Cities are those which include Rural territory within their boundaries. None of these entities have a major impact on Census data; for example, the 1990 Census identifies only 44 Independent Cities and 6 Consolidated Cities. Another term used throughout this book, though it is not official Census nomenclature, is autonomous cities—those which do not fall under the jurisdiction of surrounding MCDs.

Technical Aspects of Census Geography

This chapter has introduced basic geographic concepts and terminology, including the major Governmental and Statistical Units used in the Census. Taken together with the discussion of geographic procedures discussed in Chapter 3 and descriptions of maps and other geographic products described in Chapters 8 and 9, the reader should have a good overview of important geographic aspects of the Census. Though complex, much of the discussion has been somewhat simplified. Without delving too deeply into details, the following section introduces several key technical aspects of the Bureau's geographic operation, with an emphasis on the remarkable TIGER database.

The TIGER System

TIGER, an acronym for Topologically Integrated Geographic Encoding and Referencing system, is the new digital (computer-readable) database that automates the Bureau's geographic activities. What began as a project to streamline Census operations developed into a nationwide, computerized map of the United States. Actually, TIGER is not an electronic map, but a cartographic database—a digital record of map features.

NEW IN '90

The debut of TIGER is without question the most ambitious, exciting, far-reaching, and eagerly awaited aspect of the 1990 Census. Prior to 1990, the Bureau's Geography Division performed many complex and detailed tasks by hand. This meant little geographic data was available to Census users in machine-readable form. An exception was the GBF/DIME (Geographic Base File/Dual Independent Map Encoding) database, which provided address ranges for Blocks within the Urbanized portions of Metropolitan Areas. Although GBF/DIME represented more than 60% of the population, it covered only 2% of U.S. land area. For 1990, GBF/DIME has been replaced by a product called TIGER/Line Files. How is TIGER/Line better? It covers the entire country, data are more detailed, and it can be used with microcomputers. GBF/DIME was a computer tape product, available only to mainframe computer users.

TIGER is a giant connect-the-dots database which can be used to construct maps.

Planning for TIGER began in 1983 as a joint project of the Census Bureau and the U.S. Geological Survey (USGS), the nation's official mapping agency.

To put it another way, TIGER is a giant connect-the-dots database which can be used to construct maps.

TIGER covers all territory in the United States, Puerto Rico, the U.S. Virgin Islands, and the Outlying Areas of the Pacific. The database system has three major components: files describing physical features and political/statistical boundaries; data on postal geography (ZIP Code Areas and address ranges by Block); and the topological structure linking these features together. Topology is a branch of mathematics dealing with the relationship of points, line segments, and polygons in a two-dimensional plane. TIGER files contain no actual Census data; their content is geographic only, designed to be used in conjunction with other data products.

As described in Chapter 3, massive effort is required to support the geographic operations of the decennial Census, including mapmaking, geocoding, and Block numbering. Formerly, such activities were undertaken from scratch for each new Census and completed largely by hand. Moreover, separate operations were conducted in isolation, despite their interrelated nature. The result was many labor intensive projects, sprinkled

with unavoidable errors and inconsistencies among various geographic products, not to mention duplication of effort. The need was seen for more accurate, timely, efficient, and versatile geographic operations.

Mapmaking provides an excellent example of the frustrations inherent in the Bureau's manual system. For the 1980 Census, local governments and planning agencies provided the Bureau with base maps for their areas. These maps were received in all conceivable sizes and formats. To create standard Census products, the Bureau's cartographers literally spread maps on the floor, matched their edges with those of neighboring maps, and redrew them by hand. As a result, inconsistencies arose across the various map products; the same geographic entity might show slightly different boundaries depending on which Census map was used. Most geocoding (assigning correct geographies to individual Census Questionnaires) was also conducted manually for 1980. Geographic operations for the 1980 Census took four years, 1,600 employees, and the cooperation of 200 local agencies to complete. The result was 32,000 map sheets and 2.5 million hand-numbered Census Blocks. In contrast, the TIGER system produced 1.3 million map sheets for 1990, with all 7 million Blocks numbered automatically. Although TIGER also required four years to develop, it can be updated continuously, meaning the Bureau no longer must begin each decade's geographic operations from scratch.

Planning for TIGER began in 1983 as a joint project of the Census Bureau and the U.S. Geological Survey (USGS), the nation's official mapping agency. The system was designed to meet the requirements of both organizations. Ninety-eight percent of the territory covered by TIGER was created by digitizing USGS 1:100,000 scale maps. Features for the Urbanized portions of Metropolitan Areas was obtained from the Bureau's GBF/DIME files, and remaining information was acquired from various other map sheets. Work on the system began in 1984 and was completed in 1987. In that year, the

Q&A

So TIGER improves the Census Bureau's geographic operations. Why is everyone else so excited about it?

TIGER covers the entire United States, presents unparalleled detail in a topologically consistent format, and will provide ongoing updates, making it the de facto national standard for any Geographic Information System (GIS). All major software for mapmaking and GIS programs are now written to accommodate TIGER. By importing TIGER extracts into other computer programs, users can create customized thematic or boundary maps, relate Census data to those maps, superimpose their own data onto maps, and locate addresses in larger geographies. TIGER is not simply a product for use with the Census; it is the premiere database for all GIS users. Applications for TIGER data are virtually limitless, from market research to transportation planning to environmental analysis. Subsets from the TIGER database are available in a variety of extracted files, on magnetic tape and CD-ROM. With justifiable pride, the Bureau calls TIGER a present to the nation in celebration of the Census's 200th anniversary.

resulting database was updated and corrected with input from local agencies.

The TIGER database has three record categories, describing three types of features: points, line segments, and polygons. Each record lists numerous attributes for its respective feature. Included are the feature's name (e.g., a street name), alternate names where applicable, various classification codes, latitude/longitude coordinates, and links to Governmental and Statistical Units. Census Blocks within Metropolitan Areas show ZIP Code information and address ranges between cross streets (for each side of the street). TIGER line segments describe political and statistical boundaries as well as such physical features as rivers, railroad tracks, and power lines. Many schools, churches, and other selected landmarks are shown. Polygons include such features as parks, airports and forests. Curved line segments terminate in "shape points" indicating they are not straight. All records are topologically linked through pointers.

NEW IN '90

TIGER's precision improved the accuracy of land area measurements for 1990. TIGER also enabled the Bureau to provide more detailed measurements for water area. The 1980 Census measured only inland water bodies, such as lakes, reservoirs, rivers, and canals. 1990 measurements also include coastal waters, such as bays and inlets; the Great Lakes; and territorial waters out to a three-mile limit. These changes affect the comparability of data between 1980 and 1990. The increased accuracy of measurements, combined with more comprehensive coverage of water areas, result in significant reductions of land area for some localities. In other words, users should not attribute all of the change in land area to annexations, boundary shifts, or actual land erosion.

Area Measurements

TIGER makes it possible to calculate area measurements for every geographic entity in the Census. Land area is reported in Census products for geographic entities at all Summary Levels except ZIP Code Areas. Census Tracts and Blocks consisting of crews of merchant or military vessels always have zero land area because they are not actual geographic entities.

Printed Census Reports list land area in both square kilometers and square miles, as shown earlier in Figure 6-3. CD-ROMs and other electronic products present areas in square kilometers only.

Census Tip

Square kilometers may be divided by 2.59 to convert an area measurement to square miles. This can be demonstrated by the numbers shown in Figure 6-3. Morrow County's land area of 2,032.8 square miles is equivalent to 5,265.1 square kilometers divided by 2.59.

Measurements of water areas are shown in electronic Census products only. By definition, Census Blocks do not include water within their boundaries; therefore, the water area of a Block is always zero. Tracts, however, can contain water areas, and some Tracts are composed entirely of water. Census Tracts containing water area only are designated with a 0000 number.

Geographic Boundaries

The process of determining geographic boundaries was described briefly in Chapter 3. Boundaries for most Governmental Units are established by state and local authorities. Current information is obtained by the Bureau via ongoing Boundary and Annexation Surveys. The 1990 Census reflects boundaries legally in effect on January 1, 1990.

NEW IN '90

Nearly half of all Incorporated Places experienced boundary changes since the previous Census. Changes in county and County Subdivision bounds were less common, but many did occur; even American Indian and Alaska Native Areas were subject to change. Governmental boundaries changed as a result of annexation, merger, disincorporation, and similar legal or political actions. For example, a real estate developer might petition to have a new subdivision annexed by a town so the residents could utilize that town's water and sewer lines. Boundaries of Statistical Units also changed. Many Metropolitan Areas were redefined by the OMB based on population growth and changing commuting patterns. The bounds of Urbanized Areas and Census Designated Places were redrawn based on changing settlement patterns. More often than not, the names of such redrawn entities remained the same, so users should be wary when comparing 1990 data to 1980.

Boundaries of Metropolitan Areas are determined by the U.S. Office of Management and Budget, based on population size and commuting patterns. All other Statistical boundaries are established by the Census Bureau, usually in cooperation with state and local agencies or local committees. Because Urbanized Areas are determined ac-

Can I use TIGER data to draw my own maps?

Yes, but the map quality will depend upon the sophistication of the software used. Each TIGER record is a string of computer codes describing latitude and longitude coordinates of map points and their characteristics. To convert TIGER code into lines on a map, specialized software is required. The Bureau publishes a series of CD-ROM products, called TIGER/Line Files, which allow microcomputer users to create customized maps, but early versions of the CD-ROM contained no software whatsoever. A revised edition, released in 1994, contains a computer program called LandView. LandView allows the user to draw simple boundary maps, down to the Block Group level, but it offers no capabilities for creating thematic maps based on Census data. More advanced map-making can be done only by utilizing the TIGER/Line Files in conjunction with commercially-produced mapping software. More will be said about LandView in Chapter 8.

cording to population density, their boundaries are established by the Bureau alone.

 ## Census Tip

The "User Notes" section of the Population and Housing Unit Counts Reports for each state (1990 series CPH-2) provides county-by-county lists of all 1990 boundary changes for counties, County Subdivisions, and Places within that state.

Geographic Codes

One or more numeric codes are assigned to every high-level geographic entity in the Census. These geographic codes do not appear in printed Census Reports, but they are convenient for accessing and manipulating data on CD-ROMs and other machine-readable products. They are also crucial for GIS-related activities, such as drawing boundary maps or creating thematic maps. The Bureau utilizes two different numbering systems for the decennial Census: FIPS codes and GICS codes. FIPS, an acronym for Federal Information Processing Standards, is the standard geographic coding scheme used by all federal agencies. FIPS codes are unique identification numbers; think of them as Social Security numbers for geographic entities. They are assigned by the National Institute of Standards and Technology (NIST), formerly known as the National Bureau of Standards. The GICS system (Geographic Identification Code Scheme) is devised by the Bureau itself. The GICS system also assigns "Descriptive Codes" to certain entities to classify them by size or type. GICS numbers are generally referred to as "Census codes."

The NIST assigns FIPS numbers in such a way that most geographic entities within a particular state will appear in a single alphabetical list. For example, FIPS numbers are assigned in alphabetical sequence for Places and County Subdivisions, even though they represent two different Summary Levels. The Census Bureau assigns GICS codes so that entities appear in alphabetical order according to Summary Levels within state or regional hierarchies.

Both code structures vary in length: FIPS codes range from two digits to five digits; GICS codes run from one digit to four digits. In both cases, the codes for localities are only unique within a single state. For example, many states contain a Place or County Subdivision whose FIPS code is 65000. The codes become unique nationwide by adding the two-digit state code as a preface to the locality's five-digit code (e.g., 4865000 to represent a locality in Texas).

Depending on the type of Unit, the decennial Census uses the FIPS code, GICS code, or both. The Bureau utilizes FIPS codes for Congressional Districts, counties, and Metropolitan Areas. GICS codes are assigned to Census Divisions and Regions, Urbanized Areas, and Voting Districts. Both numbering systems are used to identify American Indian and Alaska Native Areas, County Subdivisions, and Places.

A complete guide to FIPS codes appears in a series of *FIPS Publications,* sold by the National Technical Information Service (NTIS). The complete listing of 1990 Census codes and relevant FIPS codes appears in the *1990 Geographic Identification Code Scheme,* released by the Bureau in CD-ROM and magnetic tape formats. The structure and format of Census codes and FIPS codes can also be found in the data dictionary portion of the technical documentation for the appropriate CD-ROM and magnetic tape products. Researchers who seek the appropriate codes for a specific geographic entity can utilize the GO software which comes with the CD-ROM version of most Summary Tape File products. Simply select the "Geographic Identifiers" section from the Table of Contents for the desired entity. (More will be said about the GO software in Chapter 8.)

The Bureau utilizes two different numbering systems for the decennial Census: FIPS codes and GICS codes.

Summary

Accurate geography is essential to the Bureau's enumeration and tabulation procedures; without good geography, the Census won't contain good data.

Geography is the cornerstone of the Census because its statistics are spatial—all Census data must be linked to a particular land area to have meaning. Accurate geography is essential to the Bureau's enumeration and tabulation procedures; without good geography, the Census won't contain good data. Likewise, proper understanding of Census geography is essential for correct interpretation and use of the numbers. Even the seemingly simple task of choosing the appropriate table in a printed Report (or the necessary Summary Level in a CD-ROM database) presumes familiarity with Census geography.

It's not unusual for Census users to feel overwhelmed by geographic concepts and terminology. After carefully reading this chapter, you may still feel hopelessly lost on certain topics. How can a Metropolitan Area have more than one Central City? When is a "place" not a Place? What's the difference between a Block Group and a Block Numbering Area? A Split Tract and a Divided Tract? An Urbanized Area and an Urban territory? A Minor Civil Division and an Incorporated Place? A town and a township? Rational people might conclude it's better to focus on the big picture and not sweat over the details. The problem then becomes how to decide which details are unimportant. The general concepts introduced at the beginning of the chapter affect all levels of Census geography, and are worth reviewing. Figures 6-1, 6-5, 6-16, and 6-17 may be helpful in sorting out key geographical relationships.

Serious users of Census data should consult the detailed geographic definitions found in the Bureau's *1990 Census of Population and Housing Guide: Part B. Glossary,* or in "Appendix A" of every print Report and CD-ROM File.

Beyond these suggestions, what generalities can be made? That's difficult to say. The difference between an Independent City and a Consolidated City is totally irrelevant if neither is encountered in your Census research. If you plan to concentrate on Census data in a single state or local area, then many types of geography will never crop up, and the numerous exceptions and differences among the states cease to be a concern.

Census Tip

An excellent way to become more comfortable with the concepts in this chapter is to put them in local perspective. By matching Census terminology with familiar local examples, Census geography will become clearer.

Unfortunately, if you need to compare data from a variety of states, the learning process becomes more complicated. Never assume that the principles governing your state's geography will apply elsewhere. In a particular state, is a town an Incorporated Place or an MCD? Do MCDs in that state serve as general-purpose governments or is their role more limited? Are Places in the state autonomous from their surrounding MCDs, subordinate to them, or is the pattern mixed? Does the state even have MCDs, or does the Bureau assign CCD boundaries? As demonstrated throughout the chapter, rules and practices governing Statistical and Governmental Units vary considerably across the country. The geographic structure of an unfamiliar state can be quite baffling without careful study. The comparisons listed in Figures 6-10 and 6-11 summarize some of the major differences among the states. For detailed comparisons, consult *A Guide to State and Local Census Geography,* published jointly in 1993 by the Bureau and the Association of Public Data Users. It provides concise descriptions of the geographic entities found in each state, together with explanations of their legal relationships to one another within the state.

All Census publications are careful to identify the type of geographic unit for every cited entity. The listings in Figure 6-13 provide a good example: Oxford County, Bethel town, Lincoln plantation, and so on. Even longtime residents of an area can make such erroneous assumptions as mistaking a well-known CDP for an Incorporated Place. Sometimes a place name itself can be confusing. For example, many entities with "Village" in their name are not villages at all; if Jones Village is actually a township, Census publications will identify it as "Jones Village township." (This explains the apparent redundancy of a designation such as "Junction City city.") Accurate and consistent labelling of geographic entities is a hallmark of all Census products.

Another suggestion is to use printed Census Reports to compare hierarchical and alphabetical listings covering the same localities. Tracing the indentations in a hierarchical table is an excellent way to identify the relationships among specific entities. Tables appearing in CD-ROM products do not show indentations; instead, numeric Summary Level codes are assigned to designate hierarchical relationships. Unless the user is familiar with the geographic structure of a state, or is comfortable with the numeric codes assigned to each Summary Level, it may make sense to consult a print Report before using the corresponding CD-ROM. Likewise, hierarchical tables are often helpful for showing component parts of an larger entity, as seen in Figure 6-6.

Little has been said in this chapter about Census maps. The Bureau produces innumerable maps, as separate map sheets and as appendices to printed data products; both types will be discussed in Chapter 9. It probably goes without saying that maps are the best way to verify the boundaries of a geographic entity. Careful map reading can also shed light on split geographies and other geographic relationships in a particular state.

Census Tip

Individual Census Tracts, BNAs, Block Groups, and Blocks are not given unique names; they are identified solely by number. The only way to determine the boundaries of these smaller Summary Levels is to consult an appropriate Census map.

Finally, it is useful to remember rules of thumb when dealing with Census geography, but beware of exceptions to the rules. For example, boroughs are Incorporated Places, except for Alaska and New York. Metropolitan Areas with population greater than one million are called CMSAs, yet political leaders in some eligible MAs have declined to adopt the CMSA designation. These, and similar exceptions can cause unexpected problems for the Census user.

Let's revisit a question posed early in the chapter: Must Census geography be so confusing? Perhaps not. Certain aspects of the Bureau's geographic structure result from the inherent space limitations of printed Reports. To save space in prior Censuses, the Bureau was forced to emphasize some geographies over others, and responded by creating somewhat artificial distinctions. CD-ROM products have changed this for the 1990 Census, with the same detail reported for almost all geographic Summary Levels. Alas, many old rules are firmly entrenched in Census procedures. The proliferation of misleading terminology probably could be simplified by the Bureau, given a bit more thought. Nevertheless, as this chapter has attempted to explain, there are reasons behind the complexity in most cases. The more you use Census publications, the more familiar you'll become with the Bureau's geography. Believe it or not, much of this will become second nature if you use the Census regularly.

it is useful to remember rules of thumb when dealing with Census geography, but beware of exceptions to the rules.

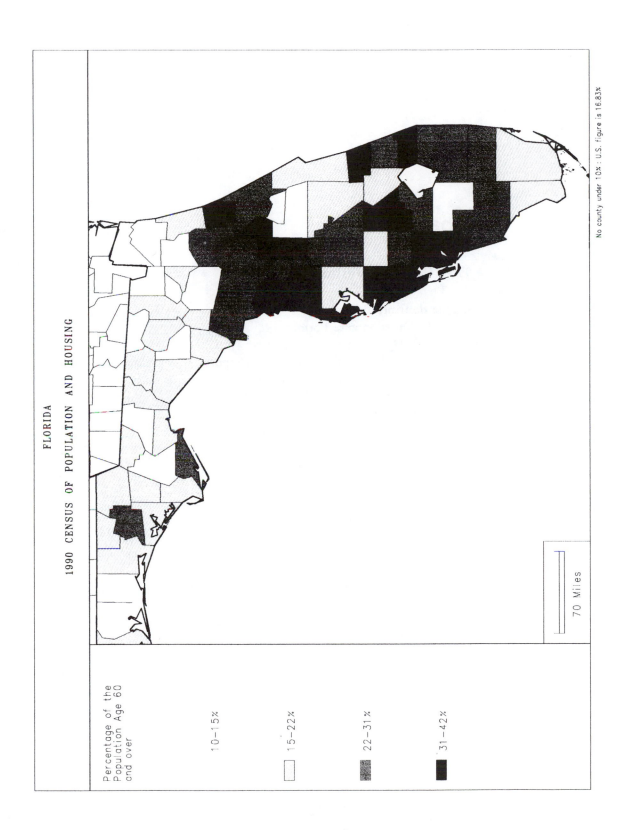

FLORIDA

1990 CENSUS OF POPULATION AND HOUSING

Percentage of the
Population Age 60
and over

10-15%

15-22%

22-31%

31-42%

70 Miles

No county under 10% : U.S. figure is 16.83%

Figure 6-18
Example of thematic map produced from 1990 Census data using commercial GIS software

Chapter 7

1990 Census Questionnaire

1990 Census Questionnaire

ALL CENSUS DATA flow from the questions asked on the Short and Long Forms, so Questionnaire content is a logical starting point for understanding the meaning of Census data. This chapter begins with a brief section providing background information on the Questionnaire. The remainder of the chapter explores each Item on the Questionnaire, describing its subject matter, the response categories, any changes from the 1980 Questionnaire, the main purpose or intent of the question, and the decades during which a question of this type has appeared on the Census Form. Readers may wish to refer to the actual text of the 1990 Questionnaire and Instructions, reproduced in Appendix C.

Questionnaire Background

The following sections introduce the basic Questionnaire format, compare significant differences between the 1980 and 1990 Forms, and discuss additional questions which were tested for 1990 but not used.

Questionnaire Format

The actual title of the 1990 Census Questionnaire is the *Official 1990 U.S. Census Form*. The Short Form version contains seven population questions and seven housing questions. The Long Form version contains the Short Form questions, plus 26 additional population questions and 19 additional housing questions. The Long Form was sent to a sample of the total population. Both versions include detailed instructions to respondents.

The Bureau refers to each numbered question as a Census Item. Population questions are identified numerically (Item 2, Item 12, etc.), while housing questions are designated by the letter H, then a number (Item H6, etc.). Certain Items are subdivided into related parts (Items 24a and 24b).

On both the Short and Long Forms, population questions appear first, followed by housing questions. Population questions

Why not handle all numeric questions with multiple-choice responses?

Standardized response categories limit the Bureau's ability to perform numeric calculations. Write-in responses allow the Bureau to tabulate data using various numeric increments, and to recast data in different forms. Write-in numbers also offer the capability to calculate more precise medians, means, and quartile values. With no reporting of discrete values, tabulations would reflect only those few choices specified on the Questionnaire.

Several Items on the 1990 Questionnaire are not intended for tabulation, but are included for purposes of identification, definition, or screening.

describe the characteristics and relationships of individual persons, while Housing questions describe the Housing Unit itself. This distinction is blurred in some cases because a housing question can pertain to the Household (all persons living in the Housing Unit.) For example, Vehicles Availability (Item H13) is a housing question because it counts the total number of vehicles owned by anyone in the Household, and is not attributed to specific individuals. Similarly, Year Moved In (Item H8) pertains to the Householder, but the question is designed to measure housing turnover.

Respondents must use a black lead pencil to complete the Questionnaire. Most Items direct the respondent to fill in an answer bubble called a FOSDIC circle. (The black rectangles appearing throughout the *Official Form* direct the FOSDIC equipment to the sections of the form which must be scanned.) Certain Items include boxes for write-in responses.

Items requiring numeric answers are handled in one of three ways. Some provide multiple-choice responses listing different number ranges (e.g., $20,000 to $24,999; $25,000 to $29,999). Examples include Items dealing with Income, Contract Rent, and Housing Value. A second method, used only for Items 5a and 5b (covering Age and Year of Birth), ask respondents to "bubble in" each digit in the number. Other questions, such as the Items on Utilities Costs (H20), require write-in responses.

Several Items on the 1990 Questionnaire are not intended for tabulation, but are included for purposes of identification, definition, or screening. The entire first page of the *Official 1990 U.S. Census Form* is devoted to a single two-part identification question. **Household Composition (Item 1a)** asks the respondent to list the names of every person living in that Housing Unit on April 1, 1990. Detailed instructions describe who should be counted as a Household member. This question serves several purposes. First, it explains the Census concept of Household and encourages the respondent to include nonfamily Household members, such as boarders, who might otherwise be overlooked. Second, it requires respondents to identify each Household member by name, enabling Enumerators or other Bureau employees to conduct necessary follow-up activities more easily. Individual names of Household members have been recorded in every Census since 1850.

Place of Usual Residence (Item 1b) identifies any Housing Units comprised entirely of residents whose usual address is elsewhere. As discussed in Chapter 5, such Housing Units are counted as Vacant, even though they are inhabited at the time of the Census. This question safeguards against a double-count of people who maintain more than one address.

Related questions are asked as part of the Housing Census. The **Coverage Screener**

(Item H1) is a two-part question which asks whether the respondent is unsure of any answers given on Item 1. **Item H1a** asks whether the respondent omitted anyone from the list of Household members who might be part of the Household. **Item H1b** asks whether anyone was included who might not belong based upon Census guidelines. Both parts require respondents to write the person's name and the reason they are unsure. Several examples of atypical residency (a newborn baby still at the hospital, a visitor staying in the Household temporarily) are provided to clarify the question's intent. Because Census residency guidelines are complex and difficult to interpret, Item H1 enables Bureau editors to verify that Household members have been identified correctly. Items 1 and H1 are asked of 100% of the population. Both are designed as coverage improvement questions. Taken together, they ensure the Bureau misses as few people as possible, and that everyone is counted in the correct location. To guarantee confidentiality, personal names are not entered into the Basic Record Tapes.

Several other screening questions are asked. The **Age Screener (Item 16)** asks each person whether he or she was born before April 1, 1975. Item 16 appears on the Questionnaire because all subsequent population questions (Items 17 through 33) are limited to persons 15 years of age or older. The **Value and Rent Screener (Item H5)** is a two-part question which enables the Bureau to create more appropriate measures of Housing Value and Contract Rent by excluding certain types of property from the calculations. **Property Size (Item H5a)** asks whether a single-Unit house or mobile home sits on ten or more acres of property. **Business Residence (Item H5b)** asks whether a business or medical office is located on the property. By excluding business residences and large real estate parcels from certain calculations of Housing Value or Contract Rent, the Bureau can provide a more realistic picture of housing finances for typical single-Unit homes. The Business Residence question was first asked in 1940,

while the Property Size screener has appeared on every Census since 1960.

 Census Tip

In Census tabulations, "Value of *Specified* Owner-Occupied and For-Sale Housing Units" excludes mobile homes, multi-Unit buildings, Business Residences, and single Units located on ten acres or more. Condominiums are included in this tabulation only if they are single-Unit detached buildings or single-Unit attached structures (e.g., townhouses). In most Census publications, Value of mobile homes is reported separately. Contract Rent and Gross Rent of *Specified* Renter-Occupied Units exclude single-Unit homes on ten or more acres.

1990 Questionnaire Changes

Most Census users will never know how close the 1990 Questionnaire came to being deeply slashed. In keeping with the provisions of the Paperwork Reduction Act and its amendments, the U.S. Office of Management and Budget had recommended a vast reduction in the number of questions proposed by the Bureau. The OMB intended to eliminate approximately half of the sample questions, and downgrade many of the complete-count questions to sample status. The agency further recommended that the sampling rate be significantly reduced. As described in Chapter 3, vocal opposition of Census users across the country, together with the subsequent intervention of Congressional leaders, preserved the integrity of the 1990 Questionnaire. The *Official 1990 Census Form* is fundamentally similar to its 1980 counterpart—few questions are new, and few existing questions have been deleted.

Virtually every Questionnaire Item experienced some change in wording, whether

---

By excluding business residences and large real estate parcels from certain calculations of Housing Value or Contract Rent, the Bureau can provide a more realistic picture of housing finances for typical single-Unit homes.

The *Official 1990 Census Form* is fundamentally similar to its 1980 counterpart—few questions are new, and few existing questions have been deleted.

those revisions appeared in the question it-self, the response categories, or the accompa-nying instructions. Many changes merely updated relevant date ranges or dollar values to reflect the effects of inflation and the passage of time. Others were designed to make wording more understandable. Figure 7-1 lists the 1990 Items which underwent little or no change. The list distinguishes between Items which are essentially the same as they were in 1980 and Items with minor wording changes or updates. More than half of all 1990 Census Items fall into these two categories.

Certain changes were more subtle, affect-ing only the scope of the Universe to be counted. For example, a variety of 1980 housing questions applied only to what was then termed Year-Round Housing Units. Included in this category were Items relating to Boarded-Up Units, Duration of Vacancy, Plumbing and Kitchen facilities, Water Sup-ply, and Sewage Disposal. For 1990, these questions pertain to all Housing Units.

The following discussion summarizes the most significant changes to the 1990 Ques-tionnaire. Throughout the chapter, other differences are described on a question-by-question basis.

New Questions and New Response Categories

Much of the new material for 1990 reflects the Bureau's concerns for measuring shifting social and economic patterns. Some changes were implemented by adding new response categories or by revising definitions, as shown in Figure 7-2. Changes in response catego-ries may seem minor, but they allow the Bureau to capture important new informa-tion. Perhaps the most noteworthy changes involve new realities in Household compo-sition, such as the addition of Unmarried Partner, stepchild, grandchild, and foster child as relationship options in Item 2. The ques-tion on Educational Attainment formerly asked the highest grade attended; on the 1990 Questionnaire, Item 12 asks the high-

QUESTIONS UNCHANGED FROM 1980 TO 1990

Comment Category:

A. Question essentially the same.
B. Minor updating of response categories or question wording.

Population Questions

Item	Subject	Comment Category
1	Coverage Screening	A
3	Sex	A
6	Marital Status	A
8	Place of Birth	B
13	Ancestry	B
14	Prior Residence	B
15	Language Spoken at Home	B
16	Age Screening	B
18	Work Disability	A
20	Children Ever Born	A
21	Work Status/Hours Worked Last Week	A
22	Place of Work	A
25	Temporary Absence from Work	A
26	Looking for Work/Available to Accept	A
27	Year Last Worked	B
31	Work Experience	A
33	Total Income	A

Housing Questions

Item	Subject	Comment Category
H1	Coverage Screening	B
H3	Number of Rooms	A
H5	Value Screening	B
H6	Housing Value	B
H7a	Monthly Rent	B
H8	Year Moved In	B
H11	Complete Kitchen Facilities	B
H12	Telephone in Unit	B
H15	Source of Water	A
H16	Sewage Disposal	A
H19	Farm Residence	B
H21	Real Estate Taxes	A
H23a	Presence of First Mortgage	A
H23c	Mortgage Payment Includes Taxes	A

Figure 7-1

est grade completed and the degrees earned. Item 32 (Sources of Income) specifies a new category for income from pension plans. Solar energy is a new response category for Type of Heating Fuel (Item H14). To clarify Questionnaire wording on Housing Tenure, Item H4 now asks residents to specify whether

QUESTIONS REVISED FOR 1990

Type of Change Made:

A. Change in response categories.
B. Substantial change in wording.
C. Change in guidelines or definition.
D. Downgraded to sample question.
E. Portions of Item upgraded to 100% question.

Population Questions

Item	Subject	Type of Change
2	Household Relationship	A
4	Race	A B C
5	Age	A
7	Hispanic Origin	A B C
9	Citizenship	A C
10	Year of Entry	A
11	School Enrollment	A
12	Educational Attainment	A
17	Veteran Status	A B
23	Journey to Work	A
28	Industry	A
29	Occupation	C
30	Class of Worker	A
32	Sources of Income	A

Housing Questions

Item	Subject	Type of Change
H2	Type of Structure	A B E
H4	Tenure	A
H9	Number of Bedrooms	C
H10	Complete Plumbing Facilities	A D
H13	Availability of Vehicles	A
H14	Cost of Heating Fuel	A
H17	Year Structure Built	A
H18	Condominium Status	D
H22	Property Insurance	B
H23b	Monthly Mortgage Payment	B C
H23d	Mortgage Payment Includes Insurance	B
H24	Subordinate Mortgage	B

Figure 7-2

A few questions from 1980 did not appear on the 1990 Questionnaire.

barriers to working or to using public transportation. In 1990, a new question (Item 19) asks whether the disability prevents the person from caring for him- or herself in the home or in leaving the home. A new question on Departure Time for Work (Item 24a) enhances the Bureau's ability to report commuting information. The 1980 question asked only the amount of travel time; the added Item for 1990 captures information about peak commuting hours. The third new population question is Item 17c, Total Years of Active-Duty Military Service. The Bureau adopted this enhancement to meet program needs of the Veterans Administration.

To gather more specific data on housing costs, new housing questions deal with Subordinate Mortgages Payments (Item H24b), Mobile Home Shelter Costs (Item H26), and Condominium Fees (Item H25). Item H7b, designed to measure the characteristics of elderly persons living in congregate housing, asks whether rent payments include the cost of meals.

Deletions and Status Downgrades

A few questions from 1980 did not appear on the 1990 Questionnaire. Several were deleted because data users evinced little interest in keeping them. Others were axed during extensive negotiations with the OMB. The government's goal was to keep the cost of data collection and tabulation, as well as the burden on respondents, to a minimum. Deleted Items consisted of five population questions and eight housing questions. Figure 7-4 provides a complete list of the deleted Items and their subject matter.

Two of the canceled questions were replaced by others with a similar purpose. The disability question relating to public transportation was replaced by a broader question dealing with respondents' ability to care for themselves in the home and to leave the home. The sample question on Number of Units at This Address duplicated much of the data gathered by the complete-count

they own their homes "free and clear" or with a mortgage.

Seven Items, listed in Figure 7-3, are completely new to the 1990 Questionnaire. None represent dramatic changes in the types of data collected by the Bureau. Instead, they are designed to capture more detailed information on traditional characteristics. In 1980, questions about handicapped individuals asked whether people's disabilities presented

NEW QUESTIONS FOR 1990

Item Number	Subject	Question Type
Population Questions		
17c	Total Years of Active-Duty Military Service	Sample
24a	Departure Time for Work	Sample
19	Disability: Activity Limitation	Sample
Housing Questions		
H7b	Meals Included with Rent (Congregate Housing)	100%
H24b	Monthly Payments on Subordinate Mortgages	Sample
H25	Condominium Fees	Sample
H26	Mobile Home Shelter Costs	Sample

Figure 7-3

question on Building Type. A third question, designed to identify boarders living in Housing Units separate from their landlords, was dropped because it proved to be unreliable. Rewording of Item H1 helped ameliorate the loss of this question.

The remaining questions were dropped to make room for new questions. They were targeted for deletion because they lacked legislative mandates, and because strong program needs could not be identified. In the case of energy-related questions (fuel for cooking, fuel for hot water, type of heating equipment, and detailed car pool arrangements), shifting priorities played a role in their deletion. In other instances, the Bureau found little support from data users to save the jeopardized Items. In the case of Marital History, existing data from other surveys were deemed adequate for most users' needs.

> **The remaining questions were dropped to make room for new questions. They were targeted for deletion because they lacked legislative mandates, and because strong program needs could not be identified.**

NEW IN '90

The deletion of certain housing questions from the 1990 Questionnaire has a more profound impact than corresponding deletions of population Items. Useful measures of housing quality or value–the presence of elevators, air conditioning, and total number of bathrooms–were removed at the behest of the OMB. The most controversial of the housing deletions was the question about Type of Heating Equipment, which had received broad support from data users.

A more subtle change, shown earlier in Figure 7-2, is the "demotion" of certain complete-count questions to the sample Questionnaire. Two Items were affected in this way: Condominium Status and Complete Plumbing Facilities.

Questions Tested But Not Used

The Questionnaire planning process (described in Chapter 3) involves input from numerous sources. Many organizations lobby the Bureau to add new Items to the Questionnaire, but unless petitioners can demonstrate how the proposed question relates to government programs or serves broad public needs, such requests are not considered seriously. Each decade, for example, the Bureau receives requests to collect data on religious affiliation, types of appliances owned, and number of pets in the Household, but such questions cannot be justified by legislative or program needs. However, many new questions recommended by the Interagency Working Groups, the Federal Agency Council, and other planning organizations are explored in a variety of field tests.

New Items for 1990, such as Meals Included in Rent (Item H7b) and Departure Time for Work (24a), underwent rigorous testing before appearing on the *Official Census Form*. Other questions were tested in various formats, but never appeared on the final Questionnaire. Many of these were designed to collect more detailed information on existing Census topics.

The Bureau tested a variety of Items relating to persons holding more than one job, including questions about the Occupations and Industries involved. One test Item asked multiple job holders the number of hours worked at the principal job. By subtracting this response from the total hours worked at all jobs, the Bureau could tabulate the number of hours worked at second or third jobs. These questions were eventually rejected because they were too complex, taking up substantial space on the Questionnaire.

1980 QUESTIONS DROPPED FROM 1990 QUESTIONNAIRE

Population Questions

QUESTION: Number of Weeks Looking for Work in Reference Year.
PURPOSE: Collect data on "Discouraged Workers."
WHY DROPPED: New in 1980. Data of poor quality, not useful.

QUESTION: Detailed Question on Car Pool Arrangements.
PURPOSE: Measured whether car pooler was driver, shared driver, or passenger.
WHY DROPPED: New in 1980. No longer needed.

QUESTION: Marital History.
PURPOSE: Measured number of times married, whether first spouse died, and date of first marriage.
WHY DROPPED: Existing survey data sufficient. No need for data at small levels of geography.

QUESTION: Activity Five Years Ago.
PURPOSE: Whether respondent was in school, Armed Forces, or working at a job.
WHY DROPPED: No demonstrated need.

QUESTION: Transportation Disability.
PURPOSE: Indicated whether respondent had disability which prevented use of public transportation.
WHY DROPPED: Replaced by new question on activity limitation.

Housing Questions

QUESTION: Independent Access to Unit from outside.
PURPOSE: Defined whether respondent lived in separate Housing Unit.
WHY DROPPED: Did not provide reliable data. Replaced by new wording to Item H1.

QUESTION: Number of Units at This Address.
PURPOSE: Captured data on total Units in apartment buildings.
WHY DROPPED: Replaced by 100% question on type of building.

QUESTION: Number of Stories in Building.
PURPOSE: General measure of housing conditions.
WHY DROPPED: Limited need; no strong support among data users.

QUESTION: Presence of Elevator.
PURPOSE: Measure of housing quality.
WHY DROPPED: Limited need; no strong support among data users.

QUESTION: Number of Bathrooms.
PURPOSE: Additional measure of Housing Value; also measured Bathrooms per person.
WHY DROPPED: Limited need; no strong support among data users.

QUESTION: Presence of Air Conditioning.
PURPOSE: Measure of energy usage and housing quality.
WHY DROPPED: Limited need; no strong support among data users.

QUESTION: Availability and Type of Heating Equipment.
PURPOSE: Measure of energy usage and housing quality.
WHY DROPPED: Received broad support from data users, but dropped in compromise with OMB.

QUESTION: Fuel for Cooking; Fuel for Hot Water.
PURPOSE: Measure of energy usage.
WHY DROPPED: No longer necessary.

Figure 7-4

An expanded version of Means of Travel to Work was tested. Rather than asking only the means used most, this version asked respondents to differentiate between principal means and other methods. Results proved unreliable. As described in Chapter 5, the Bureau also tested a variety of questions to capture data on multiple residence. These proved unreliable and too complex.

Test questions about social characteristics included Place of Parents' Birth, and Vocational Education. Strong support was demonstrated for the Item on Parent's Place of Birth (which had been a Census question from 1880 through 1970), but room was available on the Questionnaire for only one question on Ancestry. Three different versions of a Vocational Education question were tested, including one which specified certificates or diplomas from programs lasting three or more months. Results were very unreliable.

Disability questions underwent extensive testing, resulting in a new question about Activity Limitations (Item 19). Questions relating to children's disabilities, the prevalence of specific conditions, the ability to drive, and the main cause of disability were explored but not used.

Test Censuses included several new questions on Source of Income, including separate categories for alimony and unemployment insurance. Of these, the query about Pension Income (Item 32g) was the only one to appear on the 1990 Questionnaire. The Bureau also tested questions on sources of Noncash Benefits, such as food stamps, and health and retirement benefits provided by employers or unions.

Test Censuses explored three housing topics. The most extensive tests involved Household equipment. One question asked how many working smoke detectors were present in the Unit. Another expanded the categories for Vehicles Available, adding motorcycles, mopeds, campers, and heavy trucks. None of these Items received strong support from users. Other test questions investigated the number of persons living in public housing or receiving public rent subsidies. Two Items explored new methods of measuring housing quality. One asked about the presence of holes in the floor; the other asked whether a furnace or other source of heating had broken down for six consecutive hours or more during the winter months. Similar questions are asked in the Bureau's biennial *American Housing Survey*.

Test questions failed to make the *Official Census Form* for various reasons. In some cases, results proved too unreliable in a self-administered survey. For example, respondents would answer differently in a follow-up interview than when they received the Questionnaire. In other cases, the topic was too complex, requiring extensive multi-part questions to gather meaningful data. For the most part, the Bureau abandoned proposed questions for lack of space. For every new question, an existing Item would most likely be deleted. Without strong support from data users, new Items were not approved.

Population Questions

The population portion of the Census consists of seven questions asked of 100% of the population, plus an additional 26 sample questions. The subject matter can be divided into three broad areas: general demographic data, social characteristics, and economic characteristics.

General Demographic Characteristics

The general portion of the Population Census asks the respondent to identify every member of the Household and describe fundamental demographic characteristics of each one. Figure 7-5 summarizes the content of these questions and lists their Item Numbers on the Questionnaire. General characteristics include Relationship to Householder, Age, Sex, Marital Status, Residence Five

Disability questions underwent extensive testing, resulting in a new question about Activity Limitations (Item 19).

The population portion of the Census consists of seven questions asked of 100% of the population, plus an additional 26 sample questions.

**POPULATION QUESTIONS:
GENERAL DEMOGRAPHIC DATA**

Personal Characteristics

Item 2	Relationship to Householder	Short Form
Item 3	Sex	Short Form
Item 5	Age	Short Form
Item 6	Marital Status	Short Form
Item 14	Residence Five Years Ago	Long Form
Item 20	Children Ever Born	Long Form

Race and Ethnic Origin

Item 4	Race	Short Form
Item 7	Spanish/Hispanic Origin	Short Form
Item 13	Ancestry	Long Form

Figure 7-5

Separate response categories now enable Census users to better analyze Family composition, including the prevalence of "blended families."

Years Ago, and Children Ever Born. Three additional questions cover ethno-cultural background: Race, Hispanic Origin, and Ancestry.

Personal Characteristics

Questions dealing with respondents' personal characteristics represent a mixture of complete-count and sample Items. Residence Five Years Ago and Children Ever Born are sample questions. All others are 100% Items.

Relationship to Householder (Item 2) is asked of every person in the Household except Person 1, who is the Householder. The question asks how the Household member is related to Person 1, and provides responses for Relatives and Nonrelatives. Seven response categories are listed for Relatives:

- ▸ husband/wife
- ▸ natural-born or adopted son/daughter
- ▸ stepson/stepdaughter
- ▸ brother/sister
- ▸ father/mother
- ▸ grandchild
- ▸ other

Respondents are instructed to write down a specific relationship when "other" is selected. Two changes in response categories appear in

the 1990 Questionnaire. For 1980, grandchildren were tabulated under the "other" category, and stepchildren were counted together with natural and adopted children. Separate response categories now enable Census users to better analyze Family composition, including the prevalence of "blended families."

Item 2 provides four additional categories for Nonrelatives: roomer, boarder, or foster child; housemate or roommate; Unmarried Partner; and other Nonrelative. Foster child was added to the list in 1990 to reinforce the Bureau's definition of foster children as Nonrelatives. As discussed in Chapter 5, Unmarried Partner is a new concept for 1990, intended to collect data on cohabiting couples. The 1980 Questionnaire employed a single category for "housemate/roommate."

Questions about Household Relationship have been asked on every Census since 1880. Because the Enumeration process is Household-based, a question of this type is the only means of capturing data on Families. Results are tabulated to show the various types of Household and Family composition introduced in Chapter 5.

Sex (Item 3) is perhaps the most straightforward question on the *Official Form*, requiring no accompanying instructions. Male and Female are the only response categories. Gender is a fundamental demographic characteristic, considered an important part of a person's identity. The presence of Item 3 on the Questionnaire also enables the Bureau to cross-tabulate other characteristics by gender, including Income and Occupation. A question on Sex has been asked on every Census.

Age (Item 5) measures each person's age at last birthday and their year of birth. In both cases, respondents fill in the appropriate FOSDIC circles for each digit in the number. Accompanying instructions explain that infants under the age of one year should be designated "00" years old.

Age is a fundamental component of personal identity. By collecting data about Age, the Bureau can measure social and economic differences by age groups. This allows Census users to plan programs for the elderly, forecast future demands on the Social Security and health care systems, assess needs for current and future preschool programs, and similar age-dependent types of analyses. A variety of special tabulations in Census products provide data about particular age groups. For example, many tables present data on the characteristics of persons age 65 or over who live alone. An Age question has been asked since 1790, though early Censuses captured data in age ranges rather than individual years of age.

Marital Status (Item 6) identifies persons as Now Married, Widowed, Divorced, Separated, or Never Married. Individuals whose only marriage was legally annulled are instructed to indicate Never Married. Marital status is another basic demographic characteristic, providing an important measure of changes in living arrangements over time. A question of this type has been asked on every Census since 1880.

 Census Tip

Although the question is asked of every person in the Household, data on marital status are tabulated only for persons age 15 years or older. Because married children under the age of 15 are excluded from the tabulation Universe, they are neither Married or Never Married--they are simply not counted in these categories.

Residence Five Years Ago (Item 14) is a two-part question which identifies the location of each Household member's prior residence, if any. Item 14a asks whether the person lived in this house or apartment on April 1, 1985. Response categories are "Yes,"

NEW IN '90

The 1980 Questionnaire required respondents to indicate month of birth as well as year. Omission of this response category for 1990 resulted in certain inaccuracies relating to age data, especially for children under one year in age.

"No," and "Born after April 1, 1985." Individuals in the latter category are excluded from the tabulation. If the answer is "Yes," Item 14b instructs respondents to write the state or country of prior residence. For prior locations within the United States, the county and city or town must also be indicated, as well as whether the address was situated within that town or city's legal limits. Instructions for Item 14 are lengthy, reflecting the importance of collecting specific data on this topic. Persons who moved away from the present address and subsequently returned are instructed to answer "Yes" (lived at same address). Persons now living in a different apartment within the same building are instructed to indicate "No" (different address).

Item 14 is designed to collect data on migration patterns in the United States. By asking for specific locations, this Item enables demographers to analyze state-to-state and county-to-county population movement, as well as migration between cities and suburbs or Urban and Rural areas. Migration data are important for analyzing the direction of population flow. If an area experiences significant population growth, demographers and planners can determine the locations from which new entrants have come. Conversely, areas which are losing population can be studied to determine the destinations of people who are leaving. Migration data are an essential component for intercensal population estimates and for projections of future population changes. Data files from the U.S. Internal Revenue Service provide statistical information on internal migration, but only the Census offers detailed characteristics of recent movers. A question relating to

Item 14 is designed to collect data on migration patterns in the United States. By asking for specific locations, this Item enables demographers to analyze state-to-state and county-to-county population movement, as well as migration between cities and suburbs or Urban and Rural areas.

NEW IN '90

The word "Race" appeared nowhere in the wording of the 1980 question on this topic. Respondents were simply given a list of racial categories from which to choose. Consequently, the presence of country-specific racial categories caused confusion among some respondents, who wrote the name of an Ancestry group under the "Other" category. The Bureau ameliorated this problem by reintroducing the word into the language of the 1990 question.

Item 20 provides a measurement of Fertility, which is an important characteristic for the study of trends in population change.

prior residence has been asked on every Census since 1940. The 1950 question specified place of residence one year prior to the Reference Date; all other Censuses measured migration over five-year spans.

Children Ever Born (Item 20) asks women in the Household how many babies they have ever borne. Thirteen FOSDIC categories are provided, ranging from None to Twelve or More. Respondents are instructed to count any children who died shortly after birth or who no longer live in the Household. Excluded from the total are miscarriages and stillborn children, as well as adopted, foster, or step children. This question is asked of all women age 15 years or older, regardless of marital status.

Item 20 provides a measurement of Fertility, which is an important characteristic for the study of trends in population change. It enables the Bureau to publish comparable Fertility rates by Age, Income level, Educational Attainment, and other social or economic characteristics. Data for small levels of geography enable demographers and health officials to compare Fertility trends from one local area to another. The United Nations also requires member-nations to report Fertility data on a recurring basis. Children Ever Born was asked in Censuses from 1890 through 1910, and on every Questionnaire since 1940.

Race and Ethnic Origin

Conceptual differences among Race, Hispanic Origin, and Ancestry are discussed at length in Chapter 5. The following section briefly describes the three Questionnaire Items dealing with these concepts. Ancestry is a sample question; the remaining two are asked of the entire population.

Race (Item 4) provides response categories for White; Black; American Indian, Eskimo, Aleut, Inuit; and Other Race; as well as ten categories for various Asian or Pacific Islander groups, including a new category for "Other API." The Item provides spaces for three write-in responses: Indian tribe, Other API, and Other Race. The question instructs respondents to circle a single Race the person considers himself or herself to be. As discussed in Chapter 5, Item 4 underwent significant testing and evaluation before the final version was accepted. Both the question and the accompanying instructions were

Q&A

Why is Marital Status asked separately from Household Relationship?

Item 6 is the only means of collecting data on the status of persons who are not married. Also remember that Item 1 only indicates a marital relationship between the Householder and another member of the Household. As described in Chapter 5, other married persons can live within the Household, either as members of a Subfamily or as Unrelated Individuals. Finally, if the Householder's spouse does not list that address as the Place of Usual Residence (i.e., spouses living apart from one another), Item 1 would fail to recognize the Householder's marital status.

reworded substantially, and new categories were provided for Inuit and Other API, including a write-in response for the latter.

In addition to being a common demographic variable in the United States, and a fundamental component of personal description, Race is a required Census topic. It is mandated by numerous civil rights laws, including the Voting Rights Act and P.L. 94-171 itself. Racial data are used in legislative redistricting, compliance with Affirmative Action guidelines, and in monitoring economic and social disparities among racial groups. Some version of this Item has appeared on every Census.

Spanish/Hispanic Origin (Item 7) identifies individuals who come from a Spanish-speaking country or are descended from persons who came from such a country. The question is asked of all persons, regardless of Race, Ancestry, or citizenship. (The difference between Race and Hispanic Origin is explained in Chapter 5.) Item 7 provides the following response categories:

- ▸ No (not Spanish/Hispanic)
- ▸ Yes, Mexican, Mexican-Am., Chicano
- ▸ Yes, Puerto Rican
- ▸ Yes, Cuban
- ▸ Yes, Other Spanish/Hispanic

Persons indicating the latter response are instructed to write the name of a specific Hispanic group, such as Salvadoran or Dominican.

Wording of Item 7 and its Instructions were revised for 1990, including the addition of a write-in category for Other Hispanic, and the provision of numerous examples. Wording emphasizes the requirement of all persons, including non-Hispanics, to answer this question. Item 7 is mandated by the Spanish Census Act (P.L. 94-311). It was first asked as a five-percent sample question in 1970, then became a complete-count question for 1980.

Ancestry (Item 13) collects data on individuals' roots or ethnic origin, generally based

POPULATION QUESTIONS: SOCIAL CHARACTERISTICS		
Birthplace, Citizenship, and Language		
Item 8	Place of Birth	Long Form
Item 9	Citizenship	Long Form
Item 10	Year of Entry	Long Form
Item 15	Language Spoken at Home	Long Form
Education		
Item 11	School Enrollment	Long Form
Item 12	Educational Attainment	Long Form
Disability		
Item 18	Work Disability	Long Form
18a	Work Limitation	
18b	Work Prevention	
Item 19	Activity Limitations	Long Form
19a	Mobility Outside the Home	
19b	Personal Care Limitation	
Military Service		
Item 17a	Veteran Status	Long Form
17b	Period of Service	Long Form
17c	Total Years of Service	Long Form

Figure 7-6

on ancestors' homeland(s) before arriving in the United States. Census definitions pertaining to Ancestry are introduced in Chapter 5. Wording of Item 13 was revised to incorporate the phrase "ethnic origin" and to provide additional examples. Instructions emphasize that religious affiliation is not an Ancestry category. Ancestry data from the Census is intended for use by any ethnic group seeking special consideration or redress under equal opportunity laws.

Ancestry was added as a new Census topic in 1980, to cover ethno-cultural groups not designated under Race or Hispanic Origin. Prior to 1980, partial data on ethnic origin was tabulated by summing responses to the questions on Place of Birth and Parent's Place of Birth. The resulting data measured first and second generation immigrants only. Questions pertaining to each parent's country of birth appeared on every Census from 1880 through 1970. A question about

Ancestry data from the Census is intended for use by any ethnic group seeking special consideration or redress under equal opportunity laws.

"mother tongue" (the language spoken during early childhood) was asked from 1920 through 1940, and for 1960 and 1970.

Social Characteristics

Another major grouping within the Population Census is broadly described as social characteristics. Figure 7-6 summarizes the content of these questions and lists their Item Numbers on the Questionnaire. Social characteristics cover the following subject areas: Birthplace, Citizenship, and Language; Education; Disability; and Military Service.

Birthplace, Citizenship, and Language

Four Questionnaire Items focus on characteristics of the foreign-born population. All Items in this category are sample questions.

Place of Birth (Item 8) is a write-in question asking the U.S. state or foreign country where each person was born. Census tabulations count people as Native or Foreign-Born. Country names used in answering Item 8 should reflect national boundaries at the time of the Census, not borders in existence when the person was born. Instructions urge respondents to answer as specifically as possible. For example, persons should indicate Scotland rather than United Kingdom, or Trinidad rather than West Indies. Respondents are instructed to distinguish between Ireland and Northern Ireland, South Korea and North Korea, etc. Place of Birth data provide useful information for analysis of Immigration policies. A question of this type has been asked on every Census since 1850.

Citizenship (Item 9) groups the nation's residents into two main categories, Citizens and Noncitizens. Citizens are further classified into one of five subcategories: born in the United States, born in a U.S. territory, born abroad of American parent or parents, and Naturalized Citizen. Although the Census distinguishes between Citizens and Noncitizens, no questions are asked regarding the legal status of Noncitizens. Collecting data on illegal aliens would be virtually impossible, and any attempt to do so would adversely effect overall response rates.

The 1980 version of this Item was asked only of the Foreign-Born population, assuming all Natives were citizens by birth. The 1990 version is asked of all persons in the Census sample, regardless of their Place of Birth. Results from Item 9 are combined with age data to conduct voter registration analysis. Citizenship data can also be used to measure the eligible population for government programs which limit participation to U.S. citizens only. A question relating to citizenship was asked on the Censuses of 1820, 1830, 1870, 1890 through 1930, and 1950. A citizenship question was asked in 1960, but only of New York State residents. The Item has appeared on every subsequent Census beginning with 1970.

For each person whose Place of Birth was outside the United States, **Year of Entry (Item 10)** asks when the person came to this country to stay. Persons who have entered the country more than once are instructed to indicate the most recent year. Because this Item also covers U.S. citizens born abroad,

NEW IN '90

Place of Birth instructions for the 1980 Census required respondents to indicate the mother's residence at time of birth. Post-Census evaluation determined that most respondents either misunderstood the 1980 instructions or disregarded them. Guidelines for 1990 require individuals to indicate the place where the birth actually occurred. Because Place of Birth is measured at the state or national level, this minor change in definition affects few individuals.

Collecting data on illegal aliens would be virtually impossible, and any attempt to do so would adversely effect overall response rates.

Place of Birth data provide useful information for analysis of Immigration policies.

the word "immigration" is not used. Ten response categories are provided, compared to the six given in 1980. The earliest period is "Before 1950;" the most recent is "1987 to 1990."

Census Tip

For the Foreign-Born population, Year of Entry measures migration occurring any time after the person's birth, as opposed to Prior Residence (Item 14), which measures recent migration only.

The detailed response categories for Item 10 allow demographers to identify different waves of immigration and to conduct more accurate cohort analysis when studying net migration. A question of this type appeared on Censuses from 1890 through 1930, and has been asked on every Census since 1970.

Language Spoken at Home (Item 15) is a three-part question about respondents' ability to speak English. **Item 15a** asks whether the person speaks a language other than English in the home. If the person does so sometimes or always, he or she is instructed to answer "Yes." If the person does not speak a foreign language, or knows a language but does not speak it in the home, the appropriate answer is "No." **Item 15b** asks foreign- language speakers to write the name of the language. If more than one non-English language is spoken in the home, respondents are instructed to choose the one used most. If two languages are spoken equal amounts, respondents are told to indicate the language learned first. **Item 15c** asks how well the person speaks English. The response categories are "Very Well," "Well," "Not Well," and "Not at All."

Item 15 is similar to a corresponding question asked in the 1980 Census, with a slight variation in the wording of one response category. In 1980, the wording was, "No, speaks only English." For 1990, the response simply reads, "No."

Language Spoken at Home is used to identify the number of people who have difficulty speaking English. Such information is especially important at the local level to help plan special education programs, design disaster preparedness plans, and provide language assistance to voters. With the exception of 1950, a question relating to spoken language has appeared on every Census since 1890. Ability to speak English was asked from 1890 through 1930 and again in 1980 and 1990. Respondents were asked to identify a language other than English on Questionnaires appearing in 1890, 1910, and from 1980 to date. A question about "mother tongue," defined as the language spoken during early childhood, was asked from 1920 through 1940, and again in 1960 and 1970.

Education

The Population Census lists two Education questions: School Enrollment and Educational Attainment. Both Items are sample questions.

School Enrollment (Item 11) measures the number of persons attending school at the time of the Census. The question asks whether the person has attended "regular school" at any time between February 1, 1990 and April 1. The Bureau's definition covers nursery school, kindergarten, elementary school, or any school or program leading to a high school diploma or college degree. Trade or business schools are excluded, as are employee training programs. Three response categories are offered: "No," "Yes, Public School or College," and "Yes, Private School or College." For 1980, the responses further divided private schools into church related and not church related. Legislative analysis for the 1990 Census indicate no program needs for data on church-affiliated schools, so this differentiation was dropped.

Item 11 is utilized in a variety of government funding programs, as well as for education planning. Results are particularly important for studying the characteristics of high school dropouts, and for identifying local areas with large numbers of dropouts. Questions about school enrollment have been asked on every Census since 1850.

Educational Attainment (Item 12) asks how much schooling a person has completed and the highest degree received. Seventeen response categories are given, from "No school completed" to "Doctorate." Item 12 represents a major departure from the manner in which this topic had been treated in the past. The 1980 Questionnaire asked the highest grade attended or the number of years of college attended, as opposed to degrees received. In keeping with this approach, the 1980 question provided responses for each year of school, from "Nursery School" through "Eight or More Years of College." The 1990 question does not list individual grades, but makes the distinction between school attended and school completed. For example, new categories state "Twelfth Grade, No Diploma" and "Some College, But No Degree." The response for "High School Graduate" also incorporates equivalency degrees, such as the GED. Categories are quite specific, including "Associate Degree--Occupational Program" and "Associate Degree--Academic Program."

> **Census Tip**
>
> Due to the significant changes made to the 1990 response categories for Item 12, data on Educational Attainment are considered more meaningful than in the past. However, the resulting statistics are not strictly comparable to numbers gathered in 1980, especially those relating to individuals who attended college.

Item 12 is used for human resource planning and Labor Force analysis. For example, relationships between Educational Attainment and Income can be studied. Data are tabulated for various age groups. Common reporting formats are "Age 18 and Older," "Age 25 and Older," and "Age 16 to 19." Questions on Educational Attainment have been asked on every Census since 1940. From 1840 through 1930, the Bureau simply asked respondents whether they could read and write.

Disability

The Disability portion of the Questionnaire underwent extensive testing for 1990. As a result, the Census now captures more detailed data about disabled persons than ever before. Both Disability Items are sample questions.

Work Disability (Item 18) is a two-part question concerning physical, mental, or other health conditions lasting six months or more which affect the person's ability to work. **Work Limitation (Item 18a)** asks whether this condition limits the amount or kind of work the person can perform. Accompanying guidelines define Work Limitation as a condition limiting either the choice of occupation or the amount of work which can be accomplished in a given amount of time. **Work Prevention (Item 18b)** asks whether the disability prevents the person from holding a job.

With one exception, Item 18 is similar to the corresponding question asked on the 1980 Questionnaire. The 1980 question included a third part which asked whether the disability limited or prevented the person from using public transportation. For 1990, this topic has been replaced by Item 19, described below.

Work Disability data are used to assess program needs in such areas as physical rehabilitation and vocational training, to enforce antidiscrimination laws, and to help the Veterans Administration plan its facilities. A question of this type has appeared on every Census since 1970. Related questions were asked on numerous Censuses in the nineteenth and early twentieth centuries. Deaf, dumb, or blind persons were tabulated from 1830 through 1890, and again in 1910.

Educational Attainment (Item 12) asks how much schooling a person has completed and the highest degree received.

The Census now captures more detailed data about disabled persons than ever before. Both Disability Items are sample questions.

Persons identified as "insane or idiotic" were counted from 1840 through 1890. "Maimed or crippled" persons were counted in 1880 and 1890, and the 1890 Census sought to identify persons afflicted with a chronic disease or illness.

Activity Limitations (Item 19) is a second two-part question concerning Disability. Item 19 deals with physical, mental, or other health conditions lasting six months or more which affect the person's personal activities. **Mobility Outside the Home (Item 19a)** asks whether the condition limits the person's ability to leave the home to shop, visit the doctor, or perform similar tasks. **Personal Care Limitation (Item 19b)** asks whether the condition affects the person's ability to take care of personal needs, such as bathing or dressing. Personal Care Limitation is defined loosely and includes conditions which cause the person to take additional time or exert extra effort to perform personal activities. Data on Activity Limitations are affected significantly by the self-identification principle. Item 19 is new for 1990.

Military Service

Military Service (Item 17) is a three-part question concerning service in the United States Armed Forces. This is a sample question. **Veteran Status (Item 17a)** asks adult respondents whether they have ever served on active military duty. Response categories were revised for 1990 to include the National Guard or military Reserves, and to differentiate between those currently serving and those serving in the past. Reserve and National Guard service counts only if the person was called up for active duty other than training. **Period of Service (Item 17b)** provides eight response categories for dates served, including the Vietnam era. Respondents are instructed to designate as many periods as applicable. A new question about **Total Years of Service (Item 17c)** asks respondents to indicate the total number of years served. It was added to the 1990 Questionnaire to

conform to statistics collected by the U.S. Veterans Administration (VA), and because certain benefits are limited to Veterans who have served a minimum of two years.

Although the VA compiles its own statistics, Item 17 appears on the Census Questionnaire to address the need for small-area data. Results from Item 17 are used primarily by the VA and Veterans' organizations to evaluate characteristics of their service population and to select sites for new facilities and programs. Item 17 is asked of persons age 15 or older, but the Bureau tabulates results only for respondents age 16 or older. A question relating to veterans has been asked on numerous Censuses. An Item in 1840 identified military pensioners, and questions in 1890 and 1910 focused on veterans of the Civil War. A more inclusive question about Veteran Status has appeared on every Census since 1930, but the Bureau published minimal data on this topic prior to 1960.

Economic Characteristics

The final portion of the Population Census deals with economic conditions of all Household members age 15 or older. Figure 7-7 summarizes the content of these questions and lists their Item Numbers on the Questionnaire. Economic characteristics cover the following subject areas: Employment Status and Work Experience; Industry, Occupation, and Class of Worker; Place of Work and Journey to Work; and Income. Certain economic characteristics have been measured by the Census as far back as 1820. However, a

Data on Activity Limitations are affected significantly by the self-identification principle. Item 19 is new for 1990.

Certain economic characteristics have been measured by the Census as far back as 1820.

NEW IN '90

The 1990 Census statistics on Veterans are the first to include persons who served in the United States Merchant Marine during World War II.

POPULATION QUESTIONS: ECONOMIC CHARACTERISTICS

Employment Status

Item 21a	Work Status Last Week	Long Form
Item 25	Temporary Absence from Work	Long Form
Item 26a	Looking for Work	Long Form
Item 26b	Available to Accept Work	Long Form

Work Experience

Item 31a	Worked in 1989	Long Form
Item 31b	Weeks Worked in 1989	Long Form
Item 31c	Usual Hours Worked per Week	Long Form

Other Labor Force Characteristics

Item 21b	Actual Hours Worked Last Week	Long Form
Item 27	Year Last Worked	Long Form

Industry, Occupation, and Class of Worker

Item 28	Industry	Long Form
28a	Employer's Name	
28b	Kind of Business	
28c	Industry Sector	
Item 29	Occupation	Long Form
29a	Type of Occupation	
29b	Job Duties	
Item 30	Class of Worker	Long Form

Place of Work and Journey to Work

Item 22	Place of Work	Long Form
Item 23	Means of Transportation	Long Form
Item 24	Travel Time	Long Form

Income

Item 32	Source of Income	Long Form
Item 33	Total Income in 1989	Long Form

Figure 7-7

supplemental Unemployment Schedule used with the 1930 Census Questionnaire was the first to delve into such matters in greater detail.

Employment Status and Work Experience

As described in Chapter 5, Employment Status is a complex concept requiring extensive clarification. A lengthy list of Census questions measures whether adult respondents meet the government's definition of Labor Force participation. Additional ques-

A lengthy list of Census questions measures whether adult respondents meet the government's definition of Labor Force participation.

tions on Work Experience capture information on the Experienced Unemployed or help the Bureau tabulate earnings information more accurately. The Census is the only source of detailed Employment data for small areas. Results are used by the U.S. Bureau of Labor Statistics to devise sampling methods for on-going Employment surveys. Numerous federal assistance programs, such as the Job Training Partnership Act, also incorporate Census data on Employment Status.

All Items in this category are sample questions. Depending on the question, respondents are instructed to use the Reference Year (1989) or the Reference Week (the week prior to the time the Questionnaire is being filled out). Although the Items are asked of persons age 15 or older, most are tabulated only for those age 16 or older.

Employment Status is determined according to responses received on five separate questions. **Work Status Last Week (Item 21a)** asks whether the person worked at any time in the previous week. The Bureau counts both full and part-time work (including paper routes or baby sitting), as well as unpaid work for a family business. **Temporary Absence from Work (Item 25)** asks whether the person was temporarily absent from work during the Reference Week. Temporary Absence includes short-term illness, vacations, labor disputes, and temporary layoffs. Seasonal workers who did not work during the Reference Week are not counted as temporarily absent. Persons answering "Yes" to either Item 21a or Item 25 are counted as Employed.

Looking for Work (Item 26a) asks whether the person has looked for work within the previous four weeks. Looking for Work is defined as active job seeking, including registration with an employment service, attending job interviews, or preparing for self-employment. **Available to Accept Work (Item 26b)** asks whether the person could have taken a job during the Reference Week if one had been offered. Respondents are instructed to answer "No" to Item 26b if they are already employed,

To be counted as Unemployed, a person must answer "No" to Items 21a and 25 and answer "Yes" to Items 26a and 26b.

if they are laid off and expecting to return to work within 30 days, if they are temporarily ill, or if they are unable to accept employment due to school, child care responsibilities, or similar constraints. To be counted as Unemployed, a person must answer "No" to Items 21a and 25 and answer "Yes" to Items 26a and 26b. (For more information about Employment Status, refer to the discussion in Chapter 5.) Items 21a, 25, and 26 have been asked on every Census since 1930. Censuses from 1930 through 1950 also asked how many weeks the unemployed person had been looking for work.

Recent Work Experience (Item 31) is a three-part question which measured the amount of work performed during the Reference Year. **Worked in 1989 (Item 31a)** asks whether the person worked (as defined by Item 21a) at any time during 1989. Respondents are instructed to answer "Yes" even if they worked only a few days during the year. This Item has been asked on every Census since 1960. **Weeks Worked in 1989 (Item 31b)** asks respondents to write the total number of weeks worked. Every week is counted, no matter how minimal the work experience during that week. This Item has been asked on every Census since 1940. Censuses from 1880 through 1910 asked respondents the number of months they had been unemployed during the Reference Year. **Usual Hours Worked per Week (Item 31c)** asks how many hours per week the person usually worked during 1989. This Item has been asked only since 1980. Answers to Item 31 are used by the Bureau to calculate hourly and weekly earnings.

Actual Hours Worked Last Week (Item 21b) asks how many hours the person worked during the Reference Week. Respondents are instructed to add the total number of hours worked at all jobs, including overtime, but to subtract any time off due to vacations, holidays, or illness. Item 21b has appeared on every Census since 1940.

Year Last Worked (Item 27) asks respon-

dents to indicate the year they last worked, based on the definition given in Item 21a. Seven response categories are provided, including "Never Worked." Item 27 serves two purposes. Any Unemployed person who has worked at any time after 1984 is counted as Experienced Unemployed. This response category is tabulated in a variety of Census reports, such as the *Equal Employment Opportunity File*. The question also serves as a screening device for Items 28 through 30, which are restricted to the Employed, the Experienced Unemployed, and members of the Armed Forces. Item 27 has been asked on every Census since 1960.

Industry, Occupation, and Class of Worker

Three Questionnaire Items deal with employment characteristics of the Employed, the Experienced Unemployed, and members of the Armed Forces. Responses to all three Items are based on the Reference Week, except for the Experienced Unemployed, who must indicate characteristics of the job last worked. Persons working at more than one job are instructed to answer based on the job worked most. Items 28 through 30 are sample questions and all are asked of persons age 15 or older.

Industry (Item 28) is a three-part question which asks respondents to identify the type of business in which their employer is engaged. **Kind of Business (Item 28b)** identifies the employer's main business activity. Respondents are asked to be as specific as possible. Instructions suggest, for example, that "petroleum refining" is a better response than "oil company." The remaining two parts are used to help the Bureau assign correct Industry Codes to incomplete or ambiguous responses. In many cases, the answer to **Employer's Name (Item 28a)** can be checked against the Bureau's file of Establishment names, compiled as part of the Economic Census program, to verify Kind of Business. **Industry Sector (Item 28c)**

Industry (Item 28) is a three-part question which asks respondents to identify the type of business in which their employer is engaged.

Occupation (Item 29) is a two-part question which identifies the nature of the work a person performs.

Commuting patterns also form the basis of federal definitions of Metropolitan Statistical Areas

offers further clarification by asking respondents to indicate whether the employer is engaged in manufacturing, retailing, wholesale trade, or other activities. Item 28 has been asked on every Census since 1910. Rudimentary versions appeared in the Censuses of 1820 and 1840.

Occupation (Item 29) is a two-part question which identifies the nature of the work a person performs. **Type of Work (Item 29a)** asks respondents to name their occupation. Specific responses are solicited. Instructions suggest citing "carpenter's helper" rather than "helper," for example. **Job Duties (Item 29b)** asks respondents to briefly describe their most important activities or job duties. The Bureau uses answers to Item 29b to clarify ambiguous responses. In certain cases, responses to Item 28 also help the Bureau assign accurate Occupational Codes.

Data from Items 28 and 29 are used by the Bureau of Labor Statistics to make occupational projections, identify potential areas of labor shortages, and perform similar Labor Force analyses. Occupational Data for smaller areas, cross-tabulated by Sex, Race, and Hispanic Origin, are also used for monitoring Affirmative Action plans. Questions relating to Occupation have been asked on every Census since 1850.

Class of Worker (Item 30) asks the legal or organizational status of the respondent's employer. The following eight response categories are given:

- Private, for profit
- Private, not-for-profit
- Local government
- State government
- Federal government
- Self-employed, not incorporated

- Self-employed, incorporated
- Working without pay in family business or farm.

A variation of this Item has appeared on every Census since 1910.

Place of Work and Journey to Work

Three Questionnaire Items deal with workers' commuting patterns. Resulting data are used for transportation planning, including needs assessment for mass transit systems, highway construction, and parking lots. The Federal Emergency Management Authority utilizes this data to estimate day-time population figures cited in emergency evacuation plans. Commuting patterns also form the basis of federal definitions of Metropolitan Statistical Areas (described in Chapter 11) and the U.S. Labor Department's Labor Market Areas. All three Items pertain to the Reference Week, and are asked only of persons who answer "Yes" to Item 21a (Work Status Last Week). Items 22 through 24 are sample questions.

Place of Work (Item 22) identifies the location of the employee's workplace. Respondents are asked to write the street address; city, town, or post office; county; state; and ZIP Code. A space is also provided to indicate whether the location falls within the legal limits of the city or town. If the exact address is not known, the building name, office park, or nearest cross-street can be cited. Respondents are instructed not to use mailing addresses or Post Office Boxes. This question has been asked on every Census since 1960.

Journey to Work (Items 23-24) captures data on transportation modes and commuting time. **Means of Transportation (Item 23a)** asks how the person travelled to work during the Reference Week. Twelve response categories are provided, covering such options as walking, bicycle, taxicab, and bus. If several modes were used in the daily Journey to Work, or if respondents used different means on different days, they are instructed to select the mode which covered the longest total distance. Response categories were slightly modified for 1990. Options for car, truck, and van were combined into a single category. Options for bus and streetcar, formerly combined, were separated for 1990, and a new category was created for ferry boat. This Item has appeared on every Census since 1960.

Private Vehicle Occupancy (Item 23b) was asked of all persons who utilized a car, truck, or van in their Journey to Work. The question asks how many people usually rode in the vehicle. Eight responses are listed, ranging from "Drove alone" to "Ten or more people." Persons who typically dropped off their children on the way to work, or were driven to work by a spouse or roommate who then returned home, were instructed to select "Drove alone." Item 23b first appeared in 1980.

Travel Time to Work (Item 24b) asked how many minutes it took the person to reach work during the Reference Day. Guidelines instructed respondents to specify average door-to-door travel time. This question was introduced on the 1980 Questionnaire. **Time of Departure (24a)** is a new Item for 1990. It asks respondents to write the time they usually left home to go to work. Instructions emphasized citing the time of departure, not the time work began. Respondents were also asked to specify AM or PM. Data from Item 24a, coupled with results from Item 24b, allow transportation planners to identify peak travel times.

Income

Two Questionnaire Items provide detailed data on personal Money Income. (Census Bureau definitions of Income are explained in Chapter 5.) Both Items pertain to the Reference Year, and both are asked of every Household member age 15 or older. Items 32 and 33 are sample questions.

Source of Income (Item 32), an eight-part question, asks respondents to indicate whether particular types of Income were received. If so, respondents must write the annual dollar amount. The following Income Sources are listed.

- ▸ Wages, salary, commissions, bonuses, or tips from all jobs (**Item 32a**).
- ▸ Self-employment Income from nonfarm businesses (**Item 32b**).
- ▸ Farm self-employment Income (**Item 32c**).
- ▸ Interest, dividends, net rental Income, royalty Income, or Income from trusts or estates (**Item 32d**).
- ▸ Social Security or Railroad Retirement (**Item 32e**).
- ▸ Supplemental Social Security Income, AFDC, or other public assistance Income (**Item 32f**).
- ▸ Retirement, survivor, or disability pensions (**Item 32g**).
- ▸ Any other sources of Income regularly received (**Item 32h**).

NEW IN '90

Although Item 23b was similar to the corresponding question seen in the 1980 Questionnaire, less information was collected on Private Vehicle Occupancy for 1990. The 1980 Census included an additional question about carpool arrangements. Persons who did not drive alone were asked whether they shared driving, always drove others, or rode as a passenger only. This question was introduced as a result of the energy crisis of the 1970s, and was judged unnecessary for 1990.

If several modes were used in the daily Journey to Work, or if respondents used different means on different days, they are instructed to select the mode which covered the longest total distance.

The sum of Items 32a, 32b, and 32c comprise total earnings. Item 32a is reported as a gross amount, before any deductions for taxes or other payroll withholdings. Items 32b and 32c are reported as net amounts, also before taxes. The major change in this question for 1990 is the designation of pensions as a separate Income category.

Item 32 serves two purposes. The obvious application is to allow analysts to cross-tabulate Source of Income by Age, Race, Total Income, or other demographic variables. A second, more subtle purpose is to improve the accuracy of Total Income figures. Because respondents are required to list different Income Sources separately, they are less likely to overlook particular categories, such as interest, unemployment compensation, or child support payments.

order to calculate Total Income for Households and for Families.

As described in Chapter 5, Total Income is also used to calculate the number of Unrelated Individuals and Families who fall below their respective Poverty thresholds, and to determine their characteristics and geographic distributions. Data from Item 33 are incorporated into numerous allocation formulas for federal funding. Marketers and other data users also rely heavily on Total Income figures for many types of analysis. Although Source of Income has appeared as a Census question since 1940, a separate Item for Total Income has been included only since 1980.

Because respondents are required to list different Income Sources separately, they are less likely to overlook particular categories, such as interest, unemployment compensation, or child support payments.

Housing Questions

The Housing portion of the Questionnaire consists of seven questions asked of 100% of the population, plus an additional 19 sample questions. Housing subjects can be grouped

Census Tip

The Bureau's guidelines on Reference Dates have an important impact on how Total Income figures are interpreted. If a person living in the Household on April 1, 1990 was not a Household member during all or part of 1989, that person's Income is still counted toward the Household total. Alternately, if a person living in the Household during 1989 is not a Household member on April 1, their Income is not included in the Household total, even though the Household may have enjoyed the benefits of that Income.

Total Income in 1989 (Item 33) asks respondents to sum all amounts listed in Item 32 and write the total. Because Items 32b, 32c, and 32d involve net amounts, these may have been reported as losses. If so, they are subtracted from Total Income. Persons who received no Income in 1989 mark a FOSDIC circle for "None." The Census Bureau combines amounts from Item 33 for individual Household members in

---

HOUSING QUESTIONS: OCCUPANCY AND STRUCTURE

Housing Occupancy

Item B	Type of Unit	Short Form*
Item C1	Vacancy Status	Short Form*
Item C2	Unit Boarded Up	Short Form*
Item D	Months Vacant	Short Form*
Item H4	Tenure	Short Form
Item H8	Year Moved In	Long Form
Item H18	Condominium Status	Long Form
Item H19	Farm Residence	Long Form
H19a	Acreage	
H19b	Agricultural Sales	

Structural Characteristics

Item H2	Type of Building/Units in Structure	Short Form
Item H3	Number of Rooms	Short Form
Item H9	Number of Bedrooms	Long Form
Item H17	Year Structure Built	Long Form

*Question completed by Enumerator.

Figure 7-8

into three broad categories covering Occupancy and Structure; Plumbing, Equipment, and Fuels; and Financial Characteristics.

Occupancy and Structure

The first portion of the Housing Census covers a variety of Items dealing with housing occupancy and structural characteristics. Figure 7-8 summarizes the content of these questions and lists their Item Numbers on the Questionnaire. Occupancy measures Vacancy Status, Housing Tenure, Year Moved In, and Housing Utilization. Structural characteristics include Type of Building, Units in Structure, Number of Rooms, Number of Bedrooms, and Year Structure Built.

Housing Occupancy

Three Questionnaire Items, completed by Census Enumerators, identify characteristics of Vacant Housing Units. (Enumeration procedures for Vacant Units are introduced in Chapter 4. Vacancy guidelines and concepts, including Usual Residence Elsewhere, are discussed in Chapter 5.) Four additional Items, completed by residents of Occupied Housing Units, focus on Tenure and Utilization Characteristics. Tenure is a complete-count Item, as are the Vacancy Items answered by Bureau employees. All others are sample questions.

A section of the *Official Form*, marked "For Census Use Only," contains the four Items relating to Vacant Units. Enumerators use **Item B (Type of Unit)** to distinguish between "regular" Vacant Units and those which are Vacant because their occupants list a Place of Usual Residence Elsewhere. **Vacancy Status (Item C1)** classifies Vacant Units by category: For Rent; For Sale; Rented or Sold, Not Occupied; For Seasonal, Recreational, or Occasional Use; and Other Vacant. **Unit Boarded-Up (Item C2)** provides a "Yes/No" option to indicate whether the Vacant Unit is boarded-up. **Months Vacant (Item D)** lists six response categories, from "Less Than One Month" to "24 or More Months." Item C1 first appeared on the 1940 Census Questionnaire and Item D was introduced in 1960. Items B and C2 were first used in 1980.

Tenure (Item H4) distinguishes between Owner-Occupied and Renter-Occupied Housing Units. Owner-Occupied dwellings can be owned by the Householder or by anyone else in the Household. Item H4 employs four response categories, two for each type of Unit. Owner-Occupied Units are divided into those owned with a mortgage and those owned free and clear. Renter-Occupied Units are divided into those rented

How does Year Moved In (Item H8) differ from Residence Five Years Ago (Item 14)?

Residence Five Years Ago is a population question because it pertains to each member of the Household. It is designed to measure migration, the movement of people from one place to another. Year Moved In is a housing question because it pertains to the Householder only, and because it is designed to measure housing turnover. Item H8 is not concerned with where people came from, as is Item 14, but with how long they have lived in the present location. In fact, Item H8 does not address length of residence of individual Household members, only with the Householder. To put it another way, the focus of Item 14 is people, while the focus of Item H8 is the Housing Unit.

Q&A

Why does the Questionnaire contain two different Items relating to the size of the property on which the Housing Unit stands?

The question on Acreage (Item H19a) should not be confused with Item H5a, the Property Size Screener. Item H5a, which asks whether the Unit is located on ten or more acres of land, is designed to exclude large properties from certain calcula- tions of average Housing Value and Contract Rent. Item H19a, which asks whether the Unit is located on less than one acre, is part of the screening mechanism used to identify members of the Farm Population.

for cash and those Occupied without pay- ment of rent. The response category for "Owned free and clear" is new for 1990.

Item H4 serves several broad purposes. First, homeownership is a general indicator of economic well-being. By cross-tabulating Tenure with Household Income or other economic, social, or demographic character- istics, economists can study housing affordability. Second, rates of homeownership serve as partial measures of local area housing quality and neighborhood stability. Third, Tenure data are a prerequisite for analyzing statistics on housing costs, which are also collected by the Census. For example, the Bureau of labor Statistics relies on Tenure data from the Census to design sampling methodology for the Consumer Price Index. Tenure data have been collected in every Census since 1890.

Year Moved In (Item H8) asks when the Householder moved into the house or apart- ment. Response categories list six date ranges, beginning with "1959 or earlier" and ending with "1989 or 1990." Item H8 collects data on housing turnover, which is an important measure of neighborhood stability. This question has been asked on every Census since 1960.

Condominium Status (Item H18) asks whether the Housing Unit is a condominium, defined as a house or apartment which is individually owned, but whose common areas

(grounds, hallways, recreational facilities) are jointly owned by all members of the condo- minium association. Condominium Status was first asked in the 1980 Census, reflecting the increasing popularity of this type of ownership arrangement. Item H18 enables the Bureau to collect data on the character- istics of condominiums, including statistics on Vacant condominiums and Renter-Oc- cupied condominiums.

Farm Residence (Item H19) is a two-part question used to identify Housing Units which are farms. **Acreage (Item H19a)** asks whether the house is situated on property of less than one acre.

Agricultural Sales (Item H19b) asks the annual dollar amount of all sales of agricul- tural products produced on the property. Agricultural products are defined as crops, fruits, vegetables, nuts, livestock, or livestock products. Response categories list six sales ranges, including "None" and "$1 to $999." Respondents who did not live on the prop- erty for the entire Reference Year are asked to estimate an annual amount for 1989. Item H19b does not deal with Net Farm Income, which is a personal Income characteristic mea-

> By cross-tabulating Tenure with House- hold Income or other economic, social, or demo- graphic characteris- tics, economists can study housing affordability.

NEW IN '90

Condominium Status was a com- plete-count question in 1980. For 1990, the Item was downgraded to a sample question. For this reason, Value of Condominiums cannot be tabulated separately in complete- count publications.

sured by Item 32c. Nor does it capture detailed data on agricultural production, which is measured by the quinquennial *Census of Agriculture* and by numerous surveys conducted by the Department of Agriculture. The primary purpose of Item 19b is to determine whether a Housing Unit meets the Bureau's definition of Farm Residence. In Census tabulations for Rural areas, Housing Units are designated as either Farm or Nonfarm.

The Bureau defines Farm Residence as any single-Unit house or mobile home located on one acre or more and which produces $1,000 or more in annual Agricultural Sales. As discussed in Chapter 5, all Group Quarters and multi-Unit Housing Units are excluded from the definition, regardless of their other characteristics. The government uses Farm Residence to determine eligibility for a variety of assistance programs provided by such agencies as the Farmers Home Administration, the Agricultural Extension Service, and the Department of Health and Human Services. Resulting Census data are also used by rural sociologists, agricultural economists, and other social scientists and planners studying characteristics of the Farm Population. Questions on the Farm Population have appeared on every Census since 1890. The Bureau introduced current definitions in 1960; in prior decades, farms were defined based on self-identification.

Structural Characteristics

Four Questionnaire Items describe the physical characteristics of each dwelling. Of these, the Items on Units in Structure and Number of Rooms are complete-count questions. The remaining two Items are sample questions.

The Bureau has employed a diversity of structural questions since the first Housing Census in 1940, but the attention devoted to this topic has diminished in recent decades. Certain Items have disappeared because they are no longer pertinent. For example, Censuses from 1940 through 1970 asked about the availability of electric lights in the home.

Other questions have been dropped because of the Bureau's inability to demonstrate program needs, or because sufficient information can be obtained through sample surveys. For example, the 1970 Census included an Item relating to basement type, the 1980 Census inquired about passenger elevators in buildings of 4 stories or more, and Censuses from 1960 through 1980 contained a question on the number of bathrooms in the Unit.

Building Type/Units in Structure (Item H2) asks respondents to describe the building in which they live. Ten response categories distinguish among various types of single-Unit and multi-Unit buildings. The following Building Types are listed:

▸ Mobile Home or Trailer
▸ One-Family House Detached from Any Other
▸ One-Family House Attached to One or More Houses
▸ Other

As the choices suggest, row houses and duplexes are counted as single-Unit (attached) dwellings if each Unit is separated from its neighbors by walls extending from ground to roof. The remaining six categories describe multi-Unit buildings by size, ranging from

The Bureau defines Farm Residence as any single-Unit house or mobile home located on one acre or more and which produces $1,000 or more in annual Agricultural Sales.

The Bureau has employed a diversity of structural questions since the first Housing Census in 1940, but the attention devoted to this topic has diminished in recent decades.

NEW IN '90

The 1980 Questionnaire used two separate Items to capture data on Building Type and Units in Structure. A sample question was virtually identical to 1990's Item H2, except the "Other" category was worded "boat, tent, van, etc." A complete-count question asked the number of Units at This Address, providing nine response categories for buildings of one to nine apartments or Living Quarters, plus a remaining category for "ten apartments or more." For 1990, the question on Units at This Address was deleted, and the Item covering Building Type/Units in Structure was upgraded to a complete-count question. In the process, some reporting detail was lost for buildings of less than ten Units.

**HOUSING QUESTIONS:
PLUMBING, EQUIPMENT, AND FUEL**

Plumbing

Item H10	Complete Plumbing Facilities	Long Form
Item H15	Source of Water	Long Form
Item H16	Sewage Disposal	Long Form

Equipment and Fuels

Item H11	Complete Kitchen Facilities	Long Form
Item H12	Telephone	Long Form
Item H13	Vehicles Available	Long Form
Item H14	Fuel Used Most for Heating	Long Form

Figure 7-9

buildings with two apartments to those with 50 or more apartments.

Item H2 reports basic characteristics of Housing Unit composition and structure. Results are used to measure housing density, which is important for land-use analysis, zoning regulation, and transportation planning. The response category for mobile home or trailer also enables the Bureau to exclude this type of Unit from certain calculations of Housing Value. A question of this type has been asked on every Census since 1940. A category for mobile homes was added in 1950.

Number of Rooms (Item H3) asks how many Rooms are present in the house or apartment. Bathrooms, porches, balconies, foyers, halls, and half-rooms are excluded from the count. Item H3 lists nine response categories, ranging from "One Room" to "Nine or More Rooms." In addition to reporting a basic characteristic of Housing Unit structure, Item H3 measures overcrowding, which is an important indicator of housing adequacy. Results are used to evaluate the need for new housing and to determine federal funding for various housing programs. Number of Rooms has appeared on every Census since 1940.

Number of Bedrooms (Item H9) asks how many Bedrooms are present in the Housing Unit. Respondents are instructed

> *In addition to reporting a basic characteristic of Housing Unit structure, Item H3 measures overcrowding, which is an important indicator of housing adequacy.*

to count any Room which is intended for use as a bedroom, regardless of its present use. As described in Chapter 5, this definition differs from the one used in the 1980 Census. The Department of Housing and Urban Development uses Number of Bedrooms as a means of categorizing rental property. Average rents, used to establish fair market values for housing subsidies, are calculated based on Number of Bedrooms. This Item has appeared on every Census since 1960.

Year Structure Built (Item H17) asks the approximate date the structure was first built. Renters are instructed to consult with the owner or building superintendent before answering this question. Wording for Item H17 is essentially unchanged from 1980, though date ranges are updated and a response category of "Don't Know" appears for the first time. The earliest category remains "1939 or Earlier." This Item is used to determine the age of the nation's housing stock, an important measure for both urban planning and market research. This question has been asked on every Census since 1940.

 Census Tip

By dividing the number of Rooms in the Unit by the number of persons in the Household, the Bureau calculates a ratio of Persons per Room. Any Housing Unit with a ratio higher than one Person per Room is defined as overcrowded.

Plumbing, Equipment, and Fuels

The next topical grouping within the Housing Census covers Plumbing, Household Equipment, and Heating Fuels. Figure 7-9 summarizes the content of these questions and lists their Item Numbers on the Questionnaire. Plumbing questions measure the presence of Complete Plumbing Facilities,

NEW IN '90

The question on Complete Plumbing Facilities (Item H10) was downgraded to a sample question for 1990. The 1980 version of this Item was also more detailed, asking whether some but not all facilities were available, and asking whether the facilities were available for exclusive use of the Household or shared with others. Despite the fact that fewer than 3% of the nation's Housing Units lacked Complete Plumbing Facilities in 1980, the Bureau, together with many housing experts, felt this topic should remain a complete-count Item for 1990. After extensive negotiations with the Office of Management and Budget, the Item's status was downgraded.

conditions. This topic has been included on every Census since 1940. From 1940 through 1970, three separate Items covered the availability of running water, a flush toilet, and a bathtub or shower. The concept of Complete Plumbing Facilities was introduced in 1980.

Source of Water (Item H15) asked respondents to indicate which of the following means are used to supply water to the Household:

▸ A Public Water System
▸ An Individual Drilled Well
▸ An Individual Dug Well
▸ Some Other Source.

Drilled wells are differentiated from dug wells by their size. A drilled well is approximately 1.5 feet in diameter, while a dug well is wider. Households which share a well with other Housing Units are instructed to indicate "Public System" if the well is shared by five or more Units.

Data are used to study geographic patterns of water quality, land use, health conditions, and other environmental planning issues. Questions about Source of Water have been asked on every Census since 1940.

Source of Water, and Sewage Disposal. Household Equipment is an eclectic category encompassing Complete Kitchen Facilities, Telephone, and Vehicles Available. The Fuels Item focuses on the type of Heating Fuel used most.

Plumbing

Plumbing questions, most of which have been asked since the first Housing Census in 1940, were reduced significantly for 1990.

Plumbing questions, most of which have been asked since the first Housing Census in 1940, were reduced significantly for 1990. Few Housing Units in the United States lack a source of water, a means of sewage disposal, or indoor plumbing facilities, but these characteristics remain important measures of housing quality. All three Plumbing Items are sample questions.

Complete Plumbing Facilities (Item H10) asks whether the Housing Unit possesses hot and cold piped water, a flush toilet, and a bathtub or shower. If *any* of these three fixtures are lacking, respondents are instructed to answer "No." To be counted, plumbing must be located inside the house or apartment.

The presence of Complete Plumbing Facilities is a fundamental measure of housing quality. Resulting Census data are used to identify neighborhoods with substandard housing and potentially unhealthy living

Sewage Disposal (Item H16) asks whether the Housing Unit is connected to a public sewer, a septic tank or cesspool, or whether other means of sewage disposal are employed. Item H16 provides data for use in sanitation planning and related environmental health concerns. This question has been asked on every Census since 1960.

Equipment and Heating Fuels

Four Items relate to Household equipment and home heating fuels. All are sample questions.

Items on the 1990 Questionnaire relating to Household equipment are limited, but earlier Censuses included a variety of questions about availability of specific appliances in the home, as shown by the list below:

▸ Radios	1930 - 1970
▸ Refrigerators	1940 - 1950
▸ Televisions	1950 - 1970
▸ Food freezers	1960
▸ Clothes washers	1960 - 1970
▸ Clothes dryers	1960 - 1970
▸ Air conditioners	1960 - 1980
▸ Dishwashers	1970

Such questions were intended to measure economic well being and to provide data for analyzing and forecasting residential energy requirements. All have been eliminated or replaced with broader, more encompassing questions.

Each Census since 1960 has asked all respondents to list a telephone number where they can be reached by an Enumerator if necessary. This information is used to improve data quality and coverage only. Phone numbers are not entered into the Bureau's computer records, nor are these responses tabulated in any way.

Complete Kitchen Facilities (Item H11) asks whether the Housing Unit includes a sink with piped water, a range or cook stove, and a refrigerator. All three facilities must be present in order to qualify as Complete. Portable cooking equipment is excluded from the definition. Facilities need not be located in the same Room, but they must be present within the house, apartment, or mobile home. Item H11 is a measure of housing quality, since Units without Complete Kitchen Facilities are less suitable for occupancy. Data from Item H11 are also used to plan Meals on Wheels programs and similar services. Some version of this Item has appeared on every Census since 1940. The 1940 Questionnaire inquired about refrigerators, and the 1950 Form added a second question

about kitchen sinks. The 1960 Census simply asked, "Do you have a kitchen or cooking equipment?" The present wording was introduced in 1970.

Telephone in Unit (Item H12) asks whether a telephone is available within the house or apartment. This subject was introduced as a sample question in 1980. For 1990, the Bureau sought to upgrade the status of Item H12 to a complete-count question, but proponents of this revision failed to demonstrate sufficient program needs to justify the change. Access to telephone service is a measure of economic well-being, and data from Item H12 can also help health, social, and emergency service workers identify population groups or neighborhoods where significant numbers of Households are unreachable by phone. This information serves another important purpose. Survey designers in the government and the private sector rely upon small-area data on telephone access to establish valid sampling methodologies for telephone surveys.

Although this sample Item first appeared in 1980, each Census since 1960 has asked all respondents to list a telephone number where they can be reached by an Enumerator if necessary. This information is used to improve data quality and coverage only. Phone numbers are not entered into the Bureau's computer records, nor are these responses tabulated in any way.

Q&A

Why can't the Bureau use the phone numbers listed on the Census Questionnaires to tabulate data on Telephone in Unit?

Every Census Questionnaire, both Long Form and Short Form, includes a space for respondents to designate a phone number where they can be reached for enumeration follow-up. Even if the Bureau decided to use these responses for tabulation purposes, the results would not be meaningful. Because many people list a work number where

they can be reached during the day, and because those with no phone may list a neighbor's or a relative's phone, this information provides no means to identify which respondents have a telephone in the Household. For 1990, Telephone in Unit remains a sample question.

Vehicles Available (Item H13) asks how many automobiles, vans, or trucks of one-ton capacity or less ar kept at home for use by members of the Household. Eight response categories are given, from "None" to "Seven or More." The 1980 Questionnaire contained two Items relating to Vehicles Available: one for cars, and one for vans and trucks. For 1990, the Items were combined to reflect the growing popularity of vans and light trucks for personal transportation. Data on commercial use of trucks and vans are collected by the quinquennial *Census of Transportation*.

 Census Tip

Item H13 does not measure vehicle ownership. Respondents are instructed to include leased vehicles and employer-provided vehicles available for Household use. Vehicle counts also exclude cars, vans, and trucks which are owned by Household members but are unavailable for use because they are located elsewhere or are not in running order.

Item H13 enables transportation planners, environmental analysts, and others to construct statistical models relating traffic volume to the number of Households or to Household types. A question on automobiles was introduced in 1960. The scope was expanded to include trucks and vans in 1980.

Fuel Used Most for Heating (Item H14) asks Householders to indicate the fuel used most for heating the house, mobile home, or apartment. Nine response categories are listed, including piped gas, bottled gas, electricity, and coal. A category for solar energy was added to the 1990 Questionnaire. A single response must be selected, reflecting the fuel used most. Renters who do not pay utility bills are instructed to ask landlords or building superintendents. Census data on Household fuel usage, combined with statistics

from other sources, allow government agencies and utility companies to make projections of future energy needs. The Census has collected data on type of heating fuel in every decade since 1940.

> # NEW IN '90
>
> The 1980 Census included additional questions on fuels for cooking and hot water. A cooking fuel question appeared on every Census from 1940 through 1980. A water heating question was introduced in 1960. These Items were eliminated from the 1990 Questionnaire, suggesting decreased interest in energy conservation data. The U.S. Energy Information Administration also conducts ongoing surveys of household fuel consumption.

Financial Characteristics

The final section of housing questions, covering various financial characteristics, is the most extensive and complex part of the Housing Census. Figure 7-10 summarizes the content of these questions and lists their Item Numbers. Homeowners are asked to estimate property Value, while renters (or landlords, in the case of Vacant Units) are asked to indicate Rent Paid or Rent Asked. Both owners and renters must respond to questions on Costs of Utilities and Fuels. Homeowners are also asked to supply data on a variety of additional housing costs.

Housing Value and Contract Rent

1990 Census Items on Housing Value and Rent Paid are complete-count questions. As described earlier in the chapter, the Bureau also asks a screening question (Item H5) pertaining to Value and Rent. This enables the Bureau to calculate Housing Value and

For 1990, the Items were combined to reflect the growing popularity of vans and light trucks for personal transportation.

Homeowners are asked to estimate property Value, while renters (or landlords, in the case of Vacant Units) are asked to indicate Rent Paid or Rent Asked.

HOUSING QUESTIONS:
FINANCIAL CHARACTERISTICS

Housing Value and Rent Paid

Item H5	Value and Rent Screener	Short Form
H5a	Property Size	
H5b	Business Residence	
Item H6	Value of Property	Short Form
Item H7	Rent Paid	Short Form
H7a	Monthly Rent	
H7b	Meals Included in Rent	

Costs of Utilities and Fuels

Item H20a	Electricity	Long Form
Item H20b	Gas	Long Form
Item H20c	Water	Long Form
Item H20d	Fuels	Long Form

Homeowners' Selected Shelter Costs

Item H23	First Mortgage	Long Form
H23a	Presence of First Mortgage	
H23b	Monthly Payment	
H23c	Taxes Included	
H23d	Insurance Included	
Item H24	Subordinate Mortgages	Long Form
H24a	Presence of Junior Mortgage	
H24b	Monthly Payment	
Item H21	Real Estate Taxes	Long Form
Item H22	Fire, Hazard, and Flood Insurance	Long Form
Item H25	Monthly Condominium Fee	Long Form
Item H26	Mobile Home Shelter Costs	Long Form

Figure 7-10

Contract Rent for different categories of Housing Units. Some calculations are based on responses from all Housing Units, while others exclude such categories as Business Residences and Units located on ten acres or more, which would otherwise inflate the figures for typical single-Unit homes and apartments.

Value of Property (Item H6) asks respondents to indicate their estimate of the current market value of the property, including the land and all buildings on it. Item H6 pertains to all Owner-Occupied and "Vacant, For Sale" Housing Units, including condominiums and mobile homes. Respondents who own the structure but rent the land upon

which it is situated are asked to estimate the value of the land as well. The Questionnaire provides 25 response categories, beginning with $5,000 increments but expanding to broader increments as the dollar amounts increase. The highest category for 1990 is "$500,000 or More."

Item H6 is appropriate for many purposes by all types of data users, including real estate developers and agents, market researchers, and urban planners. A question on Housing Value has appeared on every Census since 1930.

Contract Rent (Item H7) is asked of all Renter-Occupied Housing Units and all Vacant Units which are For Rent at the time of the Census. Data for Occupied Units are reported as Rent Paid, while data for Vacant Units are reported as Rent Asked. **Monthly Rent (Item H7a)** instructs respondents to indicate the total monthly amount paid to the landlord, regardless of whether the amount includes utilities, furnishings, or additional services. Twenty-six responses are listed, ranging from "Less Than $80" to "$1,000 or More." Data from Item H7a are used for a variety of government purposes. HUD uses the results to determine rent subsidies for public assistance programs, while the Department of Defense relies on these numbers to determine housing allowances for members of the Armed Forces. Questions on Contract Rent have been asked on every Census since 1930.

Meals Included in Rent (Item H7b) is a new question for 1990. Item H7b asks whether the cost of meals is included in monthly rent payments. If tenants must contract with the landlord for a monthly meal plan in order to live in the building, they are instructed to answer "Yes." This question serves two broad purposes. It provides data users with more meaningful information on rental costs, and it enables the Bureau to tabulate statistics on congregate housing.

Item H7b asks whether the cost of meals is included in monthly rent payments. If tenants must contract with the landlord for a monthly meal plan in order to live in the building, they are instructed to answer "Yes."

Costs of Utilities and Fuels

The Bureau has asked decennial questions about Utilities Costs since 1940 and questions on Fuel Costs since 1950. Early versions of this Item were asked of Renter-Occupied Housing Units only. Beginning with 1980, the scope was broadened to include Owner-Occupied Units. The Item is divided into four parts, as shown below. All are sample questions.

▸ Electricity (Item H20a)
▸ Gas (Item H20b)
▸ Water (Item H20c)
▸ Oil, Coal, Kerosene, Wood, etc. (Item H20d)

The questions are asked of Renter-Occupied and Owner-Occupied Housing Units. Renters are instructed to report only the amounts paid in addition to the Contract Rent. Condominium owners are asked to report only amounts paid in addition to the Condominium Fee. Owners and Renters living in the Unit less than a full year are asked to estimate annual costs based on amounts paid to date.

The 1990 Questionnaire contains six additional Items relating to homeowners' costs, reflecting the diversity of housing arrangements found in the United States.

NEW IN '90

The 1980 Questionnaire asked respondents to report average monthly costs for both gas and electric. The 1990 Questionnaire asks for total annual costs, which the Bureau then divides by twelve to obtain a monthly average. The change was instituted because many respondents had simply listed the amounts from their most recent monthly bills, which resulted in overstated or understated amounts due to seasonal variations in utility costs.

Costs of Utilities and Fuels are added to data reported on other Census Items to calculate housing costs for owners and renters. For renters, Item H20 is added to Contract Rent to determine Gross Rent. For owners, H20 is added to the sum of miscellaneous other Items to determine Homeowners' Selected Shelter Costs, as described in the next section. In both cases, resulting data are used to compare the total amount spent on housing. For example, both the Federal Housing Administration and the Veterans Administration compare total housing costs to Household Income to establish mortgage eligibility thresholds.

Census Tip

Contract Rent is a complete-count question and is tabulated in complete-count publications. Gross Rent is derived from Item H7a (a complete-count question) and Item H20 (a sample question), so it is tabulated in sample publications.

Selected Monthly Owner Costs

The 1990 Questionnaire contains six additional Items relating to homeowners' costs, reflecting the diversity of housing arrangements found in the United States. All six Items are sample questions. When the relevant responses for each Household are added together with the results of Item H20, the resulting sum is called Selected Monthly Owner Costs. The term "Selected" is used because the amounts exclude irregular or unanticipated costs, such as maintenance and repair.

First Mortgage (Item H23) is a four-part question which inquires about the existence and characteristics of the property's senior mortgage. Item H23a was asked from 1890 through 1920, and in 1940, 1950, 1980, and 1990. Items H23b and H23c were introduced in 1940 and did not reappear until 1980. Item H23d was first asked in 1980.

Presence of First Mortgage (Item H23a) asks whether a mortgage or similar debt exists on the property. **Monthly Payment (Item H23b)** asks the Homeowner to indicate the monthly dollar amount paid on this

NEW IN '90

Questions about insurance, real property taxes, mortgage payments, and other components of Selected Monthly Owner Costs were asked of a different population during the previous Census. In 1980, these questions did not apply to Business Residences, homes located on ten or more acres, condominiums, mobile homes, or apartments in multi-Unit buildings. For 1990, all of these categories except multi-Unit buildings were included.

mortgage. **Taxes Included (Item H23c)** asks whether the payment listed in H23b includes the real estate taxes assessed against the property. The two response categories are "Yes," and "No, Paid Separately or Taxes Not Required." **Insurance Included (Item H23d)** asks whether the payment listed in H23b includes payments for fire, hazard, or flood insurance on this property. The two responses are "Yes," and "No, Paid Separately or No Insurance." For 1990, the wording of H23d was changed to include flood insurance.

Subordinate Mortgages (Item H24), a two-part question, relates to any second or junior mortgages on the property. Item H24a appeared on the 1940 Questionnaire and was reintroduced in 1980. Item H24b is new for 1990.

Presence of Junior Mortgage (Item H24a) asks whether one or more junior mortgages or home equity loans are secured by this property. The "home equity" wording was added for 1990.

Presence of Junior Mortgage (Item H24a) asks whether one or more junior mortgages or home equity loans are secured by this property. The "home equity" wording was added for 1990. **Monthly Payment (Item H24b)** asks the homeowner to specify the sum of all monthly payments on subordinate mortgages or to indicate no regular payments are required.

Real Estate Taxes (Item H21) asks the homeowner to specify the total annual real estate taxes assessed on this property, regardless of whether they are included in the mortgage payment. (If taxes are not included

in mortgage payments, as indicated by Item H23c, the Bureau divides the response to Item H21 by twelve, then adds it to Selected Monthly Owner Costs. Otherwise, the amount is already reflected in Item H23b.) This question was introduced in 1980.

Fire, Hazard, and Flood Insurance (Item H22) asks the annual payment for insurance on this property, regardless of whether the amount is included in the mortgage payment. The results of Item 22 are tabulated in similar fashion to those of Item H21. This question was introduced in 1980. The phrase "flood insurance" was added to the wording for 1990.

Monthly Condominium Fee (Item H25) asks the monthly dollar amount of any Condominium Fee paid on this property. A Condominium Fee is a charge assessed by the Condominium Owners' Association to pay for the maintenance, repair, and improvement of common areas, or the provision of similar membership services.

Mobile Home Shelter Costs (Item H26) asks mobile home owners to specify the total annual cost for personal property taxes, site rent, registration fees, and license fees paid on this home and site. Item H26 excludes any real property taxes assessed on the site. If the respondent owns the land upon which the mobile home is situated, the cost of real estate taxes is captured by Items H21 and H23c.

NEW IN '90

For 1980, Mortgage Payments included both first and second mortgages in a single amount. For 1990, the two types of payments are reported separately. As a consequence, data users should exercise care in making comparisons between the two decades.

NEW IN '90

Questions on Condominium Fees (Item H25) and Mobile Home Shelter Costs (Item H26) are new for 1990. Both were added to make Selected Monthly Owner Costs more reflective of different types of housing arrangements in the United States. In most data tables for Owner Costs, amounts are shown separately for Specified Owner-Occupied Units, Owner-Occupied Condominiums, and Owner-Occupied Mobile Homes.

Summary

Accurate interpretation of data demands a deeper knowledge of Questionnaire content—the wording of questions, the instructions given to respondents, and the response categories offered.

Understanding the Census requires users to become familiar with the questions asked. More important, accurate interpretation of data demands a deeper knowledge of Questionnaire content—the wording of questions, the instructions given to respondents, and the response categories offered.

Census Tip

To assist data users, a facsimile of the 1990 Questionnaire and Instructions is reproduced as an appendix to every printed Census Report. The Short Form is reproduced in all publications containing complete-count data; the Long Form is reproduced in Reports containing sample data.

Chapter 5 stressed the importance of understanding Census terms and concepts. Careful reading of Glossary entries is one means of grasping the Bureau's specialized terminology, but such understanding is strengthened by studying the actual Questionnaire Items. The exact nature of Census data on persons with disabilities becomes clear by scanning the wording of Items 18 and 19 and their accompanying Instructions.

Certain Items are themselves part of the defining process, determining whether a person is counted in a particular category. For example, a home is defined as a Farm only if it resides on more than one acre of land and its residents sold $1,000 or more of agricultural goods during the year (Item H19). Similarly, persons are counted as Unemployed only if they are not institutionalized, and they are 15 years of age or older, out of work, currently looking for a job, and available to accept work if it is offered (Items 1, 16, 21a, 25, and 26).

Viewing the response categories can help to explain complex topics or subtle distinctions. The difference between Relatives and Nonrelatives becomes clear by looking at the responses to Item 2. Users can identify the components of Selected Monthly Owner Costs by perusing Items H21 through H26.

The wording of questions and response categories also determines the amount of detail reported in Census publications. Looking for Census data on the number of students enrolled in parochial schools is fruitless for 1990 because no separate categories appear on the Questionnaire. Item 11 asks only whether the attended school is public or private, not its affiliation. Frequent referral to the Questionnaire while using Census publications will improve the user's ability to interpret data correctly.

Cartoon appearing in August 18, 1860, issue of *The Saturday Evening Post*. Courtesy: Library of Congress.

THE GREAT TRIBULATION.

CENSUS MARSHAL.—"I jist want to know how many of yez is deaf, dumb, blind, insane and idiotic—likewise how many convicts there is in the family—what all your ages are, especially the old woman and the young ladies—and how many dollars the old gentleman is worth!"

[Tremendous sensation all round the table.]

Chapter 8

CD-ROM Products

Chapter 8

CD-ROM Products

A COMPLETE COLLECTION of 1990 Census publications presents an arresting sight: more than 100 linear feet of shelf space, comprised of approximately 850 individual reports. Even more remarkable is the fact that this impressive array of printed books represents only about 10% of the total 1990 Census output. By far the majority of 1990 tabulated data appears in electronic form only.

While many Census users may be more familiar or comfortable with print publications, this chapter begins the discussion of the Bureau's 1990 products by introducing electronic data files. This approach makes sense for several reasons:

- all print products are derived from electronic files
- printed reports are designed to answer only the most frequently requested data needs
- electronic products often provide more subject detail

- electronic products provide more geographic detail
- technological innovations make electronic files more accessible than ever before
- electronic products are released prior to their print counterparts
- the Bureau considers CD-ROM the primary dissemination medium for 1990 data.

Published products of the 1990 Census take a variety of forms, both electronic and otherwise. Regardless of format, all of them emanate from the same source: the Bureau's primary statistical and geographic databases. This chapter focuses on files released as CD-ROMs, the most popular medium for 1990 data. Chapter 9 looks at the varied assortment of print Reports, sheet maps, and microfiche products issued by the Bureau. For those interested in alternative sources of Census information, Chapter 14 introduces other electronic formats, including time-sharing databases and Internet sites.

NEW IN '90

For users of the 1980 Census, electronic access to data required a large computer (a mainframe or minicomputer) and the technical expertise to retrieve information from computer tapes. Electronic access to 1990 data is more affordable, easier to deal with, and more widely available than ever, thanks to the Bureau's CD-ROM products, expanded offerings on its *CENDATA* online system, and the increasing availability of Census files found on Internet sites.

The Census on CD-ROM

The primary advantage of CD-ROM is its tremendous storage capacity compared to traditional magnetic media.

One of the greatest success stories of the 1990 Census was the debut of user-friendly, desktop access to computerized data files, offered through Compact Disc-Read Only Memory (CD-ROM) technology. CD-ROM is an optical recording medium employing a 4.75 inch diameter disc made of polycabonate plastic, covered with a reflective aluminum coating and a protective lacquer. Each disc contains three miles of spiral track similar to that found on a phonograph record. The track is scored with several billion pits to record data. A laser beam from a CD-ROM player reads data from the disc. The pits disperse light; the unscored areas (lands) reflect light.

The primary advantage of CD-ROM is its tremendous storage capacity compared to traditional magnetic media. A single disc can hold 650 megabytes of data. It would take 900 diskettes at 720K, or four reels of magnetic tape (2400 feet, 6250 bps) to hold an equivalent amount. To put it another way, a CD-ROM disc contains the same amount of data as 275,000 pages of print, which translates into approximately 65 linear feet of bound Census volumes.

CD-ROM technology is ideally suited to the massive data files generated by the 1990 Census. *STF 3A* alone comprises 30,000 megabytes of data, and is published on 61 separate discs.

The Bureau and CD-ROM Development

The Census Bureau was the first federal agency to adopt CD-ROM technology as a standard data dissemination medium, and it remains the government's largest producer of CD-ROM products. The Bureau began exploring the feasibility of this medium early in the decennial planning process. Although commercially-produced compact disc databases were still fairly rare in the mid-1980s, the Bureau created *Test Disk #1* in June, 1986. The test product contained a variety of files, including selected data from the

Q&A

What equipment is required to use Census data on CD-ROM?

Users wishing to access Census Bureau CD-ROMs will need a DOS-based microcomputer with a minimum of 640K RAM, operating under MS-DOS version 3.0 or higher. A software enhancement called Microsoft CD-ROM Extensions (mscdex.exe) is also required, though this package is automatically included with MS-DOS version 6.0 and higher.

Most important, users will need a CD-ROM player and a SCSI interface board (a drive controller) to read the discs. Newer models of microcomputers often are sold with built-in CD players and the peripherals necessary to run them, making the transition to CD-ROM technology less daunting than in the past.

1980 *STF 3B* tapes and intercensal population and income estimates. *Test Disk #1* was evaluated for one year at 39 sites, including four of the Bureau's Regional Offices, two State Data Centers, two universities, and 30 Patent Depository Libraries. (The latter sites were chosen because the Commerce Department was investigating the possibility of distributing patent and trademark data on CD-ROM.) The test disc had limited capabilities. Most evaluators found it frustrating to use, but considered the technology promising nevertheless.

As late as June, 1987, the Bureau viewed magnetic tape, paper, and microfiche as the "big three" data dissemination methods, with CD-ROM, online access, and floppy diskette designated for minor roles only. Response from data users at the Local Public Meetings was mixed, since many people were unfamiliar with the compact disc format and most federal Depository Libraries and State Data Center affiliates had limited microcomputer resources at that time. Despite such reservations, a tentative decision was made to produce *STF 1A* and *STF 3A* on CD-ROM.

Meanwhile, product testing continued. The Bureau mastered *Test Disk #2*, containing the 1982 *Census of Agriculture* and the 1982 *Census of Retail Trade*, in April, 1988. The product was sent to 143 Depository Libraries

> **By August, 1989, the Bureau acknowledged CD-ROM as the primary publication medium for 1990 products.**

with stated experience using CD-ROMs. Later it was distributed to all Depositories and sold to other data users. By May of that year the Government Printing Office had agreed to publish federal documents on CD-ROM, and in June the Bureau announced that major products from the 1987 Economic Census and the 1990 decennial Census would appear on compact disc. By August, 1989, the Bureau acknowledged CD-ROM as the primary publication medium for 1990 products.

What caused this gradual policy reversal? The advantages of CD-ROM were too significant to ignore. Aside from its superior storage capabilities, compact disc technology provides a more cost-effective means of producing and distributing Census data. The format is also more durable and more manageable than paper reports or magnetic tape. CD-ROM distribution offers the potential to dramatically speed the release of Census data to the public. Theoretically, discs can be issued within three-to-five weeks of original tape production. For data users, CD-ROM brings large Census files to desktop computers, with more geographic and subject detail than ever before. Customers can now manipulate Census data using familiar software products, such as dBASE and Lotus 1-2-3, or the Bureau's own "no frills" software. An added benefit is the ease of storing the discs themselves. Print reports and computer tapes both require extensive shelving to hold a large collection of Census titles. An equivalent amount of CD-ROM files can be stored easily in a desk drawer, filing cabinet, or desktop display case. To the 1990 product-planning staff, the bottom line was clear: CD-ROM technology allowed the Bureau to distribute larger quantities of data to greater numbers of users, faster and at lower cost.

NEW IN '90

The primary dissemination medium for 1980 was the printed report, despite the availability of more extensive data on magnetic tape and microfiche. Although the Bureau recognizes that some users will continue to prefer paper products, CD-ROM files are now considered the principal means of releasing Census data. This change in focus has received enthusiastic support from the general public. In a 1993 survey of data users, the Bureau asked which medium would be the preferred method of accessing future data products. More than 1,100 users responded. The results overwhelmingly favored compact disc technology: 94% selected CD-ROMs, 45% chose print Reports, and 10% indicated magnetic tape. (Respondents could cite more than one medium in their answer.)

Standard Features of Census CD-ROMs

CD-ROM products containing 1990 Census data can be classified into three broad

Q&A

Why doesn't the Bureau invest additional resources into developing enhanced software programs?

The issue of CD-ROM software was examined in great detail during the 1990 product planning process. Evaluators of Test Disk #1 urged the Bureau to provide database management or spreadsheet capabilities to enhance the value of the new storage technology. However, any efforts which the Bureau took to develop professional-quality software could only be achieved at the expense of resources which would otherwise be used to tabulate and distribute the data files themselves. Faced with a tradeoff between more data and better software, the Bureau wisely opted for data. After all, the private sector could develop software, probably better than the government could, but only the Bureau could tabulate Census results. The majority of data

users agreed with this decision, based on comments received at Local Public Meetings and other feedback mechanisms during the planning process.

A second, more political consideration should also be mentioned. Officials in the U.S. Office of Management and Budget remain sensitive to concerns of government competition with private-sector data producers. Lobbying groups such as the Information Industry Association are quick to object to government-issued software, stating that federal data agencies should limit their publishing efforts to production of raw statistics only. At the time the 1990 Census products were designed, value-added software was typically viewed as the province of commercial publishers.

---

categories: summary data files, microdata files, and geographic information files. Summary data files are the most familiar to Census users. These include the many *STF* series, plus more specialized files, such as the *Special Tabulation on Aging* and the *Equal Employment Opportunity File*. Microdata files contain a sampling of completed Questionnaires in their entirety, stripped of any personal identification characteristics. These products, issued as a series of *Public Use Microdata Samples*, are designed for detailed statistical analysis. Geographic information files are generated from the Bureau's TIGER system, described in Chapter 6. These include descriptive map outline files, called *TIGER/Line Files*, as well as geographic reference files such as the *TIGER/Census Tract Street Index*.

Most 1990 Census files are available in CD-ROM format. Figure 8-1 shows a list of the major 1990 CD-ROM products and indicates some of their basic characteristics. As of December, 1995, 220 discs are available for sale, with another five or so to be issued before the 1990 publishing cycle is completed. Considering the tremendous stor-

age capacity of each disc, this constitutes a truly impressive data library. Most CD-ROM products can be purchased at a cost of $150 per disc, with discounts for multi-disc sets. The *TIGER/Line Files* cost $250 per disc. The total cost of the entire 1990 Census collection is substantial (more than $19,000), but dramatically cheaper than magnetic tape. Users can find virtually complete CD-ROM collections at major Depository Libraries and Census Bureau Regional Offices. Smaller collections can be found at State Data Centers, Business & Industry Data Centers, and other libraries and Census assistance centers. More will be said about obtaining CD-ROM products in Chapter 10.

Census CD-ROMs are designed for novice users as well as more sophisticated data analysts. In the words of former Bureau director Barbara Everitt Bryant, CD-ROM technology "democratizes" access to Census data. Most 1990 CD-ROMs come with an easy-to-use software package loaded right on the disc. *TIGER/Line Files* come equipped with software called LandView, while *PUMS* discs contain a program called QuickTab.

Census CD-ROMs are designed for novice users as well as more sophisticated data analysts. In the words of former Bureau director Barbara Everitt Bryant, CD-ROM technology "democratizes" access to Census data.

Major CD-ROM Products: 1990 Census

TITLE	UNIVERSE	PRIMARY GEOGRAPHY	# OF DISCS	ON-DISC SOFTWARE
STF 1A	100%	Block Group	17	GO
STF 1B	100%	Blocks	10	GO
STF 1C	100%	nation	1	GO
STF 1D [a]	100%	CDs	2	GO
STF 3A	sample	Block Group	61	GO
STF 3B	sample	ZIP Codes	3	GO
STF 3C	sample	national	2	GO
STF 3D [a]	sample	CDs	2	GO
PL P4-171	100%	Blocks	10	GO
EEO File	sample	national	2	GO
SSTFs	sample	national	38[b]	GO
AOA File	sample	various	22	GO
County-to-County Migration Flow Files	sample	County	2	GO
CHAS	sample	various	1	GO
PUMS 5%	sample	PUMAs	7	CrossTab
PUMS 1%	sample	PUMAs	2	CrossTab
TIGER/Line	—	all	44	LandView
GICS	—	all	1	GO
Census Tract Street Index	—	Tracts	6	GO

[a] On both discs, STF 1D and STF 3D appear together on same disc. One disc covers the 103rd Congress, the other the 104th Congress.
[b] publication in progress as of 12/95.

Figure 8-1

Summary Tape Files include a program called GO, which provides easy menu access to preformatted data tables. GO demands no prior database management skills, no understanding of STF file structure, and no knowledge of other technical matters; it is strictly "point and shoot" software. The tradeoff for easy use is limited searching power. GO only allows retrieval of standardized tables. Users requiring customized tabular displays or basic data manipulation capabilities can use another Bureau-produced program called EXTRACT. More will be said about GO, EXTRACT, and LandView later in the chapter.

All of the Bureau's software programs offer limited search, retrieval, and display capabilities. Sophisticated computer users will find commercially produced software preferable for complex analysis of Census data. For example, relatively affordable mapping programs, such as GeoSight FactFinder (Sammamish Data Systems, Inc.) and MapInfo (MapInfo Corporation) outperform LandView in virtually every aspect. In most situations, popular database management programs and spreadsheet packages manipulate STF data and perform computations better and faster than the Bureau's own EXTRACT program.

When creating CD-ROM products, the Bureau has striven as much as possible to adopt an "open architecture" policy. Although most of its CD-ROM titles come with government-produced "bare bones" software, the discs can also be used with other computer programs. *TIGER/Line Files* are compatible with many leading GIS or mapping products. *PUMS Files* can be used with well-known statistical analysis packages, such as SPSS (the Statistical Package for the Social Sciences). Early on, 1990 product planners decided to format the files using a popular, commercially available programming language. Borland International, Inc.'s dBASE language was chosen because it was the best-selling database manager at the time and because it was compatible with many other programs. Most summary data files are issued in standard *.**dbf** format, for use with dBASE, FoxPro, Clipper, Paradox, or other database managers. Many spreadsheet programs, such as Lotus 1-2-3 and Quattro Pro, can read *.**dbf** files directly; other spreadsheets have conversion utilities that translate database files into a format they can read.

1990 Technical Documentation is product-specific for each CD-ROM title. A com-

NEW IN '90

Prior to 1990, computer tape users were the prime readers of Technical Documentation for Census files. Although documentation for each tape product was available for sale to other Census customers and was distributed to Depository Libraries, it was largely ignored by print and microform users. Widespread use of 1990 CD-ROM titles has made the current editions of the Technical Documentation indispensable resources for all data analysts. Even print users will find the 1990 Technical Documentation helpful, because it contains descriptions of geographic file structure, detailed lists of the codes used to categorize individual responses, and other important background information.

The Technical Documentation for each title provides the Data Dictionary for the files (described in Chapter 13), detailed table outlines, and other indispensable guides to file structure. Analysts wishing to use EXTRACT or commercial database management programs (such as dBASE) to create customized reports will need to consult the Technical Documentation in order to work with these large, complex files.

Summary Tape Files on CD-ROM

The Bureau publishes the bulk of the 1990 Census results in two Summary Tape File (STF) series, arranged according to the Questionnaire Items from which the data were tabulated. Figure 8-1, shown earlier, compares some of the distinguishing features of the various titles in the Summary Tape File series. The STF number indicates the subject content of the file; the letter-suffix designates the geographic specificity. The most important distinction when differentiating the contents of the Summary Tape

plete set of relevant documentation files is located on the disc itself, found on a directory called \DOCUMENTS. These files appear in ASCII format and can be viewed or printed directly, or imported to a word processing program. The Bureau also sells print versions of the Technical Documentation reports for about $15 apiece. A free copy of the relevant report is included with every CD-ROM purchase.

Q&A

What ever happened to *STF 2* and *STF 4*?

STF 2 and *STF 4* are unavailable in CD-ROM format. Because they are such large files, and because they present subject breakdowns more specialized than most users require, the products are issued on magnetic tape (reel or cartridge) only. *STF 2* provides detailed subject breakdowns for complete-count data. *STF 4* offers in-depth subject coverage of sample data.

The four STF files offer a trade-off between subject detail and geographic detail. *STF 1* and *STF 3* contain basic subject coverage for all geographic levels treated by the Census. *STF 2* and *STF 4* contain more extensive subject coverage, but for fewer geographic levels. For

example, *STF 1*, covering complete-count Items, contains 982 data cells for each geographic entity. *STF 2*, covering the same complete-count Items in greater detail, can contain as many as 41,561 data cells for each geographic entity. To make such a massive file manageable, geographic coverage is restricted. While *STF 1* presents data for Block Groups (*STF 1A*) and Blocks (*STF 1B*), none of the *STF 2* files go below the Census Tract or BNA level. Despite the restricted geographic coverage, *STF 2* files are still more than twice as large as their *STF 1* counterparts. *STF 2* and *STF 4* are described in greater detail in Chapter 14.

Files is whether they contain complete-count data or sample data. *STF 1* is based on those questions asked of all respondents. This complete-count data is derived from several sources: all Questionnaire Items from the Short Form; the first seven Population Items and the first seven Housing Items from the Long Form; and the 100% Items from various Special Count forms (ICRs, MCRs, and SCRs). *STF 3* presents sample data only: the sample Items from the Long Form and from the Special Count forms. Sample responses are then weighted to represent the total population.

STF Basics

The Bureau issued two broad groupings of 1990 Summary Tape File products on CD-ROM: *STF 1* and *STF 3*. These files were chosen for broader distribution because they were the most popular files of the previous Census addressing the most frequently requested data needs. The two product grouping are divided into subfiles with one-letter suffixes, such as *STF 1A*. The contents of the individual subfiles are described later in the chapter, as are the differences between the two major groupings.

 Census Tip

When seeking complete-count data, use *STF 1* subfiles. When seeking sample data, use *STF 3* subfiles.

Geographic distinctions among the STF subfiles are somewhat blurred because geographic coverage overlaps across products, as shown in Figure 8-2. The *STF 1A* and *STF 3A* products consist of "state-specific" files providing data for most Governmental and Statistical Units within a state, down to the Block Group level. The *STF 1C* and *STF 3C* products are nationwide files. They focus on larger geographies, beginning at the national level and continuing down to Places with population of 10,000 or more. *STF 1D* and

GEOGRAPHIC COVERAGE OF SUMMARY TAPE FILES

Summary Level	STF 1	STF 3
United States/Regions/Divisions	C	C
Amer. Indian/Alaska Native Areas[1]	A B C D	A C D
States	A B C D	A B C D
Congressional Districts		
101st Congress	A B	—
103rd & 104th Congresses	D	D
Metropolitan Areas[1]	B C	A C
Urbanized Areas[1]	B C	A C
Urban/Rural	B C	A C
Counties	A B C D	A B C D
Places (by population size)		
10,000 or more	A B C D	A C D
less than 10,000	A B	A
County Subdivisions		
all MCDs and CCDs	A B	A
MCDs of 10,000 or more[2]	C D	C D
MCDs under 10,000[3]	C	—
Census Tracts or BNAs	A B	A
Block Groups	A B	A
Blocks	B	—
ZIP Code Areas	—	B

[1] Data for that part of Area within state boundary only, except for C subfiles, which provide Area totals.
[2] 12 states where MCDs serve as general purpose governments.
[3] MCDs in Metropolitan Areas of New England states only.

Figure 8-2

STF 3D concentrate on Congressional Districts. The "B" subfiles represent unique geographies. *STF 1B* provides complete-count data for Census Blocks; *STF 3B* provides sample data for five-digit ZIP Code Areas.

Appendix D, located at the back of this book, provides a complete list of tables found in *STF 1* and *STF 3*. The listings indicate the table number, title, matrix layout, Universe measured, and number of data cells for each table. For example, Table P12 in *STF 1*, "Race (5) by Sex (2) by Age (31)," is presented in a 5 x 2 x 31 matrix, resulting in 310 data cells. This means that data for each of five racial categories are divided into two

The *STF 1A* and *STF 3A* products consist of "state-specific" files providing data for most Governmental and Statistical Units within a state, down to the Block Group level. The *STF 1C* and *STF 3C* products are nationwide files.

What does the reference to "Universe" mean in the STF data tables?

The Universe of coverage represents the total set of persons or Housing Units described in the table. It is an important characteristic of every table. A particular table may be describing only a subset of the total possible Universe, a situation illustrated by numerous examples listed in Appendix E. For example, Table P13 in *STF 1* ("Sex by Age") is based on a Universe of "persons of Hispanic Origin;" sex-by-age breakdowns for the total population are not found in Table P13 because Non-Hispanics are excluded from its Universe.

A second reason to note the relevant Universe is to verify the *type* of entity being measured. The table may not count people at all; instead, it may focus on Households, Families, Housing Units, or other measures. Once again, these may represent only a subset of the possible totality. For example, Table H42, "Units in Structure," measures Vacant Housing Units only.

Misinterpreting the Universe of coverage is a common mistake made by Census users, and examples of such pitfalls are shown in Chapter 10.

sexes; then the ten Race/sex categories are each divided into 31 age groupings. The Universe of coverage is "all persons." Figure 8-3 shows that portion of Table P12 covering the 31 age breakdowns for males in the racial category "American Indians, Eskimos, and Aleuts." The same categories are repeated nine more times for the remaining Race/sex groupings.

 Census Tip

All STF products on CD-ROM indicate the Universe being measured in a particular table. This information is found at the top of every table.

Data within a table can be presented in a variety of ways, including total counts for specific characteristics, frequency distributions, medians, means, and even aggregate values. For example, Table P81 in *STF 1*, "Aggregate Income in 1989," calculates the sum of Incomes received by all persons within a specific geographic entity, which may total in the millions or billions of dollars, depending on the area size. In contrast, Table P80 tabulates the number of Households falling

within each of 25 Income ranges, and Table P80A cites a single figure for median Household Income.

Another category of table found in Summary Tape Files is the Imputation table, which indicates the percentage of responses in a particular Universe for which the Bureau provided replacement numbers for "missing" answers on the Questionnaires. Imputation tables shown in Summary Tape Files are quite detailed, covering individual Questionnaire Items in specific geographic areas. Each table indicates the percentage of answers which were Allocated and the percentage which were Substituted. Imputation tables are essential for analyzing the quality of Census data for a given geographic entity. A fuller discussion of the Imputation process, together with examples from Imputation tables, can be found in Chapter 10.

Summary Tape Files are organized geographically. Tables within STF products are arranged by geographic levels, called Summary Levels. For example, Summary Level 040 may represent states, while Summary Level 050 represents counties. Some tables are presented in hierarchical fashion. Where subordinate levels of geography cross the boundaries of a higher level, only a portion

Tables within STF products are arranged by geographic levels, called Summary Levels.

Example of an STF Matrix (Table P12, *STF 1A*)

1990 Census Of Population And Housing Summary Tape File 1A

040 Wisconsin
    160 Green Bay city

AGE
American Indian, Eskimo, or Aleut males

Under 1 year	30
1 and 2 years	80
3 and 4 years	64
5 years	41
6 years	30
7 to 9 years	89
10 and 11 years	53
12 and 13 years	51
14 years	22
15 years	20
16 years	24
17 years	20
18 years	14
19 years	25
20 years	25
21 years	22
22 to 24 years	86
25 to 29 years	106
30 to 34 years	97
35 to 39 years	89
40 to 44 years	55
45 to 49 years	39
50 to 54 years	34
55 to 59 years	16
60 and 61 years	7
62 to 64 years	8
65 to 69 years	16
70 to 74 years	9
75 to 79 years	4
80 to 84 years	4
85 years and over	2

[Remainder of Table not shown. Data repeated for female American Indians, and for four additional racial groups (each of the sexes).]

Figure 8-3

For each geographic entity covered in the database, *STF 1* presents 101 separate data tables.

of the smaller level is shown. For example, if cities cross county boundaries, data are provided for only that part of the city which lies within the individual county. An alternative arrangement is the "inventory" presentation. Here, separate tables list each geographic entity within a particular Summary Level alphabetically. The inventory tables provide data for total entities, regardless of the borders they cross. Depending on the user's data needs, he or she can choose between a hierarchical presentation or an alphabetical listing for any given Summary

Level. For example, Summary Level 080 may represent the portion of a Census Tract within a Place (hierarchical), while Summary Level 140, shown in separate tables, represents the total Census Tract (inventoried). More will be said about Summary Levels later in the chapter.

Summary Tape File 1

The group of subfiles constituting *STF 1* provide fundamental population and housing characteristics tabulated from the complete-count Items on the Questionnaire. Population Items represent the number of inhabitants, their age, Race, sex, marital status, and Hispanic Origin status, plus Household size and type, and Family size and type. Housing Items represent the number of Housing Units, number of Units in the structure, number of Rooms, Tenure, Value, Contract Rent, Vacancy characteristics, and Persons per Room.

For each geographic entity covered in the database, *STF 1* presents 101 separate data tables. The tables are broken down as follows: 29 tables citing population characteristics, 52 tables citing housing characteristics, and 20 Imputation tables (12 population and 8 housing). The tables are identical in *STF 1A*, *STF 1C*, and *STF 1D*; the difference from one subfile to another is in the levels of geography covered. Because *STF 1B* covers nearly seven million Census Blocks in the United States, its CD-ROM version is only a small extract of the full tape file, presenting only a single table for each geographic entity. Part One of Appendix D provides a complete list of tables found in *Summary Tape File 1*, with the exception of *STF 1B*.

STF 1A (17 discs).

These state-specific files provide geographic hierarchies within each state, down to the Block Group level. *STF 1A* covers states, counties, County Subdivisions, Places, Census Tracts/Block Numbering Areas, and Block Groups, plus the pre-Census Congressional

District boundaries of the 101st Congress. The portions of American Indian Areas and Alaska Native Areas falling within an individual state's boundaries are also shown. Tables are presented in hierarchical arrangement as well as inventory style. Because *STF 1* is smaller than *STF 3*, neighboring states are often grouped together on one disc.

STF 1C (1 disc).

The single disc for *STF 1A* presents complete-count data for the United States, its Census Regions and Divisions, the states, Urban/Rural summaries, Metropolitan Areas, Urbanized Areas, Alaska Native and American Indian Areas, counties, and Places of 10,000 or more people. For those states where Minor Civil Divisions serve as general purpose governments, MCDs of 10,000 or more persons are shown. *STF 1C* also provides data for MCDs of less than 10,000 inhabitants in the New England states.

STF 1B Extract (10 discs).

STF 1B and *Public Law 94-171 Data* are the only 1990 CD-ROM products which provide statistics at the Block level. *STF 1B* also covers states, counties, County Subdivisions, Tracts/BNAs, Block Groups, and those portions of American Indian Areas, MAs, and UAs within the individual state's boundaries. It is the Census Block data, however, which makes this file unique. The *STF 1B Extract* is the only CD-ROM from *Summary Tape File 1* whose table structure differs from the outline shown in Part One of Appendix D. In fact, *STF 1B* provides only a single data table for each Census Block. The table is designed to provide a profile of commonly requested population and housing characteristics. *STF 1B* presents a total of 21 data cells for every entity covered, compared with the 982 data cells found in each of the other *STF 1* files. These 21 population and housing characteristics are shown in Figure 8-4. Like *STF 1A*, the *STF 1B Extract* files group data for neighboring states together on one disc.

 Census Tip

Users seeking more extensive data at the Block level must use the tape version of *STF 1B*.

STF 1D (2 discs, includes *STF 3D*).

Complete-count data for Districts of the 103rd Congress, reflecting new boundaries based upon the 1990 Census, are published here. (A second disc provides the same data for CDs of the 104th Congress.) Those portions of the following geographies which fall within each District are also shown: counties, Places of 10,000 or more, County Subdivisions of 10,000 or more (in some states only), Alaska Native Areas, and American Indian Areas. Summary Levels below the state level are keyed to Congressional Districts. For example, data for Places (or parts of Places) are tabulated within CD boundaries only. *STF 3D* is published as a separate database on each *STF 1D* disc.

STF 1B and *Public Law 94-171 Data* are the only 1990 CD-ROM products which provide statistics at the Block level.

Summary Tape File 3

The group of subfiles constituting *STF 3* provide population and housing characteristics tabulated from the sample Items on the Questionnaire. On the population side, this includes a diversity of Items relating to Ancestry, Nativity, language, education, Labor Force status, Income, travel to work, and other social and economic characteristics. On the housing side, it includes Items relating to utilization, structure and equipment, Tenure, and finance. A summarized list of sample Items is shown in Figure 1-4, located in Chapter 1. For more detailed descriptions of these Items, consult Chapter 7.

For each geographic entity covered in the database, *STF 3* presents 278 separate data tables. Tables are broken down as follows: 135 tables citing population characteristics, 78 tables citing housing characteristics, and 65 Imputation tables (43 population and 22 housing). The tables are identical in all four subfiles: *STF 3A, STF 3B, STF 3C,* and *STF 3D.* The difference from one subfile to another is in the levels of geography covered. Readers are again directed to Appendix D, where Part Two provides a complete list of tables found in *STF 3.*

Data from the sample responses are weighted to provide estimates of the total population. In this context, several unique data tables deserve special mention. Table P1, "Persons," presents the estimated number of inhabitants based on the sample survey. Table P3, "100-Percent Count of Persons," presents the actual Census count taken from *STF 1.* Table P2 shows the "Unweighted Sample Count of Persons" and Table P3a indicates the "Percent of Persons in the Sample." From these tables, users can easily compare the results of the sample estimates with the actual count. Tables H1, H3, H2, and H3a provided similar data for the total number of Housing Units. Chapter 10 discusses the Bureau's sampling methods in greater detail, together with measures of sampling variability.

Block Characteristics Shown on *STF 1B Extract*

HOUSING CHARACTERISTICS

Total Housing Units

Units in Structure:
  1 Unit Detached or Attached
  10 or More Units

Mean Number of Rooms

Owner Occupied Housing Units

Renter Occupied Housing Units

Mean Value (Specified Owner-Occupied Housing Units)

Mean Contract Rent (Specified Renter-Occupied Units with occupant paying rent)

Housing Units With 1.01 or More Persons Per Room:
  Total Occupied
  Renter Occupied

POPULATION CHARACTERISTICS

Total Persons

Persons by Race:
  White
  Black
  American Indian, Eskimo, or Aleut
  Asian or Pacific Islander

Persons of Hispanic Origin

Age:
  Persons Under 18
  Persons 65 years and over

Persons In Occupied Housing Units

Housing Unit Occupants:
  One-Person Households
  Family Householder, No Spouse Present, with 1 or More Persons under age 18

Figure 8-4

STF 3A (61 discs).

Geographic coverage is similar to *STF 1A,* but for sample data. *STF 3A* does not provide tables for Districts of the 101st Congress, as *STF 1A* does. However, it covers the portions of Metropolitan and Urbanized Areas within each state—two levels which are not found on *STF 1A.* Each disc contains data for a single state. Larger states, such as New York and California, require two or three discs to

NEW IN '90

The 1990 *STF 3* files are composed of approximately 3,300 data cells for each geographic entity. This triples the size of 1980's 1,126 data cells. The larger size is caused by increased detail within tables, as well as by new tables not shown in the 1980 product. For example, the 1980 edition provided 17 categories in each of its Income distribution tables, while the 1990 edition offers 25 categories. Similar detail has been added to tables dealing with distribution ranges for age, educational attainment, Units in structure, and other subjects. New tables provide additional coverage of Household Income, language spoken, education and employment status for teenagers, and numerous characteristics of the elderly population. The total number of Income tables alone more than doubled from 1980 to 1990.

The popularity of CD-ROM has caused the Bureau to rethink some of its original publishing plans.

provide complete coverage. When a state is split in this manner, each disc covers a range of counties within the state, including every applicable geographic level within those counties. State-wide totals are reproduced on every disc in the state set.

STF 3C (2 discs).

A two-disc nationwide set offering identical geographical coverage to *STF 1C.* Disc one provides tables for every applicable Summary Level except Urbanized Areas. Disc two covers UAs only.

STF 3B (3 discs).

This is the only CD-ROM product to show data at the five-digit ZIP Code level. Tables also show the county portions of ZIP Code Areas where ZIP Codes cross county boundaries. The discs are arranged in numerical ZIP Code order: disc one covers ZIP Codes from 0 to 3, disc two covers ZIP Codes ranging from 4 to 6, and disc three covers 7 through 9. For example, data for ZIP Code 48103 (Ann Arbor, Michigan) will be found on disc two.

STF 3D (2 discs, includes *STF 1D*).

Contents of the combined *STF 1D/STF*

3D discs were described earlier. The two files exist as separate databases on both discs. The first covers the 103rd Congress for both Files; the second provides revisions for the 104th Congress. Revised data reflect the six states which undertook additional redistricting for the 1994 elections. *STF 3D* covers the same geographic levels as STF 1D, but for sample data. It contains the same data tables found on other *STF 3* products.

Other CD-ROM Products

A variety of other 1990 products have been released in CD-ROM format. A few, such as the *Public Law 94-171 Data* files, were designed for a very specific purpose. Others, such as the *Equal Employment Opportunity File,* serve a multitude of uses. The popularity of CD-ROM has caused the Bureau to rethink some of its original publishing plans. Although the *TIGER/Line Files* were recognized as a unique and vital resource, the original CD-ROM version required the use of commercial mapping software. Largely in response to public demand, the Bureau released a revised edition, complete with its own software, in early 1994.

As of December, 1995, nearly all CD-ROM products from the 1990 Census had been released. The following product descriptions focus on those titles which have enjoyed the widest distribution. Two additional products—the *County-toCounty Migration Files* and the *Comprehensive Housing Affordability Strategy*—are described in an addendum following Chapter 8.

NEW IN '90

STF 3B on CD-ROM represents the first time the Bureau has issued decennial data at the ZIP Code level as a widely accessible Census product.

Public Law 94-171 Data

Federal law directs the Census Bureau to provide the governors of the 50 states with total population counts for states and local areas within one year of the Census date, to be used for redistricting purposes. (The redistricting process is described in Chapter 2.) The resulting statistics, issued as a series of reports entitled *Public Law 94-171 Data*, represent the first publications to be released following the decennial Census. The law specifies only that total population counts be provided; additional data requirements are negotiated by the Census Bureau and the states. Reports are issued in multiple formats: computer tapes, CD-ROM discs, printouts, and even floppy diskettes. Reports for counties, Places, and some MCDs are also available as *CENDATA* files. The CD-ROM version appears as a ten-disc set.

Tabulations are shown for every political geography within the state, including counties, Places, MCDs, Congressional Districts, Voting Districts (for the 46 states which participated in the program), and American Indian/Alaska Native Areas. Data are also provided for Tracts or BNAs, and for Block Groups and Blocks. Tables list total population and persons 18 years of age and older; both categories are further divided into five racial groups, plus persons of Hispanic Origin. Four sets of tables are presented, arranged in different geographic hierarchies, but the same population characteristics are repeated in each table.

In addition to Summary Tape Files, the Bureau produced numerous CD-ROM titles which focus on specific topics. These fall into three broad product groupings: the *Subject Summary Tape Files* series, the *Equal Employment Opportunity File*, and published results of the Special Tabulation Program.

NEW IN '90

Public Law 94-171 Data provided complete-count statistics for small-area geographies far sooner than in any previous Census. The series, issued from January to March of 1991, offered the first look at basic 1990 demographic characteristics for Census Tracts, Block Groups, and Blocks. For this reason, it was eagerly awaited by Census users of all types, not just government officials charged with state and local redistricting.

Despite its value as an early data product, the CD-ROM version of *Public Law 94-171 Data* is difficult to use. Because it was one of the first compact discs issued by the Bureau, the page-turning software is extremely crude. For example, each geographic entity is represented by its database code rather than its actual name. When *STF 1A* was released later in 1991, *Public Law 94-171 Data* became virtually obsolete except for users seeking certain Block-level statistics not found on the *STF 1B Extract* discs.

Subject-Oriented Discs

In addition to Summary Tape Files, the Bureau produced numerous CD-ROM titles which focus on specific topics. These fall into three broad product groupings: the *Subject Summary Tape Files* series, the *Equal Employment Opportunity File*, and published results of the Special Tabulation Program.

Subject Summary Tape Files

The last data files created by the Bureau each decade are called *Subject Summary Tape Files* (*SSTFs*). These products provide more detailed cross-tabulations by topic, with each title in the series focusing on a single subject. Some titles provide population data; others report on housing characteristics. The *SSTF* series covers large geographic areas only—in most cases limited to the United States, Census Regions and Divisions, and states. The Bureau originally proposed 40 *SSTF* titles for 1990: 30 population files and 10 housing files. The total number was later reduced to 22, due to budget limitations. It is possible that some of the canceled products will be reinstated later in the decade, should additional funds become available.

Figure 8-5 shows a list of the 1990 *SSTF* titles, together with their publication status as of December, 1995. Twenty titles have been issued on magnetic tape, with the remaining two scheduled for release in 1996.

The Bureau will publish a CD-ROM version for every *SSTF* tape it produces. As of this writing, all but five have appeared In most cases one disc will be issued for each SSTF title. The exceptions are SSTF 4 and SSTF 22, both of which appeared as three-disc sets, and SSTF 7, which appeared on eight discs. SSTF 6 and SSTF 12 were issued as a combined product on one disc. All discs contain GO software (written specifically for each product).

Although each *SSTF* title is devoted to a single topic, the subject detail and the complexity of cross tabulations are impressive. For example, *SSTF 1, The Foreign-Born Population of the United States*, contains 66 population tables and 10 housing tables. Cross-tabulations are frequently represented by four- and five-way matrices. Table PB58, "Citizenship by Year of Entry by Poverty Status by Family Type and Presence of Children, is a typical example. For each of the 48 possible "Place of Birth" categories, this table presents a 2 x 5 x 2 x 12 matrix (2 citizenship categories, 5 Year of Entry categories, etc.). This means Table PB58 contains 11,520 data cells, each of which is repeated for every geographic entity in the file. Viewed from this perspective, it is easy to see why the *SSTF* titles cover so few Summary Levels.

Subject Summary Tape Files

SSTF 1	Foreign Born Population of the U.S.[1]
SSTF 2	Ancestry of the Population in the U.S.[1]
SSTF 3	Persons of Hispanic Origin in the U.S.[1]
SSTF 4	Characteristics of Adults with Work Disabilities, Mobility Limitations, or Self-Care Limitations.[1]
SSTF 5	Characteristics of the Asian and Pacific Islander population of the U.S.[1]
SSTF 6	Education in the United States.[1,4]
SSTF 7	Metropolitan Housing Characteristics.[1]
SSTF 8	Housing of the Elderly.[1]
SSTF 9	Housing Characteristics of New Units.[1]
SSTF 10	Mobile Homes.[1]
SSTF 11	Language Use in the United States.[2]
SSTF 12	Employment Status, Work Experience, and Veteran Status.[1,4]
SSTF 13	Characteristics of American Indians by Tribe and Language.[1]
SSTF 14	Occupation by Industry.[1]
SSTF 15	Geographic Mobility for Metropolitan Areas.[3]
SSTF 16	Fertility.[1]
SSTF 17	Poverty Areas in the United States.[1]
SSTF 18	Condominium Housing.[1]
SSTF 19	The Older Population in the United States.[3]
SSTF 20	Journey to Work in the United States.[2]
SSTF 21	Characteristics of the Black Population.[2]
SSTF 22	Earnings by Occupation and Education.[1]

[1] Released on tape and CD-ROM.
[2] Tape released; CD-ROM not yet issued as of 12/95.
[3] Neither tape or CD-ROM released as of 12/95.
[4] SSTF 6 and SSTF 12 issued together on single disc.

Figure 8-5

Equal Employment Opportunity File

Chapter 2 explained the use of Census data for evaluating Affirmative Action plans and for monitoring compliance with other Equal Employment Opportunity programs. The primary 1990 Census product for these purposes is the *Equal Employment Opportunity File*, also called the *Census/EEO File*, to distinguish it from statistical compilations issued by the U.S. Equal Employment Opportunity Commission itself. This Census report has been published in multiple formats, including magnetic tape, CD-ROM, and microfiche. The files are also available in their entirety on *CENDATA*. Users looking

The Bureau originally proposed 40 *SSTF* titles for 1990: 30 population files and 10 housing files. The total number was later reduced to 22, due to budget limitations.

for paper products can order customized printouts from the Bureau's Customer Services office.

The CD-ROM version consists of two discs released in March, 1993. The file covers all states, counties, Metropolitan Areas, and Places of 50,000 inhabitants or more. MCDs of 50,000 or more are covered for the 12 states in which they serve as general-purpose governments. Occupational data are presented for 512 categories, organized into six summary groups; summary groups are then subdivided into 13 "major groups." The basic structure of the Bureau's occupational classification system is shown in Chapter 5, Figure 5-2. Occupational codes 903 through 905, representing military occupations, are excluded from the *Equal Employment Opportunity File* because its Universe is limited to the Civilian Labor Force.

For every geographic entity in the database, the *Equal Employment Opportunity File* presents six tables: three with occupational data, and three with educational data. The first set shows the 512 occupational categories by sex, Race, and Hispanic Origin. The three occupational tables are structured as follows:

Occupational data are presented for 512 categories, organized into six summary groups; summary groups are then subdivided into 13 "major groups."

NEW IN '90

The occupational classification system used in 1990 is largely the same as the one used during the previous decade, but some categories have been added to reflect changes in the Labor Force. Examples of new classification codes are managers in food serving and lodging establishments, managers in service organizations, family child care providers, and early childhood teacher's assistants. Users may wish two consult the printed guides to 1990 Census occupational codes, available in two volumes: the *Alphabetical Index of Industries and Occupations*, and the *Classified Index of Industries and Occupations*.

Table 1 Detailed occupation by sex.
Table 2 Detailed occupation by sex, Hispanic Origin, and Race.
Table 3 Detailed occupation by sex and Race.

Figure 8-6 compares the data presentations for Tables 2 and 3, using the example of lawyers (occupational code 178) in Hamilton County, Ohio. Notice Table 3 subtracts Hispanic persons from their respective racial categories and reports them as a distinct minority group. In this case, 15 lawyers (all male) are Hispanic. By comparing the two tables, it can be seen that all 15 Hispanic lawyers reported their Race as White, as shown by the following calculation:

$$15 + 2,145 = 2,160$$

The second set of tables shows educational attainment for seven age groups, once again by sex, Race, and Hispanic Origin. The three educational tables are structured as follows:

Table 4 Educational attainment by sex.
Table 5 Educational attainment by age, sex, Hispanic Origin, and Race.
Table 6 Educational attainment by age, sex, and Race.

Figure 8-7 shows the first part of Table 5 for Hamilton County. Once again, Hispanics are not double-counted by Race; the racial breakdowns are for Non-Hispanics only. In this table, the first column reports Hispanic Persons, the remaining five columns report Non-Hispanics by Race. The second part of the table (not shown) covers the female population, repeating the same age breakdowns for each category of educational attainment by Race and Hispanic Origin. These tables are not occupationally specific. They report educational attainment for the entire

Civilian Labor Force in Hamilton County.

Readers should note that, although the basic six tables listed above can be found on the CD-ROM version of the *EEO File*, the GO software displays them in a slightly different order. Users of the EXTRACT program will find the tables arranged exactly in the order described here.

🔆 Census Tip

The *Equal Employment Opportunity File* and its spinoff products are the only widely distributed Census publications containing detailed occupational data for 1990. Two *Subject Summary Tape Files* intended to cover occupational characteristics and occupation by industry were both canceled. Users seeking additional statistics must turn to *STF 4* on tape.

The Special Tabulation Program

For a fee, the Census Bureau will produce customized reports for government agencies, other organizations, or individuals. This service, called the Special Tabulations Program, is described in greater detail in Chapter 10. Most of the reports created under this program do not appear as standard Census products because they are compiled under contract with private customers.

When another federal agency contracts for a Special Tabulation, the results may be published, either by the Census Bureau or the contracting agency. To date, the Bureau itself has published more than 20 STP products. All are available on magnetic tape, but only two have been released as CD-ROM products using GO software: the *Special Tabulation on Aging* and the *Comprehensive Housing Affordability Strategy*.

A contracting agency may elect to publish its own Special Tabulation File based on 1990 Census data, but as of this writing, only two agencies have done so: the U.S. Department of Transportation, and the U.S. Edu-

cation Department. It is beyond the scope of this book to explore these non-Census products, but it is appropriate to mention them briefly. The Department of Transportation asked the Bureau to tabulate detailed Journey-to-Work data for use by transportation planners. The resulting product, called the *Census Transportation Planning Package* (*CTPP*), was published by the U.S. Bureau of Transportation Statistics. The CD-ROM version, issued on 12 discs, comes with specialized display software called TransVU-CTPP. It contains special tabulations on

A contracting agency may elect to publish its own Special Tabulation File based on 1990 Census data, but as of this writing, only two agencies have done so: the U.S. Department of Transportation, and the U.S. Education Department.

Occupational Tables from the *Equal Employment Opportunity File*

EEO Table 3:

1990 EEO File
040 Ohio
    050 Hamilton County
DETAILED OCCUPATION BY SEX BY RACE
UNIVERSE: Civilian Labor Force
    Lawyers (178):

	Male	Female
White:	2160	583
Black:	47	7
American Indian, Eskimo, or Aleut:	0	0
Asian or Pacific Islander:	20	9
Other race:	6	0
TOTAL:	2233	599

EEO Table 2:

1990 EEO File
040 Ohio
    050 Hamilton County
DETAILED OCCUPATION BY SEX BY HISPANIC ORIGIN AND RACE
UNIVERSE: Civilian Labor Force
    Lawyers (178):

	Male	Female
Hispanic Origin:	15	0
White, not of Hispanic origin:	2145	583
Black, not of Hispanic origin:	47	7
American Indian, Eskimo, or Aleut, not of Hispanic origin:	0	0
Asian or Pacific Islander, not of Hispanic origin:	20	9
Other race, not of Hispanic origin:	6	0
TOTAL:	2233	599

Figure 8-6

Educational Attainment Table from *Equal Employment Opportunity File*

040 Ohio
 050 Hamilton County

EDUCATIONAL ATTAINMENT BY AGE BY SEX, HISPANIC ORIGIN, AND RACE
UNIVERSE: Civilian Labor Force

MALE

Age Group/ Education	HISPANIC	White	NOT HISPANIC Black	American Indian/Eskimo	Asian/ Pacific Islander	Other Race
Not high school graduate:						
16 to 19 years:	59	6152	1630	13	42	23
20 to 24 years:	0	2677	893	14	18	6
25 to 29 years:	31	2794	1069	19	27	9
30 to 34 years:	16	2692	1016	14	12	0
35 to 39 years:	18	1919	776	21	20	0
40 to 69 years:	44	11798	3820	77	54	0
70 years and over:	0	584	250	0	0	0
TOTAL: 38607	168	28616	9454	158	173	38
High school graduate (includes equivalency):						
16 to 19 years:	14	1923	535	0	6	0
20 to 24 years:	27	6062	1722	18	15	0
25 to 29 years:	30	7355	1919	0	41	0
30 to 34 years:	35	7735	1955	29	10	7
35 to 39 years:	27	5642	1636	8	42	0
40 to 69 years:	40	15539	3882	13	141	6
70 years and over:	0	439	49	0	13	0
TOTAL: 56915	173	44695	11698	68	268	13
Some college or associate degree:						
16 to 19 years:	18	1798	242	8	13	0
20 to 24 years:	121	8927	1427	20	155	0
25 to 29 years:	71	7880	1517	4	86	8
30 to 34 years:	50	8414	1932	0	44	0
35 to 39 years:	30	7790	1918	39	58	0
40 to 69 years:	42	17283	2942	18	110	0
70 years and over:	0	685	50	0	0	0
TOTAL: 63700	332	52777	10028	89	466	8
Bachelor's degree:						
16 to 19 years:	0	0	0	0	0	0
20 to 24 years:	39	3204	193	0	131	0
25 to 29 years:	53	7456	634	0	114	6
30 to 34 years:	73	6062	643	0	130	0
35 to 39 years:	32	5827	432	0	45	9
40 to 69 years:	91	15562	1105	2	182	10
70 years and over:	0	337	24	0	0	0
TOTAL: 42396	288	38448	3031	2	602	25
Graduate or professional degree:						
16 to 19 years:	0	0	0	0	0	0
20 to 24 years:	0	144	26	0	12	0
25 to 29 years:	61	1760	116	0	114	0
30 to 34 years:	50	3253	174	0	241	0
35 to 39 years:	38	4143	167	5	139	0
40 to 69 years:	122	12715	658	7	506	16
70 years and over:	0	572	22	0	12	0
TOTAL: 25073	271	22587	1163	12	1024	16

FEMALE

Age Group/ Education	HISPANIC	White	NOT HISPANIC Black	American Indian/Eskimo	Asian/ Pacific Islander	Other Race

[tables repeated for Female population; not shown here]

Figure 8-7

place of work, travel-time to work and commuting flows for various levels of geography.

The National Center for Education Statistics (NCES), an agency of the U.S. Department of Education, requested a Special Tabulation containing Census data at the School District level. The resulting *School District Data Book* was issued on more than 40 CD-ROM discs, complete with its own customized software. After long delays, the first volumes of this eagerly awaited product began shipping in December, 1994. The database combines 1990 Census data on school enrollment and population by School District with Department of Education data on School District finances. It covers all public School Districts in the United States.

Special Tabulation on Aging (22 discs).

Although designed and sponsored by the U.S. Department of Health and Human Services' (DHHS) Administration on Aging, the *Special Tabulation on Aging* is published by the Census Bureau. File specifications were prepared by a committee representing 650 federal, state, and local agencies which serve the elderly. The official report number of this file is *STP 14*, but it is commonly referred to as the *AOA File*, after its sponsoring agency.

The *Special Tabulation on Aging* covers a diversity of frequently requested Summary Levels: states, counties, Metropolitan Areas, Urbanized Areas, American Indian and Alaska Native Areas, Places of 2,500 or more, and, for the 12 states where Minor Civil Divisions serve as general-purpose governments, MCDs of 2,500 or more. Several Summary Levels are divided into their Urban and Rural components as well.

The *AOA File* also covers a unique geographic construct, called the Planning and Service Area (PSA). As mandated by the Older Americans Act, PSAs are designated by the agency in each state responsible for regulating services to the elderly. PSAs vary in land area and population. In most states, they consist of single counties or groups of counties. The largest sub-state grouping, located in Kansas, encompasses 28 counties. In eight states with smaller populations, the PSA consists of the entire state. In some cases, a PSA is comprised of a single large city, groups of cities and MCDs, or an Indian Reservation. Within each state, PSAs are assigned consecutive numbers (PSA 1, PSA 2, and so on), but in several states the Areas are given letter designations (PSA A, PSA B, etc.). At the time of the 1990 Census, the nation was divided into 668 PSAs. A complete list of them, including their component parts, can be found in Appendix H of the Technical Documentation for the *AOA File*.

The *Special Tabulation on Aging* is based on 1990 sample data, and presents extraordinarily detailed population and housing characteristics for elderly persons. The file is enormous, containing 483 population tables and 228 housing tables for every geographic entity covered. A variety of characteristics are tabulated, with an emphasis on those especially important to agencies and organizations which provide services to the elderly. Among the population Items are Household Type; Work Disability, Self-Care, and Mobility Limitations; Income and Poverty Status; Ability to Speak English; and Veteran Status. Housing Items include Selected Monthly Owner Costs, Telephone and Vehicle Availability, and Meals Included in Rent. A unique feature of the *AOA File* is the inclusion of numerous tables containing data on Low-Income Status. The DHHS establishes its own Low-Income thresholds similar to the Poverty benchmarks used by the Census Bureau. The *AOA File* tabulates data for persons living above and below the Low-Income level, as well as for persons living above and below the Poverty level. Low-Income Status is described briefly in the Technical Documentation to the file. More detailed definitions and methodology (as it pertains to the 1990 Census) can be found in the February 16, 1990 issue of the *Federal Register*.

The *Special Tabulation on Aging* is based on 1990 sample data, and presents extraordinarily detailed population and housing characteristics for elderly persons.

The *AOA File* tabulates data for persons living above and below the Low-Income level, as well as for persons living above and below the Poverty level.

The primary value of the *Special Tabulation on Aging* is its incredible subject detail. Most tables are repeated for each of six age groups:

- 60 to 64 years
- 65 to 69 years
- 70 to 74 years
- 75 to 79 years
- 80 to 84 years
- 85 years and over

Some tables also provide data for two additional age groups: 55 to 59 years, and under 55 years.

Because the files focus on a limited number of Census Items, most tables offer extensive cross-tabulations. The following examples will illustrate the richness of the subject content:

- Sex by Household Type by Ability to Speak English
- Hispanic Origin by Race by Educational Attainment
- Low-Income Status by Mobility and Self-Care Limitation
- Poverty Status by Race by Social Security Income
- Mobility Limitation Status by Telephone in Unit

Like the *Subject Summary Tape Files* series, the detailed presentations created for the *Special Tabulation on Aging* often result in four- and five-way cross-tabulations.

The Bureau has issued the *AOA File* as two subfiles, following the nomenclature used in the Summary Tape File products. *STP 14A* consists of state-specific tables, while *STP 14C* contains national data and nationwide comparisons. *STP 14A* appears on 21 discs, arranged by the OMB's ten Standard Federal Administrative Regions (not to be confused with the Bureau's own Census Regions). *STP 14C* was released as a single disc. Like the Bureau's other summary data products, the *Special Tabulation on Aging* contains the Bureau's GO software on the CD-ROM discs themselves. As of this writing, Auxiliary Files for use with EXTRACT have not been created, but the Bureau intends to issue them in the future. The discs are less expensive than most 1990 CD-ROMs. A single disc sells for $50, while the entire set can be purchased for $500.

Public-Use Microdata Sample Files

With hundreds of tables to choose from, it might seem that *STF 1* and *STF 3* offer ample data for all but the most demanding Census users. Those seeking more detailed population and housing characteristics can turn to the various titles in the *Subject Summary Tape Files* series, or to such specialized products as the *EEO File* and the *AOA File*. However, when it comes to cross-tabulations of subject variables, standard Census products provide limited solutions. Researchers expecting to find a table citing earnings of Black females by individual occupation and age, or similar multiple relationships, will be disappointed. Users requiring detailed characteristics of a particular subgroup in the population—children with mobility limitations, the rural unemployed, adults with no high school diploma, etc.—will find little help in the decennial Census products, especially for local geographies. Because summary data products contain aggregated statistics, CD-ROMs and print Reports can only provide cross-tabulations which the Bureau has compiled in its standard tables. Even though *STF 3* contains 278 tables, its tabulations focus on the most commonly articulated data needs. For example, *STF 3* presents more than 50 tables relating to Personal Income by amount and source, yet this barely scratches the surface of the pos-

When it comes to cross-tabulations of subject variables, standard Census products provide limited solutions.

Because summary data products contain aggregated statistics, CD-ROMs and print Reports can only provide cross-tabulations which the Bureau has compiled in its standard tables.

NEW IN '90

Prior to the 1990 Census, *PUMS* data were available only as computer tape products. 1990 also marks the first time *PUMS*-specific software has been available for the novice user.

sible relationships between Income and other characteristics. Standard Census tables typically cross-classify topics using two (sometimes three) data Items at a time, with the second and third categories usually being age and sex. Some characteristics are also classified a fourth way—by Race or Hispanic Origin—because separate tables repeat the same Items for particular segments of the population (i.e., different Universes).

Clearly, the Bureau cannot publish multiple cross-classifications for every population and housing characteristic, even if such tables were limited to large geographies: the possible combinations would be astronomical. For users with specialized analytical needs, one solution is to contract with the Bureau for a Special Tabulation report. In most cases, users will find it much more appropriate (and affordable) to create their own customized reports employing one of the Bureau's published microdata products. Microdata refers to untabulated Questionnaire responses, stripped of all personal identifiers. Researchers can employ such files to perform all manner of customized tabulations. Because microdata files represent a collection of completed Questionnaires, access to the files offers users a close substitute to conducting a sample survey of their own. Using published microdata files for a given geographic area enables researchers to retabulate the raw data in any form they desire.

Microdata products containing 1990 Census Questionnaires are published as *Public Use Microdata Sample* (*PUMS*) *Files*. These products contain various samples of individual Household Questionnaires in their entirety. To preserve confidentiality, the Bureau deletes any information which might be used to reveal the identity of an individual person, Family, or Household.

For 1990, the Bureau compiled three separate *PUMS Files*, each one covering a different sample of the population. All three products are based on data received from Households completing the Long Form Questionnaire. The first *PUMS File* contains Questionnaires for 1% of all Households complet-

ing the Long Form, the second contains Questionnaires for 5% of the Long Form Households, and the third is a 3% subsample. The Households represented in each of the three Files are mutually exclusive from one another. In other words, once a Household has been randomly selected for one of the three *PUMS Files*, it is removed from the pool before the other *PUMS* Households are selected.

 Census Tip

The percentages designated in each of the *PUMS* titles do not represent the proportion of the total population, since only 17% of all Households received the 1990 Long Form. To put it another way, the *PUMS 5% File* refers to a 5% subsample of the original 17% sample, not 5% of all Households.

When creating *PUMS Files*, the Bureau takes several steps to ensure confidentiality of individual Questionnaires. First, as already mentioned, all personal names are removed from the file. Second, each Questionnaire is stripped of specific address information and other geographic identifiers, such as Block and Tract numbers. Third, a small number of Questionnaire Items are deleted from every Record, most notably the Place of Work question. And fourth, certain response categories are also deleted. An example is Personal Income greater than $140,000.

The three *PUMS Samples* utilize a geographic construct found in no other Census products. This unique Statistical Unit is called a Public Use Microdata Area (PUMA). PUMAs are large geographies, consisting of territory containing a minimum of 100,000 inhabitants. PUMA boundaries within each state are determined by the individual State Data Centers, following guidelines established by the Bureau. In less populated areas, each PUMA consists of a single county, or several counties whose combined population exceeds 100,000. In heavily-populated areas

---

Clearly, the Bureau cannot publish multiple cross-classifications for every population and housing characteristic, even if such tables were limited to large geographies: the possible combinations would be astronomical.

The three *PUMS Samples* utilize a geographic construct found in no other Census products. This unique Statistical Unit is called a Public Use Microdata Area (PUMA).

Q&A

How do the three *PUMS Samples* differ from one another?

Aside from the distinct, non-overlapping subsamples used in constructing the files, the three *PUMS* titles differ in two other respects: geographic coverage, and type of Household. The *PUMS 5% Sample* is a county-based product, and its PUMAs do not cross state boundaries. The *PUMS 1% Sample* focuses on Metropolitan Areas, and its PUMAs may cross state boundaries. In this Sample, Metropolitan Areas with fewer than 100,000 inhabitants are paired together. The PUMA 3% Sample is a special file. It utilizes the same PUMAs found in the *PUMS 5% Sample*, but the subsample is comprised entirely of Households containing at least one member who is age 60 or older (the responses from other members of the Household are also included, however).

For this reason, it is called the "Elderly File." Because this Sample was sponsored by government agencies serving the aged, it contains an additional level of geography—the same Planning Service Areas found on the Bureau's *Special Tabulation on Aging*.

How does the user determine which Sample is best? The choice depends on the purposes of the study. However, researchers studying a narrowly-defined Universe, such as employed men age 65 or older, will benefit from using the largest Sample possible. In fact, since the three products are mutually exclusive, they can be combined to create a single 9% Sample.

(counties with more than 200,000 inhabitants), the territory is divided into two or more PUMAs. In the latter case, such a PUMA may consist of a single large Place (a city, CDP, etc.) or a combination of smaller Places and surrounding Census Tracts outside the Place boundaries. Tracts are the smallest component of any PUMA.

PUMAs are designated by five-digit numbers. The first three digits represent the basic PUMA identification, while the final two digits are "sub-PUMA" numbers, used to designate PUMAs which are subdivisions of a single Place or county. For example, the city of Phoenix, Arizona is divided into eight PUMAs, numbered 00101 through 00108. Some states choose not to use "sub-PUMA" numbers to identify subdivided counties. PUMA numbering across the United States is not unique, but PUMA numbers are unique within an individual state. In other words, PUMA 1700 may be found in many states, but New York State will contain only one PUMA 1700.

The three *PUMS* products are available on computer tape, but only two of them can be found on CD-ROM. The *PUMS 5% Sample*

> **Two types of Records can be found on the files: Housing Records and Person Records.**

was released on seven CD-ROM discs; the *PUMS 1% Sample* is a two-disc set. The *PUMS 3% Sample* (the Elderly File) will not be published in CD-ROM format.

Each file in the *PUMS 5% Sample* represents a single state. The state files are subdivided by PUMA number. Two types of Records can be found on the files: Housing Records and Person Records. A Housing Record contains data on the characteristics of a single Housing Unit, while a Person Record contains data on an individual person. Each Household is represented by a single Housing Record, plus a Person Record for each member of the Household. All records for a Household are linked by a common Serial Number. The *PUMS 5% Sample* contains 136 variables for Person Records and 117 variables for Housing Records. Files are stored in fixed-format ASCII text.

In addition to the actual data files, each *PUMS* disc contains software and the Technical Documentation files. Technical Documentation includes a Data Dictionary file, various code lists, and a complete list of all PUMAs and their component parts. A special file, called **puma2dsk.exe**, enables users

Sample QuickTab Table: Frequency Distribution

Data file: Buffalo, NY PUMA 03001
Record: PERSON-RECORD

Universe: AGE-SINGLE	>	35	
AND	SEX	=	Female
AND	YEARSCH	>	10

Weight: PWGT1

Item: OCCUP

Values Percent:	Frequency				Cumulative	
	:Total:	Pcnt:	%Def.:	%Valid:	Total:	
Manag/Professional ....:	2112	35.4	35.4	49.4:	2112	35.4
Technical/Sales ....:	1513	25.4	25.4	35.4:	3625	60.8
Service ....:	277	4.6	4.6	6.5:	3902	65.5
Farming/Fishing ....:	-	-	-	-:	3902	65.5
Craft/Repair ....:	25	.4	.4	.6:	3927	65.9
Laborer/Operator ....:	332	5.6	5.6	7.8:	4259	71.4
Armed Forces ....:	-	-	-	-:	4259	71.4
Not in LF ....:	19	.3	.3	.4:	4278	71.8
NA ....:	1683	28.2	28.2	-:	5961	100.0
Undefined ....:	-	-	-	-:	5961	100.0

Item: YEARSCH

Values Percent:	Frequency				Cumulative	
	:Total:	Pcnt:	%Def.:	%Valid:	Total:	
None ....:	-	-	-	-:	0	.0
Nursery............. ....:	-	-	-	-:	0	.0
Kindergarten.......... ....:	-	-	-	-:	0	.0
Grade 1 to 4 ....:	-	-	-	-:	0	.0
Grade 5 to 8............ ....:	-	-	-	-:	0	.0
Grade 9 ....:	-	-	-	-:	0	.0
Grade 10 ....:	-	-	-	-:	0	.0
Grade 11 ....:	-	-	-	-:	0	.0
Grade 12/No Dipl....... ....:	-	-	-	-:	0	.0
HS Diploma ....:	-	-	-	-:	0	.0
College-No Degree ....:	2667	44.7	44.7	44.7 :	2667	44.7
Assoc-Occupation ....:	630	10.6	10.6	10.6 :	3297	55.3
Assoc-Academic ....:	679	11.4	11.4	11.4 :	3976	66.7
Bachelor's Degree ....:	1074	18.0	18.0	18.0 :	5050	84.7
Master's Degree ....:	695	11.7	11.7	11.7 :	5745	96.4
Professional Degree ....:	157	2.6	2.6	2.6 :	5902	99.0
PhD Degree ....:	59	1.0	1.0	1.0 :	5961	100.0
NA ....:	-	-	-	-:	5961	100.0
Undefined ....:	-	-	-	-:	5961	100.0

Figure 8-8

to extract data for a specific PUMA from the CD-ROM to the hard drive of their micro-computer.

Researchers can tabulate and analyze data on the *PUMS Files* using statistical software packages such as SAS and SPSS. However, the CD-ROM contains a very elementary microdata manipulation program called QuickTab. QuickTab was designed by the Census Bureau's International Statistical Programs Center, with funding from the U.S. Agency for International Development. The goal was to create a tool which the Bureau could use to train government de-mographers in third-world nations.

QuickTab actually consists of two separate programs: FREQ and CROSSTAB. The FREQ program allows users to create customized frequency distribu-tions based on the raw microdata. The CROSSTAB program allows users to construct three-way cross-tabulations.

QuickTab actually consists of two separate programs: FREQ and CROSSTAB. The FREQ program allows users to create cus-tomized frequency distributions based on the raw microdata. The CROSSTAB program allows users to construct three-way cross-tabulations. Both programs are surprisingly simple to use. Menus and on-screen prompts guide the user through every step in the process. At each stage in the search, the two QuickTab programs present lists of variables from which to choose.

 Census Tip

The Census Bureau has issued an infor-mative, step-by-step guide to loading and using the QuickTab program. The guide, entitled *Accessing Public Use Microdata Using QuickTab*, is available from the Bureau's Data User Services Division.

Both programs also provide users with the capability to define their own population segment for further analysis.

Both programs also provide users with the capability to define their own population segment for further analysis. For example, QuickTab can be used to extract all Person Records for Black males, age 25 and older, with no high school diploma. The FREQ and CROSSTAB programs can then be used to analyze the characteristics of this user-defined Universe.

It is beyond the scope of this book to provide detailed instructions on the use of QuickTab. However, a brief look at a few representative tables generated by the two QuickTab programs will demonstrate the capabilities of the system. In the following examples, the user has defined a Universe consisting of females older than 35 who have received one or more college degrees or who have completed some college courses without receiving a degree. The geographic coverage is PUMA 03001 in New York State, repre-senting a portion of the city of Buffalo. The Universe and geographic coverage are indi-cated at the top of every table. (Note: **YEARSCH > 10** refers to category 10 for the Educational Attainment variable, covering persons who have completed high school or obtained a GED. The Technical Documen-tation for the *PUMS Files* provides a com-plete list of the codes for response categories.) In these examples, the searcher has instructed QuickTab to weight the results to provide estimates for the entire Universe. Based on the 1990 *PUMS 5% Sample*, the Census Bureau estimates that 5,961 women over the age of 35 in PUMA 3001 have completed more than a high school education.

Figure 8-8 shows two tables generated from the FREQ program. The first table presents a frequency distribution by occupa-tional category; the second provides frequen-cies by year of schooling. No values are shown below the college level (i.e., the first ten categories) because persons without col-lege experience were excluded from the Universe. Note that the values for each in-terval are presented two ways: as actual amounts and as percentages. According to Figure 8-8, an estimated 2,112 of the women in the designated Universe are in managerial or professional occupations, representing 35.4% of that Universe. However, 28.2% of the respondents fall into the "Not Appli-cable" (NA) category.

Figure 8-9 shows a portion of a table generated by the CROSSTAB program. Here

Sample QuickTab Table: Cross-Tabulation

Data File: Buffalo, NY PUMA 03001
Record: PERSON-RECORD

.... Universe:		AGE-SINGLE	>	35
....		AND	SEX	= Female
....		AND	YEARSCH	> 10

Weight: PWGT1

Count: OCCUP by MARITAL by YEARSCH

		Total:	Now Marr:	Widowd:	Divorced:	Separt:	Never Marr:

Total

Total	:	5961:	2217	803	1151	440	1350
Manage/Professn	:	2112:	716	158	513	195	530
Technical/Sales	:	1513:	597	176	307	97	336
Service	:	277:	176	-	39	39	23
Farming/Fishing	:	-:	-	-	-	-	-
Craft/Repair	:	25:	-	-	-	17	8
Laborer/Operator	:	332:	39	17	48	41	187
Armed Forces	:	-:	-	-	-	-	-
Not in LF	:	19:	19	-	-	-	-
NA	:	1683:	670	452	244	51	266

Count: OCCUP by MARITAL by YEARSCH

		Total:	Now Marr:	Widowd:	Divorced:	Separt:	Never Marr:

Master's Degree

Total	:	695:	198	28	120	94	255
Manage/Professn	:	547:	157	-	120	60	210
Technical/Sales	:	33:	19	-	-	-	14
Service	:	-:	-	-	-	-	-
Farming/Fishing	:	-:	-	-	-	-	-
Craft/Repair	:	-:	-	-	-	-	-
Laborer/Operator	:	22:	22	-	-	-	-
Armed Forces	:	-:	-	-	-	-	-
Not in LF	:	-:	-	-	-	-	-
NA	:	93:	-	28	-	34	31

Figure 8-9

Although QuickTab is simple to operate, searchers must have a strong grasp of Census concepts to use it properly.

the same 5,961 women are shown in a three-way cross-tabulation, indicating Occupation by Marital Status by Educational Attainment. The top portion of the table displays occupation and marital status for the entire Universe. The bottom portion shows the same relationships for women with Master's Degrees. Additional sections (not shown in Figure 8-9) cite occupational characteristics and marital status for the remaining educational categories. In this Figure, numbers are displayed in cardinal form, but the user could have instructed CROSSTAB to present results as percentages.

Although QuickTab is simple to operate, searchers must have a strong grasp of Census concepts to use it properly. They must also consult the Technical Documentation to identify Field Names and response codes, both of which are unique to *PUMS*. QuickTab is an extremely basic program. It offers no capability to conduct regression analysis or statistical testing of any kind. Furthermore, it is designed for viewing and printing the created tables, not to further manipulate the data. For example, extracted tables cannot be imported into a spreadsheet. However, QuickTab represents the first opportunity for novice users to access *PUMS Files* directly. The ability to define a customized Universe, create frequency tables, and generate three-way cross-tabulations offers researchers many new analytical opportunities.

TIGER/Line Files

The Bureau has created several geographic reference tools in CD-ROM format. The *Geographic Identification Code Scheme* (*GICS*) was released in the summer of 1994. It contains all of the Geographic Identifier tables seen in the STF products, but reproduces them on a single convenient disc. Another useful tool, the *TIGER/Census Tract Street Index*, was released in early 1995. For most Census users, however, the *TIGER/Line Files* are the most important geographic product.

TIGER, the Bureau's comprehensive geographic database, was introduced in Chapter 6. *TIGER/Line Files* are a subset of the larger system, designed to allow users to plot their own maps. In addition to *TIGER/Line* data, the CD-ROM discs contain the relevant sections of a related product called the *TIGER/Geographic Name File*. This database links the labels for all named geographic entities with their corresponding TIGER codes.

Several editions of the *TIGER/Line Files* have been released, with subsequent versions superseding earlier ones. A "Pre-Census" edition, issued on CD-ROM in mid-1990, was based on geographic information compiled during the Bureau's Pre-Census Local Review Program. A second CD-ROM version, released in the second half of 1991, reflected the boundaries in place at the time of the Census, utilizing data from the January, 1990 Boundary and Annexation Survey. Neither of these versions provided mapping software on the discs. A third edition, called the *1992 TIGER/Line Files*, was issued on compact disc during the first half of 1994.

1992 TIGER/Line File (44 discs.)

The revised *1992 TIGER/Line Files* incorporate numerous improvements over previous versions. The most notable enhancement is the provision of map display software, called LandView, on the discs themselves. LandView is described in detail later in the chapter. The 1992 revision also updates geographic data in several important respects. First, more street address data are included. The 1990 files covered address-ranges for approximately 50 million Households. The 1992 files cover 80 million addresses, an increase of 60%. Address coverage is limited to standard city/suburban style addresses; Households in Rural areas are excluded, as are those using post office boxes. All but 73 counties in the United States now have some address coverage in the *TIGER/Line Files*. Coverage varies by county. The Technical Documentation provides a complete list of U.S. counties, showing the approximate address coverage for each.

A second geographic enhancement is the addition of boundary information for the following Summary Levels not found in the earlier versions: Congressional Districts for the 103rd Congress, School Districts; Urbanized Areas; and Urban/Rural designations. Third, the 1992 files encompass numerous boundary corrections based on Post-Census review programs. A final enhancement is the provision of supplementary information on Governmental Units, showing boundary changes which occurred between 1990 and 1992, based on results of the 1992 Boundary and Annexation Survey. Despite the presence of the latter updates, standard boundaries in the 1992 Files continue to

TIGER/Line Files are a subset of the larger system, designed to allow users to plot their own maps.

The 1990 files covered address-ranges for approximately 50 million Households. The 1992 files cover 80 million addresses, an increase of 60%.

reflect the status of Governmental Units as of January 1, 1990, in order to correspond with 1990 Census tabulations. Polygons for entities whose boundaries have changed since 1990 can be displayed using Record Type G.

 Census Tip

The 1992 *TIGER/Line Files* replace all previous versions. Earlier editions are now obsolete.

TIGER/Line data are organized into files, with each file covering a single county or county-equivalent. The 1992 files are issued on CD-ROM in 44 discs. Some discs contain the complete files for a single state, while others combine data for several smaller states. Larger states with complex geographies, such as Texas, Florida, and California, are issued in multi-disc sets.

CD-ROM Software

Although the Census Bureau is not in the software design business, it does provide basic programs to make its CD-ROM products usable to the general public. QuickTab, the program designed specifically for use with the *PUMS Files*, was introduced earlier in the chapter. The following sections describe the Bureau's other three programs for use with 1990 Census discs. LandView was created to view and print maps using data from the *TIGER/Line Files*. The remaining two programs, called GO and EXTRACT, have much broader applications.

The GO Programs

GO is the collective name for a group of programs which allows users to browse Census Bureau CD-ROMs, locate specified, preformatted tables on the disc, view those tables, and print or download their contents.

This type of data retrieval software is known as a "page turning" program because it allows the user to treat the database as though it were a series of tables in a printed book. It is often referred to as "point and shoot" software because it requires no prior knowledge on the part of the user.

GO was developed by the Systems and Programming Staff of the Bureau's Data User Services Division, using Nantucket Corp.'s Clipper software. An early version of GO appears on the *Public Law 94-171 Data* discs. More sophisticated versions can be found on all STF discs, all CD-ROM versions of the *Subject Summary Tape Files*, the *Equal Employment Opportunity File*, and the *Special Tabulations on Aging*. The GO software is loaded on the CD-ROM disc itself. To run the program, users follow a simple two-step process. First, change the logged disk drive to the drive on which the compact disc is loaded (for a single-disc CD player, this is usually designated drive **D:** or drive **L:**). Next, type the word **go**; after a pause of a few seconds, the opening GO menu will appear. The **go** command executes a batch file on the disc which then runs the Clipper program written specifically for that CD-ROM product (hence the name GO).

Census Tip

Users with insufficient memory on their microcomputers can run an abbreviated version of GO, offering limited retrieval capabilities. To utilize this program, type "go lite" at the logged disk drive instead of "go."

GO software is product-specific, though it is similar in appearance from one Census file to another. Certain features, while useful in one product, do not function in others, or do so somewhat differently. In *STF 1A*, *STF 1B*, and *STF 3A*, for example, the user locates a specific Tract number by using the <F1> function key. In *STF 3B*, the <F1> key is a "state locator," indicating which of the four

Summary of Important GO Features

Feature	Description	Files Available
<Esc>	Pressing the "Escape" key returns the user to the previous step in the menu hierarchy.	All
Browse	Used once a specific geographic entity has been selected. Displays other data tables for that entity; also displays data for other entities within the same Summary Level.	All
Keyword	Used once a specific geographic entity has been selected. Displays an alphabetical list of subject keywords. Selecting a keyword retrieves the table or tables relating to that topic.	STF 3, AOA File
Glossary	Used once a data table has been displayed. Provides abbreviated definition of the subject term(s) shown on the table.	STF 3, AOA File
[F-1]	Searches for a specific Census Tract by its Tract number.	STF 1A, 1B STF 3A
[A-Z]	Moves to the first letter in an alphabetic list; used to locate a state, county, or Place name in a lengthy list.	All except STF 1D/3D AOA File
Print table	Allows user to print entire table being viewed. Can be printed to a printer (on paper) or to a file (on diskette).	All
Print single line	Same capability as above, but instead of printing entire table for one geographic entity, it prints a single data element for all entities at that Summary Level.	All except EEO File
Copy	Copies file to diskette (or hard drive) in delimited form, complete with database coding. Can be copied in various software-specific formats.	All
<Ctrl> <Home>	"Start over" feature. Returns user to the "Select Summary Level" menu.	STF 3, AOA File
<End>	Ends session and exits GO software.	All

Figure 8-10

Utilizing the GO software is fairly straightforward, and the command line found at the bottom of every screen indicates which features can be used from that screen.

discs contain data on a particular state. The Bureau revises the GO software with each new product release, incorporating improvements suggested by data users. The "Keyword," "Glossary," and "Start Over" features do not appear on *STF 1* products, for example, but are found on later releases. Figure 8-10 describes some of the more widely-used features of the GO programs, indicating the

major CD-ROM files on which they can be found. The Figure pertains to the STF products, the *EEO File*, and the *Special Tabulation on Aging*. The GO programs for titles in the *SSTF* series are significantly different, and will be described later in this section.

Utilizing the GO software is fairly straightforward, and the command line found at the bottom of every screen indicates which features can be used from that screen. For example, when the [A-Z] feature is shown on the command line, the user can enter a single letter to move the cursor to another point in an alphabetical list of geographic names. Cursor movement is accomplished in the traditional manner, using the **<PgUp>**, **<PgDn>**, and arrow keys. The **<Enter>** key is used to select a highlighted option. The **<Esc>** key is used to return to the previous menu. Repeatedly pressing **<Esc>** allows the user to gradually back out of the program, one menu at a time. Pressing **<End>** immediately exits the GO software. The "Start Over" feature, **<Ctrl><Home>**, returns the user to the beginning menu, called the "Select a Summary Level" screen. The "Start Over" command is not available on early versions of the GO software.

GO is designed to replicate the steps a searcher would take when using printed Census reports. Once the appropriate disc has been chosen, the first step is to determine the desired level of geography. The next step is to identify a specific geographic entity, and finally, to choose a particular data table by topic. The GO program presents a series of menus which are displayed sequentially until the desired data table is shown. After the user chooses a Summary Level, a specific geographic entity can be selected. To view data for the city of Minneapolis, the user would select the Summary Level for Place totals, then choose "Minneapolis" from an alphabetic list. Depending on the disc product and the Summary Level being used, GO may provide intermediate menus before the actual geographic entity can be selected. On *STF 1A*, for example, the user must make three menu selections when seeking data for Minneapolis, because *STF 1A* contains data for several states on a single disc. In this case, the user would select "Place (totals)," "Minnesota," and then "Minneapolis."

The first screen presented by the GO program is the "Select a Summary Level" menu. (The *EEO File* and the *SSTF* titles employ an exception to this format because data on those discs are presented for a few Summary Levels only.) As described earlier, a Summary Level can appear in "inventory" format (alphabetically), or in hierarchical fashion. GO presents both formats in a single menu. When viewing an inventory presentation, the user can type the first letter of the entity's name, and the cursor will move to its vicinity in the alphabetical list. When viewing a hierarchical format, the user is presented with a series of submenus, displaying successive levels in the hierarchy.

The importance of understanding geographic relationships, as defined by the Census Bureau, cannot be overemphasized. In order to identify the necessary Summary Level from the GO menu, users must be familiar with the Bureau's geographic concepts.

Census Tip

Data for false MCDs (described in Chapter 6) are shown twice in the Summary Level groupings: once under their actual Summary Level, such as Place or American Indian Reservation, and once under the County Subdivision level. For example, "autonomous" cities are listed as Places and as County Subdivisions. The repeated tables are redundant, included to ensure that component parts within the geographic hierarchy sum to the total of the next higher level.

An example of a typical Summary Level menu, taken from *STF 3A*, is shown in Figure 8-11. Choices with no indentations

---

Summary Level Menu, STF 3A

1990 Census of Population and Housing Summary Tape File 3A

040 New Jersey

SELECT A SUMMARY LEVEL

State	040
Place (totals)	160
County (parts)	155
Consolidated city (totals)	170
County (totals)	050
Census tract/block numbering area (totals)	140
Block group (totals)	150
County subdivision (MCD/CCD) (totals)	060
Place (parts)	070
Census tract/block numbering area (parts)	080
Block group (parts)	090
American Indian Reservation, etc.	2??
Metropolitan Statistical Area	3??
Urbanized Area	4??

-Scroll PgDn/PgUp-Page   Enter-Select Esc-Reset End-Quit

Exhibit 8-11

---

indicate an inventory format. Indentations indicate options utilizing a hierarchical structure. By following the indentations upward on the menu, the user can determine successively larger geographies within which the subordinate levels are presented. In Figure 8-11, Block Group totals (Level 150) fall within Census Tract totals (Level 140), which in turn fall within county totals (Level 050).

Another example from Figure 8-11 will help differentiate between the two types of geographic presentation. Place-level data can be found in three separate menu options. Summary Level 160 offers an inventory listing, representing Places in their entirety. Summary Level 155 is a hierarchical presentation used for Places which cross county boundaries; Level 155 divides "split Places" into their component county parts. Summary Level 070 presents data for parts of Places which fall within a specified County Subdivision. Here the user must first select a particular County Subdivision before seeing a submenu with a list of Place names. Users who wish to see data for Place totals

> **In order to identify the necessary Summary Level from the GO menu, users must be familiar with the Bureau's geographic concepts.**

should select Level 160, while persons wishing to see various component parts of a Place should choose Levels 155 or 070.

Once a specific geographic entity has been selected, the GO user will see a complete list of subject tables for that entity—in effect, a Table of Contents. GO constructs the same set of tables thousands of times on each disc, tabulating results for every geographic entity in the database. After the user highlights the desired table number from the menu and presses <Enter>, GO "turns the page" to the requested table.

> **Once a specific geographic entity has been selected, the GO user will see a complete list of subject tables for that entity—in effect, a Table of Contents.**

Figure 8-12 shows the first two screens of subject menus for *STF 1A*. As with most other Summary Tape Files, the first two menu items are unnumbered. The top line, labeled "General Profiles," provides one or more data tables containing summarized data on a variety of topics, many of which are presented in the form of percentages, medians, or means. This is an extremely convenient feature, offering the user a brief overview of the geographic entity under investigation. *STF 1* files provide a single General Profile for every entity. *STF 3* files are much more extensive, requiring four separate Profiles for every entity.

The second line of the Subject menu, labeled "Geographic Identifiers," provides a detailed list of the geographic codes pertaining to the entity described. This menu item also displays data on the total land area and water area (in square kilometers) for that entity. Beginning with the third line, tables are listed in numeric order, just as they appear in Appendix D of this book. All Imputation Tables are also listed on the GO menus, once again in the numeric order shown in Appendix D.

The examples given in Figure 8-12 help illustrate a limitation of early versions of the GO software. Only the title of each table and its table number can be seen on the GO menus. Because titles can be vague, and because two or more tables may have the same or similar titles, these menus may be confusing. GO does provide additional clues, however. Two tables often have the same title because they utilize an identical format but cover two different Universes. In these situations, the GO menus easily differentiate between the two. As the cursor or highlighter bar moves from one line to the next on the GO menu, the Universe for each data table appears at the top of the menu screen. For example, Tables P15, P21, and P23 are all labeled "Household Type and Relationship." Figure 8-12, which shows the cursor positioned at Table P21, indicates the Universe for this table is Persons under 18 years of age. Moving the cursor to the line

---

Table of Contents Menus, *STF 1A*

1990 Census Of Population And Housing Summary Tape File 1A

040 Alabama
160 Birmingham City

GENERAL PROFILE	
GEOGRAPHIC IDENTIFIERS	
PERSONS	P001
FAMILIES	P002
HOUSEHOLDS	P003
URBAN AND RURAL	P004
SEX	P005
RACE	P006
DETAILED RACE	P007
PERSONS OF HISPANIC ORIGIN	P008
HISPANIC ORIGIN	P009
HISPANIC ORIGIN BY RACE	P010
AGE	P011

-Scroll PgDn/PgUp-Page Enter-Select   Esc-Reset   End-Quit

Tab P021 Universe: Persons under 18 years

RACE BY SEX BY AGE	P012
SEX BY AGE	P013
SEX BY MARITAL STATUS	P014
HOUSEHOLD TYPE AND RELATIONSHIP	P015
HOUSEHOLD SIZE AND HOUSEHOLD TYPE	P016
PERSONS IN FAMILIES	P017
PERSONS PER FAMILY	P017A
AGE OF HOUSEHOLD MEMBERS BY HOUSEHOLD TYPE	P018
RACE OF HOUSEHOLDER BY HOUSEHOLD TYPE	P019
HOUSEHOLD TYPE	P020
HOUSEHOLD TYPE AND RELATIONSHIP	**P021**
RELATIONSHIP AND AGE	P022
HOUSEHOLD TYPE AND RELATIONSHIP	P023

-Scroll PgDn/PgUp-Page Enter-Select   Esc-Reset   End-Quit

Figure 8-12

How can GO users obtain more detailed descriptions of each table's contents without looking at the table itself?

Each table's matrix structure, shown in Appendix D, provides useful clues about the table's content. For example, Tables P6 and P7 from *STF 1* both focus on racial characteristics. Based on their titles and matrix configuration, Table P7 appears to be more detailed. Table P6 contains five data cells, so the user can correctly assume that it tabulates the number of persons in each of the Bureau's five broad categories of Race. Table P7 contains 25 data cells, which suggests it contains racial breakdowns beyond the five major categories. Figure 8-13 shows Table P7 for Erie County, New York. As the user may have guessed, it presents totals for the five racial categories, plus 20 additional subcategories.

An even better guide to table content can be found in each file's Technical Documentation. In addition to the List of Tables shown in Appendix D, the Technical Documentation includes a detailed Table Outline, listing the specific tabulation categories found in every table. Figure 8-14, taken from the Technical Documentation to *STF 3*, describes the contents of several tables relating to Income and Earnings. Table P89, with a total of two data cells, shows two tabulation categories: the number of Households with Earnings, and the number without. Table P88, with 63 data cells in a 7 x 9 matrix, shows nine Income categories repeated for seven age groups.

Frequent users of the GO software may find it helpful to photocopy (or download and print) extra sets of the complete Table Outlines for *STF 1* and *STF 3*.

---

for P15 shows that table covers all persons, while the Universe for Table P23 is persons 65 and over. Still, with 100 or more tables listed on each menu, the lack of additional descriptive information can be frustrating, forcing the user to "peek" at the actual tables to determine where needed data can be found.

Figure 8-13 shows several standard features seen in all GO tables. GO always indicates the Summary Level and the name of the geographic entity at the top of each table. In Figure 8-13, it indicates Level 050 (county totals) for Erie County, New York. GO also displays the coverage Universe at the top of every table; in this case, the Universe is all Persons.

Two additional features are worth noting. Indentations in the left-hand column show the relationships among subcategories and their broader groupings. "Japanese" is a subcategory of "Asian," which in turn is a subcategory of "Asian or Pacific Islander." The sum of all the numbers within a given indented grouping will equal the amount shown on the first non-indented line above it. For

GO always indicates the Summary Level and the name of the geographic entity at the top of each table.

example, the 11 items in the group which begins with the line for "Chinese" will sum to the total for "Asian." A second feature common to the GO tables is the numbers shown in parentheses in the left-hand column. These represent the unique code numbers assigned to each response category for tabulation purposes. As seen in this example, tabulations are often based on the sum of several response categories. A complete list of the codes can be found in the Technical Documentation.

Unlike tables found in the Bureau's print publications, GO tables are limited to two-dimensional grids. Figure 8-3, shown earlier in the chapter, illustrates this limitation. Because Table P12 in *STF 1* presents a three-way matrix (Race by Sex by Age), the data must be presented in a series of two-way matrices: Sex by Age, shown five times (for each of the five racial categories). In some instances, these repeated matrices are presented in a single table, as in Table P12. In other cases, the tables are presented as submenus. Table 14 in *STF 3* (described in

Part Two of Appendix D) presents the same matrix, Race by Sex by Age, for Sample Data. Rather than showing the ten breakdowns in a single table, they are presented as ten separate submenus, indicated in Appendix D as Tables 14A through 14J.

Certain GO programs contain additional search features to assist users. The Keyword command, found on *STF 3* and *AOA* discs, allows the user to quickly identify all tables containing a specified keyword. After the user types the first letter of the desired keyword, GO displays a list of words beginning with that letter. For example, a searcher looking for *STF 3* tables which contain data

The Keyword command, found on *STF 3* and *AOA* discs, allows the user to quickly identify all tables containing a specified keyword.

for Condominiums would type **C**, then scan the list for the desired word. After selecting "Condominium" from the displayed keywords, the user would see a list of all relevant tables dealing with the topic of Condominiums (four tables, in this case). Any one of the tables can then be chosen for viewing. Similarly, after selecting the keyword "Male," the searcher would see a list of 36 tables which provide breakdowns by sex. The Keyword feature is especially useful for persons with little knowledge of Census terminology. By utilizing the Keyword command, the searcher doesn't need to know that data on the homeless are listed under Group Quarters tables, or that statistics on the self-employed are found under Class of Worker. The Keyword list for *STF 3* is selective, but covers more than 350 terms. These include words from the table titles (e.g., Aggregate, Median, Occupation) as well as words from the individual response categories (e.g., Hungarian, Widowed, Nonrelative).

Another useful feature found on later versions of GO is the Glossary command. Within a specific data table, the user can type "G" to display a pop-up window with a brief definition of various terms used in the table.

Virtually all GO programs contain the Browse function, which allows users to scan the contents of many tables without constantly Escaping back to previous menus. Within a specific table, Browse allows the user to compare a single data item for many geographic entities, or to display the same table for subordinate Summary Levels in a geographic hierarchy.

The Print command in the GO programs is analogous to photocopying a page from a paper Report. This command will reproduce a single table in its entirety, and is far more efficient than pressing the **<Print Screen>** key. The Print feature can also be

---

Detailed Race Table, *STF 1A*

1990 Census Of Population And Housing Summary Tape File 1A

040 New York
050 Erie County

DETAILED RACE
Universe: Persons
White (800-869, 971) 831,903
Black (870-934, 972) 109,852
American Indian, Eskimo, or Aleut (000-599, 935-970, 973-975):
    American Indian (000-599, 973) 5,563
    Eskimo (935-940, 974) 22
    Aleut (941-970, 975) 15
Asian or Pacific Islander (600-699, 976-985):
    Asian (600-652, 976, 977, 979-982, 985):
        Chinese (605-607, 976) 2,616
        Filipino (608, 977) 619
        Japanese (611, 981) 610
        Asian Indian (600, 982) 2,745
        Korean (612, 979) 1,661
        Vietnamese (619, 980) 700
        Cambodian (604) 101
        Hmong (609) 1
        Laotian (613) 315
        Thai (618) 79
        Other Asian (601-603, 610, 614-617, 620-652, 985) ... 687
    Pacific Islander (653-699, 978, 983, 984):
        Polynesian (653-659, 978, 983):
            Hawaiian (653, 654, 978) 38
            Samoan (655, 983) 8
            Tongan (657) 4
            Other Polynesian (656, 658, 659) 1
        Micronesian (660-675, 984):
            Guamanian (660, 984) 33
            Other Micronesian (661-675) 0
        Melanesian (676-680) 0
        Pacific Islander, not specified (681-699) 2
Other race (700-799, 986-999) 10,957

Figure 8-13

Unless the user renames each file as the table is downloaded, GO will write over the previous file.

used to download individual tables to a diskette. After typing **P**, the user sees two menu choices: "Print to printer" (on paper) or "Print to file" (on diskette). Downloading using the Print function will capture the table in ASCII text, exactly as it displays on screen. GO automatically adds a file extension (.PRN) to the downloaded file name unless the user specifies an alternative extension name. Any additional tables must be

downloaded one at a time. GO does not append a newly downloaded table to an existing one. Unless the user renames each file as the table is downloaded, GO will write over the previous file. Printing to a disk is useful for incorporating Census tables into the text of a word processing document—a technique which was employed to create many of the Figures in this chapter.

Users who wish to import Census data into a software program which performs mathematical or statistical operations must employ the Copy command. Like the Print command, this function also downloads data from a single table, but does so in comma delimited form, complete with standardized labels for every column and row in the table. The Copy function offers users a choice of several formats based on the type of software into which the data will be imported: statistical packages, spreadsheets, or database managers. The Copy command does not work with the General Profiles, but is operable with all numbered tables.

Selected Entries from *STF 3* Table Outline

Table	Title (Matrix)	Data Cells
P88. AGE OF HOUSEHOLDER (7) BY HOUSEHOLD INCOME IN 1989 (9)		63

Universe: Households with householder of Hispanic origin

        Under 25 years:
                Less than $5,000
                $5,000 to $9,999
                $10,000 to $14,999
                $15,000 to $24,999
                $25,000 to $34,999
                $35,000 to $49,999
                $50,000 to $74,999
                $75,000 to $99,999
                $100,000 or more
        25 to 34 years:
                (Repeat HOUSEHOLD INCOME IN 1989)
        35 to 44 years:
                (Repeat HOUSEHOLD INCOME IN 1989)
        45 to 54 years:
                (Repeat HOUSEHOLD INCOME IN 1989)
        55 to 64 years:
                (Repeat HOUSEHOLD INCOME IN 1989)
        65 to 74 years:
                (Repeat HOUSEHOLD INCOME IN 1989)
        75 years and over:
                (Repeat HOUSEHOLD INCOME IN 1989)

P89. EARNINGS IN 1989 (2)   2
Universe: Households
                With earnings
                No earnings

P90. WAGE OR SALARY INCOME IN 1989 (2)		2

Universe: Households
                With wage or salary income
                No wage or salary income

P91. NONFARM SELF EMPLOYMENT INCOME IN 1989 (2)		2

Universe: Households
                With nonfarm self employment income
                No nonfarm self employment income

Figure 8-14

 Census Tip

To download a table in text format, exactly as it is displayed on screen, use the "Print to File" command, not the "Copy File" command.

The GO programs are designed to present data tables for a single geographic entity. Users who wish to view comparative tables for multiple entities can utilize GO to perform this function, albeit in a limited manner. After selecting the Print option, choose "Single item for several areas." The program will then prompt you to highlight the line you wish to print. The resulting table, printed to paper or dis-

Using the Single-Line Print Feature

1990 Census Of Population And Housing Summary Tape File 1A

Geography:
    040 New York
    050 Erie County

Data Item:
DETAILED RACE
Universe: Persons

Asian or Pacific Islander (600-699, 976-985):
    Asian (600-652, 976, 977, 979-982, 985):
        Filipino (608, 977)

Albany County	401	Niagara County	109
Allegany County	18	Oneida County	240
Bronx County	3,497	Onondaga County	563
Broome County	277	Ontario County	32
Cattaraugus County	23	Orange County	504
Cayuga County	30	Orleans County	9
Chautauqua County	56	Oswego County	75
Chemung County	50	Otsego County	27
Chenango County	40	Putnam County	111
Clinton County	150	Queens County	22,324
Columbia County	21	Rensselaer County	160
Cortland County	30	Richmond County	3,516
Delaware County	18	Rockland County	2,996
Dutchess County	326	St. Lawrence County	71
Erie County	**619**	Saratoga County	140
Essex County	14	Schenectady County	130
Franklin County	24	Schoharie County	7
Fulton County	25	Schuyler County	7
Genesee County	29	Seneca County	21
Greene County	14	Steuben County	51
Hamilton County	0	Suffolk County	3,040
Herkimer County	21	Sullivan County	68
Jefferson County	207	Tioga County	29
Kings County	5,776	Tompkins County	194
Lewis County	24	Ulster County	141
Livingston County	43	Warren County	25
Madison County	46	Washington County	27
Monroe County	531	Wayne County	33
Montgomery County	19	Westchester County	2,820
Nassau County	4,316	Wyoming County	21
New York County	8,116	Yates County	7

Figure 8-15

kette, will display the chosen data Item for every entity at the specified Summary Level, as long as it falls within the hierarchy's domain. Examples include every Block Group within a chosen Tract or every County Subdivision within a county. Figure 8-15 provides an example of such a printout. It was generated from the data in Table P7 of *STF 1A* (shown earlier in Figure 8-13). GO prompts the user to highlight the desired line from the table. In this example, the user has selected "Filipinos," the seventh line of data in Figure 8-13. The "print single item" feature will then create a table showing the number of Filipinos for all entities in the designated Summary Level. Because the base table covers Erie County, New York, the program will retrieve the Summary Level for counties. The newly created table shows data for all 62 counties in New York State. Although this command can be extremely useful, it is limited to one demographic or housing variable at a time. Users wishing to create more complex tables must use the Bureau's EXTRACT program, or consider commercially-produced database or spreadsheet software.

Although the GO programs are similar from one CD-ROM title to another, they are product-specific, and certain files have unique search or display features. The *STF 1B* program contains a "Zero Block" command. In its default mode, the GO program for this file displays data for only those Blocks containing one or more Housing Units. By typing Z, the user switches to the "Zero Block" mode, which displays a list of the Blocks in the selected Block Group which have no Housing Units. Of course no population or housing data are shown for these Blocks because no inhabitants live there.

The GO program for *STF 3B* displays data at the ZIP Code level only. A specific ZIP Code can be searched numerically by entering it directly from the keyboard, or it can be selected from a list of alphabetical place names. Unlike other Summary Tape Files, *STF 3B* does not display component parts of larger geographies. Although a ZIP Code Area may cover several Places or County Subdivisions, selecting any of those names from the alphabetic list will retrieve the same table—showing data for the entire ZIP Code Area.

Another example of a unique GO command can be found on the combined *STF 1D/3D* disc. Because this product represents two separate databases on a single disc, the user must specify which database is desired. Instead of simply typing **go** to begin the program, the user must specify **go stf1** or **go stf3**.

The GO programs found on the recently issued *SSTF* products look somewhat different than previously seen versions. In place of a Browse feature, the program allows users to switch from one Summary Level to another or to flip from one sub-table to another (e.g., from citizen to non-citizen, French to German, etc.). Instead of a Keyword command, the *SSTF* discs offer a Subject Locator. Instead of moving to the first letter of an alphabetical list, the Subject Locator takes the searcher directly to a specified word or phrase. This function is case-sensitive, however, so users must be careful when typing a query. Another excellent enhancement is the ability to browse any Technical Documentation file without leaving the GO software. Despite these improvements, the GO programs found on the *SSTF* titles lack certain useful features, such as a context-specific Glossary command.

GO offers important benefits to novice Census users: it is easy to operate; it requires minimal training or instruction; it selects needed Summary Levels and geographic entities simply and efficiently; and it brings users to specified data tables fairly rapidly. GO's principal disadvantage is its inflexibility. It displays standard, preformatted tables only, and provides limited searching capabilities. Users who desire more sophisticated data manipulation may want to investigate the Bureau's EXTRACT software.

EXTRACT

EXTRACT is a public-domain software product which selects, reorganizes, displays, and extracts data from Census CD-ROMs. It allows users to manipulate the dBASE-formatted files on a particular CD-ROM product without actually owning Borland's dBASE software. EXTRACT can be used by itself, or in conjunction with other software tools. Because the program is menu-driven, it requires only a rudimentary understanding of database management concepts. However, experienced users of Database Management Systems will learn EXTRACT much more quickly than neophytes.

EXTRACT was designed by two employees of the Bureau's Economic Census Division, and was originally intended for internal use within the Division. It was ultimately included on the 1987 *Economic Census* discs, and on other CD-ROM titles from the Eco-

GO offers important benefits to novice Census users: it is easy to operate; it requires minimal training or instruction; it selects needed Summary Levels and geographic entities simply and efficiently; and it brings users to specified data tables fairly rapidly.

EXTRACT is a public-domain software product which selects, reorganizes, displays, and extracts data from Census CD-ROMs.

nomic Census Division. Following its success on economic data products, EXTRACT has become equally popular as a means of accessing 1990 Census data.

EXTRACT operates with virtually any Census CD-ROM file stored in *.dbf format, including all of the STF titles. To run EXTRACT, the program must be installed on the hard drive of the user's microcomputer. EXTRACT also requires a set of specially constructed support files and database indexes (known collectively as Auxiliary Files), and the Data Dictionary for the product being used. Unlike GO, not all of the necessary components for using EXTRACT can be found on the CD-ROM itself. Chapter 13 describes the components of the EXTRACT system, discusses how to obtain the required EXTRACT files and programs, and explains how to install them on a hard drive.

A detailed exploration of EXTRACT's capabilities, together with a step-by-step example of an EXTRACT search, can be found in Chapter 13. For now, a brief comparison of GO and EXTRACT will illustrate some of the basic tasks which EXTRACT performs. When using GO, the searcher selects a Summary Level of geography, identifies the desired geographic entity, then selects a preformatted data table from a list. With EXTRACT, the searcher also selects a Summary Level, then selects *one or more* geographic entities. Instead of choosing a preformatted table, the searcher then designs a customized table, containing as many data fields as he or she desires. EXTRACT's Main Menu consists of ten functional areas. In the following example, it is sufficient to know Menu Option 1 (Select Items) and Option 2 (Select Records) perform the most significant tasks in building a search; the remaining functions refine the search and print or download results.

Suppose you wish to create a table comparing certain ethnic characteristics for five cities of comparable size in Indiana. *STF 3A* for Indiana is published on two discs, making statewide comparisons difficult. *STF 3C* is a better choice for this search, because it

---

Example of a Customized Table Produced with EXTRACT

1990 Census STF 3C, Polish Ancestry
Five Cities in Indiana

ANPSADPI	POP100	P0330019	P0340019	STF307-> P0310012
Evansville city	126272	664	259	23
Fort Wayne city	173072	2369	982	99
Gary city	116646	1651	419	367
Hammond city	84236	10029	2702	1408
South Bend city	105511	12645	2669	2157

Key to column headings:

ANPSADPI– AREA NAME — /PSAD Term/Part Indicator
POP100 Population Count (100%)
P0330019 First Ancestry: Polish
P0340019 Second Ancestry: Polish
STF307->P0310012 Language spoken 5+: Polish (645)

Figure 8-16

---

provides sample data for all large cities in the United States. To keep matters relatively simple, let's focus on four variables: total population; the number of persons reporting their first Ancestry as Polish; those whose second Ancestry is Polish; and the number of persons who speak Polish in the home.

EXTRACT's Menu Option 1 selects variables from a list. Field locations can be found by scanning the Table Locator files on EXTRACT, or by consulting the Technical Documentation for *STF 3*. Here, the four Items you need are identified by the following field names: POP100, P0330019, P0340019, and P0310012.

Although the data request is fairly simple, the structure of the STF database adds complexity to the search. Because the four fields actually appear on three separate subfiles on the CD-ROM, they must be searched one at a time. The results of the three searches can then be merged into a single table, using Menu Options 3 and 4. Option 3 is also used to assign labels to every line on the combined table. These tasks are described in greater detail in Chapter 13.

EXTRACT operates with virtually any Census CD-ROM file stored in *.dbf format, including all of the STF titles.

Taking time to become familiar with the program is a worthwhile investment, because EXTRACT offers much greater control over database output.

Next, Option 2 selects the necessary Summary Level (SUMLEV 160, "State-Place"), chooses the appropriate state (Indiana), and specifies the five records wanted: the cities of Evansville, Fort Wayne, Gary, Hammond, and South Bend. The resulting table, reproduced in Figure 8-16, displays the 20 data values in four columns and five rows, with an additional column for Place names.

Now let's say the searcher wants to modify the table to create a new column showing the total number of persons reporting Polish Ancestry. EXTRACT provides the capability of summing the two Ancestry fields (P0330019 and P0340019). This is accomplished by the "User-defined Item" function found in Menu Option 1. The modified table is not shown in Figure 8-16.

To obtain similar results using GO, the searcher would employ the "Print Single Item" feature for each of the four fields, creating four separate tables. Unfortunately, each of the tables would include all other Places in the state. The GO user would then need to download the tables to another software program, delete a considerable amount of unwanted data, and merge the four edited tables. Unless the results were imported into a spreadsheet or a database program, the user would be unable to sum the values in the two Ancestry fields, a task which EXTRACT handles easily.

The advantage of GO is that it locates the desired tables painlessly. The searcher needs no knowledge of STF file structure. In contrast, proficient use of EXTRACT demands reasonable familiarity with Census file structure, field locations, and Summary Level codes. Although the example cited above may appear complicated to the novice searcher, it represents a fairly basic EXTRACT search. With a little practice, a finished table, such as the one shown in Figure 8-16, can be compiled relatively quickly (assuming the correct Summary Level has been chosen).

Based on the above demonstration, the difference in performance between the two programs may not appear terribly dramatic.

Proficient use of EXTRACT demands reasonable familiarity with Census file structure, field locations, and Summary Level codes.

This is because the hypothetical searcher wanted a very small, simple table. Even so, both programs required multiple steps and the use of merged files. For more complex needs, EXTRACT is far superior, creating customized tables with less effort. In many situations, it accomplishes tasks that GO cannot, such as selecting only those records which meet specified numeric requirements. Taking time to become familiar with the program is a worthwhile investment, because EXTRACT offers much greater control over database output. Readers interested in learning more about EXTRACT's capabilities and how to utilize them should consult Chapter 13.

LandView

LandView is an elementary mapping program designed specifically for use with the *TIGER/Line Files*. The software itself is a modified version of another program called MARPLOT. MARPLOT was written by the Environmental Protection Agency and the National Oceanic and Atmospheric Administration to assist local disaster preparedness officials in mapping hazardous chemical sites.

LandView draws upon data in the *TIGER/Line Files* and the *TIGER/Geographic Name Files* to create actual maps on screen. It allows the user to perform basic mapping functions: drawing outline maps, labelling map features, re-scaling map size, drawing radii around a central point, calculating map distances and areas, locating specific entities on the map, and printing simple maps on paper. In order to perform more sophisticated TIGER/Line functions, such as drawing thematic maps or conducting address matching, users must turn to more powerful commercial software packages.

LandView cannot operate from the CD-ROM itself; it must be installed on the hard drive of the computer. The program should be installed on a directory called LandView. Once installation has been completed, follow these steps to run the program:

The LandView software cannot read *TIGER/Line* files directly; they must be extracted from the disc and translated into LandView format.

1. Switch to the LandView directory on the hard drive.
   (Type **cd landview** and press <Enter>.)

2. Start the program.
   (Type **landview** and press <Enter>.)

The program can be operated using combinations of Function and Control keys, but users will find it much simpler to employ a Mouse.

The opening menu for LandView offers three options. Option One, "Creating a LandView Map," is used to copy *TIGER/Line* data from the CD-ROM onto the hard drive, in LandView format. (This time-consuming process is described below.) Option Three, "Display a LandView Reference View," is used to display a list of previously created files (called Reference Views) which have been saved by the user. Option Two, "Dis-play a LandView Map," is where actual mapping activities take place.

The LandView software cannot read *TIGER/Line* files directly; they must be extracted from the disc and translated into LandView format. In other words, not only must the LandView program itself be installed on the hard drive, so too must the required TIGER data be copied onto the hard drive. Once this is done, the LandView files for a specific county can be saved, to be searched, manipulated, displayed, and/or printed in a variety of ways whenever needed.

TIGER/Line records are organized by county; each file on the CD-ROM provides mapping data for a single county. Once LandView copies an individual county file onto the hard drive, it is called a LandView Map. The user can copy as many Map files as the computer's disk space will allow. Multiple counties can be shown in a single

Q&A

How does the user transfer TIGER/Line files to LandView?

The first option on the LandView opening menu is "Create a LandView Map." After selecting this option, follow these steps:

1. Choose a state from the displayed list.
2. Select one or more counties from the subsequent list.
3. Place the *TIGER/Line* disc for that state in the CD drive.
4. Press **<F10>** to begin creating the map(s).

TIGER/Line files are quite large, ranging anywhere from four megabytes to 200 megabytes. Depending on the speed of the computer, a typical county Map will require at least several hours to create. (The LandView program will list the file size for each county and will estimate the completion time for downloading, using a formula of one hour per 16 megabytes, based on the speed of a 33 megahertz machine.) For larger files, it is recommended to start the process at the end of the day, leaving the program running overnight. Once a Map file has been created, it can be used over and over again.

Because each LandView Map contains so much data, a single county can occupy considerable space on the hard drive. Unless a particular Map is used regularly, a good idea is to compress the files using a standard software program, such as PKZIP. The compressed files can then remain on the hard drive, waiting to be "unzipped." If the files still take up too much room in their compressed state, users can try an alternate method; instead of zipping the files on the hard-drive, use a disk backup program, such as Fastback Plus, to transfer file contents to a series of floppy diskettes for future use. Either of these compression techniques allow the user to avoid the time-consuming process of recopying a Map from the CD-ROM every time it is needed.

LandView Maps focus on the Block Group level. Although corresponding Tract numbers are identified, boundaries for Tracts are not shown explicitly.

LandView users can create a variety of Reference Views, which are used for comparative purposes. A common use of this feature is to show the position of the main View within its larger surrounding territory.

Map only if the counties share a common border.

An individual LandView Map represents the geographic boundaries and map features contained in the *TIGER/Line* file for that county. Because the files are so extensive, LandView does not display the entire county Map. Instead, the user creates a specified "Map View," which may show selected features for the entire county, or more detailed features for a smaller area. *Figures 8-17 and *8-18 illustrate typical LandView displays, based on the Map for Erie County, New York. The specific Map Views relate to the town of Grand Island, a large, heavily populated island situated in the Niagara River between Buffalo and Niagara Falls. The larger maps on the left side of both Figures are called the Main Map View. The smaller maps in the upper right corners are Reference Views. The sidebars on the lower right can display selected population and housing characteristics for a specified Block Group (shown in Figure 8-17), or the command options (shown in Figure 8-18 as a Mouse menu). The status line across the top of the screens identify the map scale, its dimensions, the latitude and longitude of the cursor position, and the county name.

LandView users can create a variety of Reference Views, which are used for comparative purposes. A common use of this feature is to show the position of the main View within its larger surrounding territory. Another use is to display the same territory with different map features highlighted. Reference Views can also be employed to save a particular Main Map View which the user may wish to display at a future date. Reference Views can be transferred to the Main Map View, and vice versa. The user displays a list of all previously created Reference Views by selecting Option Two from the opening LandView Menu.

The Reference View in Figure 8-17 shows the outline for the entire town of Grand Island, with the position of the Main View indicated by the small square on the southeast side of the island. The Reference View

in Figure 8-18 consists of the entire county outline, devoid of roads, overlays, and other map features. The tiny square in the northwest portion once again indicates the position of the Main Map View. The large darkened area represents the coastal waters of Lake Erie, while the darkened line flowing north represents the Niagara River.

LandView Maps focus on the Block Group level. Although corresponding Tract numbers are identified, boundaries for Tracts are not shown explicitly. Users seeking Tract level maps will be better served by consulting the printed Tract maps described in Chapter 9 or by using the *TIGER/Line Files* in conjunction with commercial mapping software. In Figure 8-17, the bold lines in the Main Map View represent Block Group boundaries. The quadrangle in the lower right, identified with the numbers **007302 -2** represents Block Group 2 in Census Tract 7302. This Map View also shows Block Groups 1 and 6 in their entirety, together with portions of surrounding BGs. The figure on the second line within each Block Group (P=678, etc.) indicates the total population for that area.

Landview does not display boundary lines for individual Blocks, nor does it identify Block numbers. However, LandView does show streets, which usually serve as Block boundaries, so viewers can get a general sense of Block layout within a particular BG. Returning to Figure 8-17, the largest polygon within BG 2 appears to be a single Block, including the narrow extension on the upper left side. But without consulting printed Block maps, there is no way to verify this assumption, nor to determine that this particular polygon represents Block 205. LandView users should be cautioned not to rely on displays below the Block Group level for another reason: Block boundaries are not always streets. In some cases, railroad tracks or other demarcations serve as additional boundaries. In other cases, a sparsely populated Block may cross several streets. Taking the example of Block 205 mentioned above, the small triangle in the lower left section of

Block Group 2 is also part of the larger Block, even though the diagonal line represents a road. Once again, users seeking maps at the Block level will find the necessary detail on printed Block maps described in Chapter 9.

Major functions of the LandView program are summarized in Figure 8-19, which also reproduces LandView's principal Mouse menu. These functions allow the user to reset the map scale, reposition or re-center the map, hide or show various map features and overlays, identify specific features, display Census information, and change the colors or cross-hatching shown in the display. Each time a menu setting is changed, LandView redraws the Map View on screen. It is beyond the scope of this book to explain every feature of LandView, but descriptions of major functions will offer an idea of how the program works.

The Scale menu is very important because increasing or decreasing the map size can improve its legibility dramatically. The Map

View in Figure 8-18 has been scaled at 1" = 0.2 miles, creating a map which covers less than two square miles (1.30 miles x 1.26 miles). Re-scaling can be accomplished by several methods: incrementally, using LandView's "Size Box;" directly, by resetting the scale value; or indirectly, by resetting the dimensions of the Main Map Display. Users can also employ LandView's Place Marker to re-scale the map between two designated end points.

Another way to enhance legibility is to hide unwanted map features, especially at larger map scales. Map Views become crowded as more features are shown. LandView displays two types of map features: Base Map Layers and Map Overlays. Base Map Layers consist of "line objects" from the *TIGER/Line Files*, such as geographic boundaries, roads, railroads, and rivers. Map Overlays can be line objects, points, or polygons. They represent parks, small water bodies, monuments, and other special features which can be displayed

Each time a menu setting is changed, LandView redraws the Map View on screen.

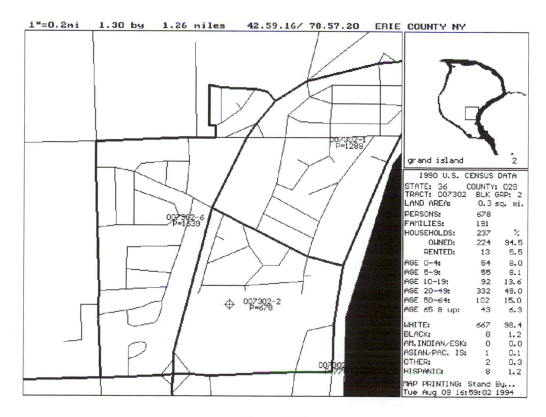

Figure 8-17

on top of the base map.

Overlay and Display are the principal menu functions which control which features are shown on the Map View. A user may wish to show state and interstate highways, while hiding railroads, county roads, and local streets. The Display function adjusts the appearance of Base Map features such as these. Similarly, the user may want to highlight airports and hospitals, while hiding other Overlay features. The Overlay function controls these displays. (In Figures 8-17 and 8-18, the Overlay function was used to darken the surrounding water bodies.)

Users can choose between two label displays when showing Base Map Layers: street names or Census Block Groups. The Map View in Figure 8-17 is displaying Block Group labels; Figure 8-18 shows the same View with street names identified. It is possible to display Block Group labels and street names simultaneously, but in most cases the Map View becomes illegible. As the Figures

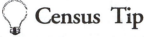

Census Tip

Users should hide all Map Overlays, street names, and Block Group numbers at the beginning of every LandView session. This will increase the speed of the program as it redraws Map Views on screen, looks for street addresses, and performs other basic functions. If Overlays and other details are desired in the final view, reinstate them as the last step before printing.

Overlay and Display are the principal menu functions which control which features are shown on the Map View.

illustrate, one technique to get around this limitation is to print two Map Views of the same land area: one showing Block Group numbers, the other showing street names. Block Group boundaries can be shown in outline form (as in Figures 8-17 and 8-18), with pattern fill (cross-hatching, etc.), or color fill.

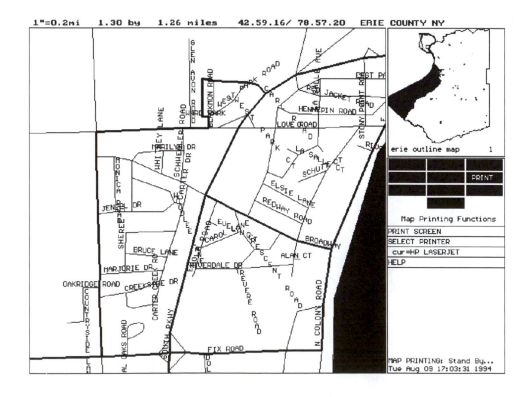

Figure 8-18

Another important LandView feature is the ability to search for specified entities. This is accomplished using the various Find commands located on the Position menu. Among other options, the Position menu allows users to search for specific Place names, street names, street intersections, address ranges, or Overlay Objects. Find commands do not work for Tract or Block Group numbers, ZIP Codes, or names of County Subdivisions. The most effective means of pinpointing a location on the Map is to search for a particular street intersection. Once this is done, the Map View can be re-scaled and/or re-centered to display the surrounding area to best advantage.

Two of the most ingenious LandView functions are found on the Census menu. The software reproduces brief population and housing profiles for all Block Groups on the LandView file itself. Data are taken from the *STF 1A* files and reproduced on the *TIGER/Line* discs. When a LandView Map is created, the Census profiles for all Block Groups in the county are copied onto the user's hard drive. A standard *STF 1A* display is shown in the lower right corner of Figure 8-17. LandView Maps contain 18 basic Census variables, some of which are shown both as totals and percentages. Notice this display window also indicates the Tract number and Block Group number for the highlighted entity.

A second feature of the Census menu is its ability to temporarily leave LandView and move directly to the GO program on an *STF 3A* disc covering the county in question. (Unlike the *STF 1A* profiles, *STF 3A* data are too extensive to copy onto the *TIGER/Line* discs directly, even in abbreviated form. LandView's Census menu links the contents of two databases—a *TIGER/Line* Map and the full *STF 3A* file.) The user need only place the appropriate *STF 3A* disc in the CD-ROM player and highlight the appropriate menu option on LandView. The software takes the user directly to the tables for the specified Block Group without having to move through the tedious hierarchy of Summary Level menus. After viewing the needed data on *STF 3A*, the user can Escape back to the LandView Map.

 Census Tip

Conducting a LandView search by street intersections is an excellent way to locate and identify specific Tract or Block Group numbers without consulting printed maps. LandView's Census menu then takes the user directly to the *STF 3A* tables for the selected Block Group.

Compared to commercially produced mapping software, LandView is an extremely limited program. Users may be frustrated by its inability to create maps for Tracts, Blocks, ZIP Code Areas, or School Districts. Another limitation is the rough appearance of the finished product. As seen in Figures 8-17 and 8-18, line segments appear as jagged lines, even when they are reproduced with high quality laser printers. Although the size of the Map View can be adjusted, the resulting printouts are very small. Larger formats can only be created with special enlarging equipment. For many users, LandView's biggest limitation is its inability to create thematic maps showing spatial representations of population and housing characteristics. The program is designed to produce outline maps, showing geographic boundaries and basic map features. On the positive side, LandView is not difficult to learn, and requires little understanding of mapping concepts. Regular users will find added benefits, such as LandView's ability to locate and identify street intersections, and to quickly retrieve Census data from STF files. For individuals and organizations unable to afford a more sophisticated program, LandView offers fast and easy access to a wealth of data found on the *TIGER/Line Files*.

The most effective means of pinpointing a location on the Map is to search for a particular street intersection. Once this is done, the Map View can be re-scaled and/or re-centered to display the surrounding area to best advantage.

A second feature of the Census menu is its ability to temporarily leave LandView and move directly to the GO program on an *STF 3A* disc covering the county in question.

Summary

With so many Census products available on CD-ROM, the most significant hurdle for novice users may be deciding which disc is best for the needs at hand. Choosing the right CD-ROM is an important step in the search process. In some instances, a print Report may be simpler or more efficient than its CD-ROM counterpart. Chapter 10 offers more detailed suggestions for data retrieval strategies, but for now, a few brief guidelines are in order. As with any Census product, the first decision is determining whether the subject matter under investigation is a complete-count Item or sample Item. This governs whether data will be found in *STF 1* or *STF 3*.

Census Tip

For each of the two STF products on CD-ROM, the table numbering is identical for the A and C subfiles. The 101 tables in *STF 1A* are exactly the same as those in *STF 1C*; likewise, the 278 tables in *STF 3A* are identical to those in *STF 3C*.

Next the user must identify which CD-ROM subfile covers the needed geographic level. Users seeking data at the national level, or who need to compare different entities across several states, should utilize *STF 1C* and *STF 3C*. Users examining smaller geographies within a single state should turn to *STF 1A* and *STF 3A*. For more specialized geographies, the choice is usually obvious. Data at the ZIP Code level can only be found on *STF 3B*. Census Block data are available only on *STF 1B*, and Congressional District data are located only on the combined *STF 1D/STF 3D* disc. Users searching for more detailed subject treatment than the Summary Tape Files provide can turn to specialized products, such as the *AOA File*, the *SSTF* series, or the *Equal Employment Op-*

portunity File. In most cases, users must accept the tradeoff between subject detail and geographic specificity.

Because geographic coverage may overlap across several subfiles, sometimes several products can serve the same purpose. Although *STF 1C* and *STF 3C* are generally associated with large geographies, both provide coverage of Places with populations of 10,000 or more. Similarly, Block Group data is found on *STF 1B* as well as *STF 1A*, and state-level tables exist on virtually every CD-ROM product. Consult Figure 8-2 for assistance in comparing geographic coverage across products.

Users must be wary of a potential trap relating to certain geographic coverages. *STF 1A* and *STF 3A* are state-specific files, a situation which presents problems when dealing with geographies that cross state borders. For these geographies *STF 1A* and *STF 3A* present data only for that portion of the entity which falls within the state boundary.

Census Tip

When seeking data for Metropolitan Areas, Urbanized Areas, or American Indian Areas, it is safest to use *STF 1C* and *STF 3C*. These files provide total area coverage for geographies which cross state boundaries.

Selecting the proper software product to use with the various CD-ROM publications is another concern. The Bureau's own software is fairly basic, but extremely affordable and easy to obtain. GO and CrossTab are surprisingly easy to use, while LandView and EXTRACT require time and effort to master. QuickTab and LandView were designed for use with specific Census products, but GO and EXTRACT can be used with many different discs. GO is best suited to retrieve profiles of a single geographic entity, while EXTRACT is designed to create customized

---

In some instances, a print Report may be simpler or more efficient than its CD-ROM counterpart.

Users seeking data at the national level, or who need to compare different entities across several states, should utilize *STF 1C* and *STF 3C*. Users examining smaller geographies within a single state should turn to *STF 1A* and *STF 3A*.

tables and to compare characteristics of multiple entities. Heavy users of Census data, particularly those with sophisticated retrieval needs, may prefer commercially-produced database management, spreadsheet, or mapping software. But even these searchers will find appropriate uses for the Bureau's own software. In most cases, for example, EXTRACT is the best means of creating a customized subset of Census data to import into another software package.

Regardless of which CD-ROM publication is chosen and which software package is utilized, proper use requires an understanding of Census geography and subject terminology. CD-ROM technology makes retrieval of 1990 Census products faster, more convenient, and more powerful than ever before, but it remains the responsibility of the Census user to interpret the resulting information correctly.

LandView Mouse Menu

SCALE	POSITION	DISPLAY
IDENTIFY	OVERLAYS	PRINT
REF VIEW	OPTIONS	CENSUS
	EXIT	

Summary of Menu Functions

SCALE — Re-scales Map View by scale value, by dimensions, by "size box," or between two end points.

POSITION — Changes position on Map View by re-centering map or repositioning the Place Marker. Also finds specific locations by Place name, street intersection, etc.

DISPLAY — Redesigns Map View by hiding or showing various features, such as street names, Block Group labels, or all Overlays. Also resets colors, highlights a specified street, and draws circles.

IDENTIFY — Identifies the name and attributes of a specific Base Map feature or Overlay Object. Also displays legend of map feature icons, and calculates map distances and areas.

OVERLAYS — Used to hide or show specified Overlay categories individually, and perform specialized Overlay control functions.

PRINT — Prints or downloads currently displayed Map View. Also configures LandView for use with printer.

REF VIEW — Locates a previously saved Reference View, switches Views, displays a Reference View in the Main View window, or displays a Map View as a Reference View.

OPTIONS — Changes various Map settings, including distance units (from miles to kilometers) and latitude/ longitude (from decimals to degree-minutes-seconds).

CENSUS — Displays *STF 1A* profile window, and allows user to view data from *STF 3A* discs. Also displays Tract and Block Group numbers on the Map View and displays BGs with pattern fill or color fill.

Exhibit 8-19

Addendum to Chapter 8

DESCRIPTIONS OF THE following three CD-ROM products were inadvertently omitted from the main text of Chapter 8. The *TIGER/Census Tract Street Index* is a geographic reference File. The *Comprehensive Housing Affordability Strategy Database* is a product of the Special Tabulation Program. The *County-to-County Migration Flow File* is a unique "Special Project" of the Census Bureau. All three utilize GO software.

TIGER/Census Tract Street Index (6 discs)

The Bureau's *Census Tract Street Index* (*CTSI*) links residential street addresses to their corresponding Tracts and ZIP Codes. The product was designed to help users comply with government regulations which require matching addresses to Census Tracts. For example, the Home Mortgage Disclosure Act requires banks and other mortgage lenders to report statistics on their lending patterns by Census Tract. *CTSI* provides that capability by allowing users to search for specific street names.

The CD-ROM product is generated from the TIGER system. Because TIGER is updated on a continuing basis, and because regulatory needs for Street/Tract matching are ongoing, the Bureau plans to issue several revised discs before the next decennial Census. Version 2 of *CTSI* was released in December, 1994. With each revision, boundaries for Places and ZIP Code Areas will reflect those in effect at the time the new version is compiled. For example, Version 2 reflects Place boundaries as of January,

1992; ZIP Codes as of July, 1993; and Metropolitan Areas as of June, 1993. Tract boundaries always refer to those in effect at the time of the Census. A second advantage of updating is the inclusion of additional address ranges. Version 1 covered approximately 58% of all residential addresses in the United States; Version 2 incorporates 69%.

Version 2 contains nearly six million Records, each describing a particular range of address numbers. Approximately 74 million addresses are encompassed within these Records, covering nearly every county in the United States. For each address range, *CTSI* displays the following Fields, as shown below: street name; low and high addresses in the range; side of street; Tract or BNA number; ZIP Code; and Place name or MCD name.

Street Name	Low	High	Side	Tract	ZIPCode	Area Name
Alcott St	1	99	Both	0008.02	02134	Boston city

Users can also retrieve more detailed Geographic Identifiers, including FIPS or GICS codes for the county and Metropolitan Area in which the address range is located.

CTSI is issued as a six-disc set, with each disc covering several states. Discs includes product-specific GO software. GO prompts the user to select a state, then to use the "Match" function to select one of the following criteria: a street name, a county, a ZIP Code, a Place name, or an MCD. Users can then browse an alphabetical list of street names within the selected category, or they can specify a particular street.

The Bureau's *Census Tract Street Index* (*CTSI*) links residential street addresses to their corresponding Tracts and ZIP Codes. The product was designed to help users comply with government regulations which require matching addresses to Census Tracts.

Users can also retrieve more detailed Geographic Identifiers, including FIPS or GICS codes for the county and Metropolitan Area in which the address range is located.

Comprehensive Housing Affordability Strategy Database (1 disc)

CHAS is a Special Tabulation File created by the Census Bureau for the U.S. Department of Housing and Urban Development. It reports housing affordability information based on HUD guidelines, using sample data from the 1990 Census. *CHAS* covers all states and counties in the United States, plus all Places and Minor Civil Divisions with population of 10,000 or more. Twenty-two tables display housing characteristics by Tenure, Rent or Value, Household type, inadequacy of facilities, and number of Bedrooms. The latter is a basic measure of Housing Unit size which HUD uses as eligibility criteria in its public assistance programs. Characteristics are cross-tabulated by Race, Hispanic Origin, Household Income (five categories), and affordability level (four categories).

Household type on *CHAS* is broken out in the following special categories: Elderly Households (containing two or more members, one of whom is 62 or older); small Family Households (with two-to-four members); and Large Family Households (containing five or more members). Income is reported as a percentage of HAMFI, which stands for HUD Adjusted Median Family Income. Affordable housing is measured as any Unit which costs no more than 30% of the Household's monthly Income to rent or no more than 2.5 times their annual Income to purchase. "Problem housing" is defined as Units which lack complete kitchen or plumbing facilities, which have a "persons per Room" ratio greater than 1.00, or which place a high cost burden on their occupants.

County-to-County Migration Flow Files (2 discs)

This remarkable product traces the direction of migration in and out of each county, as well as providing detailed population characteristics for movers and nonmovers. The Title is not part of the *STF* or *SSTF* series, nor is it a Special Tabulation. It is designated *Special Project 312* (*SP 312*, for short). The File is issued as a two-disc set. The first disc tabulates data on out-migration; the second covers in-migration. The File is based on responses to Questionnaire Item 14, which asked where each Household member lived in April of 1985. Results are used to study migration patterns and to help local governments, businesses, and other organizations analyze the characteristics of people moving into and out of their counties.

The GO software prompts users to select a state and county for the 1990 location, as well as a state and county for the 1985 location. The Out-Migration File links each person's 1985 location to their 1990 destination; the In-Migration File links the 1990 residence to the person's prior (1985) location. Data are also presented for nonmovers.

Each disc consists of the same 26 tables: 5 unnumbered tables which report general characteristics of migrating individuals; and 21 numbered tables showing multi-level cross-tabulations. The extent of these cross-tabulations can be seen from the titles of the tables themselves, as shown in Figure 8-21. For example, users can determine Race by sex by age by employment status by college enrollment. Characteristics represent each person's 1990 responses. The Universe is limited to persons age 5 and above, for obvious reasons.

With so many cross-tabulations, the potential size of a single table is enormous. Each table is then repeated for every intersection of county by current and prior residence. To save disc space, *SP 312* does not display categories with zero responses. Although Table 8 can have a maximum of 990 cells (5 x 2 x 9 x 11), the actual number will vary for each Record, depending on the number of Fields with no persons who met that characteristic. (The five summary tables represent an exception to this rule, however.)

Despite the Bureau's efforts to minimize each table's size, the nature of the cross-tabulations cause individual tables to run on for several pages. The GO software handles this by breaking each table into parts. Users

---

Household type on *CHAS* is broken out in the following special categories: Elderly Households (containing two or more members, one of whom is 62 or older); small Family Households (with two-to-four members); and Large Family Households (containing five or more members).

County-to-County Migration Flow Files traces the direction of migration in and out of each county, as well as providing detailed population characteristics for movers and nonmovers.

then press function keys to switch to various parts of the table. Figure 8-20 reproduces a small portion of Table 4 of the Out-Migration File. It shows various characteristics of persons who moved from Erie County, New York to Broward County, Florida (Note: only the first four age groupings are shown in the Figure). In this example, the table segment reports data for White males only. If the user wishes to see corresponding numbers for Black males, she would press [F-3]. To see Household and Tenure characteristics by age for White females, she would press [F-4]. In this manner, each Race/sex category can be viewed one at a time.

COUNTY TO COUNTY OUT-MIGRATION FLOW FILES

PLACE OF RESIDENCE IN 1985   PLACE OF RESIDENCE IN 1990
   New York (036)   Florida (012)
   Erie County (029)   Broward County (011)

Table 4: RACE by SEX by AGE-2 by HOUSEHOLD TYPE by TENURE-1
Universe: Persons 5 years and over in households

White (Race class 1 of 5 classes)
Male (Sex class 1 of 2 classes)

5 to 9 years	
Married-couple family	
Owner-occupied housing unit	30
Other family with female householder	
Renter-occupied housing unit	12
10 to 14 years	
Married-couple family	
Owner-occupied housing unit	32
Renter-occupied housing unit	11
15 to 19 years	
Married-couple family	
Owner-occupied housing unit	23
Renter-occupied housing unit	21
Other family with male householder	
Owner-occupied housing unit	12
20 to 24 years	
Married-couple family	
Renter-occupied housing unit	11
Other family with male householder	
Renter-occupied housing unit	16
Non-family household	
Owner-occupied housing unit	9
Renter-occupied housing unit	32

Figure 8-20

LIST OF TABLES: COUNTY-TO-COUNTY MIGRATION FLOW FILES

Table	Title (matrix)	Maximum # of data cells
1.	RACE(5) BY HISPANIC ORIGIN(2) BY SEX(2) BY AGE(18)	360
2.	RACE(5) BY SEX(2) BY PLACE OF BIRTH AND CITIZENSHIP(68)	680
3.	HISPANIC ORIGIN(3) BY SEX(2) BY PLACE OF BIRTH AND CITIZENSHIP(68)	408
4.	RACE(5) BY SEX(2) BY AGE(12) BY HOUSEHOLD TYPE(4) BY TENURE(2)	960
5.	HISPANIC ORIGIN(3) BY SEX(2) BY AGE(12) BY HOUSEHOLD TYPE(4) BY TENURE(2)	576
6.	RACE(5) BY AGE(12) BY HOUSEHOLD TYPE(4) BY POVERTY STATUS(3)	720
7.	HISPANIC ORIGIN(3) BY AGE(12) BY HOUSEHOLD TYPE(4) BY POVERTY STATUS(3)	432
8.	RACE(5) BY SEX(2) BY AGE(9) BY INCOME IN 1989(11)	990
9.	HISPANIC ORIGIN(3) BY SEX(2) BY AGE(9) BY INCOME IN 1989(11)	594
10.	RACE(5) BY SEX(2) BY AGE(12) BY POVERTY STATUS(3) BY TENURE(2)	720
11.	HISPANIC ORIGIN(3) BY SEX(2) BY AGE(12) BY POVERTY STATUS(3) BY TENURE(2)	432
12.	RACE(5) BY SEX(2) BY AGE(9) BY EDUCATIONAL ATTAINMENT(7)	630
13.	HISPANIC ORIGIN(3) BY SEX(2) BY AGE(9) BY EDUCATIONAL ATTAINMENT(7)	378
14.	RACE(5) BY SEX(2) BY AGE(8) BY EMPLOYMENT STATUS(4) BY COLLEGE ENROLLMENT(2)	640
15.	HISPANIC ORIGIN(3) BY SEX(2) BY AGE(8) BY EMPLOYMENT STATUS(4) BY COLLEGE ENROLLMENT(2)	384
16.	RACE(5) BY SEX(2) BY AGE(8) BY EMPLOYMENT STATUS(4) BY POVERTY STATUS(3)	960
17.	HISPANIC ORIGIN(3) BY SEX(2) BY AGE(8) BY EMPLOYMENT STATUS(4) BY POVERTY STATUS(3)	576
18.	SEX(2) BY AGE(8) BY OCCUPATION(13) BY POVERTY STATUS(3)	624
19.	SEX(2) BY AGE(8) BY INDUSTRY(17) BY POVERTY STATUS(3)	816
20.	RACE(5) BY SEX(2) BY AGE(12) BY TENURE(6)	720
21.	HISPANIC ORIGIN(3) BY SEX(2) BY AGE(12) BY TENURE(6)	432

Figure 8-21

Chapter 9

Print Reports and Maps

Print Reports and Maps

TWO HUNDRED YEARS ago, the first decennial Census publication consisted of a single title, about fifty pages in length. Compare this with the print products of the 1990 Census, which comprise more than 1,000 separate Reports, totaling over 300,000 pages. As mentioned in Chapter 8, this prodigious output represents a small fraction of the data available from the 1990 tabulations, but it is an important resource nevertheless. This chapter introduces the complete product line of 1990 print Reports and maps. It focuses on those publications produced using the traditional medium of paper and ink, as opposed to the various electronic formats described in Chapters 8 and 14.

Before describing the individual publications and their contents, the chapter begins with a discussion of the Bureau's 1990 publication structure: how the basic Series are organized, the sequence in which they are released, and how the individual tables are arranged. The chapter concludes with comparisons of print Reports to CD-ROM Files, plus a summary of publication changes from 1980 to 1990.

Publication Basics

Print products of the decennial Census are called Census Reports. They are designed to provide answers to the most frequently asked demographic inquiries. The format of decennial Census Reports varies from decade to decade, but their basic arrangement is surprising consistent. This massive body of Census publications follows a logical pattern, so an overview of its organization will help the user to become familiar with locating data more quickly.

Publishing Structure

The Bureau issues its decennial Reports in three broad Series: the first covers only population data, the second deals with housing data, and the third is a combined Series containing summary data of both types. These three components are designated as the *Census of Population* (*CP* Series), the *Census of Housing* (*CH* Series), and the *Census of Population and Housing* (*CPH* Series). Figure 9-1 lists all of the Titles issued under the three Series, and indicates their key characteristics. As with the Bureau's CD-ROM products, the most important distinguishing characteristic of each Report is whether its tables contain complete-count data or sample data. In most cases, an individual Report contains one or the other, not both.

As with the Bureau's CD-ROM products, the most important distinguishing characteristic of each Report is whether its tables contain complete-count data or sample data.

💡 Census Tip

Two Report Titles, *CPH-3* and *CPH-4*, contain complete-count data *and* sample data in the same publication, which can cause confusion for Census users. More will be said about this unusual situation in Chapter 10.

Within each of the three main Series, the Bureau may also produce *Subject Reports* and/or *Supplementary Reports*. Both are considered specialized or ancillary publications, rather than being part of the main body of statistical products. Often they are among the most complex publications to produce. As such, they are usually the last Census products to appear during the decennial publication cycle.

Before continuing, let's take a moment to define some publication-related terminology. As used in this chapter, "Series" refers to one of the three main components of the publication program: *CP*, *CH*, or *CPH*. "Title" refers to a specific group of publications within a Series. For example, *Population and Housing Unit Counts* and *Summary Social, Economic, and Housing Characteristics* are each specific Titles within the *CPH* Series. The terms "Report" and "Volume" are used interchangeably in this chapter, and refer to a specific subtitle within a Census Title. *Population and Housing Unit Counts: Alaska*, containing data for the state of Alaska, is an example of a specific Report within the *Population and Housing Unit Counts* Title. (Readers should note that the Bureau often refers to publication Titles as "Series" or as "Volumes." *CPH-2* may be called the *Population and Housing Unit Counts* Series or even as Volume 2 of the *Census of Population and*

Q&A

How do *Supplementary Reports* differ from *Subject Reports*?

These two types of publications are fairly similar, so it is easy to confuse one with the other. *Subject Reports*, which appear in both the *CP* and *CH* Series, are designed to provide in-depth analysis of a single topic at the national level, such as characteristics of adults with disabilities, or housing characteristics of mobile homes. By limiting coverage to the nation as a whole, these Reports can explore a topic in greater detail, providing numerous cross-tabulations.

Supplementary Reports may appear as part of all three main Series. Like *Subject Reports*, they focus on a single topic, but instead of offering enormous subject detail for a single geographic entity, they provide a few summary statistics for many geographic entities. They are meant to provide comparative statistics for topics which may not be addressed by standard Census products.

A specific example may clarify the distinction. A *Subject Report* entitled *Ancestry of the Population of the United States* is a massive 750-page document which tabulates a broad array of population and housing characteristics for each Ancestry Group, but only at the national level. *Detailed Ancestry Groups for States* is a slim, 90-page *Supplementary Report* which tabulates a handful of basic Ancestry statistics for each of the 50 states.

PRINT REPORTS, 1990 CENSUS

Report Number	Series name	Universe	Number of Vols	Number of tables
CPH-1	Summary Population and Housing Characteristics	100%	54	18
CPH-2	Population and Housing Unit Counts	sample	54	24
CPH-3	Population and Housing Characteristics for Census Tracts and BNAs	100% & sample	395	46
CPH-4	Population and Housing Characteristics for Congressional Districts	100% & sample	52	35
CPH-5	Summary Social, Economic, and Housing Characteristics	sample	54	23
CPH-6	Social, Economic, and Housing Characteristics (Outlying Areas)	100%	4	126
CPH-S	Census of Population and Housing Supplementary Reports	100% & sample	2	varies
CP-1	General Population Characteristics	100%	57	83
CP-2	Social and Economic Characteristics	sample	57	235
CP-3	Population Subject Reports	sample	7	varies*
CP-S	Census of Population Supplementary Reports	100% or sample	**	varies
CH-1	General Housing Characteristics	100%	57	76
CH-2	Detailed Housing Characteristics	sample	57	105
CH-3	Housing Subject Reports	sample	1	281
CH-4	Residential Finance	sample	1	137

_* See Figure 9-13 for a list of Reports and their sizes.
** Some publications not yet issued as of 12/95.

Figure 9-1

Housing. To avoid confusion, this Chapter will always use the "Title" designation.)

Almost all Census Reports appear in a geographic arrangement. Most Titles consist of 54 separate Reports: one for each state, plus one United States summary Volume and three Volumes covering certain state-equivalents (the District of Columbia, Puerto Rico, and the American Virgin Islands). Several Titles contain three additional Reports, covering the following geographies: American Indian Reservations and Alaska Native Areas; Metropolitan Areas; and Urbanized Areas.

The Bureau identifies all its publications with a unique Report Number, each composed of several segments identifying the Series, Title, Volume, and Section. As an example, Report Number *CH-2-34* represents the New York State Volume of *Detailed Housing Characteristics,* which is a Title within the *Census of Housing* Series. The first segment of the Report Number refers to the Series, the middle segment refers to the Title, and the third segment identifies the specific Report, as outlined below.

Segment	Number	Name
Series:	CH	Census of Housing
Title:	2	Detailed Housing Characteristics
Volume:	34	New York

For many Reports, the amount of data is so extensive it cannot be published in a single book. In these instances, a specific Volume is divided into two or more separate books, called "Sections." Using the example of *Detailed Housing Characteristics* once again, the New York Report consists of 966 numbered pages, issued in two Sections. The respective Report Numbers are *CH-2-34-1* and *CH-2-34-2.* In contrast, the corresponding Volume for Montana (*CH-2-28*) contains far fewer pages, so it is not issued in Sections.

Geographic numbering is consistent across most Titles, with the number 2 representing Alabama, 6 representing California, and so on. Just as *CH-1-34* is the Report Number for the New York Volume of *General Housing Characteristics,* *CP-1-34* is the Number for the New York Volume of *General Popu-*

lation Characteristics. However, this consistency applies only to those Titles which are issued on a state-by-state basis; exceptions to the rule are *CPH-3, CPH-6, CP-3, CH-3,* and the two *Supplementary Reports* Titles.

The Census Bureau requires several years to produce the complete set of Reports for a decennial Census. *CPH-1,* constituting the first Reports from the 1990 enumeration, began to appear in October, 1991. By September, 1994, the Bureau had issued nearly all of the basic Reports, including the massive Volumes of the *CP-2* and *CH-2* Titles. By August, 1995, all of the previously intended Volumes had been released, including the more specialized *Subject Reports* and *Supplementary Reports.*

The Bureau releases its print products on a flow basis. Because Reports are generated from the *Summary Tape Files,* the publication schedule follows that of the *STF* CD-ROM products. Tables based on complete-count data are easier to produce than those based on sample data, so complete-count Titles are issued sooner. For example, *CPH-1* (based on *STF 1*), was issued before *CPH-5* (based on *STF 3*). Similarly, Reports containing basic, abbreviated data appear before the more complex Reports containing detailed data. This is why *CPH-5* was released before *CP-2. CPH-5* is generated from the simpler tables found in *STF 3,* while *CP-2*

NEW IN '90

Print Reports of the 1980 Census also appeared in three Series, but the Report numbering was slightly different. For example, instead of calling the population Series the *Census of Population,* the Bureau named it the *Population Census.* The three basic Series types were thus designated *PC, HC,* and *PHC,* instead of *CP, CH,* and *CPH.* Certain 1980 Titles were also subdivided by letter designations called "Chapters." For example, *PC-1, Characteristics of the Population,* appeared in four subtitles denoted as Chapters A, B, C, and D. *Chapter A* was entitled *Number of Inhabitants, Chapter C* was *Economic and Social Characteristics,* and so forth. These Chapter designations had been utilized for many decades, but for 1990, the Bureau abandoned the more complex nomenclature in a welcome attempt to simplify Report numbering.

derives from the detailed tables found in *STF 4.*

Within a given Title, individual Reports are also issued on a flow basis. Less populous states and states with less complex geographies are processed first.

Geographic Coverage

Paper Census Reports tend to cover fewer geographic Summary Levels than do the

The Census Bureau requires several years to produce the complete set of Reports for a decennial Census.

Q&A

Is it really necessary to devote so much attention to Report Numbers?

Printed Census Volumes are routinely identified by their Report Numbers. Experienced Census users are more likely to refer to *CPH-5* than to its full name, *Summary Social, Economic, and Housing Characteristics.* The nomenclature also offers a simple way to determine whether a Title contains population data, housing data, or both. And most important, the numbering provides instant differentiation between complete-count data and sample data.

Regular users of Census Reports soon learn that *CPH-1, CPH-2, CP-1,* and *CH-1* contain complete-count data, while *CPH-5, CP-2,* and *CH-2* contain sample data. Although it may seem confusing at first, employing the Report Numbers is far more convenient and meaningful than trying to remember distinctions among the full names of the various publications.

NEW IN '90

The need to wait four years for detailed data is obviously one of the most serious drawbacks of the decennial Census. The 1980 publication pattern was similar, with initial Reports appearing in late 1981, and taking another three years to complete the main cycle. In 1990, however, the Bureau modified the contents of its Census Titles to ensure that the most sought-after data appeared first. For example, if a geographic entity crosses state boundaries (e.g., a federal Indian Reservation) the portion lying outside a particular state is omitted from that state's Report. For the same reason, data on Metropolitan Areas and Urbanized Areas were omitted from the individual state Reports for most Census Titles, and were released later as separate Reports covering the entire country.

Every United States Summary Report includes data for each of the 50 states, for each Metropolitan Area, for each Urbanized Area, and for each American Indian or Alaska Native Area (AI/ANA).

Summary Tape File products on CD-ROM. The most noticeable omissions are the fact that *STF 1B* and *STF 3B* have no print counterparts. In other words, neither Census Blocks or ZIP Code Areas can be found in the various print Titles. The Block Group is another conspicuously absent Summary Level. The Bureau avoids ZIP Code statistics because of the unstable nature of ZIP Code Area boundaries. The primary reason for the other two omissions is the sheer number of entities at both Levels: the 1990 Census tabulates data for more than 225,000 Block Groups and 6.96 million Blocks. The number of volumes necessary to provide even summary statistics for this many entities would be staggering to contemplate.

NEW IN '90

For the 1980 Census, data at the Block and Block Group levels appeared only on magnetic tape and microfiche. The microfiche product containing Block data was entitled *Block Statistics* (*PHC 1*). Block Group data could be found on the microfiche summaries derived from *STF 1A* and *STF 3A*. All three of these microform products were canceled for 1990 due to the popularity and convenience of the corresponding CD-ROM titles.

Beyond these obvious omissions, a few general comments can be made about geographic coverage in the print Reports. Readers can consult Figure 9-2 to see how major Titles in the three Report series cover the different Summary Levels. The Figure also shows certain patterns of coverage across the Titles. With the exceptions of *CPH-3* and *CPH-4*, all of the Titles listed in Figure 9-2 include a United States Summary Report. These are useful not only because they tabulate data at the national, Regional, and Divisional levels, but also because they provide extensive lists of other Summary Levels across the country. This makes nationwide comparisons extremely easy. For example, every United States Summary Report includes data for each of the 50 states, for each Metropolitan Area, for each Urbanized Area, and for each American Indian or Alaska Native Area (AI/ANA). In contrast, the state-specific Reports for these Titles either ignore MAs, UAs, and AI/ANAs, or they limit tabulations to only those portions of the Areas which fall within the state's boundaries. The United States Summary Volumes are always numbered as the first Report within each Title. For example, The United States Volume for *CPH-2*, *Population and Housing Counts*, is Report Number *CPH-2-1*.

 Census Tip

Some of the most useful and convenient comparisons of various entities across the country can be found in the United States Summary Report for *CPH-2*. However, subject coverage in this Report is limited to total population, total Housing Units, land area, and population and housing densities.

In addition to the United States Summary Reports, *CP-1*, *CP-2*, *CH-1*, and *CH-2* each include the following three special Reports:

Report 1A   American Indian and
                   Alaska Native Areas

Geographic Coverage of Selected 1990 Census Reports

Summary Level	CPH Series					CP Series		CH Series	
	1	2	3	4	5	1	2	1	2
United States	x^1	x^1			x^1	$x^{1,4,5}$	$x^{1,4,5}$	$x^{1,4,5}$	$x^{1,4,5}$
Regions/Divisions	x^1	x^1			x^1	$x^{1,4}$	$x^{1,4}$	$x^{1,4}$	$x^{1,4}$
All states	x^1	x^1			x^1	$x^{1,4}$	$x^{1,4}$	$x^{1,4}$	$x^{1,4}$
Single State	x	x		x	x	x	x	x	x
Metropolitan Areas	x^1	$x^{1,2}$	x		x^1	$x^{1,5}$	$x^{1,5}$	$x^{1,5}$	$x^{1,5}$
Urbanized Areas	x^1	$x^{1,2}$			x^1	$x^{1,5}$	$x^{1,5}$	$x^{1,5}$	$x^{1,5}$
American Indian/Alaska Native Areas	$x^{1,2}$			x^3	$x^{1,2}$	$x^{1,2,4}$	$x^{1,2,4}$	$x^{1,2,4}$	$x^{1,2,4}$
Congressional Districts (103rd Congress)				x					
Counties	x	x	x	x^3	x	x	x	x	x
County Subdivisions									
MCDs in 12 States				$x^{3,6}$	x	x^7	x	x^7	
MCDs in MCD states9	x	x			x	x^8		x^8	
CCDs	x	x			x	x^8		x^8	
Places (by population)									
10,000 or more	x	x			x	x	x	x	x
2,500 or more	x	x	x	x^3	x	x	x	x	x
1,000 or more	x	x			x	x		x	
Under 1,000	x	x			x				
Census Tracts/BNAs			x						

1   Areas totals reported in United States Summary volume.
2   Volumes for individual states tabulate only that portion of the area which lies within the state boundaries.
3   Shows only those portions of the area which lie within each Congressional District.
4   Detailed data for this level appear in all volumes of the following special Report category:
     American Indian/Alaska Native Areas   CP1-1A, CP2-1A, CH1-1A, CH2-1A
5   Detailed data for this level appear in one or both of these special Report categories:
     Metropolitan Areas   CP1-1B, CP2-1B, CH1-1B, CH2-1B
     Urbanized Areas   CP1-1C, CP2-1C, CH1-1C, CH2-1C
6   Entities with populations of 10,000 people or more only.
7   Entities with populations of 2,500 people or more only.
8   Abbreviated data reported in a single table only.
9   Those states where MCDs serve as general-purpose governments: Connecticut, Maine, Massachusetts, Michigan, Minnesota, New Hampshire, New Jersey, New York, Pennsylvania, Rhode Island, Vermont, and Wisconsin.

Figure 9-2

Report 1B   Metropolitan Areas
Report 1C   Urbanized Areas

For example, *CP-1-1A* is the special Report on American Indian and Alaska Native Areas within the *General Population Characteristics* Title. Each of these special Reports provides far more subject detail for its respective Summary Level than can be found in the United States Summary Report for the same Title.

Coverage of Places depends on size of Place. All print Reports listed in Figure 9-2 provide data for Places of 10,000 people or more, and most Reports provide summary data for Places of 2,500 or more. Coverage of smaller Places is less readily available. Likewise, coverage of MCDs and CCDs is fairly limited, except for the 12 states where MCDs serve as general-purpose governments.

💡 **Census Tip**

CPH 1, *CPH 2*, and *CPH 5* offer the most extensive coverage for Places and County Subdivisions of all the printed publications. They are the only print Titles which tabulate population and housing characteristics for Places with fewer than 1,000 people, and the only Titles which provide a variety of characteristics for MCDs or CCDs in all states. However, none of the *CPH* Titles offer the amount of subject detail found in the *CP* or *CH* series. Researchers seeking in-depth statistics for these Summary Levels will be better served by using the CD-ROM versions of *STF 1A* and *STF 3A*.

The two print Titles which cover specialized Summary Levels are *CPH-3* and *CPH-4*. The former is the only print publication dealing with Census Tracts, and the latter is the only one which covers Congressional Districts.

Census users may find it helpful to note parallel geographic coverage across certain pairs of print Titles. *CPH-1* and *CPH-5* offer

identical coverage of Summary Levels. Similarly, *CP-1* provides the same geographic coverage as *CH-1*, and *CP-2* is identical in coverage to *CH-2*.

Report Formats

Although each Census Report may contain several hundred tables, the Bureau strives to present information in a consistent manner from one Report to another, and even from one Title to the next. Understanding the basic pattern of table reporting will help the user to locate needed data more rapidly.

Parts of a Census Table

Before discussing the Bureau's approach to table presentation in its print Reports, a slight detour is necessary to describe the various parts of a standard Census table. The nomenclature introduced here will be used throughout the rest of the chapter and in Chapter 10.

Census tables consist of four major sections: the heading, the boxhead, the stub, and the data field. Figure 9-3, taken from *CH-1* (*General Housing Characteristics*), illustrates the various parts.

The heading contains the descriptive information found at the top of the page. Within the heading is the table number (in the example, Table 31), the title ("Occupancy, Structural, and Utilization Characteristics of Housing Units with a White Householder: 1990"), and a headnote, which provides additional information to qualify or explain the Table's scope and content. Users should note that the Table's title can provide important information about the Universe of coverage (in this case, Housing Units with White Householders) and time period (1990).

The boxhead is the section appearing below the heading. It describes the content of each vertical column. The boxhead consists of individual column heads ("Inside Urbanized Area," "Outside Urbanized Area," etc.) as well as spanners, which transcend a single

Coverage of Places depends on size of Place. All print Reports listed in Figure 9-2 provide data for Places of 10,000 people or more, and most Reports provide summary data for Places of 2,500 or more. Coverage of smaller Places is less readily available.

Although each Census Report may contain several hundred tables, the Bureau strives to present information in a consistent manner from one Report to another, and even from one Title to the next.

Parts of a Statistical Table

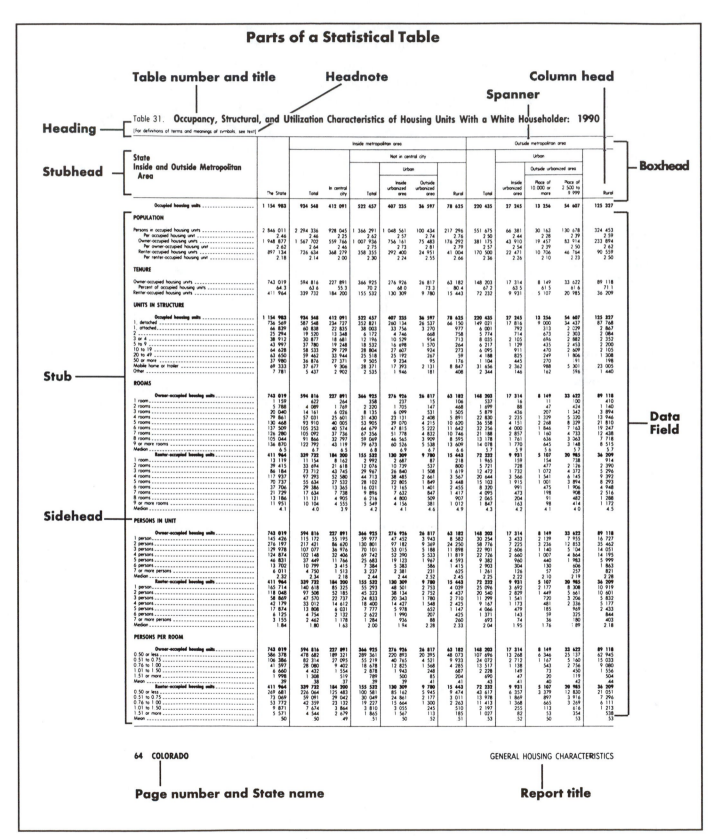

Figure 9-3

column. Spanners are used to organize the information within the columns, classifying related data into groups so that subtotals can be provided. Notice that spanners can be used in multiple levels. The reader starts at the top of the boxhead and works down to see how columns relate to one another.

Figure 9-3 shows three spanners in the uppermost level: "The State," "Inside Metropolitan Areas," and "Outside Metropolitan Areas." For any row, the sum of the latter two columns equals the state total, because the two categories are mutually exclusive. For example, the first row of data under "Tenure" shows the number of Owner-Occupied Housing Units. The values in the "Total" columns for the first spanner level, representing all Occupied Housing Units inside and outside Metropolitan Areas, sum together as follows:

594,816 + 148,203 = 743,019

The next level in Figure 9-3 is a bit more confusing, because the spanners do not cover every grouping. In this case, the following four subgroups are represented:

- Inside Metropolitan Area; In Central City
- Inside Metropolitan Area; Not in Central City
- Outside Metropolitan Area; Urban, outside Urbanized Area
- Outside Metropolitan Area; Rural

Several of the level-two spanners are further subdivided. For example, "Not in Central City" is divided into "Total," "Urban," and "Rural." This third level is divided once again, so that "Urban," is classified according to Housing Units which lie "Inside Urbanized Areas" and those lying "Outside Urbanized Areas." Four levels of data in a single table may seem confusing, but this type of layout allows the user to make quick comparisons, to view subtotals, and to understand how various parts relate to the whole. Such complexity cannot be displayed in the typical two-dimensional grids used in most of the Bureau's CD-ROM products.

Of course, the manner in which the Bureau arranges the spanners in a particular table will not suit every user's needs. In Figure 9-3, the user must add the values from two separate columns to obtain the total number of Housing Units in Rural areas: those from Rural territory within Metropolitan Areas, and those from Rural territory outside Metropolitan Areas.

The third part of every table, called the stub, consists of the descriptive information shown in the left-most column. The stub describes the contents of the horizontal rows. At the top of every stub is the stubhead, which further summarizes the content of the table. For virtually all tables found in 1990 Census Reports, the stubhead identifies the geographic coverage of each table. In Figure 9-3, the stubhead indicates coverage for the entire state, plus summary data for Metropolitan territory and Nonmetropolitan territory.

Just as column headings are grouped together with spanners, individual rows within the stub are grouped together by sideheads, which serve the same purpose. Sideheads are represented within the stub by boldface type. In Figure 9-3, the stub is divided into six parts, covering such topics as "Tenure," "Units in Structure," and "Persons Per Room." Here again a table may display multiple levels of sideheads. The major categories are designated with upper-case letters, while subgroups within the sidehead are designated in lower-case. Figure 9-3 shows the section on "Rooms" divided into two subgroups: "Owner-Occupied Housing Units" and "Renter-Occupied Units." The sum of these two values equals the total of all Occupied Housing Units, shown in the first row of the table.

Within sections of the stub, data may also be organized by use of indentations. For example, under the "Population" sidehead, we can see that 2,846,011 people live in Housing Units (as opposed to Group Quarters). Of these, 1,948,877 people live in Owner-Occupied Units and 897,134 live in

Spanners are used to organize the information within the columns, classifying related data into groups so that subtotals can be provided.

Just as column headings are grouped together with spanners, individual rows within the stub are grouped together by sideheads, which serve the same purpose.

Renter-Occupied dwellings. The indentations in the stub indicate the smaller numbers are subsets of the larger.

The final portion of every Census table represents the meat of the table—the data fields. This is the interior portion of the table, containing the actual data values. As with the Bureau's CD-ROM tables, the intersection of a specific row and column is called a data cell.

Arrangement of Data Tables

The comparison to CD-ROM products is further complicated by the fact that one table in a print product actually provides the equivalent of several CD-ROM tables on a single page. Where CD-ROM tables generally cover a single topic, tables in print Reports usually cover many related topics.

Printed Census Reports utilize more complex table sequences than those seen in most CD-ROM Files. Census CD-ROM products repeat a single table many times. The Bureau's GO software reproduces the same table layouts for every geographic Summary Level, for individual geographic entities within each Summary Level category, and in some cases, for specifically defined subsets (Universes) within the entire population. For example, Table H13 in the *STF 1* databases, shown in Figure 9-4, shows the distribution of all Housing Units by number of Rooms in the Unit. The table is repeated several thousand times within a single CD-ROM File—once for every city, township,

Census Tract, or other entity in the database. The user never sees these hundreds of repetitions, because the GO program only retrieves the specific entity which the user has selected.

Tables within print Reports are also repeated many times, but in a slightly different fashion. Instead of creating a separate table for each geographic entity, all entities within a specific Summary Level are listed in a single table, as shown in Figure 9-5, taken from Table 50 of *CH-1*. What the print Reports *do* repeat are tables for every relevant Summary Level, and for selected subgroups (Universes) of the total population. For example, the exact format for Table 50 can also be seen in Table 14 (which provides state totals) and Table 59 (which covers Places with populations of 10,000 persons or more).

The comparison to CD-ROM products is further complicated by the fact that one table in a print product actually provides the equivalent of several CD-ROM tables on a single page. Where CD-ROM tables generally cover a single topic, tables in print Reports usually cover many related topics. It takes four CD-ROM tables from *STF 1* to cover the same topics displayed in Figure 9-5, as the following comparison shows.

CH-1 sidehead	*STF 1* table
Rooms	H13
Duration of Vacancy	H40
Persons in Unit	H18
Persons per Room	H22

Note that the data for Householders age 65 or older, shown at the bottom of Figure 9-5, do not appear in *STF 1* tables, because *CH-1* is actually derived from *STF 2*, which has no direct CD-ROM counterpart.

The repetition of tables in the print Reports follow fairly stable patterns. The first table is presented at the state level, then repeated for smaller Summary Levels (e.g., counties, large Places, smaller Places). Once all the necessary iterations of the first table have been completed, a second table appears, which in turn is repeated for every relevant

---

Table H13, *STF 1A* for Colorado

1990 Census Of Population And Housing Summary Tape File 1A

    040 Colorado
    050 Kiowa County

ROOMS
Universe: Housing units

1 room	5
2 rooms	20
3 rooms	65
4 rooms	176
5 rooms	217
6 rooms	159
7 rooms	96
8 rooms	66
9 or more rooms	74

Figure 9-4

Table 50. Utilization Characteristics: 1990 — Con.

[For definitions of terms and meanings of symbols, see text]

County	Kiowa County	Kit Carson County	Lake County	La Plata County	Larimer County	Las Animas County	Lincoln County	Logan County	Mesa County
ROOMS									
All housing units	**878**	**3 224**	**3 527**	**15 412**	**77 811**	**6 975**	**2 204**	**7 824**	**39 208**
1 room	5	15	53	582	961	216	16	50	364
2 rooms	20	89	140	735	2 872	350	29	225	1 275
3 rooms	65	222	391	1 412	5 919	693	183	625	3 192
4 rooms	176	587	685	3 456	15 661	1 570	474	1 468	8 463
5 rooms	217	662	831	3 620	13 933	1 717	529	1 867	8 995
6 rooms	159	548	616	2 529	12 055	1 223	351	1 339	7 165
7 rooms	96	401	366	1 426	9 803	579	235	885	4 455
8 rooms	66	296	200	808	7 431	312	175	616	2 649
9 or more rooms	74	404	245	844	9 176	315	212	749	2 650
Median	5.3	5.6	5.1	4.9	5.5	4.9	5.3	5.3	5.2
Owner-occupied housing units	**453**	**1 984**	**1 534**	**7 818**	**44 297**	**3 634**	**1 276**	**4 654**	**23 534**
1 room	–	2	4	61	46	16	4	1	34
2 rooms	4	17	15	128	345	39	3	27	153
3 rooms	15	53	74	400	1 031	135	24	119	679
4 rooms	56	265	208	1 292	4 510	643	214	606	3 184
5 rooms	110	422	378	2 019	7 554	1 051	313	1 125	5 735
6 rooms	97	389	325	1 635	8 538	838	248	959	5 463
7 rooms	69	290	220	1 045	7 867	425	162	680	3 680
8 rooms	49	227	147	612	6 311	253	132	517	2 267
9 or more rooms	53	319	163	626	8 095	234	176	620	2 339
Median	5.9	6.1	5.8	5.5	6.5	5.4	5.8	6.0	5.9
Renter-occupied housing units	**204**	**801**	**848**	**4 158**	**26 175**	**1 787**	**541**	**2 324**	**12 716**
1 room	2	8	19	173	745	79	9	42	200
2 rooms	4	48	73	388	2 242	149	11	149	948
3 rooms	23	105	163	701	4 135	334	101	391	2 112
4 rooms	41	197	222	1 225	9 032	467	136	592	4 444
5 rooms	54	144	177	854	4 694	385	118	540	2 565
6 rooms	32	105	108	455	2 461	216	65	271	1 333
7 rooms	21	82	43	197	1 350	91	49	159	607
8 rooms	11	58	19	78	774	31	25	82	282
9 or more rooms	16	54	24	87	742	35	27	98	225
Median	5.1	4.8	4.3	4.2	4.2	4.2	4.6	4.5	4.2
DURATION OF VACANCY									
Vacant-for-sale-only housing units	**7**	**43**	**60**	**188**	**991**	**107**	**73**	**154**	**526**
Less than 2 months	–	4	5	42	227	10	7	21	103
2 up to 6 months	2	10	17	51	341	16	10	34	142
6 or more months	5	29	38	95	423	81	56	99	281
Vacant-for-rent housing units	**19**	**98**	**148**	**453**	**1 381**	**245**	**81**	**258**	**797**
Less than 2 months	3	25	39	209	641	52	30	58	376
2 up to 6 months	2	26	47	158	495	47	9	70	245
6 or more months	14	47	62	86	245	146	42	130	176
PERSONS IN UNIT									
Owner-occupied housing units	**453**	**1 984**	**1 534**	**7 818**	**44 297**	**3 634**	**1 276**	**4 654**	**23 534**
1 person	108	457	351	1 449	7 593	890	310	1 052	4 508
2 persons	182	820	515	2 922	16 511	1 354	523	1 851	9 605
3 persons	59	249	278	1 340	7 649	564	152	644	3 609
4 persons	57	271	247	1 290	8 219	457	183	669	3 711
5 persons	36	126	110	563	3 101	229	79	307	1 433
6 persons	9	44	22	175	860	88	23	101	459
7 or more persons	2	17	11	79	364	52	6	30	209
Median	2.15	2.15	2.31	2.34	2.38	2.18	2.13	2.19	2.26
Renter-occupied housing units	**204**	**801**	**848**	**4 158**	**26 175**	**1 787**	**541**	**2 324**	**12 716**
1 person	69	259	305	1 380	8 585	696	208	867	4 465
2 persons	49	179	224	1 285	8 783	433	125	600	3 568
3 persons	22	123	123	684	4 198	270	71	349	2 018
4 persons	42	126	115	504	2 878	213	80	296	1 624
5 persons	16	71	58	204	1 151	110	38	148	690
6 persons	5	28	16	60	386	42	13	41	225
7 or more persons	1	15	7	41	194	23	6	23	126
Median	2.17	2.29	2.03	2.04	2.01	1.96	2.00	1.99	2.03
PERSONS PER ROOM									
Owner-occupied housing units	**453**	**1 984**	**1 534**	**7 818**	**44 297**	**3 634**	**1 276**	**4 654**	**23 534**
0.50 or less	354	1 565	1 084	5 202	34 302	2 592	990	3 609	17 523
0.51 to 0.75	58	239	268	1 463	6 938	570	171	644	3 852
0.76 to 1.00	37	140	151	905	2 529	373	103	334	1 795
1.01 to 1.50	4	30	20	169	407	73	9	58	265
1.51 or more	–	10	11	79	121	26	3	9	99
Mean	.40	.39	.43	.46	.40	.44	.39	.40	.42
Renter-occupied housing units	**204**	**801**	**848**	**4 158**	**26 175**	**1 787**	**541**	**2 324**	**12 716**
0.50 or less	136	504	495	2 418	16 640	1 039	353	1 513	7 842
0.51 to 0.75	34	145	175	803	5 018	320	90	401	2 454
0.76 to 1.00	29	108	143	710	3 566	324	82	319	1 890
1.01 to 1.50	5	31	23	146	643	70	12	71	394
1.51 or more	–	13	12	81	308	34	4	20	136
Mean	.47	.51	.54	.54	.52	.54	.49	.50	.54
Occupied housing units	**657**	**2 785**	**2 382**	**11 976**	**70 472**	**5 421**	**1 817**	**6 978**	**36 250**
HOUSEHOLDER 65 YEARS AND OVER									
Occupied housing units	**216**	**776**	**350**	**2 086**	**11 104**	**1 783**	**573**	**1 849**	**8 607**
1-person households	101	350	171	871	4 633	823	284	893	3 663
Mean number of persons per room	.30	.28	.29	.33	.31	.35	.29	.30	.32
Units in structure:									
1, detached or attached	180	664	309	1 499	7 694	1 446	443	1 498	5 857
2 or more	12	49	27	261	2 259	192	48	240	1 560
Mobile home, trailer, or other	24	63	14	326	1 151	145	82	111	1 190
Specified owner	117	498	268	1 090	6 389	1 033	281	1 078	4 779
Mean value (dollars)	36 500	46 200	45 800	93 000	88 300	44 100	42 000	43 900	65 900
Specified renter	30	82	32	355	2 425	358	93	339	1 839
Mean contract rent (dollars)	179	178	225	284	335	145	161	183	253
With meals included in rent	–	–	–	6	172	2	–	–	3
Mean contract rent (dollars)	–	–	–	875	836	157	–	–	808
No meals included in rent	23	71	28	296	2 129	295	87	306	1 693
No cash rent	7	11	4	53	124	61	6	33	143

Figure 9-5

Summary Level. For example, Table 5 might cover Veterans Status at the state level. Tables 6 through 8 would then cover the same topic, using the same table format, but for other Summary Levels. Table 9 would then switch to a completely different topic, such as Disability Status at the state level, then repeat in Tables 10 through 12 for the remaining Summary Levels. Within this basic structure, tables can be further repeated for subgroups of the total population, usually for specific Racial or Hispanic Origin groups. When this happens the pattern of repetition works as follows:

Topic A; State; All persons
Topic A; State; Whites
Topic A; State; Blacks
Topic A; State; [remainder of Race/Hispanic tables]

Topics B-D; State; same Racial repetition as above

Topic A; Counties; All persons
Topic A; Counties; Whites
Topic A; Counties; Blacks
Topic A; Counties; [remainder of Race/

Hispanic tables]

Topics B-D; Counties; same Racial repetition as above.

These patterns can become confusing because of numerous Summary Levels in a single Report, multiple Racial/Hispanic breakdowns, or both. The situation is further muddled by the fact that similar types of data may be found in several table formats. For example, let's return to the case of number of Rooms in Housing Units, a type of statistic which the Bureau calls a Housing Utilization Characteristic. *STF 1* data on number of Rooms can be found in a single table, shown earlier in Figure 9-4. In *CH-1*, similar information appears in five different table formats, each of which is repeated for various Summary Levels and population Universes, creating a total of 31 separate iterations. Two of those formats have already been seen in earlier exhibits. Figure 9-3 shows a table format entitled "Occupancy, Structural, and Utilization Characteristics." Figure 9-5 shows a format called "Utilization Characteristics." Notice that the table devoted exclusively to Utilization data offers a

Within this basic structure, tables can be further repeated for subgroups of the total population, usually for specific Racial or Hispanic Origin groups.

Q&A

Why do similar statistics appear in so many different table formats? Why doesn't the Bureau simply repeat the same format for every Summary Level and every population Universe?

Actually, the same format is repeated for as many iterations as possible. Variations occur for numerous reasons. The major reason is that more subject detail is provided for the biggest Summary Levels, with less subject detail for smaller Levels. This is due in part to confidentiality concerns, in part to save space, and in part because such detail may be unwarranted for smaller geographies. For example, it may be perfectly appropriate to show the number of Filipino and Vietnamese persons at the state or county level, but for most Places with fewer than 2,500 inhabitants, an aggregate number for all Asians is sufficient.

The other notable reason is that the same data Item can be presented in myriad combinations, and a single format does not suit all Census users. The Bureau presents a variety of formats for the same topic in an attempt to address as many of the most common types of data needs as possible. For example, some users are interested only in the characteristics of Occupied Housing Units, while others want data for all Units, whether Occupied or Vacant. By providing a variety of reporting formats for the same topic, the Bureau offers data for different Universes, different subtotals, and different cross-tabulations. This approach enables users to compare related topics in numerous ways.

Example of Table Repetitions in print Reports:
"Number of Rooms" Tables in *CH-1*

	"Utilization Characteristics."	
Table title:	**"Utilization Characteristics."**	
Data reported:	Frequency distribution for 9 size-categories; 1 median value.	
Universe(s):	All Units; Owner-Occupied Units; Renter-Occupied Units.	

Repetitions:

Table Numbers	Geographic Summary Level	Racial/Hispanic Detail
14	State: Urban/Rural	All persons
29	State: Metro/Non-Metro	All persons
50	Counties	All persons
59	Places: 10,000 +	All persons

	"Occupancy, Structural, and Utilization Characteristics."	
Table title:	**"Occupancy, Structural, and Utilization Characteristics."**	
Data reported:	Frequency distribution for 9 size-categories; 1 median value.	
Universe(s):	Owner-Occupied Units; Renter-Occupied Units.	

Repetitions:

Table Numbers	Geographic Summary Level	Racial/Hispanic Detail
16-21	State: Urban/Rural	5 Race tables 1 Hispanic table
31-36	State: Metro/Non-Metro	5 Race tables; 1 Hispanic table
43	State Total	22 Racial categories
45	State Total	Hispanic by type
47	State Total	Race x Hispanic Origin
52	Counties	5 Races; 1 Hispanic
54	Counties	22 Racial groups*
56	Counties	Hispanic by type
61	Places: 10,000 +	5 Races; 1 Hispanic
63	Places: 10,000 +	22 Racial groups*
65	Places: 10,000 +	Hispanic by type
74	American Indian Areas	All Persons

	"Utilization and Financial Characteristics."	
Table title:	**"Utilization and Financial Characteristics."**	
Data reported:	Frequency distribution for 9 size-categories; 4 median values.	
Universe(s):	All Housing Units.	

Repetitions:

Table Number	Geographic Summary Level	Racial/Hispanic Detail
68	Places: 2500-9999	All Persons

	"Occupancy, Structural, and Financial Characteristics."	
Table title:	**"Occupancy, Structural, and Financial Characteristics."**	
Data reported:	Frequency distribution for 9 size-categories; 1 median value.	
Universe(s):	Occupied Housing Units.	

Repetitions:

Table Numbers	Geographic Summary Level	Racial/Hispanic Detail
69	Places: 2500-9999	5 Races; 1 Hispanic
70	Places: 2500-9999	22 Racial groups*
71	Places: 2500-9999	Hispanic by type

	"Selected Housing Characteristics."	
Table title:	**"Selected Housing Characteristics."**	
Data reported:	2 median values.	
Universe(s):	Owner-Occupied Units; Renter-Occupied Units.	

Repetitions:

Table Number	Geographic Summary Level	Racial/Hispanic Detail
72	Places: 1000-2499	All Persons

*Based on Bureau's reporting threshold's for individual Races.

Figure 9-6

bit more subject detail for this topic. The table in Figure 9-5 shows number of Rooms for All Housing Units (whether Occupied or Vacant), plus subtotals for Owner-Occupied Units and Renter-Occupied Units. The user can calculate Utilization Characteristics for Vacant Units by adding the two subtotals for Occupied Units, then subtracting the result from the total of All Units. The table in Figure 9-3 provides subtotals for Occupied Units only, offering no data for All Housing Units, and no way to calculate numbers for Vacant Units.

To see just how many ways a typical Report might tabulate statistics on the same topic, lets continue with the example of the Questionnaire Item dealing with number of Rooms. Figure 9-6 compares the five basic table formats in *CH-1* which present data on Housing Utilization Characteristics, including frequency distributions for number of Rooms. Only one of the five formats is devoted exclusively to Utilization data. The others tables compare Utilization figures to some combination of other categories, such as Occupancy, Structural, or Financial characteristics.

 Census Tip

The smaller the geographic Summary Level, the less subject detail is provided in print Reports.

For each format, Figure 9-6 specifies the Universe of coverage and the number of response categories provided. In most cases, the tables cite the same nine categories— "1 Room," "2 Rooms," and so on up to "9 or more Rooms." Within each format, Figure 9-6 compares the geographic Summary Levels and the Racial/Hispanic breakdowns shown on individual tables. From the sequence of table numbers, the reader can see the pattern of repetition described earlier. One can also see that only one table (Table 72) provides data on number of Rooms for Places with less than 2,500 population, and that this table is the least detailed on the list.

What makes the print Reports appear more difficult to use is that every table repetition is visible to the reader. With the Bureau's CD-ROM products, the GO software "hides" the thousands of available tables until the user specifies the type of information desired. Actually, the table selection process is identical for print Reports and CD-ROMs. Both formats require the user to take the following steps:

1. **Determine the appropriate title to use.**
2. **Select the desired Summary Level.**
3. **Identify the subject matter required.**
4. **Locate the specific geographic entity or entities.**

The GO software guides searchers through this process one step at a time, unlike the print Reports, which leave the user to his or her own devices. Locating the required data from among such a confusing array of table formats and iterations can be challenging, but the task is made easier by several finding aids included in every Census Report. More will be said about these aids later in the chapter.

Before leaving the topic of table arrangement, two special types of tables should be mentioned: Summary Tables and Supplemental Tables. One or more Summary Tables can be found at the front of most print Reports, and in some cases, throughout the Report. These serve the same purpose as the unnumbered General Profile tables which the GO software creates at the beginning of most CD-ROM Files. Summary Tables are designed to present a quick profile of each geographic entity by presenting key population and/or housing characteristics, usually in the form of percentages and median values. Figure 9-7 shows one of the Summary Tables found at the beginning of the *CP-2* Reports. Using 15 columns, this table presents summary data on Nativity, Mobility, Language Spoken at Home, school enrollment, educational attainment, and fertility.

within any given Title, table numbering will be identical from one Report to the next.

Summary Tables are designed to present a quick profile of each geographic entity by presenting key population and/or housing characteristics, usually in the form of percentages and median values.

Census Tip

Since most Census tables do not tabulate percentages, the various Summary Tables are an excellent source of such handy measurements. Otherwise, users must calculate their own percentages.

Supplemental Tables appear at the back of print Reports, and provide technical information evaluating the quality of the data tables. Every Report contains Imputation Tables which specify the percentage of responses for each Item which were Substituted or Allocated by the Bureau. Additional Supplemental Tables, found only in those Census Titles which are based on sample data, provide specific information on the sampling rates and confidence bounds for every geographic entity covered in the Report. More will be said about these specialized tables in Chapter 10.

Perhaps the most important pattern of table presentation which users should remember is that within any given Title, table numbering will be identical from one Report to the next. In other words, if Table 116 of the Delaware Report for *CP-2* is "Occupation of Employed Persons for Selected Racial Groups," then Table 116 will have the exact same title and format in the *CP-2* Reports for New Jersey, Maryland, and each of the other states. The United States Summary Volumes are the only Reports for which this rule does not hold true.

Guides and Appendices

In addition to the data tables, all Census Reports contain large amounts of additional information to help users locate and understand needed information. These consist of several finding aids located at the front of the Report, plus a series of Appendices at the back.

Table 1. Summary of Social Characteristics: 1990

[Data based on sample and subject to sampling variability, see text. For definitions of terms and meanings of symbols, see text]

State / Urban and Rural and Size of Place / Inside and Outside Metropolitan Area / County / Place and [In Selected States] County Subdivision [2,500 or More Persons]	All persons — Total	All persons — Percent foreign born	Persons 5 years and over — Foreign born persons—Percent entered 1980 to 1990	Native persons—Percent born in State of residence	Percent living in different house in 1985	Percent living in different State or abroad in 1985	Percent who speak a language other than English at home — Total	And do not speak English "very well"	Persons enrolled in elementary or high school—Percent in private school	Persons 16 to 19 years—Percent not enrolled in school and not high school graduate	Persons 18 to 24 years—Percent enrolled in college	Persons 25 years and over — Percent high school graduate or higher	Percent with bachelor's degree or higher	Persons under 18 years—Percent living with two parents	Children ever born per 1,000 women 35 to 44 years
The State	1 003 464	9.5	36.9	70.0	42.6	13.6	17.0	7.0	13.4	11.1	42.5	72.0	21.3	73.4	1 789
URBAN AND RURAL AND SIZE OF PLACE															
Urban	863 427	10.5	37.5	70.4	42.8	14.0	18.7	7.9	13.9	11.7	42.3	70.4	20.2	71.3	1 781
Inside urbanized area	824 524	10.7	37.7	70.8	42.4	13.7	19.1	8.1	14.2	12.4	39.7	70.2	20.0	71.0	1 780
Central place	305 476	16.0	50.1	66.5	50.4	20.1	27.7	13.0	15.8	14.7	46.1	63.5	18.5	57.8	1 855
Urban fringe	519 048	7.6	22.4	73.2	37.8	10.0	14.1	5.3	13.2	10.6	34.0	73.7	20.8	79.4	1 743
Outside urbanized area	38 903	5.1	28.8	61.6	51.3	19.9	9.9	3.0	7.6	4.0	72.5	76.1	25.1	77.6	1 805
Place of 10,000 or more	16 612	6.5	19.1	63.9	44.5	18.0	13.5	4.4	9.9	18.7	25.0	73.3	19.2	78.8	1 808
Place of 2,500 to 9,999	22 291	4.1	40.1	63.9	56.2	21.4	7.2	1.9	5.7	1.1	84.3	78.8	30.8	76.4	1 802
Rural	140 037	3.3	24.0	67.9	41.1	11.5	6.9	1.7	10.6	6.7	44.1	82.1	27.9	85.0	1 826
Place of 1,000 to 2,499	6 208	1.3	–	72.0	41.8	12.2	3.8	.7	14.4	8.9	33.2	74.9	18.7	84.2	2 202
Place of less than 1,000															
Other rural	133 829	3.4	24.5	67.7	41.1	11.5	7.1	1.7	10.4	6.6	44.6	82.4	28.3	85.0	1 813
Rural farm	1 124	6.5	21.9	65.9	28.5	4.9	12.6	2.8	11.5	–	31.9	84.1	28.2	75.6	1 220
INSIDE AND OUTSIDE METROPOLITAN AREA															
Inside metropolitan area	928 129	9.9	37.1	72.1	41.7	12.5	17.8	7.4	13.7	11.4	43.4	71.0	20.5	73.1	1 785
In central city	277 249	17.1	50.5	68.8	49.7	19.0	29.7	14.1	16.2	15.9	46.6	61.3	17.1	57.4	1 864
Not in central city	650 880	6.8	22.8	73.4	38.4	9.8	12.8	4.6	12.6	9.1	41.6	74.7	21.9	80.3	1 758
Urban	526 197	7.7	22.6	74.4	37.9	9.5	14.1	5.3	13.1	9.6	40.8	73.2	20.6	78.9	1 737
Inside urbanized area	487 294	7.9	22.3	75.5	36.8	8.7	14.5	5.5	13.5	10.7	35.2	73.0	20.3	79.0	1 733
Outside urbanized area	38 903	5.1	28.8	61.6	51.3	19.9	9.9	3.0	7.6	4.0	72.5	76.1	25.1	77.6	1 805
Rural	124 683	3.3	24.6	69.1	40.6	11.1	7.1	1.7	10.8	6.8	45.2	81.5	27.4	85.1	1 830
Outside metropolitan area	75 335	4.3	30.0	45.9	53.3	27.1	7.7	2.1	9.6	6.6	32.3	85.0	30.4	77.4	1 830
Urban	59 981	4.5	32.0	42.6	55.3	30.2	8.3	2.4	9.8	6.7	32.1	84.7	30.1	75.6	1 843
Inside urbanized area	59 981	4.5	32.0	42.6	55.3	30.2	8.3	2.4	9.8	6.7	32.1	84.7	30.1	75.6	1 843
Outside urbanized area	–	–	–	–	–	–	–	–	–	–	–	–	–	–	–
Place of 10,000 or more	–	–	–	–	–	–	–	–	–	–	–	–	–	–	–
Place of 2,500 to 9,999	–	–	–	–	–	–	–	–	–	–	–	–	–	–	–
Rural	15 354	3.5	19.8	58.6	45.6	14.8	5.6	1.1	8.8	5.8	33.5	86.1	31.4	84.1	1 785
COUNTY															
Bristol County	48 859	11.1	19.3	58.6	40.1	13.3	18.2	7.3	17.7	8.0	48.4	73.9	27.4	85.7	1 852
Kent County	161 135	4.3	16.0	77.9	36.8	7.4	8.0	2.4	12.6	9.1	29.1	76.8	20.5	79.6	1 769
Newport County	87 194	4.4	25.7	39.3	49.0	25.2	8.6	2.4	12.1	6.4	32.6	82.8	30.1	77.5	1 828
Providence County	596 270	12.5	40.9	75.0	42.7	13.2	22.5	9.9	14.5	13.9	41.8	67.0	18.3	68.6	1 776
Washington County	110 006	4.0	33.9	63.1	46.7	16.3	6.9	1.9	8.1	4.9	62.6	82.8	29.1	81.7	1 818
PLACE AND COUNTY SUBDIVISION															
Barrington CDP	15 849	4.5	34.1	53.8	34.3	13.7	7.6	1.1	14.7	4.2	43.5	88.9	46.4	91.1	1 933
Barrington town	15 849	4.5	34.1	53.8	34.3	13.7	7.6	1.1	14.7	4.2	43.5	88.9	46.4	91.1	1 933
Bristol town	21 625	16.4	17.3	60.9	43.4	14.8	26.4	11.8	24.2	8.3	55.8	65.0	19.7	84.7	1 680
Bristol CDP	21 625	16.4	17.3	60.9	43.4	14.8	26.4	11.8	24.2	8.3	55.8	65.0	19.7	84.7	1 680
Burrillville town	16 230	2.1	5.4	75.8	42.0	10.0	8.3	2.1	12.3	9.6	21.2	70.6	15.9	84.0	1 780
Central Falls city	17 637	27.7	49.2	73.5	50.9	15.8	51.3	26.0	15.1	29.8	15.6	46.9	5.7	58.6	2 216
Charlestown town	6 478	2.2	8.4	62.9	45.7	16.4	3.7	.8	1.5	3.9	33.3	86.0	23.5	79.9	1 574
Coventry town	31 083	2.8	14.1	80.5	34.4	5.1	7.5	2.3	10.8	9.5	27.8	74.4	14.2	83.2	1 890
Cranston city	76 060	7.3	22.1	82.7	37.0	6.1	13.7	4.6	12.7	14.4	32.8	74.0	21.1	77.4	1 611
Cumberland town	29 038	8.5	17.9	73.7	38.2	11.6	18.1	7.1	8.6	13.5	33.3	74.7	22.5	86.7	1 862
Cumberland Hill CDP	6 379	4.3	13.0	68.8	46.8	20.7	17.5	5.6	11.9	8.8	34.4	80.1	29.3	91.8	1 669
East Greenwich town	11 865	4.5	20.1	57.3	43.3	16.8	6.9	1.5	9.6	1.1	48.0	89.8	44.2	86.6	1 789
East Providence city	50 380	14.7	18.0	77.0	34.4	7.5	22.3	10.1	13.8	13.9	28.3	66.9	16.0	76.7	1 746
Exeter town	5 461	2.5	32.4	71.7	39.6	7.5	6.6	.9	7.0	8.9	23.6	76.2	23.7	84.3	1 742
Foster town	4 316	2.3	–	75.7	35.0	7.6	4.0	.8	12.7	1.3	33.6	81.9	24.3	82.8	1 945
Glocester town	9 227	2.1	6.3	83.1	32.0	5.5	5.2	.7	10.0	6.9	39.4	82.8	23.4	81.8	1 715
Greenville CDP	8 303	4.0	11.3	77.2	36.1	8.1	5.1	.6	15.4	15.6	40.0	84.7	27.3	85.4	1 601
Hopkinton town	6 873	2.3	20.0	70.0	41.5	11.5	4.4	1.6	7.1	12.0	34.5	79.5	18.3	85.0	2 152
Jamestown town	4 999	2.7	14.6	62.6	43.0	12.4	5.3	.8	21.8	10.0	51.0	89.0	41.7	80.0	1 455
Johnston town	26 542	4.3	11.8	87.9	31.0	4.4	11.2	4.4	17.8	10.3	32.6	66.8	13.5	77.8	1 620
Kingston CDP	6 504	6.8	61.9	36.8	82.8	44.5	9.7	3.1	1.8	–	98.0	95.8	69.4	85.6	1 709
Lincoln town	18 045	5.2	8.0	82.0	34.7	5.7	16.3	4.0	6.4	7.8	34.0	76.1	22.6	82.5	1 884
Little Compton town	3 339	2.9	–	32.0	35.5	14.3	4.3	1.1	7.6	2.3	45.3	86.0	33.6	83.9	1 570
Melville CDP	4 426	3.4	49.0	6.7	91.4	36.1	10.0	4.0	2.4	14.0	5.6	96.2	35.1	96.8	2 123
Middletown town	19 500	5.1	28.3	39.9	59.0	35.6	9.7	3.2	9.4	10.1	14.7	85.0	27.6	82.1	1 975
Narragansett town	14 985	3.3	39.6	63.0	52.7	17.6	6.6	1.3	8.0	5.8	76.0	87.2	37.1	79.8	1 746
Narragansett Pier CDP	3 658	1.5	18.2	61.2	54.0	12.3	6.9	.5	6.1	–	63.8	84.3	34.8	73.3	2 100
Newport city	28 227	5.2	37.1	46.6	58.1	30.3	8.0	2.3	10.9	4.5	42.6	84.1	32.2	62.5	1 771
Newport East CDP	11 080	5.2	21.0	53.6	46.5	16.3	9.7	2.9	11.5	10.0	22.3	81.6	26.0	73.2	1 776
North Kingstown town	23 801	2.8	23.0	63.4	40.2	11.1	4.9	1.0	10.3	3.4	35.8	86.2	30.8	82.6	1 838
North Providence town	32 090	8.0	25.0	84.1	35.4	8.1	15.6	5.4	17.1	10.2	29.8	70.8	20.4	81.1	1 486
North Providence CDP	32 090	8.0	25.0	84.1	35.4	8.1	15.6	5.4	17.1	10.2	29.8	70.8	20.4	81.1	1 486
North Smithfield town	10 497	4.3	10.4	77.8	32.0	6.7	18.4	5.4	10.1	2.9	38.2	71.5	20.8	85.3	1 863
Pascoag CDP	4 995	3.0	8.1	77.0	43.0	10.9	10.2	2.5	10.2	14.4	15.7	65.4	12.3	79.8	1 759
Pawtucket city	72 644	17.7	34.7	77.3	41.9	10.9	28.4	13.5	19.5	20.2	22.5	61.6	13.1	68.9	1 783
Portsmouth town	16 817	3.0	17.9	38.4	43.4	20.0	6.6	1.6	11.8	6.9	30.0	86.3	34.7	90.2	1 874
Providence city	160 728	19.6	58.2	63.0	54.8	24.6	30.5	16.6	17.2	13.7	57.6	62.8	21.6	50.6	1 911
Richmond town	5 351	1.6	28.6	72.0	43.4	6.1	3.3	.8	6.9	5.4	38.5	80.9	24.1	86.0	1 746
Scituate town	9 796	2.4	15.8	82.5	35.5	5.1	4.4	1.4	5.7	5.8	27.9	83.8	27.3	86.6	1 667
Smithfield town	19 163	3.5	11.4	71.2	40.5	15.6	5.3	.9	11.9	4.1	75.6	80.8	25.2	86.5	1 680

Figure 9-7

LIST OF STATISTICAL TABLES

Figure 9-8

Finding Aids

The front matter of every printed Report includes a table of contents, a "List of Statistical Tables," a "Table Finding Guide," a section of "User Notes," and a preface entitled, "How to Use This Census Report." The table of contents is quite brief, and simply indicates the titles and page numbers for all the front matter and appendices. Of greater value is the List of Statistical Tables, an example of which is reproduced in Figure 9-8. This important tool lists the table number, title, stubhead, and starting page number for every data table in the Report. The List is useful in a variety of ways. Table titles are fairly descriptive, so users can consult the List to determine the broad topics and Universes covered by each table. Because the stubheads specify the Summary Levels for every table, the List of Statistical Tables is also helpful for determining which tables

The front matter of every printed Report includes a table of contents, a "List of Statistical Tables," a "Table Finding Guide," a section of "User Notes," and a preface entitled, "How to Use This Census Report."

TABLE FINDING GUIDE

Subjects by Type of Geographic Area and Table Number

Subjects covered in this report are shown on the left side, and types of geographic areas are shown at the top. For definitions of area classifications, see appendix A. For definitions and explanations of subject characteristics, see appendix B. Race and Hispanic origin are indicated with reference letters in parentheses after the table numbers. When a range of table numbers is shown together with a reference letter, there is one table for each race and Hispanic group. Reference letters for population counts and characteristics by race and Hispanic origin are:

(A) White; Black; American Indian, Eskimo, or Aleut; Asian or Pacific Islander; Hispanic origin; White, not of Hispanic origin
(B) American Indian, Eskimo, Aleut, All Asian, Chinese, Filipino, Japanese, Asian Indian, Korean, Vietnamese, Cambodian, Hmong, Laotian, Thai; All Pacific Islander, Hawaiian, Samoan, Guamanian
(C) Mexican, Puerto Rican, Cuban, Other Hispanic origin, Dominican, Central American, Costa Rican, Guatemalan, Honduran, Nicaraguan, Panamanian, Salvadoran, South American, Argentinean, Chilean, Colombian, Ecuadorian, Peruvian, Venezuelan, All other Hispanic origin
(D) Race by Hispanic origin

Subject	The State			County		Place and (in selected States) county subdivision[1]		American Indian and Alaska Native area[2]
	Total	Urban, rural, size of place, and rural farm	Inside and outside metropolitan area	Total	Rural or rural farm	10,000 or more	2,500 to 9,999	
SUMMARY CHARACTERISTICS	1-3, 8-13(A)	1-3, 8-13(A)	1-3, 8-13(A)	1-3, 8-13(A)	...	1-3, 8-13(A)	1-3, 8-13(A)	14-16
POPULATION COUNTS BY RACE AND HISPANIC ORIGIN	4-5(A-D)	4(A-D)	5(A-D)	6(A-D)	214(A), 218(A)	7(A-D)	7(A-D)	...
SOCIAL CHARACTERISTICS								
Age	20, 34, 45(A), 110(B), 119(C), 128(D)	20, 56-61(A)	34, 56-61(A)	140, 151(A)	215, 219	169, 180(A)	196	222
Ancestry	17, 31	17	31	137	...	166	195	...
Disability	20, 34, 45(A), 111(B), 120(C), 129(D)	20, 62-67(A)	34, 62-67(A)	140, 152(A)	216, 220	169, 181(A)	197	223
Education:								
School enrollment and type of school, educational attainment	22, 36, 47(A), 111(B), 120(C), 129(D)	22, 62-67(A)	36, 62-67(A)	142, 152(A), 160(B), 163(C)	215, 219	171, 181(A), 189(B), 192(C)	197, 205(A), 208(B), 211(C)	223
Fertility (children ever born)	21, 35, 46(A), 110(B), 119(C), 128(D)	21, 56-61(A)	35, 56-61(A)	141, 151(A), 160(B), 163(C)	215, 219	170, 180(A), 189(B), 192(C)	196, 205(A), 208(B), 211(C)	222
Household and family characteristics:								
Household type and relationship	21, 35, 46(A), 110(B), 119(C), 128(D)	21, 56-61(A)	35, 56-61(A)	141, 151(A)	215, 219	170, 180(A)	196	222
Selected living arrangements, unmarried partner households	21, 35, 46(A), 110(B), 119(C), 128(D)	21, 56-61(A)	35, 56-61(A)	141, 151(A)	...	170, 180(A)	196	222
Family type by presence of own children	21, 35, 46(A), 110(B), 119(C), 128(D)	21, 56-61(A)	35, 56-61(A)	141, 151(A), 160(B), 163(C)	215, 219	170, 180(A), 189(B), 192(C)	196, 205(A), 208(B), 211(C)	222
Language:								
Language spoken at home (detailed list)	18, 32	18	32	138	...	167	...	...
Language spoken at home by ability to speak English	18, 32	18	32	138	...	167	195	...

See footnotes at end of table.

TABLE FINDING GUIDE   II-1

Figure 9-9

cover the level of geography desired. The List of Statistical Tables is also extremely useful for determining the pattern of table repetition followed by the Report in question.

As helpful as the List of Statistical Tables may be, experienced Census users typically turn to another reference aid first—the Table Finding Guide. This invaluable tool provides a cross-referenced index to the subject variables and geographic Summary Levels covered by an individual Report, leading the user to the specific table he or she seeks. In some instances, the Table Finding Guide also distinguishes among the various population and housing Universes contained in the tables.

Figure 9-9 presents a typical Table Finding Guide, in this case taken from *CP-2*. The Guide lists subject variables in alphabetical order in the left-most column. The remaining columns link the specified subject to the different Summary Levels found in each table.

The letters shown in parentheses following certain table numbers indicate these tables are limited to one or more subgroups in the population. For population variables, these subgroups usually pertain to specified Racial groups or Spanish Origin groups. For housing variables, the subgroups relate to the Race/Hispanic Origin of the Householder, or in some cases, to the Vacancy Status of the Unit. Table numbers with no letter refer to tables which cover All Persons (or in the case of housing characteristics, to All Housing Units).

According to Figure 9-9, users seeking age data at the county level can find it in Tables 140 and 151. The former provides totals for the entire population, while the latter offers breakdowns by seven major categories of Race and Hispanic Origin. Tables 215 and 219 provide age data for parts of each county only. Table 215 tabulates data for the Rural portion of every county which contains Rural territory, while Table 219 covers an even smaller segment—the Rural Farm population in each relevant county.

Census Tip

A "Composite Table-Finding Guide," covering every 1990 print Report issued through July, 1994, can be found in a publication called *Subject Index to the 1990 Census of Population and Housing.* This useful guide is not a Census Bureau product, but a commercial publication issued by Epoch Books in 1996 as a companion to *Understanding the Census.* The "Composite Table-Finding Guide" provides a single alphabetical index to every subject variable cited in the Bureau's original Table Finding Guides. Each subject is then subdivided by summary level.

Depending on the size and complexity of the Report, a Table Finding Guide may go on for several pages. The Guide for *CP-2*

requires three pages to index every table in the Report.

Additional Prefatory Material

Two sections found at the beginning of every Report provide additional explanatory material. The first section, entitled, "How to Use This Census Report," offers a diversity of useful information. Included here are instructions on how to use the Table Finding Guides, an illustrated description of the parts of a statistical table, and a summary of the numerous appendices found at the back of every Report. This section also lists standard abbreviations for commonly encountered geographic terms, and a guide to the symbols used in Census tables. For the reader's convenience, the following brief list identifies some of the most frequently seen symbols and abbreviations.

... Subject is not applicable for this entity.

(NA) Not available.

- The value in the data field is zero, or in the case of a percentage, the value rounds to less than one percent.

(pt.) This symbol is used in connection with geographic areas in hierarchical tables. It indicates that the listed value corresponds only to that portion of the entity which falls within the boundaries of the next highest Summary Level.

The second prefatory section is called "User Notes." This commentary describes characteristics unique to a particular Report or alerts users to changes or corrections which were made too late to appear in the tables themselves. Some notes can be seen in virtually every Report. For example, after analyzing the 1990 Census results, the Bureau determined that respondents tended to round their age upward by one year if their birthday occurred soon after April 1, so the implications of this phenomenon are discussed in a User Note. Other notes may apply to all Reports in a Title, such as the explanation of the Bureau's reporting thresholds for Racial

---

Sidebar (left margin):

Depending on the size and complexity of the Report, a Table Finding Guide may go on for several pages. The Guide for *CP-2* requires three pages to index every table in the Report.

The second prefatory section is called "User Notes." This commentary describes characteristics unique to a particular Report or alerts users to changes or corrections which were made too late to appear in the tables themselves.

and Hispanic breakdowns. (More will be said about thresholds and complementary thresholds in Chapter 10.) In some cases, a User Note may pertain to a single Report only.

The "User Notes" section for *CPH-2* is especially important; in each state Report, it lists all boundary changes which occurred following the 1980 Census, as well as a brief description of the geographic categories particular to that state. The United States Summary Report for *CPH-2* also provides useful comments about comparing geographic information nationwide.

Appendices

Every Census Report contains six Appendices, labeled A through G, as follows:

A Area Classifications
B Definition of Subject Characteristics
C Accuracy of the Data
D Collection and Processing Procedures
E Facsimiles of Respondent Instructions and Questionnaire Pages
F Data Products and User Assistance
G Maps

Five of these (all except Appendix E and G) can also be found in the "Documents" subdirectory of every *STF* product on CD-ROM.

Appendix A provides extensive definitions and commentary about the geographic terms used in the Census. The text of this Appendix is identical in every Report. Appendix B serves as a glossary for nongeographic terms used in the particular Report, and includes discussions of the comparability of each term or concept with previous Censuses. The content of Appendix B varies from one Report Title to another, because the glossary covers only those terms used in the actual publication. Definitions in the *CP* series describe population concepts, while those in the *CH* series focus on housing terminology. Furthermore, Reports which are derived from the Long Form Questionnaire provide more definitions because these Reports cover many

more subject variables than their Short Form counterparts. For example, Appendix B is much longer in *CH-2* than in *CH-1*.

Appendix C discusses such technical aspects of the Census as Confidentiality Edits, Allocation and Substitution of the data, and sources of error in the data. The version of Appendix C found in Titles generated from the Long Form Questionnaire is more detailed because these Reports contain sample data and are subject to sampling error. In sample Reports, these additional sections discuss the Bureau's estimation procedure, its sample design, the calculation of standard errors, and the generation of confidence intervals. All of these concepts will be discussed in Chapter 10.

Appendix D offers a brief introduction to procedural concepts which affect the interpretation of Census data. Such concepts include the Bureau's residency rules, methods used to count persons away from home, and various other data collection and processing procedures.

Census Tip

Some publication information appearing in Appendix F contains slight errors (especially comments relating to print Reports and CD-ROM products) because the text was written before all 1990 publication plans were finalized.

Appendix E provides a facsimile of the 1990 Census Questionnaire, together with the accompanying instructions for respondents. Complete-count Titles (e.g., *CPH-1*, *CP-1*, *CH-1*) reproduce the Short Form; sample Titles (*CPH-5*, *CP-2*, *CH-2*) reproduce the Long Form. (Note: For the reader's convenience, a facsimile of the Long Form is also provided in Appendix C of *Understanding the Census*.)

Appendix F summarizes the major 1990 Census publications, including magnetic tape Files, CD-ROM products, print Reports, microfiche sets, maps, and various reference

The "User Notes" section for *CPH-2* is especially important; in each state Report, it lists all boundary changes which occurred following the 1980 Census, as well as a brief description of the geographic categories particular to that state.

Appendix B serves as a glossary for nongeographic terms used in the particular Report, and includes discussions of the comparability of each term or concept with previous Censuses.

guides. Appendix F also offers suggestions on sources of additional Census information, all of which will be discussed in Chapter 10.

Finally, Appendix G contains detailed outline maps for all geographic entities appearing in the particular Report. More will be said about these maps later in the chapter.

Census of Population and Housing Series

Titles in the *CPH* Series combine population data and housing data in a single Report. *CPH* Titles offer easy-to-use summary data, or provide coverage of specialized geographies not found in other Reports.

Titles in the *CPH* Series combine population data and housing data in a single Report. *CPH* Titles offer easy-to-use summary data, or provide coverage of specialized geographies not found in other Reports. *CPH-1* contains summary population and housing data from the complete-count Questionnaire Items. *CPH-5* serves the same function for sample data. *CPH-2* is an extremely convenient Title focusing on historical comparisons of population counts and Housing Unit counts, plus measurements of land area and population density. The remaining three Titles in the *CPH* Series deal with specialized geographies. *CPH-3* contains summary population and housing data for Census Tracts. *CPH-4* accomplishes the same function for Congressional Districts, while *CPH-6* covers the Outlying Areas of the Pacific.

The first of the 1990 print Reports Series to be issued was *CPH-1*, entitled *Summary Population and Housing Characteristics*.

 ## Census Tip

CPH-1 and *CPH-2* provide complete-count data. *CPH-5* provides sample data. *CPH-3* and *CPH-4* contain both complete-count and sample data in the same publication.

Figure 9-2 (shown earlier) compares geographic coverage among the major Titles in the *CPH* Series. Note that data for Block Groups and Blocks are not tabulated for any of these Reports.

Individual Titles in the *Census of Population and Housing* Series are described in greater detail below.

Summary Population and Housing Characteristics (CPH-1)

The first of the 1990 print Reports Series to be issued was *CPH-1*, entitled *Summary Population and Housing Characteristics*. It was designed to provide a small selection of the most frequently requested population and housing variables taken from the Short Form Questionnaire. The tables are generated from *STF 1A* for the state-specific Reports and from *STF 1C* for the United States Summary Volume.

CPH-1 contains 18 data tables: 9 population tables and 9 housing tables. Pairs of tables actually contain duplicate information, arranged in two different formats. The odd-numbered tables present information in a geographic hierarchy. The even-numbered tables show the same data, arranged alphabetically by place name. For example, Table 1 contains tabulations for age by sex, with geographic entities listed hierarchically (county, County Subdivision, and Place). Table 2 provides the same data for age by sex, with all County Subdivisions and Places in a single alphabet.

Figure 9-10 is taken from Table 6 of the *CPH-1* Report for Massachusetts. Because it is an even-numbered table, it lists towns and cities in alphabetical order. The corresponding odd-numbered table (Table 5, not shown) displays the same data, but groups statistics for the city of Cambridge together with the other localities in Middlesex County. This approach allows users to locate quick information for a single geographic entity (a town, city, etc.) or to obtain an overview of all neighboring areas in a specified vicinity (e.g., all the municipalities and CDPs within a county). The final two tables (17 and 18) show population and housing data for American Indian/Alaska Native Areas.

Table 6. Household, Family, and Group Quarters Characteristics: 1990—Con.

[For definitions of terms and meanings of symbols, see text]

State County Place and [In Selected States] County Subdivision	Persons in households	All house-holds	Family households			Nonfamily households		Householder living alone		Persons per—		Persons in group quarters		
			Total	Married-couple family	Female house-holder, no husband present	Total	Total	65 years and over Total	Female	Household	Family	Total	Institu-tionalized persons	Other per-sons in group quarters

PLACE AND COUNTY SUBDIVISION—Con.

Buzzards Bay CDP, Barnstable County	2 612	1 036	714	542	122	322	265	118	91	2.52	3.02	638	88	550
Cambridge city, Middlesex County	81 769	39 405	17 575	12 177	4 212	21 830	16 686	3 755	2 888	2.08	2.90	14 033	1 269	12 764
Canton town, Norfolk County	18 244	6 605	4 879	4 084	603	1 726	1 440	713	576	2.76	3.28	286	284	2
Carlisle town, Middlesex County	4 333	1 457	1 257	1 146	75	200	153	53	41	2.97	3.19	–	–	–
Carver town, Plymouth County	10 564	3 585	2 878	2 447	326	707	591	361	275	2.95	3.32	26	17	9
Centerville CDP, Barnstable County	8 930	3 696	2 618	2 173	362	1 078	879	439	352	2.42	2.86	260	228	32
Charlemont town, Franklin County	1 249	483	323	269	42	160	133	56	33	2.59	3.21	–	–	–
Charlton town, Worcester County	9 371	3 147	2 542	2 216	235	605	463	155	112	2.98	3.33	205	190	15
Chatham CDP, Barnstable County	1 810	905	485	412	59	420	370	213	168	2.00	2.67	106	64	42
Chatham town, Barnstable County	6 358	3 023	1 916	1 649	193	1 107	975	583	470	2.10	2.62	221	178	43
Chelmsford CDP, Middlesex County	32 167	11 455	8 970	7 592	1 058	2 485	1 997	730	577	2.81	3.20	221	208	13
Chelmsford town, Middlesex County	32 162	11 453	8 968	7 590	1 058	2 485	1 997	730	577	2.81	3.20	221	208	13
Chelsea city, Suffolk County	27 944	10 553	6 522	3 817	2 182	4 031	3 207	1 416	1 067	2.65	3.31	766	618	148
Cheshire town, Berkshire County	3 479	1 291	969	827	112	322	251	101	67	2.69	3.12	–	–	–
Chester town, Hampden County	1 280	464	356	304	34	108	89	44	32	2.76	3.16	–	–	–
Chesterfield town, Hampshire County	1 048	360	283	252	17	77	52	19	14	2.91	3.28	–	–	–
Chicopee city, Hampden County	55 281	22 625	15 303	11 538	3 035	7 322	6 403	3 122	2 436	2.44	3.01	1 351	399	952
Chilmark town, Dukes County	650	286	170	143	20	116	82	27	20	2.27	2.84	–	–	–
Clarksburg town, Berkshire County	1 745	655	514	451	44	141	123	73	57	2.66	3.03	–	–	–
Clinton town, Worcester County	13 127	5 320	3 481	2 584	647	1 839	1 538	647	509	2.47	3.08	95	95	–
Clinton CDP, Worcester County	7 922	3 263	2 060	1 489	404	1 203	1 014	502	422	2.43	3.09	21	21	–
Cochituate CDP, Middlesex County	5 953	2 167	1 679	1 446	174	488	390	192	157	2.75	3.13	93	93	–
Cohasset town, Norfolk County	6 963	2 563	1 915	1 641	204	648	531	251	206	2.72	3.18	112	97	15
Colrain town, Franklin County	1 753	623	478	383	72	145	116	56	42	2.81	3.17	4	–	4
Concord town, Middlesex County	15 293	5 693	4 264	3 736	399	1 429	1 131	513	413	2.69	3.09	1 783	1 680	103
Conway town, Franklin County	1 529	554	421	364	38	133	96	41	29	2.76	3.12	–	–	–
Cordaville CDP, Worcester County	1 530	517	424	383	31	93	66	28	22	2.96	3.23	–	–	–
Cotuit CDP, Barnstable County	2 364	1 008	714	626	59	294	242	120	92	2.35	2.77	–	–	–
Cummington town, Hampshire County	785	317	209	189	14	108	83	34	22	2.48	3.03	–	–	–
Dalton town, Berkshire County	7 053	2 627	1 944	1 660	244	683	584	309	235	2.68	3.17	102	94	8
Danvers town, Essex County	23 254	8 813	6 435	5 310	854	2 378	1 973	852	691	2.64	3.12	920	634	286
Danvers CDP, Essex County	23 254	8 813	6 435	5 310	854	2 378	1 973	852	691	2.64	3.12	920	634	286
Dartmouth town, Bristol County	25 100	9 190	7 107	6 018	839	2 083	1 815	1 119	937	2.73	3.15	2 144	180	1 964
Dedham town, Norfolk County	23 349	8 490	6 404	5 082	1 023	2 086	1 754	917	737	2.75	3.21	433	346	87
Dedham CDP, Norfolk County	23 349	8 490	6 404	5 082	1 023	2 086	1 754	917	737	2.75	3.21	433	346	87
Deerfield town, Franklin County	4 973	1 995	1 383	1 183	145	612	498	191	149	2.49	3.00	45	45	–
Dennis CDP, Barnstable County	2 633	1 124	764	650	95	360	314	179	152	2.34	2.85	–	–	–
Dennis town, Barnstable County	13 726	6 194	4 002	3 253	611	2 192	1 883	1 095	887	2.22	2.74	138	138	–
Dennis Port CDP, Barnstable County	2 775	1 352	755	560	156	597	509	280	233	2.05	2.67	–	–	–
Dighton town, Bristol County	5 575	1 927	1 566	1 328	178	361	313	179	134	2.89	3.24	56	22	34
Douglas town, Worcester County	5 430	1 889	1 481	1 264	143	408	343	186	135	2.87	3.29	8	–	8
Dover CDP, Norfolk County	2 163	722	595	526	59	127	101	43	33	3.00	3.30	–	–	–
Dover town, Norfolk County	4 898	1 643	1 394	1 273	95	249	199	88	67	2.98	3.22	17	–	17
Dracut town, Middlesex County	25 594	8 992	7 010	5 794	906	1 982	1 584	611	464	2.85	3.25	–	–	–
Dudley town, Worcester County	8 955	3 387	2 552	2 120	330	835	719	363	273	2.64	3.09	585	–	585
Dunstable town, Middlesex County	2 236	692	593	545	33	99	69	26	18	3.23	3.50	–	–	–
Duxbury CDP, Plymouth County	1 637	594	469	419	40	125	110	56	43	2.76	3.14	–	–	–
Duxbury town, Plymouth County	13 751	4 625	3 788	3 306	382	837	718	393	315	2.97	3.34	144	140	4
East Bridgewater town, Plymouth County	10 969	3 593	2 921	2 444	364	672	536	253	185	3.05	3.42	135	135	–
East Brookfield town, Worcester County	2 033	721	575	492	60	146	122	71	54	2.82	3.18	–	–	–
East Brookfield CDP, Worcester County	1 396	504	393	328	50	111	92	55	44	2.77	3.16	–	–	–
East Dennis CDP, Barnstable County	2 584	1 129	797	673	106	332	295	196	157	2.29	2.74	–	–	–
East Douglas CDP, Worcester County	1 945	763	526	423	67	237	213	132	95	2.55	3.13	–	–	–
East Falmouth CDP, Barnstable County	5 577	2 244	1 635	1 222	346	609	490	236	172	2.49	2.88	–	–	–
Eastham town, Barnstable County	4 462	1 908	1 344	1 117	178	564	456	224	186	2.34	2.77	–	–	–
Easthampton town, Hampshire County	15 509	6 170	4 165	3 332	618	2 005	1 598	674	535	2.51	3.06	28	–	28
East Harwich CDP, Barnstable County	3 828	1 585	1 180	1 035	126	405	344	225	172	2.42	2.79	–	–	–
East Longmeadow town, Hampden County	12 970	4 670	3 754	3 250	382	916	835	582	429	2.78	3.15	397	395	2
Easton town, Bristol County	18 474	6 436	5 009	4 260	575	1 427	1 136	422	347	2.87	3.29	1 333	125	1 208
East Pepperell CDP, Middlesex County	2 296	770	600	487	92	170	120	26	5	2.98	3.41	–	–	–
East Sandwich CDP, Barnstable County	3 171	1 179	898	794	85	281	217	102	8	2.69	3.10	–	–	–
Edgartown town, Dukes County	3 033	1 297	779	647	100	518	399	140	111	2.34	2.96	29	19	10
Egremont town, Berkshire County	1 229	515	343	300	35	172	139	56	34	2.39	2.93	–	–	–
Erving town, Franklin County	1 372	525	385	327	46	140	112	48	37	2.61	3.07	–	–	–
Essex CDP, Essex County	1 507	599	414	347	44	185	161	76	57	2.52	3.06	–	–	–
Essex town, Essex County	3 260	1 284	887	745	97	397	326	124	65	2.54	3.07	–	–	–
Everett city, Middlesex County	35 318	14 528	9 421	6 675	2 157	5 107	4 313	1 589	1 532	2.43	3.05	383	224	159
Fairhaven town, Bristol County	15 851	6 359	4 393	3 561	644	1 966	1 710	928	753	2.49	3.04	281	261	20
Fall River city, Bristol County	90 952	37 303	24 758	18 115	5 520	12 545	11 225	5 751	4 618	2.44	3.06	1 751	1 288	463
Falmouth CDP, Barnstable County	3 855	1 983	970	764	155	1 013	897	520	425	1.94	2.72	192	172	20
Falmouth town, Barnstable County	27 307	11 274	7 720	6 137	1 264	3 554	2 970	1 439	1 123	2.42	2.92	653	360	293
Fiskdale CDP, Worcester County	2 189	836	586	472	96	250	209	105	55	2.62	3.17	–	–	–
Fitchburg city, Worcester County	39 040	15 363	10 167	7 420	2 144	5 196	4 244	2 033	1 554	2.54	3.11	2 154	673	1 481
Florida town, Berkshire County	742	266	215	184	17	51	47	19	14	2.79	3.15	–	–	–
Forestdale CDP, Barnstable County	2 739	901	749	653	72	152	103	31	24	3.04	3.32	94	–	94
Fort Devens CDP	6 301	1 772	1 704	1 586	73	68	65	–	–	3.56	3.64	2 672	–	2 672
Middlesex County	1 306	368	351	330	12	17	16	–	–	3.55	3.65	–	–	–
Worcester County	4 995	1 404	1 353	1 256	61	51	49	–	–	3.56	3.63	2 672	–	2 672
Foxborough town, Norfolk County	14 419	5 262	3 946	3 259	528	1 316	1 082	293	329	2.74	3.21	218	217	1
Foxborough CDP, Norfolk County	5 590	2 442	1 510	1 187	246	932	772	221	170	2.29	2.91	116	116	–
Framingham town, Middlesex County	61 362	25 113	16 014	12 687	2 568	9 099	7 109	2 165	1 778	2.44	3.03	3 627	1 982	1 645
Framingham CDP, Middlesex County	61 367	25 115	16 014	12 687	2 568	9 101	7 109	2 165	1 778	2.44	3.03	3 627	1 982	1 645
Franklin town, Norfolk County	21 183	7 406	5 801	4 940	648	1 605	1 267	513	415	2.86	3.27	912	80	832
Franklin CDP, Norfolk County	9 053	3 448	2 443	1 966	366	1 005	842	418	342	2.63	3.17	912	80	832
Freetown town, Bristol County	8 414	2 722	2 294	1 984	228	428	347	152	103	3.09	3.38	108	100	6
Gardner city, Worcester County	19 032	7 979	5 177	3 982	931	2 802	2 376	1 156	901	2.39	2.98	1 093	1 018	75
Gay Head town, Dukes County	201	82	54	43	9	28	22	15	5	2.45	2.94	–	–	–
Georgetown town, Essex County	6 327	2 178	1 743	1 514	161	435	359	202	157	2.90	3.28	57	41	16
Gill town, Franklin County	1 583	617	445	389	34	172	151	55	30	2.57	3.05	–	–	–

Figure 9-10

Census Tip

When seeking data for a specific Place in *CPH-1*, use the even-numbered tables, because a Place can cross other political boundaries. The odd-numbered tables are useful for identifying hierarchical relationships, for specifying the portion of an entity which falls within the borders of a larger Governmental Unit, and for comparing geographic entities within a single county. These guidelines also hold true for *CPH-5*, which uses the same table-numbering system.

CPH-1 is entitled "Summary Characteristics" because it focuses on the most basic demographic variables, with no cross-tabulations or subject detail. For example, Racial breakdowns are presented for the five basic categories of Race only, not for the more detailed subcategories. Summary population characteristics consist of total population, age distribution in 12 age groups, median age, sex, Race (by five basic categories), Hispanic Origin, Non-Hispanic population by Race, 14 basic variables dealing with Households and Families (e.g., number of Households, persons in Households, and persons in Group Quarters), and population density. Summary housing characteristics consist of number of Housing Units, Units in structure (six categories), mean number of Rooms, Occupied and Vacant Housing Units, Units with more than one person per Room, Vacancy by type, Tenure, Value of Specified Owner-Occupied Units (in six ranges, plus median, upper quartile, and lower quartile), Contract Rent (in five ranges plus median and quartile values), and number of Units with meals included in rent. An additional table shows number of Occupied Housing Units by Race and Hispanic Origin or Householder.

Geographic coverage includes state totals, counties, County Subdivisions, Places, American Indian Areas, and Alaska Native Areas. Users should note that data in the state-specific Volumes are restricted to areas which fall within the state's boundaries. If a federal Indian Reservation crosses state lines, only the portion within the specified state will be reported.

CPH-1 is useful because it highlights the most significant demographic characteristics and relationships, so the user seeking quick facts doesn't become bogged down in unwanted detail. For this reason, *CPH-1* tends to report totals, averages, and ratios instead of complete frequency distributions. Figure 9-10 illustrates the amount of salient information which is presented in a single table. In this case, Table 6 shows key characteristics of Households, Families, and the Group Quarters population. The table shows that the Buzzards Bay Census Designated Place, located in Barnstable County, Massachusetts, contains 1,036 Households. Of these, 714 are Family Households (e.g., Families) and the remaining 322 are Nonfamily Households. Within these two spanners, each category is further described according to the various column heads. Here again tables focus on the most frequently requested characteristics, such as single-person Households ("Householder Living Alone"), and Female Householder, No Husband Present.

CPH-1 is a new Title for 1990. Its closest equivalent in 1980 was the complete-count tables found in *Summary Characteristics for Governmental Units* (*PHC-3*).

Summary Social, Economic, and Housing Characteristics (CPH-5)

The Bureau designed *CPH-5* to provide key sample data for population and housing characteristics, in much the same way as *CPH-1* covers complete-count data. It is arranged in exactly the same format as *CPH-1*, with alternating odd- and even-numbered tables showing a hierarchical geographic display in the odd numbers, followed by an

CPH-1 is useful because it highlights the most significant demographic characteristics and relationships, so the user seeking quick facts doesn't become bogged down in unwanted detail.

The Bureau designed CPH-5 to provide key sample data for population and housing characteristics, in much the same way as CPH-1 covers complete-count data.

Historical Coverage Shown in *CPH-2*

Characteristic Covered	Summary Level	Decades
Total Population	United States*	1790 +
	Regions/Divisions*	1790 +
	states	1790 +
	Urban/Rural	1790 +
	Metropolitan Areas*	1970 +
	counties	1940 +
Housing Units	United States*	1790 +
	Regions/Divisions*	1940 +
	Urban/Rural	1950 +
	Metropolitan Areas*	1970 +
	states	1940 +
	counties	1940 +
Land Area/Density	United States*	1790 +
	states	1970 +
	counties	1970 +
	County Subdivisions	1970 +
	Places	1970 +
Population Change	United States*	1790 +
	Regions/Divisions*	1790 +
	states*	1790+
Population Distribution	Regions/Divisions*	1790 +
	states*	1790 +
Population Rankings	Regions/Divisions*	1970 +
	states*	1970 +
	Urban/Rural by Region*	1970 +
	Urban/Rural by state*	1970 +
	% change by Region*	1970 +
	% change by state*	1970 +
	Places within state	1980 +
	Largest Incorp. Places*	1790 +
% Change Housing Units	United States*	1940 +
	Regions/Divisions*	1940 +
	states*	1940 +
Housing Distribution	United States*	1940 +
	Regions/Divisions*	1940 +
	states*	1940 +
Housing Unit Rankings	Regions/Divisions*	1970 +
	states*	1970 +
	Urban/Rural by Region*	1970 +
	Urban/Rural by state*	1970 +
	% change by Region*	1970 +
	% change by state*	1970 +
	Places within state	1980 +
	Largest Incorp. Places*	1940 +
Congressional Representation	United States*	1789 +
	Regions/Divisions*	1789 +
	states*	1789 +

* shown in United States Summary volume only.

Figure 9-11

alphabetical display in the even numbers. *CPH-5* contains 18 data tables: nine population and nine housing. It covers the same geographic Summary levels as *CPH-1*: the state total, counties, all County Subdivisions, and Places. Once again, the final two data tables focus explicitly on American Indian Areas and Alaska Native Areas.

Although *CPH-5* only provides 18 tables, it offers an impressive diversity of salient summary data, with representative numbers from virtually every sample question. Population characteristics include Disability status, educational attainment, Income, Poverty status, Labor Force status, Language Spoken at Home, travel to work, Nativity, place of birth, school enrollment, veteran status, and Migration. Housing characteristics cover Gross Rent, condominium status, Tenure, heating fuel, number of Bedrooms, kitchen and plumbing facilities, mortgage status, year structure built, source of water, type of sewage disposal, and availability of telephone and vehicles.

Users should note that all *CPH-5* Volumes contain several inaccurate tables. *Summary Tape File 3*, from which *CPH-5* was derived, contained tabulation errors which were not discovered until after the Files were published. The errors deal with the following variables: weeks worked in 1989; usual hours worked; mobility limitations; and self-care limitations. The magnetic tape and CD-ROM versions of *STF 3* were republished, but the cost of reprinting all of the paper Reports was prohibitive. Instead, the Bureau issued a series of separate errata Reports containing the corrected data for each state. The affected sections, reprinted in these errata pages, incorporate revised data for Tables 5, 6, 7, and 8. Anyone ordering a *CPH-5* Report automatically receives the amended pages as well.

CPH-5 is a new Title for 1990. Its closest equivalent in 1980 was the sample-data tables found in *Summary Characteristics for Governmental Units* (*PHC-3*).

Population and Housing Unit Counts (CPH-2).

The only Census publication to contain extensive historical data is *CPH-2*, entitled *Population and Housing Counts*. Data are generated from the *STF 1* Files. For major geographic levels, *CPH-2* provides comparative historical data for total population, Housing Unit count, land area, and population density. Some figures date back to 1790, while others describe the most recent three decades (1970-1990) only. The individual state Reports show comparisons for geographic entities within the state. The United States Summary Report provides historical comparisons for the entire country, the fifty states, Metropolitan Areas, the most populous Incorporated Places, and other large geographies. The United States Summary Report also contains a variety of unique comparison tables, such as percent changes in population and housing between decades, and population distribution over time. Figure 9-11 shows the years of coverage for each demographic characteristic and Summary Level.

CPH-2 gives historical comparisons for every current geographic entity which existed at the time of the previous Census, whether or not the Area Name was the same. Users should be careful to note that geographic boundaries can change significantly over time. In some cases, *CPH-2* does not cite historical data. If an entity did not exist during a previous Census, the table will cite three dots (...) in the affected decades. Likewise, if an entity's territory later extended into another county or County Subdivision, the affected parts will be represented by three dots for prior decades. If the opposite phenomenon has occurred (a previously existing entity has split into two new entities), the values for prior decades will be designated "NA."

Another important symbol is an "r" preceding certain 1980 counts. This symbol

indicates that the statistic appearing in the original 1980 Census Reports was either erroneous, or was revised subsequent to its publication in the 1980 Census. Because *CPH-2* is the only major Census product which provides historical comparisons, it is the only Title which uses this symbol.

One of the most useful features of *CPH-2* is the guide to geographic boundary and name changes, found in the "User Notes" section of every Report. For each county in the state, "User Notes" list all geographic changes which occurred following the 1980 Census. Among the listed changes are boundary annexations and detachments, new Incorporated Places, deleted CDPs, and geographic name changes. To assist the user, all statistical tables in *CPH-2* utilize a dagger symbol to indicate which entities have undergone boundary changes since the 1980 Census. *CPH-2* is the only Census Report which provides this important historical information.

 Census Tip

CPH-2 is by far the most convenient source for locating data on total population, Housing Unit counts, land area, and population density for principal Summary Levels within a state (or in the case of the United States Summary Report, for all states).

Except for the historical comparisons, land areas, and population/housing densities, most data cited in *CPH-2* can be found in other Census Reports. For this reason, the Title tends to be overlooked by many data users. However, *CPH-2* is especially valuable for ready-reference purposes. Researchers seeking the most basic demographic variables and persons wishing to make quick comparisons across geographies will find it extremely easy to use. *CPH-2* is also one of the few print Reports containing data on Metropolitan Areas and Urbanized Areas. Reports for in-

CPH-2 gives historical comparisons for every current geographic entity which existed at the time of the previous Census, whether or not the Area Name was the same.

CPH-2 is also one of the few print Reports containing data on Metropolitan Areas and Urbanized Areas.

dividual state's cite MA and UA data only for the portions of those Areas which fall within the state's boundaries. However, the United States Summary Report provides data for all Metropolitan and Urbanized Areas in their entirety.

Another useful feature of *CPH-2* is the collection of tables showing the distribution of population, Housing Units, and land area by type and size of geographic entity. For example, several tables distinguish population distributions by Urban/Rural, Metropolitan/Nonmetropolitan; Inside Places/ Outside Places, and so on. Distributions are also shown by size of Place, according to 14 size categories. Distribution by geographic category allows analysts to obtain a better picture of population and housing concentrations and the types of communities in which people live.

The United States Summary Report for *CPH-2* is particularly important because it provides a diversity of comparative tables for all states, counties, Metropolitan Areas, Urbanized Areas, and large Places. This Volume is one of the only Census publications to show nationwide rankings by size. Among the more interesting comparisons are counties ranked by population and housing counts; and Metropolitan Areas ranked by population, housing, and population density. This Volume also contains data on the number of geographic entities by size and

The United States Summary Report for *CPH-2* is particularly important because it provides a diversity of comparative tables for all states, counties, Metropolitan Areas, Urbanized Areas, and large Places. This Volume is one of the only Census publications to show nationwide rankings by size.

type, making it especially useful for understanding the relative importance of the various Governmental Units and how they differ across states. The United States Summary Volume offers several tables relating to Congressional apportionment. The official Apportionment Population for the United States and for the fifty states can be found here, as well as a historical table showing the number of Congressional Representatives by state for every decade from 1789 to the present.

Population and Housing Characteristics for Census Tracts and Block Numbering Areas (CPH-3).

The purpose of *CPH-3* is quite clear: it is the only print Report from the 1990 Census to contain data at the Tract or BNA level. As discussed in Chapter 6, Census Tracts are found in Metropolitan Areas, while Block Numbering Areas (BNAs) represent the equivalent of a Tract in Nonmetropolitan counties. In addition to Tracts or BNAs, *CPH-3* presents data for Metropolitan Areas, county totals, and large Places, but the focus of the publication is the Tract level. *CPH-3* contains 43 data tables: 24 covering population characteristics and 19 dealing with housing. It is also one of the only Census publications, print or electronic, to contain complete-count data and sample data in the same Report. Tables 1 through 15 provide complete-count figures; tables 16 through 43 provide estimates from the sample survey. Complete-count data come from *STF 2A*, while sample data come from *STF 4A*.

CPH-3 consists of 395 separate Reports, plus accompanying maps for each. One Report is published for every MSA and PMSA, plus an additional 52 Reports arranged by state or state-equivalent. The 52 statewide Reports present data for Block Numbering Areas (BNAs) for the Nonmetropolitan counties in the state. The Report Numbers follow

---

NEW IN '90

Population and Housing Counts (CPH-2) is a new publication for 1990. Nevertheless, much of the data on population, land area, and population density found in CPH-2 are similar to statistics shown in a 1980 Report entitled *Number of Inhabitants (Chapter A of PC-1)*. The 1980 publication provided historical comparisons for the two previous decades only, while many of the tables in the 1990 publication date back four decades or more. Housing counts for 1980 were published in *General Housing Characteristics (Chapter A of HC-1)*. The historical comparisons for housing data, as well as the tabulations of housing density, are completely new for 1990.

an alphabetical arrangement. All the state-wide Reports appear first, followed by the individual Metropolitan Area Reports, running from Abilene, Texas to Yuma, Arizona. The only discrepancy from the alphabetical arrangement relates to PMSAs, which are grouped within their CMSAs. For example, Volumes for the Los Angeles, CA CMSA, which is comprised of four separate PMSAs, is numbered in the following manner:

215A	Anaheim-Santa Ana PMSA
215B	Los Angeles-Long Beach PMSA
215C	Oxnard Ventura PMSA
215D	Riverside-San Bernardino PMSA

To help users locate the appropriate publication for a desired Metropolitan Area, every *CPH-3* Report contains a complete alphabetical list of all the Volumes within this Title, together with the Report Number for each.

To help users locate the appropriate publication for a desired Metropolitan Area, every *CPH-3* Report contains a complete alphabetical list of all the Volumes within this Title, together with the Report Number for each.

NEW IN '90

The 1990 Census is the first to assign Tract or BNA Numbers to every county and county-equivalent in the United States. As such, it is the first Census to create Tract/BNA maps and Tract-level tabulations covering the entire country. In 1980, the supplemental state Reports for *Census Tracts* provided data only for those states or counties which contracted with the Bureau to create Nonmetropolitan Tracts. For 1990, the supplemental state Reports cover all territory not already included in one of the state's Metropolitan Areas. Therefore, the total output of 1990 maps and Reports is much more extensive than ever before.

Many of the tables in *CPH-3* are repeated several times for different Universes. In most cases, the sequence is repeated six times, covering the following groups: All Persons; Whites; Blacks; American Indians, Eskimos, and Aleuts; Asians and Pacific Islanders; and Hispanics. In two instances, a seventh version is provided, covering White Non-Hispanics. For example, data on Means of Transportation to Work (Table 17), are repeated for the various Racial/Hispanic groups in tables 20, 22, 24, 26, 28, and 30; each of

these tables is identical except for the Universe covered.

All tables list geographic entities in a consistent fashion. They display subject variables in the stub (representing rows of data) and geographic entities in the headers (representing columns). Tables are arranged in hierarchical fashion. The first columns always display totals for the Metropolitan Area and its component counties. Within each county, separate columns show totals for all Places with populations of 10,000 people or more. Tract-level hierarchies are then displayed in the following manner:

- ▸ Totals for Split Tracts within County A
- ▸ Tracts by Place, within County A, including portions of Split Tracts
- ▸ The remaining Tracts (those lying outside large Places), including portions of Split Tracts within County A
- ▸ Above pattern repeated for remaining counties.

Figure 9-12 shows a typical example of this geographic pattern for the Lima, Ohio MSA. An important feature of every *CPH-3* Report is the pair of Comparability Tables which appear at the beginning of the publication, immediately preceding the data tables. Both Comparability Tables show the relationship between 1990 Tract boundaries and their corresponding 1980 boundaries, but only for those Tracts which have experienced significant changes. Table A lists 1990 Tracts, together with their 1980 counterparts. Table B offers a reverse view, listing 1980 Tracts, with their 1990 counterparts.

 Census Tip

Tract Comparability Tables are useful for alerting the user to situations where significant boundary changes have occurred. However, the best way to determine the exact nature of those changes is to compare the Tract maps for both decades.

Table 19. Income and Poverty Status in 1989: 1990—Con.

[Data based on sample and subject to sampling variability, see text. For definitions of terms and meanings of symbols, see text]

Census Tract or Block Numbering Area	Totals for split tracts/BNA's in Allen County—Con.						Lima city, Allen County			
	Tract 118	Tract 123	Tract 124	Tract 126	Tract 130	Tract 137	Tract 109 (pt.)	Tract 110 (pt.)	Tract 112 (pt.)	Tract 113 (pt.)
INCOME IN 1989										
Households	933	1 704	1 171	983	1 897	545	419	707	6	–
Less than $5,000	33	68	80	70	99	77	9	31	–	–
$5,000 to $9,999	8?	155	208	159	211	82	4	51	–	–
$10,000 to $14,999	76	169	203	120	224	34	14	63	–	–
$15,000 to $24,999	1?7	430	250	290	372	151	44	200	–	–
$25,000 to $34,999	146	406	219	171	358	83	80	101	6	–
$35,000 to $49,999	242	341	156	114	361	63	117	153	–	–
$50,000 to $74,999	132	128	43	59	210	45	55	96	–	–
$75,000 to $99,999	8	7	5	–	39	10	53	12	–	–
$100,000 or more	98	–	7	–	23	–	43	–	–	–
Median (dollars)	36 958	25 872	17 316	20 013	25 932	20 594	43 878	25 545	33 750	–
Mean (dollars)	48 443	27 345	21 862	22 158	29 646	23 503	59 043	29 945	33 100	–
Families	694	1 274	752	664	1 176	400	335	493	6	–
Median income (dollars)	41 3?5	29 123	23 333	23 438	32 924	25 132	46 307	24 830	33 750	–
Males 15 years and over, with income	879	1 515	899	774	1 538	460	750	567	1 310	–
Median income (dollars)	25 921	18 194	13 194	15 431	19 386	18 088	8 854	23 375	2 500–	–
Percent year-round full-time workers	53.0	54.5	43.7	39.3	46.4	47.4	34.5	64.0	11.3	–
Median income (dollars)	36 32?	25 250	20 474	20 870	29 246	21 528	43 249	32 355	15 469	–
Females 15 years and over, with income	866	1 660	1 079	981	1 792	500	484	625	6	–
Median income (dollars)	10 256	7 970	8 524	7 736	9 696	6 731	9 278	10 313	8 750	–
Percent year-round full-time workers	28.4	25.7	35.8	26.9	26.1	29.2	28.5	36.0	–	–
Median income (dollars)	18 295	14 781	14 265	14 185	16 556	19 559	20 192	16 062	–	–
Per capita income (dollars)	19 561	10 184	9 166	9 200	12 601	7 619	15 739	12 036	3 378	–
INCOME TYPE IN 1989										
Households	933	1 704	1 171	983	1 897	545	419	707	6	–
With earnings	726	1 304	881	681	1 304	418	372	609	6	–
Mean earnings (dollars)	49 300	27 633	23 494	22 252	30 555	24 288	53 180	29 925	32 000	–
With Social Security income	332	548	313	429	842	178	94	148	–	–
Mean Social Security income (dollars)	8 456	8 595	7 436	7 674	7 963	6 909	9 882	8 607	–	–
With public assistance income	30	115	146	47	158	74	11	52	–	–
Mean public assistance income (dollars)	2 360	3 651	3 656	2 595	3 346	4 123	7 506	2 554	–	–
With retirement income	157	372	172	224	572	105	66	104	–	–
Mean retirement income (dollars)	7 055	6 324	4 778	8 530	7 190	4 870	9 417	6 290	–	–
MEAN FAMILY INCOME IN 1989 BY FAMILY TYPE										
Families (dollars)	55 612	30 262	25 572	25 927	35 984	27 547	66 558	30 206	33 100	–
With own children under 18 years (dollars)	60 194	29 368	23 448	25 859	36 504	24 088	49 249	25 202	33 100	–
No own children under 18 years (dollars)	52 605	31 038	28 159	25 971	35 639	33 313	80 423	35 975	–	–
Married-couple families (dollars)	57 614	32 534	29 268	29 230	39 968	31 314	73 427	37 200	33 100	–
With own children under 18 years (dollars)	66 365	34 474	29 831	31 056	41 577	29 479	54 981	36 082	33 100	–
No own children under 18 years (dollars)	51 821	31 102	28 671	28 119	38 822	33 977	87 735	38 037	–	–
Female householder, no husband present (dollars)	33 062	18 007	17 037	16 732	20 114	13 549	33 287	13 218	–	
With own children under 18 years (dollars)	21 559	13 756	10 185	16 607	12 858	6 528	19 718	11 464	–	
No own children under 18 years (dollars)	41 210	28 144	26 908	16 802	23 767	35 665	45 085	20 426	–	
POVERTY STATUS IN 1989										
All Income Levels in 1989										
Families	694	1 274	752	664	1 176	400	335	493	6	–
Householder worked in 1989	524	992	600	455	854	269	297	387	6	–
With related children under 18 years	296	645	422	274	509	256	159	269	6	–
With related children under 5 years	108	242	184	104	189	111	48	148	6	–
Married-couple families	605	1 050	513	460	921	304	277	334	6	–
Householder worked in 1989	464	829	416	314	684	217	239	262	6	–
With related children under 18 years	256	499	264	174	402	186	124	143	6	–
With related children under 5 years	92	195	146	75	145	73	48	68	6	–
Female householder, no husband present	41	176	205	152	218	83	43	138	–	–
Householder worked in 1989	35	122	156	95	139	45	43	104	–	–
With related children under 18 years	23	124	130	68	94	63	27	116	–	–
With related children under 5 years	6	36	38	17	44	31	–	70	–	–
Unrelated individuals for whom poverty status is determined	288	569	513	378	789	188	103	329	–	–
Nonfamily householder	239	430	419	319	721	145	84	214	–	–
65 years and over	108	233	134	155	427	56	26	23	–	–
Persons for whom poverty status is determined	2 338	4 515	2 791	2 293	4 425	1 699	1 194	1 768	24	–
Persons under 18 years	517	1 261	769	503	1 032	618	354	532	12	–
Related children under 18 years	517	1 259	769	503	1 024	618	354	532	12	–
Related children 5 to 17 years	370	891	549	332	754	434	280	349	–	–
Persons 65 years and over	367	748	360	460	975	161	136	127	–	–
Persons 75 years and over	151	266	167	201	444	63	49	61	–	–
Income in 1989 Below Poverty Level										
Families	29	92	115	83	95	83	–	66	–	–
Percent below poverty level	4.2	7.2	15.3	12.5	8.1	20.8	–	13.4	–	–
Householder worked in 1989	8	54	66	41	41	37	–	44	–	–
With related children under 18 years	18	73	100	49	60	71	–	66	–	–
With related children under 5 years	10	24	43	6	34	36	–	49	–	–
Married-couple families	19	34	29	18	35	34	–	–	–	–
Householder worked in 1989	8	19	19	11	25	16	–	–	–	–
With related children under 18 years	8	15	19	12	9	22	–	–	–	–
With related children under 5 years	–	–	13	–	9	14	–	–	–	–
Female householder, no husband present	–	52	76	54	54	49	–	66	–	–
Householder worked in 1989	–	29	37	19	16	21	–	44	–	–
With related children under 18 years	–	52	71	26	45	49	–	66	–	–
With related children under 5 years	–	18	30	–	25	22	–	49	–	–
Unrelated individuals	49	112	142	86	133	82	11	48	–	–
Nonfamily householder	29	58	95	62	112	48	9	17	–	–
65 years and over	–	51	14	27	95	12	–	–	–	–
Persons	116	428	475	321	388	381	11	232	–	–
Percent below poverty level	5.0	9.5	17.0	14.0	8.8	22.4	9	13.1	–	–
Persons under 18 years	19	179	184	86	111	186	–	110	–	–
Related children under 18 years	19	177	184	86	111	186	–	110	–	–
Related children 5 to 17 years	8	148	128	80	73	106	–	68	–	–
Persons 65 years and over	15	51	24	54	133	36	–	–	–	–
Persons 75 years and over	–	27	14	20	92	18	–	–	–	–
Ratio of income in 1989 to poverty level:										
Persons below 50 percent of poverty level	96	245	176	113	177	201	11	86	–	–
Persons below 125 percent of poverty level	212	593	605	396	685	529	21	397	–	–
Persons below 200 percent of poverty level	491	1 488	1 302	960	1 202	1 015	80	714	–	–

Figure 9-12

Tract Comparability Tables list only the most notable boundary changes, including 1980 Tracts which were divided into two or more 1990 Tracts; 1980 Tracts which were subsequently merged into one; and Tracts where boundary changes affected more than 2.5% of the Tract's population.

Tract Comparability Tables list only the most notable boundary changes, including 1980 Tracts which were divided into two or more 1990 Tracts; 1980 Tracts which were subsequently merged into one; and Tracts where boundary changes affected more than 2.5% of the Tract's population. The list excludes Tracts in cases where no changes occurred; where changes affected fewer than 2.5% of the population; or for areas where Tracts were defined for the first time in 1990. These tables appear only for those counties containing Tracts (i.e., they exclude all counties consisting of Block Numbering Areas).

The 1990 *CPH-3* Reports are similar in content, format, and geographic scope to their 1980 equivalent, entitled *Census Tracts* (*PHC-2*). The main difference is the inclusion of data tables for Block Numbering Areas for 1990.

Population and Housing Characteristics for Congressional Districts of the 103rd Congress (CPH-4)

Representation for the 103rd Congress, which began in January 1993, was determined by reapportionment and redistricting activities which took place following the 1990 Census. All states underwent redistricting for the 103rd Congress, with the following minor exceptions:

▸ seven states comprised of a single Congressional District each (Alaska, Delaware, Montana, North Dakota, South Dakota, Vermont, and Wyoming); and

▸ Maine, which did not complete its redistricting until 1993.

CPH-4 provides 1990 Census data for the redrawn Congressional District boundaries, which were in effect for the Congressional election of November, 1992. The actual dates when redistricting took effect vary for every state. The effective dates for individual states

CPH-4 provides 1990 Census data for the redrawn Congressional District boundaries, which were in effect for the Congressional election of November, 1992.

can be found on the map legend shown in Appendix G of the respective *CPH-4* Volumes. (Chapters 2 and 12 of *Understanding the Census* provide additional information about reapportionment and redistricting activities.)

 Census Tip

The United States Summary Volume for *CPH-3*, called the *Finders Guide to Census Tract Reports* (*CPH-3-1*), does not publish comparative statistical tables for the nation. Instead, it provides an alphabetical list of counties and Places within each state, together with the *CPH-3* Report Number which covers that area. For example, a quick check of the index indicates that data for Census Tracts in St. Cloud, Florida can be found in *CPH-3-252*, which covers the Orlando MSA. Place-level indexing is limited to areas with a population of 10,000 or more, because *CPH-3* does not tabulate data for smaller Places.

Geographic coverage in *CPH-4* focuses on the Congressional Districts themselves. Most tables provide data for the entire state and for every Congressional District in the state. In the seven states which contain a single District, *CPH-4* lists statistics for that single District alone.

Selected tables also provide data for the portions of counties, general-purpose County Subdivisions, and Places which fall within each District. Four special tables present data for the portions of American Indian Areas and Alaska Native Areas which fall within each District. All Volumes of *CPH-4* contain outline maps of the Congressional District boundaries within that state. The Bureau also reproduces CD boundary maps and name indexes for all 50 states in a special Census publication entitled *Congressional District Atlas: 103rd Congress of the United States.*

CPH-4 contains 17 population tables and 15 housing tables. Coverage is fairly broad, representing approximately 35 population variables and 31 housing variables. Items range from basic information, such as age, voting age, Race, citizenship, and housing Tenure, to detailed Items, such as Ancestry, Class of Worker, Disability status, and plumbing facilities. Nearly all variables are cross-classified by major Racial group and by Hispanic Origin.

CPH-4 is one of the few 1990 Titles which includes complete-count data and sample data in the same Report. Tables 1 through 12 represent complete-count data, while Tables 13 through 32 cover sample data. Data are obtained from *STF 1D* (the complete-count File) and *STF 3D* (the sample File).

Social, Economic, and Housing Characteristics [Outlying Areas of the Pacific] (CPH-6)

The four Volumes published as *CPH-6* contain summary data for the Outlying Areas of the Pacific: Guam, American Samoa, the Republic of Palau, and the Commonwealth

of the Northern Mariana Islands. *CPH-6* presents data for the statistical equivalents of states, counties, County Subdivisions, and Places. Geographic terminology in these Areas varies considerably from the designations used in the United States. The equivalent Units for counties are called "states" in Palau, "municipalities" in the Northern Marianas, and "districts" in American Samoa; county-equivalents do not exist in Guam. The Outlying Areas of the Pacific contain no Metropolitan Areas, and therefore contain no Census Tracts. However, each territory is completely divided into Block Numbering Areas. Unlike the other state-equivalents, BNA data for the four territories are not published in *CPH-3*.

💡 Census Tip

The Outlying Areas in the Caribbean—Puerto Rico and the American Virgin Islands—receive the same Census coverage as each of the 50 states, and thus do not appear in *CPH-6*. In any print Title issued on a state-by-state basis, Puerto Rico appears as Report 53 and the Virgin Islands is Report 55. No publications are issued using Report Number 54.

All residents of the Outlying Areas of the Pacific received the Long Form Questionnaire, which means that no Questionnaire Items are sample Items. In other words, information on such topics as Income, Labor Force status, educational attainment, and Disability status, which appear as sample data for the 50 states, Puerto Rico, and the U.S. Virgin Islands, are published as complete-count Items in the Outlying Areas of the Pacific.

All residents of the Outlying Areas of the Pacific received the Long Form Questionnaire, which means that no Questionnaire Items are sample Items. In other words, information on such topics as Income, Labor Force status, educational attainment, and Disability status, which appear as sample data for the 50 states, Puerto Rico, and the U.S. Virgin Islands, are published as complete-count Items in the Outlying Areas of the Pacific.

CPH-6 contains 126 tables: 99 of them cover population topics, and the remaining 27 deal with housing variables. The Reports are fairly detailed, providing at least some data for every Item appearing on the Long Form. Unlike *CPH-1* and *CPH-5*, this Title

NEW IN '90

The 1980 counterpart to *CPH-4* was issued in two phases. *Congressional Districts of the 98th Congress (PHC-4)*, provided Census data based on redrawn boundaries in effect for the November, 1982 Congressional elections. Ten states (California, Hawaii, Louisiana, Maine, Mississippi, Montana, New Jersey, New York, Texas, and Washington) conducted additional redistricting for 1984. The Bureau then published phase 2, entitled *Congressional Districts of the 99th Congress*, for those ten states only.

A similar situation occurred following the 1990 Census. Six states (Georgia, Louisiana, Maine, Minnesota, South Carolina, and Virginia) conducted additional redistricting for the 104th Congress. Revised data appear on CD-ROM only. These revisions have not yet appeared as part of *CPH-4*.

is not limited to summary characteristics. For example, users of *CPH-6* can find age by single years, detailed breakdowns for Language Spoken at Home, and fairly specific response categories for occupational groups. Geographic detail is also good, with most variables tabulated for the local equivalents of counties, County Subdivisions, and Places. *CPH-6* does not tabulate data for BNAs, Block Groups, or Blocks.

Another unexpected benefit of *CPH-6* is the presence of subject cross-tabulations. Fully one-half of the tables contain cross-tabulations by one or more variables, but these detailed tables are limited in geographic coverage to the total Outlying Area. Cross-tabulated characteristics focus on age, Place of Birth, Race, Ancestry, Educational Attainment, Labor Force status, and Income. Examples include educational attainment by Income, Disability Status by age, and citizenship by Place of Birth.

Census of Population and Housing Supplementary Reports (CPH-S)

The Bureau has produced two Supplementary Reports in the *CPH* Series for 1990, though more may be issued before the decade

draws to a close. The first, entitled *Metropolitan Areas as Defined by the Office of Management and Budget, June 30, 1993* (*CPH-S-1-1*), is a unique Report. It is the only publication of the 1990 Census to provide population counts for the Metropolitan Areas which were redefined as a result of the 1990 Census. As explained in Chapter 11, OMB revises its official list of Metropolitan Areas each decade, based on the Census Bureau's analysis of commuting patterns from the decennial Census. The process takes several years, and in this case, OMB released its revised list on June 30, 1993.

NEW IN '90

1990 represents the first Census for which the Bureau published information on Outlying Areas of the Pacific as a separate Title. For 1980, Reports for each Outlying Area appeared as state-equivalent Volumes within the two main Census Titles: *Characteristics of the Population* (PC-1), and *Characteristics of Housing Units* (HC-1). As with the Reports for each of the 50 states, the Volumes for Outlying Areas were issued in parts, called Chapters (Chapters A-D for population data, and Chapters A-B for Housing data). As in the 1990 Census, all inhabitants of the Outlying Areas of the Pacific received the Long Form in 1980. Content and coverage between the two decades is quite similar. The main difference is greater geographic detail for 1990 versus slightly more detailed response categories for 1980.

The Bureau has produced two Supplementary Reports in the *CPH* Series for 1990, though more may be issued before the decade draws to a close.

Q&A

Where can I find additional data for the Outlying Areas of the Pacific?

CPH-6 is the only print Title providing decennial Census figures for Guam, American Samoa, Palau, and the Northern Mariana Islands. This Title presents fairly detailed statistics, but not as extensively as the major 1990 Reports for the 50 states. The only other data source for these three Areas can be found on magnetic

tape, in the form of *Summary Tape File 1* and *Summary Tape File 3*. Neither one is divided into Subfiles A, B, and C; instead, each exists as a consolidated Outlying Areas File. The Bureau issued no CD-ROM products for the Pacific Outlying Areas in 1990.

CP-1 provides detailed tables for complete-count population data. CP-2 contains detailed tables for sample data, and CP-3 represents specialized *Subject Reports* based on sample data.

Census Tip

All other 1990 publications relating to Metropolitan Areas are based on the MA definitions which were in place at the time of the Census. *CPH-S-1-1* is the only 1990 Census product which provides statistics for the post-Census Metropolitan boundaries and definitions.

CPH-S-1-1 contains 12 statistical tables providing a broad range of summary characteristics for individual Metropolitan Areas. Subject content is fairly similar to *CPH-3*, and like the *CPH-3* Volumes, this Report

includes both complete-count and sample data in a single publication. Users who wish to compare characteristics of the revised 1992 Metropolitan Areas with those of the 1990 MAs should consult the United States Summary Volumes for *CPH-1* and *CPH-5*.

The other *CPH Supplementary Report* for 1990 is called *Urbanized Areas of the United States and Puerto Rico* (*CPH-S-1-2*). It provides a single table for each state, displaying the following characteristics for every Urbanized Area and its component parts: total population, total Housing Unit count, land area, population density, and housing density. Detailed UA boundary maps for each state are also shown.

Census of Population Series

Detailed population data are found in the three Titles of the *Census of Population* Series, designated by *CP* Report Numbers. *CP-1* provides detailed tables for complete-count population data. *CP-2* contains detailed tables for sample data, and *CP-3* represents specialized *Subject Reports* based on sample data. *CP-1* and *CP-2* are each issued in 57 Volumes: 53 Volumes covering the individual states and state-equivalents; a United States Summary Volume; and three Volumes covering Metropolitan Areas, Urbanized Areas, and American Indian and Alaska Native Areas. *CP-3* is issued in seven Volumes, arranged by topic.

Census Tip

Use *CP-1* to locate complete-count data and *CP-2* for sample data. The complete-count Items shown in *CP-2* are provided for comparative purposes only, and represent estimates, not actual counts.

NEW IN '90

The purpose of the *CPH Supplementary Reports* for 1980 were much different. The 1980 Title, called *Advance Estimates of Social, Economic, and Housing Characteristics*, was designed to publish sought-after summary statistics in advance of the detailed Titles in the *Population Census* (*PC-1-C*) and *Housing Census* (*HC-1-C*). The Title consisted of a single Report containing sample data for states and for larger Metropolitan Areas, plus 50 state-specific Reports containing sample data for all counties and for all MCDs and Places with populations greater than 25,000. The need for these "Advance Reports" was eliminated in 1990 with the creation of *CPH-5*, and through rapid dissemination of Census results via the *CENDATA* online system.

For 1990, the Bureau also unveiled another Census Title designed for rapid release of newly-tabulated data. Called *Selected Population and Housing Data Paper Listings* (*CPH-L*), it consists of over 150 Reports of varying size. Topics are extremely specific, as indicated by such titles as *The Nursing Home Population* and *Twenty Place of Work Destinations for Counties*. Geographic coverage also varies, ranging from state-by-state comparisons to smaller areas within a single state. Tables in these Reports often present data as ranked lists by size or percent change. The Reports in this Title are not available from the Government Printing Office; they must be ordered directly from the Census Bureau. A list of specific titles and prices can be found in the Bureau's annual *Census Catalog and Guide*.

Q&A

The *CPH Supplementary Report* for Urbanized Areas seems to duplicate data which are easily found in other Census Reports. Does it provide any unique information?

The state tables in *CPH-S-1-2* utilize the same format found in Table 23 of the individual state Volumes of *CPH-2*. However, the *CPH-2* Reports provide tabulations for only that portion of a UA which falls within the state's boundaries. Table 51 of the United States Summary Volume for *CPH-2* shows the Area totals for UAs which cross state boundaries, but does not provide detail for component parts of each UA. The *Supplementary Report* combines aspects of both tables in a single Report. A second useful element of *CPH-S-1-2* is the provision of detailed UA boundary maps for the entire country. State-specific maps can be found in the individual Volumes of *CPH-2*, but a single collection of maps is reproduced only in the Supplementary Report. UA maps are not published in the United States Summary Volumes for *CPH-1*, *CPH-2*, or *CPH-5*, nor do they appear in the special Urbanized Area Reports of the Census of Population (*CP-1-1C* and *CP-2-1C*). And unlike the various United States Summary Volumes, this *Supplementary Report* includes data for Puerto Rico.

The features described above are designed largely for convenience and offer little information which is unique. However, *CPH-S-1-2* is the only Census Report which focuses on comparative data for the component parts of Extended Cities. (Readers may remember from Chapter 6 that Extended Cities are Places within Metropolitan Areas which contain a significant amount of Rural territory. The portion which lies outside the boundary of the Urbanized Area represents the Rural component.) Other Census publications show the Urban and Rural components of Extended Cities, but don't explicitly indicate that the entity represents such an unusual geographic construct. Table 9 of *CPH-S-1-2* provides the only readily available guide to all Extended Cities in the United States.

Neither *CP-1* or *CP-2* have a CD-ROM equivalent. Both are generated from *Summary Tape Files* which exist in magnetic tape format only.

Figure 9-2, shown earlier, compares geographic coverage among the major Titles in the *CP* Series. Note that data for Congressional Districts, Census Tracts, Block Groups, and Blocks are not tabulated in any of these Reports.

Neither *CP-1* or *CP-2* have a CD-ROM equivalent. Both are generated from *Summary Tape Files* which exist in magnetic tape format only. However, **some** of the tables published in *CP-1* and *CP-2* can be found (in full or partial form) in various CD-ROM products. Tables from *CP-1* correspond in part to those from *STF 1A* and *STF 1C*. Tables from *CP-2* correspond in part to selected tables from *STF 3A* and *STF 3C*. More specific comparisons between various print Reports and CD-ROM products will be made at the end of this chapter.

General Population Characteristics (*CP-1*).

CP-1 tabulates detailed population characteristics based on questions asked of the entire population (all population Items from the Short Form, plus those from the complete-count portion of the Long Form). Data are generated from *Summary Tape File 2*, which is available on magnetic tape only, and has no CD-ROM equivalent. Each *CP-1* Report contains 83 tables, including two Imputation Tables.

CP-1 covers a fairly broad range of geographic Summary Levels, but focuses predominantly on the state, counties, and larger Places (including MCDs in the 12 states where they serve as general-purpose governments). A handful of tables cover American

Indian/Alaska Native Areas, but only for that portion of an Area which falls within the state's boundaries. A few tables present data for Places with populations in the 1,000 to 2,499 range, but Places with fewer than 1,000 persons are omitted from this Title. *CP-1* presents a single table which covers County Subdivisions in the 38 states where they do not serve as general-purpose governments.

Subject coverage is fairly narrow, limited to the following topics: total population; population in Households and Group Quarters; Group Quarters population by type of Quarters; age (in single years and groups of years); Household size and relationships; age of Householder; Family size and type; and marital status. The important contribution made by *CP-1* is that most tables are cross-tabulated by one or more of the following characteristics: sex, Race/Hispanic Origin, or age.

The Table Finding Guides for *CP-1* list 10 different table formats for cross-tabulations by Race/Hispanic Origin, plus one format which presents totals for the entire population. Some formats compare many Races in a single table, while others focus on a single Racial or Hispanic group. The following list summarizes the eleven categories and indi-

cates the letter codes used to identify them in the Table Finding Guides.

A All Persons
B White
C Black
D American Indian/Eskimo/Aleut
E Asian/Pacific Islander
F Hispanic
G White, not Hispanic
H detailed breakdowns for Native Americans (3 categories) and for Asian/Pacific Islanders (15 categories)
I Hispanic Origin by type (Mexican, Puerto Rican, Cuban, Other)
J Race by Hispanic Origin
K 15 additional Asian/Pacific Islander categories not shown in Format H.

Formats A through G provide cross-tabulations for virtually every subject variable in the Reports, and are presented for all Summary Levels. Formats I through J present cross-tabulations for many of the subject variables, but not always for every Summary Level; the smaller the level, the less detailed the cross-tabulations. Format K presents cross-tabulations for total population counts only, and only for the largest Summary Levels.

The 1980 equivalent of *CP-1* was *Chapter B* of *PC-1*, which had the same name: *Gen-*

The Table Finding Guides for *CP-1* list 10 different table formats for cross-tabulations by Race/Hispanic Origin, plus one format which presents totals for the entire population.

Q&A

What type of detail does *CP-1* provide which cannot be found in *CPH-1*?

The major features of *CP-1* are the extensive cross-tabulations and the increased number of response categories. Virtually all characteristics in *CP-1* are cross-tabulated according to the major Racial and Hispanic categories, and many tables present Racial and Hispanic cross-tabulations for even more detailed breakdowns, such as Japanese (as a Race) or Cubans (as a Hispanic type). Several tables also provide cross-tabulations by age or sex.

Added detail in response categories include age by

single-years, plus much more detail on Household and Family composition (e.g., age of Householders, presence of children in the Family, and Household relationships of the elderly).

Why would anyone prefer using *CPH-1*? Because many people find that *CPH-1* presents summary data more conveniently, making it easier to locate basic information. *CPH-1* also covers more geographic entities, including Places with population under 1,000 inhabitants, and all MCDs and CCDs.

eral Population Characteristics. Subject content was virtually identical, though the 1990 Reports are slightly more detailed.

Social and Economic Characteristics (CP-2).

Reports in this Census Title focus on Items taken from the Long Form Questionnaire. Data are derived from *Summary Tape File 4*, which is available on magnetic tape only, and has no CD-ROM equivalent. *CP-2* Reports are huge, each containing 235 tables, including five Imputation Tables.

Because *CP-2* contains greater subject detail, it offers slightly less geographic coverage than *CP-1*. It provides no statistics for Places with fewer than 2,500 persons. Like *CP-1*, coverage of County Subdivisions is limited to the 12 states where MCDs serve as general-purpose governments, but in this case, no tabulations are made for MCDs with fewer than 2,500 persons.

Subject coverage is enormous and wide-ranging, dealing with every sample Item on the population side of the Census Questionnaire. Where *CPH-5* offers a handful of summary tables, *CP-2* explores each sample variable in considerable detail. Equally impressive is the number of response categories listed for each Item. To cite a few examples, relevant tables in *CP-2* show responses for 46 industry categories, 46 occupations, 88 Ancestry groups, 94 countries of birth, and 26 languages or language groups.

Like its corresponding complete-count Title, *CP-2* cross-tabulates data for specialized Racial and Hispanic Universes. Because of the enormity of subject detail, these cross-tabulations are less ambitious than those found in *CP-1*. Instead of ten additional table formats, *CP-2* utilizes four (plus the basic format covering all persons regardless of Race or Hispanic Origin). These special formats are listed below, together with the letter codes used in the Table Finding Guides to differentiate them from one another.

A   four major Racial groups (White; Black; American Indian, Eskimo, or Aleut; and Asian or Pacific Islander), plus two Hispanic categories (Hispanic Origin; and White, Non-Hispanic).

B   three categories of Native Americans, plus 15 categories of Asian/Pacific Islander.

C   20 categories of Hispanic Origin, from Puerto Rican to Venezuelan.

D   Race by Hispanic Origin.

Each of the five formats is employed for every subject reported at the state level. Most subjects tabulated at the county and Place levels utilize each of the formats except for type D, "Race by Hispanic Origin." *CP-2* also provides separate tables focusing on characteristics of persons age 60 and older.

The 1980 equivalent of *CP-2* was *Chapter C* of *PC-1*, entitled *General Social and Economic Characteristics*. Subject coverage was virtually the same, but the 1990 Reports are much more detailed, especially concerning the number of response categories shown.

Population Subject Reports (CP-3).

CP-3 is based on the *Subject Summary Tape Files* (*SSTFs*) described in Chapter 8. Each *CP-3* Report focuses on a different subject, but in greater detail than the tabulations created for *CP-1* or *CP-2*. Most *CP-3* Re-

Because *CP-2* contains greater subject detail, it offers slightly less geographic coverage than *CP-1*.

NEW IN '90

The 1980 *Census* contained an additional sample Report called *Detailed Population Characteristics* (*Chapter D* of *PC-1*), not to be confused with the 1990 Title of the same name. *Chapter D* provided complex cross-tabulations and detailed response categories, but displayed data only for states and for Metropolitan Areas containing a population of 250,000 or more. This Title was canceled for 1990—in part because users showed little interest, and in part because the 1990 *CP-2* Title displays greater detail than its 1980 equivalent.

Subject Reports, 1990 Census

Number	Title	Source	Geography	Tables	Pages
Population Subject Reports					
CP3-1	Foreign Born Population	SSTF 1	U.S.	7	506
CP3-2	Ancestry of the Population	SSTF 2	U.S.	7	744
CP3-3	Persons of Hispanic Origin	SSTF 3	U.S.	7	356
CP3-4	Education in the United States	SSTF 6	U.S.; states	7	824
CP3-5	Asians and Pacific Islanders	SSTF 5	U.S.	7	336
CP3-6	Characteristics of the Black Population	SSTF 21	U.S.; states[1]; MAs[2]	63	499
CP3-7	Characteristics of American Indians by Tribe and Language	SSTF 13	U.S.; Regions; Divisions; states; MAs	28	1571
Housing Subject Report					
CH3-1	Metropolitan Housing Characteristics	SSTF 7	U.S.	281	432

[1] 17 states only; each consisting of 900,000 or more Black inhabitants.

[2] 13 Metropolitan Areas only; each consisting of 400,000 or more Black inhabitants.

Figure 9-13

ports limit their geographic coverage to the United States only. Several Reports provide additional coverage for other highly populated Summary Levels, such as Census Regions, Divisions, states, or Metropolitan Areas. A complete list of *CP-3* Reports is

NEW IN '90

For 1980, the Bureau published 15 *Population Subject Reports*, compared to the seven issued so far for 1990. However, the Bureau plans to release 15 population-oriented *SSTF* products on CD-ROM for 1990, covering most of the same topics addressed in the prior decade. During the 1980 Census cycle, *Subject Reports* which had been slated for cancellation were reinstated when additional money was found. The last *Subject Report* in the 1980 Series was published in 1989. It is possible that several unanticipated 1990 Reports will appear between 1996 and 1999.

shown in Figure 9-13. Not all population Files in the *SSTF* series have print counterparts, as can be seen by comparing Figure 9-13 with Figure 8-5 in the previous chapter.

The Bureau considers the *CP-3* and *CH-3* Titles to be the least essential Reports of the decennial Census. As such, they are the last to be published, and the first to be slated for cancellation when the agency encounters problems with its budget for decennial products. The Bureau originally planned to issue one Report for each 1990 *SSTF* population product, for a total of 30 *CP-3* Reports. This number was subsequently reduced to 15 Reports after half of the original *SSTF* products were themselves canceled. In early 1994, the Bureau announced that only seven of the 15 *SSTF* population Files would be translated into print Reports. By mid-1995, all seven had been published.

Because of the detailed nature of *Population Subject Reports* and the amount of cross-tabulations they provide, the tables found within this Title tend to be lengthy and complex. Figure 9-14 shows a fairly typical *Subject Report* table, taken from *CP-3-2* (*Ancestry of the Population in the United States*). It describes a variety of social characteristics for each of 75 different Ancestry groups. Within each Ancestry category, statistics are further broken down by Nativity (native and foreign born). Data for the foreign-born population are then cited by citizenship and year of entry to the United States. The table is so detailed it requires a two-page spread to include all the columns for each geographic entity; Figure 9-14 reproduces the second part of this two-page display only. Five levels of classification within the boxhead make the table fairly challenging to read. The number 359 in the first leftmost data cell of Figure 9-14 indicates that 359 persons of Estonian Ancestry in the United States age three years or older and enrolled in school are foreign-born naturalized citizens. This particular table runs for 101 pages.

CP-3 Reports are fairly similar to their CD-ROM counterparts in content, geo-

Table 3. Social Characteristics of Selected Ancestry Groups by Nativity, Citizenship, and Year of Entry: 1990 —Con.

[Data based on sample and subject to sampling variability, see text. Ancestry is based on first ancestry reported. For definitions of terms and meanings of symbols, see text]

United States	Estonian—Con. Foreign born—Con.						Finnish	
	Naturalized			Not a citizen				
		Year of entry			Year of entry			
	Total	1980 to 1990	Before 1980	Total	1980 to 1990	Before 1980	All persons	Native
SCHOOL ENROLLMENT AND TYPE OF SCHOOL								
Persons 3 years and over enrolled in school	359	25	334	218	163	55	116 072	112 916
Preprimary school	-	-	-	8	8	-	8 301	8 234
Public school	-	-	-	-	-	-	5 291	5 267
Elementary or high school	47	11	36	126	115	11	69 837	68 704
Public school	47	11	36	92	81	11	65 185	64 104
College	312	14	298	84	40	44	37 934	35 978
Public college	227	6	221	56	19	37	31 048	29 692
Persons 3 years and over enrolled in school	359	25	334	218	163	55	116 072	112 916
3 and 4 years	-	-	-	8	8	-	3 056	3 045
5 to 14 years	8	8	-	91	82	9	54 686	54 139
15 to 17 years	3	3	-	25	25	-	16 533	16 092
18 and 19 years	6	6	-	-	-	-	9 806	9 570
20 to 24 years	6	6	-	16	9	7	12 436	11 991
25 to 34 years	14	8	6	7	7	-	9 529	8 836
35 years and over	328	-	328	71	32	39	10 026	9 243
EDUCATIONAL ATTAINMENT								
Persons 18 to 24 years	12	6	6	40	24	16	44 604	43 502
High school graduate (includes equivalency)	6	6	-	7	-	7	12 323	12 022
Some college or associate degree	6	-	6	12	9	3	22 085	21 604
Bachelor's degree or higher	-	-	-	14	8	6	3 837	3 712
Persons 25 years and over	8 111	38	8 073	1 638	355	1 283	317 014	296 726
Less than 5th grade	93	-	93	63	2	61	2 111	1 339
5th to 8th grade	460	-	460	160	10	150	19 266	16 679
9th to 12th grade, no diploma	693	12	681	171	24	147	29 335	27 142
High school graduate (includes equivalency)	1 883	6	1 877	388	71	317	97 216	92 805
Some college, no degree	1 578	5	1 573	339	61	278	65 713	62 648
Associate degree, occupational program	204	-	204	59	10	49	15 319	14 032
Associate degree, academic program	277	7	270	25	12	13	11 469	10 688
Bachelor's degree	1 512	8	1 504	220	88	132	50 872	48 263
Master's degree	847	-	847	115	34	81	17 982	16 385
Professional school degree	306	-	306	51	18	33	4 870	4 411
Doctorate degree	258	-	258	47	25	22	2 861	2 334
Females 25 years and over	4 523	26	4 497	945	203	742	169 044	155 926
Less than 5th grade	49	-	49	40	2	38	1 072	568
5th to 8th grade	259	-	259	109	10	99	9 812	8 104
9th to 12th grade, no diploma	422	12	410	99	24	75	15 644	14 102
High school graduate (includes equivalency)	1 258	6	1 252	241	41	200	55 803	52 689
Some college, no degree	961	-	961	188	36	152	34 936	33 033
Associate degree, occupational program	138	-	138	29	10	19	8 707	7 775
Associate degree, academic program	181	-	181	14	7	7	6 944	6 412
Bachelor's degree	684	8	676	134	45	89	25 192	23 573
Master's degree	358	-	358	46	5	41	8 183	7 342
Professional school degree	143	-	143	23	11	12	1 891	1 659
Doctorate degree	70	-	70	22	12	10	860	669
ABILITY TO SPEAK ENGLISH								
Persons 5 years and over	8 144	55	8 089	1 794	486	1 308	437 200	414 786
Speak a language other than English	5 771	43	5 728	1 299	354	945	54 159	39 523
5 to 17 years	11	11	-	94	94	-	3 286	2 410
18 to 64 years	2 474	25	2 449	613	216	397	24 857	15 743
65 to 74 years	1 361	-	1 361	314	31	283	12 903	11 285
75 years and over	1 925	7	1 918	278	13	265	13 113	10 065
Do not speak English "very well"	2 181	12	2 169	692	249	443	13 206	7 475
5 to 17 years	-	-	-	94	94	-	774	432
18 to 64 years	334	5	329	163	118	45	5 781	2 908
65 to 74 years	598	-	598	199	24	175	2 947	2 082
75 years and over	1 249	7	1 242	236	13	223	3 704	2 053
ABILITY TO SPEAK ENGLISH IN HOUSEHOLD								
Persons 5 years and over in households	7 980	55	7 925	1 782	486	1 296	426 407	405 167
In linguistically isolated households	1 569	7	1 562	427	178	249	6 093	3 216
5 to 17 years	-	-	-	60	60	-	272	84
18 to 64 years	158	-	158	105	81	24	2 017	810
65 to 74 years	418	-	418	141	24	117	1 759	1 180
75 years and over	993	7	986	121	13	108	2 045	1 142
DISABILITY STATUS OF CIVILIAN NONINSTITUTIONALIZED PERSONS								
Persons 16 to 64 years	4 063	40	4 023	1 012	349	663	298 987	284 654
With a mobility or self-care limitation	192	-	192	8	-	8	7 608	7 199
With a mobility limitation	29	-	29	2	-	2	2 556	2 485
With a self-care limitation	131	-	131	-	-	-	3 304	3 042
Persons 65 to 74 years	1 782	-	1 782	348	39	309	38 191	35 720
With a mobility or self-care limitation	298	-	298	119	9	110	3 934	3 650
With a mobility limitation	38	-	38	37	-	37	1 663	1 589
With a self-care limitation	188	-	188	51	-	51	1 146	991
Persons 75 years and over	2 151	7	2 144	328	13	315	28 754	24 736
With a mobility or self-care limitation	940	7	933	149	8	141	7 184	5 721
With a mobility limitation	279	-	279	84	-	84	3 391	2 755
With a self-care limitation	334	7	327	36	8	28	1 069	824
VETERAN STATUS								
Male civilian veterans	1 301	-	1 301	38	-	38	58 661	57 280
Percent of civilian males 16 years and over	36.2	-	36.4	5.3	-	7.0	33.8	34.6
Female civilian veterans	2	-	2	12	-	12	3 007	2 926
Percent of civilian females 16 years and over	.1	-	.1	-	-	-	.2	.2

ANCESTRY

Figure 9-14

NEW IN '90

The 1980 Census contained 20 *CP Supplementary Reports,* many of which were slim pamphlets. These provided nationwide comparisons for a single topic, ranging from *Gross Migration for Counties: 1975 to 1980* to *Detailed Occupation of the Experienced Civilian Labor Force by Sex.* For 1990, the need for these Reports was filled in part by the creation of a new Title, described earlier in the chapter, called *Selected Population and Housing Data Paper Listings* (CPH-L).

CH-1 provides detailed tables for complete-count housing data. **CH-2** contains detailed tables for sample data, and **CH-3** represents specialized *Subject Reports* based on sample data.

graphic coverage, subject detail, and cross-tabulation. The primary difference is the CD-ROM Files provide more response categories for many subjects, and in some cases, offer slightly more geographic detail. *CP-3-7,* entitled *Characteristics of American Indians by Tribe and Language,* serves as a typical example. It corresponds to *SSTF 13,* a CD-ROM product of the same name. Both versions tabulate an extensive array of population and housing characteristics for American Indians and Alaska Natives by tribal groupings and by individual tribes. Both present data for the United States, Regions and Divisions, the 50 states, and individual Metropolitan Areas. *CP-3-7* contains 28 tables showing a total of 37 broad subject categories. *SSTF 13* treats the same topics, but does so in 88 tables. The *SSTF* database handles fewer topics on a single table, which accounts for most of the difference in size, but most *SSTF* tables are a bit more detailed than those in the print Report. For example, *SSTF* tables present tribe-specific Poverty data for five separate age groups, while the print version offers breakouts for two age groups only. Similarly, *SSTF 13* tabulates Poverty statistics for five categories of Unrelated Individuals, while *CP-3-7* shows only two.

Census of Population Supplementary Reports (CP-S)

The Bureau has issued two *CP Supplementary Reports* for 1990, though others may appear before the decade ends. The first is entitled *Detailed Occupation and Other Char-*

acteristics from the EEO File for the United States (CP-S-1-1). This brief Report cites employment totals for 511 occupations, cross-tabulated by sex, Race, and Hispanic Origin. It provides similar sex/Race cross-tabulations for industry categories and for educational attainment. Coverage is limited to the national level. As its name suggests, this Report is derived from the *EEO File,* described in Chapter 8.

 Census Tip

The designation of *Population Subject Report* is a slight misnomer, since most Reports in the *CP-3* series also tabulate selected housing characteristics. However, the percentage of housing data is fairly small. For example, *CP-3-6,* (*Characteristics of the Black Population*) contains 63 tables, four of which are housing tables. The only *CP-3* Report which contains no housing data is *CP-3-4, Education in the United States.*

The second Report is called *Detailed Ancestry Groups for States (CP-S-1-2),* and it contains three brief tables showing state-by-state totals for every Ancestry Group tabulated by the Census. It also provides several analytical tables showing percent distributions of the largest Ancestry Groups in the nation.

Census of Housing Series

Detailed housing data are found in the three Titles of the *Census of Housing,* designated by *CH* Report Numbers. *CH-1* provides detailed tables for complete-count housing data. *CH-2* contains detailed tables for sample data, and *CH-3* represents specialized *Subject Reports* based on sample data. *CH-1* and *CH-2* are each issued in 57 Volumes: 53 Volumes covering the individual states and state-equivalents; a United States Summary Volume; plus three Volumes covering Metropolitan Areas, Urbanized Areas, and American Indian and Alaska Native Areas. *CH-3* is issued in one Volume.

Census Tip

Use *CH-1* to locate complete-count data and *CH-2* for sample data. Complete-count Items shown in *CH-2* are provided for comparative purposes only, and represent estimates, not actual counts.

Figure 9-2, shown earlier, compares geographic coverage among the major Titles in the *CH* Series. Note that data for Congressional Districts, Census Tracts, Block Groups and Blocks are not tabulated for any of these Reports.

Neither *CH-1* or *CH-2* have a CD-ROM equivalent. Both are generated from *Summary Tape Files* which exist in magnetic tape format only.

Neither *CH-1* or *CH-2* have a CD-ROM equivalent. Both are generated from *Summary Tape Files* which exist in magnetic tape format only. However, *some* of the tables published in *CH-1* and *CH-2* can be found (in full or partial form) in various CD-ROM products. Tables from *CH-1* correspond in part to those from *STF 1A* and *STF 1C*. Tables from *CH-2* correspond in part to selected tables from *STF 3A* and *STF 3C*. More specific comparisons between the print and CD-ROM products will be made at the end of this chapter.

General Housing Characteristics (CH-1)

CH-1 tabulates detailed housing characteristics based on questions asked of the entire population (all housing Items from the Short Form, plus those from the complete-count portion of the Long Form). Data are generated from *Summary Tape File 2*, which is available on magnetic tape only, and has no CD-ROM equivalent. Each *CH-1* Report contains 76 tables, including two Imputation Tables. It covers the same geographic Summary Levels found in *CP-1*, and it uti-

CH-1 provides more subject detail than can be found in the housing tables from CPH-1, but CPH-1 offers greater geographic coverage for smaller Summary Levels

lizes the same ten table formats for cross-tabulations by Racial group and Hispanic Origin.

CH-1 tabulates data for a reasonably small number of subject variables, including the following topics: Units in structure; Vacancy Status (including breakouts for Boarded-Up Units); Vacancy rate; duration of Vacancy; age of Householder; persons in Unit; number of Rooms; persons per Room; Tenure; Value; Contract Rent; and Units which include meals with rent. Separate tables provide housing details for Units with Householders age 65 or older.

CH-1 provides more subject detail than can be found in the housing tables from *CPH-1*, but *CPH-1* offers greater geographic coverage for smaller Summary Levels (Places with fewer than 1,000 inhabitants, plus County Subdivisions in all states).

CH-1 is virtually identical in overall content to its 1980 counterpart, which was also called *General Housing Characteristics*. However, the 1990 version provides more subject detail, with nearly 50% more tables than its predecessor.

Detailed Housing Characteristics (CH-2)

Reports in this Census Title focus on Items taken from the Long Form Questionnaire. Data are generated from *Summary Tape File 4*, which is available on magnetic tape only, and has no CD-ROM equivalent. *CH-2* contains 105 tables, including five Imputation Tables. It covers the same geographic Summary Levels found in *CP-2*, and it utilizes the same four table formats for cross-tabulations by Racial group and Hispanic Origin.

The 1980 equivalent of *CH-2*, which was also called *Detailed Housing Characteristics*, is similar in most respects. It contains almost the same number of tables and covers the same Summary Levels, but the response categories are less detailed. As a result, the 1990 Reports are nearly twice the size of their 1980 counterparts.

Housing Subject Reports (CH-3)

The Bureau has released one *Housing Subject Report* for 1990, and has no plans to issue others at this time. The Report is called *Metropolitan Housing Characteristics* (*CH-3-1*). It provides extremely detailed cross-tabulations for characteristics of Housing Units in Metropolitan Areas. *CH-3-1* contains 281 tables which offer a level of subject detail not found in any other *Census of Housing* Report. The table titles are themselves quite complicated, such as "Selected Housing Characteristics of Renter-Occupied Housing Units, for Married-Couple Families with Related Children and with a White Not of Hispanic Origin Householder, by Age of Householder."

Over 30 major housing Items are each cross-tabulated with the following other characteristics: Units in structure; year built; year Householder moved in; size of Household; Household Income; Value; and Selected Monthly Owner Costs. All of these relationships are then cross-tabulated by Race/Hispanic Origin of Householder, and all but the latter two are further cross-tabulated by Tenure. This results in a four-way tabulation of Subject A by Subject B by Race/Hispanic Origin by Tenure.

 ## Census Tip

The Table Finding Guide for *CH-3-1* provides an excellent grid showing all of the cross-tabulations available in the Report, and on which tables they can be found.

Additional tables cross-tabulate most of these 34 housing characteristics by Household Composition/Family Type, then further by Race/Hispanic Origin of Householder, age of Householder, and Tenure, creating a set of five-way cross-tabulations. For example, Table 242 of *CH-3-1* answers the question, "How many Hispanic, female Householders age 25-34, living alone, who own their own home, have Household Income of $50,000 or more?"

Because of this extensive subject detail and cross-tabulation, *CH-3-1* presents statistics for the entire United States only. The Report also provides a series of additional tables showing the same relationships for the portion of United States land area lying inside Metropolitan Areas, and within this subset, for that portion which lies inside Central Cities. No tabulations are given at the state level, or for smaller geographies, such as counties or cities.

The corresponding CD-ROM product for *CP-3-1* provides much greater geographic detail. It appears as *SSTF 7* and is issued as a set of eight discs. *SSTF 7* contains the same subject coverage and cross-tabulations as the print Report, but does so for each state and for every Metropolitan Area in the United States.

NEW IN '90

For 1980, *Metropolitan Housing Characteristics* did not appear as a *Housing Subject Report*, but as a separate Title in the *Housing Census Series* (HC-2). The Bureau issued the 1980 *Metropolitan Housing Characteristics* Title as several hundred individual Reports, with one for each of the following entities: the United States; the 50 states; and every Metropolitan Area. The United States Summary Volume for 1980 is similar in format, content, and subject detail to the CP-3-1 Report for 1990. The individual 1980 Reports for states and Metropolitan Areas have been replaced by the CD-ROM File for *SSTF 7*.

For 1980, the Census Bureau issued five *Housing Subject Reports*. None of these will be released as print Reports for 1990 unless additional money becomes available later in the decade. Two have been issued as *SSTF* databases only, and three have been completely canceled.

Residential Finance (CH-4)

The final Title in the 1990 Census of Housing is a single Volume entitled *Residential Finance*. It is similar to a *Housing Subject Report* in that it provides detailed cross-tabulations for one topic, in this case for mortgage-related information. However, it differs from the Subject Reports because its figures are not derived from the decennial Census. By law, the Bureau is directed to conduct a separate sample survey, called the Residential Finance Survey, in conjunction with every decennial Census. Its purpose is to collect additional data on the financing of privately-owned residential property. The survey for 1990 took place in stages throughout 1991 and utilized a nationwide sample of 70,000 addresses.

CH-4 contains 137 data tables, most of which cross-tabulate the characteristics of mortgages and home-equity lines of credit with the demographic characteristics of the homeowners (e.g., age, Income, previous homeownership) and with the housing characteristics of the financed Units (Value, year built). Much of the subject detail is unique to this Report, including breakdowns by type of mortgage (Veterans Administration loan, insured conventional loan, Adjustable Rate Mortgage, etc.). It also provides analyses of income property, comparing rental receipts to ownership costs and Housing Unit Value.

A major difference between *CH-4* and other housing Reports from the 1990 Census is that *CH-4* measures data for the entire property, while other Reports focus on individual Housing Units. A 50-Unit apartment building would be counted as 50 Housing Units by regular Census Reports, but as a single building in *Residential Finance*.

The 1980 Report for Residential Finance was similar in most respects. However, the scope of the 1990 Report was expanded to include Condominium Units and Mobile Homes, and to incorporate statistics on home-equity lines of credit.

The Bureau generates all 1990 Census maps from its extensive TIGER database system.

A major difference between *CH-4* and other housing Reports from the 1990 Census is that *CH-4* measures data for the entire property, while other Reports focus on individual Housing Units.

NEW IN '90

The 1980 Census included an additional survey Report entitled *Components of Inventory Change*. Like *Residential Finance*, it was conducted as a separate survey in conjunction with the decennial Census, and it was mandated by law. The survey measured changes in the quantity of housing stock over time due to new construction, conversions, other additions, and demolitions. This Report will not be published for 1990.

Maps and Microfiche

Print Reports are not the only nonelectronic products issued by the Census Bureau. The following sections describe the basic map and microfiche products available for 1990.

Census Maps

The Bureau generates all 1990 Census maps from its extensive TIGER database system, described in Chapter 6. These maps are designed specifically for use with decennial data products (both print Reports and electronic Files). They are called outline maps because they do not summarize Census data, but simply identify the boundaries referred to in the Bureau's many statistical products.

The Bureau prints many of its map series using electrostatic plotters located in the Regional Offices. Customers purchase the plotted maps directly from the Census Bureau, which produces them on a per-order basis. Other Census maps are published by the Government Printing Office, either as sheet maps or as appendices to paper Census Reports. These are ordered through the GPO as one would order most standard Census products.

Data users can also generate their own crude boundary maps using the Bureau's LandView software (described in Chapter 8), or they can create more sophisticated maps using commercially produced GIS software.

Plotted Map Sheets

The Bureau accepts orders for a diversity of electrostatic map products, but the most common series are listed below.

- ▸ American Indian/Alaska Native Area Maps
- ▸ Urbanized Area Boundary Maps
- ▸ Voting District Outline Maps
- ▸ County Subdivision Outline Maps
- ▸ County Block Maps

Most maps consist of one or more 36" by 42" flat sheets. Each series consists of outline maps showing the boundaries of various geographic entities, the names or identifying numbers of each entity, and a variety of visible features, such as rail lines, rivers, and parks. The smaller the Summary Level, the larger the map scale and the more detailed the features. For example, Block maps are extremely detailed. In addition to identifying Block outlines and Block Numbers, they show all street names, boundaries of all Governmental Units, and numerous physical features.

All maps cost $5.00 per sheet, plus a $25

processing fee per order. A complete set of Block Maps for a single county typically costs several hundred dollars, depending on the size of the county.

Printed Maps and Map Sets

Nearly all paper Census Reports also include a set of 8½" by 11" outline maps, issued as Appendix G of the Report. Because of their smaller size, these maps are typically divided into sections. While a County Outline Map for an individual state may fit on a single page, a County Subdivision Map for that state will require many pages to display in its entirety. Maps found in Appendix G generally describe every geographic entity covered in the particular Report. The most common Summary Levels are counties, County Subdivisions, Metropolitan Areas, Urbanized Areas, and American Indian/Alaska Native Areas.

The United States Summary Volume for *CPH-2* also includes several thematic maps printed in color. These include a historical map showing the acquisition of territory by the United States (indicating admission dates for the 50 states), and a 200-year history of the country's mean population center.

Because Tract and BNA maps require considerable detail, users find them frustrating to use when divided into 8½" by 11" sections. For this reason, the accompanying maps for *CPH-3* are not reproduced as an appendix to each Report, but appear as separate sets of folded map sheets, each sheet being 36" by 48". The maps are sold in county sets, with five or more map sheets per county, depending on its size. Tract or BNA maps are available for every county in the United States.

In the early stages of the decennial cycle, before any printed maps had been published, the Bureau sold electrostatically plotted Tract maps on demand. Now that Tract and BNA maps are available as printed items from the GPO, the Bureau no longer creates them on demand.

NEW IN '90

Block Maps for 1980 were issued in paper and microfiche formats, both of which were standard GPO publications. The microfiche version proved extremely impractical, so it was discontinued for 1990. Customers must now order 1990 sheet maps for Census Blocks directly from the Bureau.

Microfiche Products

In prior Censuses, microfiche products played a more important role than in 1990. At one point in the 1990 product planning process, Bureau officials decided to cancel nearly all microfiche publications because CD-ROM technology made microforms obsolete. This decision was later rescinded, and now customers can order a microfiche version of virtually any paper Report. None of these products can be purchased through the Government Printing Office, however. They must be special-ordered through the Census Bureau. The Bureau's annual *Census Catalog and Guide* provides price and ordering information. A microfiche symbol can be found next to every Report in the *Catalog* which is also available in microformat.

NEW IN '90

One of the best-kept secrets of the 1980 Census was the availability of extensive microfiche Reports derived from the *Summary Tape Files*. The Bureau issued four 1980 microfiche products containing extracts taken directly from the *Summary Tape Files: STF 1A, STF 1C, STF 3A,* and *STF 3C.* The *STF 1* products provided two-page data summaries for every relevant geographic entity, while the *STF 3* products offered six-page profiles. The total size of these products was gargantuan: a complete national set of fiche for *STF 3A* alone comprised more than 900,000 pages. *STF 1A* and *STF 3A* comprised the only easily accessible 1980 Census publications containing population and housing characteristics displayed down to the Block Group level. Because of the popularity of 1990 CD-ROM Files and the sheer size of the microfiche Reports, they were canceled for 1990.

Making Sense of Print Reports

With so many Reports to select from, the novice Census user may find it difficult to recognize distinctions among them. Understanding the basic structure of the Bureau's publishing system is one way become comfortable with this bewildering array of products. Using the *Subject Index to the 1990 Census of Population and Housing,* is another. Chapter 10 offers a variety of tips for devising a search strategy. The following sections offer two additional ways to make sense of the publishing maze. For researchers, librarians, and other data users familiar with the publications of the 1980, one method is to compare 1990 Reports to their counterparts from the previous decade. A second method, for those who feel comfortable with the Bureau's basic CD-ROM products, is to compare the Reports to their closest electronic counterparts and then identify elements which are unique to each.

Changes in Publications from 1980 to 1990

Much of the publication structure established for the 1980 remains intact for 1990, but differences in Report names, publication numbers, and formats are inevitable. Making direct comparisons can be difficult in some cases, because certain 1990 publications represent bits and pieces taken from several 1980 Titles. Figure 9-15 compares major 1990 Titles to their closest 1980 counterparts.

Many of the Report Titles for 1990 are virtually identical in content to their 1980 counterparts. For example, *CH-1* and *CH-2* are basically the same as the two major Titles of the 1980 *Housing* (called *Chapter A* and *Chapter B*, respectively). *CPH-3* and *CPH-4* are also unchanged from their 1980 equivalents.

CPH-1 and *CPH-5* are new Titles for 1990, but they provide much of the same data seen previously in a single publication called *Summary Characteristics of Governmental Units (PHC-3).* This popular and convenient 1980 title cited 80 summary characteristics from both the complete and sample counts. It covered the same geographic en-

Comparison of 1990 and 1980 print Reports			
1990 Title		**1980 Title**	
Number	Name	Number	Name
CPH-1	Summary Population and Housing Characteristics	PHC-3	Summary Characteristics for Governmental Units
CPH-2	Population and Housing Unit Counts	PC-1-A	Number of Inhabitants
CPH-3	Population and Housing Characteristics for Census Tracts	PHC-2	Census Tracts
CPH-4	Population and Housing Characteristics for Congressional Districts	PHC-4	Congressional Districts of the 98th Congress
CPH-5	Summary Social, Economic, and Housing Characteristics	PHC-3	Summary Characteristics for Governmental Units
CPH-6	Social, Economic, and Housing Characteristics [Outlying Areas of the Pacific]	—	included in main Titles (PC-1 and HC-1)
CPH-S	CPH Supplementary Reports	PHC-S	PHC Suppl. Reports
CP-1	General Population Characteristics	PC-1-B	General Population Characteristics
CP-2	Social and Economic Characteristics	PC-1-C	General Social and Economic Characteristics
CP-3	Population Subject Reports	PC-2	Pop. Subject Reports
CP-S	Population Supplementary Reports	PC-S	Pop. Suppl. Reports
CH-1	General Housing Characteristics	HC-1-A	General Housing Characteristics
CH-2	Detailed Housing Characteristics	HC-1-B	Detailed Housing Characteristics
CH-3	Housing Subject Reports	HC-3	Housing Subject Reports
CH-4	Residential Finance	HC-5	Residential Finance

Figure 9-15

tities as *CPH-1* and *CPH-5*, including Places with fewer than 1,000 inhabitants and all County Subdivisions regardless of size. Because of its popularity and overall usefulness, the Bureau decided to expand the subject content and release it as two separate Titles

for 1990.

Separate publications focusing on Metropolitan Areas, Urbanized Areas, and American Indian/Alaska Native Areas are also new for 1990 (the so-called 1A, 1B, and 1C Reports which appear in the *CP* and *CH* Series). In the past, this data appeared as part of the individual state Reports in the *Population* and the *Housing* . Because the Bureau tabulates data on a flow basis state-by-state, and because many MAs and UAs cross state boundaries, their inclusion in individual state Reports tended to slow down the publication process. To resolve this problem, the Bureau decided to include only the portions of these Areas within a state's boundaries, and publish separate Reports containing MA and UA totals.

Another new Title for 1990 is *CPH-2*, designed to provide historical data in a single publication. *CPH-2* replaces *Chapter A* of *Characteristics of the Population*, which was called *Number of Inhabitants*. *CPH-2* also includes historical housing data, a new feature for 1990.

Just as several 1990 publications are new, certain 1980 products have been discontinued. The most noticeable cancellation is *Chapter D* of *Characteristics of the Population*. This Chapter, called *Detailed Population Characteristics*, provided complex four- and five-way cross-tabulations on a variety of subjects, but only for states and large Metropolitan Areas. Although *Chapter D* is now gone, the 1990 *CP-2* Title (which basically replaces the 1980 *Chapter C*) provides numerous cross-tabulations not found in its 1980 counterpart.

The Bureau has produced a 1990 edition of *Metropolitan Housing Characteristics*, but only at the national level. For 1980, 374 additional Volumes covered individual states and MAs. These print Reports were canceled for 1990, but they exist in CD-ROM format as *SSTF 7*.

For 1980, the Bureau issued two Titles called "Advance Reports." These were designed to provide quick release of key summary characteristics for the most popular Summary Levels prior to publication of the more detailed main Reports. *PHC-V* contained advance summaries for complete-count data, while *PHC-S* dealt with sample data. Both Titles became obsolete with the creation of two improved products for 1990, known as *CPH-1* and *CPH-5*. Although these 1990 Titles were actually designed to replace a different 1980 product (namely, *PHC-3*), their rapid dissemination served the same purpose as the old "Advance Reports."

Many of the canceled print Titles have merely been replaced by more detailed and convenient CD-ROM products. The 1980 microfiche Title called *Block Statistics* (*PHC-1*), was canceled for 1990. However, the 1990 *STF 1B Extract* Files are identical to the old microfiche product in nearly every respect. Similarly, the Bureau decided to issue fewer printed *Subject Reports* for 1990, but the impressive list of *SSTF* products on CD-ROM addresses this deficiency more than adequately. Finally, the little-known, but extremely useful 1980 microfiche versions of *STF 1* and *STF 3* have also been superseded in 1990 by their CD-ROM counterparts.

Subtler publication differences between 1980 and 1990 can also be found. As described in Chapter 7, many of the Questionnaire Items for 1990 contained more detailed response categories, and many of the 1990 Reports reflect this greater detail. The basic organization of Titles within each of the three Series is more straightforward and logical than in the past and many small touches make Reports easier to use. For example, the Bureau has significantly improved the all-important Table Finding Guides for 1990.

Despite the changes outlined above, the fundamental structures of the two decennial Censuses are remarkably similar. Users seeking to conduct comparative analyses across the decades should be comfortable moving from one to the other.

Comparing Print Reports and CD-ROM Products

It takes several dozen print Reports to convey the same information found on a single Compact Disc. Furthermore, 1990 CD-

Many of the Questionnaire Items for 1990 contained more detailed response categories, and many of the 1990 Reports reflect this greater detail.

Q&A

If the CD-ROM products offer so many advantages, why did the Bureau decide to issue print Reports for 1990?

The primary answer relates to the lengthy lead times necessary in the decennial planning process. Deliberations regarding product formats began in the mid-80s, when CD-ROM technology was in its infancy. Test discs issued by the Bureau in 1986 and 1988 were crude and cumbersome to use. Bureau employees created the easy-to-use GO software only after the 1990 publication process was well under way, and it was not until 1992 that the Bureau decided to include GO on most CD-ROM products. Hardware constraints presented another obstacle to CD-ROM implementation. As late as 1988, few CD-ROM players were available in GPO Depository Libraries, State Data Center Affiliate offices, or government agencies. Due

to these factors, the Bureau received clear and overwhelming feedback during the Local Public Meetings phase of the planning process: data users wanted to see as many print Reports as possible.

Will we see paper Reports for the 2000 ? It is too soon to tell at this juncture. It seems highly probable that print Reports will continue to exist, though the Bureau will most likely produce fewer Titles. In various circumstances, users will still find a particular Report more convenient than its CD-ROM counterpart. And for complex tables, especially those showing multiple cross-tabulations, a printed page can convey information much more concisely than the two-dimensional grids found in CD-ROM products.

ROM products are easy to use, convenient, powerful, and affordable. For these reasons, the Bureau considers its CD-ROM products to be the primary dissemination medium for 1990 data. Not surprisingly, planners, demographers, librarians, and other regular users of data have indicated to the Bureau that CD-ROM is the preferred means of accessing information. Nevertheless, paper Reports do offer certain advantages, and in some instances, provide unique data not found in their CD-ROM equivalents.

Advantages of Table Design in Print Reports

One potential advantage offered by print Reports is greater convenience for users in certain situations. In fact, most 1990 print products were designed with this purpose in mind. Tables in the print Reports focus on the most frequently requested data relationships. A researcher who requires a very specific type of information on a recurring basis may find it simpler to keep a single paper Volume at his or her desk. For example, *CPH-3* is ideally suited to provide summary characteristics at the Tract level, and it combines data tables found in two electronic sources: *STF 1A* and *STF 3A*.

Table layout offers another advantage for many users. The GO software found on the CD-ROM versions of *STF* products presents data for one geographic entity at a time. In contrast, tables from the print Reports generally provide comparable data for many entities on a single page. GO does offer the capability of displaying some geographic comparisons, but on a limited basis only. Print Reports can also be useful for showing relationships among different Summary Levels of Geography, such as counties and Minor Civil Divisions. GO tables are arranged by individual Summary Level, and users must employ EXTRACT to create files which incorporate multiple Summary Levels on a single Table.

Tables in the print Reports focus on the most frequently requested data relationships.

Even experienced data users are surprised to learn that certain print Reports contain statistics not found in any of the CD-ROM publications.

Census Tip

print Reports can be especially useful for helping the user to decipher the hierarchical and jurisdictional relationships among various Summary Levels in a specific state.

The same advantage holds true for subject-oriented relationships. Most GO tables are limited to a single topic, but print Reports are much more flexible. The use of multiple columns allows printed tables to present comparable topics on a single page. When table formats utilize columns for geographic entities rather than for subject variables, print Reports achieve the same effect by employing indentations and bold-face print in the table stubs, displaying several sub-tables on a single page, as shown in Figures 9-5, 9-12, and 9-14.

Another advantage relating to table layout is that CD-ROM tables are limited to two-dimensional presentations. More complex cross tabulations must be accomplished by limiting a table's Universe, or by making the user choose subsections of a table in a two-step selection process. Print Reports suffer from no such limitations; three- and four-way cross tabulations are not uncommon. This effect is usually achieved by dividing the boxhead at the top of a table into spanners and column heads. Examples of this technique are especially prevalent in *CP-3*, *CH-3*, and *CH-4*.

Unique Data Found in Print Reports

Convenience and the ease of displaying comparable data are not the only advantages afforded by print Reports. Even experienced data users are surprised to learn that certain print Reports contain statistics not found in any of the CD-ROM publications. The main reason is shown Figure 9-16: several print publications are generated from the *STF 2* and *STF 4* databases, which are available on magnetic tape only and have no CD-ROM equivalents.

Unique data derived from *STF 2* and *STF 4* can be described in three categories: historical comparisons; cross-tabulations by detailed Racial and Hispanic breakdowns, and greater detail in tabulated response categories. Historical comparisons for total population and housing counts can be found in *CPH-2*, which is generated from the *STF 2* tapes. In most cases, this retrospective data spans many decades; a few tables actually provide total counts all the way back to 1790.

 Census Tip

CPH-2 **is the only print or CD-ROM product for the 1990 which provides historical data for many decades, but does so only for the most basic population and housing data.**

The time-series information found in *CPH-2* is fairly limited. Researchers wishing to locate sources comparing detailed population and housing data across the decades can turn to nondecennial publications, such as the *Statistical Abstract of the United States* or *Historical Statistics of the United States*, or they can examine the decennial Census decade by decade.

The most obvious difference in subject detail between the *STF* CD-ROM products and the *CP* or *CH* Series is the extensive cross-tabulations by Race and Hispanic Origin. To be sure, *STF 1* and *STF 3* provide separate tables for subgroups of the population, but these are typically limited to the five major Racial groups and to Hispanic Origin. The print Reports also provide separate tables for these specific Universes, but they offer additional detail as well. *CP-1, CP-2, CH-1,* and *CH-2* all cross-tabulate data for the three American Indian/Eskimo/Aleut subcategories, for ten additional Asian subcategories, and for three Pacific Islander subcategories.

Source Files for 1990 Census Reports	
Print Series	**Source Tapes**
CPH-1	STF 1A, STF 1C[1]
CPH-2	STF 1B, STF 1C[1]
CPH-3[2]	STF 2A, STF 4A
CPH-4[2]	STF 1D, STF 3D
CPH-5	STF 3A, STF 3C[1]
CPH-6	STF 1 (Pacific)[3], STF 3 (Pacific)[3]
CP-1	STF 2B, STF 2C[1]
CP-2	STF 4B, STF 4C[1]
CP-3	SSTFs
CH-1	STF 2B, STF 2C[1]
CH-2	STF 4B, STF 4C[1]
CH-3	SSTFs

[1] STF "C" subfiles used to generate the United States Summary volumes, and where they exist, the summary volumes for Metropolitan Areas, Urbanized Areas, and American Indian/ Alaska Native Areas.

[2] These print Reports combine sample data and complete count data in a single publication.

[3] Special STF subfile covering Pacific Outlying Areas. The Long Form questions were asked of 100% of the population.

Figure 9-16

CP-1 and *CH-1* report many tables for four subcategories of the Hispanic population (Mexican, Puerto Rican, Cuban, and Other); *CP-2* and *CH-2* do the same, plus certain tables provide additional breakdowns for 15 additional Hispanic subcategories, as seen in Figure 9-17, taken from Table 60 of the *CH-2* Report for Arizona. (Note: Table 60 requires a two-page display to show all Hispanic categories; Figure 9-17 reproduces the first half of this display only.) Such detail is provided for most geographic Summary Levels, but only for those entities which meet the Bureau's standard population thresholds

The most obvious difference in subject detail between the *STF* CD-ROM products and the *CP* or *CH* printed Series is the extensive cross-tabulations by Race and Hispanic Origin.

Table 60. Occupancy, Fuel, and Structural Characteristics of Housing Units With a Householder of Hispanic Origin by Type: 1990

[Householders of Hispanic origin may be of any race. Threshold is 50 persons. Data based on sample and subject to sampling variability, see text. For definitions of terms and meanings of symbols, see text]

State	Mexican	Puerto Rican	Cuban	Other Hispanic	Dominican (Dominican Republic)	Central American	Costa Rican	Guatemalan	Honduran	Nicaraguan
Occupied housing units	**162 590**	**2 755**	**674**	**15 455**	**77**	**1 719**	**109**	**482**	**153**	**181**
TENURE										
Owner-occupied housing units	88 800	1 252	383	8 064	46	570	63	120	37	53
Renter-occupied housing units	73 790	1 503	291	7 371	31	1 149	46	362	116	128
YEAR STRUCTURE BUILT										
Owner-occupied housing units	88 800	1 252	383	8 064	46	570	63	120	37	53
1989 to March 1990	1 336	70	4	269	9	51	–	35	–	–
1985 to 1988	8 205	321	101	1 034	8	101	14	4	12	21
1980 to 1984	9 728	228	59	1 158	–	70	–	8	21	–
1970 to 1979	25 581	349	111	2 218	29	106	11	15	–	19
1960 to 1969	14 799	120	42	1 322	–	103	20	5	–	8
1950 to 1959	16 251	122	39	1 242	–	66	12	16	4	5
1940 to 1949	6 932	25	27	463	–	40	6	23	–	–
1939 or earlier	5 968	17	–	378	–	33	–	14	–	–
Renter-occupied housing units	73 790	1 503	291	7 371	31	1 149	46	362	116	128
1989 to March 1990	1 087	27	14	123	–	22	–	15	–	–
1985 to 1988	10 385	272	108	1 485	–	154	6	36	29	–
1980 to 1984	12 642	311	51	1 448	–	202	35	43	47	12
1970 to 1979	17 699	461	53	1 751	17	304	–	110	32	54
1960 to 1969	11 814	243	16	1 102	12	187	–	50	8	33
1950 to 1959	9 840	123	13	755	–	120	–	53	–	6
1940 to 1949	5 332	61	20	396	2	142	–	45	–	20
1939 or earlier	4 991	5	16	311	–	18	5	10	–	3
BEDROOMS										
Owner-occupied housing units	88 800	1 252	383	8 064	46	570	63	120	37	53
None	744	–	–	53	–	–	–	–	–	–
1	7 129	83	46	635	7	68	8	7	–	9
2	21 945	199	67	1 928	6	129	9	40	–	7
3	44 946	536	136	3 849	24	233	26	37	21	30
4	12 651	391	105	1 318	9	80	8	–	16	7
5 or more	1 385	43	29	301	–	60	12	36	–	–
Renter-occupied housing units	73 790	1 503	291	7 371	31	1 149	46	362	116	128
None	6 308	152	23	835	12	197	–	57	9	40
1	23 793	443	120	2 657	12	488	21	182	53	21
2	28 829	554	102	2 587	17	358	20	87	38	47
3	12 934	271	36	1 136	–	98	5	36	16	20
4	1 753	83	8	140	2	6	–	–	–	–
5 or more	173	–	2	16	–	2	–	–	–	–
SOURCE OF WATER										
Public system or private company	156 144	2 729	651	15 081	77	1 699	109	475	153	181
Individual drilled well	5 484	26	23	322	–	20	–	7	–	–
Individual dug well	479	–	–	22	–	–	–	–	–	–
Some other source	483	–	–	30	–	–	–	–	–	–
SEWAGE DISPOSAL										
Public sewer	141 222	2 582	592	13 712	69	1 574	109	417	149	158
Septic tank or cesspool	20 273	173	66	1 651	8	134	–	65	4	15
Other means	1 095	–	16	92	–	11	–	–	–	8
KITCHEN FACILITIES										
Complete kitchen facilities	161 384	2 722	666	15 337	77	1 707	109	478	153	173
Lacking complete kitchen facilities	1 206	33	8	118	–	12	–	4	–	8
HOUSE HEATING FUEL										
Utility gas	87 780	977	257	6 351	31	724	34	210	38	71
Bottled, tank, or LP gas	7 390	75	24	622	–	37	–	30	–	–
Electricity	62 457	1 692	393	7 938	46	932	75	229	115	102
Fuel oil, kerosene, etc.	278	–	–	18	–	–	–	–	–	–
Coal or coke	16	–	–	17	–	–	–	–	–	–
Wood	2 720	3	–	435	–	5	–	5	–	–
Solar energy	96	–	–	8	–	–	–	–	–	–
Other fuel	106	–	–	5	–	5	–	–	–	–
No fuel used	1 747	8	–	61	–	16	–	8	–	8
VEHICLES AVAILABLE										
None	19 446	272	71	1 694	20	240	–	62	44	49
1	60 924	1 119	194	5 962	26	672	41	209	52	43
2	56 942	1 076	305	5 396	21	602	28	174	50	62
3	18 818	222	90	1 725	10	149	16	37	7	20
4	4 856	43	14	530	–	44	12	–	–	7
5 or more	1 604	23	–	148	–	12	12	–	–	–
YEAR HOUSEHOLDER MOVED INTO UNIT										
Owner-occupied housing units	88 800	1 252	383	8 064	46	570	63	120	37	53
1989 to March 1990	11 282	312	44	1 272	17	146	–	50	8	5
1985 to 1988	23 438	450	178	2 392	6	188	28	17	25	30
1980 to 1984	13 973	188	73	1 355	–	79	–	11	–	12
1970 to 1979	22 091	254	70	1 854	23	144	35	32	4	6
1960 to 1969	9 528	21	18	635	–	–	–	–	–	–
1959 or earlier	8 488	27	–	576	–	13	–	10	–	–
Renter-occupied housing units	73 790	1 503	291	7 371	31	1 149	46	362	116	128
1989 to March 1990	41 977	912	199	4 734	19	800	31	256	77	106
1985 to 1988	22 356	489	67	2 076	12	283	15	82	14	22
1980 to 1984	5 627	68	18	358	–	59	–	24	25	–
1970 to 1979	2 637	34	7	170	–	7	–	–	–	–
1960 to 1969	600	–	–	16	–	–	–	–	–	–
1959 or earlier	593	–	–	17	–	–	–	–	–	–
PLUMBING FACILITIES BY PERSONS PER ROOM										
Owner-occupied housing units	88 800	1 252	383	8 064	46	570	63	120	37	53
Lacking complete plumbing facilities	715	10	8	78	–	–	–	–	–	–
1.01 or more	305	–	8	30	–	–	–	–	–	–
Renter-occupied housing units	73 790	1 503	291	7 371	31	1 149	44	362	116	128
Lacking complete plumbing facilities	1 046	24	–	95	–	26	–	18	–	8
1.01 or more	656	11	–	32	–	12	–	4	–	8

DETAILED HOUSING CHARACTERISTICS

ARIZONA 77

Figure 9-17

for the Universe in question. To read more about population thresholds in Reports, consult Chapter 10.

The purpose of this detail is not simply to report total population or housing counts, but to cross-tabulate population and housing characteristics by Race and Hispanic Origin. For example, Table H9 of *STF 1A* displays housing Tenure by five categories of Race, plus Race by Hispanic Origin. *CH-1* does the same, but also offers breakdowns for 20 additional Racial subcategories and four additional Hispanic subcategories. *CH-2* does all of the above, then cross-tabulates Tenure by 15 additional Hispanic subcategories. What does this mean for users? *STF 1A* reports Tenure for Asians and Hispanics, but not for Koreans and Mexicans. Yet researchers can find the latter two breakouts easily in *CH-1* or *CH-2*; refer to Figure 9-17 for a typical display of Hispanic Origin detail, including Guatemalans, Hondurans, and other less common categories.

The difference in detail for response categories is less clear, and depends on the subject. Sometimes the print Reports provide more detail; other times the reverse is true. For example, *CP-2* tabulates data for 48 occupational categories, while *STF 3* does so for 13 broader groupings. Conversely, *STF 3* reports 13 categories for travel time to work (the duration of the commute), while *CP-2* reports only six categories. Distinctions in the level of subject coverage must be examined on a case-by-case basis. Figure 9-18 uses the example of Language Spoken at Home to illustrate the subject detail found in *CP-2* versus *STF 3A*. The CD-ROM product provides three table numbers relating to language: P28, P29, and P31. An unnumbered table entitled "Profile of Social Characteristics" also provides brief summary data on this topic. *CP-2* provides two basic tables dealing with language, each of which is repeated for various geographies and population Universes.

Some aspects of coverage are identical in *CP-2* and *STF 3A*. As summarized in example 7 of Figure 9-18, both products pro-

Comparison of Subject Detail for Language Spoken at Home: *CP-2* and *STF 3A*

No.	Characteristic	STF 3 Table	CP-2 Table	Which Better?	Explanation
1	Total persons who speak English only	P31	18	same	data identical
2	Total persons who speak lang. other than English	P31*	20	CP-2	no need to calculate
3	Total persons who do not speak English very well	P28*	20	CP-2	no need to calculate
4	Percent who speak other language	P31*	1	CP-2	no need to calculate
5	Percent who do not speak English very well	P28*	1	CP-2	no need to calculate
6	Total # of English-speaking Households	P29	–	STF 3	CP-2 does not provide
7	Detailed language spoken at home	P31	18	same	tables are identical
8	Persons who speak English only, by age	P28	20*	either	must calculate CP-2, but gives 4 age grps.
9	Persons who speak language other than English, by age	P28*	20	CP-2	CP gives 4 age grps; no need to calculate
10	persons who do not speak English very well, by age	P28*	20	CP-2	CP gives 4 age grps; no need to calculate
11	Language spoken, by ability to speak English	P28*	18	CP-2	CP gives 4 language groups; 4 ability groups
12	Language spoken, by ability to speak English, by age	P28	–	STF 3	CP-2 does not provide
13	Households speaking language other than English, by language	P29*	–	STF 3	CP-2 does not provide
14	Total persons linguistically isolated	P30*	20	CP-2	no need to calculate
15	Persons in ling. isolated Households, by age	P30*	20	CP-2	CP gives 4 age grps; no need to calculate
16	Persons in ling. isolated Households, by age, by language	P30	–	STF 3	CP-2 does not provide
17	# of linguistically isolated Households	P29	–	STF 3	CP-2 does not provide
18	Linguistically isolated Households, by language group	P29	–	STF 3	CP-2 does not provide

Figure 9-18

Q&A

How can I determine which format is better for my needs: print Reports or CD-ROM?

Unfortunately, the answer depends on your circumstances. In one situation CD-ROM may be best, while in another, paper products will be preferred. The most basic factor in such format decisions is whether the needed data can be found. If one format fails to cover a particular Summary Level, or doesn't offer the degree of detail required, then the other format must be explored. Another factor to consider is data presentation. When extensive profiles of a single entity are needed, the CD-ROM approach may be best. When numerous entities are being compared, print Reports may be easier to consult, especially for users who are unfamiliar with EXTRACT or related software products.

In many situations, the choice boils down to a matter of personal preference, since either format will address the particular data request quite nicely. Some people feel more comfortable with the CD-ROM products, while others prefer traditional sources.

Personal preferences aside, one format will not always replace the other, at least for the 1990. In one situation, you may need a CD-ROM database, but the very next day you may find that only a print Report can satisfy a particular request. For most researchers, building a complete collection for the entire United States, whether in print or CD-ROM, is impractical and/or cost-prohibitive. However, regular users would be well-advised to purchase both formats for the geographic areas which they work with most frequently.

---

vide the exact same list of specific languages spoken; each product lists 26 languages or language groups. Differences in format are fairly minor in other cases. For example, *CP-2* generally cites total counts, while *STF 3A* users must usually add individual values to calculate the total (as shown in examples 2, 3, 9, 10, 14, and 15). For certain topics, *CP-2* offers a greater number of tabulation categories. For example, *CP-2* typically cites age levels for linguistic characteristics in four groupings, while *STF 3A* uses only three (see examples 8, 9, 10, and 15). Similarly, when tabulating Ability to Speak English, *CP-2* uses four choices: very well; well; not well; or not at all. In contrast, *STF 3A* offers only three categories, combining "not well" and "not at all" into a single response.

Does this mean that *CP-2* always offers more response categories than *STF 3A*? Actually, in some instances the situation is reversed. Before disregarding the utility of *STF 3A* completely, consider examples 12, 13, 16, 17, and 18 in Figure 9-18. In these situations, *STF 3A* cites detailed data which the print Report simply cannot provide. In example 12, Table P28 from *STF 3A* pro-

vides a three-way tabulation, linking Ability to Speak English with Language Spoken at Home (Spanish, Asian, or Other), for each of three age groups. *CP-2* provides a two-way tabulation only, linking Ability to Speak English with age, but not with language spoken.

As Figure 9-18 demonstrates, it is difficult to make generalizations when comparing the level of subject detail between the two products. This is also true when comparing *CP-1* and *STF 1A*, or when comparing *CH-1* or *CH-2* to their corresponding *STF* products. The reason for this is that these four print Titles have no direct CD-ROM equivalents.

Advantages of CD-ROM Files over Print Reports

Of course the CD-ROM products offer important advantages of their own, not the least of which are convenience, ease of use, and compact storage. Perhaps the greatest benefit of using CD-ROM over print is the more extensive geographic detail, including Blocks, Block Groups, and ZIP Code Areas (none of which can be found in print Re-

Perhaps the greatest benefit of using CD-ROM over print is the more extensive geographic detail, including Blocks, Block Groups, and ZIP Code Areas.

ports), plus County Subdivisions and small Places (both of which receive minimal treatment in print). *STF 1A* and *STF 3A* also provide much more subject detail at the Tract level than can be found in *CPH-3*.

The GO software provides numerous advantages, such as the ability to search for needed tables by subject keywords and the ready availability of online definitions for subject and geographic terminology. For more sophisticated users seeking to create customized tables or conduct comparative analyses, the ability to work with EXTRACT or other Database Management Systems is another clear plus.

Summary

As is the case with CD-ROM products, the fundamental question which users must ask about print Reports is how to make sense of the voluminous output of data. And once again, the best answer is to look for similarities and differences among the major Titles. For example, the *CPH* Series offers brief summary data, while *CP* and *CH* Series provide much greater subject detail. The most important difference to remember is which Reports contain complete-count data, which contain sample data, and which have both. Figure 9-1 provides a useful review of these differences. Regular users of the CD-ROM products will find it helpful to relate various print Titles to the corresponding *STF* databases from which they are derived. Figure 9-16 summarizes these relationships. The levels of geographic coverage are another important feature which helps determine which Title to use. For example, Tract data can be found in *CPH-3* only, while *CPH-4* is the only Report which covers Congressional Districts. Researchers seeking data for Metropolitan Areas, Urbanized Areas, or American Indian/Alaska Native Areas are best served using the specialized Reports within the *CP* and *CH* Series, rather than the regular Reports for individual states. Comparisons of geographic coverage can be found

in Figure 9-2.

Users should also remember the basic tradeoff between subject detail and geographic detail. *CP-2* offers far less geographic coverage than *CP-1*, because *CP-2* deals with many more subject variables. The same relationship holds true for *CH-2* as it compares to *CH-1*. Additional tips for choosing and using the appropriate Census product, whether CD-ROM disc or print Report, will be introduced in Chapter 10. For now, readers should simply remember that the various print Titles follow a set pattern, which becomes more familiar through repeated use of the products.

Regular users of the CD-ROM products will find it helpful to relate various print Titles to the corresponding *STF* databases from which they are derived.

156. 1990 Census Detailed Cross-Tabulations for the U.S. Virgin Islands. $33.

Census Questionnaire Content, 1990 (1990 CQC)

See abstract number 1624.

New! (1610) 📖 ▦

Metropolitan Areas as Defined by OMB, June 30, 1993 (1990 CPH-S-1-1)

Data time span—1990.

Geographic areas covered—United States; regions; divisions; States; metropolitan areas (MA's) defined by OMB, June 30, 1993; central cities; and metropolitan counties and county equivalents.

Subject content—Similar to *Population and Housing Characteristics for Census Tracts and Block Numbering Areas* (1990 CPH-3) (see abstract number 1603). However, the subjects differ somewhat in level detail (that is, the number of categories shown for such topics as age), and the smallest geographic units reports are metropolitan areas (MA's), "inside central city," "outside central city," central cities, and metropolitan counties and county equivalents. General maps of metropolitan and other areas are included.

*GPO Stock No. 003-024-08738-3.
Section 1, 864 pp.; Section 2, 875 pp. 1994.
$42 a set.
Contact Customer Services for the latest ordering information. Also available on microfiche from Customer Services.*

New! (1611) 📖 ▦

Urbanized Areas of the United States and Puerto Rico (1990 CPH-S-1-2)

Data time span—1990, with some comparative data for 1980.

Geographic areas covered—United States; regions; divisions; States; Puerto Rico; and urbanized areas (zonas urbanas in Puerto Rico), their central places and urban fringes (shown separately and within State, county, and subcounty boundaries); and extended cities (that is, those extending into rural areas).

Subject content—Shows number of inhabitants and housing units, compared with land area, to indicate population and housing density. Density and area are measured in square miles and kilometers, with tables including total area as well as land area.

The report includes population and housing units in several residential contexts. In addition to areas specifically named, the report includes summaries by type of area. For example, the report cross-tabulates population counts for the area inside and outside of metropolitan areas in the United States and Puerto Rico, by size of place. Similarly, the

report summarizes urban and rural data for extended cities.

Maps showing urbanized areas in context are included.

*GPO Stock No. 003-024-07511-3.
Section 1 of 2, 409 pp.; Section 2 of 2, 380 pp. 1994. $43 a set.
Contact Customer Services for the latest ordering information. Also available on microfiche from Customer Services.*

New! (1624) 📖

We Asked . . . You Told Us. Census Questionnaire Content, 1990 (1990 CQC)

Subject content—Presents, in each of a series of brochures, data for the United States for a few related questions from the 1990 census questionnaires. The report provides the information graphically in maps, charts, and excerpts from questionnaires.

A series of reports in progress. Pages vary. Published beginning in 1992. Single copies free, additional copies $1 each. Report numbers 2, 5, 8 to 11, and 27 were listed in the 1994 Catalog/Guide. Contact Customer Services for the latest ordering information. Not available on microfiche.

2. Household Relationship.

3. Gender. 2 pp.

5. Age. 2 pp.

6. Marital status. 2 pp.

8. Type of Housing and Tenure. 2 pp.

9. Number of Rooms and Bedrooms. 2 pp.

10. Year Moved In and Year Structure Built. 2 pp.

11. Value of Home and Monthly Rent. 2 pp.

12. Place of Birth, Citizenship, and Year of Entry. 4 pp.

13. Education. 4 pp.

15. Residence in 1985. 2 pp.

16. Language Spoken at Home. 2 pp.

20. Employment Status. 2 pp.

25. Complete Plumbing and Kitchen Facilities. 2 pp.

26. Telephone and Vehicle Availability. 2 pp.

27. Home Heating Fuels. 2 pp.

Population

New! (1626) 📖 ▦

Social and Economic Characteristics (1990 CP-2)

Data time span—1990.

Geographic areas covered— United States, regions, divisions, metropolitan areas (MA's), urbanized areas (UA's), and American Indian and Alaska Native areas (AIANA's) in the first four summary volumes; in the remaining volumes: States (total and inside and outside metropolitan

and urban areas), counties (total and inside and outside rural and rural farm areas), county subdivisions of 2,500 or more (for some States), incorporated and other places of 2,500 or more population, and State portions of AIANA's; and Puerto Rico and the Virgin Islands of the United States.

Subject content—Presents sample data from the Census of Population. Sample data include general topics covered in the 100-percent count and additional topics collected on a sample basis. (This printed report is derived from Summary Tape File (STF) 3A.)

The report provides data on the following general 100-percent population topics: age, family, Hispanic origin, household relationship, marital status, race, and sex. The report shows data on age in 17 categories, suggesting the degree of detail on general population topics.

The report also cites additional subjects found only in sample population data. These cover social and economic topics. Social topics include the following: ancestry; disability; education (enrollment and attainment); fertility; language spoken at home; migration (residence in 1985); place of birth, citizenship, and year of entry into the United States; and veteran status. The report profiles educational attainment in 11 categories, for example.

Economic topics include the following: income in 1989; labor force (including employment and unemployment); occupation, industry, and class of worker; place of work and journey to work; and work experience in 1989. Income data, aside from poverty, are shown by type of income and family. The report provides, for instance, 11 categories for household income.

The items above are generally shown by race and Hispanic origin; otherwise, the report rarely cross-classifies topics.

A series of 57 paperbound reports for each of the following areas: the United States (4 reports), the 50 States, the District of Columbia, Puerto Rico, and the U.S. Virgin Islands. Published 1993-94. For all reports the price is $2,495.50. Contact Customer Services for the latest ordering information. Also available on microfiche from Customer Services.

1. United States. 598 pp. $37. GPO Stock No. 003-024-07508-3.

1A. American Indian and Alaska Native Areas (Section 1 of 2, 948 pp.; Section 2 of 2, 1,166 pp.). $53 a set. GPO Stock No. 003-024-07509-1.

1B. Metropolitan Areas (Section 1 of 6, 824 pp.; Section 2 of 6, 940 pp.; Section 3 of 6, 916 pp.; Section 4 of 6, 952 pp.; Section 5 of 6, 816 pp.; Section 6 of 6, 868 pp.). $66 a set. GPO Stock No. 003-024-07510-5.

Figure 9-19
Sample page from Census Catalog and Guide

Chapter 10

Finding and Using Census Data

Finding and Using Census Data

THE FUNDAMENTAL objectives of using Census publications are to locate needed statistics, to understand their meaning, and to apply them properly to the situation at hand. Everything discussed in the previous chapters has been presented with these objectives in mind. Mastering the Census requires several levels of understanding. The key components of this understanding are outlined below, together with the chapters in which they are discussed.

1. Develop a general idea of how the Bureau collects, processes, and tabulates data (Chapter 4).
2. Study important subject concepts and Census-specific terminology (Chapter 5).
3. Learn about relevant geographic concepts, especially those pertaining to the locality you are researching (Chapter 6).
4. Examine the Census Questionnaire to become familiar with the specific questions asked and the way in which they

are phrased (Chapter 7 and Appendix D).
5. Determine the structure of the Bureau's publication program, and the basic formats used in major publications (Chapters 8, 9, and 14).

Chapter 10 builds upon these topics and provides additional tips for locating Census statistics and using them properly. The chapter begins with an introduction to obtaining needed publications, whether by purchasing them or by using various Census libraries. Sources of assistance are also described including help from the Bureau's Regional Offices and through the State Data Center Program. The subsequent section offers suggestions for developing a search strategy when using Census publications, whether in print or electronic formats. Next, major factors affecting the accuracy and reliability of Census data are described, including sampling limitations and sources of coverage error. The final section explores some of the pitfalls researchers may encounter when using Cen-

Q&A

How do customers contact the Census Bureau or GPO to purchase publications?

Both agencies accept purchase orders via mail, telephone, telefacsimile (fax), or electronic mail. Credit card orders (VISA or Mastercard) are accepted. Both agencies support deposit accounts for customers who anticipate an ongoing need for Census products. The Government Printing Office also operates GPO Bookstores in 24 cities throughout the United States.

The Bureau's annual *Census Catalog and Guide* contains GPO and Census Bureau order forms, together with more detailed instructions for placing orders with both agencies. Another convenient resource is the "Market Place" section of the Census

Bureau's Internet Web server. The Internet site is described in Chapter 14.

When in doubt, customers can contact the agencies by telephone to obtain information on current prices and availability. The numbers are listed below.

Superintendent of Documents
U.S. Government Printing Office
(202) 512-1800

Customer Services
U.S. Bureau of the Census
(301) 457-4100

---

sus publications. Examples of common mistakes are provided.

Obtaining Census Publications and Assistance

Chapters 8, 9, and 14 describe an extensive collection of 1990 Census products in various formats, but they do not discuss the mundane issue of acquiring the desired documents. How can Census users obtain specific printed Reports, CD-ROM products, or magnetic tapes? The following sections explore this concern from several viewpoints: purchasing Census products for personal use; contracting with the Census Bureau for specialized data services; and using Census publications housed in the collections of libraries and other organizations.

Purchasing Census Publications

Depending on the type of publication, decennial Census products must be ordered through either the U.S. Government Print-

ing Office (GPO) or the Bureau itself. The GPO handles orders for standard print publications, such as the Reports in the *CP*, *CH*, and *CPH* Series. The Bureau handles orders for electronic data products (magnetic tape, CD-ROM, or diskette), as well as for microfiche products and technical documentation for electronic files. The appropriate source for ordering maps depends on map format. As described in Chapter 9, maps which are published using standard commercial printing methods can be ordered from the GPO. For example, the sheet maps for Census Tracts and Block Numbering Areas (which accompany the *CPH-3* Title) can be obtained from the GPO. Electrostatically plotted maps, which are produced on demand, must be ordered directly from the Bureau itself.

The Census Bureau also sells older publications which are no longer in stock at the Government Printing Office. Any "out-of-stock" publication for the 1990 Census can be obtained from the Bureau as a microfiche reprint or as a paper "blow back" photocopied from the microfiche.

The Census Bureau issues ongoing catalogs and census guides in print and electronic formats. These guides provide detailed de-

> **The GPO handles orders for standard print publications, such as the Reports in the *CP*, *CH*, and *CPH* Series. The Bureau handles orders for electronic data products (magnetic tape, CD-ROM, or diskette), as well as for microfiche products and technical documentation for electronic files.**

scriptions of each product available for sale: subject content, geographic coverage, time span, format, size, price, and source for ordering. Listings for GPO publications include the Stock Number for each item. The two primary sources of catalog information are described below, together with brief descriptions of their electronic counterparts.

The *Census Catalog and Guide*

The Bureau publishes this indispensable resource annually, in the summer of each year. It contains descriptions and ordering information for current Census publications of all types, including products from the decennial Census, the various Economic Censuses, and a diversity of ongoing survey programs. Coverage includes paper Reports, microfiche, CD-ROM, diskettes, and magnetic tape files. Products issued as part of the decennial Census program appear in a separate section of the *Catalog*. The *Catalog* utilizes icons to indicate the various formats in which each product is made available, and employs a notation to highlight which products are new since the previous *Catalog*. Items identified by a GPO Stock Number must be ordered from the GPO; all other materials are supplied by the Bureau.

Although each annual *Catalog* focuses on the products issued during the previous year, some of the annual editions are cumulative. For example, the 1989 edition covers all publications listed in the prior *Catalogs* from 1980 through 1988. The 1994 edition includes all listings seen in the *Catalogs* issued from 1990 through 1993. A new cumulation began with the 1995 *Catalog*.

In addition to actual product listings, the *Census Catalog and Guide* provides a number of helpful finding tools and supplementary materials. A section entitled "Product Overview" describes the scope and structure of the Bureau's publishing program, and provides summary tables outlining the types of publications available. Another section reproduces the subject menus from *CENDATA*, the Bureau's online database service. Two indexes make it relatively easy to locate specific Census products in the *Catalog*: one is arranged by publication title; the other by subject.

What makes the *Census Catalog and Guide* stand out as an exceptional reference tool is Appendix B, "Sources of Assistance." This section provides an updated directory of departments within the Census Bureau, and lists other Census-related organizations. This section includes entries for the Census Bureau's Regional Offices, the State Data Centers for the 50 states, hundreds of local Data Center Affiliates around the country, over 1,400 Depository Libraries, GPO bookstores located in major cities, and several other important information resources.

The *Census Catalog and Guide* has no direct electronic equivalent, but most of the information contained therein can be found on the Census Bureau's Internet Web page. Catalog information is located in the "Market Place" section of the Home Page, and is updated approximately once per month; directory information from Appendix B is found in the "Ask the Experts" section. *CENDATA* does not provide an electronic version of the *Catalog*, but it does reproduce

---

Census Tip

Users wishing to maintain a comprehensive guide to retrospective Census publications must pay attention to the cumulation pattern of the annual *Census Catalog and Guide*. In some cases, previous years are superseded, and may be thrown away, but in other years, important cumulations must be kept. For recent publications, the cumulative editions appeared in 1989 and 1994. The Bureau also published a massive historical guide in 1973, entitled *Bureau of the Census Catalog of Publications: 1790-1972*. No cumulations were published covering the years 1973 through 1979.

[Margin notes:]

Items identified by a GPO Stock Number must be ordered from the GPO; all other materials are supplied by the Bureau.

What makes the *Census Catalog and Guide* stand out as an exceptional reference tool is Appendix B, "Sources of Assistance." This section provides an updated directory of departments within the Census Bureau, and lists other Census-related organizations.

many of the directories found in Appendix B. *CENDATA* and the Bureau's Web server are both described in greater detail in Chapter 14.

The *Monthly Product Announcement*

The Bureau updates the annual *Catalog and Guide* with a free newsletter entitled the *Monthly Product Announcement* (*MPA*). It provides product descriptions and price information for new Census publications as they are released. Each issue also contains a section called "Looking Ahead," which highlights major products due to be released shortly. An order form can be found at the back of every issue. As an added feature, *MPA* sometimes reprints brief articles or reference guides relating to Census publications. A schedule of upcoming training programs offered by the Bureau is also published periodically.

The *Monthly Product Announcement* is also available in electronic form. The electronic version is distributed sooner than its paper counterpart. The most recent three issues can be found on the Bureau's Internet Web site: click on the "Market Place" section of the Home Page, then look for the section entitled, "Recently Released Products." The Web site offers two versions of *MPA*: the HTML edition, and a Portable Document Format version (which reproduces the actual page layout and typeface seen in the paper version). The HTML version is not uploaded to the Web server as rapidly as the graphic version. *CENDATA* also provides the most recent three months of *MPA*, but in ASCII text. *CENDATA* also offers a separate section containing daily updates to the monthly newsletter.

Users wishing to be placed on the mailing list to receive the paper edition of this useful newsletter can contact the Bureau's Customer Services office by phone. Users can also choose to receive an electronic copy automatically every month via e-mail. To

---

NEW IN '90

Customers can now place orders for Census products by e-mail with the Government Printing Office or the Census Bureau, depending on the type of product.

Orders for printed publications can be placed electronically through an Internet service called GPO Access. The easiest means of locating this service is through the Census Bureau's own Internet Web server. The Bureau has created a hypertext link to the GPO catalog and order-placing sections of GPO Access for the convenience of Census customers.

Orders for CD-ROM products, magnetic tapes, or other specialized publications can be placed electronically with the Census Bureau. Customers can either send a message to **orders@census.gov** or they can use the "Market Place" section of the Census Bureau's Internet Web page.

Whether ordering through the Government Printing Office or the Census Bureau, Web users can simply click on the "Order" icon found in most individual catalog entries. Customers are then instructed to fill out an electronic order form, citing the necessary Stock Number and price information. Customers must also provide their Deposit Account number or credit card information before an order can be processed.

---

subscribe to this free service, send a message to Majordomo@census.gov. The body of the message should say **subscribe product-announce**, followed by your complete e-mail address. The Bureau's Web server offers a simpler approach. It contains a section that will transmit the necessary "subscribe" message by simply clicking on that option.

The Bureau updates the annual *Catalog and Guide* with a free newsletter entitled the *Monthly Product Announcement* (MPA).

Special Services from the Census Bureau

In addition to its regular selection of publications and databases, the Census Bureau offers several specialized options for data users whose needs may not be met by standard products. Both of these options—the User Defined Areas Program and the Special Tabulations Program—involve customized tabulations based on customer specifications.

User-Defined Areas Program

Despite the diversity of geographic levels for which Census data are produced, standard Census geography does not meet the needs of all data users. Users can create their own geographic boundaries by combining Census Blocks and summing Block data. Unfortunately, such aggregations have limited value because sample data are not tabulated at the Block level. To circumvent this limitation, organizations can pay the Bureau to perform standard tabulations for customized geographies based on groupings of individual Census Blocks as specified by the contracting party. The Bureau calls this service the User-Defined Areas Program (UDAP).

UDAP customers use Block maps provided by the Bureau to outline the boundaries of their desired territory. UDAP boundaries are created through the aggregations of whole Blocks, but the resulting area can cross Block Groups, Tracts, counties, or other geographies if the customer wishes. The Bureau then utilizes unpublished computer tapes to generate a standard set of tables, including complete-count and sample data. UDAP pricing is based on two components: map preparation and data tabulation. The larger the land area, the greater the cost, but the fees are not excessive. An organization requesting the aggregation of 1,000 Blocks and five separate map sheets would pay $300

For a fee, the Census Bureau will create customized subject reports based on 1990 Census returns. This service is called the Special Tabulation Program (STP).

for map preparation and $500 for data tabulation.

The Bureau marketed the 1990 User-Defined Area Program to government agencies, nonprofit organizations, businesses, and private individuals. For example, local governments could design UDAP boundaries to obtain data for police precincts, sewer districts, municipal planning areas, or even post-redistricting Voting Districts. Nonprofit and business organizations could utilize the program to identify social, economic, and housing characteristics of their service areas, marketing territories, or sales districts. Census Blocks may not conform exactly to a UDAP customer's desired geographic area, but because Blocks are so small, UDAP configurations usually will be close approximations.

 ## Census Tip

The 1990 UDAP Program was a special service which the Bureau offered for a limited time. Due to lack of demand, the program was canceled in 1994. A similar service existed during the 1980 Census, and another may be offered following the 2000 Census.

Special Tabulation Program

For a fee, the Census Bureau will create customized subject reports based on 1990 Census returns. This service is called the Special Tabulation Program (STP). Such reports can be costly and are typically commissioned by other government agencies or by large corporations. Resulting reports usually involve standard Census geographies, such as states, counties, or Metropolitan Areas, but they provide subject detail or cross-tabulations not found in regular products covering the same Summary Levels. For example, the Department of Housing and Urban Development (HUD) may need certain detailed housing variables reported at

---

NEW IN '90

For 1980, the User Defined Areas Program was called the Neighborhood Statistics Program. The 1980 program was identical in purpose to UDAP, but was free of charge and was available only to governmental organizations. Because the program was free to requesting governments, it was more widely used than the 1990 UDAP Program. Microfiche reports based on the 1980 Neighborhood Statistics Program were actually published as a standard Report series, and could be purchased by any interested individuals. Results of 1990 UDAP reports were not published by the Bureau; instead, they were provided to the contracting party only.

Q&A

What is the difference between the UDAP and STP Programs?

Generally speaking, UDAP (a service which is no longer offered) provided standard summary statistics for customized geographies. In contrast, STP reports provide detailed, customized subject tabulations for standard geographies.

the Block Group level. *STF 3A* provides Block Group data, but its subject coverage is less detailed than HUD desires. *STF 4* provides necessary subject detail, but not at the Block Group level. The solution is a Special Tabulation which combines the features of both Files. Because the Bureau maintains the Basic Record Tapes which contain individual Questionnaire results, new tabulations can be created to meet requestors' needs.

Since the Bureau undertakes Special Tabulations at the behest of a fee-paying organization, the results of the project are given to the contracting party. But if a Special Tabulation provides information which might be useful to a broader audience, the Census Bureau may decide to publish the results for others to use as well. As described in Chapter 8, an *STP File* called the *Special Tabulation on Aging* was commissioned by the U.S Agency on Aging (AOA). The results were deemed so useful that the Bureau published this *AOA File* on CD-ROM, complete with accompanying GO software. However, most published *STP Files* are available only as magnetic tape or diskette files. A representative list of STP products available in these formats can be seen in Figure 14-8, found in Chapter 14.

The Bureau's responsibility does not end with collecting, tabulating, and publishing data; the agency also wants data users to locate specific statistics when needed and to utilize them properly.

Other Sources of Census Data

Researchers in need in Census data can purchase their own copies of publications or databases through one of the means described above. Census users can also obtain online access to Census databases, either through the fee-based *CENDATA* service or the Bureau's Internet Web server, both of which are introduced in Chapter 14. Several additional options are available for obtaining needed data, or for requesting assistance in using and understanding Census statistics. The following sections discuss some of the more helpful options, including the Bureau's Regional Offices, the State Data Center Program, the Federal Depository Library Program, and the National Clearinghouse for Census Data Service.

Assistance from the Census Bureau

Census users can turn to the Bureau itself for all kinds of advice and assistance in locating and using the agency's data products. Assistance comes from two sources: employees at Bureau headquarters in and around Suitland, Maryland; and the Bureau's 12 Regional Offices.

Although the Census Bureau is a fairly large, far-flung government agency with many different divisions, it fosters a strong commitment to customer service among all its employees. The Bureau's responsibility does not end with collecting, tabulating, and publishing data; the agency also wants data users to locate specific statistics when needed and to utilize them properly. Bureau employees are happy to answer all types of questions, from the general to the specific, and from elementary to highly sophisticated. Whether the user has questions about the release date for a new product, how to use the Bureau's

Recognizing that the Bureau and its Regional Offices do not possess sufficient resources to handle all of the queries posed by Census users throughout the nation, the Data User Services Division established a separate network of information resources at the local level.

software, the legislative redistricting process, how the OMB defines Metropolitan Areas, or current developments for the 2000 Census, someone at the Bureau will usually be able to provide an answer.

The State Data Center Program

Recognizing that the Bureau and its Regional Offices do not possess sufficient resources to handle all of the queries posed by Census users throughout the nation, the Data User Services Division established a separate network of information resources at the local level. The network, called the State Data Center Program (SDC), was inaugurated in 1978. Within a few years of the network's creation, Data Centers existed in each of the 50 states and in most of the Outlying Areas. The Census Bureau supplies

organizations in the SDC Program with print Reports, CD-ROM products, and magnetic tapes at no cost. In return, participating

 Census Tip

In most cases, employees at the Bureau's headquarters facilities will not provide actual data from published Reports or databases. Instead, they will direct the user to various sources of published information, such as Depository Libraries or local State Data Center Affiliates. In addition to this referral service, Bureau employees will answer specific questions relating to technical aspects of Census procedures and methodology, or help users to interpret Census concepts and terms correctly.

Q&A

How can I contact the right person to ask a specific Census question?

For many years, the Census Bureau maintained a Data User Services Division (DUSD) which served as the focal point for fielding customer requests. Within DUSD, the Customer Services office handled order requests for Census publications, while other DUSD employees fielded other information requests, maintained the electronic Bulletin Board System, and so on. As *Understanding the Census* was going to press, the Bureau announced that it will be disbanding the DUSD, and dividing its functions among other Divisions within the organization. Following this reorganization, the simplest method of initiating contact is to call the Bureau's Customer Services office, which now serves as the focal point for all information referral.

Another means of making contact is to telephone a specific employee or department directly. The Bureau maintains an updated telephone directory which is published in a variety of sources. It can be found in the "Sources of Assistance" section of the *Census Catalog and Guide* and it is also published annually (usually in February or March) in the Bureau's monthly newsletter entitled *The Census and You*. One of the most convenient sources of current phone numbers is the "Ask the Experts"

section of the Bureau's Web server. Here the user can browse a list of "Frequently Called Numbers" or can search for subject experts by topic. Similar listings can be found through the *CENDATA* online service.

The Bureau offers another source of assistance through the Information Officers employed at its 12 Regional Offices (ROs). The cities in which permanent ROs are located can be found in Figure 10-13, located at the end of the chapter. Information Officers can answer specific questions by telephone or they can refer callers to other sources of local Census information. Regional Offices are open to the public, and researchers can stop in to use the collections of print Reports and CD-ROM products. Information Officers may also be available to make presentations at area workshops and conferences. A directory of the Regional Offices and their phone numbers can be found in the annual *Census Catalog and Guide* or the "Ask the Experts" section of the Bureau's Web server. Each of the Regional Offices also maintains its own Web page, with appropriate links from the Bureau's Web server.

organizations agree to make Census data available to the public, and to assist Census users with information requests.

Under the SDC Program, the Census Bureau designates an organization in each state to act as the Lead Agency to administer the program within that state. In most states, the Lead Agency is an executive department within state government—typically an agency dealing with commerce, labor, budget, or planning. In several states, the state library serves as the Lead Agency. In approximately ten states, the Lead Agency is a university. In a few states, Lead status is shared by two agencies.

The Lead Agency can designate one or more additional organizations to serve as statewide "Coordinating Agencies." Lead Agencies and Coordinating Agencies are entitled to receive all Census products for their state. The Lead Agency also appoints Data Center Affiliates to provide assistance at the local level. Each Affiliate specifies a local area which it agrees to service (usually one or more counties). In turn, Affiliates receive Census publications covering their service area. The organizational structure of SDC Affiliates varies from state to state, but in most cases Affiliates are libraries (public or academic), government planning agencies (county or regional), universities, or regional councils of government.

In 1988, the Bureau expanded the SDC Program to incorporate a second, newly created structure called the Business and Industry Data Center (BIDC) network. The BIDC Program fulfills several goals: to expand the network of Affiliates beyond the traditional types of SDC organizations; to provide access to other Census products besides demographic resources; and to actively reach out to the business community. SDC/BIDC Affiliates now include Chambers of Commerce, Small Business Development Centers, Private Industry Councils, and other economic development organizations, as well as other nonprofit organizations serving business needs.

SDC/BIDC services vary from one organization to another. Lead Agencies typically publish state and county profiles based on the Bureau's magnetic tape products or other statistical sources. Many Lead Agencies maintain a staff of professional demographers who generate population projections for the state or who work with the Bureau's Federal-State Cooperative Program for Population Estimates. Some Lead Agencies handle information requests from the public, while others refer queries to the appropriate SDC Affiliate. Lead Agencies also work with the Census Bureau during the decennial planning process, and they may coordinate training programs for Affiliate members and for local governments.

Census Tip

Some SDC Affiliates maintain necessary resources to generate customized tables from magnetic tapes, but many do not. The same is true for customized tables generated from CD-ROM products (using EXTRACT or other database management software) or for thematic maps based on TIGER/Line Files (using GIS software). Readers should also remember that many Affiliates collect data for their service area only.

The types of services provided by local SDC Affiliates also vary. Most Affiliates allow researchers to utilize their collection of publications and CD-ROMs within the office. Many publish demographic and economic profiles for their service area. Most handle telephone requests, and will supply brief information over the telephone, or will send a reasonable number of data tables at no charge. However, Lead Agencies and Affiliates may charge fees to cover their service costs. Fees can range from small charges for printing or photocopying to more extensive billing for staff time. The latter is especially true for organizations which provide cus-

Under the SDC Program, the Census Bureau designates an organization in each state to act as the Lead Agency to administer the program within that state.

In 1988, the Bureau expanded the SDC Program to incorporate a second, newly created structure called the Business and Industry Data Center (BIDC) network.

tomized tables or maps generated from magnetic tapes or CD-ROM products.

National Census Information Centers

A more recent information network is the National Census Information Center (NCIC) program. The Bureau sponsors NCICs to encourage demographic research relating to minority groups and to facilitate the dissemination of Census data to nonprofit minority organizations. The Bureau has designated five organizations as National Census Information Centers:

- the National Urban League (New York, NY)
- the National Council of La Raza (Washington, DC)
- the Southwest Voter Research Institute (San Antonio, TX)
- the INDIANnet Information Center (Seaside, CA)
- the Asian American Health Forum (San Francisco, CA)

The purpose of the Centers is to conduct demographic research on issues affecting minority populations and to publish topical statistical profiles and analytical reports. Each of the Centers maintains a resource library and can provide various information services upon request. As with the SDC Program, each of the national agencies can designate local or regional Affiliate Centers.

Depository Libraries

The Federal Depository Library Program provides an invaluable resource for Census users. Approximately 1,400 public, college, and university libraries in the United States have been designated as GPO Depositories— at least one library in every Congressional District. These libraries can receive GPO publications free of charge, on the condition that they make these publications available to the general public. The GPO publishes government documents on behalf of virtually all federal agencies, including the Bureau of the Census. In fact, the GPO is the largest publisher in the United States, issuing nearly 50,000 titles each year.

At the state level, 53 libraries have been designated as Regional Depositories. This means they receive and retain all publications issued by the GPO under the Depository Library Program. Regional Depositories serve as a resource of "last resort" for the other libraries in their region. The majority of libraries in the program are Selective Depositories, which means they can determine which categories of GPO publications they wish to receive. Some Selective Depositories receive only 10% of all Depository documents, but many receive 50% or more.

Census publications are among the most frequently requested documents in many Depository Libraries, and most institutions in the Federal Depository Program select at least some Census products, including CD-ROM databases. Depository librarians are familiar with basic Census concepts, geography, and terminology, and are happy to help data users locate needed Census tables. Some librarians even specialize in Census information, and may provide advice and instruction on using EXTRACT, GIS programs, or other software for data manipulation and presentation.

Approximately 1,400 public, college, and university libraries in the United States have been designated as GPO Depositories—

Depository librarians are familiar with basic Census concepts, geography, and terminology, and are happy to help data users locate needed Census tables.

> ## NEW IN '90
>
> National Census Information Centers are new for the 1990 Census. At present, approximately 20 NCIC Affiliates have been established, with plans to expand the program to include 50 Affiliates.

💡 Census Tip

As with the State Data Center Program, the amount of information and level of service will vary from one Depository Library to another. However, the largest Depositories offer "one-stop shopping," and are among the best resources for locating Census products for all 50 states in one location.

A comprehensive list of all 1,400 Depository Libraries can be found in the annual *Census Catalog and Guide*. Another convenient directory is provided by *GPO Access*, the Government Printing Office's Internet database system. *GPO Access* includes a component called the Federal Locator, which allows users to search by state or by telephone Area Code to identify the Depository Library nearest to them. This feature of *GPO Access* is also searchable directly from the Census Bureau's Web server. It can be found in two sections of the Bureau's Web site: the "Market Place," and "Ask the Experts."

National Clearinghouse for Census Data Services

The Bureau has established another information network of interest to Census users. Unlike the SDC and NCIC programs, this network is not sponsored by the Bureau. Participating agencies have no direct ties to the federal government, they receive no free data products from the Bureau, nor are they are obligated to provide any public services. The network, called the National Clearinghouse for Census Data Services, is merely a referral list of organizations which can provide various Census-related services for a fee. Any organization may apply to the Bureau for Clearinghouse status. Most Clearinghouse participants are commercial firms, but some are nonprofit institutions. The types of services offered by these organizations vary greatly, and include customized data extracts from Census tapes, access to proprietary databases, demographic market research, population estimates and projections, mapping services, and training. The Bureau provides a list of codes to designate the types of services offered by each organization. In previous years, the list of Clearinghouse organizations was published in the Bureau's *Census Catalog and Guide*, but no longer. The current list can be received free of charge by contacting the Census Bureau's Customer Services office.

Census Search Strategies

To many novice Census users, the most frustrating aspect of working with this enormous body of data is learning how to locate specific statistics quickly and efficiently. *Understanding the Census* has stressed the importance of learning Census methodology, concepts, geography, and terminology. Gaining such knowledge requires effort and preparation, of course. Can someone simply open up a Census Report or CD-ROM product and start using it? Yes, but they will spend more time searching for needed data and figuring out what the numbers mean. A more important concern is that failure to understand key concepts will lead to the likelihood of interpreting data incorrectly.

Experienced Census users employ systematic search strategies, whether they do so consciously or not. No single strategy will work for every Census query, but certain decision rules can be applied. How can beginning users develop an awareness of important search guidelines? Studying Census documentation or reading other guides and textbooks (like *Understanding the Census* or the Bureau's own *1990 Census of Population and Housing Guide*) will certainly help. The best way to develop research skills is through practice. The more one uses Census publications, the easier it becomes to locate needed data.

The Search Process

Sooner or later most Census users ask, "Isn't there some better way to locate the proper publication and table without plowing haphazardly through innumerable publications?" The honest answer is sometimes there is no simple way to find the data you need. Proficient researchers develop their own shortcuts, but in most cases, search time can be reduced by dividing the process into logical steps.

STEPS IN LOCATING CENSUS DATA

A. Preliminary Steps.
　　1. Verify that the question is asked by the decennial Census.
　　2. Verify that the geographic Summary Level is covered by the Census.

B. Choosing the Appropriate Publication
　　1. Determine whether it is a sample or complete-count Item.
　　2. Determine whether it is a population or housing question.
　　3. Select the appropriate format (Print or CD-ROM).
　　4. Match the needed Summary Level to the proper publication.

C. Locating the Proper Table(s).
　　1. Translate question into Census terminology.
　　2. For print sources:
　　　　a. Determine the required geographic Summary Level.
　　　　b. Utilize the **Table Finding Guide** to locate likely tables.
　　3. For CD-ROM sources using the **GO** software:
　　　　a. Select proper Summary Level.
　　　　b. Scan the list of tables or use the keyword search feature.

Figure 10-1

Figure 10-1 outlines key steps in the search process. This is not the only model which one can use, nor is it applicable for every situation, but it offers a sensible means to approach decennial Census publications. The intent of this outline is to offer suggestions on how to begin the search and how to make the task less intimidating. The following sections elaborate upon this outline, offering tips on how best to approach most Census inquiries. To simplify the process, this model assumes users will be consulting either print Reports or CD-ROM Files. Chapter 14 introduces other publication formats, including magnetic tape, Internet files, and online databases, but print and CD-ROM still remain the most heavily used and comprehensive resources for Census research.

Preliminary Search Steps

The first step in the search process is to verify whether the information sought is available from the decennial Census. Searching for data on religion will be fruitless because nothing about religion appears on Census Questionnaires. A common misconception held by many novice data users is that Census coverage includes so-called vital statistics—

The first step in the search process is to verify whether the information sought is available from the decennial Census.

the number of births and deaths in a given period. Although birth and death rates are an important aspect of demographic analysis, neither characteristic is tabulated by the decennial Census.

 Census Tip

Birth and death statistics are published at the national, state, county, and Metropolitan Area levels by the National Center for Health Statistics. Their annual publication, called *Vital Statistics of the United States,* tabulates figures for number of births, birth rates, characteristics of mother and child, number of deaths, death rates, and cause of death.

In some instances, determining whether a topic is covered by the decennial Census is not as straightforward as one might suppose. For example, the Census collects no data on the structural or financial characteristics of Group Quarters. In fact, the Census doesn't even report the **number** of Group Quarters in the United States. Since GQs are excluded from the Bureau's definition of Housing Units, they are not described in any housing publications or tables. Statistics **are** reported for the number and characteristics of people living in Group Quarters, however.

A related issue is whether the Census tabulates data in the manner and detail a user requires. For example, information on college enrollment can be found in the Census, but not broken down by academic major. Data on persons with disabilities can be found, but not by type of disability. When designing sample surveys, public opinion pollsters and market researchers need to know what percentage of the population can be reached at home by telephone. The Census tabulates data on how many Households have telephones, but not how many persons live in those "telephone Households," nor whether the phone numbers are listed or unlisted. If you intend to use the Census on a regular basis, familiarize yourself with the Census Questionnaire, which is reproduced in Appendix C. Chapter 7 describes each Questionnaire Item in detail.

A second preliminary step involves identifying the required level of geography. This decision affects later steps in the search process, but also determines whether the information can be found in the Census at all. The decennial Census tabulates data for more types of geography than any other statistical program, but certain Summary Levels are simply not covered. For example, users seeking population figures for School Districts need not bother with the decennial Census unless they are willing to approximate District boundaries by summing component Tracts and Block Groups. A better source of population statistics at the School District level would be the National Center for Education Statistics' *School District Data Book*, a massive CD-ROM series which includes special tabulations from the 1990 Census.

Choosing the Proper Publication

Once the user has verified that the sought-after subject matter and geographic coverage are likely to be found in the Census, the next task is to determine the best publication in which to locate the desired data. The first step in selecting the appropriate Census Report or database is to determine whether the required Items are from the complete enumeration or the sample survey. Figure 1-4 (shown in Chapter 1) summarizes the questions asked on the Long and Short Forms. Based on this information, the researcher can then determine which Census Reports should be consulted. To recap the contents of the major products, 100% data will be found primarily in three print Reports (*CPH-1*, *CP-1*, and *CH-1*) and three CD-ROM Files (*STF 1A*, *STF 1B*, and *STF 1C*). The remaining publications contain sample data only, or in a few cases (*CPH-3*, *CPH-4*, and the *STF 1D/STF 3D* disc) a combination of complete-count and sample data in a single publication.

The next step outlined in Figure 10-1 may seem unnecessary, but disregarding it can result in wasted time and energy. Census publications are organized by type of data, and it is important to determine whether the characteristic being sought is a population Item or a housing Item. This is particularly important when using print Reports: the *CP* Series covers population Items, the *CH* Series covers housing Items, and the *CPH* Series provides summary data for both. The distinction is also important for CD-ROM products. Even though most CD-ROM Files contain population and housing Items in the same database, the tables are arranged by type. The **P** tables cover population characteristics, while the **H** tables deal with housing variables.

Determining the difference between population and housing characteristics may appear simple, but in some cases it will require a moment's thought. Information on people living in Group Quarters is a population question, for example, as is information on Household characteristics. Household Income is a population Item, but rent as a percentage of Income can be found in the housing tables. Sometimes the distinctions between housing and population are even less obvious. Data on the number of vehicles owned by people in a Household is a housing question, while data on how people travel to work is a population question.

The third step in selecting a specific publication is to determine the best format to use: print or CD-ROM. In many situations, needed data can be found easily in either format. In such cases, the resulting decision may be based on matters of personal preference or convenience. Some users are more comfortable with print Reports, while others find CD-ROM Files much easier to use. Many times the choice is determined by the types of resources near to hand. Table layouts or database structure can also play a role in the decision. Users seeking to construct a profile of a single geographic entity may find CD-ROM more appropriate, while those

The first step in selecting the appropriate Census Report or database is to determine whether the required Items are from the complete enumeration or the sample survey.

Determining the difference between population and housing characteristics may appear simple, but in some cases it will require a moment's thought.

seeking to compare many entities in a single table may prefer print formats. CD-ROM databases offer an additional advantage for users willing to learn how to manipulate the Bureau's EXTRACT software: some tables are best constructed on a customized basis, using EXTRACT or similar database management programs.

Certain types of subject detail may be found only in one format or the other. *CPH-2* (a print Report) is the only 1990 Census publication which offers historical comparisons for basic population and housing characteristics.

One of the drawbacks to CD-ROM tables is that subtotals are seldom provided. For example, *CP-1* and *STF 1* both provide tables which report age by sex for single years of ages, but *CP-1* also summarizes this data in five-year age intervals. CD-ROM users can employ EXTRACT to calculate their own subtotals, but many users will find the print Reports easier to handle in this regard.

A problem unique to print Reports is the issue of publication thresholds. This restriction affects cross-tabulations by Race and Hispanic Origin in the following publications: *CP-1*, *CP-2*, *CH-1*, and *CH-2*. In tables which provide breakdowns by Race and/or Hispanic Origin, data for a particular subgroup will be omitted if the total number of persons in that subgroup fall below a threshold established by the Bureau. For example, if the reporting threshold for counties were 400 persons, cross-tabulations for Hispanic subgroups would be omitted for counties containing fewer than 400 Hispanic persons. The size of the threshold varies according to Summary Level and topic. For each affected table, the specific threshold is listed in a headnote for the table.

Blanket comparisons between print and CD-ROM formats are difficult to make. In some cases, a CD-ROM File will provide greater detail, while in others, a print Report will offer the better solution. Generally speaking, *STF* databases provide more detailed geographic coverage, while the *CP* and *CH*

print Reports offer greater subject detail and more cross-tabulations. However, as discussed in Chapter 9, this distinction does not always hold true. Some CD-ROM tables offer more detailed response categories than their closest printed counterparts. The best advice one can follow is to choose one format or the other based on the considerations outlined above, then simply plunge in. If the resulting tables do not display data in the exact manner needed, then the user may wish to explore another format.

 Census Tip

Publication thresholds should not be confused with the pre-1990 concept of suppressing data to protect confidentiality. These 1990 thresholds have been established simply to save space in print Reports. The omitted data can be obtained by using the electronic counterparts to the affected print sources. The Bureau did not issue the corresponding electronic products (*STF 2* and *STF 4*) in CD-ROM format, however; they are available on magnetic tape only.

The final step in selecting a particular Census publication is to match the desired geographic Summary Level to the publication which provides that coverage. Sometimes geography is not a major concern because the Bureau tabulates data for the desired Summary Level in many different products. Data at the state and county levels can be found in nearly every major Census publication. In other situations, a particular Summary Level can be found only in one or two specialized products. For example, data at the Tract level appear only in *STF 1A, STF 3A*, or *CPH-3*. Statistics for Congressional Districts of the 103rd and 104th Congress are published in *STF 1D/STF 3D* and in *CPH-4* only. In some cases, geographic coverage is even format-specific. Census figures for ZIP Code Areas can only be found in *STF*

3B; data at the Block level are reported only in *STF 1B*; Block Group statistics are found only in *STF 1A* and *STF 3A*. Most print Reports exclude CCDs, nonfunctioning MCDs, and Places with fewer than 1,000 inhabitants.

A related issue when selecting a specific publication is determining whether to use a nationwide product or a state-specific product. Nationwide products are appropriate when seeking data at the national level, when examining entities which cross the boundaries of a single state (such as certain Metropolitan Areas and American Indian Areas) or when comparing similar entities in different states. Each of the major print Report Titles includes a "United States Summary Volume." The comparable products in CD-ROM format are *STF 1C* and *STF 3C*.

The fastest way to determine which publication is best suited to coverage of a particular Summary Level is to consult a table which compares geographic coverage. A geographic guide to CD-ROM products can be found in Figure 8-2 (in Chapter 8). A corresponding table for print Reports can be seen in Figure 9-2 (in Chapter 9).

Locating a Specific Table.

Once the appropriate publication has been identified, the user must locate a specific table (or tables) in which the needed statistics are presented. This involves the intersection of two factors: the geographic Summary Level and the subject characteristic being sought. The first step in this process is to match the required characteristic to the appropriate terminology used by the Census. This step may not be necessary for certain commonly understood concepts, such as age, Race, sex, or Marital Status. As discussed in Chapters 5 and 7, the Bureau uses specialized terminology unique to the Census. Matching the desired subject to its official Census terminology is often an important step, especially to Census newcomers. Figure 10-2 provides a selective list of specialized Census terms and the general concepts to which they per-

---

Translating Census Language

POPULATION CHARACTERISTICS

Data Sought:	Census Language:
Carpooling	Means of Transportation to Work (general); Private Vehicle Occupancy (specific)
Commuting patterns	Place of Work; Travel Time to Work
Country of birth	Nativity
Dual-income Family	Labor Force Status of Family Members
Employed (Currently)	Labor Force Status (general); Employment Status (specific)
Employed (Previous Year)	Work Status in 1989
Ethnic group	Ancestry
Families with children	Family Type by Presence of Children
Female head of Family	Family Type (general);
Female Householder, No Husband Present	(specific)
Fertility	Children Ever Born
Gay couples	Unmarried Partners
Geographic mobility (Migration patterns)	Residence in 1985
Government employees	Class of Worker
Head of Household	Householder
Homeless persons	Persons in Emergency Shelters; Persons in Visible Street Locations
Immigration	Foreign-Born: Year of Entry
Institutional population	Group Quarters Type
Mother tongue	Language Spoken at Home
Self-employed	Class of Worker
Student employment	School Enrollment & Labor Force Status
White-collar workers	Occupation
Unemployment	Labor Force Status
Welfare recipients	Income Type
Vietnam-era Veteran	Period of Military Service

HOUSING CHARACTERISTICS

Data Sought:	Census Language:
Age of house	Year Structure Built
Bathrooms	Complete Plumbing Facilities
Congregate housing	Meals Included in Rent
Home ownership	Tenure
Housing turnover	Year Householder Moved
Overcrowded housing	Persons per Room
Seasonal housing	Vacancy Status
Size of building	Units in Structure
Utilities Costs	Gross Rent; Monthly Owner Costs

"General" refers to terms which incorporate this concept together with other related characteristics.
"Specific" refers to terminology used for this concept alone.

Figure 10-2

tain. Census words and phrases can sound completely nonsensical, especially when taken out of context. Prime examples are "Children Ever Born," which refers to a woman's lifetime childbearing history, and "Class of Worker," which distinguishes between private and public sector employees.

For certain characteristics, the Bureau has no specific measures, but data users can employ related concepts to locate information. For example, the Bureau does not use the term "Homeless," but the Census does count persons in Emergency Shelters and persons Visible in Street Locations. Combining the two categories provides the closest approximation to a count of homeless persons. Similarly, no Census publications use the phrase "white-collar worker," but researchers can sum various occupational groups to meet their own definition of the term. In some instances, the Bureau enables data users to analyze complex or subjective characteristics by providing a diversity of indicative measurements. The decennial Census does not provide a definition of substandard housing, but a variety of statistics can be used to identify areas with significant housing problems: Housing Units lacking complete plumbing facilities, age of the structure, duration of Vacancy, Boarded-Up Status, and so on.

A complicating factor is the fact that similar characteristics are often grouped together and described under more general terms. For example, the phrase "Work Status in 1989" refers to three specific topics: whether the person was employed or unemployed in the previous year; the average number of weeks an employed person worked in that year; and the "usual" number of hours worked per week.

Two finding tools can be helpful in translating Census terminology: the Table Finding Guides (in print Reports), and the keyword search feature (found in many of the CD-ROM products). For example, the Census tabulates two measures relating to commuters who carpool as a means of travel to work: the total number of workers who

carpool; and a frequency distribution based on number of persons in the carpool. A third, less direct measurement calculates average persons per vehicle, including people who drive alone. All three measurements can be found in *CP-2*, in a table entitled "Geographic Mobility, Commuting, and Veteran Status." Most users would guess that "commuting" might include information about carpooling, but the catchall nature of the table's title might cause confusion. The Table Finding Guide to *CP-2* actually utilizes the term carpooling, making it much simpler to locate the needed table. Under "Economic Characteristics," the user sees a heading for "Commuting," which is further divided into subtopics, including "Means of Transportation and Carpooling."

Carpool data can be found on two separate tables in *STF 3*: "Means of Transportation to Work," which includes the total number of workers who carpool; and "Private Vehicle Occupancy," which shows the frequency distribution by number of riders in the carpool. By scanning the list of tables for *STF 3*, some users would guess that carpooling information might be found under "Means of Transportation to Work," but the meaning of "Private Vehicle Occupancy" is not terribly obvious. However, searching the keyword list for the word "Carpool" will automatically retrieve both these tables.

It helps to understand broad categories of population and housing concepts, as presented in Chapter 7. Population Items are grouped into categories such as Social Characteristics and Economic Characteristics, then subdivided into such groupings as Educational data, Labor Force data, or Income data. Housing Items are classified into such categories as Occupancy, Structural, and Financial Characteristics.

Once a searcher has identified the appropriate Census language, the quest for individual tables can begin. The process is similar whether using print Reports or CD-ROM Files. For both approaches, the user must find a table which covers the needed subject

---

For certain characteristics, the Bureau has no specific measures, but data users can employ related concepts to locate information.

Two finding tools can be helpful in translating Census terminology: the Table Finding Guides (in print Reports), and the keyword search feature (found in many of the CD-ROM products).

Each CD-ROM table focuses on an individual topic, while a single table in a print Report typically covers a variety of related characteristics.

matter for the required Summary Level. Geographic terminology plays a critical role here as well, which is why it so important for Census users to develop a firm understanding of key geographic concepts.

In the case of print Reports, the best way to link a subject table to the needed Summary Level is to use the Table Finding Guides found at the beginning of every Report. Because each table focuses on a particular Summary Level, the Table Finding Guides link specific population or housing characteristics to the sought-after geography. The final step is to identify the value for the specific geographic entity.

In the case of CD-ROM tables, the process is similar, but more directed. The GO soft-

ware forces users to select an appropriate Summary Level before any tables can be viewed. Next, the software prompts them to select a specific geographic entity from within that Summary Level. Finally, GO displays a complete list of tables available for that entity. Most of the CD-ROM products include a keyword search feature, which allows the user to look for specific tables by topic. Some of the earlier Files (notably the *STF 1A* discs) do not offer this feature, so users must scan through the complete list of tables to locate the appropriate data.

The other noticeable difference between CD-ROM products and print Reports is that each CD-ROM table focuses on an individual topic, while a single table in a

Q&A

What if the required information is not found by following these steps?

The decennial Census cannot tabulate every conceivable variation of the statistics it gathers. Sometimes users must accept that the data they seek is simply not available in the form they desire. One recourse is to be willing to use a different breakdown. Useful information may be available in a similar form, or may be reported for a different Summary Level. The following options may also help in certain situations.

1. Determine whether a specialized publication may help where standard ones do not. Sources of detailed data include the *Special Tabulation on Aging*, the *Equal Employment Opportunity File*, the various *Subject Reports* or *SSTF* discs, and the many *CPH-L* printouts.
2. Calculate your own values from published data. Sometimes the required figures can be obtained by adding, subtracting, or dividing other numbers. For example, a median figure may not be reported, but you can calculate a mean value by dividing the aggregate figure by the relevant number of observations. Numerous aggregate tables can be found in the *STF* products on CD-ROM. Be careful to make appropriate calculations, however. Always consult

documentation or speak to experts to ensure you are utilizing the proper numbers.

3. Use another characteristic as a surrogate measure. For example, Income is not tabulated at the Block level, but Housing Value and Contract Rent are. Therefore, financial housing characteristics might serve as appropriate indicators of Household Income.
4. Hire someone to generate customized tables from *STF 2* or *STF 4*.
5. Consider diskette or magnetic tape products from the Special Tabulations Program. Although you may not possess the in-house resources to utilize these Files, you should be able to locate someone who can. If an *STP* File contains the type of data you require, the results may be well worth the extra effort or expense.
6. Look into the possibility of calculating your own cross-tabulated estimates using the *PUMS Files*.
7. Ask experts at the Bureau, its Regional Offices, the State Data Centers, or others sources introduced earlier. Needed data may be available in a source unknown to you, or experts may suggest a viable alternative to the specific measure you seek.

print Report typically covers a variety of related characteristics. For this reason, locating specific tables in CD-ROM products may be easier. The title of each print table is usually more general than its electronic counterpart. Let's return to the example of "Work Status in 1989," described earlier. *CP-2* contains a series of tables entitled "Additional Labor Force Characteristics and Veterans Status." The table is repeated ten times. Each iteration utilizes the same table layout, but covers a different combination of geographic Summary Level and Race/Hispanic Origin Universe. The table layout incorporates the following six topics, identified by separate sideheads in the table stub.

▶ Labor Force Status of Family Members
▶ School Enrollment and Labor Force Status
▶ Class of Worker
▶ Work Status in 1989
▶ Workers in Family
▶ Veteran Status

Each of these "subtables" can be located fairly easily through the Table Finding Guide located in the front of *CP-2*. In contrast, *STF 3* presents these six topics in a series of individual tables. For example, "Work Status in 1989" can be found in Table P75, which indicates whether the person was employed or unemployed; P76 cross-tabulates Usual Hours Worked by Total Weeks Worked. Data in both tables are broken down by sex.

Step-by-Step through the Search: A Case Study

Tracing a specific query through the search process may be the best means of putting this topic in perspective. As an example, consider someone who requires data on Household and Family Income for persons age 60 or older. In particular, the researcher needs to know the median Income for Households headed by a person in that age group. Furthermore, he would like to see these figures broken down by Income by Race, by His-

panic Origin, and by Household or Family type. The researcher would also like to know how many Households in this category fall below the Poverty Level. Data are needed at the county level for selected counties in Georgia.

Answers to the preliminary steps are fairly straightforward. The decennial Census does include a Questionnaire Item dealing with Income. It is likely that the Bureau tabulates this data for Households and Families, and that median values are presented. The Census also tabulates data pertaining to Poverty. It remains to be seen whether statistics are broken down by age of Householder, but many Census tables focus on characteristics of the elderly population, so the chances are good. Whether such figures are cross-tabulated by Race, Hispanic Origin, and Family type is uncertain. Virtually all Census Items are reported at the county level, so geography should not be a problem.

Income characteristics are asked on the Long Form Questionnaire, so the user must limit the search to sample publications. Income is a population question, so it can be found in *CP-2* as well as *STF 3*. Since the researcher seeks fairly detailed subject breakdowns, *CPH-5* (a summary publication) will probably be too general to be useful. The user is unsure whether the print Report or the CD-ROM would be the better source, but *CP-2* may be more likely to provide the types of cross-tabulations required. Because he needs data at the county level, any of the designated publications will meet this requirement, including *CP-2*, *STF 3A* (the state-specific disc for Georgia), and *STF 3C* (the nationwide File). Where CP-2 is concerned, the state-specific Report for Georgia is probably the better bet because the United States Summary Report is less likely to provide the subject detail needed, even though it provides data at the county level.

Translating the request into appropriate Census terminology is fairly simple. The user needs median Household Income and median Family Income, as well as statistics on

As an example, consider someone who requires data on Household and Family Income for persons age 60 or older.

Virtually all Census Items are reported at the county level, so geography should not be a problem.

Poverty Status. The key to finding the correct tables lies in the fact that the Householder must be age 60 or older.

For the sake of comparison, the user decides to examine *STF 3A* as well as *CP-2*. After loading the *STF 3A* disc for Georgia, the user searches by keyword for the term "Median." GO displays the following three tables:

P80A   Median Household Income
P107A   Median Family Income
P110A   Median Nonfamily Household
        Income

In all three cases, a single value is given for the entire population. No medians are calculated by age of Householder or Family type.

A second keyword search for the term "poverty" yields better results. Eleven tables are shown, including the following six containing age-specific breakdowns:

P117   Poverty Status by Age
P118   Poverty Status by Sex by Age
P119   Poverty Status by Race by Age
P120   Poverty Status by Age for
        Hispanic Persons
P122   Poverty Status by Age by
        Household Type
P127   Poverty Status by Age of House-
        holder by Household Type

Table P117 presents data for three relevant age groupings: persons 60 to 64 years of age; 65 to 74; and 75 or older. The remaining five tables provide totals for the latter two groupings, but not for persons age 60-64. Also note that Table 127 is the only one which focuses on age of Householder, rather than the age of all individuals in the Household, but it doesn't include the entire age range needed. In other words, none of the six provides Poverty data in the exact form the user requires.

On the off-chance that median data were somehow missed in the first keyword search, the user tries a third approach, using "Income" as a keyword. This search retrieves no less than 63 tables, including the 11 Poverty

tables and the three median Income tables uncovered previously. A quick scan of the list reveals only two new possibilities. Table P86 is entitled "Age of Householder by Household Income." Table P88 has the same title, but covers Hispanic Households only. In both cases, several Income intervals are shown for various age groups, including the 65-74 category and the 75 or older range. No median values are presented.

In an effort to be thorough (or as an act of desperation), the searcher tries several other keyword approaches, including "Elderly," "Older," and "Age of Householder," all to no avail. Despite the impressive array of Income tables found in *STF 3A*, none offer the exact breakdowns and summaries the user needs. Perhaps the print Report will offer better results.

The first step in using *CP-2* is to consult the Table Finding Guide. Under "Economic Characteristics," an entry is found for Income. According to the chart, median Income in 1989 by selected characteristics is tabulated at the county level in Tables 148, 157, 162, and 165. The first of these provides data for all persons, while the remaining three focus on specific Races and Hispanic groupings. Before leaving the Table Finding Guide, the searcher notices another category under Economic Characteristics, labeled "Older Population (60 years and over)." It appears that *CP-2* presents specific data on Income and Poverty Status for this age group. The tables in question are identified as 150 and 159.

A quick look at Table 159 shows that *CP-2* does indeed provide Income data for married-couple Families in this age group, as well as for elderly Persons Living Alone. Figures are broken down by Race and Hispanic Origin, but only if the total figures meet the Bureau's reporting thresholds. For example, statistics for Chatham County are broken out for White, Black, Asian/Pacific Islander, and two Hispanic categories, while data for Charlton County shows only White and Black. Age groupings are broken down into

Despite the impressive array of Income tables found in *STF 3A*, none offer the exact breakdowns and summaries the user needs.

and 75 and over. For each category, the table calculates the percentage of that population which falls below the 1989 Poverty Level. Unfortunately, Table 159 is deficient in several respects. First, it does not provide median Income figures. The table presents frequency distributions by Income intervals, but it provides no way for the user to determine median values. Second, it tabulates Income data only for certain types of Households and Families, namely married-couple Families and single-person Households. These two categories account for the majority of living arrangements for elderly Householders, but they ignore other types of Nonfamily Households (such as two elderly nonrelatives living together) as well as Family Households which do not consist of married couples (such as an unmarried elderly Householder whose adult child lives with him or her). Table 150 presents an identical table layout, but for all elderly persons regardless of Race or Hispanic Origin.

Returning to the more general tables which provide median Income for selected characteristics (Tables 148, 157, 162, and 165) offers little help. These tables show median Household Income for one category of elderly only: persons age 65 or older living alone. The various tables present this data by sex, Race, and Hispanic Origin, but once again it is not exactly what the searcher requires.

At this point, the researcher could accept what has been found so far, which includes a diversity of statistics for Income and Poverty Status of the elderly population. But, convinced that more specific numbers must be available somewhere, he chooses not to give up.

The next logical step is to determine whether another, more specialized Census publication might provide additional data. In this instance, the answer is, "Yes." A CD-ROM product called the *Special Tabulation on Aging* provides all manner of detailed breakdowns and cross-tabulations for the elderly population, including those characteristics the user seeks.

The next logical step is to determine whether another, more specialized Census publication might provide additional data.

For print Reports and CD-ROM Files alike, the beginning tables in each publication usually present summary data, including percentages, median values, and other meaningful comparisons.

Search Tips

A variety of general rules can aid in Census searching. First, the more detailed the information, the more likely it was asked of the 17% sample and not the full population. Second, the smaller the geographic area, the less data will be available. For example, more will be published about Florida than about Dade County, and much more will be available on Dade County than on Census Blocks within the city of Miami. An important reason for this deals with confidentiality issues; another reason has to do with sampling error. The smaller the sample, the less reliable the estimates it generates, so data may not be tabulated at smaller Summary Levels.

An important point to remember when using print publications is that the table numbers in each Report will be the same from state to state. If Table 24 of *General Population Characteristics* for Texas contains "General Characteristics by Spanish Origin," then Table 24 in the California report will be the same. However, this is not true of the United States Summary Volumes, which have a table-numbering sequence of their own. A similar relationship can be found in major CD-ROM products, but numbering for state-specific Files is actually the same as those for the United States Summary discs. Table numbering is identical for every *STF 1A* and *STF 1C* disc, regardless of the state or the Summary Level. Likewise, table numbers in *STF 3A* and *STF 3C* are always the same.

Many other tips can be given, but only a few will be mentioned to round out this discussion. For print Reports and CD-ROM Files alike, the beginning tables in each publication usually present summary data, including percentages, median values, and other meaningful comparisons. As discussed in Chapters 8 and 9, most Census publications utilize the same table format (or data matrix) to display tabulations for different segments of the population (different Universes) or for different geographic Summary Levels. Becoming familiar with the data elements of frequently repeated tables will cut down on searching time.

Finally, it helps to know that some Census characteristics are equal to others by definition. As shown in Chapter 5, the number of Households in a particular geographic entity is always equal to the number of Occupied Housing Units, which is equal to the number of Householders. Tautologies such as this can save time when you can't seem to find data one way but it is readily available in another form. This type of exercise is good for another purpose: it strengthens the user's knowledge of Census concepts and what they measure. By corroborating equivalent data which is presented on another table in different form, researchers new to the Census can make sure they understand important conceptual relationships.

Helpful Reference Tools

Census publications, whether issued as print Reports or CD-ROM products, contain their own helpful guides, indexes, and appendices. For the casual seeker of Census data, simpler, more basic resources may be all the user requires. Numerous commercial publications have been created which summarize key statistics from the decennial Census. Such resources fall outside the scope of *Understanding the Census*, but two summary publications from the Bureau itself will be described in brief fashion: the *Statistical Abstract of the United States* and the *County and City Data Book*. Detailed indexes to 1990 Census publications are less common. One such guide, designed as a companion to *Understanding the Census*, is introduced below.

Statistical Abstract of the United States

This annual compendium is probably the Census Bureau's best known and most frequently used publication. It provides data on many more topics besides the decennial

Census. Other subjects include vital statistics, health, immigration, law enforcement, education, politics, the economy, and industry. Most of the information is provided by federal agencies, but nongovernment sources are utilized also. The first section of the *Statistical Abstract* deals with population issues, and includes summary tables from the 1990 Census. Although most data are presented at the national level, some regional and state information can be found, and a few tables present population counts for large cities. Most tabulations provide both current and historical data. Each table cites the titles of the publications where the information was found, so researchers may consult the original source for greater detail. Supplementary sections include a series of state rankings and updated estimates of Metropolitan Area population. For users seeking decennial data at the national level, or looking for convenient historical comparisons, the Statistical Abstract is highly recommended. A CD-ROM version of this popular resource is available.

The Bureau also published a useful companion to the *Statistical Abstract*, called *Historical Statistics of the United States: Colonial Times to 1970*. Although the *Statistical Abstract* has been published since 1878, data in each year's edition are not necessarily comparable over long periods of time. *Historical Statistics* presents information in a single publication, with footnotes to each table indicating when definitions and methodologies have changed. A narrative history of each time series explains when data were first collected and how. A subject index to the tables and an index by time period are included.

County and City Data Book.

Another excellent compendium of summary statistics is the *County and City Data Book*, published by the Census Bureau every five years. The 1994 edition contains numerous Items from the 1990 Census, including Income, median housing Value, journey to

It helps to know that some Census characteristics are equal to others by definition.

The first section of the *Statistical Abstract* deals with population issues, and includes summary tables from the 1990 Census.

Another excellent compendium of summary statistics is the *County and City Data Book*, published by the Census Bureau every five years.

work data, and veteran status. Like the *Statistical Abstract*, the *Data Book* includes numbers from many other government agencies as well. Statistics are presented for counties and for Incorporated Places with 1990 population of 25,000 or greater. A separate section provides briefer information (1990 total population, median Household Income, and per capita Income) for Places with population of 2,500 or more. The *County and City Data Book* also provides several useful supplemental features, such as county outline maps for the 50 states, and a series of ranking tables for counties and cities. It offers convenient, single-volume access to a variety of 1990 Census measures at the county and city levels, and is also available in CD-ROM format.

The *County and City Data Book* also provides several useful supplemental features, such as county outline maps for the 50 states, and a series of ranking tables for counties and cities.

Subject Index to the 1990 Census of Population and Housing.

This resource was created to help users of the 1990 Census locate specific tables within the Bureau's major printed Reports and CD-ROM Files. It consists of three parts: a guide to tables in the print Reports; a set of indexes to *STF 1* and *STF 3* on CD-ROM; and a brief glossary of key Census terms. The index to print Reports includes a Composite Table-Finding Guide to every 1990 Census Report issued through July, 1994. This massive index provides a single alphabetical list of every subject variable cited in the individual Table Finding Guides published in the Census Reports themselves. Each subject is then subdivided by Summary Level. For the sake of consistency and to present information as clearly as possible, the Composite Guide corrects discrepancies in terminology and formatting found in the original Table Finding Guides. In the case of certain highly detailed special Reports, the Composite Guide summarizes some of the more specific topics.

The section dealing with CD-ROM databases includes an alphabetical list of tables by title, a numerical list of tables and their content, an index by subject matter, and an index by Universe of coverage. The *Subject*

Simply stated, sample data represent estimates, which are really only educated guesses.

Index to the 1990 Census of Population and Housing was compiled by librarians Cynthia Cornelius, Michael Lavin, and Jane Weintrop. It was published by Epoch Books in 1996.

Sources of Error in Census Publications

Despite the widely-acknowledged expertise of the Census Bureau in designing questionnaires, developing sample surveys, and conducting the Census, users must be aware of many potential errors and limitations inherent in Census tabulations. How accurate is the 1990 Census? Put another way, for any statistic reported in the Census, how closely does that number represent a "true value?" Whether the characteristic is a sample Item or a complete-count Item, many factors can affect the answer to that question. The following sections focus on three types of concerns affecting the accuracy and reliability of Census results: sampling methods; coverage errors, including Census undercount; and miscellaneous sources of nonsampling error, such as erroneous information supplied by respondents.

Sampling Error

Understanding the Census has consistently stressed the difference between complete-count Items and sample Items, whether talking about the Census Questionnaire itself, or tabulations presented in individual Census products. The reason for this emphasis, aside from the fact the publications tend to be organized according to complete-count or sample Items, is that sample data are subject to sampling error. Simply stated, sample data represent estimates, which are really only educated guesses. The accuracy of those estimates is dependent on how closely the composition of the sample reflects the reality of the total population. Generally speaking, the smaller the sample size (as a percentage of the total population), the less reliable the estimates it generates. The following sections discuss the Bureau's sampling methodology and explain how users can determine sampling rates for individual geographic entities, as well as how to calculate sampling variability for specific characteristics reported for those entities.

Sample Design

Only a small portion of the population receives the Long-Form Questionnaire, but some of the nation's most important and detailed population and housing characteristics are obtained from this sample. The Bureau utilizes a variable sampling scheme, based on the population size of the area surveyed. For the 1990 Census, approximately 17.7 million Housing Units received the Long-Form Questionnaire. In Governmental Units with estimated 1988 populations of 2,500 people or less, the sampling rate was one-out-of-two Housing Units. These included less populated counties, Incorporated Places, and MCDs which serve as general-purpose governments. Outside of these entities, the basic sampling area was the Census Tract or Block Numbering Area. Here, if the Tract or BNA contained a pre-Census population of fewer than 2,000 people, it was sampled at a rate of one-in-six. If it had a pre-Census population of 2,000 or more people, the rate was one-in-eight. People living in Group Quarters were sampled at a rate of one-in-six regardless of the population of the locality in which they lived.

The Bureau sampled Housing Units in American Indian/Alaska Native Areas according to the same criteria, except that population thresholds were not based on the total number of inhabitants, but on the number of American Indians or Alaska Natives living within the Area. Furthermore, pre-Census population figures for American Indian/Alaska Native Areas were taken from the 1980 Census, because no 1988 population estimates were available for these Areas.

> # NEW IN '90
>
> In 1980, 19% of all Housing Units received a sample Questionnaire. In 1980, the overall sampling rate was reduced to approximately 17%, based on limitations imposed by the U.S. Office of Management and Budget.

After the Bureau processed completed Long-Form Questionnaires, estimates were generated by assigning weights to each person and Housing Unit. Simplistically stated, if the Questionnaire came from a one-in-six sampling area, each person's responses were multiplied by six. If the Questionnaire was received from a one-in-two area, the responses were multiplied by two. (The actual weights used for individual localities were more complicated than portrayed here, based on a location-specific ratio of the total population to the number of Long-Forms received.) This variable rate increased accuracy in less populous areas, and decreased costs and respondent burden in areas of greater population density.

Although the Bureau utilized uniform sampling rates of one-in-two, one-in-six, and one-in-eight, the actual percentage of completed Long-Form Questionnaires varies across geographic entities. Discrepancies occur for a variety of reasons, including the impact of Group Quarters in a given locality and the manner in which sampling areas are defined. Every sample publication from the 1990 Census includes tables which show the specific sampling rates for every geographic entity contained in that publication. In print Reports, these tables can be found at the back of each Volume. For example, in *CPH-5*, Table 19 shows sampling rates for persons and Table 21 shows sampling rates for Housing Units. Similar tables are also provided in relevant CD-ROM Files. In *STF 3A*

For the 1990 Census, approximately 17.7 million Housing Units received the Long-Form Questionnaire.

Every sample publication from the 1990 Census includes tables which show the specific sampling rates for every geographic entity contained in that publication.

and *STF 3C*, they can be found in Table P3A (for persons) and Table H3A (for Housing Units). The overall sampling rates for the United States were 15.5% for persons (38.6 million people) and 16.0% for Housing Units (16.3 million Units).

Figure 10-3, which reproduces several related tables from the *STF 3C* Record for the city of Lackawanna, New York, illustrates how sample rates are calculated. Table P2, entitled "Unweighted Sample Count of Persons," tabulates the number of persons in Lackawanna from whom the Bureau received completed Long-Form Questionnaires. Table P3, "100-Percent Count of Persons," tabulates the actual number of persons enumerated in the Census (the complete-count value taken from *STF 1C*). Table 3A, representing the sampling rate, was calculated by dividing the value in Table P2 by the value in Table P3 (2753 ÷ 20,585). What does Table P1 present? This is the Bureau's estimate of the total population, based on the sample. For reasons which will be explained in a moment, sometimes the number in Table P1 equals the value found in P3, but sometimes it does not. As Figure 10-3, shows, the same relationships are presented in corresponding H tables for Housing Units.

Census Tip

When searching for complete-count data, always use a complete-count publication, even if estimates can be found more readily in a sample publication.

To reinforce the difference between Census estimates and complete-count values, consider the population statistics shown in Figure 10-4. The table, created by using EXTRACT, focuses on MCDs (towns) in Dutchess County, New York. It compares complete-count and sample data for two characteristics: total population and number of married-couple Families. For 12 out of the 20 towns in the county, estimates generated from the sample survey match the actual

---

Sampling Percentages from *STF 3C*

1990 Census Of Population And Housing *Summary Tape File* 3C
040 New York
161 Lackawanna city

Table P1: PERSONS
Universe: Persons
Total   20,585

Table P2: UNWEIGHTED SAMPLE COUNT OF PERSONS
Universe: Persons
Total   2,753

Table P3: 100-PERCENT COUNT OF PERSONS
Universe: Persons
Total   20,585

Table P3A: PERCENT OF PERSONS IN SAMPLE
Universe: Persons
Total   13.40

Table H1: HOUSING UNITS
Universe: Housing units
Total   8,986

Table H2: UNWEIGHTED SAMPLE COUNT OF HOUSING UNITS
Universe: Housing units
Total   1,188

Table H3: 100-PERCENT COUNT OF HOUSING UNITS
Universe: Housing units
Total   8,986

Table H3A: PERCENT OF HOUSING UNITS IN SAMPLE
Universe: Housing units
Total   13.20

Figure 10-3

100% enumeration. In the remaining eight counties, the values differ; in three cases, the estimate is slightly larger than the corresponding complete-count value, while in the remaining five, the estimate is smaller. In all eight cases, the discrepancy between the estimate and the complete-count figure is less than one percent (ranging from .05% to .89%). The differences between the estimates and complete-count values for married-couple Families are much more pronounced. Here, all 20 towns show a discrepancy between the two statistics. Furthermore, the amount of disparity is generally higher than it was for total population. The results shown here for Dutchess County are

COMPARING COMPLETE-COUNT AND SAMPLE VALUES

1990 Census STF 3A, File 01, Tables P1 - P13
Dutchess County, NY

STF300->ANPSADPI	P0010001	P0030001	POPDIF	MAR-EST	MAR100	MARDIF
Amenia town	5241	5195	0.89	912	889	2.59
Beekman town	10392	10447	-0.53	2078	1987	4.58
Clinton town	3760	3760	0.00	969	926	4.64
Dover town	7792	7778	0.18	1468	1466	0.14
East Fishkill town	22101	22101	0.00	5322	5273	0.93
Fishkill town	17655	17655	0.00	3326	3301	0.76
Hyde Park town	21219	21230	-0.05	4538	4397	3.21
La Grange town	13346	13274	0.54	3305	3276	0.89
Milan town	1895	1895	0.00	462	455	1.54
North East town	2918	2918	0.00	626	641	-2.34
Pawling town	5947	5947	0.00	1397	1392	0.36
Pine Plains town	2287	2287	0.00	502	488	2.87
Pleasant Valley town	8063	8063	0.00	1951	1897	2.85
Poughkeepsie town	40117	40143	-0.07	8523	8339	2.21
Red Hook town	9565	9565	0.00	1956	1950	0.31
Rhinebeck town	7558	7558	0.00	1530	1553	-1.48
Stanford town	3495	3495	0.00	826	825	0.12
Union Vale town	3577	3577	0.00	851	868	-1.96
Wappinger town	25973	26008	-0.14	6107	5934	2.92
Washington town	4474	4479	-0.11	1005	1001	0.40
Dutchess County	259462	259462	0.00	54908	53635	2.37

Key to column headings:

ANPSADPI– AREA NAME – /PSAD Term/Part Indicator
P0010001 Persons: Total (based on sample)
P0030001 Persons: Total (100-percent count)
POPDIF Percent Variance, Complete-Count Population and Sample
MAR-EST Sample Data, Married-Couple Families
MAR100 Complete-Count Data, Married-Couple Families
MARDIF Percent Variance, Complete-Count Married and Sample Married

Figure 10-4

not atypical by any means; such discrepancies hold true for County Subdivisions in all 50 states.

 Census Tip

Corresponding estimates in population and housing tables (for example, number of Households with a Hispanic Householder) may not match because weights for population Items are assigned independently from weights for housing Items.

Determining Sampling Variability

Sample data from the Long-Form Questionnaire are only estimates of what their actual values would have been had the Census Bureau enumerated the entire population for the characteristic being estimated. How much will such an estimate vary from its "true value" (i.e., the complete-count data)? As Figure 10-4 has shown, for Items which appear on the Short-Form Questionnaire, we can calculate the variance of these values from their corresponding estimates because we actually know both numbers. In the case of Long-Form Items, of course, a complete-count figure is not available. We can only

Q&A

When comparing corresponding statistics from complete-count and sample publications, why are the results so inconsistent?

As Figure 10-4 shows, sometimes the figures match, and sometimes they don't. Why? The answer lies in the way the Census Bureau calculates its estimates. Before assigning weights to each response on the completed Long-Form Questionnaires, the Bureau divided the nation into 54,000 "Weighting Areas," based on aggregations of Census Blocks. When creating these Weighting Areas, the Bureau strove to conform to local governmental boundaries, but this was not always possible. One reason the boundaries might not match is because Block Groups and Tracts can cross the borders of local Governmental Units. A second reason deals with sampling concerns: in order to produce reliable estimates, each Weighting Area had to contain a minimum population of 400 persons. The sampling rate for counties and Incorporated Places with fewer than 2,500 persons was one out of every two Housing Units. This means that if a Place had a total population of fewer than 800 persons, the number of persons in the sample would probably be less than 400. In these instances, the Place had to be combined with an adjoining Governmental Unit to create a larger Weighting Area.

A second factor affecting the outcome is that, when constructing its estimates, the Bureau combined different categories of related characteristics if the number of responses in the sample was too small to adequately represent the total population. Again, in the interests of reliability, it was necessary to add certain subgroups together if they were two small to stand alone. For example, unless a particular Weighting Area contained a minimum of 150 Black persons (as determined by the complete-count enumeration) and at least ten Blacks in the sample, and unless the ratio of sample responses to total count was sufficiently large, Black respondents would be combined with another Race in the sample.

1990 Weighting Areas were constructed in such a way that the Bureau always controlled the following two sample characteristics to the corresponding values from the complete-count enumeration: total population count and total number of Housing Units. In other words, if the boundaries of a particular Governmental Unit match those of its Weighting Area, the sample value for total population will equal the 100% count. The same will be true of total Housing Units. Discrepancies seen between values in the first two columns of Figure 10-4 are caused solely by the fact that the boundaries of a town differed from those of the Weighting Area of which it is a part. For characteristics other than total population and number of Housing Units, the likelihood that the estimated value differs from the complete-count value will be much higher, as Figure 10-4 illustrates.

So why does the Bureau bother to include estimates of complete-count Items in its sample publications? Wouldn't it be less confusing if sample Items were the only characteristics shown in sample publications? The answer is that certain 100% Items are needed so users can calculate percentages and make other meaningful comparisons. In order to calculate the percentage of Households where a language other than English is spoken in the home, a user must know the tabulations for Language Spoken at Home (a sample Item) as well as those for number of Households (a complete-count Item). Furthermore, in order to ensure that a proper comparison is being made, the numerator and denominator must both be estimates, even though the enumerated value is available for total number of Households.

guess how much the estimate varies from an actual enumerated value. However, statisticians tell us we can determine the probability that our estimate lies within a specified range of numbers. The key to determining these numeric ranges is a statistic known as the "standard error." Large groups of numbers exhibit particular characteristics whose probabilities can be calculated by mathematical formula. One such probability is that we can be 67% confident that the true value falls within one standard error on either side of the estimated value. If we want to be more confident, the range of values increases. For

Table 6. Employment Status and Journey to Work Characteristics: 1990 — Con.

[Data based on sample and subject to sampling variability; see text. For definitions of terms and meanings of symbols, see text]

State County Place and [In Selected States] County Subdivision	Persons 16 years and over — Total	Female	Labor force: Percent in labor force — Total	Female	Civilian labor force — Total	Percent unemployed	Workers — Total	Means of transportation to work: Percent using car, truck, or van	Percent in carpools	Percent using public transportation	Worked in 1989 — Total	Worked 40 or more weeks in 1989 — Total	Usually worked 35 or more hours per week, 50 to 52 weeks	Females with own children under 6 years — Total	Percent in labor force	Own children under 6 years in families and subfamilies, all parents in household in labor force
PLACE AND COUNTY SUBDIVISION — Con.																
Ira town, Cayuga County	1 432	725	69.2	62.5	989	6.2	914	89.9	19.3	—	1 062	801	589	108	54.6	94
Irondequoit town, Monroe County	43 277	23 616	59.7	51.4	25 808	3.7	24 319	93.7	11.2	2.3	27 999	22 258	15 547	2 560	62.1	2 052
Irondequoit CDP, Monroe County	43 225	23 585	59.7	51.4	25 767	3.7	24 298	93.7	11.2	2.3	27 958	22 217	15 524	2 552	62.0	2 046
Irvington village, Westchester County	4 952	2 652	68.8	57.7	3 406	4.0	3 193	70.2	6.1	21.3	3 763	2 860	2 147	357	50.4	245
Ischua town, Cattaraugus County	604	299	62.7	54.8	379	12.1	315	94.3	14.3	1.0	422	290	217	37	67.6	34
Islandia village, Suffolk County	2 216	1 224	75.1	67.7	1 664	4.7	1 523	92.3	7.4	5.3	1 784	1 426	996	147	59.2	83
Island Park village, Nassau County	4 012	2 197	59.9	45.3	2 402	4.3	2 264	73.4	5.3	20.1	2 639	2 077	1 524	331	36.3	130
Islip CDP, Suffolk County	14 846	7 748	69.2	59.2	10 253	4.5	9 546	89.6	11.9	7.1	11 005	8 918	6 359	1 352	49.9	841
Islip town, Suffolk County	232 298	119 687	69.5	59.9	161 384	5.0	150 141	88.7	12.1	7.1	171 005	134 706	98 222	18 491	48.4	11 938
Islip Terrace CDP, Suffolk County	4 249	2 190	74.9	66.2	3 179	5.6	2 948	90.1	9.8	6.3	3 253	2 655	1 986	370	61.1	286
Italy town, Yates County	799	399	67.5	58.9	539	5.2	490	94.3	21.2	—	587	437	274	56	67.9	69
Ithaca city, Tompkins County	26 977	13 030	51.0	51.0	13 762	4.9	12 708	42.9	8.1	5.9	22 046	8 996	4 610	818	54.0	482
Ithaca town, Tompkins County	15 269	8 217	55.2	49.3	8 412	3.3	7 996	68.8	11.3	3.4	12 105	6 459	3 564	845	52.8	503
Jackson town, Washington County	1 173	595	65.5	56.1	768	8.1	695	85.8	17.7	1.2	857	624	421	103	52.4	66
Jamesport CDP, Suffolk County	1 191	627	64.1	56.3	763	3.4	720	85.7	5.0	2.8	811	599	421	49	34.7	22
Jamestown city, Chautauqua County	26 594	14 536	60.5	50.7	16 039	8.1	14 515	86.9	16.6	2.9	16 759	12 811	8 420	2 342	57.6	1 906
Jamestown West CDP, Chautauqua County	2 210	1 192	56.8	45.0	1 255	7.0	1 159	92.8	8.7	.7	1 399	1 110	772	149	47.0	111
Jasper town, Steuben County	849	406	61.2	47.5	520	10.2	460	77.2	12.2	.2	548	423	331	83	34.9	32
Java town, Wyoming County	1 628	806	65.7	51.2	1 068	7.1	970	88.2	11.2	.2	1 155	857	584	148	48.6	91
Jay town, Essex County	1 736	916	61.1	47.8	1 061	10.8	910	89.5	19.6	—	1 190	906	664	130	44.6	76
Jefferson town, Schoharie County	923	460	55.1	47.8	509	5.7	469	85.1	11.7	2.6	559	409	279	78	44.9	42
Jefferson Heights CDP, Greene County	1 252	736	46.5	32.3	582	3.8	539	90.2	15.6	2.2	674	520	420	104	61.5	91
Jefferson Valley-Yorktown CDP, Westchester County	11 048	5 843	67.0	57.7	7 401	3.6	7 041	87.4	10.1	7.8	8 022	6 449	4 594	769	60.1	677
Jeffersonville village, Sullivan County	405	215	50.6	45.1	203	1.5	202	82.2	18.3	13.7	212	171	133	19	78.9	25
Jericho CDP, Nassau County	10 579	5 434	48.4	56.9	7 239	2.6	6 946	80.5	10.4	13.7	7 855	7 248	4 564	778	42.8	338
Jerusalem town, Yates County	2 976	1 660	60.3	50.4	1 795	3.5	1 700	76.9	13.4	—	2 176	1 499	901	177	62.1	143
Jewett town, Greene County	753	376	58.0	47.1	437	8.5	393	88.8	9.9	1.8	507	358	211	52	65.4	51
Johnsburg town, Warren County	1 813	947	63.7	54.3	1 154	10.3	1 005	88.9	13.1	—	1 234	834	528	136	64.0	108
Johnson City village, Broome County	14 002	7 657	58.4	50.7	8 183	5.1	7 629	84.1	8.4	5.4	8 887	6 952	4 776	868	58.4	690
Johnstown city, Fulton County	7 077	3 890	62.5	53.0	4 401	8.5	3 929	88.2	13.2	1.7	4 641	3 530	2 485	516	57.6	405
Johnstown town, Fulton County	5 055	2 621	62.8	50.4	3 165	6.4	2 904	93.9	14.9	.8	3 532	2 617	1 709	348	49.7	223
Jordan village, Onondaga County	968	515	64.6	57.5	623	4.7	580	93.3	12.6	1.2	677	500	360	92	62.0	87
Junius town, Seneca County	1 009	501	71.1	60.7	714	7.1	650	90.2	7.8	.6	744	554	429	83	61.4	86
Keene town, Essex County	710	404	54.9	45.8	383	4.4	359	83.6	7.5	—	420	316	199	45	64.4	33
Keeseville village, Clinton [Essex County]	1 314	695	61.3	52.2	796	7.3	726	87.1	14.5	.7	880	648	474	101	60.4	73
Clinton County	718	387	61.0	52.5	433	9.2	382	90.6	20.7	.5	480	351	259	52	67.3	34
Essex County	596	308	61.7	51.9	363	5.0	344	83.1	7.6	.9	400	297	215	49	53.1	39
Kendall town, Orleans County	1 965	953	72.2	65.1	1 418	9.6	1 244	99.3	16.9	—	1 446	1 165	847	207	75.8	211
Kenmore village, Erie County	13 523	7 480	66.7	59.1	9 022	3.6	8 566	90.8	11.1	5.7	9 601	7 565	5 226	1 090	64.1	879
Kensington village, Nassau County	886	488	64.3	54.1	570	3.0	543	67.2	11.6	22.1	630	474	336	53	52.8	36
Kent town, Putnam County	9 897	5 019	75.0	66.1	7 413	3.7	7 002	91.5	12.0	4.5	7 814	6 196	4 383	942	59.2	745
Kerhonkson CDP, Ulster County	1 289	694	63.0	49.9	794	5.2	728	88.7	13.0	.7	846	659	372	78	33.3	28
Kiantone town, Chautauqua County	1 014	509	60.7	55.5	615	3.0	581	91.9	5.5	—	659	556	398	71	59.2	58
Kinderhook town, Columbia County	1 017	560	64.8	55.5	659	3.7	626	85.1	14.2	3.7	728	530	352	70	64.3	72
Kinderhook village, Columbia County	6 179	3 252	68.0	58.6	4 194	3.0	4 014	91.3	12.8	2.2	4 436	3 466	2 409	497	65.0	428
Kingsbury town, Washington County	9 045	4 769	66.0	59.0	5 929	8.5	5 305	92.3	13.0	1.7	6 405	4 793	3 315	805	71.3	708
Kings Park CDP, Suffolk County	14 578	7 523	61.2	54.5	8 911	5.5	8 230	88.1	9.6	8.0	9 471	7 208	5 232	753	46.3	539
Kings Point village, Nassau County	4 083	1 830	51.7	41.5	2 098	2.0	1 997	68.0	9.7	22.8	2 733	1 784	1 208	174	37.4	69
Kingston city, Ulster County	18 482	10 130	62.6	54.2	11 547	5.6	10 725	85.3	12.5	3.1	12 494	9 796	6 956	1 186	56.7	968
Kingston town, Ulster County	677	349	75.6	67.0	512	3.9	487	96.9	14.2	—	539	437	322	52	65.4	38
Kirkland town, Oneida County	8 315	4 365	60.0	56.4	4 967	4.2	4 694	81.1	7.9	.6	6 243	3 996	2 609	498	70.7	461
Kirkwood town, Broome County	4 662	2 359	70.2	61.8	3 265	5.2	3 079	94.0	15.2	—	3 422	2 856	1 976	406	65.3	325
Kiryas Joel village, Orange County	3 238	1 443	36.9	20.0	1 195	7.0	1 105	46.1	18.3	22.1	1 205	987	615	798	8.0	107
Knox town, Albany County	2 027	1 073	69.9	54.9	1 416	2.5	1 365	93.6	18.2	.6	1 480	1 160	867	192	61.6	160
Kortright town, Delaware County	1 079	521	60.5	55.5	651	5.5	606	77.2	9.2	1.0	746	558	361	79	58.2	70
Lackawanna city, Erie County	16 278	8 749	56.7	49.0	9 210	8.6	8 197	88.8	13.3	6.2	9 659	7 271	5 037	1 383	65.0	831
Lacona village, Oswego County	453	221	64.0	54.8	288	5.2	273	86.4	17.6	—	316	225	160	39	51.3	38
LaFayette town, Onondaga County	3 800	1 870	71.3	67.3	2 708	3.1	2 560	92.4	11.1	1.1	2 915	2 320	1 649	321	63.6	351

example, a 95% confidence interval is ± two standard errors (actually, 1.96 SE) from our estimate.

Let's take an imaginary example to illustrate the concept. Assume that the 1990 Census estimates that the median monthly Gross Rent for selected Renter-Occupied Housing Units in County Y is $354 and the standard error associated with this estimate is 6. This means we can be 67% confident that the actual value lies somewhere in the range of $348 to $360 ($354 ± $6). If we want to be more confident, the range will widen. At the 95% confidence level, we add and subtract two standard errors, so the new range is $342 to $366 ($354 ± $12). How does one interpret these confidence intervals? If we were to take a series of new sample surveys, each time following acceptable statistical methods, then in 95% of the samples, the results would fall with two standard errors of our estimated value.

Calculating confidence intervals for Census estimates requires several steps. The best way to demonstrate the use of these formulas is by example. According to Figure 10-5, reproduced from *CPH-5*, the estimated size of the Civilian labor Force in the city of Lackawanna, New York on April 1, 1990 was 9,210 persons. The total population of the city, based on the 100% count was 20,585 people (not shown in Figure 10-5). The following steps indicate how to calculate the standard error and confidence intervals for the number of employed persons in Lackawanna.

Step 1: Calculate the "unadjusted standard error."

This number is obtained through use of one of the two mathematical formulas shown in Figure 10-6. These formulas are listed in Appendix C of every sample publication (print Reports and CD-ROM Files both). The formula appearing below Table A is used when the estimate is a total, while the formula appearing below Table B is used when the estimate is expressed as a percentage. Other formulas (not shown in Figure 10-6)

are used when the estimate appears in the form of a median, a ratio, a sum, or a difference.

The value of N for the city of Lackawanna is 20,585 (the complete-count value for the city's total population) and the value of y is 9,210. Applying the first formula shown in Figure 10-6, the value of SE(y)—the unadjusted standard error for y—is 160 persons (rounded to the nearest whole person).

The unadjusted standard error can also be approximated based on the values shown in Table A. The "estimated total" falls between 5,000 and 10,000. Choosing the 25,000 column for "size of publication area" provides a value somewhere between 140 and 170 for SE(y), according to Table A. Algebraic interpolation could then be employed to provide a better approximation, but using the formula itself is usually much simpler and will provide a more exact solution, as we have seen.

Step 2: Determine the sampling rate for your area.

Look up the sampling rate for persons in the city of Lackawanna. This rate can be found in Table P3A (shown earlier in Figure 10-3) or in a corresponding table located in a print Report. In *CPH-5*, the necessary information is provided on Table 20. According to either of these tables, the sampling rate for persons in the city of Lackawanna is 13.4%.

Step 3: Determine the "standard error design factor."

The unadjusted standard error must now be adjusted to account for the sampling design for the particular characteristic being estimated. This figure is obtained by using Table C from Appendix C in the appropriate sample Report for your state. (Table C from the *CPH-5* Volume for New York State is reproduced in Figure 10-7.) Since the sampling rate for Lackawanna has already been determined to be 13.4%, we must use the first column in Table C, "Less than 15 percent." The characteristic in which we are

Table A. **Unadjusted Standard Error for Estimated Totals**

[Based on a 1-in-6 simple random sample]

Estimated Total[1]	Size of publication area[2]													
	500	1,000	2,500	5,000	10,000	25,000	50,000	100,000	250,000	500,000	1,000,000	5,000,000	10,000,000	25,000,000
50	16	16	16	16	16	16	16	16	16	16	16	16	16	16
100	20	21	22	22	22	22	22	22	22	22	22	22	22	22
250	25	30	35	35	35	35	35	35	35	35	35	35	35	35
500	-	35	45	45	50	50	50	50	50	50	50	50	50	50
1,000	-	-	55	65	65	70	70	70	70	70	70	70	70	70
2,500	-	-	-	80	95	110	110	110	110	110	110	110	110	110
5,000	-	-	-	-	110	140	150	150	160	160	160	160	160	160
10,000	-	-	-	-	-	170	200	210	220	220	220	220	220	220
15,000	-	-	-	-	-	170	230	250	270	270	270	270	270	270
25,000	-	-	-	-	-	-	250	310	340	350	350	350	350	350
75,000	-	-	-	-	-	-	-	310	510	570	590	610	610	610
100,000	-	-	-	-	-	-	-	-	550	630	670	700	700	710
250,000	-	-	-	-	-	-	-	-	-	790	970	1 090	1 100	1 100
500,000	-	-	-	-	-	-	-	-	-	-	1 120	1 500	1 540	1 570
1,000,000	-	-	-	-	-	-	-	-	-	-	-	2 000	2 120	2 190
5,000,000	-	-	-	-	-	-	-	-	-	-	-	-	3 540	4 470
10,000,000	-	-	-	-	-	-	-	-	-	-	-	-	-	5 480

[1]For estimated totals larger than 10,000,000, the standard error is somewhat larger than the table values. The formula given below should be used to calculate the standard error.

$$SE(\hat{Y}) = \sqrt{5\hat{Y}\left(1 - \frac{\hat{Y}}{N}\right)}$$

N = Size of area

$\hat{Y}$ = Estimate of characteristic total

[2]The total count of persons in the area if the estimated total is a person characteristic, or the total count of housing units in the area if the estimated total is a housing unit characteristic.

Table B. **Unadjusted Standard Error in Percentage Points for Estimated Percentage**

[Based on a 1-in-6 simple random sample]

Estimated Percentage	Base of percentage[1]												
	500	750	1,000	1,500	2,500	5,000	7,500	10,000	25,000	50,000	100,000	250,000	500,000
2 or 98	1.4	1.1	1.0	0.8	0.6	0.4	0.4	0.3	0.2	0.1	0.1	0.1	0.1
5 or 95	2.2	1.8	1.5	1.3	1.0	0.7	0.6	0.5	0.3	0.2	0.2	0.1	0.1
10 or 90.	3.0	2.4	2.1	1.7	1.3	0.9	0.8	0.7	0.4	0.3	0.2	0.1	0.1
15 or 85.	3.6	2.9	2.5	2.1	1.6	1.1	0.9	0.8	0.5	0.4	0.3	0.2	0.1
20 or 80.	4.0	3.3	2.8	2.3	1.8	1.3	1.0	0.9	0.6	0.4	0.3	0.2	0.1
25 or 75.	4.3	3.5	3.1	2.5	1.9	1.4	1.1	1.0	0.6	0.4	0.3	0.2	0.1
30 or 70.	4.6	3.7	3.2	2.6	2.0	1.4	1.2	1.0	0.6	0.5	0.3	0.2	0.1
35 or 65.	4.8	3.9	3.4	2.8	2.1	1.5	1.2	1.1	0.7	0.5	0.3	0.2	0.2
50	5.0	4.1	3.5	2.9	2.2	1.6	1.3	1.1	0.7	0.5	0.4	0.2	0.2

[1]For a percentage and/or base of percentage not shown in the table, the formula given below may be used to calculate the standard error. This table should only be used for proportions, that is, where the numerator is a subset of the denominator.

$$SE(\hat{p}) = \sqrt{\frac{5}{B}\hat{p}(100 - \hat{p})}$$

B = Base of estimated percentage

$\hat{p}$ = Estimated percentage

Figure 10-6

Table C. **Standard Error Design Factors—New York**

[Percent of persons or housing units in sample]

Characteristic	Less than 15 percent	15 to 30 percent	30 to 45 percent	45 percent or more
POPULATION				
Age..	1.2	1.0	0.6	0.5
Sex..	1.2	1.0	0.6	0.5
Race	1.2	1.0	0.6	0.5
Hispanic origin (of any race)....................	1.2	1.0	0.6	0.5
Marital status.................................	1.2	0.9	0.5	0.4
Household type and relationship	1.4	1.1	0.6	0.5
Children ever born	2.6	2.2	1.3	1.1
Work disability and mobility limitation status ...	1.3	1.0	0.6	0.5
Ancestry	2.1	1.6	0.9	0.8
Place of birth	2.4	2.4	1.4	1.2
Citizenship	1.8	1.5	0.9	0.7
Residence in 1985	2.3	1.9	1.1	0.9
Year of entry	1.6	1.2	0.6	0.5
Language spoken at home and ability to speak English........	1.7	1.4	0.8	0.7
Educational attainment........................	1.4	1.1	0.6	0.5
School enrollment............................	1.8	1.5	0.9	0.7
Type of residence (urban/rural)	2.1	1.8	1.7	1.5
Household type	1.4	1.1	0.6	0.5
Family type..................................	1.3	1.1	0.6	0.5
Group quarters...............................	1.1	0.8	0.8	0.8
Subfamily type and presence of children........	1.3	1.0	0.5	0.5
Employment status...........................	1.3	1.0	0.6	0.5
Industry.....................................	1.4	1.1	0.6	0.5
Occupation..................................	1.3	1.0	0.6	0.5
Class of worker	1.5	1.2	0.7	0.6
Hours per week and weeks worked in 1989	1.3	1.0	0.6	0.5
Number of workers in family....................	1.4	1.1	0.6	0.5
Place of work................................	1.5	1.2	0.7	0.6
Means of transportation to work	1.5	1.3	0.7	0.6
Travel time to work...........................	1.4	1.1	0.6	0.5
Private vehicle occupancy.....................	1.5	1.3	0.7	0.6
Time leaving home to go to work	1.4	1.1	0.6	0.5
Type of income in 1989.......................	1.5	1.2	0.6	0.5
Household income in 1989.....................	1.3	1.0	0.5	0.5
Family income in 1989........................	1.3	1.0	0.6	0.5
Poverty status in 1989 (persons)	1.7	1.3	0.8	0.7
Poverty status in 1989 (families)	1.3	1.0	0.5	0.5
Armed Forces and veteran status	1.7	1.2	0.7	0.6
HOUSING				
Age of householder	1.2	1.0	0.6	0.5
Race of householder	1.2	1.0	0.6	0.5
Hispanic origin of householder.................	1.2	1.0	0.6	0.5
Type of residence (urban/rural)................	1.1	1.0	0.5	0.5
Condominium status..........................	1.3	1.1	0.5	0.5
Units in structure............................	1.2	1.1	0.5	0.5
Tenure......................................	1.2	1.0	0.6	0.5
Occupancy status............................	1.2	1.0	0.6	0.5
Value.......................................	1.2	1.0	0.5	0.5
Gross rent...................................	1.3	1.1	0.5	0.5
Household income in 1989.....................	1.3	1.0	0.5	0.5
Year structure built	1.3	1.0	0.5	0.5
Rooms, bedrooms............................	1.3	1.1	0.5	0.5
Kitchen facilities	1.4	1.0	0.6	0.5
Source of water, plumbing facilities.............	1.4	1.1	0.6	0.5
Sewage disposal.............................	1.2	1.0	0.5	0.5
House heating fuel	1.3	1.1	0.6	0.5
Telephone in housing unit.....................	1.3	1.1	0.6	0.5
Vehicles available	1.3	1.1	0.6	0.5
Year householder moved into structure	1.3	1.1	0.5	0.5
Mortgage status and monthly mortgage costs	1.2	1.0	0.5	0.5
Mortgage status and selected monthly owner costs	1.2	1.0	0.5	0.5
Gross rent as a percentage of household income in 1989	1.3	1.1	0.6	0.5
Household income in 1989 by selected monthly owner costs as a percentage of income	1.2	1.0	0.5	0.5

Figure 10-7

interested is "Employment Status," so the appropriate standard error design factor is 1.3.

Step 4: Calculate the adjusted standard error.

To obtain the appropriate standard error, multiple the unadjusted standard error (calculated in Step 1) by the result of Step 4:

$$160 \times 1.3 = 208$$

Step 5: Choose a confidence level and multiply the adjusted standard error by one of the numbers shown below:

Confidence level	Multiplier
67% confidence	1.00
90% confidence	1.65
95% confidence	1.96
98% confidence	2.58

For example, at the 95% confidence level, the confidence interval will lie within 1.96 standard errors of the estimated value, or 408 persons (1.96 x 208, rounded to the nearest whole number).

Step 6: Calculating the confidence interval.

Add the result of Step 5 to the estimated value of your characteristic to determine the upper bound of the confidence level. Subtract the result of Step 5 from the estimated value to obtain the lower bound of your confidence level.

$$9,210 + 408 = 9,618$$
$$9,210 - 408 = 8,802$$

At the 95% confidence level, the estimated number of people in the Civilian Labor Force in Lackawanna, New York on April 1, 1990 was anywhere from 8,802 workers to 9,618 persons.

The formula found below Table B in Figure 10-6 can be used to determine sampling variability when the estimate is a percentage rather than a total number. For example, according to Figure 10-5, the unemployment rate for Lackawanna was 8.6%. Apply-

ing the variance formula for percentages, we use 8.6% as the estimated percentage, and 9,210 (the estimated number of persons in the Civilian Labor Force) as the base value. The unadjusted standard error is .653. Since the sampling rate for Lackawanna is still 13.4%, and we are still considering characteristics relating to Employment Status, we use the same standard error design factor as before (1.3). The adjusted standard error becomes .849 (.653 x 1.3). At the 95% confidence level, the appropriate confidence interval is ± 1.7% (.849 x 1.96). Thus, at the 95% confidence level, the estimated unemployment rate lies between 6.9% and 10.3%.

 **Census Tip**

The most important aspect of estimating sampling variability for percentages is to determine the appropriate percentage base (B) to use in the denominator of the equation.

Coverage Errors

Another source of error affecting the quality of Census data relates to coverage concerns. Chapter 4 describes the many procedures which the Bureau employs to improve Census coverage, including various outreach programs targeting minority populations, the Vacancy Check process, and Non-Response Follow-Up. Despite the enormous resources devoted to these efforts, the Bureau is unable to collect data for some persons and Housing Units. The majority of such coverage limitations can be classified into one of three broad categories: Housing Units identified by the Bureau but which did not return a completed Questionnaire; Questionnaires which contain omissions or inconsistent information which was not corrected during the Follow-Up process; and persons and/or Housing Units which were not counted because they were not identified during Address Compilation operations or the enu-

To obtain the appropriate standard error, multiple the unadjusted standard error (calculated in Step 1) by the result of Step 4.

Despite the enormous resources devoted to these efforts, the Bureau is unable to collect data for some persons and Housing Units.

meration process. The first two problems are systematically corrected by use of a computerized editing procedure which the Bureau calls Imputation. Confidentiality concerns present another source of data error. Although confidentiality is not a coverage issue, the Bureau utilizes Imputation to address this problem also, so it will be discussed here as well. Before examining the nature of Census Imputation, the most publicized aspect of coverage error will be explored—the Census undercount.

Census Undercount

Undercount refers to the number of persons and Housing Units which go uncounted during a decennial enumeration because Census-takers do not know they exist. The Bureau measures undercount through two separate procedures—the Post Enumeration Survey (PES) and Demographic Analysis—both of which were introduced in Chapter 4. Demographic Analysis is based on the Bureau's ongoing program of population estimates. Population figures are estimated by measuring changes in the "inventory" of people through births, deaths, immigration, and out-migration. In contrast, the PES is a sample survey of 165,000 Housing Units which compares information received after the Census to the responses which the same Household provided (if any) on the decennial Questionnaire. By locating individuals who were missed by the Census itself, PES data enable the Bureau to estimate the size of the undercount and the demographic characteristics of persons uncounted. The results of both analyses for 1990 were released by the Bureau in 1991. Preliminary estimates were announced in April of that year, with slight revisions published in June and July.

The Bureau expended more resources in 1990 to reduce the undercount than in any previous Census, yet for the first decade since such measurements were taken, the undercount actually rose. Overall estimates for each decade are shown below. Data are

based on Demographic Analysis, the method which has been used consistently since 1940.

Census	Net Undercount
1990	1.8%
1980	1.2%
1970	2.7%
1960	3.1%
1950	4.1%
1940	5.4%

As the figures show, the total estimated percentage of undercount has dropped steadily from 1940 through 1980, but 1990 marks a reverse in this trend.

A more significant concern is what demographers call the differential undercount: the fact that certain segments of the population are more likely to be missed than others. Included in this group are Blacks, Hispanics, and other minorities, young males, the poor, transients, and non-English speakers. Figure 10-8 summarizes total undercount for particular segments of the population, based on data from the PES. As shown here, the net undercount for Blacks, Hispanics, and American Indians were all more than double the rate for the overall population. Data from the Demographic Analysis program show even greater disparities. According to PES estimates, the 1990 net undercount for Black males was 5.4%, while the same measure based on Demographic Analysis was 8.0%.

Another aspect of differential undercount is geographic disparity. Large Urban areas experience higher rates of undercount than do suburban and Rural areas. Compared with the national average of 2.1%, the undercount was 5.1% for Los Angeles, 2.6% for New York City, and 5.0% for Washington, D.C. It is important to remember that regardless of the methodology used, the Bureau's measure of undercount represents an estimate only. Revised PES figures, released in June of 1991, measured the undercount at 2.1%—approximately 5.3 million persons. At the 95% Confidence Level, the margin of sampling error was 0.4%. In other words, the undercount actually ranged from 1.7% to 2.5% (anywhere

Undercount refers to the number of persons and Housing Units which go uncounted during a decennial enumeration because Census-takers do not know they exist.

The Bureau expended more resources in 1990 to reduce the undercount than in any previous Census, yet for the first decade since such measurements were taken, the undercount actually rose.

POST-ENUMERATION SURVEY ESTIMATES OF TOTAL RESIDENT POPULATION: U.S. TOTAL

Race/Hispanic/ Sex Group	Resident Census Enumeration(1)	Selected PES Estimate of Population (Rounded)	Estimated Undercount Rate	Margin of Error due to Sampling(2)
[1]	[2]	[3]	[4]	
Total	248,709,873	253,979,000	2.1	0.4
Male	121,239,418	124,249,000	2.4	0.4
Female	127,470,455	129,730,000	1.7	0.4
Black	29,986,060	31,505,000	4.8	0.6
Male	14,170,151	14,974,000	5.4	0.6
Female	15,815,909	16,531,000	4.3	0.6
Non-Black	218,723,813	222,474,000	1.7	0.4
Male	107,069,267	109,275,000	2.0	0.4
Female	111,654,546	113,199,000	1.4	0.4
Other Populations of Interest				
Asian or Pacific				
Islander	7,273,662	7,504,000	3.1	0.9
Male	3,558,038	3,688,000	3.5	1.0
Female	3,715,624	3,816,000	2.6	0.9
American Indian	1,878,285	1,977,000	5.0	2.1
Male	926,056	981,000	5.6	2.2
Female	952,229	996,000	4.4	2.0
Hispanic(3)	22,354,059	23,591,000	5.2	0.8
Male	11,388,059	12,087,000	5.8	0.9
Female	10,966,000	11,504,000	4.7	0.9

(1) The population counts released are subject to possible correction for undercount or overcount. The United States Department of Commerce is considering whether to correct the counts and will publish corrected counts, if any, no later than July 15, 1991.

(2) Add to and subtract from estimated under/over count rate to obtain a 95% confidence interval.

(3) Persons of Hispanic Origin may be any race.

Source: U.S. Commerce Department Press Release, June 13, 1991

Figure 10-8

from 4.9 million to 5.7 million persons). The margin of error was much larger in some states than in others.

Before leaving the topic of Census undercount, some of its major causes should be reviewed. Two broad types of undercount typically occur: entire Housing Units (and their inhabitants, if Occupied) are completely missed; or specific individuals within a Household are omitted from the Questionnaire. The later situation, called "within Household omissions," may result from respondents who do not understand the Bureau's definitions of Household members. The types of persons most likely to be missed in these circumstances are temporary residents, boarders, and other Household members who are not part of the nuclear family. As described in Chapter 7, two Questionnaire Items (Items 1a and H1a) are specifically designed to ameliorate such occurrences, but the problem persists nevertheless. The more likely cause of "within Household omissions" is the fact that many people wish to conceal their presence from Census takers despite government assurances of confidentiality protection. Illegal aliens, persons living in overcrowded apartments which violate lease agreements or fire ordinances, and individuals concerned about losing public assistance benefits are all examples of people whom respondents might omit intentionally from the Census Questionnaire.

The Bureau's failure to identify the existence of certain Occupied Housing Units is a second major cause of Census undercount. Address Compilation is one of the most important aspects of conducting the Census. Chapter 4 describes the elaborate steps take by the Bureau to identify as many Housing Units as possible, including such follow-up activities as Recanvassing based on Post-Census Local Review. Despite these diligent efforts, Units do remain hidden from Census enumerators, largely because of the diversity of unconventional Living Quarters seen in modern America. People live in boats, shacks, garages, recreational vehicles, and all manner of other domiciles which are difficult for the Bureau to identify. Housing Units are often missed simply because they are not obvious or visible from the street. Someone who lives in a remodeled storeroom in a commercial building, and who receives mail through his employer or a post office box, probably has a home which is invisible to everyone, including the Postal Service.

Innumerable other reasons account for Census undercount, including illiteracy or inability to speak English, the prevalence of nontraditional Households, and a highly mobile population. One other situation deserves special mention, namely the homeless population. Chapter 4 briefly describes the Bureau's efforts to enumerate persons living in emergency shelters or on the street. March 21, 1990 was "Street and Shelter Night" (S-Night), when a small army of Census workers and volunteers attempted to count individuals and families with no permanent housing arrangements. Most analysts agree that, despite the Bureau's best efforts, large numbers of the homeless were not counted. The 1990 Census counted 228,372 persons on S-Night—176,638 living in Emergency Shelters and 49,734 Visible in Street Locations. Although the Bureau has been careful to stress that this number is not meant to be a measure of the homeless population, the Census figure constitutes less than 50% of the probable homeless population as estimated by such reputable organizations as the Urban Institute and the U.S. Congressional Budget Office during the late 1980s.

To evaluate the effectiveness of its procedures, the Census Bureau contracted with independent organizations to observe S-Night operations in five cities: Chicago, Los Angeles, New Orleans, New York, and Phoenix. In addition to observing the S-Night operations from unobtrusive locations, the research teams deployed decoys to act as homeless individuals in neighborhoods targeted by the Bureau for S-Night enumeration. The independent researchers also employed other evaluation methods, such as comparing the Bureau's list of homeless shelters with lists of their own devising.

Evaluation results were fairly consistent across the five cities. Enumerators did a thorough job counting people in known emergency shelters, but counting persons on the street was far from adequate. The proportion of decoys who were contacted by an enumerator ranged from 22% to 66%. The

studies also pointed out important methodological flaws which reinforced how difficult it is to count the homeless. For example, even working with community agencies, the Bureau typically failed to identify informal shelters, such as churches and other occasional refuges. The street locations targeted for S-Night enumeration were those identified in advance as having the highest density of homeless, so many persons were missed who spent the night beyond these areas. And it is likely that many homeless people intentionally avoided contact with enumerators. Some advocates for the homeless even encouraged boycotting the enumeration, fearing that the resulting undercount would be used by politicians to prove that the homeless problem in America was greatly exaggerated.

One solution to the undercount problem would be to adjust the official population count to reflect PES results. It is beyond the scope of *Understanding the Census* to explore the ramifications of this highly-charged issue, or to review the arduous history of the adjustment debate in the courts and in Congress. Although the Commerce Department Secretary ruled that no adjustments would be made to 1990 Census counts, the matter was reopened by President Clinton in 1994, and the controversy remains unresolved as of this writing.

Political issues aside, the Bureau's primary concern over adjusting the Census relates to the question of whether PES estimates are sufficiently reliable to produce more accurate

Most analysts agree that, despite the Bureau's best efforts, large numbers of the homeless were not counted.

One solution to the undercount problem would be to adjust the official population count to reflect PES results.

NEW IN '90

Despite media perceptions to the contrary, Census methods of counting the homeless were not new for 1990. The Bureau has been conducting S-Night operations for several decades. The major differences in 1990 were that the Bureau devoted far more resources to the task, that the efforts received more public attention than ever before (much of it negative, unfortunately), and that the resulting data were tabulated and published in greater detail than in previous Censuses.

sufficiently reliable to produce more accurate results than the enumerated figures. Of particular note is the fact that Census numbers have relevance only as they pertain to specific localities. If PES data were used to adjust the Census, the estimated undercount would need to be distributed across the country. In other words, the 5.3 million persons identified as undercounted must be allocated across the four million Census Blocks which the Bureau estimates were affected by undercount.

A final issue pertaining to the appropriateness of Census adjustment is the notion of overcount. 1990 PES estimates represent a net figure, because they also incorporate those persons who were inadvertently counted twice. In fact, some areas of the country actually experienced an overcount due to doublecounting or counting people in the wrong Census Blocks. The U.S. General Accounting Office garnered significant media attention in August, 1991 when the agency published the results of a study which stated that the actual number of persons missed in the 1990 Census was closer to 10 million. This conclusion is based on the Bureau's own PES data, which estimated that 4.4 million persons were either double counted (often because they had dual residences) or were fictitious people. The GAO study isn't suggesting that the Bureau's total count was actually off by 10 million persons, but rather that the geographic distribution of those persons, together with their corresponding demographic characteristics, are less reliable than the net undercount would indicate. The GAO study emphasizes a serious question raised by demographers and statisticians about the ability of the government to conduct an actual head count in our highly complex, mobile society.

Substituted Census Returns

The Bureau utilizes two types of Imputation procedures: Substitution and Allocation. Both techniques involve filling in missing information on a Questionnaire by assigning responses from other completed Questionnaires. In other words, the Bureau makes up answers by assigning characteristics from similar persons or Housing Units. Substitution takes place when a complete set of responses is assigned to a person or Housing Unit for which no data are available. Allocation occurs when only selected responses are assigned due to incomplete or erroneously-completed Questionnaires.

Substitution addresses the problem of Questionnaires which the Bureau sent out, but which were not returned or for which enumerators were unable to contact someone to interview. Substitution was employed only when all other methods failed. As described in Chapter 4, the Census Bureau makes every effort to obtain a completed Questionnaire from nonrespondents. During the Non-Response Follow-Up (NRFU) operation, enumerators attempted to contact each nonresponding Household by phone and in person. Enumerators made a maximum of three personal visits and three phone calls, all at different days and times, to every nonresponding Housing Unit. If no response was obtained at this point, enumerators fell back on the "Last Resort Method," which involved asking neighbors, building managers, postal carriers, and other potentially knowledgeable individuals to provide information on the missing address. If enumerators determined the Housing Unit was Vacant (or that it was not a residential address), it was scheduled for additional follow-up during the Vacancy Check operation. During these various procedures, approximately one-half of all Housing Units in the United States received one or more follow-up visits.

Once these procedures had been exhausted, Census Bureau computers assigned responses to the missing Housing Units. The Substitution process considers housing and population Items separately. In the case of housing characteristics, the first step was to verify Vacancy Status based on results of the Vacancy Check operation. Once a Unit had been designated Vacant as of April 1, 1990, the Substitution process assigned all the characteristics of a similar, but randomly

In fact, some areas of the country actually experienced an overcount due to doublecounting or counting people in the wrong Census Blocks.

Substitution addresses the problem of Questionnaires which the Bureau sent out, but which were not returned or for which enumerators were unable to contact someone to interview.

Q&A

How much Substitution took place in 1990?

Nationwide, 7.6% of all Housing Units underwent Substitution, but the majority of these were Vacant Units. In comparison, less than one percent (0.6%) of all persons tabulated in the 1990 Census had their characteristics assigned through Substitution. These rates vary from one location to another, but few localities experienced unusually high Substitution rates. For example, only seven states had state-wide rates greater than one percent; Massachusetts was the highest, with an average rate of 1.7%. Similarly, only six Metropolitan Areas had rates greater than two percent, and none were higher than 2.9%. These rates vary more for smaller levels of geography. For example, approximately a dozen cities with population greater than 10,000 persons experienced Substitution rates ranging from 3.0% to 5.6%.

Census users can find Substitution rates for specific geographic entities in several Census publications.

It is important to remember that, unlike other statistical programs, the decennial Census utilizes no tabulation categories to summarize Items which respondents left blank or for which they provided unusable answers.

had received a completed Questionnaire. In the case of Occupied Units, a full set of housing characteristics was assigned based on a previously processed Questionnaire. In the same manner, a full set of population characteristics was copied from a randomly selected Household.

Census users can find Substitution rates for specific geographic entities in several Census publications. The best print Titles are *CP-1* (for Substitution of persons) and *CH-1* (for Substitution of Housing Units). In state-specific Volumes, the relevant table numbers are Table 82 and 83 for *CP-1*, and Table 75 for *CH-1*. Coverage in both Titles is limited to the geographic Summary Levels shown in Figure 9-2 (presented in Chapter 9). The United States Summary Volumes of these two Titles also provide convenient nationwide comparisons of Substitution rates. These tables cover the United States, the 50 states, all Metropolitan Areas, and Places with population of 10,000 or more. The relevant table numbers for the U.S. Summary Volumes are Table 287 of *CP-1-1* and Table 203 of *CH-1-1*.

The second source for data on Substitution rates is the *STF 1* series on CD-ROM. Data can be found down to the Block Group level on the state-specific Files of *STF 1A*. Nationwide comparisons are provided on *STF 1C*. In both cases, Table P29 presents Substitution of persons, and Table H45 lists Substi-

tution of Housing Units. Neither table cites data in percentage form, but the rates can be easily calculated from the figures given.

 Census Tip

Although Substitution is not a significant problem at the national level, users studying smaller Summary Levels are advised to check Substitution rates for the localities under investigation.

Allocated Data

The second method of Imputation, called Allocation, relates to Questionnaires for which the Bureau has received incomplete responses. It is important to remember that, unlike other statistical programs, the decennial Census utilizes no tabulation categories to summarize Items which respondents left blank or for which they provided unusable answers. Instead, the Bureau assigns responses to replace "unacceptable" data. Aside from a blank response, what constitutes an unacceptable answer? In many cases, internal inconsistencies will trigger the editing process. For example, if a respondent indicated he moved into a house many years before the house was actually built, one of the two responses is obviously incorrect. Items to which a respondent answered, "Don't Know," or "NA" are also deemed unacceptable responses. Two exceptions to this rule can be seen in the 1990 Census. The only question which includes "I don't know" as a valid response is Item H17, Year Structure Built. Similarly, population Item 13, covering Ancestry, is the only question which includes a tabulation category for "No response given."

In some cases, editing for unacceptable and missing responses is handled by computer, but at the District Office level, Census clerks conducted much of the editing manually. In both cases, Questionnaires of this type were referred to the Edit Check operation, in which Households were contacted by telephone or in person to supply missing information or to correct errors and inconsistencies. Questionnaires underwent Allocation only after repeated attempts to contact the affected Households were unsuccessful.

Allocation operates in similar fashion to Substitution, except that the Bureau assigns responses only to those Items affected by unacceptable data.

Allocation operates in similar fashion to Substitution, except that the Bureau assigns responses only to those Items affected by unacceptable data. For example, if the all Items on a Household's Questionnaire were filled out properly except for Educational Attainment (Item 12) for Person 3, the Allocation procedure would assign a value for the missing response. However, Allocation can effect more than a single response or more than one person in the Household; the process generally supplies data for every unacceptable response on a given Questionnaire.

The computer editing program which governs the Allocation process is Item-specific; the computer looks for logical relationships before assigning a value.

The computer editing program which governs the Allocation process is Item-specific; the computer looks for logical relationships before assigning a value. Three major factors govern data Allocation. First, the program tries to resolve internal inconsistencies based on the person's other responses. For example, if the responses for Person 2 indicated she was female, age 45, and was the Householder's spouse, but the Item for Marital Status was left blank, the program would assign the value of "Married." A second mechanism used by the Allocation program is to compare the affected person's responses to those of the other Household members. If a child's Race was unidentified or otherwise unacceptable, the program would assign the Race of the mother. The descriptions above represent oversimplified examples of the Allocation process. For most unacceptable responses, the Bureau's Allocation program actually examines a variety of relationships to other Items on the Questionnaire.

If existing responses on the Questionnaire are insufficient for assigning a value to missing or unacceptable data, the Allocation program takes a third approach: it looks for another Questionnaire which describes a person or Housing Unit similar to that of the affected Questionnaire. Once again, a variety of characteristics are examined for each unacceptable response. For example, when assigning a value for Wages and Salary (Item 32a), the Allocation program matches the person with another respondent of the same sex, age group, Household relationship, occupation, industry, class of worker, and number of weeks worked in 1989.

Many Census publications provide information on the amount of Allocation which occurred for specific Questionnaire Items and specific geographic entities. In print Reports, these tables generally appear at the end of the Volume, and list certain key variables only. In some Imputation tables, Allocation rates and Substitution rates are combined; in other tables they are presented separately. The most detailed Imputation tables can be found on the Bureau's CD-ROM products. *STF 1A* and *STF 1C* each contain 17 Imputation tables, while *STF 3A*

NEW IN '90

1980 Census Reports included detailed Allocation tables describing virtually all Questionnaire Items, but geographic coverage was limited. 1980 print Reports provided no Allocation rates for smaller geographies, such as Blocks, Block Groups, Tracts, and Places of fewer than 1,000 population, or for CCDs and nonfunctioning MCDs. CD-ROM products for 1990 display complete Allocation tables for every geographic entity covered by the Census.

Selected Allocation Rates for the United States

Characteristic	Percent Allocated	Universe
COMPLETE-COUNT ITEMS		
Any population Item	16.2	all persons
Any housing Item	15.7	all Housing Units
Race	2.0	all persons
Hispanic Origin	10.0	all persons
Sex	1.2	all persons
Age	2.4	all persons
Household Relationship	2.6	persons in Households
Marital Status	2.0	persons 15 years or older
Rooms	4.6	all Housing Units
Units in Structure	3.0	all Housing Units
Tenure	3.1	Occupied Housing Unit
Housing Value	4.2	Specified Owner Occupied
Housing Value	19.7	Vacant, for sale
Contract Rent	4.4	Specified Renter-Occupied
Contract Rent	36.4	Vacant, for rent
Vacancy Status	8.0	Vacant Housing Units
Duration of Vacancy	22.0	Vacant Housing Units
SAMPLE ITEMS		
Any population Item	53.3	all persons
Any housing Item	57.6	all Housing Units
Place of birth	5.4	all persons
Language Spoken at Home	5.1	persons 5 years and older
Residence in 1985	4.0	persons 5 years and older
School enrollment	4.5	persons 3 years and older
Educational attainment	4.6	persons 25 years and older
Means of Transportation to Work	4.7	workers 16 years and older
Labor Force Status	3.9	persons 16 years and older
Occupation	7.1	employed persons 16 years and older
Industry	5.9	employed persons 16 years and older
Weeks worked in 1989	14.9	persons 16 years and older who worked in 1989
Personal Income	14.2	persons 15 years and older with Income in 1989
Household Income	18.9	persons 15 years and older with Income in 1989
Year structure built	23.0	Occupied Housing Units
Bedrooms	7.5	Occupied Housing Units
Plumbing facilities	1.7	Occupied Housing Units
Kitchen facilities	1.8	Occupied Housing Units
Telephone in Unit	1.9	Occupied Housing Units
Home heating fuel	2.9	Occupied Housing Units
Vehicles available	2.2	Occupied Housing Units
Year Householder moved	2.9	Occupied Housing Units
Monthly owner costs	8.7	Specified Owner-Occupied Units, with mortgage
Monthly owner costs	13.6	Specified Owner-Occupied Units, without mortgage
Gross Rent	6.6	Specified Renter-Occupied

Sources: CP-1-1 (Table 283); CH-1-1 (Table 202); CP-2-1 (Table 178); CH-2-1 (Table 259); STF 3C (Tables P128 and H72).

Figure 10-9

and *STF 3C* each contain 64.

Figure 10-9 compares national averages for Allocation rates for a variety of key population and housing variables. 16.2% of all persons answering the Short Form Questionnaire had one or more responses Allocated. At 53.3%, the comparable percentage for persons answering the Long Form is much higher. This disparity is to be expected because the Long Form contains many more Items and is a much more complicated Questionnaire. However, for specific Questionnaire Items, national Allocation rates are fairly low. This is particularly true of fairly basic characteristics, such as age, sex, and marital status. It is also clear that more complicated questions, those involving more complex Census Bureau definitions, or those which inquire about more personal characteristics are much more likely to exhibit higher Allocation rates. For example, the Bureau assigned a value for Hispanic Origin for 10% of all persons in the United States, probably as a result of general confusion about the concept. Similarly, 18.9% of all Households had their Household Income assigned by the Bureau.

 Census Tip

Allocation rates can vary enormously from one locality to another. Serious users of Census data should always take the time to examine Imputation tables for the geographic entities they study. It is important to examine both the overall rates for the entity and the Allocation rates for specific Items of interest.

Perhaps the best way to illustrate the impact of Imputation on the accuracy of Census data is to review a few specific cases. Figure 10-10 lists all Census Tracts in Erie County, New York which experienced a high rate of data Allocation for complete-count Questionnaire Items. The Bureau's EX-TRACT software (described in greater detail

Tracts in Erie County, New York with High Imputation Rates

TRACTBNA	POPIMPUTE	HSEIMPUTE	RACEIMP	HISPIMP	VALIMP	RENTIMP
13.02	36.54	41.73	7.67	22.11	25.00	5.74
14.01	35.09	50.00	0.00	31.58	0.00	12.24
14.02	31.35	53.54	1.46	25.04	4.00	10.72
15	32.09	34.09	3.89	21.93	12.30	14.02
25.01	31.91	46.24	2.66	13.30	0.00	5.56
25.02	32.08	34.21	2.77	23.86	10.27	9.57
31	30.31	31.37	3.77	21.27	14.04	10.07
32.01	41.27	39.75	2.87	25.32	17.11	13.85
32.02	37.04	37.04	1.86	22.60	19.85	20.51
34	30.84	31.29	1.81	20.11	14.04	19.25
35	30.59	30.78	2.10	19.69	11.38	13.86
40.01	30.26	32.55	2.51	19.15	11.65	19.44
40.02	32.02	87.36	2.25	21.35	14.29	14.58
64	30.69	35.69	1.91	17.03	6.00	14.44
71.01	33.37	32.82	9.75	15.07	11.11	8.23
71.02	31.89	32.90	7.38	17.14	7.69	7.01
72.01	60.88	34.66	1.62	56.89	0.00	9.95
121	30.02	32.61	5.56	17.83	18.18	8.77
148.04	60.00	33.33	0.00	0.00	0.00	0.00

Key to column headings:

TRACTBNA Census Tract/Block Numbering Area
POPIMPUTE Percentage of All Persons with Imputed Values
HSEIMPUTE Percentage of All Housing Units with Imputed Values
RACEIMP Percentage of Persons with Imputed Race
HISPIMP Percentage of Persons with Imputed Hispanic Origin
VALIMP Percentage of Owner-Occupied Units with Imputed Value
RENTIMP Percentage of Renter-Occupied Units with Imputed Rent

Figure 10-10

In fact, it is not unusual to see high overall Imputation rates as a result of one or two missing variables.

in Chapter 13), was used to identify all Erie County Tracts for which the overall Allocation rate was more than 30%. Of the 226 Tracts in the county, 21 met this condition. A second EXTRACT search identified 26 Tracts in Erie County for which more than 30% of all Housing Units experienced at least one allocated characteristic. To compare the effects of allocating the two types of characteristics, a third search identified those Tracts which had more than 30% data Allocation for both population and housing Items. (In other words, the third search identified those Tracts which appeared in both of the previous searches.) The third search, whose results are shown in Figure 10-10, identified 19 Tracts, 17 of which are located in the city of Buffalo.

Drawing conclusions based solely on simple

percentages is seldom a good idea. To obtain a clearer picture of the Imputation process, characteristics for each of the 19 Tracts must be analyzed more carefully. For example, 60% of the persons in Tract 148.04 had one or more characteristics allocated to them. But on closer examination, the high Imputation rate is due to the small size of the Tract itself. Tract 148.04 consists of three Housing Units (all of them Occupied), with a total population of ten people. By examining the Imputation tables individually, we see that six of the ten inhabitants (60%) experienced data Allocation, as well as one of the three (33.3%) Housing Units. A single population Item (age) and a single housing Item (number of Rooms) accounted for all allocated responses. None of the other responses were affected by the editing process.

A different situation explains the extremely high rate (more than 87%) of housing Imputation for Tract 40.02. This Tract contains a recently abandoned housing project. Of the 436 Housing Units in this Tract, 365 of them were Vacant at the time of the 1990 Census. 380 out of 435 Units (87.36%) experienced Allocation of one or more housing Items, and one Unit was substituted. Fully 362 of the Allocations were a result of a single Item: number of Rooms.

In fact, it is not unusual to see high overall Imputation rates as a result of one or two missing variables. To take a third conspicuous example from Figure 10-10, the high population Imputation rate for Tract 72.01 is largely due to Allocation of Hispanic Origin (56.89% allocated) and age (49.1% allocated). This Tract is located in the heart of downtown Buffalo (including the City Hall area), but it also incorporates a small residential section of mixed racial composition, containing the second-lowest median Household Income in the city. Not all of the high Imputation rates can be explained by one or two variables, however. Users are encouraged to study Imputation tables carefully before reaching conclusions based on Census data.

The Confidentiality Edit

By federal law, information provided on individual Census returns may not examined by anyone outside the Census Bureau, a restriction which Bureau employees enforce rigidly.

Chapter 1 stressed the importance of Census confidentiality. By federal law, information provided on individual Census returns may not examined by anyone outside the Census Bureau, a restriction which Bureau employees enforce rigidly. Without such guarantees, United States residents would be much less willing to provide personal information when answering the Census Questionnaire. A more subtle aspect to the confidentiality issue is the fact that data users might be able to deduce information about specific individuals or Households if the number of respondents in a given locality were fairly small. This concern is especially relevant for smaller geographic Summary Levels, such as Census Tracts, Block Groups, or Blocks. For example, if only three Hispanic Households lived in a particular Tract, the confidentiality of each of these Households might be compromised, even though Census publications sum all three together when tabulating results. The Bureau copes with this concern by utilizing a procedure known as the Confidentiality Edit.

The process is similar to that described for data Allocation: selected values for a small, random sample of Households are switched with responses for similar Households elsewhere in the state. This is done to introduce a "small amount of uncertainty" into the Census results. In other words, since data users cannot tell which Households have been switched, they cannot identify the characteristics of an individual Household no matter how few the respondents in a particular locality or within a particular subgroup of the population.

Confidentiality Edits for complete-count Items and sample Items are conducted separately. In the case of complete-count Items, the Households for which the Bureau swaps data are controlled on the following key variables: number of persons in the Household; Race; Hispanic Origin; age group (number of persons under and over 18 years); housing Tenure; Units in Structure; and

Q&A

Isn't the Imputation process just a fancy way of saying the Bureau makes up answers to missing responses?

Yes. But readers should remember the Allocation process is based on logical relationships. When values are supplied based on other data found on the Questionnaire itself, the probability is high that the assigned value is "true." When values are assigned based on the characteristics of a similar person or Household, the likelihood of erroneous information is much greater. Once again, serious users should take the time to consult relevant Imputation tables for the geographic entity being studied. This is particularly true for smaller Summary Levels, such as Tracts, Block Groups, and small Places, where Imputation rates may be surprisingly high.

The Substitution process presents a knottier problem because each substituted entity represents a fictitious person or Housing Unit. The Housing Unit exists, and the people in it may exist, but their characteristics are completely invented by Substitution. With fewer than one percent of all persons nationwide affected by Substitution, the overall impact on Census results is minimal, but housing Substitution is a more serious concern, especially for Vacant Units.

The very idea of data Imputation is shocking to many Census users, but readers should remember that the Bureau is doing nothing underhanded. Imputation rules are applied consistently, following acceptable statistical procedures, and the Bureau publishes its Imputation tables, enabling users to identify potential problem areas.

Contract Rent or Value. For each pair of Households interchanged by the Bureau, those characteristics are identical, and the remaining characteristics are swapped.

Consider the following hypothetical and simplified example of how a Confidentiality Edit might work. A particular Census Block contains three Housing Units and a total of 20 persons. One of the Households includes one person under age five and two persons age 18 to 64. This Household undergoes a partial data interchange with a similar Household in another location. The second Household has one person age 5 to 17 and two persons age 18 to 64. One person is switched in each Household: the "under 5" child in one is interchanged with the "5 to 17" child in the other. The "before and after" results for the first Census Block are shown below.

Age Distribution	Before	After
Under 5 years	3	2
5 to 17	4	5
18 to 64	10	10
65 or over	3	3
Total	20	20

The Block still contains a total of 20 persons. Of these, 13 remain age 18 or older and 7 remain younger than 18.

For sample data, the sampling process itself generally affords sufficient protection where confidentiality is concerned. The exception is for smaller Summary Levels, especially Block Groups. Wherever a Confidentiality Edit occurs for sample data, the editing program erases at least one response on a completed Questionnaire, then utilizes the Item-specific Allocation process to find a matching Household elsewhere in the state and assigns that value to the "missing" response.

For both complete-count and sample edits, the sampling rate is higher for small Summary Levels than for larger geographies. The Bureau tested the effects of Confidentiality Edits extensively before adopting the program for 1990. Because the sampling rates are small and Imputations are controlled for key variables, the quality of the resulting data remains high.

NEW IN '90

The Confidentiality Edit was used for the first time in the 1990 Census. In prior decades, data values which might compromise individual privacy were completely suppressed from Census publications. The threshold of confidentiality for any Summary Level was five Households or 15 people. For example, if only 12 Hispanics resided in a particular town, the total number of Hispanic persons in the town would not appear in any Census publications. The affected numbers would be included in larger aggregations (by subject and geography), however. In the previous example, the unreported Hispanics would be incorporated into the count for all persons at the town level, and they would also be tabulated as part of the total number of Hispanic persons for larger Summary Levels, such as the county and the state.

The major reason the Bureau no longer uses this technique is due to the problem of "complementary suppression," where additional data fields are suppressed to prevent users from inferring information about individuals or Households by subtracting reported figures from total amounts. Because complementary suppression resulted in large amounts of unpublished data, the Bureau adopted Confidentiality Edits as a more appropriate safeguard for the 1990 Census. Users now have reasonably accurate pictures of certain population and housing characteristics where none were available in the past.

Other Data Limitations

Sampling and coverage errors represent the two most significant sources of concern for Census users, but a host of other limitations affect the accuracy of Census data. Problems also occur in collecting and processing the data. Because 90% of all Questionnaires are returned in the mail, a phenomenon the Bureau euphemistically calls "fictitious answers" does happen. It is believed that the number of people who submit deliberately false answers is small, and many such answers can be caught in the editing process, but the possibility must be recognized by Census users. Enumerators themselves can make up answers due to lack of commitment or fear of visiting run-down buildings. As discussed

Because 90% of all Questionnaires are returned in the mail, a phenomenon the Bureau euphemistically calls "fictitious answers" does happen.

in Chapter 4, this problem is minimized by close supervision and monitoring of temporary Census workers and by follow-up visits in problem areas. A more likely problem is that enumerators and other temporary workers will make mistakes through a lack of understanding or insufficient training. Errors can also occur when Questionnaires are being edited and coded for entry into the computer.

Another limitation involves the Last Resort method of data collection. Readers should remember that in certain situations, responses are supplied by neighbors, landlords, or even postal carriers. In 1990, enumeration areas which experienced unacceptably high rates of Last Resort responses were recanvassed by Census workers from other District Offices. Nevertheless, the Last Resort method introduces error in Census results.

Problems caused by the nature of the questions asked are more difficult to identify. The way a question is phrased can cause confusion among respondents, and some people will fill out a Questionnaire incorrectly no matter how well it is designed or how explicit the instructions. For example, age might seem like a fairly straightforward characteristic to describe, but because many respondents misinterpreted Census instructions, 1990 age data are problematic for children younger than one year and for persons whose birthday fell near the Reference Date. A related problem is due to the Bureau's principle of self-identification. Certain self-identified characteristics have a tendency to be under or overstated, but the Bureau has little recourse but to take each respondent's word. Questions on Race, Hispanic Origin, disability, Income, and Housing Value, and even age are examples of Questionnaire Items which are subject to this phenomenon. For example, a proudly independent person with an artificial limb may not think of himself as handicapped, while someone who wears bifocals might report this as a disability.

One of the most frequently heard objections to the usefulness of the Census does not involve accuracy, but rather the timeliness of

the data. The Census is conducted only every ten years, and by the time tabulated data are released, the numbers are already several years old. The Bureau meets these problems in two ways: by releasing publications on a flow basis, as soon as results are tabulated, and by providing annual and sometimes monthly estimates for basic population and housing characteristics at the national and state levels.

Using Census Data Properly

Census statistics are consistently misinterpreted by those who use them. Knowing how **not** to use Census publications is as important as how to use them correctly. People of all types inadvertently misuse Census data everyday, just as they misuse other types of statistics. But because Census publications are such an authoritative source, and because they are so complex, the numbers are especially vulnerable to misinterpretation by data users. Readers can do little to counteract errors in the tabulations themselves other than to be aware of the possibility they exist. However, outright mistakes in using Census publications can be avoided by taking the time to understand important concepts, becoming familiar with the idiosyncrasies of table layout, and exercising due care. The following discussion highlights some of the most frequently encountered trouble spots for Census users.

One of the most common mistakes in quoting Census statistics results from incorrectly using sample data instead of complete counts. As this chapter has stressed, a cardinal rule of Census research is to use only complete count tables for complete count data. For an quick idea of which Questionnaire Items fall into each category, readers are referred to Figure 1-4 (in Chapter 1). All CD-ROM Files and most print Reports limit their coverage to one type of data or the other. The two notable exceptions are *CPH-3*, covering Census Tracts, and *CPH-4*, focusing on Congressional Districts. Each of

---

Certain self-identified characteristics have a tendency to be under or overstated, but the Bureau has little recourse but to take each respondent's word.

One of the most common mistakes in quoting Census statistics results from incorrectly using sample data instead of complete counts.

these Titles contains sample data and complete-count data in the same Report, so users must be alert to which type of table is being used. The same variable can be reported as a complete-count figure on one table and as a sample estimate on another, which can lead to different values for the same variable. In such cases the user can encounter three tables within the same publication which provide three different numbers for the same characteristic: a complete-count figure, an estimate from a population table, and an estimate from a housing table.

 Census Tip

Sample tables in *CPH-3* and *CPH-4* can be identified by the following phrase shown in small print at the top of the page: "Data based on sample and subject to sampling variability."

Novice users frequently confuse commonly encountered Census terms with related words or ideas.

The importance of understanding Census geography and terminology has been emphasized throughout the book, but it is worth repeating here. Making mistakes with Census data is inevitable when definitions and concepts are not fully understood. Certain terms are extremely easy to misinterpret. Novice users frequently confuse commonly encountered Census terms with related words or ideas. The Bureau utilizes the word "Ancestry" to describe a person's ethnic heritage, regardless of that person's place of birth, but many Census newcomers assume the term refers to the foreign-born population. Users should never make assumptions concerning the meaning of a term. An Unrelated Individual is not the same as a Single-Person Household. The Farm population does not equal the Rural population. When the Bureau uses different terminology on different tables, it is to denote subtle distinctions in meaning. For example, the terms Child, Related Child, and Own Child are used to measure different Family relationships. As described in Chapter 5, concepts such as

To guard against making unwarranted assumptions, the researcher must refer to the way questions are phrased on the Census Questionnaire as well as the definitions of terms.

Subfamilies and multiple Ancestries also lend themselves to misinterpretation. The solution is to never take terminology for granted. Make it a habit to check the glossaries found in every Census publication. In some cases, reading the definitions may not be sufficient. To guard against making unwarranted assumptions, the researcher must refer to the way questions are phrased on the Census Questionnaire as well as the definitions of terms.

To illustrate how easy it can be to misinterpret Census terminology, consider the Labor Force statistics shown earlier in Figure 10-5, taken from *CPH-5*. Since the table displays the percentage of persons in the Labor Force and the percent unemployed, it might be logical to assume that the column labelled "Workers" refers to the total number of employed persons. A quick comparison of the numbers proves that this is not the case. According to the table, Lackawanna's 1990 unemployment rate was 8.6%. It is apparent from the table spanners that the denominator for the unemployment rate is the total Civilian Labor Force: 9,210 persons for Lackawanna. If the value in the Workers column represents the number of employed persons, then the number of unemployed in Lackawanna should be 1,013 (9,210 minus 8,197). Dividing that difference by 9,210 yields a result of 11%, so something is clearly wrong here. Consulting a more detailed Report might shed light on the situation. According to Table 173 in *CP-2*, the number of employed civilians in Lackawanna is estimated at 8,421 and the number of unemployed is shown as 789. The latter figure divided by 9,210 yields an unemployment rate of 8.6%, so these seem to be the appropriate statistics. What does the number of "Workers" actually represent? Several clues are offered. First, the figure is smaller than the total number of employed persons. Second, the subheads under the "Workers" spanner relate to Means of Transportation to Work. The answer to our mystery is found by reviewing the Long Form Questionnaire itself. Item 21a asks whether the respondent worked during the Reference Week. Item 25 asks employed persons whether they were absent from work during the Reference Week due to temporary layoff, labor dispute, vacation, or illness. The number of employed civilians is obtained by adding the responses to Items 21a and 25. Number of Workers is obtained from Item 21a alone.

 Census Tip

When relationships shown in summary tables are unclear, consult tables which provide greater detail.

As described in Chapter 5, even the definition of the United States is subject to interpretation, depending upon whether one cites Resident Population, Apportionment Population, or some other measure. What is the *real* population of the United States? As Figure 10-11 demonstrates, various Census statistics can be cited as the 1990 United States population. Depending on the definition employed, each is correct. The Resident Population excludes federal civilian and military personnel stationed abroad. The Apportionment Population, used for determining state representation in Congress, includes military and governmental employees abroad, but excludes residents of the District of Columbia. When making annual comparisons for recent years, users frequently cite the Bureau's July, 1990 estimated population, rather than the April, 1990 decennial total. For historical comparisons, certain Census publications list the population of the contiguous United States, which excludes Alaska and Hawaii. Residents of Puerto Rico and the other Outlying Territories are typically not counted in United States population totals, but certain analyses may include them. The "official" 1990 population of the United States depends on the purpose at hand.

Many errors in using Census publications result from the simple mistake of reading

---

ALTERNATE DEFINITIONS OF UNITED STATES POPULATION

Possible components of total U.S. population.

A. Lower 48 states	246,444,701
B. Alaska and Hawaii	1,658,272
C. District of Columbia	606,900
D. Apportionment component of population stationed abroad	919,810
E. Total population stationed abroad	942,844
F. Outlying territories	3,862,238

Various Measures of 1990 United States Population

1. Conterminous U.S. (A only)	**246,444,701**
2. Resident Population (A + B + C)	**248,709,873**
3. Apportionment Population (A + B + D)	**249,022,783**
4. United States and Territories (A + B + C + F)	**252,572,111**
5. Population Counted by 1990 Census (A + B + C + E + F)	**253,514,955**
6. Estimated Resident Population (Bureau's July 1990 estimate)	**249,924,000**

Figure 10-11

---

tables incorrectly. A common mistake is to cite what appears to be characteristics of the whole population when the entire table covers characteristics of a specific Race or Hispanic group only. Identifying the Universe for a particular table is fairly simple, but users must make the effort. When consulting print Reports, read the title of each table to determine its Universe. For CD-ROM products, the Universe is usually shown at the top of the each table. In cases where it is not shown, the user can Escape back to the Table of

Even the definition of the United States is subject to interpretation, depending upon whether one cites Resident Population, Apportionment Population, or some other measure.

 Census Tip

The most commonly cited population figure for the United States is the Resident Population, but don't make hasty assumptions. When using Census data, be certain you understand the universe being measured.

Contents Menu, and the Universe for the highlighted table will appear at the top of the Menu. The specified Universe can also help users determine the unit of measurement shown in the table. For example, when consulting a table which shows Household relationships, if the Universe is All Persons, then the statistics being reported are persons in the Household, not the number of Households.

Census users must also exercise care when population or housing characteristics are divided into more specific subcategories. This concern is less problematic in CD-ROM products, where each table typically focuses on a single characteristic. However, the tables in print Reports usually display a variety of characteristics on a single page. Therefore, print tables are generally more complex and more susceptible to misinterpretation. Users must pay particular attention to table spanners. Once again, Figure 10-5 provides a useful example. Here, the user might mistakenly interpret the first column, labelled "Total," to represent all persons in the population. Looking at the uppermost spanner, however, we can see that the values refer only to persons 16 years or over. (This is because Labor Force participation is based upon the persons in that age group.) Spanners and subheads are not used in CD-ROM tables, making them somewhat easier to interpret.

Census Tip

The best way to read tables in print Reports is from the outside, working inward. When looking at column headings, start with the broadest spanner, then check each successively smaller level to determine how values in an individual column relate to other data on the page.

Another way in which print tables display subsets of data is through the use of indentation in the table stubs. Although the sub-divisions are indented in the stub portion of the table, their corresponding data values are not indented. As a result, careless users may double-count certain characteristics by adding the subtotal to the value of the component parts shown beneath it. Once again, this is seldom a problem for CD-ROM tables. Although they also employ indented stubs, the tables in CD-ROM products rarely include subtotals.

Table layout can also create confusion relating to Census geography. For example, users may make careless errors when different entities utilize the same name for various Summary Levels. This typically happens with Metropolitan Areas, Urbanized Areas, and their Central Cities. However, the situation can also occur when a township has the same name as a neighboring city or village. Another common mistake occurs when Tracts, Places, or even Metropolitan Areas are split by state or county lines. Depending on which table is viewed, the entire entity may be reported, or only that part included within the borders of the larger Summary Level.

Another common pitfall is the problem of misusing percentages and other comparative measures. Many Census tables provide percentages, means, and median values. It is important to determine just what percentage is being reported. Is a table with data on women workers giving the percent of all women who are in the Labor Force, or the percentage of the Labor Force consisting of women? Exercising caution in dealing with percentages is even more important when calculating your own numbers based on values in a table. The critical factor when doing so is to make sure the numerator and denominator compare what you want them to. If you are measuring the percentage of Housing Units with complete kitchen facilities, make certain the numerator and denominator are taken from the same Universe (e.g., Occupied Housing Units as opposed to All Housing Units). This type of error is especially likely to occur when comparing data from two different tables.

SUGGESTIONS FOR PROPER CENSUS USE

▶ Never use Sample publications for Complete Count data.
▶ Choose the appropriate geographic Summary Level for your needs.
▶ Study definitions of Census terminology found in appendices to print reports and CD-ROM Files.
▶ Check table titles for clues to coverage Universe and other content-related matters.
▶ Make sure you understand the universe being measured.
▶ Read relevant footnotes, headnotes, and column headings.
▶ Determine the unit of measurement being used (e.g., persons, Households, dollars, percents, etc.).
▶ When unclear on proper interpretation of data, check the wording of the Questionnaire Item and its accompanying instructions.
▶ If terminology is still unclear, the lists of codes found in the Technical Documentation for CD-ROM products can be very helpful.
▶ Read the User Notes section of any Report or database you plan to consult. These describe data limitations associated with the particular publication.

Figure 10-12

The best way to avoid potential problems in summing component parts or calculating percentages is to have a clear understanding of the relationships among important Census terms. Some of the most commonly misunderstood concepts involve the definitions of Households and Housing Units. To help users avoid making erroneous assumptions in these two areas, Figures 5-4 and 5-6 (shown in Chapter 5) depict some of the major conceptual relationships of both.

The last pitfall to be mentioned in this section pertains to comparing Census data over time. Changing definitions, methodologies, and geographic boundaries make such comparisons particularly difficult. The longer the time span, the more significant the changes. When comparing data across decades, users should make the effort to study definitions for even the most fundamental terms and concepts. To illustrate the danger of taking terminology for granted, consider the changing definition of "person." When determining whether slaves should be counted toward Congressional representation, framers of the Constitution argued along regional lines. Predictably, the South wanted to count slaves, while the North did not. The so-called New Jersey Compromise resulted in slaves

When comparing data across decades, users should make the effort to study definitions for even the most fundamental terms and concepts.

being counted as three-fifths of a person, which is how the Census treated them up to and including 1860. Enumeration of American Indians was also determined by the Constitution, which explicitly excluded "Indians not taxed." This was generally interpreted to mean those living outside white settlements. Until 1860, Indians living in settled areas were counted, but instead of being listed separately in Census publications, they were grouped with "other races." The 1860 Census showed separate tabulations for the Indian population, but those living on Reservations or in the Indian Territories continued to be excluded from the count. The 1890 Census was the first to enumerate all Indians regardless of where they lived, but those on Reservations were still excluded from the definition of "persons" for purposes of Congressional representation. It wasn't until 1940 that all Indians were considered to be "taxed," and thus included in state apportionment totals.

This section has explored some of the most common Census mistakes. Numerous additional examples could be given. The best way to minimize mistakes is to develop good research habits. Figure 10-12 summarizes some of the most important rules for proper Census use. It is probably worth mentioning that even experienced Census researchers make mistakes in interpreting data, and learning about the Census is an ongoing process.

Summary

This chapter has attempted to alert readers to sources of error inherent in the Census process, and to explain how users can evaluate the quality of specific Census figures. The discussion also suggests methods for locating needed tables quickly and efficiently, and offers tips on avoiding common Census mistakes.

The main theme of the chapter is that quality research depends upon a thorough understanding of Census concepts and methods. Hasty assumptions or careless searching

Census publications are among the best-documented statistical reports in the world.

can lead to disastrous results. This doesn't mean readers should shrink from using the Census, only that they should have a healthy respect for its complexity. Still, users of the Census have an advantage over researchers who turn to alternative sources: Census publications are among the best-documented statistical reports in the world. If all this sounds like too much for a novice to cope with, always remember that plenty of excellent glossaries and guides are available to clarify terminology and concepts, and that Census specialists are usually more than willing to answer your specific questions.

Even the broadest understanding of the decennial Census and how it works will cut down on wasted search time and erroneous results. Researchers who consult Census publications on a reasonably frequent basis will be pleased to discover how quickly such understanding falls into place.

SOURCES OF ASSISTANCE

A complete list of State Data Centers and their local affiliates, Federal Depository Libraries, and other Census-related organizations can be found in the annual *Census Catalog & Guide*. A detailed list of Census Bureau subject specialists can be found in the annual *Telephone Contacts for Data Users* or on the Bureau's Internet server. For more information about these publications, contact the Bureau's Customer Services number listed below.

CENSUS BUREAU - WASHINGTON

Bureau of the Census
Washington, D.C. 20233

Census Customer Services: (301) 457-4100

CENSUS BUREAU - REGIONAL OFFICES

Atlanta GA:
101 Marietta St., N.W.
Atlanta, GA 30303-2700
(404) 730-3833

Boston MA:
2 Copley Place
Suite 301
Boston, MA 02117-9108
(617) 424-0510

Charlotte, NC:
Suite 106
901 Center Park Dr.
Charlotte, NC 28217-2935
(704) 344-6144

Chicago, IL:
2255 Enterprise Dr.
Suite 5501
Westchester, IL 60154-5800
(708) 562-1740

Dallas TX:
Room 210
6303 Harry Hines Boulevard
Dallas, TX 75235-5269
(214) 767-7105

Denver CO:
6900 West Jefferson Ave.
Denver, CO 80227-9020
(303) 969-7750

Detroit, MI:
1395 Brewery Park Blvd.
Detroit, MI 48223-5405
(313) 259-1875

Kansas City, KS:
Gateway Tower II
Suite 600
400 State Ave.
Kansas City, KS 66101-2410
(913) 551-6711

Los Angeles, CA:
Suite 300
15350 Sherman Way
Van Nuys, CA 91406-4224
(818) 904-6339

New York, NY:
Room 37-130
Jacob K. Javits Federal Building
26 Federal Plaza
New York, NY 10278-0044
(212) 264-4730

Philadelphia, PA:
First Floor
105 South 7th St.
Philadelphia, PA 19106-3395
(215) 597-8313

Seattle, WA:
101 Stewart St.
Suite 500
Seattle, WA 98101-1098
(206) 728-5314

Figure 10-13

Chapter 11

Rules Affecting Metropolitan and Urbanized Areas

Rules Affecting Metropolitan and Urbanized Areas

THE RULES AFFECTING Metropolitan Areas (MAs) and Urbanized Areas (UAs) are extensive and complex. Chapter 6 introduced basic concepts relating to MAs and UAs, but researchers who need to work with data for these geographic constructs may wish to learn more details about them. This chapter discusses some of the rules pertaining to the following concepts for MAs and UAs: eligibility standards; Area definitions; creation of new Areas; naming conventions; and designation of Central Cities or Places. Another Statistical Unit, called the New England County Metropolitan Area (NECMA) is also introduced. The chapter concludes with a comparison of differences and similarities between MAs and UAs.

More about Metropolitan Areas

The purpose of a Metropolitan Area is to provide a standard definition for large population centers which extend beyond city limits. Metropolitan territory includes the surrounding communities which demonstrate a high degree of economic and social integration with a particular core city. MAs have been an important component of decennial data analysis since the 1950 Census. Furthermore, many government agencies, commercial firms, and nonprofit planners utilize

Metropolitan Areas as a basic unit for comparing large population and business centers in the United States. Federal and state agencies also employ MAs as a primary criterion for distributing funds to local governments. Because Metropolitan Areas serve such a wide range of important functions, the U.S. Office of Management and Budget promulgates exacting rules to govern the creation of these essential geographic constructs.

The regulations set forth by the OMB to administer the creation, classification, composition, and naming of MAs are called "Metropolitan Area Standards." The official list of MAs, which the OMB releases in accordance with its Standards, is called "Metropolitan Area Definitions." Both terms are used throughout this chapter, so it is important for the reader to remember the meaning of each. The Standards and the Definitions may undergo minor changes from year to year, but the OMB announces major changes to each of them every ten years, in conjunction with the decennial Census. It should be stressed that both the MA Standards and the MA Definitions are issued by the Office of Management and Budget, not the Census Bureau.

The regulations set forth by the OMB to administer the creation, classification, composition, and naming of MAs are called "Metropolitan Area Standards." The official list of MAs, which the OMB releases in accordance with its Standards, is called "Metropolitan Area Definitions."

OMB Standards

The fundamental criterion for establishing a Metropolitan Area is the presence of a city with a population of 50,000 or more persons. For large population centers which don't meet the 50,000 population threshold, an alternate set of rules must be met: the county must contain a minimum population of 100,000 persons (75,000 in the New England states); and it must include a Census Bureau-defined Urbanized Area.

Each Metropolitan Area consists of a single county or group of counties, except in the six New England states, where MAs are based on aggregations of cities and towns. The cities which serve as nuclei of a Metropolitan Area are called Central Cities.

Each Metropolitan Area consists of a single county or group of counties, except in the six New England states, where MAs are based on aggregations of cities and towns.

Census Tip

Many novice Census users assume incorrectly that the term Central City pertains to some core portion of a large city. In fact, each Central City consists of an entire city and should not be confused with such non-Census concepts as inner cities or downtown business districts. The adjective "Central" refers to the fact that the city serves as a hub for its Metropolitan Area.

The OMB published its current regulations governing Metropolitan Areas in the March 30, 1990 issue of the *Federal Register*. The document, entitled, "Revised Standards for Defining Metropolitan Areas in the 1990s," represents the first major change in MA Standards since January, 1980. Before issuing final guidelines, the OMB held public hearings, solicited written commentary, and met repeatedly with an interagency group called the Federal Executive Committee on Metropolitan Areas.

Census Tip

The Revised Standards issued in March of 1990 did not take effect until June, 1992. The Metropolitan Areas appearing in the 1990 Census were defined based on the OMB Standards published in January of 1980.

The 1990 Standards maintain continuity with those promulgated in prior decades. The most notable changes involve rules affecting the designation of Central Cities and Outlying Counties. The 1990 Revisions also institute a variety of technical changes, such as those relating to Central Cities whose boundaries extend beyond a single county. Another minor change (which actually went into effect on April 1, 1990) involves naming

How pronounced were the effects of the Revised 1980 Standards on the 1990 Census?

At first glance, readers may see little difference between the Metropolitan Areas tabulated by the Censuses of 1980 and 1990, but the end result was the creation of many new MAs.

Why did OMB institute these changes? The driving force was the fact that many communities were not eligible for Metropolitan status under the old Standards because they didn't have a sufficiently large Central City, even though their areas were Metropolitan in character. The 1980 Standards eased this restriction, creating more MSAs for 1990. Second, as Areas grew in size, neighboring SMSAs were merging with one another and losing their separate identities. Under the 1980 guidelines, these entities can be called CMSAs, thus reflecting their unity as massive Metropolitan Areas, while at the same time being split into component PMSAs to retain past identity. Finally, the new terminology makes it easier to distinguish the three categories of Metropolitan Areas from one another.

---

conventions. The OMB introduced the general phrase "Metropolitan Area" to provide a more encompassing term which can be used to describe MSAs, CMSAs, or PMSAs regardless of their specific type.

As described in Chapter 6, far more significant changes occurred when the OMB issued its 1980 Standards. 1980 revisions did not take effect until *after* the 1980 Census. Since the 1980 Standards govern Metropolitan Areas shown in the 1990 Census, it is these earlier rules which largely determined the differences in treatment of MAs between the two Censuses. For example, the 1980 rules introduced new nomenclature (MSAs, CMSAs, and PMSAs), eased eligibility thresholds for Metropolitan status, and authorized the division of large MAs into smaller subcategories (PMSAs).

Central Cities

The starting point for defining a Metropolitan Area is OMB's designation of one or more Central Cities for the MA. In most cases, this means the presence of a city with a minimum population of 50,000. For counties which do not meet this threshold, a smaller city is eligible, but only if it is part of an Urbanized Area, and only if the surrounding county contains 100,000 people or more. Readers should also note that a Cen-

tral City need not be a city; in a few instances, Central Cities are towns, villages, or even Census Designated Places.

Census terminology implies that each Metropolitan Area has only one Central City, but this is not always the case. In theory, an MA can have an unlimited number of Central Cities, and nearly 40% of all MSAs or PMSAs contain more than one. Every MSA and CMSA must have at least one Central City, but a few PMSAs have none.

The OMB has established six separate criteria for designating Central Cities. The first, and most obvious, is the largest city in the Metropolitan Area. The second criterion states that each additional city with a minimum population of 250,000 persons or 100,000 employed workers will also be designated as a Central City. The remaining criteria pertain to cities with a population of 15,000 or larger, and they reflect various combinations of the following characteristics: the city's size in relation to the largest Central City; the ratio of employed persons to total population; and the percentage of employed residents who also work within that city's boundaries.

OMB rules affecting the naming of Metropolitan Areas are based primarily on the Central Cities. Most MAs are named after their largest Central City, with up to two

In theory, an MA can have an unlimited number of Central Cities, and nearly 40% of all MSAs or PMSAs contain more than one.

NEW IN '90

Previous OMB Standards specified that in order to qualify for Metropolitan status, an Urbanized Area must contain a city with a minimum of 25,000 people. The 1990 Standards relax this rule: now as long as the entity meets the Census Bureau's definition of an Urbanized Area, and the surrounding county contains a minimum of 100,000 people, the OMB will designate it as a Metropolitan Area even if its largest city has a population smaller than 25,000. However, OMB Standards also state that a city must contain a minimum of 15,000 people in order to qualify as a Central City. As a result, several Urbanized counties qualify as PMSAs, yet they contain no Central Cities.

additional cities appearing in the name (e.g., Salt Lake City-Ogden, UT MSA; Albany-Schenectady-Troy, NY MSA). Metropolitan Areas may also have Central Cities which are not included in the name. For example, the Detroit, MI PMSA now contains four Central Cities, but only Detroit appears in the name. Such discrepancies are due to local considerations. The Central Cities of a Metropolitan Area are defined by the OMB alone, but the agency solicits local opinion before assigning the actual MA name. PMSAs without Central Cities are named after their component counties (e.g., Lake County, IL PMSA; Nassau-Suffolk, NY PMSA). Names of CMSAs typically identify their component PMSAs.

Component Parts of a Metropolitan Area

Each Metropolitan Area contains one or more Central Counties and may also contain additional Outlying Counties. A county is designated as "Central" if it meets one of the following two criteria:

- ▸ it contains at least one Central City; or
- ▸ at least 50% of its population lies within the Urbanized Area of the adjacent Central County.

Rules governing Outlying Counties are more complex. Basically, they are designed to

Rules governing Outlying Counties are more complex. Basically, they are designed to address the question, "How far beyond the population center should the boundaries of a Metropolitan Area extend?"

address the question, "How far beyond the population center should the boundaries of a Metropolitan Area extend?" Three characteristics affect this decision: the percentage of employed residents who commute to one of the neighboring Central Counties; the population density of the Outlying County; and the percentage of the Outlying County's population included in the neighboring Urbanized Area. If one of these characteristics is weak, then the other characteristics must compensate by being stronger. For example, if at least 50% of the Outlying County's employed residents commute to one of the Central Counties, then the population density of the Outlying County need only be 25 persons per square mile. But if 25-49% of the employed residents commute to one of the Central Counties, then the density of the Outlying County must be at least 35 persons per square mile.

Census users need not become terribly concerned about the details of these eligibility rules. Instead, they should focus on the fundamental concept affecting Outlying Counties: the commuting patterns of the working population.

 Census Tip

Because Metropolitan Areas in the New England states are based on aggregations of cities and towns, the terms Central Counties and Outlying Counties do not apply. Instead, OMB uses similar commuting guidelines to identify a "Central Core" and a group of outlying towns.

Types of Metropolitan Areas

The OMB's Revised 1980 Standards (which took effect in 1983) introduced new categories of Metropolitan Areas, together with corresponding new terminology. What was formerly known as a Standard Metropolitan Statistical Area (SMSA) is now simply called a Metropolitan Statistical Area (MSA). The largest entities, once called Standard Consolidated Statistical Areas (SCSAs) have been renamed Consolidated Metropolitan Statistical Areas (CMSAs). OMB initiated the change in nomenclature to emphasize an important new distinction: that CMSAs can now be divided into PMSAs, a Statistical Unit which has no direct pre-1983 equivalent.

In addition to the three basic types of Metropolitan Area, the OMB also classifies MAs into size levels, as follows:

- Level A—Population of 1 million or greater
- Level B—Population of 250,000 to 999,999
- Level C—Population of 100,000 to 249,999
- Level D—Population less than 100,000.

When an MSA's population reaches one million (i.e., when it becomes a "Level A" Area), it can be reclassified as a CMSA and subdivided into PMSAs. Neighboring MSAs can also merge to form a newly-defined CMSA if the territory separating them becomes sufficiently Metropolitan. For example, the Baltimore and District of Columbia MSAs became a combined CMSA in December, 1992. Merging to become a CMSA is not merely a point of civic pride; larger size can offer important economic advantages for a Metropolitan Area. Major corporations tend to focus on the largest concentrations of population, so a combined CMSA may be more likely to attract new retail outlets, corporate headquarters, or foreign investors. The newly-created Washington-Baltimore, DC-MD-VA-WV CMSA is now the fourth largest Metropolitan Area in the nation.

Local officials in a Class A MSA can decline CMSA status. Although the OMB creates all CMSAs, local Congressional delegations are now consulted before such changes are made. St. Louis, with a combined 1980 population of nearly 2.4 million, was targeted by the OMB to be divided into three PMSAs in 1983. Local residents later opposed the change, so the following year St. Louis reverted to a single, massive MSA. In 1992, four CMSAs (Buffalo, Hartford, Pittsburgh, and Providence) requested a change to MSA status. Why would the residents of a Metropolitan Area care about the distinction between MSA and CMSA? Because the perceived advantages of maintaining separate PMSA identities may be outweighed by the economic benefits enjoyed by a single MSA. For example, hospitals in Metropolitan Areas with a population of one million or more can qualify for higher Medicare reimbursement rates, so a single MSA may obtain more hospital funding than two smaller PMSAs.

The Role of Local Opinion

The Office of Management and Budget has created exacting Standards for Metropolitan

> **When an MSA's population reaches one million (i.e., when it becomes a "Level A" Area), it can be reclassified as a CMSA and subdivided into PMSAs.**

Q&A

What happens when an Outlying County is situated between the Central Counties of two different Metropolitan Areas?

Commuting patterns govern the creation of Outlying Counties. In cases where a potential Outlying County lies between two different Metropolitan Areas, it will be assigned to the MA which receives the greatest percentage of commuters. If those percentages are extremely close (within 5% of one another), the decision will be based on local preference.

The OMB Standards also address a variety of related concerns, such as two neighboring MSAs merging into a single, larger Area, and the division of CMSAs into component PMSAs.

How should data users compare the various types of Metropolitan Areas?

Discussing CMSAs and MSAs in the same analysis might be viewed as a case of comparing apples and oranges. The massive New York-Northern New Jersey-Long Island, NY-NJ-CT CMSA dwarfs the two-county Binghamton, NY MSA in all respects. Yet the Stamford, CT PMSA component of the New York CMSA has a smaller population than Binghamton. How should the different areas be compared? In common practice, when Metropolitan Areas are ranked, MSAs and CMSAs are compared directly; PMSAs, as component parts of their CMSAs, are typically excluded from such listings. However, in many situations it makes more sense to analyze data at the PMSA-level. The choice is up to the data user. Also remember that certain guidelines affecting federal funding or regulatory compliance are based on PMSAs rather than their CMSA aggregates.

The actual list of MAs, as determined by the Office of Management and Budget, is called the Metropolitan Area Statistical Definitions. The OMB makes changes to this official roster of Metropolitan Areas every year.

Areas, but these regulations also allow local preferences to play a role in certain decisions. The OMB considers an Area's Congressional delegation to be the official channel for communicating such "local opinion." However, the 1990 Standards explicitly encourage U.S. Representatives and Senators to seek input from local government officials, Chambers of Commerce, and other community groups.

The following list highlights some of the decisions about which the OMB will consider local opinion relating to Metropolitan Areas:

- designation as a CMSA (for qualifying Areas only)
- naming of MSAs, CMSAs, and PMSAs
- combining of neighboring MSAs
- assignment of Outlying Counties which are located between two different Metropolitan Areas.

For example, an MSA title consists of the name of its largest Central City, plus additional Central Cities for a maximum of three cities in the title. Local Opinion determines which, if any, of the additional cities will appear in the name. A similar situation pertains to the naming of CMSAs. When the Washington-Baltimore CMSA was created in 1992, extensive local debate swirled around its prospective title: would it be called "Baltimore-Washington" or "Washington-Balti-

more?" Once the OMB receives local input and makes its decision, the ruling will remain in effect until after the next decennial Census.

Metropolitan Area Definitions

The actual list of MAs, as determined by the Office of Management and Budget, is called the Metropolitan Area Statistical Definitions. The OMB makes changes to this official roster of Metropolitan Areas every year. New MSAs are established when Nonmetropolitan counties gain sufficient population. Outlying Counties are appended to existing Metropolitan Areas when commuting patterns change. MSAs can merge to form CMSAs. Within existing CMSAs, new PMSAs can arise, or adjoining PMSAs can merge. Metropolitan Areas also undergo name changes, partly due to population shifts affecting Central Cities and partly due to expressed preferences of local inhabitants. A complete alphabetical list of all Metropolitan Areas (MSAs, PMSAs, and CMSAs) as they existed at the time of the 1990 Census is provided in Appendix B of *Understanding the Census*.

Two factors trigger the creation of new MSAs or changes in the status of existing MAs: revised OMB Standards; and population growth or decline. The Office of Man-

OMB Standards include a "grandfather clause" for Metropolitan Areas: once the Office of Management and Budget confirms an MA based on decennial Census data, that Area remains Metropolitan even if its population subsequently falls below OMB thresholds.

agement and Budget typically announces major revisions in its Metropolitan Area Standards once per decade, as described earlier in the chapter. Metropolitan Areas shown in the 1990 Census are based on OMB Standards published in the January 3, 1980 issue of the *Federal Register*, which became effective in 1983. The March, 1990 Standards did not take effect until June of 1992.

The second factor affecting Metropolitan status is population growth or decline. If a city reaches the 50,000 population threshold, or an Urbanized Area's surrounding county attains the 100,000 mark, the OMB will designate the county an MSA. Population changes are measured by the decennial Census itself, as well as by population estimates calculated between the Censuses. The Bureau of the Census publishes intercensal estimates based on the Federal-State Cooperative Program for Population Estimates. County population estimates are calculated annually, while subcounty estimates (including cities, other Places, and Minor Civil Divisions), are issued every two years. The Bureau publishes both sets of estimates as part of its *Current Population Reports* series. Results can also be found on *CENDATA* and the Census Bureau's World Wide Web site. The latter two electronic sources are described in Chapter 14.

Even though the OMB accepts the Bureau's intercensal estimates when announcing an-

nual changes to its Metropolitan Area Definitions, an MA does not gain permanent status until its population has been confirmed by the next decennial Census.

OMB Standards include a "grandfather clause" for Metropolitan Areas: once the Office of Management and Budget confirms an MA based on decennial Census data, that Area remains Metropolitan even if its population subsequently falls below OMB thresholds. However, this clause pertains only to MAs which pass the decennial test. If a Metropolitan Area is newly defined during an intercensal period (i.e., based on population estimates), its Metropolitan status does not become permanent until its size is confirmed by the next Census. In this manner, a locality could become an MA for a brief time, only to have its status revoked following publication of the decennial Census results.

The OMB unveils major revisions to its list of MAs within two-to-three years of each decennial Census. Changes reflect the revised Standards, as well as the official population counts appearing in the Census itself. Subsequent additions to the list, together with other minor changes, are announced every year, usually in June. Major revisions based on 1990 Census tabulations were issued by the OMB on December 28, 1992, as *OMB Bulletin 93-05*, entitled "Revised Statistical Definitions for Metropolitan Ar-

Q&A

Where can I find a list of current Metropolitan Area Definitions?

The complete, official list of MA Statistical Definitions is issued annually by the Office of Management and Budget as part of its *OMB Bulletin* series. This document, which typically appears in June, must be ordered through the National Technical Information Service (NTIS), not the U.S. Government Printing Office. Lists of important changes to the MA Definitions are usually summarized in press releases from the Census Bureau. These can be found through *CENDATA*, the Bureau's World Wide Web site, or its monthly newsletter (*The Census and You*). The most accessible list of revised Metropolitan Area Definitions is published annually as Appendix II of the *Statistical Abstract of the United States.*

```
            Sample Entry from OMB "Revised Statistical Definitions
                  for Metropolitan Areas," December, 1992.

  FIPS    Area
  Code    Title        Type    Level   Definition          Central Cities

  0520    Atlanta, GA  MSA     A       Barrow County       Atlanta, GA
                                       Bartow County *
                                       Carroll County *
                                       Cherokee County
                                       Clayton County      (Marietta, GA deleted)
                                       Cobb County
                                       Coweta County
                                       DeKalb County
                                       Douglas County
                                       Fayette County
                                       Forsyth County
                                       Fulton County
                                       Gwinnett County
                                       Henry County
                                       Newton County
                                       Paulding County
                                       Pickens County *
                                       Rockdale County
                                       Spalding County
                                       Walton County

                                       (Butts County deleted)

  * added to Statistical Definition in 1992.
```

Figure 11-1

eas." Because of the number and complexity of the PMSAs in the Boston and New York CMSAs, as well as difficulties in obtaining agreement from local officials, final post-Census Definitions for these two Areas (including their component PMSAs) were not published until June, 1993. For this reason, the final list of post-Census MA Definitions can be found in *OMB Bulletin 93-17*.

Metropolitan Area Definitions for each MA consist of the following components: the title (name) of the Metropolitan Area; its type; its component counties (or in the case of a New England MA, its component cities and towns); and a list of its Central Cities. Figure 11-1 shows a sample entry from the 1992 Revised Statistical Definitions, identifying the key characteristics of the Atlanta, GA MSA. According to Figure 11-1, Atlanta is a "Class A" MSA comprised of 20 counties,

with a single Central City (Atlanta). The OMB added three counties to the Atlanta Statistical Definition in 1992, and deleted one. Marietta, Georgia was also deleted as a Central City.

Although the Bureau's 1990 list of Metropolitan Areas is based on the OMB's 1980 Standards, readers should remember that OMB's official Metropolitan Area Definitions are revised every year. The 1990 Census utilizes MA Definitions published in June, 1990—after the official Census Day, but prior to publication of any 1990 tabulations. The 1990 Definitions incorporate the cumulative changes which occurred between 1983 and 1990. Figure 6-7 (located in Chapter 6) summarizes the net effect of those changes. Yuma, Arizona was the last new Metropolitan Area created prior to the 1990 Census tabulations.

The 1990 Census utilizes MA Definitions published in June, 1990—after the official Census Day, but prior to publication of any 1990 tabulations.

New England County Metropolitan Areas (NECMAS)

Individuals who wish to make county-based comparisons between an MA in New England and an MA elsewhere can employ a Statistical Unit called the New England County Metropolitan Area, or NECMA.

Metropolitan Areas in New England differ from those in the rest of the country because they are not comprised of entire counties. Counties do not serve as general-purpose governments in the New England States, so the OMB defines New England MAs as aggregations of cities and towns. In fact, portions of New England counties often appear as parts of several Metropolitan Areas. For example, sections of Worcester County, Massachusetts appear in the following four MAs: the Boston, MA PMSA; the Fitchburg-Leominster, MA MSA; the Pawtucket-Woonsocket-Attleboro, RI-MA PMSA; and the Worcester, MA MSA.

Figure 11-2 lists the component parts of the Portland, ME MSA, a typical New England Metropolitan Area as defined by the OMB. Similar lists for larger MAs, such as Boston or Providence, can be extremely long, with many component parts.

 Census Tip

Standard publications of the 1990 Census reflect the Metropolitan Areas which existed at the time the Census was processed, but a special Report does provide tabulations based on post-Census Definitions. This printed Report, entitled *Metropolitan Areas as Defined by the Office of Management and Budget, June 30, 1993* (*CPH-S-1-1*), shows 1990 population and housing characteristics for 1993 Metropolitan Areas. It appears as part of the *Census of Population and Housing Supplementary Reports*.

Individuals who wish to make county-based comparisons between an MA in New England and an MA elsewhere can employ a Statistical Unit called the New England County Metropolitan Area, or NECMA. The OMB creates NECMAs based on MSAs and CMSAs only; PMSAs do not receive their own NECMAs. NECMAs roughly correspond to their official Metropolitan Area counterparts, but follow county boundaries rather than those of cities and towns. OMB guidelines specify that NECMAs are created in two steps: first, the entire county containing the first-named Central City of the MSA or CMSA is selected; then, the OMB adds any counties which have at least 50% of their population in the MA or CMSA identified during step one.

For example, Figure 11-2 indicates that the Portland, ME MSA consists of 15 towns and 3 cities, representing portions of Cumberland and York Counties. The MSA contains a single Central City (Portland),

COMPONENT PARTS OF A NEW ENGLAND MSA: THE EXAMPLE OF PORTLAND, MAINE

Metropolitan Area Components	Total Population	Land Area (sq. miles)
Portland, ME MSA	**215 281**	**553.1**
Cumberland County (pt.)	197 281	473.2
Cape Elizabeth town	8 854	14.8
Cumberland town	5 836	26.1
Falmouth town	7 610	29.6
Freeport town	6 905	34.7
Gorham town	11 856	50.6
Gray town	5 904	43.3
North Yarmouth town	2 429	21.2
Portland city	64 358	22.6
Raymond town	3 311	33.3
Scarborough town	12 518	47.4
South Portland city	23 163	11.9
Standish town	7 678	60.4
Westbrook city	16 121	16.9
Windham town	13 020	46.7
Yarmouth town	7 862	13.3
York County (pt.)	17 856	80.0
Buxton town	6 494	40.5
Hollis town	3 573	32.0
Old Orchard Beach town	7 789	7.4

Figure 11-2

located in Cumberland County. As a result, the Portland NECMA consists of Cumberland County in its entirety; the York county component of the MSA is not part of any NECMA, because its Metropolitan population represents a small percentage of the total MSA. The total population of the Portland MSA is 215,281 persons; its land area is 743 square miles. The population of the Portland NECMA is 243,135, with a land area of 836 square miles.

Figure 11-3 provides a complete list of 1990 NECMAs. Unlike their corresponding Metropolitan Areas, each NECMA lies within the confines of a single state. Also note that the OMB collapsed the 17 New England MSAs or CMSAs into 16 NECMAs. As with Metropolitan Areas, the OMB revises its list of NECMAs annually, though the most significant changes occur following every decennial Census. The post-Census revisions, published in *OMB Bulletin 93-05*, reduced the number of NECMAs from 16 to 12, largely as a result of consolidating counties.

Rules Affecting Urbanized Areas

Urbanized Areas are defined by the Census Bureau, not the OMB. As described in Chapter 6, the Bureau invented this Statistical Unit to distinguish between Urban and Rural territory in the vicinity of large cities. Because Metropolitan Areas are comprised of counties, and many counties include Rural portions, the Bureau devised Urbanized Areas to identify the most densely-settled land area within a Metropolitan Area. This unique construct first appeared in the 1950 Census.

An Urbanized Area consists of one or more Places and their immediately surrounding densely settled territory which together contain a minimum population of 50,000 persons. The Place or Places around which an Urbanized Area is defined can be Incorporated Places or Census Designated Places. In either case, the Bureau calls them "Central

NEW ENGLAND COUNTY METROPOLITAN AREAS (NECMAs)
(As defined by the OMB in June, 1990)

Bangor, ME
Penobscot County

Boston-Lawrence-Salem-Lowell-Brockton, MA
Essex County
Middlesex County
Norfolk County
Plymouth County
Suffolk County

Bridgeport-Stamford-Norwalk-Danbury, CT **
Fairfield County

Burlington, VT
Chittenden County
Grand Isle County

Hartford-New Britain-Middletown-Bristol, CT
Hartford County
Middlesex County
Tolland County

Lewiston-Auburn, ME
Androscoggin County

Manchester-Nashua, NH
Hillsborough County

New Bedford-Fall River-Attleboro, MA
Bristol County

New Haven-Waterbury-Meriden, CT
New Haven County

New London-Norwich, CT
New London County

Pittsfield, MA
Berkshire County

Portland, ME
Cumberland County

Portsmouth-Dover-Rochester, NH
Rockingham County
Strafford County

Providence-Pawtucket-Woonsocket, RI
Bristol County
Kent County
Providence County
Washington County

Springfield, MA
Hampden County
Hampshire County

Worcester-Fitchburg-Leominster, MA
Worcester County

Figure 11-3

Places," to enable data users to distinguish them from the "Central Cities" of Metropolitan Areas. The territory within a UA which lies outside the Central Places is called the "Urban Fringe."

 Census Tip

Tabulations for NECMAs do not appear in any major 1990 Census publications, because these entities are created by the OMB simply for the convenience of certain data users. However, such tabulations are obtained easily by adding needed figures for the component counties. The Bureau publishes the OMB's list of post-Census NECMAs in Appendix J of a *Supplementary Report* entitled *Metropolitan Areas as Defined by the Office of Management and Budget, June 30, 1993.* An annual list of revised NECMAs can be found in Appendix II of the *Statistical Abstract of the United States.*

The boundaries of an Urbanized Area include all contiguous Blocks which have a population density of at least 1,000 persons per square mile.

Generally speaking, Census Blocks serve as the fundamental component of the Urban Fringe portion of every Urbanized Area. The boundaries of an Urbanized Area include all contiguous Blocks which have a population density of at least 1,000 persons per square mile. The rules governing UAs are complex, and the Bureau incorporates numerous exceptions to the basic density guideline. For example, if 50% of the Blocks within a Place contain a minimum density of 1,000 persons per square mile, then the entire Place becomes part of the Urbanized Area, including those Blocks with lesser density. (In other words, Places play a special role in the creation of UAs.) A second exception relates to the Bureau's goal of maintaining continuous boundaries. If Blocks lying at the outer edges of a UA do not meet the minimum density guideline, but they separate certain densely settled Blocks from the main body of the UA, these sparsely settled outliers will be included in order to eliminate disconnected enclaves of territory. Other sparsely settled Blocks on the outskirts of the UA may be included if they are connected to the Urbanized Area by a main road.

As a result of these rules, the boundaries of an Urbanized Area can cross those of all other Summary Levels except Places. (An exception to this statement involves another unique Census construct called the Extended City. Extended Cities, which are described in Chapter 6, represent the only Incorporated Places whose boundaries are not completely encompassed by their surrounding UAs.) Readers need not remember the intricacies of the Bureau's Urbanized Area guidelines. Instead, they should focus on the primary purpose of the UA, which is to delineate the most densely settled territory surrounding large Places.

 Census Tip

Because Urbanized Areas do not conform to other readily identifiable geographic boundaries, Census users must consult UA maps to determine their exact configuration. Small scale maps can be found in Appendix G of the individual state volumes of *CPH-2* or in the *Supplementary Report* entitled *Urbanized Areas of the United States and Puerto Rico* (*CPH-S-1-2*). Large scale sheet maps can be ordered directly from the Census Bureau.

Figure 11-4 lists the component parts of a typical Urbanized Area, the Appleton-Neenah, WI UA. The Area consists of portions of Outagarnie and Winnebago Counties, plus a very small section of Calumet County. Appleton and Neenah cities represent the Central Places; the other components comprise the Urban Fringe. Notice that all cities and villages within the UA are included in their entirety because they are Incorporated Places. (This situation is complicated by the fact that cities in Wisconsin can cross county boundaries, which is the case with Appleton and Menasha. Nevertheless, both of these cities are completely contained within the UA boundary.) In con-

**Component Parts of an Urbanized Area:
The Example of the Appleton-Neenah, WI Urbanized Area**

Urbanized Area Components	Total Population	Land Area (sq. miles)	Population Density[1]
Appleton-Neenah, WI UA	160 918	62.1	2 794.4
In Central Place	88 914	25.6	3 620.9
Appleton city, WI	65 695	17.6	3 835.4
Neenah city, WI	23 219	8.0	3 126.3
Urban Fringe	72 004	36.6	2 179.9
Calumet County (pt.)	9 840	3.0	3 233.8
Appleton city	9 075	2.2	4 219.0
Harrison town (pt.)	692	0.6	1 153.3
Menasha city	73	0.3	250.1
Outagarnie County (pt.)	98 219	35.4	2 913.9
Appleton city	56 177	15.1	3 838.9
Buchanan town (pt.)	1 309	1.2	1 054.9
Combined Locks village	2 190	1.4	1 815.1
Grand Chute town (pt.)	11 318	6.2	1 871.3
Greenville town (pt.)	597	0.6	947.4
Kaukauna city	11 982	5.1	2 545.2
Kimberly village	5 406	1.9	3 164.9
Little Chute village	9 207	3.8	2 622.5
Vandenbroek town (pt.)	33	–	1 554.0
Winnebago County (pt.)	52 859	23.8	2 536.9
Appleton city	443	0.3	1 287.7
Clayton town (pt.)	103	0.1	1 839.8
Menasha city	14 638	5.7	3 402.0
Menasha town (pt.)	13 004	8.1	1 807.3
Neenah city	23 219	8.0	3 126.3
Neenah town (pt.)	1 452	1.6	961.1

[1] Persons per square mile.

Figure 11-4

trast, each of the towns is only partially encompassed by the UA because towns in Wisconsin are unincorporated MCDs. The UA includes only those Blocks within each town which meet the minimum density guidelines.

The column labeled Population Density lists three component entities, whose densities are less than 1,000 persons per square mile. The Calumet County portion of Menasha City is included because Incorporated Places, by definition, are represented in their entirety. Portions of the towns of Neenah and Greenville are presumably included because they fill gaps in the outer boundaries of the UA.

As with Central Cities in an MA, an Urbanized Area can have an unlimited number of Central Places. Most have anywhere from one to three Central Places, but larger UAs, such as Boston or Chicago may have seven or eight. How does the Bureau determine which Places within an Urbanized Area will serve as Central Places? If the Urbanized Area includes Central Cities of a Metropolitan Area, every Central City automatically be-

As with Central Cities in an MA, an Urbanized Area can have an unlimited number of Central Places.

Census Tip

Because Urbanized Areas are composed of Blocks, UA boundaries can split Blocks Groups (BGs). When using *STF 1A* and *STF 3A*, users should be alert to split BGs, especially in Minor Civil Divisions. Normally, the "pt." designation following a Block Group number would indicate the Block Group crossed the boundary of an Incorporated Place or CDP, but it might also mean the Block Group crosses a UA boundary. The latter situation can only be verified by using detailed Block maps and UA maps to compare the boundaries of the Block Group to those of the UA.

Metropolitan Areas consist of entire counties and are based on population size and commuting patterns, while Urbanized Areas consist of portions of counties and are based on population size and density.

comes a Central Place. However, some Metropolitan Areas do not contain a Central City, and some UAs do not contain any Metropolitan territory. In these instances, the UA's Central Place (or Places) are determined strictly by population size. The Bureau's naming conventions are also tied closely to those of the corresponding Metropolitan Area. Where a UA is located primarily within a single MA, it will have the same name. For example, the Sioux City, IA-NE-SD Urbanized Area uses the same name as the Sioux City, IA-NE-SD MSA, although

the boundaries of the two entities are not the same. If an Urbanized Area is not part of a single Metropolitan Area, it is named after one or more of its Central Places, with priority given to Incorporated Places.

Comparing MAs and UAs

Despite the fact that MAs and UAs often have the same or similar names, and that their territories overlap, it is difficult to compare the two Summary Levels directly. Each is defined by a different government agency, is based on different guidelines, and serves different purposes. Figure 11-5 summarizes some of the major differences between the two Statistical Units. The most important distinctions are that Metropolitan Areas consist of entire counties and are based on population size and commuting patterns, while Urbanized Areas consist of portions of counties and are based on population size and density. Another noteworthy difference is that the decennial Census utilizes the MA Definitions established by the OMB prior to the Census, while its UA definitions are those created by the Bureau itself after the Census is taken. Most Metropolitan Areas contain some Rural territory; by definition, Urbanized Areas contain no Rural territory whatsoever. As a result, Metropolitan Areas represent 16% of the land area in the United States, while Urbanized Areas represent less than 2%. Readers may wish to refer to the diagrams shown in Figures 6-16 and 6-17 (located in Chapter 6) for two alternate views of MA/UA relationships.

The following discussion explores some of the ways in which an Urbanized Area can interact with its corresponding Metropolitan Area. The relationships between the two are indirect, complicated, and vary from case to case. The situation is all the more confusing because most UA/MA pairs have the same or similar names. The diagram shown earlier in Figure 6-17 represents a major oversimplifi-

NEW IN '90

The phrase "Central Place" is new terminology for 1990. Earlier Censuses referred to the nuclei of Urbanized Areas as Central Cities. The new terminology was adopted to distinguish between UAs and MAs, but also to emphasize that the population center of a UA need not be a city, but can also be a town or other Incorporated Place. A Central Place can also be a statistical construct called a Census Designated Place (CDP). The Central Place of the Hyannis, MA UA is the Hyannis CDP, within the town of Barnstable. (CDPs are described in Chapter 6.)

COMPARISON OF METROPOLITAN AREAS WITH URBANIZED AREAS

Metropolitan Areas	Urbanized Areas
Defined by OMB.	Defined by Census Bureau.
New Areas defined annually.	New Areas defined decennially.
Based on commuting patterns.	Based on population density.
Definitions used in decennial Census are determined prior to Census tabulation.	Definitions used in decennial Census are determined *after* Census is tabulated.
Nucleii called Central Cities.	Nucleii called Central Places.
Minimum component: one county.[1]	No minimum component; transcends most political boundaries.
Can cross county and state lines.	Can cross, county, state, and MA lines.
Do not cross County Subdivisions.	Can cross County Subdivisions.
Easily recognizable boundaries.	No easily recognizable bounds.
Includes Rural territory.	Contains no Rural territory.
Virtually all MAs contain portions of at least one UA.	Can exist outside the bounds of a Metropolitan Area.
Encompass 78% of 1990 U.S. population.	Encompass 64% of 1990 U.S. population.
Comprise 16% of U.S. land area.	Comprise 1.7% of U.S. land area.

[1] Except in the six New England states.

Figure 11-5

Due to quirks in the rules and regulations of the OMB and the Census Bureau, a Metropolitan Area can contain more than one UA.

cation, because an Urbanized Area may cross the boundaries of its corresponding MA, and because it typically assumes the shape of an irregular, many-sided polygon, resembling some free-form drawing made on an Etch-a-Sketch.

By definition, UAs can cross county boundaries; therefore portions of a UA can extend beyond a Metropolitan Area. A UA can also comprise parts of two or more adjacent PMSAs within a CMSA.

Every CMSA contains at least one Urbanized Area, as do most MSAs. All PMSAs contain Urbanized territory within their boundaries, but many PMSAs have no Urbanized Area of their "own." The latter situ-

ation occurs where no Central Place is found within that PMSA's boundaries, but where Urbanized territory from a neighboring PMSA extends into it. One of the many examples for 1990 is the Beaver County, PA PMSA, whose Urbanized territory consists entirely of portions of the Pittsburgh, PA Urbanized Area which extend from the adjacent PMSA.

Due to quirks in the rules and regulations of the OMB and the Census Bureau, a Metropolitan Area can contain more than one UA. How can that be? If the densely populated Urban Fringes of two Central Places within the MA do not connect with one another, each is designated a separate Urbanized Area. For example, the Daytona Beach, FL MSA contains large portions of the Daytona Beach UA and the Deltona UA. For 1990, nine PMSAs and 27 MSAs each contain two or more Urbanized Areas. The most extreme case is the Riverside-San Bernardino, CA PMSA, which contains portions of five different UAs.

Even more confusing, it is possible (though rare) for an MSA to have no accompanying UA. For 1990, three MSAs exhibit this phenomenon: Bradenton, FL; Enid, OK; and Jamestown-Dunkirk, NY.

As a final variation, an Urbanized Area can be completely independent of any Metropolitan Areas. This occurs where a city and its Urban Fringe have more than 50,000 persons, but the surrounding county has fewer than 100,000 people, and thus does not qualify as an MSA. An example is Ithaca, NY, which became an Urbanized Area in 1990, but is not yet part of an MSA. The 1990 population of Ithaca's surrounding county (Tompkins) is only 94,097 and the neighboring counties are Nonmetropolitan. Figure 11-6, lists the 21 UAs which were independent of any MA as of the 1990 Census. The boundaries for these UAs lie completely outside those of any MA. Thirteen of these were newly defined based on analysis of 1990 population data.

Designation as a UA is generally the first step toward becoming an MA. When the

Q&A

Why do some MSAs contain no Urbanized territory?

Although the situation seldom arises, it is possibly for a Metropolitan Area to have no corresponding Urbanized Area. Various scenarios can account for this, but the reasons are based on the fact that MSAs and UAs are established at different points in time. In the case of Enid, OK, the OMB's "grandfather rule" comes into play. Enid, which is the nation's smallest MSA for 1990, now falls below the OMB's population thresholds for Metropolitan Areas. The city of Enid's 1990 population was under 50,000 and its county population was well below 100,000. However, because the city's 1980 population was above 50,000, Enid remains an MSA. In contrast, the Bureau reevaluates Urbanized Areas based on the most recent decennial data. Therefore, Enid lost its UA status for 1990.

A similar fluke affects the Bradenton, FL MSA. For 1990, Bradenton has no Urbanized Area which is distinctly its own; it shares Urbanized territory with the adjacent Sarasota, FL MSA. The Urbanized Area is called the Sarasota-Bradenton UA. This scenario is fairly common for PMSAs, but quite rare for MSAs. The Bradenton situation was remedied in 1992, when the OMB merged Sarasota and Bradenton into a single MSA based on 1990 commuting patterns.

1990 URBANIZED AREAS INDEPENDENT OF METROPOLITAN AREAS

Urbanized Area Title	New in 1990 [1]	MSA in 1992 [2]
Auburn-Opelika, AL		
Brunswick, GA	X	
Dover, DE	X	X
Goldsboro, NC		X
Grand Junction, CO		
Greenville, NC	X	X
Hattiesburg, MS		
Hyannis, MA	X	X [3]
Idaho Falls, ID	X	
Ithaca, NY	X	
Logan, UT	X	
Longview, WA-OR		
Missoula, MT		
Myrtle Beach, SC	X	X
Pocatello, ID		
Punta Gorda, FL	X	X
Rocky Mount, NC	X	X
Rome, GA		
San Luis Obispo, CA	X	X
Sumter, SC	X	X
Vero Beach, FL	X	

[1] Newly-designated UA in 1990.
[2] Newly-defined MSA in 1992. Does not affect 1990 Census publications.
[3] MA title: Barnstable-Yarmouth, MA MSA.

Figure 11-6

OMB announced its post-Census Metropolitan Area Definitions in December of 1992, nine "independent" UAs had gained sufficient population to be became MAs. For example, Hyannis gained MA status, but Ithaca did not.

Summary

This chapter has merely touched on some of the basic provisions of the rules and regulations affecting MAs and UAs. The OMB Standards for Metropolitan Areas may seem unduly complex, but with millions of dollars in federal aid riding on a Metropolitan designation, such guidelines must be extremely precise. And with more than 350 Metropolitan Areas currently defined, the possible combinations of individual circumstances can be quite varied.

To understand the importance of large Metropolitan Areas in the United States, consider the following facts: only 40 MAs had a 1990 population of one million or more, yet the sum of these few areas comprised 53% of the total U.S. population.

Although the rules governing the creation of Urbanized Areas are a bit more straightforward, they are equally important, since UAs serve as important definitional components of many MAs.

Users must also remain alert to a variety of pitfalls associated with these complex Statistical Units. Researchers should remember that the component parts of Metropolitan Areas may undergo considerable change from decade to decade and even year to year. For CMSAs, users must also determine whether they need data at the consolidated level or for individual PMSAs. Urbanized Areas present challenges of their own. At the very least, researchers should always consult a UA map before working with this unique type of geographic construct.

Urbanized Areas

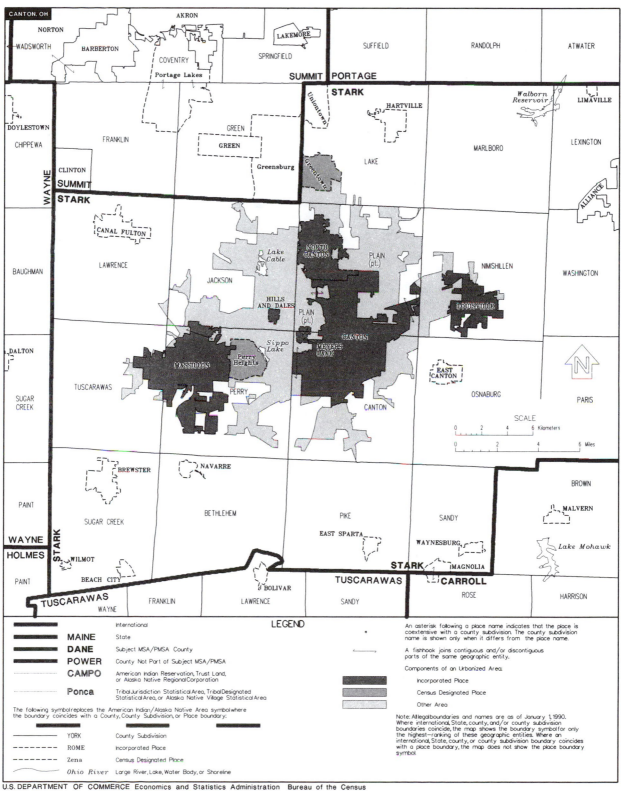

Figure 11-7
Map of Canton, Ohio Urbanized Area

Chapter 12

Congressional Apportionment Explained

Congressional Apportionment Explained

THE CONSTITUTION mandates Congressional reapportionment every ten years, but it is silent on the matter of *how* such redistribution should be accomplished. Congress itself enacts legislation which determines the actual apportionment method, and the topic has been debated fiercely at various times since the dawn of the Republic. In fact, President Washington exercised the first veto in United States history to strike down a reapportionment act. For the first 50 years, Congress simply enlarged the number of Congressional seats to accommodate the growing population; the ratio thus remained fixed at about one Representative per every 33,000 constituents. Beginning in 1840, Congress established the total number of seats prior to receiving Census results, so the number of constituents per District fluctuated each decade. Finally, in 1912, the number of Representatives was fixed at 435, where it remains today.

For apportionment purposes, the official 1990 population of the United States includes all federal government employees and military personnel stationed abroad and their dependents, but otherwise excludes the residents of such U.S. foreign territories as Puerto Rico and Guam. Residents of the District of Columbia are also excluded. The 1990 apportionment population is 249,022,783. The corresponding counts for each of the 50 states are shown in Figure 12-1.

The Apportionment Problem

Given the fixed number of seats, it is mathematically impossible to maintain Congressional Districts of equal size. This is because the Constitution imposes two restrictions:

1990 Population and Number of Representatives, by State

STATES	APPORTIONMENT POPULATION	NUMBER OF REPRESENTATIVES BASED ON THE 1990 CENSUS	CHANGE IN SIZE OF DELEGATON
UNITED STATES	249,022,783	435	...
Alabama	4,062,608	7	...
Alaska	551,947	1	...
Arizona	3,677,985	6	+1
Arkansas	2,362,239	4	...
California	29,839,250	52	+7
Colorado	3,307,912	6	...
Connecticut	3,295,669	6	...
Delaware	668,696	1	...
Florida	13,003,362	23	+4
Georgia	6,508,419	11	+1
Hawaii	1,115,274	2	...
Idaho	1,011,986	2	...
Illinois	11,466,682	20	-2
Indiana	5,564,228	10	...
Iowa	2,787,424	5	-1
Kansas	2,485,600	4	-1
Kentucky	3,698,969	6	-1
Louisiana	4,238,216	7	-1
Maine	1,233,223	2	...
Maryland	4,798,622	8	...
Massachusetts	6,029,051	10	-1
Michigan	9,328,784	16	-2
Minnesota	4,387,029	8	...
Mississippi	2,586,443	5	...
Missouri	5,137,804	9	...
Montana	803,655	1	-1
Nebraska	1,584,617	3	...
Nevada	1,206,152	2	...
New Hampshire	1,113,915	2	...
New Jersey	7,748,634	13	-1
New Mexico	1,521,779	3	...
New York	18,044,505	31	-3
North Carolina	6,657,630	12	+1
North Dakota	641,364	1	...
Ohio	10,887,325	19	-2
Oklahoma	3,157,604	6	...
Oregon	2,853,733	5	...
Pennsylvania	11,924,710	21	-2
Rhode Island	1,005,984	2	...
South Carolina	3,505,707	6	...
South Dakota	699,999	1	...
Tennessee	4,896,641	9	...
Texas	17,059,805	30	+3
Utah	1,727,784	3	...
Vermont	564,964	1	...
Virginia	6,216,568	11	+1
Washington	4,887,941	9	+1
West Virginia	1,801,625	3	-1
Wisconsin	4,906,745	9	...
Wyoming	455,975	1	...

Apportionment population for the United States includes federal government employees and military personnel stationed abroad, but excludes residents of the District of Columbia and of U.S. territories.

Figure 12-1

each state must have at least one Representative; and Districts cannot be split between two states. So how can fair representation be achieved? As shown below, the basic reallocation method seems simple.

1. Divide the national population by 435 to obtain the average size of a Congressional District.

2. To obtain each state's quota of Representatives, divide the state's population by the size of that average District.

Using the official 1990 apportionment count, the average ("ideal") size of a District is 572,466 persons. (This figure is obtained by divided 249,022,783 by 435, then rounding to the nearest whole number.)

 Census Tip

The process of allocating the number of Congressional Districts among the 50 states following every decennial Census is called apportionment. Once the Districts have been reapportioned, the states themselves determine the actual boundaries of the new Districts, in a process called redistricting. Redistricting is explained more fully in Chapter 2.

Next, divide 572,466 into each state's apportionment population to determine its quota of Congressional seats. Montana, with a 1990 population of 803,655, would receive 1.40 seats in the House of Representatives (803,655 divided by 572,466). Using the same method, California would receive 52.12 seats, New York would receive 31.52 seats, and so on. The problem lies in the fractional remainders. Should Montana's allotment be rounded up to two seats or down to one? Unfortunately, neither solution results in an equitable distribution. If Montana were to retain two seats, each District would contain 401,828 persons, which is 29.8% smaller than the ideal. If Montana's delegation were reduced to one statewide Representative, then the single District would be 40.4% larger than the ideal.

Since states cannot have fractional representation, wouldn't it be fair to split differences down the middle? Half the difference between 1 and 2 is 1.5; Montana's ideal quota of 1.4 would thus be rounded down to 1. This method utilizes the arithmetic average, or "mean," to determine the rounding point. (The arithmetic mean of two numbers is obtained by adding the two numbers together, then dividing the sum by 2.)

This solution is simple and intuitive, so of course it is not the correct answer. Although it is unlikely that most Congressional Districts will equal the ideal size, some Districts will be closer to the ideal than others. To achieve the fairest representation possible, size differences among all Districts must be minimized. Rounding at the arithmetic mean does not minimize variances, but several other statistical methods offer viable alternatives.

Over the decades, a variety of rounding techniques have been tried. Some methods favored large states, others benefitted smaller ones. With so much at stake, politicians could become extremely passionate about statistical methods. The ongoing debate came to a standstill following the 1920 Census, when 42 different reapportionment bills were introduced and none were passed. As a result, no reapportionment took place during that decade, directly violating the Constitutional mandate. In 1929, the Speaker of the House asked the National Academy of Sciences to evaluate five valid alternatives. The four prominent mathematicians conducting the study sought to identify the method which minimized variance among the Districts and was least biased toward large or small states. The recommended technique, called the Method of Equal Proportions, was the only option which met both of the following tests: it minimized the deviation between the most and the least populous Districts; and it minimized each District's variance from the nationwide average. This emphatic endorsement failed to sway Congress after the 1930

To achieve the fairest representation possible, size differences among all Districts must be minimized.

The recommended technique, called the Method of Equal Proportions, was the only option which met both of the following tests: it minimized the deviation between the most and the least populous Districts; and it minimized each District's variance from the nationwide average.

Census, but a permanent apportionment law was enacted in 1941, and the Method of Equal Proportions has been used in every decade since.

The Method of Equal Proportions

The apportionment method utilized by the Census Bureau side-steps these concerns by allocating Congressional seats one-by-one until all 435 have been filled.

The Method of Equal Proportions, also called the Hill Method, rounds up or down by utilizing the geometric mean between whole numbers. The geometric mean between two numbers is obtained by multiplying the two numbers together, then taking the square root of their product. The geometric mean between 1 and 2 is 1.4142 (the square root of 1 x 2). Using this method, Montana would still be entitled to one seat only, since its ideal quota (1.40) falls slightly below the geometric mean. Taking another example, the ideal quota for Georgia is 11.37 seats. The geometric mean of 11 and 12 is 11.4891 (the square root of 11 x 12), so the allotment is rounded down to 11 seats.

Despite the National Academy's seal of approval, the Method of Equal Proportions is not statistically neutral. Notice the fractional portion of the mean grows larger as the size of the whole numbers increase. In the case of California, with an ideal quota of 52.12, the geometric mean is 52.4976. In other words, the cut-off point for rounding upward is higher for larger states. This means as a state accumulates seats, it becomes increasingly difficult to obtain each additional one.

Think of the process as a buffet line, with Congressional seats doled out one at a time, like plates of food. Because larger states have bigger appetites (i.e., they are entitled to greater representation), they return to the front of the queue for additional "servings" more frequently than smaller states.

Another, more mechanical problem is that the sum of the allocated seats does not automatically total 435. As with other rounding methods, the total seldom equals 100%. Using the ideal District size of 572,466, the total actually comes to 438. The divisor itself must be rounded up in order for the sum of the state allocations to equal 435. In fact, there is a range of acceptable values for an ideal District size, each of which will satisfy the equation.

Allocation by Priority Value

What is the point of the Equal Proportions method if a single "ideal" District size cannot be used as a divisor? If any number within a range of values will serve equally well as the divisor, which number should be used? The apportionment method utilized by the Census Bureau side-steps these concerns by allocating Congressional seats one-by-one until all 435 have been filled. The Bureau calculates a ranked list of state claims to each seat. Priority Values, based on population size, determine the order in which the seats are distributed. But because the Constitution requires every state to have at least one Congressional District, each state starts the process with a single seat. The allocation procedure thus begins with the 51st seat.

Think of the process as a buffet line, with Congressional seats doled out one at a time, like plates of food. Because larger states have bigger appetites (i.e., they are entitled to greater representation), they return to the front of the queue for additional "servings" more frequently than smaller states. In fact, larger states can receive third, fourth, or fifth helpings before a smaller state receives its second allocation.

So where does the Method of Equal Proportions come into play? A state's rankings are not determined solely by its population, but also according to the geometric mean of its current and next seat in the round. As shown below, the Priority Value for California's second seat is 21,099,536, which outranks all other states; therefore, California receives its second seat before any other state. To see how Priority Values are assigned, follow the process through each step.

Step 1: Generate a List of Multipliers

Because every state starts with a single seat, priority ranking starts with each state's second seat. Priority Values are computed by dividing the state's 1990 population by the geometric mean of its current and next seat numbers. The geometric mean for any state's second seat would be 1.4142— the square root of (1 x 2). The geometric mean for the third seat would be 2.4495— the square root of (2 x 3)— and so on. These values are identical for every state; the geometric mean for a second seat is the same for California as it is for Montana.

Step 2 divides the geometric means into each state's population. To keep the calculations simpler, the means are first converted into their reciprocals (the number divided into 1) so they can be multiplied rather than divided. For example, the reciprocal of 1.4142 is .70710678. Multiplying any number by .70710678 will produce the same result as dividing that number by 1.4142.

The listing below shows the geometric means for the second through seventh seats, then skips to the 53rd seat to save space. California, the largest state, has an ideal quota of 52.12 seats, so we only need to calculate the geometric means up to 53. The listing also shows the reciprocal values for each geometric mean. The reciprocals are the multipliers used in the next step.

Seat Number	Geometric Mean	Reciprocal Value (Multiplier)
2	1.4142	.70710678
3	2.4495	.40824829
4	3.4641	.28867513
5	4.4721	.22360680
6	5.4772	.18257419
7	6.4807	.15430335
53	52.4976	.01904848

Step 2: Calculate Priority Values

Next, the appropriate Multiplier for each seat is applied to a state's population to determine a list of Priority Values. In the example below, the Priority Value for California's third seat is computed as follows:

.40824829 x 29,839,250 = 12,181,823.

Priority Values for California's remaining seats are calculated in similar fashion until the 52nd value is computed. The process is then repeated for all other states.

Calculating California's Priority Values				
Seat	Multiplier	x	population	= Priority Value
2	.70710678		29,839,250	21,099,536
3	.40824829		29,839,250	12,181,823
4	.28867513		29,839,250	8,613,849
5	.22360680		29,839,250	6,672,259

The table below further illustrates the process, showing Priority Values for the first several seats for each of the eight most populous states. The Values in a single column are generated by applying the same multiplier to each state's population.

State	Seat 2	Seat 3	Seat 4	Seat 5	Seat 6
CA	21,099,536	12,181,823	8,613,849	6,672,259	5,447,877
NY	12,759,392	7,366,638	5,209,000	4,034,874	3,294,461
TX	12,063,104	6,964,636	4,924,741	3,814,688	3,114,680
FL	9,194,765	5,308,600	3,753,747	2,907,640	2,274,078
PA	8,432,043	4,868,243	3,442,367	2,666,446	
IL	8,108,169	4,681,253	3,310,146	2,564,028	
OH	7,698,501	4,444,732	3,142,900		
MI	6,596,446	3,808,460			

Step 3: Assign Seats in Ranked Order

After all Priority Values have been assigned to every state, the resulting numbers are ranked in descending order. Seats are then allocated one at a time until the last has been filled. The table below shows the outcome of the first 12 rounds in the allocation process. It takes 385 rounds before the 435th seat has been filled (435 minus the first 50 which are automatically assigned).

For 1990, California received the 51st seat and New York the 52nd. As the first and second most highly populated states, this

After all Priority Values have been assigned to every state, the resulting numbers are ranked in descending order. Seats are then allocated one at a time until the last has been filled.

Cumulative Allocation Round	Seat Number	Priority Value	State	Seats Assigned for that state
First	51	21,099,536	CA	2
Second	52	12,759,392	NY	2
Third	53	12,181,823	CA	3
Fourth	54	12,063,104	TX	2
Fifth	55	9,194,765	FL	2
Sixth	56	8,613,849	CA	4
Seventh	57	8,432,043	PA	2
Eighth	58	8,108,169	IL	2
Ninth	59	7,698,501	OH	2
Tenth	60	7,366,638	NY	3
Eleventh	61	6,964,636	TX	3
Twelfth	62	6,672,259	CA	5

outcome seems logical. The 53rd seat did not go to Texas (the third most populous state), but again to California. Because of its overwhelming size, California returned to the head of the line. Texas received the 54th seat, Florida the 55th, then California returned once again for the 56th. In this way, the larger states were given additional turns before smaller states received their first.

 ## Census Tip

The Apportionment Population of the United States is used for one purpose only: Congressional reapportionment. Congressional redistricting is based upon the Resident Population, as provided to the states by the Bureau's P.L. 94-171 data.

Summary

The manner in which Congressional seats are allocated appears complex, but the arithmetic is fairly basic. The Census Bureau computes Priority Values and assigns the seats, but the procedures followed are set forth in the Apportionment Act of 1941. For the five decades preceding the 1990 Census, the process received little notoriety. Following the 1990 reallocation, however, several states filed lawsuits to protest the outcome.

Q&A

Where can Census information relating to Congressional Districts be found?

Complete-count data for Congressional District boundaries as they existed at the time of the Census (the 101st Congress) appear on *Summary Tape File 1A.* Summary statistics can be found on *Public Law 94-171 Data* files and in the May 15, 1991 issue of *U.S. Department of Commerce News*, also designated as Press Release CB 91-182, and on *CENDATA.*

Complete-count data for the redrawn boundaries of the 103rd Congress are published on *Summary Tape File 1D*; sample data appear on *Summary Tape File 3D.* (The boundaries for the 102nd Congress are the same as those in effect for the 101st.) Summary statistics for each state are published in the print Report series CPH-4, *Population and Housing Characteristics for Congressional Districts of the 103rd Congress.*

A series of 36 by 42 inch map sheets, *Congressional District State Outline Maps (103rd Congress)* can be purchased from Census Bureau Customer Services. A more convenient format for District boundaries is the two-volume *Congressinal District Atlas, 103rd Congress of the United States*, which includes a detailed Place-name index.

Because the Census focuses on the Resident Population of the United States, the Apportionment Population statistics shown in Exhibit 12-1 are not published in any of the 1990 Summary Tape Files or print Reports except for the Summary Volume for CPH-2. The numbers were released in the December 26, 1990 issue of *U.S. Department of Commerce News*, also designated as Press Release CB 90-232, and can also be found on *CENDATA.* A more detailed table is shown in *1990 Census Profile* Number 1 (March 1991), entitled *Population Trends and Congressional Apportionment.*

The arcana of statistical rounding methods occupied headlines and lawyers' briefs for several months, but in the end, the Court ruled that Congress maintained the right to determine an allocation method, so long as it was statistically defensible.

tana, whose Congressional delegation was reduced from two to one, took its case all the way to the Supreme Court. The arcana of statistical rounding methods occupied headlines and lawyers' briefs for several months. In the end, the Court decided against Montana, ruling that Congress maintained the right to determine an allocation method, so long as it was statistically defensible. The Method of Equal Proportions met that test. Massachusetts also sued the government, and its case went to the Supreme Court as well. Massachusetts objected to the inclusion of armed forces abroad in the apportionment population. (Chapter 5 describes the manner in which the overseas population was enumerated and allocated among the states.) Had resident population been used, as it had been in 1980, the state would have retained its ninth seat. The Court once again rejected the challenge and the reapportionment outcome remained unchanged. With so much at stake, however, it is likely that reapportionment will reemerge as a controversy surrounding the 2000 Census, whether in Congress, the courts, or both.

Chapter 13

Using EXTRACT

Using **EXTRACT**

THE AVAILABILITY of Census publications on CD-ROM has opened an undiscovered world of information access for thousands of researchers and data users. The widespread distribution of CD-ROM products, together with easy-to-use software such as GO, make Census Files accessible to even the most inexperienced user. However, one aspect of computerized Census retrieval remains daunting. EXTRACT, the Bureau's data extraction software for use with CD-ROMs, is one of the most bewildering and underutilized facets of the electronic Census. Many users who have struggled to master this complicated program give up after encountering frustration and confusion. Others find EXTRACT completely intimidating, and have never bothered to try it. EXTRACT is definitely not for the one-time Census user, or even the casual, sometime user. Learning the program requires an investment in time, effort, and patience. Furthermore, EXTRACT is not an elegant product, nor is it intended for complex data manipulation. To create even the most basic tables requires multiple steps.

So why should anyone bother learning to use EXTRACT? As discussed in Chapter 8, the GO programs included on most Census CD-ROMs are wonderfully simple to use, but they provide limited data retrieval and display capabilities. Although GO insulates users from the intricacies of Census File structures, it offers extremely basic, prepackaged choices only. In contrast, EXTRACT allows users to perform customized searches, and allows them to manipulate their retrieval sets in myriad ways. Among EXTRACT's more useful capabilities, it can:

- ► retrieve data from more than one table at a time
- ► customize data display
- ► select specified combinations of geographic areas
- ► identify entities which meet desired characteristics
- ► calculate percentages and subtotals
- ► combine data from several different Census discs
- ► combine 1990 data with statistics from

other Census products
- download results for use with spreadsheets and other software.

This chapter provides an introduction to the basic functions of the EXTRACT program. The discussion focuses on using EXTRACT to retrieve 1990 Census information. Although it is impossible to explore all the features of EXTRACT in such a brief presentation, the chapter also describes some of the software's more sophisticated capabilities. In order to provide a realistic idea of how the program can be used, the chapter concludes with a step-by-step case study of EXTRACT in action.

EXTRACT was designed by Paul Zeisset and Bob Marske, of the Bureau's Economic Census Division, to allow analysts at the Bureau to manipulate CD-ROM data from the Economic Census without using commercial software. Because Bureau employees found EXTRACT so useful for internal purposes, the decision was made to offer it as a public-domain software product. The program, together with the necessary Auxiliary Files to read the discs, were included on later editions of the 1987 Economic Census CD-ROM. Zeisset and Marske subsequently wrote all revised versions of the program, plus the accompanying documentation. Like GO, EXTRACT was compiled using Nantucket's Clipper software.

EXTRACT works with the most popular 1990 Census CD-ROM products: all *Summary Tape Files* and the *EEO Files*. To be EXTRACT-compatible, a Census disc must contain data stored in database (*.**DBF**) format, and the File must have corresponding EXTRACT Auxiliary Files available. *PUMS Files* and *TIGER/Line Files* are not EXTRACT-compatible because they do not exist in .**DBF** format. The *SSTF* titles and AOA Files are not EXTRACT-compatible at this time because no Auxiliary Files have been created. The latter two series contain extremely large, complex tables, but the Bureau plans to create the necessary Auxiliary Files in the future. For the purposes of illustration,

this chapter uses examples from various *STF 1* and *STF 3* products, with an emphasis on *STF 3A*.

Census Tip

For readers who learn best from a hands-on approach, Zeisset and Marske have designed an excellent set of self-paced tutorials. The tutorials can be found on most CD-ROM discs issued by the Economic Division, and are located in the "*extract*" directory. The files are stored in ASCII-text format and can be printed or downloaded from the discs. The tutorial for Summary Tape File products is called EXTUTOR4.

Census Database Structure

Data from 1990 Summary Tape Files and similar summary data products are stored on CD-ROM in database format. These databases were created using Borland International, Inc.'s dBASE III Plus format. dBASE was chosen to create the CD-ROM Files not only because it is one of the most widely-used database programs, but also because the dBASE programming language is regarded as an industry standard. In this way, the Bureau has striven to make the Census discs conform as closely as possible to the goal of "open architecture," meaning the discs can be used with a variety of common software packages. However, the EXTRACT program was written specifically for use with Census Files, so dBASE or other commercial products are not actually needed to retrieve and manipulate data from the CD-ROM discs.

Proper use of EXTRACT requires an understanding of fundamental database concepts, as well as a familiarity with the File structures found on the various Census CD-

EXTRACT works with the most popular 1990 Census CD-ROM products: all *Summary Tape Files* and the *EEO Files*.

The EXTRACT program was written specifically for use with Census Files, so dBASE or other commercial products are not actually needed to retrieve and manipulate data from the CD-ROM discs.

ROMs. The following description pertains to the summary data products introduced in Chapter 8, so readers may wish to review that material before continuing. For those unfamiliar with database management software, a brief introduction to basic terminology is presented below.

Basic Database Concepts

A database is a collection of data (words, symbols, and/or numbers) arranged in a specific order and presented in a standardized format. A relational database is one in which individual entries are linked to one another in a specified manner. Information contained in such databases can be easily retrieved, rearranged, and updated. Software products designed to create, search, and manipulate relational databases are called Database Management Systems (DBMSes). A variety of commercially produced DBMS packages, such as dBASE IV, Clipper, FoxPro, Paradox, and Lotus Approach, enjoy widespread use in the business world.

Relational databases consist of several components:

- Files
- File Segments
- Records
- Fields.

A File is another name for the database in its entirety. All *STF 1A* data for an individual state is an example of a Census CD-ROM File. Standard DBMS programs can only handle a limited amount of data in a single File; larger databases must be divided into File Segments, which are simply smaller subfiles. File Segments are arranged in tabular form, as rows and columns of words and numbers. Each row, containing data which describe a particular entity, is called a Record. Each column, containing data about a specific characteristic or attribute of that entity, is called a Field. Relational databases can include several different types of Fields, rep-

resenting different categories of data. A Character Field contains text. A Numeric Field contains numbers, which the DBMS can manipulate using arithmetic functions. A Date Field stores calendar dates; and a Logic Field denotes true/false conditions.

The difference between Records and Fields can be illustrated by a simple example. A personnel manager might create a small database containing facts about company employees. All information in the database relating to a particular person would constitute a single Record. Record 1 describes the first employee, Record 2 describes the second employee, and so on. Database Fields might include the employee's last name, first name, job title, base salary, starting date, and a "yes/no" designator indicating whether the employee belonged to the union. In this example, each Record contains six Fields. The first three are Character Fields, the fourth is a Numeric Field, the fifth is a Date Field; and the last is a Logic Field.

Electronic databases can be thought of as computerized equivalents of manual files kept on index cards. Using this analogy, the complete set of cards represents the File (or database), the sections partitioned by card dividers might represent File Segments, each index card represents a single Record, and the categories of information found on each card (the standard parts of the card) represent the Fields.

"Cell" is another term used to describe the characteristics of DBMS programs. Using the analogy of a statistical table, a cell represents the intersection of a row and a column. In the case of the personnel manager's database, he has defined six Fields, so each Record contains six cells. If the database described 100 employees, its total size would be 600 cells (six Fields times 100 Records).

When creating a relational database, each Field must be assigned a Field Name and a fixed width (the maximum number of characters which can fit in that Field) by the database creator. The Field Name itself is limited to a maximum of eight characters,

A database is a collection of data (words, symbols, and/or numbers) arranged in a specific order and presented in a standardized format.

File Segments are arranged in tabular form, as rows and columns of words and numbers. Each row, containing data which describe a particular entity, is called a Record. Each column, containing data about a specific characteristic or attribute of that entity, is called a Field.

but Field widths can be any size. In the personnel manager's employee database, the Field for employee last name might be called LNAME, with a fixed width of 30 characters. The Field for starting date might be called STRTDATE, with a fixed width of 10 characters. The actual data found in each Field of an individual Record is called its value. For example, the value of the LNAME Field for Record 1 is Jones, the value for the LNAME Field in Record 2 is Smith, etc.

DBMS software also determines the order in which Records are listed in the database. In order to arrange the File alphabetically by employee name, the program must create an index for the Records based on the values in the LNAME Field. Similarly, if the personnel manager wanted to sort the database by job title first, then by name, he must create an index using a combination of both Fields. Indexing not only controls the order in which Records appear, but allows the user to quickly search and retrieve Records according to specified characteristics.

Census File Segments, Records, and Fields

Proper use of EXTRACT requires an understanding of Census File structure, the components of Census Records, and the nomenclature used to identify those components. The following sections describe important characteristics of Census File Segments, Records, Tables, and Fields, as well as a brief review of Geographic Summary Levels. A useful guide to technical matters, called the Data Dictionary, is also introduced.

File Segments and Table Numbering

The dBASE format limits the size of every Record to a maximum of 128 Fields. Because Census Records contain so many Fields, every File must be divided into numerous File Segments. Following the naming conventions used in dBASE III, EXTRACT calls its File Segments "Catalogs." *STF 1*,

Proper use of EXTRACT requires an understanding of Census File structure, the components of Census Records, and the nomenclature used to identify those components.

STF 1, containing 982 data cells for each Record, is divided into 10 separate Segments (Catalogs). STF 3, with 3,300 data cells, is divided into 35 Catalogs.

containing 982 data cells for each Record, is divided into 10 separate Segments (Catalogs). *STF 3*, with 3,300 data cells, is divided into 35 Catalogs. Catalogs are identified by sequential numbers, as shown in Figures 13-1 and 13-2. The 35 Catalogs in each *STF 3* File range from STF300 to STF334. The first digit in the name represents the File number, so Catalog STF324 is actually Catalog 24 in *STF 3*. Two additional characters, indicating the state abbreviation, appear at the end of each Catalog name (e.g., STF315AL, STF315NY).

 **Census Tip**

The first Catalog on every Summary Tape File Product is a special geographic subfile, containing a complete list of all searchable geographic Fields, a label Field for Area Name, plus data Fields representing land areas and other geographic characteristics. These Geographic Identification Catalogs are designated by zeroes. On *STF 1A* Files, this Segment is called Catalog STF1A0. On *STF 3A* Files, the Segment is named Called Catalog STF300. The importance of the Geographic Identification Catalogs will be discussed later in the chapter.

The remaining Catalogs in each File contain the actual data tables. Tables are listed in exactly the same order in which they appear when using the GO software, with exactly the same table numbers. Population tables are identified by the letter P, Housing tables by the letter H. Figure 13-1 shows the contents of every Catalog found in *STF 1*, while Figure 13-2 lists the contents of *STF 3* Catalogs. Both Figures indicate the range of table numbers in each Catalog, together with a brief summary of the subject matter therein. A more detailed guide to all tables contained in *STF 1* and *STF 3* can be found in Appendix D of this book.

The number of tables appearing in each Catalog is determined by the size of the tables, because a single Catalog can contain 128 Fields only. Whenever possible, Catalogs are created in such a way as not to split a table across two Segments. For example, Catalog STF306 contains Tables P18 through P26, while Catalog STF307 holds Tables P27 through P32. However, some tables are so large they cannot fit in a single Catalog. As seen in Figure 13-2, Table P14 requires portions of three Catalogs: STF303-STF305.

File Segments for STF 1

(Segments are identical in STF 1A, STF 1C, and STF 1D.)

File	Tables	Subjects covered
STF1A0	P1 - P10	Geographic Identifiers; Total Population; Households; Families; Sex; Race; Hispanic Origin
STF1A1	P11 - P12	Age: Total and White
STF1A2	P12 (cont.)	Age: Black; Age: American Indian, Eskimo, Aleut (male)
STF1A3	P12 (cont.)	Age: American Indian (female); Age: Asian or Pacific
STF1A4	P12 (cont.) - P13	Age: Other Race; Age: Hispanic Origin (male)
STF1A5	P13 (pt. 2) - P19	Age: Hispanic Origin (female); Marital status; Household Type & Relationship; Household/Family size
STF1A6	P20 - P35	Household Relationship & Type by Hispanic Origin/Age; Group Quarters; Population Imputations
STF1A7	P36, H1 - H20	Population Imputations (continued); Housing: Vacancy; Tenure; Age of Householder; Rooms, Household Size
STF1A8	H21 - H40	Persons Per Room; Value; Contract Rent; Duration of Vacancy
STF1A9	H41 - H55	Units in Structure; Housing Imputations

Figure 13-1

Records and Fields

In addition to the data tables themselves, every Catalog contains a small selection of the most commonly used Geographic Identification Fields. For example, the Identification Fields common to all *STF 3* Segments are listed below:

SUMLEV	Summary Level
STATEFP	State (FIPS)
CNTY	County (FIPS)
COUSUBFP	County Subdivision (FIPS)
PLACEFP	Place (FIPS)
TRACTBNA	Census Tract/Block Numbering Area
BLCKGR	Block Group
LOGRECNU	Logical Record Number

Every Census Record contains data for a single geographic entity (e.g., the city of Dubuque, Iowa; Tract 105 in Erie County,

Pennsylvania; the Billings, Montana MSA, etc.) Data for each entity are spread across all File Segments. In other words, a Record for the Billings, Montana MSA will appear on *every* Catalog, but each Catalog will provide different information about Billings. To obtain all the available data (all database Fields) for a single Record, the user must retrieve the relevant Record from every Catalog. In order to link this information from one Catalog to another, every entity is assigned a unique identification code, called a Logical Record Number. This code is contained in the LOGRECNU Field, found in every Catalog.

Except for the Geographic Identification Fields, which have mnemonic abbreviations, database Fields are numbered sequentially within each table, and are designated by standard eight-character Field Names. For example, Table P88 in *STF3*, which cross-

Every Census Record contains data for a single geographic entity (e.g., the city of Dubuque, Iowa; Tract 105 in Erie County, Pennsylvania; the Billings, Montana MSA, etc.)

File Segments for STF 3

(Segments are identical in all STF 3 titles.)

File	Tables	Subjects covered
STF300	—	Geographic Identification Section
STF301	P1 - P13	Urban/Rural; Sex; Race; Hispanic Origin; Age (total)
STF302	P14A - P14C	Age by Sex: White; Black male
STF303	P14D - P14F	Age by Sex: Black female; American Indian, Eskimo, Aleut
STF304	P14G - P14I	Age by Sex: Asian or Pacific Islander; Other Race, male
STF305	P14J - P17	Age by Sex: Other Race, female; Age by Sex: Hispanic; Household Type & relationship
STF306	P18 - P26	Relationship and Age; Household/Family Type; Subfamily
STF307	P27 - P32	Marital Status; LanguAge Spoken at Home
STF308	P33 - P36	Ancestry; Year of Entry for Foreign Born
STF309	P37 - P51	Citizens; Fertility; Group Quarters; Migration; Place of Work
STF310	P52 - P60	Carpooling; School Enrollment; Educational Attainment
STF311	P61 - P65	School and Employment for 16-19 year olds; Veteran Status
STF312	P66 - P70	Disability; Employment Status
STF313	P71 - P76	Employment Status by Race/Hispanic Origin; Children Present
STF314	P77 - P83	Industry; Occupation; Household Income
STF315	P84 - P86	Household Income by Age of Householder: Total
STF316	P87A	Household Income by Age of Householder: White
STF317	P87B	Household Income by Age of Householder: Black
STF318	P87C	Household Income by Age of Householder: American Indian, Eskimo, Aleut
STF319	P87D	Household Income by Age of Householder: Asian/Pacific Islander
STF320	P87E	Household Income by Age of Householder: Other Race
STF321	P88 - P107A	Household Income by Age: Hispanic; Income Type; Family Income
STF322	P108 - P118	Nonfamily Income; Per capita Income; Poverty by Age and Sex
STF323	P119 - P121	Poverty Status by Age by Race/Hispanic Origin
STF324	P122 - P123	Poverty Status by Household Type & Relationship/Family Type
STF325	P124A - P124B	Poverty Status by Race and Family Type
STF326	P125 - P143	Poverty for Hispanics, by Family/Household Type; Population Imputations
STF327	P144 - P170,	Population Imputations (continued);
	H1 - H9	Housing Units; Occupancy Status; Condominiums; Tenure
STF328	H10 - H21	Tenure by Race/Hispanic Origin; Tenure by Age of Householder; Rooms; Tenure by Household Size; Units in Structure
STF329	H22 - H33	Tenure by Units in Structure; Water; SewAge; Year Built; Year Moved In; Fuel; Bedrooms
STF330	H34 - H44	Telephone; Vehicles; Kitchen; Gross Rent
STF331	H45 - H52A	Gross Rent; Rent as % of Income; Owner Costs
STF332	H53 - H59	Owner Costs by MortgAge Status/Race; Owner Costs as % Income;
STF333	H60 - H81	Housing Value; Plumbing; Housing Imputations
STF334	H82 - H92	Housing Imputations (continued)

Figure 13-2

tabulates Household Income by age of Householder, contains 63 data cells. The first cell is identified as Field P0880001 and the last is Field P0880063. The first character in a Field Name indicates whether it is a population or housing characteristic. The next three characters represent the table number, right justified with leading zeroes (e.g., H004; P107). The fifth character may represent a sub-table identification (e.g., P107A), but few tables are divided into subcategories, so in most cases the fifth character is a zero. The final three characters represent the Item number, right justified with leading zeroes. EXTRACT users must become comfortable with Field numbering conventions because data retrieval is based on these Field Names.

EXTRACT users must become comfortable with Field numbering conventions because data retrieval is based on these Field Names.

The Data Dictionary

Every 1990 CD-ROM disc includes a **document directory**, containing a set of Technical Documentation Files. Included in the directory are glossaries of subject and geographic terms, a list of tables (similar to those shown in Appendix D), and a Subject Locator index. One of the most important pieces of documentation for use with EXTRACT Files is the Data Dictionary. A complete Data Dictionary for each CD-ROM product can be found on the CD itself, and can be downloaded and printed for reference use. On most discs, an ASCII version of the Data Dictionary is located on the **document** directory, under the name TBL_MTX.ASC. The Data Dictionary also appears in the Techni-

---

Sample Entries, *STF 3A* Data Dictionary

Table number	Table (matrix)	Data dictionary reference name	Field size	Data type	Table coordinates
	P79. CLASS OF WORKER(7) [7]				
	Universe: Employed persons 16 years and over				
	Private for profit wage and salary workers	P0790001	9	N	1
	Private not for profit wage and salary workers	P0790002	9	N	2
	Local government workers	P0790003	9	N	3
	State government workers	P0790004	9	N	4
	Federal government workers	P0790005	9	N	5
	Self employed workers	P0790006	9	N	6
	Unpaid family workers	P0790007	9	N	7
	P80. HOUSEHOLD INCOME IN 1989(25) [25]				
	Universe: Households				
	Less than $5,000	P0800001	9	N	1
	$5,000 to $9,999	P0800002	9	N	2
	$10,000 to $12,499	P0800003	9	N	3
	$12,500 to $14,999	P0800004	9	N	4
	$15,000 to $17,499	P0800005	9	N	5
	$17,500 to $19,999	P0800006	9	N	6
	$20,000 to $22,499	P0800007	9	N	7
	$22,500 to $24,999	P0800008	9	N	8
	$25,000 to $27,499	P0800009	9	N	9
	$27,500 to $29,999	P0800010	9	N	10
	$30,000 to $32,499	P0800011	9	N	11
	$32,500 to $34,999	P0800012	9	N	12
	$35,000 to $37,499	P0800013	9	N	13
	$37,500 to $39,999	P0800014	9	N	14
	$40,000 to $42,499	P0800015	9	N	15
	$42,500 to $44,999	P0800016	9	N	16
	$45,000 to $47,499	P0800017	9	N	17
	$47,500 to $49,999	P0800018	9	N	18
	$50,000 to $54,999	P0800019	9	N	19
	$55,000 to $59,999	P0800020	9	N	20
	$60,000 to $74,999	P0800021	9	N	21
	$75,000 to $99,999	P0800022	9	N	22
	$100,000 to $124,999	P0800023	9	N	23
	$125,000 to $149,999	P0800024	9	N	24
	$150,000 or more	P0800025	9	N	25
	P80A. MEDIAN HOUSEHOLD INCOME IN 1989(1) [1]				
	Universe: Households				
	Median household income in 1989	P080A001	9	N	1

Figure 13-3

cal Documentation manual included with every CD-ROM purchase.

Figure 13-3 shows a typical page from the Data Dictionary of *STF 3A*. For every table in the File, it lists the title of the table, the universe of coverage, the matrix arrangement, and the total number of data cells (Fields). This basic information can also be seen in Appendix D of *Understanding the Census*. The Data Dictionary provides additional, unique information which is important to EXTRACT users. Within each table, a complete list of Fields is provided. The column marked "reference name" indicates the Field Name, as described above. The next column indicates the fixed Field width. This is followed by a column designating the type of Field (Numeric, Alphabetic, or Alphanumeric). The final column, listing the table coordinates, is used primarily with the magnetic tape products, not the CD-ROM Files. Looking at the description of Table P80, for example, we can see that it consists of 25 Fields in a single matrix, and each Field is 9 characters long.

With EXTRACT, users must take the initiative to incorporate a Summary Level into their search strategy.

Geographic Summary Levels

Chapter 8 stressed the importance of Geographic Summary Levels in all Census CD-ROM products. The GO software automatically prompts users to choose a desired Summary Level at the beginning of every search. With EXTRACT, users must take the initiative to incorporate a Summary Level into their search strategy. The process, which occurs in Option 2 of the EXTRACT Main Menu, is explained later. For now, readers should simply be aware of the organization and nomenclature of these Levels in the EXTRACT program.

Geographic Summary Levels categorize each geographic entity (i.e., each Record) in the Census database according to the type of

---

Examples of Summary Level Sequences, STF 3A

Summary Level Area	SUMLEV Code
State	040
State—County	050
State—County—County Subdivision	060
State—County—County Subdivision—Place/Remainder	070
State—County—County Subdivision—Place/ Remainder—Census Tract/Block Numbering Area	080
State—County—Census Tract/Block Numbering Area	140
State—County—Census Tract/BNA—Block Group	150
State—Place—County	155
State—Place	160
State—Metropolitan Statistical Area/Consolidated Metropolitan Statistical Area	319
MSA [no CMSAs]-State-Central City	340
MSA [no CMSAs]-State-County	329
State—CMSA—PMSA	321
CMSA—PMSA—State—Central City	341
CMSA—PMSA—State—County	331

Figure 13-4

Governmental or Statistical Unit it represents, as well as how it fits into the geographic hierarchy. Because Census users may wish to depict alternate geographic relationships, the same geographic entity can be represented as part of several different hierarchies (Summary Levels). For example, Census Tracts can be shown as they relate to their surrounding county, but they can also be portrayed in relationship to their more immediate surroundings (Places and County Subdivisions).

Each Census Subfile (e.g., *STF 1A*, *STF 1B*, *STF 1C*) presents a different assortment of Summary Levels from which to choose. Figure 13-4 shows a selection of some of the most common Summary Levels contained in *STF 3A*. Each Summary Level is designated by a unique three-digit code. The Field Descriptions indicate the hierarchy contained in that Summary Level. Hyphens separate the sequence of levels in the hierarchy. Slashes indicate geographic equivalents appearing at the same hierarchical level (e.g., Tracts are equivalent to BNAs). The first level in the sequence represents the Universe of entities which will be displayed. The last level in the sequence determines the type of entity which will be retrieved in the search. For example, Summary Level 050 (State-County) indicates the user will retrieve all counties within a single state. To illustrate the effect of different hierarchical sequences, compare Summary Levels 070 and 160. Summary Level 160 presents an alphabetical list of all Places within the state. Summary Level 070 also lists Places in the state, but they are arranged according to the County Subdivisions in which they are located. If a Place crosses the boundary of two County Subdivisions, Level 070 will divide the Place into two parts; each part will describe the portion of that Place's territory which falls within a particular County Subdivision.

The hierarchical sequence of Summary Levels also affects the indexing of Records. If the user is searching for Places within a specified county, Summary Level 160 should not be used, because the component counties

are not part of the hierarchy.

A complete list of Summary Levels available on a particular Summary Tape File product can be found in the **document** directory, in the File called **SUM_LEV.ASC**. A detailed chart depicting the searchable hierarchies for every Summary Level is contained in a File called **HOWTOUSE.ASC**.

Installing and Running EXTRACT

EXTRACT is designed to run on microcomputers equipped with a hard drive and 640 Kilobytes of RAM. In order to use EXTRACT, the following four components are needed:

- ▶ A 1990 CD-ROM product in .DBF format
- ▶ The Data Dictionary for that product (found on the CD itself)
- ▶ A fairly recent version of the EXTRACT software
- ▶ Auxiliary Files for the specific CD-ROM title.

Zeisset and Marske have written many revisions of the EXTRACT program since its public debut. Release 1.5a, for example, was issued in February, 1993. The number following the decimal in the release name indicates a major software revision. The letter indicates minor revisions to the basic program. Each major release incorporates useful search enhancements. Some releases were written to accommodate unique aspects of newly-issued CD-ROM products, such as the ZIP Code data found on *STF 3B*. Users of decennial Census discs should try to obtain the most recent EXTRACT version they can find. The search examples described in this chapter are based on the capabilities of EXTRACT Release 1.4d.

The second necessary component, called Auxiliary Files, provide the link between EXTRACT and the CD-ROM discs. They contain alphabetical and numerical indexes to their corresponding dBASE Files, allow-

Field Descriptions indicate the hierarchy contained in that Summary Level. Hyphens separate the sequence of levels in the hierarchy. Slashes indicate geographic equivalents appearing at the same hierarchical level.

Users of decennial Census discs should try to obtain the most recent EXTRACT version they can find.

A fast and simple method of obtaining the EXTRACT program (or updating an old version) is to copy it from a recent Economic Census CD-ROM. Older Economic Census discs will contain earlier versions of EXTRACT; discs with more recent release dates will contain more current versions. Most Economic discs issued after 1993 also contain Auxiliary Files for 1990 Population and Housing titles.

The following CD-ROM discs are among the best sources for obtaining the necessary Auxiliary Files for 1990 Census products:

▸ *County Business Patterns* (1991 version or later)
▸ *1992 Economic Census* (any version)

Less complete collections, together with an older release of the EXTRACT software, can be found on the *1987 Economic Census* (version 2B).

A second means of obtaining EXTRACT and individual Auxiliary Files is to download them from the Bureau's Electronic Bulletin Board, described briefly in Chapter 14. Your nearest State Data Center Affiliate or Census Bureau Regional Office may also provide assistance in acquiring needed Files.

A final resource is the nonprofit software clearinghouse operated by the University of Tennessee. For a nominal fee, the University's Institute for Electronic Data Analysis will supply diskettes with compressed versions of the requested Files. The Institute can be contacted at the following address:

Institute for Electronic Data Analysis
University of Tennessee
316 Stokley Management Center
Knoxville TN 37996
(615) 975-5311

Unfortunately, few 1990 Census discs contain the EXTRACT program or the appropriate Auxiliary Files. The needed Files must be obtained from another source before EXTRACT can be used with decennial Census products.

ing EXTRACT to locate desired Records more rapidly. They also contain Master Catalogs of the database Segments; a program which links EXTRACT to the appropriate Data Dictionary for each Catalog; label Files used to describe the contents of specific data Fields; and textual Files used to generate online help screens. One or more Auxiliary Files exists for each 1990 summary data product. The Auxiliary File for the *Equal Employment Opportunity* disc is called EEOAUXIL, for example. All *STF* titles require two separate Auxiliary Files: a general File designated STFAUX, and a product-specific File (STFAUX1A, STFAUX3C, etc.).

Because EXTRACT was designed specifically for use with the Economic Census and other products issued by the Bureau's Economic Division, the software, and the corresponding Auxiliary Files are loaded on the Bureau's Economic CD-ROMs. Unfortunately, few 1990 Census discs contain the EXTRACT program or the appropriate

Auxiliary Files. The needed Files must be obtained from another source before EXTRACT can be used with decennial Census products.

Installing EXTRACT

EXTRACT must be installed on the hard drive of the user's microcomputer. Before installing the program and its accompanying Auxiliary Files to the hard drive, the user should make a new directory called "EXTRACT," and two subdirectories designated "WORK" and "1990AUX." The **EXTRACT\WORK** subdirectory will store the user's EXTRACT work Files; the **EXTRACT\1990AUX** subdirectory becomes the location for the Auxiliary Files on the hard drive. Users can install as many 1990 Auxiliary Files as their needs require and their hard drive's storage capacity will allow. All 1990 Auxiliary Files can reside on the same subdirectory. Once the directories have been created, the EXTRACT.EXE program can be copied onto the EXTRACT directory, and Auxiliary Files can be copied onto the EXTRACT\1990AUX subdirectory.

Installing EXTRACT from the CD-ROM disc to the hard drive is a simple matter if the user has version 1.4d or later. From the default CD-ROM drive, type **install**, then follow the on-screen prompts. During installation, the user indicates which Census products are desired for use with EXTRACT, then the program automatically copies the required Auxiliary Files to the user's hard drive. The newer versions of the installation program allow users to create a customized batch menu, called EXMENU, which is used to run the various components of EXTRACT.

The Installation program on earlier versions of EXTRACT is not as straightforward. For detailed instructions, consult the EXTRACT Reference Manual, available on most Economic CD-ROM products as **EXTRACT.DOC**. Installing software obtained from the Bulletin Board or the software Clearinghouse is also tricky. Before installing the compressed Auxiliary Files onto a hard drive, the user should consult the appropriate READ.ME File for instructions.

Running EXTRACT

The start-up procedure for older versions of EXTRACT was somewhat tedious. Every time the program was run, it required the user to designate disk drive locations for the CD-ROM, the Work Files, and the Auxiliary Files. The user could create batch files to circumvent these delays, but the process wasn't obvious. The EXMENU program, available on newer versions of EXTRACT, simplifies the start-up process enormously. The File configuration is stored once, during installation process; from that point on, EXMENU takes care of the rest.

Figure 13-5 is an example of a typical EXMENU screen. The choices of databases, the names of the batch programs (EX1A, etc.) and the menu descriptions, are all de-termined by the user during installation. In this example, the installer chose to load eight different Census products, including the 1992 Economic Census and the EEO Files.

To view the EXMENU screen and run EXTRACT, the user follows four simple steps:

1. Place the required CD-ROM product in the CD player.
2. From the C: prompt, type **cd extract** and press **<Enter>**.
3. Type **exmenu** and press **<Enter>**.
4. Type the desired File name, as shown on the EXMENU screen, and press **<Enter>**. (Example: **ex3a**, **<Enter>**.)

EXTRACT will then display a welcome screen, followed by the "Choose a Catalog" Menu. The user can now select one of the listed Catalogs. Next, EXTRACT provides a brief description of the chosen Catalog. After pressing **<Enter>**, the user will see another screen entitled "Select a Data File." If the CD-ROM disc contains Files for more than one state, the user chooses the desired state; if the disc contains data for one File only, the user simply presses **<Enter>**. At this point, EXTRACT takes a few seconds to read the appropriate Data Dictionary for the chosen Catalog. Finally, EXTRACT's Main Menu will appear on the screen. The bottom right corner displays the name of the current Catalog.

Installing EXTRACT from the CD-ROM disc to the hard drive is a simple matter if the user has version 1.4d or later.

```
           EXTRACT MENU

ECON              Economic and Agricultural Censuses
           1990 Census of Population and Housing
EX1A              STF 1A (State Specific - Complete Count)
EX1B              STF 1B (Block Data - Complete Count)
EX1C              STF 1C (National - Complete Count)
EX3A              STF 3A (State Specific - Sample)
EX3B              STF 3B (ZIP Code - Sample)
EX3C              STF 3C (National - Sample)
EEO               Equal Employment Opportunity Files


C:\EXTRACT>
```

Figure 13-5

EXTRACT Basics

The EXTRACT Main Menu consists of ten functional areas. Figure 13-6 is a facsimile of the Main Menu, together with a summary of the menu features. Menu Options 1 and 2 perform the most fundamental tasks in building a search; Option 6 displays search results to the screen; the remaining functions refine the search and print or download results.

Menu selections can be chosen in any order, but logic dictates following a specific pattern when planning a search strategy. In most cases, the user will choose Options in the following order:

> ‣ Option 1 to select Items
> ‣ Option 2 to select Records
> ‣ Option 3 or Option 4 to merge Files
> ‣ Option 5 to set output format
> ‣ Option 7 or 8 to print or download

Option 6 is used throughout the search process to view results between steps.

Before walking through the basic EXTRACT functions, a look at the unedited database will provide a sense of File structure, as well as the "look" of a typical EXTRACT table. Menu Option 6 displays data on screen. Until the searcher employs Options 1 and 2 to retrieve specified data from the File, Option 6 will show the complete contents of the

entire Catalog as one gigantic table, with dozens of columns and hundreds of rows. Every data Field in the Catalog will appear in columns, while every geographic entity will display in rows. By using the arrow keys and the <PgUp> and <PgDn> keys, the user can move up, down, and across this massive table, viewing any portion desired. Of course, an unrestricted File such as this is much too large to be manageable, which is why the program is used to "extract" selected Fields and Records.

Online Documentation

The EXTRACT program contains three types of online documentation to provide assistance while using the program: Help Screens, Table Locators, and Definitions. Help Screens, retrieved either by typing H or pressing <F1>, are context-sensitive, explaining the commands or database components currently displayed on screen. Special introductory Help messages automatically display when a database Catalog is opened. They provide a general description of the Catalog contents and a brief explanation of each Menu Option. These introductory screens can also be retrieved by pressing H at the Main Menu.

Menu Options 1 and 2 perform the most fundamental tasks in building a search; Option 6 displays search results to the screen; the remaining functions refine the search and print or download results.

How does the user know which Catalog to select?

The "Choose a Catalog" Menu supplies a list of tables found in each Catalog. The descriptions are brief, looking similar to those shown in Figures 13-1 and 13-2, so they may not provide sufficient information to make a proper selection.

If the user is uncertain, two options are available: he or she can consult printed guides, such as the Technical Documentation for the product, or the List of Data Tables

found in Appendix D of this book; or, the user can turn to the online Table Locator, described later in the chapter. In either case, a Catalog must be opened before the Main Menu will display.

What if the wrong Catalog has been chosen? At any point during the search session, the user can escape to the Main Menu and select Option 9 (Return to File Selection Menu) to change Catalogs.

The Table Locator feature is helpful for determining which Catalog contains the desired data tables. From the Main Menu, type I or D—either command will work. A submenu lists separate Table Locators for *STF 1* and *STF 3*. Because *STF 3* is such a large File, its Table Locator is divided into three parts, arranged alphabetically by subject. For example, if the user seeks data on occupations, he would choose "Table Locator—Index by Subject—H to Q," and scan through the list. Under "Occupation—Employed persons 16 years and over," the Locator indicates Catalog STF314, Table 078. Cross-references to related tables are also provided.

 Census Tip

Typing *D* while highlighting the SUMLEV Field (in Options 1 or 2, or from the Main Menu) will display an abbreviated guide to the Summary Levels available on that Census product.

EXTRACT's Definition feature enables the user to determine whether the correct Fields or Record types have been chosen. The user can easily switch from a data Field to its definition by typing D. Unlike the GO program, which only displays abbreviated definitions of key terms, EXTRACT calls up the full definition for every term, taken from the Appendices to the Summary Tape Files. This includes both subject terms and geographic terms. The Definition feature enables users to scan the complete glossary, or to view a context-specific definition.

The former works from the Main Menu, while the latter is used from within Options 1, 2, or 6. By typing D from the Main Menu, the user can call up a complete alphabetical list of terms and retrieve individual defini-

---

EXTRACT MENU

1. Select ITEMS	6. Display to Screen
2. Select RECORDS	7. Print
3. Add LABELS	8. EXTRACT DATA to a file
4. Manipulate files	9. Return to FILE SELECTION menu
5. Format options	10. Advanced options
(Q to QUIT)	(<F1> for Help)

Enter option number:

Summary of EXTRACT Menu Options

1. SELECT ITEMS	Specifies which data cells will appear as columns in the user-defined table.
2. SELECT RECORDS	Specifies which records will appear as rows in the table; indicates Summary Levels as well as individual entities.
3. ADD LABELS	Adds one or more additional columns to serve as row identifiers (labels)
4. MANIPULATE	Merges data from two different files or adds additional records to existing file. Also selects existing indexes, creates new indexes, and tabulates totals and subtotals.
5. FORMAT	Creates page format (lines per page, margins) and table headings. Changes table from columnar format to paragraph (row-wise) format.
6. DISPLAY	Shows resulting table on screen. Also adjusts width of specified columns.
7. PRINT	Sends text of completed table to printer.
8. EXTRACT DATA	Downloads data from user-created table in various formats.
9. FILE SELECTION	Returns user to File Selection menu to choose a new database "catalog."
10. ADVANCED OPTIONS	Saves format options; creates new Data Dictionary; adds files to MY_FILES catalog.

Figure 13-6

tions from the list. Or, by typing **D** from a highlighted term within a menu function, the user can verify information while Selecting Items, Selecting Records, or Displaying tables on the screen, without interrupting the search process.

Selecting Items and Records

Menu Options 1 and 2 are the workhorse functions of the EXTRACT program. Utilizing them properly is critical to a successful EXTRACT search. Menu Option 1 (Select Items) is used to choose data Fields from the Catalog. It is typically used to determine which population and housing characteristics will be displayed. Menu Option 2 (Select Records) specifies the database Records to be extracted. It determines which geographic entities will be retrieved. Put another way, Option 1 creates the columns in a customized table, while Option 2 creates the rows.

Using Option 1 (Select Items)

Selecting Items via Option 1 is fairly straightforward. The key to locating the desired Items is to choose the appropriate Census Catalog. As described earlier, this can be done by consulting the Technical Documentation, or by using the online Table Locators, or by simply browsing the Catalog menus and trusting to luck.

Once the proper Catalog has been opened, the searcher can choose Option 1 from the Main Menu. EXTRACT then displays a complete list of the Fields contained in that Catalog. Now the searcher can scan the list

and place an X next to each desired Field, which in turn will be represented by a single column in the extracted database.

Figure 13-7 shows a typical screen from an Option 1 menu. In this case, the Items are taken from *STF 3A*, Catalog 314. This Catalog covers Tables P077 through P083, dealing with occupations, industry, Class of Worker, and Household Income. The menu screens display three columns: an empty column, where the searcher makes selections; the eight-character Field Names; and the Field Descriptions. Fields are arranged according to Table number. At the top of every Select Items menu is the standard list of Geographic Identifiers (not shown in Figure 13-7).

Figure 13-7 indicates the user has selected two Fields: **P0780001** (Executive, Administrative, and Managerial Occupations) and **P0780002** (Professional Specialty Occupations). The four entries containing hyphens in the Field Name column are Comment Lines, included to make the lists more readable. Comment Lines cannot be selected because they contain no data values.

Menu Option 1 (Select Items) is used to choose data Fields from the Catalog. It is typically used to determine which population and housing characteristics will be displayed. Menu Option 2 (Select Records) specifies the database Records to be extracted. It determines which geographic entities will be retrieved.

```
                          SELECT ITEMS
   (Press H for HELP)
   Enter an X next to each item to include in display.

   Use <PgUp>, <PgDn>, or < > to scroll through the list.
   TO EXIT: Press the <Esc> key.

   X     FIELD NAME          DESCRIPTION

         P0770016            Employed 16+: Professional & related svcs: other
         P0770017            Employed 16+: Public administration
         ——                  P78. OCCUPATION (13)
         –P078–                  Universe: Employed persons 16 years and over
         ——                      Managerial and professional specialty occupations:
   x     P0780001            Executive, administrative, and managerial occupations
   x     P0780002            Professional specialty occupations
         ——                      Technical, sales, and administrative support occupations
         P0780003            Technicians and related support occupations
         P0780004            Sales occupations
         P0780005            Administrative support occupations, including clerical
         ——                      Service occupations:
         P0780006            Private household occupations
         P0780007            Protective service occupations

   Options: <J>ump,<L>ocate,<W>ord search,<D>efinition,<P>review,<U>ser-defined item
```

Figure 13-7

A typical search in Option 2 consists of three steps, with on-screen prompts provided between each step.

 Census Tip

If a line remains blank when trying to place an X, it means the user is on a Comment Line used for descriptive purposes. Repositioning the cursor down to the next line containing an eight-character Field Name will move the user to the appropriate data line for marking purposes.

An extremely useful feature in Option 1 is the Preview command. Once the desired Items have been selected, the user can see what the resulting columns will look like in the extracted database, without exiting Option 1. By typing **P** and pressing <Enter>, a small display window will pop up, revealing the appearance of the extracted columns, complete with their current Field widths. The importance of this feature will become clear during the discussion of the Display command (Option 6). From the Preview window, the user can return directly to the Item list by typing **R** to Reselect Items, or can press <**Esc**> to back out to the Main Menu.

Once chosen, Option 1 selections remain unchanged throughout the search, unless they are reset or deselected, or the user ends the search. To deselect a previously marked Item, press the Space Bar while on the selected line; this erases the X.

Using Option 2 (Select Records)

Selecting the desired Records is the most complex step in an EXTRACT search and can be a difficult process for experienced and novice users alike.

Selecting the desired Records is the most complex step in an EXTRACT search and can be a difficult process for experienced and novice users alike. Option 2 is used primarily to determine the appropriate geographic entities to be retrieved, but the process is more complicated than the corresponding operation in the GO program. When using GO, the software prompts the searcher step by step, and retrieves one geographic entity (one Record) at a time. With EXTRACT, searchers have a choice. Option 2 can be used

to retrieve a single entity, or a group of entities sharing common characteristics. Choosing a particular Summary Level determines the hierarchical sequence and the domain (Universe) of the search. Most Option 2 searches actually accomplish two separate tasks: specifying a particular Summary Level, and selecting a geographic index to search.

A typical search in Option 2 consists of three steps, with on-screen prompts provided between each step.

> Step 1. Select SUMLEV Field and/or one additional geographic Field.
> Step 2. Choose a specific Summary Level (if SUMLEV was chosen).
> Step 3. Choose one or more geographic entities from a list (if a geographic Field was chosen).

The Select Records option asks the searcher to identify the variables which will appear as rows in the database, rather than columns. After choosing Option 2 from the Main Menu, the user will see the same list of subject variables and Geographic Identifiers that was shown in Option 1. However, making choices from this list is only the first step in the Select Records process. This step is unique because the choices made indicate only the types of Records to be included in the Universe from which the Record selection will ultimately be made. To emphasize this difference, EXTRACT requires that in this step, users indicate their choices by placing an **S** on each selected line, instead of the X utilized in Option 1 and in all other steps in Option 2. (In other words, on the first screen in Option 2, the user makes selections with an **S**. On subsequent screens, representing the next steps in the "Select Records" process, the user makes selections with an **X**.)

To deselect a previously-chosen Field, the user can press the Space Bar. This erases the S or X. Another way to reset the choices is to escape to the Main Menu, reenter Option 2, and make new selections. Unlike the selections in Option 1, which remain in effect throughout the search session, Option 2

Q&A

Why does EXTRACT display the same list of Fields in Option 2 as in Option 1?

If Option 2 allowed searchers to select Records based solely on geographic characteristics, the lengthy list of demographic and housing variables would be completely superfluous. However, as will be shown later in the chapter, numeric Fields can also be used for Record selection in Option 2. In short, any Field in the database can be used to select Records.

Here's the flip side of the question: why do Geographic Identifiers appear as selection choices in Option 1? Once again, because any Field in the database can be used to select Items. For example, if

a user creates a table containing many different types of Summary Levels, it would make sense to create a column identifying the geographic Level of each entity. To do so, the searcher must select SUMLEV as an Item in Option 1.

Still confused? It might help to consider the situation from another perspective. Any Field which can be selected in Option 1 can also be selected in Option 2, and vice versa. Option 1 uses the Field to create columns, while Option 2 uses the Field to create rows.

---

selections change every time the searcher invokes the Select Records function.

Figure 13-8 shows the first few listings under Option 2 for Catalog STF314. The first eight entries in Figure 13-8 represent geographic characteristics. Notice these are the same geographic choices shown earlier in the chapter. They are standard choices found in all *STF 3* Catalogs. The listings followed by an asterisk are those for which a separate Index File have been created, meaning the user can search those Files alphabetically by Field Name. Indexing speeds up retrieval time enormously.

SUMLEV, shown as the first or second Field Name on most Option 2 menus, is extremely important. This Field *must* be selected in order to specify a particular Summary Level. If SUMLEV is not selected, EXTRACT will retrieve every geographic level existing within the chosen geographic territory. In the example shown in Figure 13-8, the user has selected SUMLEV and CNTY. This tells EXTRACT the user wishes to:

a.) search for a designated Summary Level, and

b.) select a specific county or collection of counties as the domain of the retrieval set.

At this point, the user has not identified which Summary Level and which county (or counties) are wanted. Identifying the individual Summary Level and the specific county or counties takes place during the next steps. Understanding the distinction between the SUMLEV Field and the other geographic-level Fields is critical to proficient searching in Option 2.

Within Option 2, the <Esc> key must be pressed to proceed from one step to the next. In Figure 13-8, the searcher has selected SUMLEV and CNTY as the desired Fields in Step 1. After pressing <Esc>, the user will see a list of available Summary Levels from which to choose. Only one Summary Level can be selected from the list. Let's assume the user chooses Level 140, covering State-County-Census Tract/Block Numbering Area. This tells EXTRACT to retrieve only those Records which contain data summarized at the Tract/BNA level within counties.

To proceed to the final step in Option 2, press <Esc> again to see a new submenu, listing every entity (within the relevant domain) for whichever geographic category was selected in Step 1. In this case, since CNTY was chosen, EXTRACT will present

SUMLEV, shown as the first or second Field Name on most Option 2 menus, is extremely important. This Field *must* be selected in order to specify a particular Summary Level.

```
SELECT RECORDS
                        Mark with S the variable(s) to restrict.
                        ( you will be prompted for values to select )

TO EXIT:  Press the <ESC> key.
>, or <> to scroll through the list.


S     FIELD NAME    DESCRIPTION
_____
      —title—                   1990 Census STF 3A, File 14, Tables P77 - P83
S     SUMLEV        *           Summary Level
      STATEFP       -           State (FIPS)
S     CNTY          *           County
      COUSUBFP      *           County Subdivision (FIPS)
      PLACEFP       *           Place (FIPS)
      TRACTBNA      *           Census Tract/Block Numbering Area(4-digit + 2-digit suffix)
      BLCKGR        *           Block  Group
      LOGRECNU                  Logical Record Number
      ———                       P77. INDUSTRY(17)
      —PO77—                     Universe: Employed persons 16 years and over
      P0770001                  Employed 16+:  Agriculture, forestry, and fisheries
      P0770002                  Employed 16+:  Mining
      P0770003                  Employed 16+:  Construction

*   Marked variables are indexed, - denotes others with value selection menus
```

Figure 13-8

an alphabetical list of all counties in the state. Figure 13-9 reproduces a typical submenu of this type, showing a portion of the list of counties in Alabama. Now the searcher can specify one or more individual counties to retrieve. If a single county is chosen, EXTRACT will retrieve all the Tracts or Block Numbering Areas found in that county.

From within any submenu which lists actual Area Names, searchers can select a single entity, several entities, or a consecutive range of entities. By typing **R** for Range, users can designate starting and ending points in a desired range of values, but only the numeric codes for the geographic entities are retrievable by range. In Figure 13-9, for example, if the searcher wished to select all counties from Henry through Lamar, each line could be marked with an **X**, or a range search could be done on counties 067 through 075.

Perhaps the best way to understand the effect of different search strategies in Option 2 is to try a few to see what happens. Figure 13-10 illustrates the search steps taken to retrieve different categories of Records. The examples are based on *STF 3A*. For simplicity's sake, assume all Records for an entire state appear on a single disc. This means that the Universe of records on the disc represents all Records for the state. The notations S and X indicate the manner in which the selections are marked for retrieval. As you compare the

Q&A

If the SUMLEV Field is so important, why doesn't EXTRACT select it automatically?

The most common EXTRACT searches require the user to specify a Summary Level, but sometimes a SUMLEV search is not needed. In certain situations it is useful to retrieve every level of geography within a large geographic territory. By *not* selecting SUMLEV in Option 2, the EXTRACT program will do just that. For example, a user may wish to extract every geographic entity within a specified county—all the cities, townships, CDPs, Tracts,

Block Groups, and so on.

Searches of this type are particularly helpful if the user wishes to design a large database which can be used over and over again. By selecting Records for every geographic entity within a county, for example, the user has created a geographically detailed file specific to that county.

various examples, you should notice certain patterns emerging.

1. To retrieve all occurrences of a particular Summary Level in the entire state (all counties, for example, or all Places), select only the SUMLEV Field on the first screen. (By not selecting another Geographic Identifier, the user instructs EXTRACT to consider the entire Universe when seeking Summary Level Records. In this case, the Universe is an entire state.) On the next screen, specify the appropriate Summary Level (050, 160, etc.). See Examples 1, 3, and 9 in Figure 13-10.

(Note: Example 9 is a specialized variation of Example 3. The Bureau divides certain Summary Levels into subcategories, so the searcher must employ a more complicated strategy to retrieve one of these subcategories in its entirety. The Field which makes this type of search possible is named PSADC, which stands for Political and Statistical Area Designation Code. For example, a Place can be a city, a village, a town, a CDP, or so on. If the searcher only wants to retrieve cities, but not other types of Places, he must select SUMLEV 160 for Places, together with PSADC 58 for cities.)

2. To retrieve all occurrences of a particular Summary Level, but only for a specified portion of a state, select SUMLEV and the geographic category which defines the part of the state in which you are interested. On the second screen, select the desired Summary Level. The remaining screens will prompt you to specify the particular entity or entities you seek. (Examples 5, 6, 7, 8.)

3. To retrieve all Records for all Summary Levels within a specified territory, do not select SUMLEV. On the first screen, select only the category of Geographic Identifier

which you wish to define as your new Universe. On the next screen, you will be prompted to name the specific entity. All Summary Levels within that named entity will be retrieved. (Examples 10 and 11.)

4. To retrieve a single Record for a specific entity, select both the SUMLEV Field and the geographic category which applies to that entity (CNTY, etc.). On the following screens, specify the appropriate Summary Level and the entity name. (Examples 2 and 4.)

5. To retrieve two or more specific entities, utilize the same search strategy described in

```
> SELECT RECORDS   (Screen 2)

Enter a X next to each value you want to include.

>, or <> to scroll through the list.
TO EXIT: Press the <ESC> key.

    X    CNTY    DESCRIPTION

         055     Etowah, AL
         057     Fayette, AL
         059     Franklin, AL
         061     Geneva, AL
         063     Greene, AL
         065     Hale, AL
         067     Henry, AL
         069     Houston, AL
    X    071     Jackson, AL
         073     Jefferson, AL
         075     Lamar, AL
         077     Lauderdale, AL
         079     Lawrence, AL
         081     Lee, AL

To select based on a range of codes, type R
Other options: D,J,L,W, Or H<elp>
```

Figure 13-9

Selecting Summary Levels Using EXTRACT
Single-Pass Searches

(Examples using *STF 3A*)

To retrieve:	Follow these search steps:
1 All counties in the state	s SUMLEV <Esc> x 050 State-County <Esc>
2 Specific county in the state	s SUMLEV s CNTY <Esc> x 050 State-County <Esc> x [choose county name from list] <Esc>
3 All Places in the state	s SUMLEV x 160 (State-Place) <Esc>
4 Specific Place(s) in the state	s SUMLEV s Place <Esc> x 160 State-Place <Esc> x [choose Place name from list] [repeat previous step for each additional Place names wanted] <Esc>
5 All County Subdivisions in a county	s SUMLEV s CNTY <Esc> x 060 State-County-County Subdivision <Esc> x [choose county name from list] <Esc>
6 All Tracts within a county	s SUMLEV s CNTY <Esc> x 140 State-County-Tract/Block Numbering Area <Esc> x [choose county name from list] <Esc>
7 All Tracts within a County Subdivision	s SUMLEV s COUSUBFP <Esc> x 080 State-County-County Subdivision-Tract/BNA <Esc> x [choose name from the list] <Esc>
8 All Block Groups within a county	s SUMLEV s CNTY <Esc> x 150 State-County-Tract/Block Numbering Area-Block Group <Esc> x [choose county name from list] <Esc>
9 All cities in the state	s SUMLEV s PSADC <Esc> x 160 State-Place <Esc> x 58 City - place [PSADC] x 59 City- place (no description in name) <Esc>
10 All Records within a County (all Summary Levels)	s CNTY <Esc> x [choose county name from list] <Esc> [speed-up screen will appear] x 050 State-County
11 All records within a CMSA	s MSACMSA <Esc> x [choose CMSA name from list] <Esc>

(Note: this search will take longer because the MSACMSA Field is not indexed.)

Figure 13- 10

method #4, but choose several entities (either from a list or as a range of consecutive Records).

The primary purpose of Option 3 is the ability to add a Label column (also called a Table Stub) to an extracted File.

Census Tip

Selecting a specific category of Geographic Identifier restricts the domain of the search (to an individual county, Metropolitan Area, County Subdivision, or so forth). If a particular geographic Field is not selected, EXTRACT searches the entire File. For *STF 1A* and *STF 3A*, which are state-specific databases, EXTRACT will search the entire state. For *STF 1C* and *STF 3C*, which are nationwide databases, EXTRACT will search the entire country. Searchers should always be aware of the Universe from which their Record selections will be made.

The search techniques described in this section are fairly rudimentary, but Option 2 can also handle more complicated strategies. Advanced searching techniques, including "double-pass" searches and numeric screening, will be introduced later in the chapter.

Using Option 3 (Add Labels)

Option 3 (Adding Labels) offers a variety of useful File merging capabilities, some of which will be described later in the chapter. The primary purpose of Option 3 is the ability to add a Label column (also called a Table Stub) to an extracted File. It is this aspect of the Label function which we will explore now.

The best way to explain Option 3 is to demonstrate its operation. Assume a searcher has created a small EXTRACT table based on the selections shown earlier in Figures 13-7 and 13-8. He has selected Items P0780001 and P0780002, both taken from *STF 3A*, Catalog 14. For the purposes of this example, the searcher is using the CD-ROM disc covering various Florida counties, including Dade County. As seen in Figure 13-8, he has chosen SUMLEV and CNTY as the first step in the Record Selection process. In the next two steps (not shown), he has selected Summary Level 060 (State-County-County Subdivision) and Dade County. As a result, EXTRACT will retrieve two data Fields for every County Subdivision in Dade County, Florida. The extracted table is reproduced in Figure 13-11. At the bottom of the table, EXTRACT automatically lists the Field Descriptions for Items P0780001 and P0780002. What is plainly missing is a column indicating the names of the County Subdivisions shown in the table. Because the searcher did not Select **Area Name** as an Item, he has inadvertently created a list of numbers which are virtually meaningless to anyone reading the table.

Returning to Option 1, the searcher attempts to identify the appropriate Field which will supply the needed names. He remembers that geographic Fields always appear at the top of the list. Figure 13-8, shown earlier, reproduces the Geographic Identifiers for Catalog STF314. Since all of his extracted Records represent County Subdivisions, he selects COUSUBFP. But to his disappoint-

---

1990 Census STF 3A, File 14, Tables P77 - P83
Dade, FL

P0780001	P0780002
352	134
12475	8400
1975	1905
17216	13427
14662	17971
1377	1086
37241	41230
7215	7778
3232	4916
5205	3235
4877	4396
6177	4791

- -

Key to column headings:

P0780001   Executive, administrative, and managerial occupations
P0780002   Professional specialty occupations

Figure 13-11

1990 Census STF 3A, File 14, Tables P77 - P83
Dade, FL

COUSUBFP	P0780001	P0780002
91040	352	134
91482	12475	8400
91534	1975	1905
91703	17216	13427
91716	14662	17971
91729	1377	1086
92158	37241	41230
92171	7215	7778
92444	3232	4916
92470	5205	3235
92886	4877	4396
93211	6177	4791

– ·

Key to column headings:

COUSUBFP   County Subdivision (FIPS)
P0780001   Executive, administrative, and managerial occupations
P0780002   Professional specialty occupations

Figure 13-12

ment, he finds the revised table (reproduced in Figure 13-12) is little better than the first. He has added a column to identify the geographic entities, but those entities are described by numeric FIPS Codes, not their Area Names.

The Field being sought so unsuccessfully by our frustrated searcher is designated ANPSADPI, which stands for Area Name/ Political Statistical Area Description/Part Indicator, or "Area Name" for short. But a thorough scanning of the list of Fields in Catalog STF314 shows no ANPSADPI Field. On *STF 3A*, ANPSADPI can be found in one place only—Catalog STF300, the special Geographic Identifier Catalog. Contrast the brief list of geographic Fields shown earlier in Figure 13-8 with the lengthier list shown in Figure 13-13. Figure 13-13 contains the first two screens from Catalog STF300, the special Geographic Identification Segment found at the beginning of all *Summary Tape File* products. It lists every geographic Field searchable on the database, plus Fields for longitude, latitude, land area, and the vitally important Field which labels

On *STF 3A*, ANPSADPI can be found in one place only—Catalog STF300, the special Geographic Identifier Catalog.

the geographic names. (Note that the ANPSADPI Field is not shown in Figure 13-13, because it appears on the fifth screen of this Catalog 's menu.)

So how can the EXTRACT user display Area Names for data found in other Catalogs? Option 3 (Add Labels) offers the fastest and easiest solution. It is an ingenious function which automatically merges data from two different Catalogs. From the main Menu, the searcher simply chooses Option 3, and is presented with the Catalog Selection menu— a list of all *STF 3A* Catalogs. Now he can pick any Catalog, and merge data from that Segment to the one he already has open (in this case, Catalog STF314). The more complex aspects of File merger will be introduced later in the chapter; for now, we will focus on the ANPSADPI Field.

 Census Tip

In most Census CD-ROM products, the ANPSADPI Field appears only in the special Geographic Identifier Segment (the "zero" Catalog, which appears first on the Catalog Selection Menu). It is typically "buried" near the end of a lengthy list, approximately five screens from the top of the menu. An exception to this rule is *STF 1C*, where the ANPSADPI Field can be found in every Catalog.

At this point, the searcher can choose Catalog STF300. In case he has forgotten which Catalog contains ANPSADPI, the Catalog Selection menu provides additional assistance; the menu indicates that Catalog 300 contains "Area Name and geographic codes." After choosing STF300, the searcher will see a single line designated ANPSADPI. By pressing <Enter>, he will merge this Item with his existing table from STF314. The EXTRACT program is actually conducting a series of steps behind the scenes. Not only does it select ANPSADPI as an Item from Catalog STF300, but it automatically marks

```
SELECT RECORDS
    Mark with S the variable(s) to restrict
    ( you will be prompted for values to select )

TO EXIT:  Press the <ESC> key.
>, or <> to scroll through the list.

S   FIELD NAME                  DESCRIPTION
    STUSAB            -          State/US Abbreviation
S   SUMLEV            *          Summary Level
    GEOCOMP          -          Geographic Component        (Shown only for State totals)
    CHARITER                    Characteristic Iteration     (always 000 in STF 3A files)
    LOGRECNU                    Logical Record Number
    LOGRECPN                    Logical Record Part Number    (always 0001 in STF 3A files)
    PARTRECT                    Total Number of Parts in Record    (always 0001 in SFT 3A)
    ANRC             -          Alaska Native Regional Corporation
    AIANACE          -          American Indian/Alaska Native Area (Census)
    AIANAFP                     American Indian/Alaska Native Area (FIPS)
    AIANACC          -          American Indian/Alaska Native Area Class Code
    ARTLI            -          American Indian Reservation Trust Land Indicator
    BLCK                        Block                (always 000 in STF 3A files)
    BLCKGR           *          Block Group
    TRACTBNA         *          Census Tract/Bock Numbering Area (4-digit + 2-digit suffix)
    CONGDIS                     Congressinoal District (101st/102nd Congress)
    CONCITCE         -          Consolidated City (Census)
    CONCITFP                    Consolidated City (FIPS)
    CONCITCC                    Consolidated City Class Code
    CONCITSC         -          Consolidated City Size Code
    CMSA                        Consolidated Metropolitan Statistical Area
    CNTY             *          County
    CNTYSC           -          County Size Code
    COUSUBCE                    County Subdivision (Census)
S   COUSUBFP         *          County Subdivision (FIPS)
    COUSUBCC         -          County Subdivision Class Code
    COUSUBSC         -          County Subdivision Size Code
    DIVIS            -          Division

*  Marked variables are indexed, - denotes others with value selection menus
```

Figure 13-13

the same Records which the user selected earlier in Catalog 314, and links the two data sets using the unique Logical Record Number found in each Record.

Before viewing the results of the Add Label operation, let's explore some of Option 3's added capabilities. Instead of pressing <Enter> when the ANPSADPI field appeared on the screen, the user could have chosen to select additional Fields from Catalog STF300. EXTRACT provides prompts at the bottom of the screen, suggesting the appropriate steps. By pressing **M** (for Multiple Fields), the searcher indicates he wishes to add more than one Field in the merge process. Next, he presses **A** to call up a list of All Fields found in Catalog 300. For the purposes of this example, the searcher selects two Fields from the list: ANPSADPI and POP100. The latter Field contains the values for total population.

The newly revised table is shown in Figure 13-14. It shows data for all County Subdivisions in Dade County, with the Area Names displayed in column 1. Column 2 provides total population counts, also taken from Catalog STF300. Columns 3 and 4 present the occupational characteristics originally selected from Catalog STF314. For example, the Miami Beach Division of Dade County, Florida has a population of 122,672 inhabitants. Of the employed persons (age 16 and older), 7,215 people are in Executive, Administrative, or Managerial occupations, and 7,778 are in Professional Specialty occupa-

By pressing M (for Multiple Fields), the searcher indicates he wishes to add more than one Field in the merge process.

Q&A

What purpose does the ANPSADPI Field serve for Records which have no Area Names, such as Tracts, Block Groups, and Blocks?

Although Tracts and related Statistical Units are designated by numbers rather than words, their ANPSADPI Field can be useful. The numeric Codes for these entities lack important information, such as decimal points and "part" indicators. Numeric codes also insert leading zeroes, making it somewhat difficult to interpret the number correctly. In contrast, the ANPSADPI Field presents the entity's number (its "Name") in a more readable fashion. To give a simple example, the Census Code for Block Group 4 in any given Tract is simply "4." The corresponding ANPSADPI Field would be "BG 4," which is a bit more informative.

A better example can be found in the nomenclature for Census Tracts. Compare the following Census Codes and their corresponding ANPSADPIs, and the distinction will be clear.

Census Code (TRACTBNA)	Area Name (ANPSADPI)
0003	Tract 3
0501	Tract 501 (pt.)
005402	Tract 54.02

Unlike named entities (cities, counties, etc.), numerically designated entities can be displayed in extracted tables without adding Area Name labels; but adding the ANPSADPI Field provides additional information which makes the table easier to read.

tions. The remaining occupational categories were not selected for display in this table.

Tips for Selecting Items and Records

The lists presented in Menu Options 1 and 2 are usually quite lengthy, and scanning them for the desired variables can be time-consuming. EXTRACT includes several search features which help users locate Items and Records more quickly. The commands are Jump, Locate, and Word Search, and they are executed by pressing J, L, or W respectively. This set of commands performs the same functions in Option 1 and Option 2.

The Jump command moves the cursor to a specified alphanumeric Field Name on the list. The Locate command moves the cursor to a string of characters in the Field Description, but only looks for the beginning characters in that Description. Punctuation must be included in the search string exactly as it appears in the Description. The Word command moves the cursor to the first occur-

1990 Census STF 3A, File 14, Tables P77 - P83 Dade, FL

STF300->ANPSADPI	STF300->POP100	P0780001	P0780002
Everglades division	4283	352	134
Hialeah division	237725	12475	8400
Homestead division	60204	1975	1905
Kendale Lakes-Lindgren Acres division	190810	17216	13427
Kendall-Perrine division	150800	14662	17971
Key Biscayne division	8854	1377	1086
Miami division	803988	37241	41230
Miami Beach division	122672	7215	7778
Northwest Dade division	96313	3232	4916
North Westside division	75895	5205	3235
Princeton-Goulds division	97996	4877	4396
South Westside division	87554	6177	4791

Key to column headings:

ANPSADPI	— AREA NAME — /PSAD Term/Part Indicator
POP100	Population Count (100%)
P0780001	Executive, administrative, and managerial occupations
P0780002	Professional specialty occupations

Figure 13-14

J looks for codes, L looks for beginning phrases, and W looks for individual words. None of the commands are case-sensitive.

rence of the specified word or word string anywhere in the Field Description, whether it is the first word or not. J looks for codes, L looks for beginning phrases, and W looks for individual words. None of the commands are case-sensitive.

Returning to Figure 13-7, any one of the three commands could be employed to quickly locate the line for "Executive, administrative, and managerial occupations." If the code for the Field Name were known (from the Technical Documentation for *STF 3A*), the user would type J, then type **P0780001**. If the user knew the standard description for the desired Field, he could type L, then type **Executive, admini**, or as much of the beginning character string as deemed necessary. If neither the code or the standard description were known, the user could type W, then type a word that seemed likely, such as **manager** or **managerial**.

The commands operate in exactly the same manner when searching for a specific Record in Option 2. Here the features are especially useful because a complete list of geographic entities (Tract numbers within a county, Place names within a state, etc.) can be quite long. Most of the search strategies shown in Figure 13-10 could be improved by using the L command during the third step in the retrieval process.

 Census Tip

A Word search takes longer to execute than a Jump or Locate search, and can be especially slow when searching through the long lists found in Option 2. To cancel a Word search while it is in progress, type W again, then press *<Enter>*.

Choosing the appropriate geographic Field can speed up the Record Selection process enormously.

Choosing the appropriate geographic Field can speed up the Record Selection process enormously. It is particularly important to select Fields which EXTRACT has already indexed. In Option 2, an indexed Field is designated on the menu screens by an asterix.

For example, some EXTRACT Catalogs list two separate entries for County Subdivisions. COUSUBCE lists County Subdivisions by their Census codes (GICS codes), and is not indexed. COUSUBFP lists the same County Subdivisions by the government's FIPS codes, and this Field *is* indexed. To retrieve Records for one or more specific County Subdivisions quickly, the user would select COUSUBFP. The difference between the two Fields can be seen in Figure 13-13, where COUSUBFP is designated with an asterisk. EXTRACT users may also wish to explore the "Select Index" feature found in Option 4 (Manipulate Files). This allows the searcher to view a list of indexed Fields, and choose the one which best relates to the chosen SUMLEV.

Another way to speed EXTRACT retrieval is to plan effective search strategies. After selecting Records, if the searcher finds the program is taking more than five or ten minutes to retrieve the first Record or display the first screen, he or she may want to rethink their approach. Certain Record selection activities can take an hour or more to execute. Sometimes an alternate approach will speed up the process tremendously, so the user may find it advantageous to kill a slow search and start over again. (The EXTRACT program can usually be aborted by pressing <Alt> C. If this doesn't work, the only way to break a search is to press <Ctrl> <Alt> <Del>.)

Basic examples of alternate search strategies include choosing a different file (e.g., *STF 1A* instead of *STF 1C*), or selecting an indexed Field rather than an unindexed one. In some situations, it may even be better to select more Records than needed, and delete the unwanted entities after downloading. When Selecting Records, EXTRACT users should remember several guidelines:

▸ the larger and more geographically complex the selected entity, the longer it will take to retrieve the Records

▸ selecting two or more entities takes longer than selecting one entity

▶ selecting nonsequential Records can be time-consuming.

The third guideline requires explanation. When searching an Indexed File, EXTRACT stops at the first Record which meets the requested criteria. If more than one Record is sought, the CD-ROM player must search each additional Record sequentially, until a second match is found.

💡 Census Tip

When seeking two or more nonsequential Records, it is advisable to run separate searches, and merge the resulting databases later.

The third guideline requires explanation. When searching an Indexed File, EXTRACT stops at the first Record which meets the requested criteria. If more than one Record is sought, the CD-ROM player must search each additional Record sequentially, until a second match is found. Consider the case of a county-name search in an Alabama File, as shown earlier in Figure 13-9. If data for Jefferson County are sought, Option 2 will retrieve the Record relatively quickly. Similarly, if data for Jackson and Jefferson Counties are required, retrieval will be rapid because the two Records are near one another on the disc. Requesting data for Jefferson and Tuscaloosa counties will take additional time,

because the program must search the entire state File alphabetically for every county, until it locates the second Record.

Displaying, Printing, and Downloading Results

Creating customized tables is fine, but unless the user can view and save the results, the value of EXTRACT would be limited. In fact, EXTRACT offers three different methods of capturing search results: Option 6 (Displaying), Option 7 (Printing), and Option 8 (Downloading).

Using Option 6 (Display to Screen)

Option 6 allows users to view the results of their search on the screen. As mentioned earlier, by utilizing Option 6 before a search is begun, the user can view an entire Catalog. Option 6 is particularly useful as a means of checking the progress of a search in between steps, and to verify the size and appearance of a table before printing or downloading.

Q&A

What are the major differences between Selecting Items (Option 1) and Selecting Records (Option 2)?

Until readers have had an opportunity to conduct a few successful EXTRACT searches, the distinctions between these two important functions may seem confusing. This confusion is exacerbated by the identical selection menus found in both Options.

Simply stated, Option 1 creates the columns in an extracted database, while Option 2 creates the rows. Option 1 selects the Fields taken from every Record; Option 2 selects the Records themselves. The interaction between Fields and Records determines the composition of the extracted File.

In addition to their fundamental differences, the two

Options perform differently during the search process. When new selections are made in Option 1, the old choices remain in effect unless the user deletes them. In contrast, new selections in Option 2 will supersede previous ones unless the original choices are saved (Reinstated) by the user. Option 1 offers a simple one-step selection process. Option 2 presents a series of screens during the selection process. Option 1 allows the user to select as many Items from the list as he or she wishes. Option 2 permits a maximum of two selections on each pass.

Displaying results can take a minute or two, as EXTRACT painstakingly fills the screen one line at a time. The program will not return control to the user until the first screen is filled. Each screen contains 17 lines of data, representing 17 Records. To see the next group of Records, the user must employ the down-arrow key or the <PgDn> key. After paging down to a second screen, EXTRACT will once again require a moment to fill the screen. If the Record retrieval process (Option 2) was time consuming, its corresponding screen display will also be slow. It may take many minutes to fill the first screen during a complex search, especially if non-consecutive Records are retrieved.

In many cases, an extracted table will contain too many columns to fit the standard width of an 80-character screen. The left- and right-arrow keys can be used to shift the display, revealing adjacent columns. Notice also, as the cursor moves from one column to the next, EXTRACT displays the current Field Description on a status line appearing at the bottom of the screen. This is a particularly useful feature, since the searcher may have forgotten what the selected Field Names represent.

The width of each column is based on the fixed width of the Field itself, as documented in the Data Dictionary. Because Field widths are established to accommodate the largest possible values, the default setting may be larger than necessary in a given table. The ANPSADPI Field offers a good example. ANPSADPI, you may recall, contains the text of each Record's geographic name: "Talladega County, AL," "Milwaukee WI MSA," "Tract 108.02," and so forth. Because some area names are quite lengthy, the Field width is 66 characters. To shorten the width in Option 6, the user can highlight the desired column and type W. The 66 character display can be reduced to a more reasonable size, as determined by the user. If a particular Record's value in that Field is too long to fit in the reduced column, the information will be truncated. For example, if the ANPSADPI Field were reduced to 14 char-

acters, Talladega County would display as **Talladega Coun**. Before narrowing Field widths, it's a good idea to scan the column's entire contents to determine an appropriate size. Premature truncation can hide important information, such as "part" identifiers or numeric values.

Every time a column width is adjusted in Option 6, the program will take a moment to refill (rewrite) the information on the screen. The time it takes to do so can cause frustration, especially if the user wishes to adjust the widths of numerous columns. A better way to adjust column widths is through the Preview command, available only in Option 1. Because the Preview command only displays the first row in any table, adjusting the width in Option 1 is virtually instantaneous. The operation is conducted exactly as in Option 6, by typing **W** while the desired column is highlighted.

If the Preview command is so convenient, why would a searcher want to use Option 6 at all? Because Preview only shows one row of data at a time. If the searcher wants to view the complete table, Option 6 must be employed. This is particularly important for confirming whether the correct Records have been selected in the search. Whether column widths are adjusted in Option 1 or Option 6, they will remain at the adjusted setting until they are changed again, or until the user exits the program.

☿ Census Tip

Adjusting Field widths is accomplished best by using the Preview command, available in Option 1 only. But the searcher should always view results in Option 6, to ensure that columns aren't truncated too severely.

Option 6 offers one additional feature. Users can change a display from the standard columnar format to a "row-wise" format. Instead of presenting data in tables, the Fields will be listed in paragraphs. This is especially useful when the searcher has selected many Items but only a few Records. The row-wise format presents a concise profile of each geographic entity. In contrast, when the user has selected a few variables for many entities, or when he wishes to import data into a spreadsheet, the standard columnar format is preferred.

Figure 13-15 illustrates a typical row-wise display. In this example, the user selected 18 different Fields describing housing characteristics for two counties in Montana. Presenting the data in columnar format wouldn't make sense, because the resulting table would show 19 columns and two rows. By reversing the order, the searcher creates two easily comparable profiles. Notice that row-wise displays also show the full Field Descriptions rather than the eight-character Field Names.

Switching between the two formats is accomplished using the Toggle command. Typing **T** in Option 6 switches from one to another, and back again. The columnar setting is the default format in all EXTRACT programs.

Using Options 5 and 7 (Format and Print)

Printing EXTRACT Files is fairly simple. The user chooses Option 7 from the Main Menu and presses <Enter>; the program does the rest. The Print function even creates a "Key to Column Headings," describing the content of each column. Examples of column heading keys can be seen in Figures 13-11, 13-12, and 13-14, among others.

 Census Tip

Always Display the results of a search (Option 6) before printing the File. Users can abort a bad printout by pressing <*Esc*>.

Unfortunately, if the desired table is too wide to fit on the page, the spilled-over

Housing Data, Yellowstone and Missoula Counties, Montana

Catalogs STF1C7 and STF1C8

Yellowstone County

48781	Housing units, total
44689	Occupied housing units
4092	Vacant housing units
29371	Owner occupied housing units
15318	Renter occupied housing units
1735	Vacant housing units: For rent
877	Vacant housing units: For sale only
269	Vacant housing units: Rented or sold, not occupied
204	Vacant units: For seasonal, recreational, or occasional use
31	Vacant housing units: For migrant workers
976	Other vacant housing units
133	Vacant housing units: Boarded up
2.49	Persons per occupied housing unit (2 implied decimals)
62800	Median value
289	Median contract rent
602	For rent: Vacant 6 or more months
514	For sale only: Vacant 6 or more months
862	All other vacants: Vacant 6 months or more

Missoula County

33466	Housing units, total
30782	Occupied housing units
2684	Vacant housing units
18514	Owner occupied housing units
12268	Renter occupied housing units
533	Vacant housing units: For rent
274	Vacant housing units: For sale only
137	Vacant housing units: Rented or sold, not occupied
1093	Vacant units: For seasonal, recreational, or occasional use
1	Vacant housing units: For migrant workers
646	Other vacant housing units
47	Vacant housing units: Boarded up
2.47	Persons per occupied housing unit (2 implied decimals)
66200	Median value
273	Median contract rent
86	For rent: Vacant 6 or more months
132	For sale only: Vacant 6 or more months
808	All other vacants: Vacant 6 months or more

Figure 13-15

columns will wrap around to a second line, creating a jumbled mess.

Option 5 allows the user to adjust the format of the table before printing or downloading. As shown in Figure 13-16, the menu for Option 5 offers several choices for modifying the appearance of a File before printing takes place. The user can adjust the margins, the number of characters per line (to accommodate wider paper), and the

Option 5 allows the user to adjust the format of the table before printing or downloading.

number of lines per page. Choices 1 and 2 on the submenu allow users to switch between columnar and row-wise formats, which performs exactly the same function as the Toggle command in Option 6. Menu choices 3 and 4 allow users to add customized headings to the File. The resulting headings will appear on downloaded or printed files. In Figure 13-15, for example, the "first level" heading was designated "Housing Data, Yellowstone and Missoula Counties, Montana." The "second level" heading is "Catalogs STF1C7 and STF1C8."

For Printing purposes, certain reformatting tricks can be particularly useful. If the desired table is slightly wider than a standard page, the Width command can be employed to narrow each column. In some instances, a row-wise display will be preferred. Resetting the number of lines per page is particularly useful in the row-wise format. Another quick trick is to "hide" the contents of a particular Field temporarily before printing. If a specified column is not wanted, the user can reset the width to zero, which will make it disappear when the results are printed. Other tricks are more complex, and may involve downloading in ASCII-text format for subsequent editing, or creating an abbreviated MY_FILE. The latter operations are described in the next section.

Using Option 8 (Extract Data to a File)

Extracting Data to a File (Option 8) allows the user to save the results of a search session for future use. Downloading offers several advantages. One is the ability to import data into other software packages, including spreadsheets, word processors, and mapping programs. A second is the ability to create customized files which the searcher can reuse over and over again. Third, and most practical, is the ability to save work in progress. EXTRACT is a particularly unforgiving product. Certain mistakes will cause the program to crash in mid-operation. Given the likelihood that EXTRACT may "bomb

```
┌─────────────────────────────────────────────────┐
│               FORMAT OPTIONS                    │
│                                                 │
│    Type of report                               │
│                                                 │
│  1  Select columnar output   X                  │
│  2  Select row-wise output                      │
│                                                 │
│  3  Heading (1st level)                         │
│  4  Heading (2nd level)                         │
│                                                 │
│    Configure output for printer    Current values│
│                                                 │
│  5  Page width                        80        │
│  6  Number of data lines per page     60        │
│  7  Top margin                        0         │
│  8  Left margin                       0         │
│  9  Print one page at a time          N O       │
│                                                 │
│                  Press <ESC> to return to main menu│
│                                                 │
│    Enter option number:                         │
└─────────────────────────────────────────────────┘
```

Figure 13-16

out" at any moment during a reasonably complicated search, the user should build the database in stages, downloading the results at convenient breaking points. In this way, if the program crashes, the work won't be lost. A final use, discussed later in the chapter, is the ability to merge downloaded Files.

Option 8 permits downloading in four different formats, similar to those seen in the GO program. The menu choices are listed below:

1	.DBF	Database format
2	.PRN	Comma-delimited
3	.SDF	Fixed-format text
4	.TXT	Print File, with page breaks and headers

The .TXT format downloads results in ASCII-text, for use with word processing software. The .PRN format is used primarily for spreadsheet applications. The .DBF format is used for Database Management Systems, such as dBASE or EXTRACT itself. Downloading in the .DBF format has an added benefit: in addition to downloading the data File, EXTRACT will automatically create a customized Data Dictionary for the downloaded Fields and Records. If the down-

If a specified column is not wanted, the user can reset the width to zero, which will make it disappear when the results are printed.

Certain mistakes will cause the program to crash in mid-operation.

Q&A

What is a MY_FILE?

MY_FILES is the name EXTRACT gives to the collection of *.DBF Files saved on the **c:\extract\work** subdirectory. (When downloading Files using Option 9, EXTRACT will automatically save them to the default destination on the hard drive unless the user specifies an alternate location.) A MY_FILE is any downloaded File which has been saved on the **work** subdirectory in .DBF format. EXTRACT also creates a customized Data Dictionary for the new database, so the MY_FILE can be used again with EXTRACT.

Because EXTRACT prompts the user to provide a brief description of the downloaded File, the MY_FILES Catalog becomes a menu of downloaded Files which the user can retrieve at any time for further EXTRACT manipulation. The MY_FILES directory appears as the last option in the "Choose a Catalog" menu. When the user selects a MY_FILE from the list, EXTRACT treats it exactly the same as a regular Census Catalog. But instead of retrieving data from the CD-ROM, EXTRACT will search the MY_FILE located on the hard drive. By downloading large data sets as MY_FILES, the user can avoid subsequent use of the CD-ROM entirely. The retrieval process is faster and the risk of a complex search crashing the system is minimized. Additional uses for MY_FILES will become apparent later in the chapter, during the discussion of File merging operations.

---

loaded File were named **Miami.dbf**, for example, the corresponding Data Dictionary File will be called **MiamiD.dct**.

After the searcher chooses one of the four menu options, a prompt will appear, asking the user to specify the file path (drive\directory\filename) for the downloaded File. Data can be saved to the hard drive or to a floppy diskette. If a drive and directory are not specified, EXTRACT will download the File to the default work space—the c:\extract\work subdirectory which the user created when EXTRACT was installed on the computer.

 Census Tip

When naming a File, do not add a file extension. EXTRACT will automatically add the appropriate three-letter extension shown in the list above.

The advantage of downloading to the **work** subdirectory is that EXTRACT will add the downloaded File to the MY_FILES Catalog. It will also prompt the user to create a brief description of the File, which will appear in the MY_FILES menu. In this way, the user can easily return to the downloaded File at any time during a subsequent EXTRACT session.

 Census Tip

EXTRACT assigns a file name for every newly-created Data Dictionary. When naming .DBF Files for downloading as MY_FILES, the user must make sure the first seven characters in the name are unique, because EXTRACT automatically adds the letter D as the eighth character in the new Data Dictionary's name. The natural inclination, when creating a series of related Files, might be to name them sequentially: miami1, miami2, etc. EXTRACT cannot accommodate such similar names.

If a drive and directory are not specified, EXTRACT will download the File to the default work space—the c:\extract\work subdirectory which the user created when EXTRACT was installed on the computer.

Additional Search Techniques

It is beyond the scope of this book to delve too deeply into the intricacies of EXTRACT searching. But it is important to mention, however briefly, a few of EXTRACT's more sophisticated capabilities. The following presentation is divided into three parts: creating User-Defined Items, creating complex Record Selection strategies, and merging Files.

Creating User-Defined Items

With hundreds of specific Census Fields to choose from, it might seem unnecessary to create your own variables, but the need often arises. Census tables on CD-ROM seldom contain Fields for subtotals or percentages. For example, Catalog STF301 provides six categories for types of Family Household, but it doesn't provide a Field for total number of Family Households. The user must create his or her own total by adding the individual Fields together. EXTRACT provides that capability through the User-Defined Item command.

EXTRACT allows searchers to create a maximum of ten User-Defined Items during a search session. The user can return to Option 1 at any time to add new User-Defined Items. Each Item is numbered sequentially. Whenever the U command is invoked, EXTRACT will display a numbered list of the User-Defined Items which were created earlier in the search. For example, if three User-Defined Items had been created, EXTRACT will list them on the menu screen, and prompt the searcher to create number four. EXTRACT also enables searchers to designate their own Field Names and Field Descriptions for every User-Defined Item they create.

The program can handle two types of User-Defined Items: Ratios, and Free-Form Expressions. To create one, the searcher enters Option 1 (Select Items) and types U from any point on the menu screens. EXTRACT will supply a template to be used in creating the desired variable. The first template screen contains four boxes: three are used to create percentages or ratios, while the fourth is used for "Freeform Expressions."

Freeform Expressions

The most common use of Freeform Expressions is the creation of totals and subtotals. To move to the Freeform Expression box on the User-Defined template screen, the searcher presses <Enter> until the cursor is positioned in the proper box.

Fields can be added together by typing an arithmetic expression, using the + sign. For example, Table P019 (found in Catalog STF306) contains data on Family Households, including Female Householders, No Husband Present. Field P0190005 represents Female Householders, No Husband Present with children and Field P0190006 represents the corresponding category with no children. To create a new variable which represents all Female Householders, No Husband Present, the searcher would type the following notation in the Freeform Expression box:

P0190005 + P0190006

Now the searcher can press <Enter> to receive additional prompts.

The next template screen provides boxes for four additional attributes: Length, Decimal places, Field Name, and Description. To move from one box to the next, the user presses <Enter>. In the Length box, the user designates the Field width—the maximum number of characters to appear in the User-Defined Field. Under Decimal Places, the user specifies the desired number of decimal places. If this box remains empty, the resulting variable will be shown as a whole number. The designated length must provide sufficient room to contain the largest value of the desired variable, including a decimal point and decimal places, if these were selected.

The most common use of Freeform Expressions is the creation of totals and subtotals.

EXTRACT allows searchers to create a maximum of ten User-Defined Items during a search session.

Census Tip

If the assigned Length is too short to accommodate the resulting totals, EXTRACT will crash. Searchers are advised to consult the Data Dictionary to determine the maximum widths of component Fields before creating a User-Defined Item.

In the Field Name box, the user is prompted to name the newly-defined variable, using any combination of letters and numbers which are eight characters or less. The Description box allows the user to enter a descriptive phrase which explains the nature of the Field. The Description may be up to 60 characters in length. Continuing with our example, the searcher might name the Field **FMHEAD**, with an accompanying Description of **Total: Female Householders, No Husband Present**.

A range of values can be summed together by using a colon instead of a plus sign.

A range of values can be summed together by using a colon instead of a plus sign. Consider the following example, taken from Table P117, found in Catalog STF322. This table shows the number of persons who fall below the Poverty Level, with data presented by age group. Twelve age categories are shown, from P1170013 to P1170024. The Fields can be totaled as a User-Defined Item by entering the following Freeform Expression:

P1170013:P1170024

The ability to create subtotals is especially important in EXTRACT because Tables containing the desired totals may be present only in another Catalog, or not at all. This ability is critical for creating appropriate denominators for use with ratio calculations, as will be demonstrated in a moment.

Ratios and Percentages

The User-Defined Items command can also be employed to create ratios or percentages. The first three boxes in the User-Defined template screen prompt the searcher to specify a Numerator, Denominator, and a Scaling Factor. To generate percentages, the proper

The first three boxes in the User-Defined template screen prompt the searcher to specify a Numerator, Denominator, and a Scaling Factor. To generate percentages, the proper Scaling Factor would be 100.

Scaling Factor would be **100**. To create a one-to-one ratio, the Scaling Factor would be **1**. After these three boxes are filled, a new template appears, asking the searcher to designate Length, Decimal Places, Field Name, and Description—exactly the same as with a Freeform Expression.

Before continuing with the Poverty Level example, let's take a simpler illustration from *STF 1A*. Catalog STF1A0 contains tables showing the racial composition of the population. Table P006, consisting of five data Fields, shows the five broadest racial categories, with Field P0060002 representing the number of Blacks. Catalog STF1A0 also contains Field P0010001, representing the total number of inhabitants. To calculate the percentage of Blacks in the populations, the following calculation would be entered:

Numerator	P0060002
Denominator	P0010001
Scaling Factor	100

Catalog STF1A0 is atypical. In most cases, total values cannot be found as pre-determined Fields in the Catalog being searched. Returning to the example of Catalog STF322, if the user wants to calculate the percentage of persons below the Poverty Threshold, both the numerator and denominator must be created before a ratio can be computed. The numerator, representing the number of people who fall below the Poverty Level, was created earlier by entering the Freeform Expression P1170013:P1170024. But how can the desired denominator be created? The correct denominator isn't the total number of persons, but the total number of persons for whom Poverty Status is determined. (As described in Chapter 5, Poverty Status is only calculated for certain categories of the population.) Therein lies the clue. The Universe of Table P117 is indeed "Persons for whom Poverty Status is determined." Therefore, if the searcher adds up every Field found in Table P117, the resulting total will equal the required Universe. The desired denominator is represented by the expression **P1170001:P1170024**.

Percentage of Blacks, Largest Counties in Ohio

ANPSADPI	P0010001	P0060001	P0060002	PCTBLK	ALTPCT
Butler County	291479	274892	13134	4.5	4.5
Cuyahoga County	1412140	1025756	350185	24.8	24.8
Franklin County	961437	783714	152840	15.9	15.9
Hamilton County	866228	672972	181145	20.9	20.9
Lake County	215499	209879	3528	1.6	1.6
Lorain County	271126	241549	21230	7.8	7.8
Lucas County	462361	380155	68456	14.8	14.8
Mahoning County	264806	221109	39681	15.0	15.0
Montgomery County	573809	463551	101817	17.7	17.7
Stark County	367585	339421	25052	6.8	6.8
Summit County	514990	446902	61185	11.9	11.9
Trumbull County	227813	210915	15221	6.7	6.7

Key to column headings:

ANPSADPI	AREA NAME — /PSAD Term/Part Indicator
P0010001	Persons, total
P0060001	White
P0060002	Black
PCTBLK	Blacks as a percentage of the total population
ALTPCT	Alternate method of calculating percentage of Blacks

Figure 13-17

P1170001:P1170012 represents all persons above the Poverty Threshold, while P1170013:P1170024 represents all persons at or below the Threshold. The sum of the two groups represents all persons for whom Poverty Status is calculated. To summarize, the percentage of poor persons is calculated in the following manner:

Numerator   P1170013:P1170024
Denominator P1170001:P1170024
Scaling Factor 100

Newer versions of EXTRACT allow the user to incorporate previously-created User-Defined Field names in subsequent calculations.

 Census Tip

When the Universe of a given table represents the desired denominator in a ratio calculation, the easiest way to create the denominator is to sum all the values in the table.

To prove the point, return to the example taken from Catalog STF1A0, involving the percentage of Black persons. Figure 13-17

shows the appropriate values for the largest counties in the state of Ohio. The column labeled PCTBLK was calculated in the manner described above, with P0010001 as the denominator. The next column, ALTPCT, was calculated with a denominator reflecting the Universe found in Table P006 (i.e., P0060001:P0060005). The values are identical.

Newer versions of EX-TRACT allow the user to incorporate previously-created User-Defined Field names in subsequent calculations. In the earlier example, if the number of Poor persons had been calculated in a prior step and named POVNUM, the POVNUM Field could be used in the numerator of the ratio calculation.

 Census Tip

Each time Option 2 is entered, the previous selections are deleted, *unless* the R command is used to save them. This is the only way in which more than two selections can be made in Option 2. A common mistake in a double-pass search is to forget to use R, especially since no on-screen prompts are provided as a reminder.

Complex Record Selection

Successful Record selection can be challenging in the best of circumstances, but the examples provided earlier in the chapter actually constitute fairly basic search methods. Because of the nature of geographic hierarchies and the way in which EXTRACT is designed, certain searches require an additional level of complexity. The following sections introduce two specialized categories of Record selection: complex geographic retrieval, and numeric searching. In many cases, such searching requires a two-stage retrieval strategy, hereafter known as "double-pass" searching.

Double-Pass Searching

Option 2 allows users to select Records using a maximum of two Fields at a time, unlike Option 1, where users can select as many as desired (within the constraints of the dBASE format). For most searches, two selections are sufficient, but in certain situations, more than two are necessary. To get around this limitation, EXTRACT allows users to build a search in two passes (or stages). In the first pass, the user selects two variables. Once the selections have been made, the program automatically escapes to the Main Menu. The user must then reenter Option 2, type **R** (for "Reinstate"), and press **<Enter>** to save the first two selections. At this point, one or two additional selections can be made in the second pass.

The first two examples in Figure 13-18 illustrate geographic retrieval methods requiring a double-pass search strategy. To retrieve all Block Groups in a Tract, for example, it might appear sufficient to simply select **SUMLEV** and **TRACTBNA**, then designate the **150** Summary Level and choose the desired Tract. This doesn't work because Tract numbers are not unique within the

Complex SUMLEV Searching Using EXTRACT:
Record Selection Requiring Two Passes

To retrieve:	Follow these search steps:
All Block Groups in a Tract	**[first pass]** s SUMLEV s CNTY <Esc> x 150 State-County-Tract/Block Numbering Area-Block Group <Esc> x [choose county name from list] <Esc> **[second pass]** R [to reinstate previous selections] s TRACTBNA <Esc> L [type desired Tract area name; e.g. **Tract 301**] <Esc>
All Block Groups within a County Subdivision	**[first pass]** s SUMLEV s CNTY <Esc> x 090 State-County-County Subdivision-Place-Tract/Block Numbering Area-Block Group <Esc> x [choose county name from list] <Esc> **[second pass]** R [to reinstate previous selections] s COUSBFP <Esc> [scan list for desired Subdivision name; second pass takes user directly to first Subdivision in desired county] x [desired Subdivision name] <Esc>
Within a county, all Block Groups with at least one building of 50 Units or more	**[first pass]** s SUMLEV s CNTY <Esc> x 150 State-County-Tract/Block Numbering Area-Block Group <Esc> x [choose county name from list] <Esc> **[second pass]** R [to reinstate previous selections] s H0200008 50 or more <Esc> [specify minimum value of 1] <Enter> [specify no maximum value] <Enter>

Figure 13-18

search domain (the state). The sequence of Tract numbering is only unique within each county, so the same Tract Number will exist in many counties across the state. For this reason, the user must specify the County and the Tract Number, as well as the desired Summary Level. Because three selections are required, the searcher must use a second pass. (Note: EXTRACT provides an alternative to the double-pass approach for certain complex retrieval needs, but that method will not be described here. Searchers will find that a double-pass strategy is sufficient for virtually all complex Record selection requirements.)

Numeric Searching

So far, the discussion of Record selection has focused on geographic retrieval. But users may want to restrict their retrieval set to geographic entities which meet specified demographic or housing characteristics. Option 2 can also be used to restrict the domain by specified numeric characteristics. In fact, this is one of the most powerful, versatile, and useful of all EXTRACT applications.

Users can easily identify those Fields which can be searched numerically, based on indicators listed on the Option 2 menu screens. As shown earlier in Figures 13-8 and 13-13, Field Names followed by an asterisk or a hyphen are Geographic Identifiers. When these are selected, the searcher is presented with a list of all possible values in the domain, and he or she selects desired entities from the list. Any Field name *without* an asterisk or hyphen is numerically searchable, which means the user will be prompted to specify minimum and maximum desired values.

In Chapter 8, Figure 8-16 shows an EX-TRACT table with Records for four of the largest cities in Indiana (excluding Indianapolis). In that example, the Records were selected from Catalog STF3C308IN—Catalog 8 on the *STF 3C* disc for the United States. First, the user selected SUMLEV and Place. Next, Summary Level 160 (State-Place) was selected, then the desired cities were chosen from an alphabetical list. This presumes the searcher already knew the names of the desired cities. But what if the largest cities were not known?

Option 2 can be used to retrieve only those Places in Indiana with populations greater than a specified amount. Using the same Catalog (STF1A0IN), the searcher would select **SUMLEV** and **P0010001** (the numeric Field for Total population). He would

then be prompted to choose a specific Summary Level (**160**, State-Place) and a numeric range for P0010001. The first range prompt asks for a minimum value. Here the searcher might type **80000**. Then EXTRACT asks for a maximum value. To specify an open-ended range, the searcher would simply press <Enter>. Now EXTRACT will retrieve all Records in the database meeting the specified requirements: Places with total population of 80,000 or more. (If the searcher wanted to exclude Indianapolis, because it is so much larger than the other cities, he could have specified a maximum value of whatever size seemed appropriate—say, 300,000 or so.)

Numeric range searching can also be used to retrieve Records meeting a yes/no requirement. For example, if the searcher wanted to locate all Block Groups with Hispanic residents, he would select P0080001 (Persons of Hispanic Origin) and specify a minimum value of 1. This would retrieve all Block Groups containing at least one Hispanic person. The third listing in Figure 13-18 provides another example of this technique. Field **H0200008** counts the number of buildings containing 50 or more Housing Units in the structure. To identify all Block Groups in a county containing at least one large apartment building, the searcher retrieves all BGs with a minimum value of **1** in the H0200008 Field. Notice that this particular search requires two passes to execute.

EXTRACT's numeric retrieval capability can be employed to meet an amazing variety of search requirements. The following brief list offers a sample of what EXTRACT can accomplish.

- ▸ Within a state, Tracts with a median Housing Value greater than $200,000.
- ▸ Within a county, all Block Groups with 20 or more Asian inhabitants.
- ▸ Within a state, all counties with a Poverty Rate greater than 20%.
- ▸ Within a state, all counties containing more than 100 persons who are inmates

---

Option 2 can also be used to restrict the domain by specified numeric characteristics. In fact, this is one of the most powerful, versatile, and useful of all EXTRACT applications.

Numeric range searching can also be used to retrieve Records meeting a yes/no requirement.

of a Correctional Institution.

▸ Within a state, all Tracts containing Housing Units built before 1940.

Merging Files

EXTRACT provides two types of File merging capabilities: horizontal and vertical. A horizontal merge occurs when the user adds new Items from other Catalogs, with the merged appearing as added columns to Records already selected. An example of a horizontal merge was given earlier in the chapter, when Option 3 (Add Labels) was introduced.

A vertical merge occurs when the user adds new Records, often from a completely different File. A useful application of a vertical merge takes place with larger states, where *STF 3A* Files are split across several CD-ROM discs. Another use of vertical merging is to increase retrieval speed for nonconsecutive Records, especially if those Records are located in different counties. As mentioned earlier, it is usually much faster to retrieve two or more nonsequential Records separately, then merge the results. If the searcher wanted to select Block Group data for two Tracts in one county and three Tracts in another, conducting separate searches in each county would provide far faster results.

The following discussion focuses on horizontal File merging. Horizontal merging is extremely important with *Summary Tape Files* because desired population and housing characteristics may be scattered across several Catalogs. Assume for example, that a searcher wishes to create a fairly simple table with the following five variables:

▸ Number of Households
▸ Number of Families
▸ Median Household Income
▸ Median Family Income
▸ Per Capita Income

The first two variables are found in Catalog STF301; the third variable is located in Catalog STF314; and the last two are listed in Catalog STF322. The only way to extract

the data on a single table is to merge the respective Fields from the three Catalogs.

 **Census Tip**

Horizontal merging can also be used to combine different types of Census Files. Data from *STF 1* and *STF 3* can be combined horizontally, for example. Horizontal merging is also useful for combining decennial data with Items from nondecennial products, such as the *Economic Census* or the *County and City Data Book*.

In the following sections, "Base Catalog" (or "Base File") refers to the first Catalog opened by the user, before additional Catalogs are merged. The Base Catalog is created when the user initiates an EXTRACT search session. It can be changed during the session by choosing Option 9 (Return to File Selection Menu) from the Main Menu. Option 9 resets the Base File. Data from merged (secondary) Files will be appended to the Base File. When conducting merge functions, the user should remember which is the Base Catalog. As will be shown momentarily, the order in which columns are displayed in a merged table is dependent on the relationship between the Base File and the secondary Files.

EXTRACT offers two ways to merge Files. Option 3 (Add Labels) can be used for horizontal merging only. Option 4 (Manipulate Files) handles both horizontal and vertical merging.

Merging with Option 3

One way to initiate a horizontal merge is to utilize Option 3, the Add Labels feature. As discussed earlier, Option 3 can be used not only to add the Area Name Field to a table stub, but to insert additional columns of data from another Catalog. Option 3 allows searchers to merge a maximum of three Catalogs (the currently opened Catalog plus one or

EXTRACT provides two types of File merging capabilities: horizontal and vertical.

Horizontal merging is extremely important with Summary Tape Files because desired population and housing characteristics may be scattered across several Catalogs.

two "Label" Catalogs), as long as the total number of Items selected from the Label Catalogs is ten or less. For example, if two Catalogs were being merged, the user could select a maximum of ten Items from the second Catalog; if three Catalogs were being merged, the ten Items could be distributed across the second and third Catalogs in any combination (seven and three, six and four, two and eight, etc.)

To merge Files using Option 3, the searcher would open a Catalog, then select Items and Records in the usual manner. To add columns from a second Catalog, he would then choose Option 3 and select a new Catalog from the menu. If only one Item is desired, he can scan the list and select the needed Field. If more than one Item is wanted, the searcher must type **M** (for Multiple Items), **A** (to view All Items), then select the desired Fields. When the selection process is completed, the searcher presses **<Esc>** to return to the Main Menu. The selected Items from the two Catalogs are now merged in a single File. The columns selected from the Label Catalog will display first, followed by the columns from the Base Catalog.

To merge a third Catalog, the searcher can choose Option 3 a second time and select a new Catalog from the menu. A warning then flashes on the screen, advising the user to press **S** to save the previously selected Labels. He can now repeat the process to select additional Items from the third Catalog. Columns generated from the third Catalog will display after those from the second, but *before* those from the first. In other words, Label Files display before the Base File. Users should also note that Items selected from Label Files display in the order in which they were selected, unlike Base File Items, which display in the order they appear on the menu.

Merging with Option 4

Option 3 offers a simple, automatic process for horizontal merging, but this function limits users to ten new Item selections, and a maximum of three merged Files. An alter-

nate method of combining Files is available through Option 4 (Manipulate Files). This function is more complicated than Option 3, but it offers greater flexibility. Option 4 only allows searchers to merge two Files at a time, but the process can be repeating as many times as the user desires. In this way, searchers can combine data from as many Catalogs as they need, by successively merging two Catalogs at a time. As an added benefit, Option 4 permits searchers to select as many Items from each Catalog as they wish. The only limit to the process is imposed by dBASE itself—no single dBASE File can contain more than 128 columns of data.

Option 4 provides a submenu listing five separate database functions, including the ability to conduct horizontal and vertical File merges. This discussion will focus on submenu choice 3, "Merge Files Horizontally."

Once the searcher selects the choice for horizontal merging, he or she will see a complete list of available Catalogs, similar to the list seen in Option 3 (Add Labels). After the desired Catalog is chosen, EXTRACT asks how the two Catalogs will be linked. (In Option 3, this step is done automatically.) The program offers two choices:

1. by Record Number
2. by index, which the user creates.

The latter choice requires the searcher to duplicate the Record Selection process executed in the Base Catalog. Linking by Record Number is far simpler, providing both Files contain the LOGRECNU Field. LOGRECNU is the Logical Record Number, a unique number assigned to every Record in the Census databases.

After the searcher indicates the first choice, EXTRACT uses the LOGRECNU Field to match the Records in the new Catalog to those previously selected in the Base Catalog. Now the searcher will see the complete list of Items available in the second Catalog. He or she can select the desired Items from the new list, press **<Esc>**, and return to the Base

An alternate method of combining Files is available through Option 4 (Manipulate Files). This function is more complicated than Option 3, but it offers greater flexibility.

LOGRECNU is the Logical Record Number, a unique number assigned to every Record in the Census databases.

In contrast to
Option 3, merging
through Option 4
places the columns
selected from the
secondary Catalog
after columns
selected from the
Base Catalog.

Catalog. At this point, if the searcher decides to Display, Print, or Download the resulting table, it will contain the data selected from both Catalogs. In contrast to Option 3, merging through Option 4 places the columns selected from the secondary Catalog *after* columns selected from the Base Catalog.

 Census Tip

When merging Items via Option 3 (Labels), the secondary choices display first. When merging Items via Option 4 (Manipulating Files), the secondary choices display last.

If the searcher wishes to save the merged File for further manipulation in EXTRACT, Option 9 must be employed to download the data as a MY_FILE in .DBF format. Once this is done, the new MY_FILE can be retrieved again, and it can be merged with data from another Catalog, if the user wishes.

In this manner, a customized database can be constructed step by step, with each merge resulting in a more complex product, as long as the user remembers to save each interim step as a new MY_FILE.

With each new MY_FILE, the list of available Items shown in Option 1 will lengthen. Option 4 can be used to merge data horizontally in several combinations:

▸ merging Items from two different Catalogs
▸ merging Items from a Catalog and a MY_FILE
▸ merging Items from two different MY_FILES.

The best way to ensure successful merging in the latter two cases is to make sure the MY_FILES in question include the LOGRECNU Field. However, this capability is only available for EXTRACT versions 1.3e or higher. It is also a good idea to include an appropriate selection of Geographic Identifiers in the MY_FILES, be-

Q&A

What are the major differences between merge operations in Option 3 (Add Labels) and Option 4 (Manipulate Files)?

Although the two functions perform the same basic task, they do so differently. Each Option offers advantages and disadvantages.

1. Option 3 is simpler to perform and is less likely to crash in mid-operation, but it is limited in its capabilities.

2. Option 3 can be used for horizontal merging only. Option 4 can handle horizontal and vertical merges.

3. Option 3 can merge three Files at a time, Option 4 can only merge two Files at a time. Both functions enable users to merge additional Files in successive stages, but it is trickier to do so successfully in Option 3.

4. Option 3 limits users to selecting a maximum of ten secondary Items for merging. Option 4 imposes no limits on the number of secondary Items.

5. Option 3 displays the secondary columns before those selected from the Base File. Option 4 displays the secondary columns after the Base columns.

6. Option 3 displays columns in the order in which they were selected. Option 4 displays columns in the order in which they are listed in the Select Items menu.

7. Option 3 works best when linking one Catalog to another. Option 4 is the better choice for linking one MY_FILE to another.

cause EXTRACT creates a customized Data Dictionary for every File downloaded in **.DBF** format.

 ## Census Tip

When creating MY_FILES, remember to select the LOGRECNU Field as a downloaded Item, whether you think it will be needed or not. If you decide to merge data at a later time, the presence of LOGRECNU values will make matters much simpler.

Step-by-Step Extract Searching: A Case Study

A step-by-step demonstration of a more complex search will reinforce how the various EXTRACT functions can work together. This example will be easier to follow if the user mirrors the steps on his or her own computer. In this way, the effects of each operation will become clearer, and the results can be viewed on the screen. The example deals with the Birmingham, Alabama area. If the reader does not have access to the necessary File for Alabama, the same steps can be followed using the *STF 3A* disc for another state. Simply choose a Metropolitan county familiar to you.

Bear in mind that this case study is designed to illustrate a diversity of EXTRACT functions. As such, it is more involved and time-consuming, utilizing many features in a single session. A more typical EXTRACT search would be far simpler, utilizing far fewer steps in the process.

In this case study, a county planner wants to compile a list of Census Tracts in Jefferson County, Alabama in which the Median Household Income is $42,500 or greater. Then, for those same Tracts, she would like to compare Income data to the percentage of

adults holding a graduate or professional degree. Creating the extracted File requires a variety of EXTRACT operations, including double-pass Record retrieval, numeric searching, creation of User-Defined Items, creation of MY_FILES, and merging of Files. The completed EXTRACT table is shown in Figure 13-19, which appears later in the chapter.

To create the table, the searcher must first place the appropriate *STF 3A* disc in the CD player. From the C: prompt, she types **cd extract**, to change to the EXTRACT directory on the hard drive. Then, by typing **exmenu**, she can call up the batch menu which lists the Census Files available for searching. From here, she can select the appropriate exmenu option to open the *STF 3A* program.

Now the searcher sees the "Choose a Catalog" menu. Briefly consulting the Technical Documentation, she discovers that Median Household Income is reported on Table 80A, which, according to EXTRACT's Catalog Menu, is located on Catalog STF314 (i.e., File Segment 14). After choosing Catalog STF314, the EXTRACT Main Menu appears on screen.

Selecting Items and Retrieving Records

From the Main Menu, the searcher chooses Option 1 to Select Items. She now sees a complete list of all data Fields located within this Catalog, including Geographic Identification Fields. She can scan through the list, looking for the table containing Median Household Income, but the desired table doesn't appear until six screens down the list. Since she already knows the table number, a faster approach involves the Jump command. By typing **J**, entering the desired table number (**P080A**), and pressing **<Enter>**, she will move quickly and directly to that table. Median Household Income is identified by Field name P080A001. Placing an **X** next to the Field name, the searcher selects this Item to appear in her table. Pressing **<Esc>** returns her to the Main Menu.

The next step involves Option 2, Select Records. A new list of Field names now appears, identical in every respect to the list displayed under Option 1. The searcher wants to retrieve those Census Tracts in Jefferson County with Median Household Income of $42,500 or greater. This operation requires two passes using Menu Option 2. In the first pass, all Tracts in Jefferson County are retrieved by executing the following steps:

```
s SUMLEV
s CNTY
<Esc>
x Summary Level 140 (State-County-Tract)
<Esc>
L Jefferson
<Enter>
x 073 Jefferson, AL
<Esc>
```

The system will then take a few seconds to extract the set and return to the Main Menu.

At this point, it might be a good idea to add labels to the File and view the results, just to make sure the search was run correctly. The searcher enters Option 3 to Add Labels. From the Catalog list, she chooses Catalog STF300. A single line will appear on the screen for the Area Name Field (ANPSADPI). At this point she could press **<Enter>** to add the Name labels to the extracted table and return once again to the Main Menu. Instead, she decides to add two fields from Catalog STF300. Since STF300 also contains the POP100 Field, representing the total number of inhabitants, she decides to include this Field in her extracted File. To select more than one column in Option 3, the user types **M** for multiple fields, then **A** to display a complete list of available fields in the Catalog. (On-screen prompts provide guidance.) She can now page down to the fifth screen, where she sees the desired Fields: ANPSADPI and POP100. Pressing **<Enter>** on each highlighted line will select these

Fields as Labels. Pressing **<Esc>** returns her to the Main Menu.

The searcher can now use Option 6 to Display the results, though it will take a few seconds to fill the screen.

The resulting table shows a list of all Tracts in Jefferson County, Alabama, arranged in numeric order. At this point, the table contains three columns: the ANPSADPI Field, containing the Tract names; the POP100 Field; and Field P080A001, showing Median Household Income for every Tract. The third column came from Catalog STF314. The first two columns, taken from Catalog STF300, were merged using Option 3.

The searcher must now conduct a second pass in Option 2 to narrow the set to those Tracts with a high Median Household Income. Option 2 is chosen once again, but now the searcher must type **R** to Reinstate the previously selected Records. A confirmation message which reads, "Previous selection criteria reinstated" will appear on the screen. The searcher is now free to select a maximum of two additional search criteria. Instead of selecting a geographic Field, she will locate the appropriate demographic Field by Jumping to Table P080A. She then places an **S** next to Field P080A001 (Median Household Income) and presses **<Esc>**. Because P080A001 is a numeric Field, EXTRACT prompts the user to specify a range of values. As a minimum value, the searcher types **42,500** and presses **<Enter>**. To leave the maximum value open-ended, she simply presses **<Enter>** a second time. Once again the system will take a moment to retrieve the qualifying Records and return to the Main Menu.

Option 6 can be used once again to verify the results so far. Now the searcher sees a much briefer list, consisting of 15 Tracts, each of which has a Median Income of $42,500 or more. (Note: if the reader uses a different county for this exercise, the resulting number of Tracts will differ.) By pressing **<Esc>**, the Main Menu appears once more.

The searcher must now conduct a second pass in Option 2 to narrow the set to those Tracts with a high Median Household Income. Option 2 is chosen once again, but now the searcher must type R to Reinstate the previously selected Records.

Creating MY_FILES

At this point, the searcher decides to save the extracted File for additional manipulation. The best way to do this is by creating a MY_FILES extract. Before leaving Catalog STF314, however, she may want to retrieve some additional data Items for the MY_FILE. Since the searcher is interested in Household Income, and because she may later wish to calculate various percentages, she decides to select every Field in the Household Income table. After entering Option 1 (Select Items), she can either scan the list for the appropriate table, or jump directly to Table P080. She can now select every Field in the table by placing an X next to each line. The table contains 25 separate Fields (P0800001 through P0800025), providing Household Income distribution in intervals of varying dollar amounts (shown earlier in Figure 13-3).

One more Field is required if the searcher plans to merge her MY_FILE with other extracted Files. She must select LOGRECNU, the Field containing the unique Logical Record Number for each entity. Now her resulting MY_FILE can be merged easily with other Files. At this point, it would be a good idea to use the Preview command to make sure all necessary Fields have been selected. The resulting window should display 28 columns, containing Area Name, Total Population, Median Household Income, and 25 Income ranges.

The first MY_FILE

After escaping to the Main Menu once again, the searcher can choose Option 8 to Extract data to a File. She would then enter choice 1 (.DBF format), press <Enter>, and name the File. If the File path is not specified, EXTRACT will save it to the default work space on the hard drive. She names the File **Medinc**, and enters the following File description: "Tracts in Jefferson County with High Median Income."

Now the searcher would like to retrieve data on educational attainment for the same

15 Tracts. Using the Table Locator (The I command) from the Main Menu, she discovers the required table, covering persons age 25 or older, is found in Catalog STF310. At this point, she could chose Option 9 to change Files, open Catalog 310, select the same Records as before, select the necessary Items from Table P057 (Educational Attainment), and download it as a second MY_FILE. The two MY_FILES could then be merged into a single database, as long as both of the original Files included the LOGRECNU Field.

A faster solution would be to open the first MY_FILE (Medinc.dbf), merge it with Catalog STF310, and then download the merged database as a new MY_FILE. The decision depends upon whether the searcher will be using the Files again in the future, and on the order in which she wishes the columns to appear in the merged table. For this example, the searcher will follow the second, faster option.

Merging the MY_FILE with Another Catalog

From the Main Menu, the searcher can re-open the Medinc database by choosing Option 9. The MY_FILES Catalog appears at the end of all the standard *STF 3* Catalogs. After opening the MY_FILES Catalog, a complete list of all MY_FILES currently found on the hard drive will now appear. Once the Medinc database has been opened, the searcher will see a new Main Menu.

Now comes the time to use Option 4 (Manipulate Files). The system prompts the user to select the desired operation, and the searcher indicates choice 3, a horizontal merge. Next she is prompted to open a Catalog for the new File to be merged. In this case, it is Catalog 310. As a final step in the merging process, EXTRACT asks how the two Files are related. Since Medinc contains the LOGRECNU Field, the searcher indicates choice 1, "By way of Record Number," then types **LOGRECNU** as the Record Number expression. Records from the two Files are

The two MY_FILES could then be merged into a single database, as long as both of the original Files included the LOGRECNU Field.

Household Income and Educational Attainment
Tracts with High Median Income, Jefferson County, AL

ANPSADPI	POP100	P080A001	HIGHINC	HSEHLDS	HIPCT	P0570007	GRADPCT
Tract 59.07	2199	44183	419	1276	32.8	108	7.3
Tract 107.03	2216	43617	499	1100	45.4	268	16.5
Tract 108.02	3331	76932	904	1485	60.9	481	21.3
Tract 108.03	6498	48904	1560	3316	47.0	841	18.7
Tract 108.04	2861	81696	865	1253	69.0	493	24.3
Tract 108.05	7720	67630	1871	3813	49.1	1178	23.4
Tract 111.04	6779	46842	1346	3725	36.1	238	5.6
Tract 128.01	6552	44074	1440	3711	38.8	785	17.1
Tract 129.03	6436	66120	1501	3111	48.2	799	19.9
Tract 129.05	4178	54077	1007	1718	58.6	572	18.7
Tract 129.06	5958	46305	1297	3182	40.8	701	17.6
Tract 129.07	3559	46648	846	2102	40.2	511	19.2
Tract 144.03	8567	56592	1923	4418	43.5	838	15.0
Tract 144.06	4785	58761	1175	2499	47.0	534	16.3
Tract 144.07	3158	50104	739	1377	53.7	251	10.8

– ·

Key to column headings:

ANPSADPI	— AREA NAME — /PSAD Term/Part Indicator
POP100	Population Count (100%)
P080A001	Median household income in 1989
HIGHINC	Number of Households with Income gt 42,499
HSEHLDS	Total Number of Households
HIPCT	Percentage of Households with Income gt 42499
P0570007	Persons 25+: Graduate or professional degree
GRADPCT	Percentage of Persons 25+ with Grad/Prof Degrees

Figure 13-19

What the searcher must do is create the appropriate User-Defined Items, then extract a new MY_FILE, containing only the Fields she really wants to display.

now merged, and the searcher can select the desired Items from Catalog 310 to include in a new, smaller File. Choosing Option 1 (Select Items) from the Main Menu, she places X's next to Fields 0570001 through 0570007, representing the seven categories of educational attainment. Escaping to the Main Menu, Option 8 can be employed once again to create a new MY_FILE containing the merged data, which she calls **Eduinc**.

Creating User-Defined Items

The new File, Eduinc.dbf, contains all the data on Household Income and Educational Attainment which our searcher needs to create her final table. Two problems arise with the File in its present state. First, with 25 columns on Household Income, seven col-

umns on educational levels, and one column each for Median Income, LOGRECNU, and Area Name, the table is too unwieldy for presentation purposes. Second, it contains no subtotals or percentages, which she needs to provide proper analysis. What the searcher must do is create the appropriate User-Defined Items, then extract a new MY_FILE, containing only the Fields she really wants to display.

She decides that the following User-Defined Items would be helpful:

▸ total number of Households
▸ number of Households with Income of $42,500 or more
▸ percentage of Households with Income of $42,500 or more
▸ percentage of persons age 25 or older who have earned graduate or professional degrees.

Let's walk through the steps necessary to create the last category only. To calculate the required percentage, the searcher must divide the number of adults with graduate or professional degrees (Item P0570007) by the total number of persons age 25 or older. Since the Universe for Table P057 is "Persons age 25 years or more," the needed total is obtained by summing all seven Items in the table. From Option 1 (Select Items), the searcher types **U**, for User-Defined Item. In the box for numerator, she types **P0570007** and presses **<Enter>**. In the box for denominator, she types **P0570001:P0570007**, and presses **<Enter>**. In the box for Scaling Factor, she types **100** and presses **<Enter>** again. She is then prompted to specify the Field width, the number of decimal places, and the Item's Field Name and Description. She decides to call it **GRADPCT**, and types "Percentage of Persons Age 25+ with Grad/Prof Degrees" as the description.

The same process is followed to create the remaining Fields. Total number of Households, which the searcher calls **HSEHLDS**, is calculated by summing Fields P0800001 through P0800025. The number of Households with Income of $42,500 or more, which she calls **HIGHINC**, is obtained by adding Fields P0800016 through P0800025. And the percentage of all Households meeting the searcher's definition of high income is calculated by dividing HIGHINC by HSEHLDS. This last Item is designated **HIPCT**.

The searcher can now extract one final MY_FILE, containing exactly the data Items she wants to display. Option 1 or 6 can be used to adjust the column widths, and Option 5 can create a new title for the extracted table. EXTRACT performs all of the operations described above very rapidly because the searcher is using a MY_FILE, not the CD-ROM. The final results of her efforts can be seen in Figure 13-19.

As the reader may have noticed in the example above, EXTRACT allows a great deal of flexibility in determining the order in which complex operations are executed. Which is better: creating separate MY_FILES first, then merging them; or merging two Catalogs, then creating the MY_FILE? The answer depends on the circumstances, but both choices present potential problems. When manipulating data before extracting to a MY_FILE, the user runs the risk of crashing the program and losing all the data before it can be downloaded. When downloading first, the danger lies in forgetting to include key Items in the extracted Files, making further manipulation and merging difficult or impossible. Neither problem is insurmountable—the user is simply forced to start over again. No matter how carefully the operation is planned, no matter how experienced the EXTRACT user, searchers will still encounter unexpected and inexplicable problems.

Users should plan the order in which they execute operations for another reason: the order governs the manner in which columns are displayed.

1. Label Files appear first, with Items listed in the order they were chosen.
2. The Base File appears next, with Items listed in the order they appear on the menu.
3. Files merged via Option 4 appear next, with Items listed in the order they appear on the menu.
4. Within each File, User-Defined Items appear last, after all Items selected from the menu.

Census Tip

When creating User-defined ratios, users must be careful to choose the proper denominator. As described in Chapter 10, ratios involving an estimate as a numerator should also employ an estimate in the denominator.

Summary

To look at Figure 13-19, the reader wouldn't necessarily realize the number of EXTRACT steps required to create it. In retrospect, some might wonder whether the results are worth the effort. Might it not have been simpler (if not faster) to copy the information by hand from the printed Census Reports, or from the CD-ROM using GO software? Percentages and totals could be obtained with a calculator, or the data could be entered by hand into a spreadsheet. By EXTRACT standards, the creation of Figure 13-19 is fairly complicated. With practice, of course, many of the steps become second nature. And readers should remember that describing the process keystroke-by-keystroke makes it appear a bit more lengthy and more involved than it truly is. Still, it's difficult to dispute that the process of creating Figure 13-19 was cumbersome and frustrating.

 Census Tip

The watchword of EXTRACT searching is KISS—Keep It Simple, Stupid. If a search strategy can't be accomplished with a minimal number of operations, it should be broken down into a series of smaller searches which can then be merged.

EXTRACT is frequently criticized for being slow, clumsy, tedious, and unforgiving. It can also be difficult to learn, especially for users unfamiliar with database management and Census File structure. Remember, however, EXTRACT was never intended as an end-user product and it was not developed by professional programmers. Although each new software release offers welcome improvements, EXTRACT will never have the appearance or performance of a premiere commercial DBMS package. The program has an infuriating propensity to crash at the slightest provocation. Lengthy retrieval requests can freeze the program, requiring a reboot to break the

search. And a host of lesser annoyances and peeves could be listed here by any veteran user. The determined and experienced EXTRACT searcher learns to compensate for the program's limitations.

So, let's return to the question posed earlier in the chapter: if EXTRACT is such a limited program, why use it at all? Perhaps the most important benefit of EXTRACT is its Record Selection capability. If done properly, the process can scan through thousands of geographic entities, retrieving only those which meet the user-specified characteristics. The MY_FILES capability is also important. For users who anticipate a need to manipulate data for the same city, county, or collection of counties in a variety of ways over a period of time, the creation of MY_FILES enables them to return to the same data set over and over again. EXTRACT allows them to retrieve the tables they need, merge them together in a new database, and download the results to a hard drive. The resulting MY_FILES then take the place of the CD-ROM itself, providing the user with faster access to frequently requested information, which in turn can be further manipulated using the EXTRACT program itself.

EXTRACT is frequently criticized for being slow, clumsy, tedious, and unforgiving. It can also be difficult to learn, especially for users unfamiliar with database management and Census File structure.

Perhaps the most important benefit of EXTRACT is its Record Selection capability. If done properly, the process can scan through thousands of geographic entities, retrieving only those which meet the user-specified characteristics.

Chapter 14

Internet Resources and Other Electronic Products

Internet Resources and Other Electronic Products

CD-ROM PRODUCTS provide users with direct and easy access to huge amounts of detailed Census data. However, CD-ROM is not the only electronic medium through which the Census Bureau releases its publications. Researchers with access to large computer systems can utilize the Bureau's many magnetic tape products for 1990. For some specialized Files, magnetic tape remains the only source of information.

Users can also obtain varying amounts of 1990 Census data by tapping into remote electronic databases. For the sake of this discussion, Census Files which do not reside on the user's own microcomputer, mainframe, or Local Area Network will be referred to as online resources. Online Census data can take several forms. The oldest of these is a timesharing system, called *CENDATA*, which is offered through commercial database vendors. Users can also access electronic Bulletin Board Systems operated by the Bureau itself, or by various State Data Centers. The newest and most exciting wrinkle

in remote access is the ability to locate, view, and download 1990 Census Files via the Internet.

This chapter describes each of these electronic options and compares their advantages and disadvantages. It is beyond the scope of the book to describe Internet concepts and search methods in detail, but for the benefit of readers who are unfamiliar with the Internet, a few basic terms will be defined.

Internet Resources

Agencies of the United States government are among the most prolific and reliable providers of statistical data accessible through the Internet, so it should be no surprise that the Census Bureau has embraced this new medium with great enthusiasm. In April, 1994 the Bureau established an Internet host site, but the service was not widely publicized until the spring of 1995. By that time, the number and diversity of Files had increased dramatically. Now, thousands of users connect to the Bureau's Internet server every month, and the agency views the Internet as a major vehicle for data dissemination.

Internet Basics

The Internet is a worldwide computer network consisting of thousands of smaller networks which are linked to one another. Each of these networks employs a common set of telecommunications standards which allows the different computer systems to recognize and "understand" one another. Local institutional networks are linked to regional networks, which in turn are connected to larger "backbone" networks. All of these networks are connected through high-speed data transmission lines. Special devices, called "routers," determine the most efficient pathway for sending a transmission on its journey through the networks.

The Internet is analogous to a worldwide phone system which allows different phone companies to connect and communicate with one another. Instead of communicating by voice, users communicate by sending digital messages with their computer keyboards. The beauty of the Internet is that all types of computers, regardless of their manufacturers and operating systems, can communicate

The Internet is analogous to a worldwide phone system which allows different phone companies to connect and communicate with one another.

Q&A

How can I obtain Internet access?

Generally speaking, Internet connections take one of two forms: continuous access through leased (dedicated) telecommunications lines, or dial-up access through regular telephone lines. Most large organizations (universities, government agencies, business corporations, etc.) maintain leased lines for full-time Internet access. If your school or work site has Internet access, you probably do also. Simply ask your organization's system administrator how you can get "plugged in."

What about connecting to the Internet as an "unaffiliated" individual? A diversity of commercial services have emerged to provide dial-up access to the Internet. Popular online vendors, such as CompuServe and America Online, now offer basic Internet services. Regional telecommunications networks, such as NYSERNET and CERFNet also offer Internet access. A variety of new companies, sometimes called Network Service Resellers, now specialize in providing Internet access to local customers.

How much does Internet access cost? If you are connecting via a dedicated line at your work place, your employer is paying the costs, which are generally quite expensive. Personal (nondedicated) access is more affordable. Commercial Internet providers typically charge individuals a monthly service fee, which varies according to the level of access you select and the amount of time you spend on the system. As of this writing, basic Internet access begins at about $15.00 per month. Would-be Internet customers should investigate their options before selecting a service provider. Many excellent books and magazine articles describe the pros and cons of the different types of Internet providers, and suggest questions you should ask when comparison shopping. A visit to your local public library is usually a good place to start.

If you live in a community which sponsors a local Free-Net, this is an excellent way for beginners to explore the Internet. Free-Nets provide Internet access either at no cost to the subscriber, or at very low costs. They are sponsored by universities, public libraries, or other nonprofit organizations as a community service, usually with the help of grants from local companies. They are maintained solely through the efforts of hard working volunteers. The types of services offered by a Free-Net may be limited, and users may experience difficulties in making a connection during busy times of the day, but this option offers a friendly, affordable way for the novice 'Net surfer to get his or her feet wet.

More than 20,000 computer networks, representing millions of individual computers, are connected to the Internet worldwide.

Where Gopher takes a linear, hierarchical approach, the Web offers a more free-form alternative, allowing the user to jump from one related concept to another with no pre-established sequence.

with one another by virtue of using standard telecommunication protocols. Participation in the Internet continues to grow at a staggering rate. More than 20,000 computer networks, representing millions of individual computers, are connected to the Internet worldwide. As of this writing, nearly every country on the planet enjoys some type of Internet access.

Another advantage of the Internet is that it utilizes client/server architecture. This means client software (Gopher, Lynx, Mosaic, Netscape, etc.) resides on the user's system and manages the details of navigating the Internet, retrieving data, and displaying the results. Furthermore, once a particular document is retrieved, it resides on the user's system until the connection is broken. This frees each host site to act more efficiently as a data "server."

Readers should note that the Internet is not an entity, nor is it maintained by a single organization. Each local and regional network is operated and managed independently from the others. Furthermore, each host site determines what data it will offer, and what links it will provide to other sites. As a result, the Internet's highly decentralized, somewhat disorganized structure, coupled with its ever-changing nature, can be a source of frustration to the user. As an example, interesting and useful data sites may disappear without warning, or they may change addresses overnight.

A variety of widely-used computer programs have been created to help users navigate on the Internet. These navigational tools help the user locate needed Internet hosts (servers) and connect to them quickly and easily without knowing their actual Internet addresses. Gopher, created at the University of Minnesota, is a menu-based system. It presents a series of hierarchical menus which take the user step by step through a sequence of data screens, and can even take the user from one server to another, depending on the types of linkages created by the administrator of the individual Gopher site.

A newer, and more popular navigational

tool is called the World Wide Web (also known as the Web, WWW, or W3). The Web program was first developed at the European Laboratory for Particle Physics (CERN) in Geneva, Switzerland. Instead of providing information as a series of menus, the Web presents pages of narrative containing hypertext links. A computer mouse is used to "point and click" on highlighted words or phrases. When the user selects a highlighted portion of the text, the Web software moves immediately to a new page of text containing the desired information. The World Wide Web and Gopher protocols are similar in that links may point to other sections on the host server, or they may connect to other Web servers or Gophers located anywhere in the world. The two programs differ in the way in which they organize information. Where Gopher takes a linear, hierarchical approach, the Web offers a more free-form alternative, allowing the user to jump from one related concept to another with no pre-established sequence. This complex, interconnected approach is analogous to the design of a spider's web: the user can choose any number of pathways to move from Point A to Point B.

Another way to obtain information via the Internet is through a protocol called Anonymous File Transfer Protocol, or FTP. This is a means of finding large archives of data files located on a remote computer and copying them for local use. The Anonymous designation refers to the fact that users do not need to be affiliated or registered with the host archive to copy its files; instead, they can log in as a guest, usually by typing the word "anonymous" to identify themselves. Once the user is connected to the remote FTP site, the **dir** command will display the root directory for the site, which lists the various subdirectories contained in the archive. Users then employ the **get** command to copy individual files, including the important **readme** files, which provide useful explanatory matter and instructions for using the actual data files.

Gopher, the World Wide Web, and FTP

Q&A

How can I locate a particular Web server if I don't know its URL?

If a searcher doesn't know the specific URL for a desired site, he or she can locate it using one of many Web search engines. These take one of two general forms. Web directories, list useful Web sites according to topic or geographic location. For example, Yahoo (at **http://www.yahoo.com**) provides an extensive guide to thousands of sites, arranged into broad categories, from business to recreation. Under the Yahoo category of "Social Science," the user can select "Data Collections" as a subcategory, then view a list of useful statistical sites pertaining to the social sciences, including various hosts providing Census data.

A second type of search engine allows users to locate desired sites by keyword. Examples of popular keyword engines include WebCrawler and Lycos. Using directory-based or keyword services such as these, searchers can identify and connect to relevant Web sites if their URLs are not known, or even if the name of a sponsoring organization is not known.

---

each utilize various standardized computer conventions. Standards employed by the Web include HyperText Transfer Protocol (HTTP), which supports the hypertext linkages on the Internet; HyperText Markup Language (HTML), a means of creating Web pages by assigning labels (tags) to each major segment of a hypertext document; and Uniform Resource Locators (URLs), a standardized address system for connecting to individual servers.

 Census Tip

The URL protocol can also be used to make connections to Gopher sites. For example, the University of Missouri at St. Louis, whose library offers some interesting Census data, can be reached at: *gopher://umslvma.umsl.edu.*

To connect to a particular Web server, the user must type the site's Uniform Resource Locator. A URL consists of a string of characters which identifies the server's unique domain name (the computer's address), the location of the particular resource on the computer, and the type of Internet navigational tool it employs (HTTP, Gopher, FTP, etc.). Web sites incorporate the designation **http://** as part of the URL. For example, the URL for Harvard Business School's Web site is **http://www.hbs.harvard.edu**. The domain portion of the name is **hbs.harvard.edu**. The last segment of the domain name indicates the type of institution (educational, government, commercial, etc.) or the country in which it is located.

Users can open specific files on the Web in several ways. Taking a general approach, they can connect to a site's "Home Page," then browse through the links provided to specific files. For example, the Home Page for *Info Louisiana*, a state-government sponsored Web server, can be accessed by typing the following URL: http://www.state.la.us. Among the many files residing on the *Info Louisiana* server are those of the Louisiana State Data Center, which provides a variety of 1990 Census tables and other demographic statistics for the state. From the Home Page, the user can click on a link to "Louisiana Profiles," then click again on a link to "Demographic and Census Information." Further links provide a series of "Detailed Population Reports," including extracts of selected tables from *STF 4.* As an alternate pathway from the Home Page, users can choose the "Topic Index" and browse through an alphabetical list of specific files relating to Ancestry, Poverty, and other topics.

To connect to a particular Web server, the user must type the site's Uniform Resource Locator.

The Census Bureau maintains an Internet site which utilizes the HTTP (World Wide Web) and FTP protocols.

A more direct approach can be taken if the user knows the directory path and file name for desired files on a server. Instead of viewing a general description of *Info Louisiana*, users can type a more specific URL for the Home Page of the State Data Center itself:

http://www.state.la.us/state/census/census.htm.

The Center's profile of 1990 Ancestry statistics for Louisiana can be found at

http://www.state.la.us/state/census/prof22.htm.

Searchers retrieve information on the Web by using client programs called "Web browsers." Some browsers, like Lynx, are text-based programs. Others, like Mosaic and Netscape, provide a Graphical User Interface, which means that the user can retrieve photographs and other graphic images in addition to plain text.

The Census Bureau Web Server

The Census Bureau maintains an Internet site which utilizes the HTTP (World Wide Web) and FTP protocols. During the early stages of developing its Internet service, the Bureau also maintained a Gopher server, but by mid-1995 the agency announced that it could no longer afford to support two versions of the same data sets. Although the Gopher server remains accessible as of this writing, no new Files are being added, and the Bureau plans to disband this site in the immediate future. Meanwhile, the Web version continues to grow and improve daily.

Users can connect to the Bureau's Web server at the following URL:

http://www.census.gov.

Figure 14-1 shows the Home Page for the Bureau's Web site. It is organized into eight general categories, plus a welcoming message

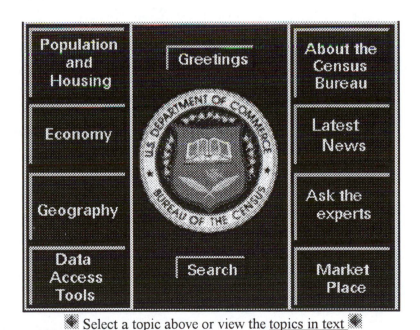

Select a topic above or view the topics in text

| Pop Clocks | Data Maps | Genealogy | Radio Broadcasts | Other topics
| Archie | HTTP Files | FTP Files | BBS | Excellent Sites |
| Employment Opportunities |

Figure 14-1

The most dramatic feature of the Web site's "Population and Housing" section is a powerful research tool called "Census LOOKUP."

Another useful feature of this section is a series of links to the Web servers at Census Bureau Regional Offices, State Data Centers, and other Census-related organizations.

from the Bureau's Director and a keyword search engine. The brief text portion at the bottom of the Home Page offers additional subject categories, including the Bureau's Population Clock, a section on genealogy, a guide to current job openings in the agency, and a link to the Bureau's electronic Bulletin Board System.

The "Latest News" section reproduces the text of press releases from the Census Bureau. "Ask the Experts" provides a telephone directory for Census Bureau employees, listed by specialty as well as by name. This section also allows the user to post general questions to the Bureau's staff via e-mail. Another useful feature of this section is a series of links to the Web servers at Census Bureau Regional Offices, State Data Centers, and other Census-related organizations. This section also provides a link to a search engine which can identify the nearest Depository Library by ZIP Code, courtesy of the Government Printing Office's *GPO Access* Web server.

"Market Place" provides online catalogs of Census products available for sale, whether from the Bureau itself or the Government Printing Office. Major sections include an electronic version of the current issue of the *Monthly Product Announcement* (called "Recently Released Products" on the Web site) and a more comprehensive catalog entitled "Current Census Products and Services." The latter section is organized according to type of publication or service: CD-ROMs, print Reports, magnetic tape, and Fastfax subscriptions. Users can place orders for most products listed in the "Market Place," either with the Bureau or the GPO, depending on the type of publication.

The "Population and Housing" section contains selected statistical tables taken from the 1990 Census, from various current surveys, from current population estimates and projections, and from two of the Bureau's most popular general reference tools: the *County and City Data Book* and the *Statistical Abstract of the United States.* This section also provides Web access to the many FTP files in the Bureau's data archive.

The most dramatic feature of the Web site's "Population and Housing" section is a powerful research tool called "Census LOOKUP." LOOKUP is a project of the University of California's Lawrence Berkeley National Laboratory (LBNL). The project, called the University of California CD-ROM Information System, was funded by grants from the U.S. Department of Energy, with additional support provided by the Census Bureau and the University of California. Over 300 Census Bureau CD-ROMs were loaded on a file server, together with custom-designed search software. The Web version of LOOKUP first appeared in August, 1994 and is the world's largest Internet site of government-produced CD-ROM data. Because of the heavy traffic anticipated for this service, it is available on three different Web servers: one at the Bureau, one at the Department of Energy, and one at the Berkeley Laboratory. Each of the sites duplicates the full program, accessing all 300 CD-ROM products.

The LOOKUP software emulates basic functions of the Bureau's own GO software. Users select a specific CD-ROM title, then choose a state and a geographic Summary Level. The program then prompts them to choose one or more table numbers from the Table of Contents of that CD-ROM product. Unlike the GO software, LOOKUP allows users to customize their data output by specifying how many tables will be combined in a single file.

Geographic Summary Levels offered via LOOKUP are less comprehensive than can be found on the CD-ROM products themselves. LOOKUP searches are limited to the nation, states, counties, Places, Metropolitan Areas, Urbanized Areas, Congressional Districts, and ZIP Code Areas.

Funding for the project actually ended on September 30, 1995. The Berkeley Laboratory has requested new funding from a variety of sources, including the Bureau and the Government Printing Office. Meanwhile, the Bureau is working on an improved successor to the LOOKUP system, called the

Census Open Server (COS). The ability to conduct Internet searches in any of the major CD-ROM products of the 1990 Census is a marvelous service for users who have no ready access to a complete CD-ROM library. As of this writing, the fate of the LOOKUP project is uncertain, but it is likely to continue in one form or another.

The "Geography" section of the Web server provides another remarkable software system called the TIGER Mapping Service (TMS). TMS allows users to construct *TIGER/Line File* maps on the Internet. It consists of several components, some of which were developed for the Bureau under contract. The primary TMS services are a mapping engine, which generates maps on request, and a map browser, which allows users to view the resulting map online. The Geography section of the Web server also offers a United States Gazetteer. Here the user can enter a Place name, and the program will retrieve a TIGER/Line map for that Place. As of this writing, all of the components of TMS are undergoing upgrades to make them faster, more powerful, and easier to use.

Another feature found in the Geography section is DataMap, which provides map-based searching links to the LOOKUP program. From the online map of the United States, the user clicks on an individual state.

The "Geography" section of the Web server provides another remarkable software system called the TIGER Mapping Service (TMS). TMS allows users to construct *TIGER/Line File* maps on the Internet.

Once the state map appears, a specific county is chosen, then the user is offered a choice of CD-ROM products to search: *STF 1A, STF 3A, USA Counties,* or *County Business Patterns.* After a selection is made, the LOOKUP software prompts the user to choose desired tables from a list.

The final segment of the Web site, called "Data Access Tools," repeats several of the links found under the "Population" and "Geography" sections: the DataMap, the Census LOOKUP program, the TIGER Mapping Service, and the U.S. Gazetteer.

Other Internet Web Sites

Numerous nongovernmental Internet sites have loaded portions of various 1990 Census Files on their own servers, using either the HTTP or the Gopher protocol. It is beyond the scope of this chapter to explore the topic in depth, but several representative sites will be described briefly.

A logical source of Census data on the Internet would be the State Data Centers themselves. As of this writing, only 11 Data Centers have established Web servers, but more are sure to follow. The Louisiana State Data Center's Web site, introduced earlier in the chapter, is typical of this type of resource.

Q&A

How can I access *CENDATA* Files?

Users with a microcomputer, modem, and any communication software package can make the necessary connection to one of *CENDATA*'s host vendors. Both hosts are also accessible via the Internet. Regardless of the method of telecommunications, a subscription to one of the host systems is required. To inquire about subscription costs, contact the database providers at these numbers:

CompuServe (800) 848-8199
DIALOG (800) 334-2564

The vendor assigns an individual user code and password to each subscriber. Subscribers also receive system documentation and a local telephone number which connects with the vendor's telecommunications network. Once logged on, CompuServe subscribers can access the database by typing "Go CENDATA." DIALOG subscribers should type "Begin CENDATA" to utilize the menu-driven version, or "Begin 580" to access the command version.

In addition to summary data from the 1990 Census, this site provides a variety of other demographic, social, and economic data series from state and federal agencies. The Bureau's own Web server maintains links to each of the active State Data Center Web pages.

Another common provider of Census data on the Internet is the University community. Two examples of fairly extensive data servers can be found at the University of Missouri-St. Louis and the University of Michigan. Both are Gopher servers. The URLs for these two sites are:

> gopher://umslvma.umsl.edu and
> gopher://una.hh.lib.umich.edu.

Most Web servers which contain 1990 Census data focus on information for a single state or even an individual city or county. One of the few independent sites which offers summary data for all states can be found at the Columbia Online Information Network (COIN). COIN is a joint project of the University of Missouri-Columbia, the City of Columbia, the Columbia Public Schools, and the Daniel Boone Regional Library System. COIN operates a Gopher server with an extensive data collection, including extracted *STF 3* tables for all states, counties, and Metropolitan Areas in the United States, and for every Place with a population of 25,000 or more. The COIN files have become extremely popular on the Internet, and many other Web and Gopher sites across the country have established links to COIN's Census tables. The URL for COIN's Census collection is:

gopher://gopher.coin.missouri.edu:
70/11/reference/census.

Varying amounts of 1990 Census data can be found on hundreds of Internet sites, from Maine to California. At the present time, no one has compiled a comprehensive directory of these resources. The Census Bureau actively encourages universities and other research centers to mount data files containing Census figures for their own state or region.

In this manner, the Bureau hopes to distribute responsibility for maintaining such massive Internet files among many organizations. As the Internet continues to evolve, and as more and better directories, search engines, and other guides are created, the amount, variety, and usefulness of Census-oriented Web sites can only increase.

CENDATA

CENDATA is an interactive online database produced and maintained by the Bureau but distributed by several commercial timesharing services. *CENDATA* provides immediate access to a variety of Census publications as they are issued, including press releases from the Bureau; new product announcements and ordering information; guides to Bureau services; and an impressive selection of data products from the *Current Population Report* series, from economic surveys and censuses, and from the decennial Census itself. The

As the Internet continues to evolve, and as more and better directories, search engines, and other guides are created, the amount, variety, and usefulness of Census-oriented Web sites can only increase.

NEW IN '90

CENDATA underwent significant improvements following the 1990 Census; the amount of online data has increased dramatically, and the system's search and display capabilities have been enhanced. Although *CENDATA* first became available in 1984, very little data from the 1980 decennial Census was ever loaded online. The system was created primarily to provide timely access to the Bureau's current economic statistics as they were released throughout each month; demographic information was not a priority during the early years. The Bureau added intercensal population estimates, as well as ongoing data summaries from the Current Population Survey, but as late as 1989, decennial figures from 1980 comprised only one percent of *CENDATA* Records. With the addition of 1990 Census Files, the total size of the database has nearly quadrupled. As of July, 1994, *CENDATA* contained 356,000 Records; more than 84% of these consisted of 1990 Census figures. Throughout the first half of the decade, as each new 1990 publication was released, the Bureau considered *CENDATA* to be an important vehicle for providing speedy access to eagerly-awaited data.

database is available from two leading online service providers (also called "vendors" or "hosts"): DIALOG (owned by Knight-Ridder Information Services, Inc.), and CompuServe (owned by CompuServe, Inc.). On DIALOG, the database can be searched two ways: through a series of menu offerings, or as a more powerful command-based system. On CompuServe, the database is menu-driven only. Both vendors offer printing and downloading capabilities.

Both host systems update their *CENDATA* Records daily. Data Files typically appear on the DIALOG and CompuServe menu versions within hours of their official release. Users of DIALOG's command-driven database should note, however, that this version is not updated until the end of each business day.

CENDATA offers access to selected 1990 Census Files only. For example, 35 data tables from *STF 1A* are provided, with coverage of the 50 states, all counties and Places, and those County Subdivisions which serve as general-purpose governments in 12 states. Approximately 80 data tables were loaded from *STF 3A*, covering similar geographies. Other decennial Files include fairly complete P.L. 94-171 Records and a comprehensive version of the *EEO Files*. Numerous special tables provide summary characteristics at the national and state levels; rankings of states, counties, and cities; and similar comparative data. *CENDATA* contains important press releases relating to the 1990 Census, such as Secretary of Commerce Mosbacher's 1991 decision not to adjust Census enumerations for differential undercount. The online service also provides glossaries of subject and geographic terms, a complete list of Metropolitan Area Definitions, 1990 "User Notes," and related reference data. Figure 14-2 lists a sampling of the major decennial Files which can be found on *CENDATA*.

It should be noted that *CENDATA* is not the only commercially available database which provides decennial Census results. Demographic research firms such as CACI Marketing Systems, Claritas, and Market

Statistics, Inc., each incorporate decennial Census figures in their online databases. Such services are beyond the scope of *Understanding the Census* because the decennial statistics contained in these databases consti-

---

Selected *CENDATA* Files Relating to the 1990 Census

SUBJECT	MENU OPTION
American Indian Population by Tribes for U.S. and States	16.10.3
American Indians, Eskimos, or Aleuts, 1990 Census Counts	16.10.4
Ancestry Groups for U.S., Regions, and States	16.10.9
Census Data (1990) for U.S., Regions, & Division	18.7.1-4
Age by Race by Sex for All Persons	18.7.1
Number of Households by Race	18.7.2
Tenure by Race of Householder	18.7.3
Population by Age for All Persons	18.7.4
Census Terms, 1990	18.11
Counties with Population over 100,000, Ranked by Size	8.11
Economic, Social, and Housing Portraits—STF 3A	18.2.2-12
Education and Language Data for States	16.7.1
Equal Employment Opportunity File (EEO), 1990	18.3
Foreign-Born by Place of Birth for U.S. and States	16.10.8
Geographic Entities of the U.S., 1990 Census	16.5.1
Hispanic Population Groups, 1990 Census Counts	16.10.2
Housing Highlights from the 1990 Census	11.12
Language Spoken at Home and Ability to Speak English	16.7.1.7
Metropolitan Area Definitions	8.7
Metropolitan Areas, Population by Race	16.10.6
Nursing Home Population	16.6.6
Occupation by Sex, Race, & Hispanic Origin (EEO)	18.2.1
Outlying Areas of the Pacific, STF 1 Data	18.2.14.5
Outlying Areas of the Pacific, STF 3 Data	18.2.12
P.L. 94-171 Population by Race and Hispanic Origin and Housing Unit Counts, States, Counties, and Places	18.6
Persons in Emergency Shelters and Observed on Streets	18.2.15.11
Population by Race and Hispanic Origin	18.2.13.1
Population Counts for Places	18.10
Population Counts for States and Counties	18.9
Post-Enumeration Survey Estimates for States	18.2.15.3
Press Releases With 1990 Census Data	18.2
Puerto Rico & Its Municipios, Population Counts (STF 1)	18.2.14.5
Puerto Rico, Social, Economic, & Housing (STF 3A)	18.2.12.4
Racial Groups, 1990 Census Counts	16.10.7
Rankings of Counties and Selected Places by Race	8.17
Ranking of Cities Over 100,000 by Population	8.8.4
Representatives, Number of by State, 1990 Census	8.16.2
Residential & Overseas, Population by State	8.6.5
States Ranked by Selected Social, Economic, and Housing Characteristics: STF 3A	8.4
Summary Tape File 1, States, Counties, Places	18.5
Summary Tape File 3A, States, Counties, Places	18.4

Figure 14-2

CENDATA Main Menu

1 Census Bureau Products, Services, and Contacts
2 What's New in CENDATA
3 U.S. Statistics at a Glance
4 Press Releases
5 *Census and You* (Selected Articles)
6 Product Information
7 CENDATA User Feedback
8 Profiles and Rankings
9 Agriculture Data
10 Business Data
11 Construction and Housing Data
12 Foreign Trade Data
13 Governments Data
14 International Data
15 Manufacturing Data
16 Population Data
17 Genealogical and Age Information
18 1990 Census Information

Exhibit 14-3

---

tute a small portion of the total product; the majority of the information found on such systems consists of proprietary estimates and projections of household demographics and purchasing behavior. A more important distinction is that these databases are designed and compiled by commercial firms, while *CENDATA* is a product of the Census Bureau itself—the service is simply distributed through commercial suppliers.

The Menu Version

The menu version of *CENDATA*, found on both DIALOG and CompuServe, is extremely easy to use. The Main Menu, reproduced in Figure 14-3, lists 18 general subject areas from which to choose, covering topics as diverse as genealogical information and agricultural statistics. Menu numbers M1, M5, and M6 focus on user assistance, announcing and describing the Bureau's data products and services and explaining how to obtain them. Menu M2 announces the latest Files which can be found on *CENDATA*. Selection M1.3 is especially useful; it provides a detailed alphabetical index to all current *CENDATA* Files on every menu. (Figure 14-2 was adapted from this menu selection.)

After choosing an option from the Main Menu, users will see a submenu listing the topics found within that category. The menus for options M16 and M18 are shown in Figure 14-4. To retrieve data from the *Equal Employment Opportunity Files*, the user would select option 3 from Menu 18 (referred to in *CENDATA* shorthand as M18.3). Depending on the complexity of the File, the user

may be presented with additional submenus. The menu presentations may or may not resemble those seen in the GO programs on CD-ROM. *CENDATA* menus for the *EEO File* provide a good example. Instead of listing four broad options, as the GO software does, the *CENDATA* menus list the six underlying *EEO* tables described in Chapter 8. (In other words, the user will see the same file structure visible through the EXTRACT software.) Once the *CENDATA* user selects the type of table desired, the system presents a series of menus for geographic Summary Level, followed by specific choices for state, county, and/or Place names.

A complete *CENDATA* Record for a single geographic entity can be quite lengthy, even though the online version of the Files are usually subsets of their CD-ROM counterparts. An *STF 3* Record, containing 85 of the original 262 tables, is still 40 pages in length. Users may choose to download the entire File, but the cost of retrieving such a large online Record is not trivial, especially if multiple geographies are selected. For this reason, 1990 Census Files on *CENDATA* are also available as individual tables. Locating specific tables requires the user to navigate through numerous menu levels. To retrieve the table on Language Spoken at Home for a specific geographic entity requires six additional menu choices within the M18 menu group. Despite the cumbersome nature of menu searching, *CENDATA's* response time is fast, most menus are organized logically, and online instructions are easy to follow.

Users who know the exact menu location of the data they need can bypass intermediate menu screens by entering the table's specific "address." Figure 14-2 indicates that 1990 data on the nursing home population can be found in M16.6.6. Entering this location code, complete with decimal points, will retrieve the Record directly.

Decennial information can be found on a variety of *CENDATA* menus, but the bulk of it appears on menus M18, M16, and M8. M8 reproduces various ranked lists, state profiles, and subject-oriented *Statistical Briefs*.

CENDATA's command version (File 580), available exclusively on DIALOG, is not as easy to use as the menu versions, but it offers faster, more powerful searching capabilities.

CENDATA Sub-Menus

Menu 16 - POPULATION

1   Introduction to the Population Statistics Program
2   Population of Counties: 1990 and 1980
3   Population Estimates and Projections
4   Household Estimates
5   Population Growth and Distribution
6   Households, Families, Marital Status, and Child Care
7   School Enrollment, Educational Attainment, and Language Use
8   Labor Force, Income, Noncash Benefits, Pensions, and Poverty
9   Voting Patterns and Registration
10 Ethnic Data
11 Other Population Topics

Menu 18 - 1990 CENSUS DATA AND INFORMATION

1   1990 Census Information
2   Press Releases With 1990 Census Data
3   Equal Employment Opportunity (EEO)
4   Income, Education, Labor Force & Housing Characteristics (STF 3)
5   Persons, Families, Households & Housing Units (STF 1)
6   Race, Hispanic, & Housing Unit Counts
7   1990 Census Data for the US, Regions, & Divisions
8   Post-1990 Certifications
9   1990 Population Counts for States & Counties
10 1990 Population Counts for Places
11 1990 Census Terms (Definitions and Explanations)
12 User Notes

Figure 14-4

M16 focuses on current population data, such as intercensal estimates for states, counties, and County Subdivisions, but it does reproduce subject-oriented tables from the 1990 Census, plus decennial data on special geographies such as American Indian Areas. M16 is also a good source for 1980 data comparisons. M18 is devoted exclusively to the 1990 Census. Here is where the *CENDATA* versions of *STF 1* and *STF 3A* can be found. Although menu M4 contains the text of important press releases issued by the Bureau, news releases related to the 1990 Census are found on M18.2.

The Command Version

CENDATA's command version (File 580), available exclusively on DIALOG, is not as easy to use as the menu versions, but it offers faster, more powerful searching capabilities.

Keyword searching, coupled with the use of DIALOG's coding system, allows users to locate specific press releases, *Statistical Briefs*, or other narrative Records by identifying words or word combinations in the text and/or title of the Record. It is beyond the scope of this book to provide detailed instructions for command-level searching on DIALOG, but a few examples will illustrate how *CENDATA* searches can be executed on File 580. To retrieve information about the Census undercount, as measured by the Bureau's 1991 Post-Enumeration Survey, the user can enter the following search statement:

ss post (w) enumeration/ti and py=1991 and sh=18

This instructs the host computer to retrieve the phrase "post enumeration" in the title of a Record, but only for documents published in 1991 and only for Records located in menu group 18 (called "section heading" 18 in DIALOG's command version). The search retrieves four Records: three containing narrative and/or data from the Bureau's June 13, 1991 announcement, plus a subsequent message from the Commerce Department Secretary. User's can print or download the complete Records, brief citations, or even excerpts using DIALOG's Keyword in Context (KWIC) display format.

The command version can also locate specific data tables by using DIALOG's coding system. To retrieve the *STF 3* tables for the city of Phoenix, Arizona, the searcher can enter:

ss lv=city and st=az and phoenix/ti and sf=stf3

The lv code indicates the Summary Level of geography, st specifies the state postal code, and sf selects the desired Census subfile. The search statement also requests occurrences of the word "phoenix" in the title of the Record, to ensure that the table's contents focus on Phoenix. As in the menu version, the complete *STF 3* Record is 40 pages long. Indican invoke DIALOG's **Report** command to create a customized table or spreadsheet comparing specific characteristics from the *STF 1* File. A complete list of Field labels can be displayed online by typing **help rpt 580** and following the on-screen directions.

Through experience, *CENDATA* searchers will discover other DIALOG commands and features which are particularly useful in File 580. For example, the **Expand** feature is essential for identifying specific codes; by typing **expand lv=**, the searcher will see a list of the summary levels which are searchable on the system. Figure 14-5 lists some searching tips which are particularly useful for File 580. Regular *CENDATA* searchers will also want to purchase the 50-page *Reference Guide to CENDATA on DIALOG*, which can be ordered directly from Knight-Ridder.

Comparing *CENDATA* to the Bureau's Web Site

CENDATA appears to offer many of the same types of information which can be found on the Bureau's World Wide Web server: extracts of 1990 data Files, news releases, summaries of current demographic and economic surveys, telephone directories of Bureau employees, and catalog listings for Census products available for sale. In fact,

CENDATA appears to offer many of the same types of information which can be found on the Bureau's World Wide Web server.

vidual tables can be downloaded using standard format options created by DIALOG. The "Language Spoken at Home" table is requested as Format 52. (A complete list of the standard format numbers is obtained by typing **help fmt 580**.)

DIALOG's Report feature can be used to generate customized tables comparing selected characteristics for multiple geographic entities, but only for subfiles *STF 1* and *STF 3*. Each data cell in the *Summary Tape File* tables is assigned a Field label which can be used to construct these customized Reports. For example, the searcher can create a set of complete-count tables for all counties in New York State by entering the following command:

ss st=ny and lv=county and sf=stf1

The resulting set can then be ranked in descending order by total population by using DIALOG's **Sort** command. Then the searcher

CENDATA Search Tips

MENU VERSION

• Print or download copies of frequently used menus and submenus.

• Bypass menu levels by entering a required table's menu number.

• Remember that numbering within each menu is subject to change.

• Check CENDATA's "What's New" section.

COMMAND VERSION (DIALOG ONLY)

• Print list of standard formats.

• Print list of report formats.

• Don't print entire table unless it is really needed.

• Use **SF** feature to select data file.

• Use **SH** feature to choose menu category.

• Use DIALOG's free database of the month to print out the list of CENDATA report codes and format numbers.

• Although total population is the only field which is searchable numerically, data can be downloaded in spreadsheet format and further manipulated offline.

• Plan your search before going online.

• Utilize DIALOG search codes.

• Use standard formats and customized reports to tailor output to your needs and to reduce costs.

• Browse search results in free formats before downloading full records.

• Truncate county and city names when searching, or search by FIPS codes.

ALL VERSIONS

• To avoid page breaks when printing or downloading, set the retrieval format to continuous scrolling. (On both DIALOG versions, type **set v 0**; on CompuServe, the command is **S**.

Figure 14-5

CENDATA does provide certain types of data not found on the Web server.

the Bureau's Web site seems to offer more than CENDATA, including such features as the ability to order Census publications online, fairly sophisticated map-drawing capabilities, and the convenience of hypertext links to non-Census resources. Access cost is a more significant issue to consider when comparing the two resources. CENDATA users must first become subscribers to CompuServe or DIALOG. Furthermore, CENDATA imposes additional charges each

time the database is searched. Compare this with the Bureau's Web site, which is available to anyone with access to the Internet and a Web browser. For most users, connecting to the Bureau's Web server costs nothing beyond the regular fees paid to obtain general Internet services, and for modem users, modest telephone charges.

The obvious question is, "Why would anyone prefer CENDATA to the Web site?" The answer, as of this writing, is that CENDATA does provide certain types of data not found on the Web server. The best example is the EEO Files, which are available in their entirety on CENDATA, but are not found on the Bureau's Web pages at all. DIALOG's command version offers special search and display capabilities which the Web server does not. The command version of CENDATA allows users to create customized comparative tables of STF data for multiple geographic entities, and to rank results alphabetically or by size. The Web site does offer the capability to create customized table formats for individual geographic entities, but only due to the University of California's LOOKUP service (the future of which is uncertain as of this writing). Finally, the command version of CENDATA provides more retrospective information than the Web site, including older press releases and older articles from The Census and You.

Until the advent of the University of California's LOOKUP project, CENDATA was the only place to obtain easy access to STF data for virtually every major geographic entity in the United States.

The world of online information access undergoes constant change, and the pace of that change has been exceedingly rapid in recent years. Many CENDATA users continue to connect to the service because they are already DIALOG or CompuServe customers, and because they have become familiar with the database. Oddly enough, usage of CENDATA actually increased in 1995, probably due to the growth of CompuServe's subscriber base. As the Bureau's Web server continues to grow and improve, it seems

Will the Census Bureau continue to support *CENDATA*?

As *Understanding the Census* goes to press, the future of the Bureau's involvement in *CENDATA* is undecided. One fact is clear, however: the Bureau now considers its Web server as the primary means of disseminating online information. Fewer Files are being added on *CENDATA* and some existing Files are not being updated. It's highly likely that the Bureau will decide to discontinue direct data updates to *DIALOG* and *CompuServe* in the near future. However, it is also probable that one or both of the online vendors will continue to maintain and update *CENDATA* without the Bureau's assistance, by simply downloading files from the Bureau's own Web pages and reformatting them for use on their systems. The World Wide Web has not made *CENDATA* obsolete, but it does provide stiff competition. To the extent that DIALOG and/or CompuServe can add value to the basic data files—through easier, more powerful searching capabilities or through more flexible table formatting options—the commercial versions may continue to be a viable alternative to the Bureau's own services.

reasonable to assume that more *CENDATA* customers will gravitate to the World Wide Web.

The *Census Bereau/BEA Electronic Forum*

The major difference between the *Electronic Forum* and the Bureau's other online services is that the *Forum* allows subscribers to post messages and questions to the BBS, which can then be read and responded to by all other subscribers.

Another means of obtaining remote access to Census data is through an electronic Bulletin Board System (BBS), sometimes called a Remote Bulletin Board System (RBBS). The Census BBS is operated by the Census Bureau's Data User Services Division, in cooperation with another Commerce Department agency, the Bureau of Economic Analysis (BEA). Its current name is the *Census Bureau/BEA Electronic Forum*, but it was formerly known as the *Census Bureau/BEA Electronic Bulletin Board*. Like *CENDATA* and the Bureau's Internet Web server, the *Electronic Forum* offers news releases, product announcements, and data sets for downloading. It also provides the latest editions of the EXTRACT software and the appropriate Auxiliary Files for using EXTRACT with various CD-ROM products. The major difference between the *Electronic Forum* and the Bureau's other online services is that the *Forum* allows subscribers to post messages and questions to the BBS, which can then be read and responded to by all other subscribers. The most frequent non-Bureau posters to the *Forum* tend to be professional data users from universities, government agencies, corporations, and other research organizations, but all types of subscribers are welcome, from novice to expert.

The *Electronic Forum* is organized into Special Interest Groups (SIGs), which focus on particular topics. Users may subscribe to as many SIGs as they like. The ten SIGs are listed below:

<1> Open Forum (General Information)
<2> 1990 Census
<3> TIGER
<4> Economic Surveys from the Census
<5> CD-ROM Software and Products
<6> Census of Agriculture
<7> Population Estimates and Projections
<8> Industry Surveys
<9> Survey of Income and Program Participation (SIPP)
<0> 1992 Economic Census

Each SIG is maintained by a Bureau specialist, who posts general announcements, responds to queries posted to the Group, and refers more specialized queries to other experts in the Bureau. SIG subscribers can also read formal Bureau notices, called Bulletins.

The major function of the BBS is its capability to send messages or questions to a particular SIG. These postings can be read by any SIG subscriber, and often result in extended discussions involving many individuals. Queries range from the general ("How do I download files?" or "Where can I purchase a CD-ROM product?") to extremely detailed questions about a specific data set. Questions may be answered by the Bureau's SIG specialist, by other employees at the Bureau, by Affiliates of the Bureau's State Data Center program, or by knowledgeable subscribers who have experience with the topic at hand. As with other electronic forums, readers soon recognize the most frequent and reliable posters to the Group.

Activities on the BBS are carried out by typing single-letter commands: **R** to read mail, **L** to leave a message on a particular SIG, **D** to download, and so forth. One of the most helpful functions for reading new messages is the Quickscan command, which allows the reader to browse a list of message headings and mark the most pertinent ones for later reading.

Another feature found within every SIG is the ability to download data files and software programs from the Census Bureau. These files are currently arranged into four categories:

- ▸ Census Bureau File Lists
- ▸ 1992 Economic Census File Lists
- ▸ CD-ROM Software File Lists
- ▸ Statistical Abstract Highlights File Lists

Many of the files found in these categories are identical to those seen in the FTP section of the Bureau's Web site. In fact, files on the Web server are posted on the *Electronic Forum* before they appear anywhere else.

Web users may find the *Electronic Forum* cumbersome in comparison. Like all Bulletin Board Systems, it requires practice before becoming familiar with its various commands and capabilities. However, the system is fairly easy to use, and it provides an unrivaled mechanism for sharing thoughts, questions, and concerns with a large audience of serious Census users.

> **Another feature found within every SIG is the ability to download data files and software programs from the Census Bureau.**

Q&A

How can I subscribe to the *Electronic Forum*?

Users can connect to the Bureau's BBS via modem by dialing (301) 763-7554. For most areas of the country, this involves a long-distance phone call. The Bureau does not support access through a toll-free number or local packet-switching networks, such as Sprintnet. Except for the telephone costs, the BBS service is free.

Users can avoid long-distance charges by accessing the *Electronic Forum* through the Internet. The connection is made by invoking the **Telnet** command to the following address: **cenbbs.census.gov**. Internet users who prefer the Web protocol to Telnet can connect to the *Electronic Forum* directly from the Bureau's Home Page. At the present time, Web access to the BBS is limited. Web users can read files posted on the Board, but cannot send or receive e-mail.

Regardless of the means of access, the first time a user connects to the Bureau's *Electronic Forum*, the system asks for the user's full name, city, and state. Incomplete names and aliases are not accepted. The user then selects a password which will be used during each subsequent logon session. First-time users do not obtain full access to the system until they register as a subscriber. To register, the user simply types **R**, presses <ENTER>, and answers a few simple questions. For further information or assistance with connecting to the *Electronic Forum*, users can call the Bureau at (301) 457-1242.

Census Tip

Some State Data Centers maintain independent Bulletin Board Systems with current demographic information about their state. To find out whether a particular State Data Center operates its own BBS, contact the organization directly. A complete list of phone numbers for SDC Lead Agencies can be found in the annual *Census Catalog and Guide*.

Magnetic Tapes

Summary data tapes from the decennial Census were first sold to data users following the 1970 Census. Now the Bureau issues virtually all of its 1990 data products on magnetic tape. For any of these tapes, users can specify whether reels or cartridges are desired. Most tape products, including *STF 1A*, *STF 3A*, and the *TIGER/LINE Files*, are issued on a state-by-state basis. Tapes are priced by File size: $1.25 per megabyte, with a minimum charge of $175 for each order. For example, *STF 1A* for California contains approximately 664 megabytes of data and is priced at $830. *STF 1A* for Delaware, which contains a mere 18 megabytes, is priced at the minimum amount of $175. However, a single order placed for both states would only cost $852.50. The annual *Census Catalog and Guide* provides prices and specifications for every tape product.

Using tape files requires considerable computer resources. Minimum system requirements include the appropriate equipment (tape drives, processor, etc.), as well as personnel to operate and maintain the system. Usage also presumes the researcher is proficient at manipulating machine-readable numeric files. Users can employ commercially-produced general-purpose statistical software from such companies as SPSS Inc.,

the SAS Institute Inc., or BMDP Statistical Software Inc.; or they can write their own coding to merge files and reformat tables. Regardless of the software or programming language employed, Census tape products must be used in conjunction with the Bureau's supporting documentation, including the all-important Data Dictionaries described in Chapter 13. The Bureau provides machine-readable Data Dictionary Files with all its tapes.

For magnetic tape products which have a CD-ROM counterpart, the content and structure of the databases are almost always identical in both versions, except that tape products do not utilize the .dbf format. Chapter 8 describes decennial Census products on CD-ROM, so the discussion won't be repeated here. However, a reasonable number of 1990 Files have no CD-ROM equivalents, and must be utilized on tape. A list of selected products issued only in tape form can be found in Figure 14-6. Readers who wish to see a concise list of products available in both formats (CD-ROM as well as tape) should consult Figures 8-1 and 8-5. The following discussion focuses on a few of the most notable products issued solely on tape: *STF 2*, *STF 4*, and the *MARS Files*.

Summary Tape Files 2 and 4

These two *Summary Tape File* products cover the same Questionnaire Items found in *STF 1* and *STF 3*, but offer much greater

For magnetic tape products which have a CD-ROM counterpart, the content and structure of the databases are almost always identical in both versions, except that tape products do not utilize the .dbf format.

Major Data Files Available Only as Magnetic Tape Products

File Number	Title or Description	Print Equivalent
STF 2A	complete-count data for Tracts	CPH-3
STF 2B	complete-count data for small Places	CP-1, CH-1
STF 2C	complete-count data for the nation	CP-1, CH-1
STF 4A	sample data for Tracts/BNAs	CPH-3
STF 4B	sample data for small Places	CP-2, CH-2
STF 4C	sample data for the nation	CP-2, CH-2
STF-S-1	Population and Housing Unit Counts	CPH-L-1
STF-S-2A	MARS File (Tracts/BNAs)	none
STF-S-2B	MARS File (MCDs)	none
STF-S-3	MARS File (Counties)	none
STF-S-4	MARS File (Places)	none
STF-S-5	Number of Workers by County of Residence by County of Work	none
STF 420	Place of Work for 20 Destinations	none
—	Residential Finance Survey	CH-4
STP Files	see Figure 14-8 for details	none

Figure 14-6

STF 2 tabulates complete-count data (analogous to STF 1), while STF 4 provides sample data (analogous to STF 3).

subject detail. *STF 2* tabulates complete-count data (analogous to *STF 1*), while *STF 4* provides sample data (analogous to *STF 3*). Subject detail in these tape products takes three forms: tabulation of additional response categories; more detailed reporting for Race and Hispanic Origin categories; and more cross-tabulation of topics.

Where *STF 1* and *STF 3* often summarize responses in broader aggregations, *STF 2* and *STF 4* tend to tabulate data for individual response categories. For example, *STF 3* reports Ancestry by 36 ethnic categories; *STF 4* does so for 106 Ancestry groups. The hallmark of these two tape products is the prodigious amount of detail relating to Race and Hispanic Origin. *STF 1* and *STF 3*

provide only a few tables which are cross-tabulated by Race and/or Hispanic Origin; the detailed tape products do so for several hundred tables. Furthermore, the breakdowns by Race and Hispanic Origin are far more detailed. *STF 1* and *STF 3* typically report data for five Race categories and two Hispanic Origin categories. Many of the tables in *STF 2* and *STF 4* cover 48 or more categories of Race/Hispanic Origin. In addition to cross-tabulation by Race, *STF 2* and *STF 4* also offer extensive cross-tabulation by such other characteristics as age, sex, Household type, and Housing Tenure.

 Census Tip

Readers who wish to obtain a better sense of the subject detail found in *STF 2* and *STF 4* may wish to examine the four major printed Census Reports derived from these tape products: *CP-1*, *CH-1*, *CP-2*, and *CH-2*. These four titles are described in Chapter 9.

STF 2 and *STF 4* are each divided into three subfiles designated by the letters A, B, and C. Within each of the two main Summary Files, the subject content and table numbering are virtually identical; the subfiles denote different levels of geographic coverage. In other words, *STF 2A*, *STF 2B*, and *STF 2C* all provide the same subject arrangement, but each focuses on a different group of geographic Summary Levels. The pattern is similar to that of the *STF 1* and *STF 3* subfiles described in Chapter 8, except that neither of the two tape products include a subfile D. Figure 14-7 compares the geographic scope of the six tape products. *STF 2A* and *STF 4A* are state-specific Files which focus on data at the Tract or BNA level. These subfiles also present data for the individual state, its counties, Places with 10,000 or more population, and the portions of Metropolitan Areas which fall within the state's boundaries. *STF 2B* and *STF 4B* are also state-specific products, but they focus on

NEW IN '90

Five *Summary Tape Files* were produced for the 1980 Census. 1990 Census planners decided to cancel *STF 5* due to limited interest expressed by data users. *STF 5* provided complex, three- and four-way cross-tabulations of detailed social, economic, and housing characteristics for large geographies (primarily states and Metropolitan Areas). *Subject Summary Tape Files* from the 1990 Census partially replace data formerly found in *STF 5*. Users wishing to create more complex cross-tabulations for 1990 must perform their own calculations using the Bureau's *PUMS Files*.

Another change for 1990 is the creation of a separate tape product called *Place of Work 20 Destinations File* (*STF 420*). This product compares place of residence to place of work for every county, large Place or MCD, and Tract/BNA in the United States. The top 20 destinations are listed for each origin. For 1980, this information was included as part of *STF 4*.

ties, and large Places. MCDs are covered, but once again, only for the 12 general-purpose states.

As with other Census products, these magnetic tape files offer a tradeoff between geographic detail and subject detail. *STF 2* and *STF 4* provide more subject content than *STF 1* and *STF 3*, but they do so by covering fewer geographic Summary Levels. *STF 1* and *STF 3* include every category of Census geography, but *STF 2* and *STF 4* do not. The following list represents the most prominent Summary Levels omitted from *STF 2* and *STF 4*:

- ▶ Blocks
- ▶ Block Groups
- ▶ ZIP Code Areas
- ▶ Census County Divisions (CCDs)
- ▶ MCDs in states where they do not serve as general-purpose governments
- ▶ Small Places (under 1,000 population for *STF 2*; under 2,500 for *STF 4*)
- ▶ Congressional Districts.

The file structures for *STF 2* and *STF 4* are further complicated by the fact that every subfile contains two types of Records: "Level A" Records present tables for the total population for each geographic entity; "Level B" Records present tables for the total population, then repeat the same tables for component Race and Hispanic Origin groups within the population. For example, a table containing data on school enrollment for the Eskimo

small Places: 1,000 population or above for *STF 2B*, and 2,500 or above for *STF 4B*. Other Summary Levels included in every "B" subfile are the state, its counties, and the portion of American Indian/Alaska Native Areas which fall within its boundaries. These Files also present data for Minor Civil Divisions, but only for the 12 states for which MCDs serve as general-purpose governments. *STF 2C* and *STF 4C* provide nationwide coverage: the United States, the 50 states, Metropolitan Areas, Urbanized Areas, Coun-

Q&A

Why didn't the Bureau issue *STF 2* and *STF 4* products on CD-ROM?

The primary reason is that CD-ROM is intended to disseminate the most heavily requested Census products, and few data users require the amount of subject detail found on *STF 2* or *STF 4*. The other reason pertains to the size and complexity of the files. Even with reduced geographic coverage, *STF 2* is more than twice the size

of *STF 1*, and *STF 4* is nearly three times the size of *STF 3*. With the two levels of Record types, the enormous number of table repetitions and the presence of numerous cross-tabulations, the complexity of the file structure would certainly tax the ability of the GO software on CD-ROM.

GEOGRAPHIC COVERAGE OF *STF 2* AND *STF 4*

Summary Level	STF 2	STF 4
United States/Regions/Divisions	C	C
American Indian/Alaskan Native Areas	B¹ C	B¹ C
States	A B C	A B C
Metropolitan Areas	A¹ C	A¹ C
Urbanized Areas	C	C
Counties	A B C	A B C
County Subdivisions		
MCDs in 12 states²	B⁶ C⁴	B⁵ C⁴
MCDs in 6 states³	B C	B C
Places with 10,000 or more population	A B C	A B C
Places with population between 2,500 and 9,999	B	B
Places with population between 1,000 and 2,499	B	–
Census Tracts or BNAs	A	A

¹ Data for that part of Area within state boundary only.
² States where MCDs serve as general-purpose governments: CT, ME, MA, MI, MN, NH, NJ, NY, PA, RI, VT, WI.
³ Only for MCDs located within Metropolitan Areas of the six New England states.
⁴ Population of 10,000 or more.
⁵ Population of 2,500 or more.
⁶ Population of 1,000 or more.

Figure 14-7

As the name suggests, the *MARS Files* "modify" 1990 Census data for Age and Race.

population represents a "Level B" record type, while the corresponding table for school enrollment of the entire population represents a "Level A" Record. *STF 2A* and *STF 4A* provide a maximum of 10 repetitions for "Level B" tables. *STFs 2B* and *2C* present as many as 34 repetitions for "Level B" Records. *STFs 4B* and *4C* contain the same array of 34 repetitions, plus an additional 15 repetitions for "Other Hispanic" breakdowns.

STF 2 represents an extremely large data

set, and *STF 4* is even larger. To put the size in perspective, consider the fact that every *STF 4* product contains 465 tables: 203 "Level A" tables and 263 "Level B" tables. In contrast, *STF 3* products each contain a total of 262 tables. This comparison doesn't convey the full enormity of the size difference without considering that each of *STF 4*'s "Level B" tables can be repeated a maximum of 48 times for specific components of the population.

STF 2C and *STF 4C* are each issued as single products covering the entire nation. *STFs 2A, 2B, 4A,* and *4B* are all state-specific products, issued for each of the 50 states, the District of Columbia, Puerto Rico, and the U.S. Virgin Islands. The number of reels or cartridges varies from state to state for each product. The Bureau tabulates no *STF 2* or *STF 4* data for the Outlying Areas of the Pacific.

The *MARS Files*

A completely unique product group from the 1990 Census is the so-called *MARS Files*. The acronym stands for *Modified Age/Race, Sex, Hispanic Origin Files*. As the name suggests, the *MARS Files* "modify" 1990 Census data for Age and Race. Why? For two reasons. Race data are modified to conform to the Office of Management and Budget's federal standards. *OMB Circular 15* stipulates that when federal agencies report statistics by Racial groups, they must do so for the following four categories: White, Black, Asian/Pacific Islander, and American Indian/Eskimo/Aleut. (This guideline also pertains to nonfederal organizations seeking federal funds.) Unfortunately, the decennial Census tabulates data for a fifth category, designated "Other." As explained in Chapter 5, "Other" is more than a miscellaneous catchall. By definition, the Census Bureau counts Multi-Racial individuals who do not specify their component Races as "Other." The Census tabulates Hispanics who mistakenly indicate some type of Hispanic Origin as a category

Q&A

Do the MARS modifications for Race have any relationship to the issue of differential undercount in the Census?

No. Do not confuse the Bureau's *MARS* allocations with the issue of adjusting decennial Census figures to reflect undercount. The *MARS Files* compensate for the large numbers of persons who are "mistakenly" counted as "Other Race." This is strictly a problem of misreporting by respondents who did not understand (or were unwilling to comply with) Census definitions. The Census undercount is a more fundamental matter. Proposals to adjust the Census count are intended to address the issue of individuals who were not counted at all in the Census.

The *MARS Files* simply redistribute the total number of persons counted by the Census, placing them into different categories. Any adjustment for differential undercount would actually add persons to the total population. To put it another way, *MARS* data do not affect the official population count of the United States; the reallocated figures found in the *MARS Files* are used primarily by organizations and individuals seeking federal funds under specific grant programs. In contrast, any proposal to adjust the official Census figures to compensate for uncounted individuals would have more far-reaching ramifications. For example, such an adjustment would affect the distribution of federal funds to the states and localities across-the-board, rather than on a program-by-program basis.

---

of Race in the same manner. Because the OMB does not recognize a category for "Other," the decennial Census under-represents the number of individuals whom the government would otherwise consider to be non-White. The Bureau rectifies this problem in the *MARS Files* by allocating all persons in the "Other" category to one of the four remaining Race groups.

Census Tip

Nearly 10 million persons identified themselves as "Other Race" in the 1990 Census. Over 95% of these people were also Hispanic. Hispanic Origin is not a type of Race, because a Hispanic Person can be of any Race.

The *MARS Files* assign each "Other Race" person to a new category by comparing them to another person in the same Census Block who reported the same response category for Hispanic Origin.

The second reason for modifying data in the *MARS Files* deals with the age component of the allocation process. Respondents whose birthdays occurred shortly after Census Day tended to round their age up by one year. This was a particularly common problem for parents who responded for children under the age of one year. Another source of misreporting was persons who indicated their age as of the date they filled out the Census Questionnaire, instead of their age on Census Day. The Bureau employed another algorithm to reallocate age data to compensate for these situations, based on birth-year data reported to the National Center for Health Statistics. Age adjustments in the *MARS Files* are much more common than reassignment of Race. Approximately 100 million people had their age reallocated, but the net effect was negligible at larger Summary Levels because the adjustments tended to offset one another.

The Bureau issues *MARS Files* as four separate tape products, all with a designation of *STF-S*. *STF-S-2A* reports *MARS* data for states, counties, and Census Tracts/BNAs. *STF-S-2B* covers states, counties, and Minor Civil Divisions, but only for the 12 states where MCDs serve as general-purpose gov-

Because the OMB does not recognize a category for "Other," the decennial Census under-represents the number of individuals whom the government would otherwise consider to be non-White.

ernments. *STF-S-3* reports data for all states and counties in the United States. *STF-S-4* tabulates results for all Places in the United States with population of 2,500 or more. The latter three products are each issued as a single tape covering the entire country. *STF-S-2A*, containing Tract and BNA data, is issued as a set of nine tapes organized by Census Division.

Subject content for the four Files is identical. Age and Race are both cross-tabulated by sex and Hispanic Origin. Age data are reported for single years.

The Special Tabulation Program

The Census Bureau produces customized tabulations for government agencies and other organizations on a cost-recovery basis. Those products deemed to have broad interest are offered for sale to the general public and are listed in the Bureau's annual *Census Catalog and Guide*. To date, only two 1990 STP Files have been issued in CD-ROM format: *STP 14, (Special Tabulation on Aging)* and *CHAS (Comprehensive Housing Affordability Strategy)*. Figure 14-8 lists the other *STP Files* currently available on magnetic tape.

Readers should note that the *STP Files* shown in Figure 14-8 can also be ordered on CD-ROM, but the compact disc versions are extremely limited. Unlike the Bureau's standard CD-ROM products, these discs can be damaged fairly easily through normal usage. Furthermore, these discs are not produced in **.dbf** format, so they cannot be utilized with EXTRACT or with commercially-produced Database management software, nor do they include GO, the Bureau's page-turning software. The Records on these CD-ROMs are exact replicas of the magnetic tape files; the discs are intended strictly as a storage medium, not as an end-user data retrieval product. *STP 14* and *CHAS*, which were issued as standard CD-ROM products (complete with GO software), are the only exception to these limitations as of this writing.

File	Format	Title
		***Special Tabulation Program Files* on Magnetic Tape or Diskette**
STP 2	tape	Place of Work by Industry, Earnings, and Education File. (Uses 1990 Definitions for Metropolitan Areas. See also STP 73.)
STP 4	tape	Poverty Status of Persons in Families File. (Focuses on American Indian/Alaska Native Areas. See also STP 7.)
STP 5	tape	Veterans Characteristics File. (Published as 14 subfiles.)
STP 7	tape	Poverty Status of Persons in Families File. (Focuses on counties, functioning MCDs, and Places. See also STP 4.)
STP 8	tape	Women, Infants, and Children File.
STP 19	tape	HUD 1990 Block Group Program: Block-Group Level File.
STP 23	diskette	Industry and Occupation and Modified Age-Race-Sex File. (See also STP 24.)
STP 24	diskette	Industry and Occupation and Modified Age-Race-Sex File. (See also STP 23.)
STP 25	both*	Housing Characteristics File.
STP 26	both*	Occupation (Detailed) by Selected Characteristics File. (See also STP 27.)
STP 27	both*	Occupation (Detailed) by Selected Characteristics File. (See also STP 26.)
STP 30	tape	Occupation (Detailed) by Industry and Class of Worker File.
STP 54	tape	Poverty Status in 1989 of Housing Units File.
STP 62	tape	Characteristics of Households and Housing Units File.
STP 73	tape	Place of Work by Industry, Earnings, and Education File. (Uses 1993 Definitions for Metropolitan Areas. See also STP 2.)
STP 86	both*	Substandard Housing and Income and Poverty Status in 1989. (See also STPs 95 and 129.)
STP 89	diskette	Characteristics of Displaced Homemakers and Single Parents File.
STP 95	both*	Substandard Housing and Income and Poverty Status in 1989. (See also STPs 86 and 129.)
STP 129	both*	Substandard Housing and Income and Poverty Status in 1989. (See also STPs 86 and 95.)
STP 144	diskette	Children in Poverty in 1989. (See also STP 145.)
STP 145	diskette	Children in Poverty in 1989. (See also STP 144.)

Note: STP 14, Special Tabulation on Aging, is available on CD-ROM and magnetic tape.

* "Both" indicates availability on magnetic tape and diskette.

Figure 14-8

Summary

Making sense of the vast array of electronic products for the 1990 Census is daunting, especially considering the variety of formats which the Bureau supplies. For most users, CD-ROM will be the most popular electronic medium. CD-ROM products are particularly appropriate for data tables which will be consulted repeatedly over time or used heavily for briefer durations.

In some cases, no choice is offered to the user because the Bureau provides certain products on magnetic tape only. Examples include *STF 2*, *STF 4*, and the *MARS Files*. It is likely that users who dealt with tape files in the past will continue to do so with the 1990 products. Census users without the resources and knowledge to manipulate data on magnetic tape may quickly dismiss the likelihood of ever utilizing such products. However, researchers without the requisite computer resources can pay a fee to an affiliate of one of the following two Census networks: the National Clearinghouse for Census Data Service, or the State Data Center system. These networks, which were introduced in Chapter 10, can create customized tables from magnetic tape products for a fee. Not all participants in the networks have tape extraction capabilities, and not all provide fee-based services.

Online databases are much easier to access than magnetic tape, and are less expensive than building a large CD-ROM collection. Perhaps the best use of online Census products is to obtain basic Census data for geographic areas which lie beyond the user's normal research territory. Aside from utilizing the CD-ROM collections of large Depository Libraries, few users will have immediate access to data products for states outside their immediate area. And if all a user needs is the occasional summary table, it makes little sense to invest in a large personal library of CD-ROMs or print Reports. Online Census products can provide summary tables quickly and affordably. Online resources also offer the fastest means of obtaining newly released Census information, whether it be data tables or administrative announcements. The ability to search for keywords in the text of online documents offers another important advantage.

Users can obtain online access to Census Files in one of three ways: via the Bureau's Internet Web server; by registering as a subscriber to its *Electronic Forum*; or through the commercial *CENDATA* service. Each method is fairly easy to use and requires a minimum investment in hardware. The amount and types of data seem fairly similar on all three systems, yet each one offers certain benefits. The primary advantage of the Bulletin Board System is its interactive capability. Users can send queries and comments to individuals at the Census Bureau, who will then reply in prompt fashion. Like other electronic bulletin boards, discussion lists, Internet news groups, or other online forums, the Bureau's BBS creates an electronic community, where Census users of varying levels of expertise can share their knowledge, experience, and opinions, or can post questions for the membership at large.

The primary advantages of the Bureau's Web server are its convenience and low cost to access. Its HTTP protocol allows users to move from one data file to another quickly and easily, as well as the ability to automatically connect to related Web sites for which the Bureau has created hypertext links. In contrast, *CENDATA* imposes additional usage costs, but the system is also easy to use. *CENDATA* contains data tables not found on the other systems, it is available to individuals without Internet capabilities, and the command version on DIALOG provides more powerful searching and downloading capabilities.

CENDATA and the Bureau's Web site have both experienced tremendous improvement since their initial development, a fact which is most noticeable in the area of decennial Census offerings. Although

CD-ROM products are particularly appropriate for data tables which will be consulted repeatedly over time or used heavily for briefer durations.

Perhaps the best use of online Census products is to obtain basic Census data for geographic areas which lie beyond the user's normal research territory.

CENDATA made its debut in 1978, significant amounts of decennial data did not appear on the service until the early 1990s. Similarly, large files of decennial data did not appear on the Web page until the Bureau provided access to the University of California LOOKUP project. Although the immediate future of that project remains in doubt at this time, it appears likely that the Bureau will continue to offer Web access to large amounts of *STF* data in one form or another.

It is fairly apparent that the Bureau's Web page is becoming the preferred method of remote access for many Census users, though the *Electronic Forum* and *CENDATA* remain popular. As indicated earlier in the chapter, the future of *CENDATA* is in doubt. The Bureau is also reevaluating the future role of the *Electronic Forum* in relation to the Internet. Given the rapid changes which the Internet has undergone in recent years, including the fleeting popularity of the Gopher protocol, it is likely that the Bureau's Web site will also undergo unpredictable changes in the years ahead. For the moment, it remains a truly remarkable resource, enabling users to keep abreast of the latest news and data files from the Bureau, and to quickly retrieve 1990 Census data from the convenience of home or office.

It is fairly apparent that the Bureau's Web page is becoming the preferred method of remote access for many Census users, though the *Electronic Forum* and *CENDATA* remain popular.

Appendix A

Acronyms and Initialisms Used in this Book

ACF	— Address Control File
AFDC	— Aid to Families with Dependent Children
AHS	— American Housing Survey
AI/ANA	— American Indian/Alaska Native Area
ANPSADPI	— Area Name Field (used with EXTRACT)
ANRC	— Alaska Native Regional Corporation
ANV	— Alaska Native Village
ANVSA	— Alaska Native Village Statistical Area
AOA	— U.S. Administration on Aging
API	— Asian or Pacific Islander
APDU	— Association of Public Data Users
APOC	— Advance Post Office Check
BBS	— Bulletin Board System
BEA	— U.S. Bureau of Economic Analysis
BG	— Block Group
BIDC	— Business and Industry Data Centers
BNA	— Block Numbering Area
BRT	— Basic Record Tape
CAPP	— Census Awareness and Products Program
CCD	— Census County Division
CD	— Congressional District
CDP	— Census Designated Place
CD-ROM	— Compact Disc-Read Only Memory
CENSPAC	— Census software for use with magnetic tape (1980)
CH	— Census of Housing (publication series)
CMSA	— Consolidated Metropolitan Statistical Area
COM	— Computer-Output Microform
CP	— Census of Population (publication series)
CPH	— Census of Population and Housing (publication series)
CPS	— Current Population Survey
CSAC	— Census Statistical Areas Committee
CTPP	— Census Transportation Planning Package
DEC	— Digital Equipment Corporation
DHHS	— U.S. Department of Health and Human Services

DIME	— Dual Independent Map Encoding (1980)
DO	— District Office
DUSD	— Data User Services Division of the Census Bureau
ED	— Enumeration District (1980)
EEO	— Equal Employment Opportunity
EEOC	—U.S. Equal Employment Opportunity Commission
ENIAC	—Electronic Numerical Integrator and Calculator
ESL	— English as a Second Language
FACT-90	— Film and Automated Camera Technology
FIPS	— Federal Information Processing Standard
FOSDIC	— Film Optical Sensing Device for Input to Computers
FTP	— File Transfer Protocol
FY	— Fiscal Year
GAO	— U.S. General Accounting Office
GBF	— Geographic Base File
GED	— General Equivalency Diploma
GICS	— Geographic Identification Code Scheme
GPO	— U.S. Government Printing Office
GQ	— Group Quarters
GU	— Governmental Unit
HTTP	— Hypertext Transport Protocol
HUD	— U.S. Department of Housing and Urban Development
ICR	— Individual Census Report
IWG	— Interagency Working Group
LPM	— Local Public Meetings program
MA	— Metropolitan Area
MCD	— Minor Civil Division
MCR	— Military Census Report
MIS	— Management Information System
MO/MB	— Mailout/Mailback method
MPA	— *Monthly Product Announcement*
MPO	— Metropolitan Planning Organization

MSA	— Metropolitan Statistical Area	UT	— Unorganized Territory
NCCDS	— National Clearinghouse for Census Data Services	VA	— U.S. Veterans Administration
		VTD	— Voting District
NCES	— National Center for Education Statistics	WWW	— World Wide Web
NCIC	— National Census Information Centers	ZIP	— Zone Improvement Plan [for U.S. mail]
NCS	— National Content Survey		
NECMA	— New England County Metropolitan Area		
NIST	— National Institute of Standards and Technology	(1980)	indicates terminology used in the 1980 Census.
NSP	— National Services Program		
NRFU	— Non-Response Follow-Up		
NTIS	— National Technical Information Service		
OMB	— U.S. Office of Management and Budget		
OMR	— Optical Mark Recognition		
PES	— Post-Enumeration Survey		
P.L.	— Public Law		
PMSA	— Primary Metropolitan Statistical Area		
PSA	— Planning and Service Area		
PSA	— Public Service Announcement		
PSADC	— Political/Statistical Area Designation Code		
PUMS	— Public Use Microdata Samples		
RBBS	— Remote Bulletin Board System		
RCC	— Regional Census Center		
RO	— Regional Office		
SCR	— Shipboard Census Report		
SCSA	— Standard Consolidated Statistical Area (1980)		
SDC	— State Data Centers		
SIG	— Special Interest Group		
SIPP	— Survey of Income and Program Participation		
SMSA	— Standard Metropolitan Statistical Area (1980)		
SOC	— Standard Occupational Classification		
SPSS	— Statistical Package for the Social Sciences		
SSTF	— Subject Summary Tape File		
STF	— Summary Tape File		
STP	— Special Tabulation Program		
SU	— Statistical Unit		
SUMLEV	— Summary Level Field (used with EXTRACT)		
TAR	— Tape Address Register		
TDSA	— Tribal Designated Statistical Area		
TIGER	— Topologically Integrated Geographic Encoding and Referencing		
TJSA	— Tribal Jurisdiction Statistical Area		
TMS	— TIGER Mapping Service (on the Internet)		
UA	— Urbanized Area		
UDAP	— User-Defined Areas Program		
UNIVAC	— Universal Automatic Computer		
URL	— Uniform Resource Locator		
USGS	— U.S. Geological Survey		
USPS	— United States Postal Service		

Appendix B

Metropolitan Areas and Their Components
as of June, 1990

[Each Metropolitan Area is shown as it existed at the time of the Census, using the OMB's June, 1990 Definitions. Listings are arranged alphabetically. For relationship of PMSAs to their CMSAs, see the CMSA entry. Population is cited as of April 1, 1990. Figures are rounded to the nearest thousand. Totals may vary from the sum of their component parts due to rounding.]

1990 Population (1,000)

Abilene, TX MSA	120
Taylor County	120
Akron, OH PMSA	658
Portage County	143
Summit County	515
Albany, GA MSA	113
Dougherty County	96
Lee County	16
Albany-Schenectady-Troy, NY MSA	874
Albany County	293
Greene County	45
Montgomery County	52
Rensselaer County	154
Saratoga County	181
Schenectady County	149
Albuquerque, NM MSA	481
Bernalillo County	481
Alexandria, LA MSA	132
Rapides Parish	132
Allentown-Bethlehem-Easton, PA-NJ MSA	687
Carbon County, PA	57
Lehigh County, PA	291
Northampton County, PA	247
Warren County, NJ	92

Altoona, PA MSA	131
Blair County	131
Amarillo, TX MSA	188
Potter County	98
Randall County	90
Anaheim-Santa Ana, CA PMSA	2,411
Orange County	2,411
Anchorage, AK MSA	226
Anchorage Borough	226
Anderson, IN MSA	131
Madison County	131
Anderson, SC MSA	145
Anderson County	145
Ann Arbor, MI PMSA	283
Washtenaw County	283
Anniston, AL MSA	116
Calhoun County	116
Appleton-Oshkosh-Neenah, WI MSA	315
Calumet County	34
Outagamie County	141
Winnebago County	140
Asheville, NC MSA	175
Buncombe County	175

Athens, GA MSA	156
Clarke County	88
Jackson County	30
Madison County	21
Oconee County	18
Atlanta, GA MSA	2,834
Barrow County	30
Butts County	15
Cherokee County	90
Clayton County	182
Cobb County	448
Coweta County	54
De Kalb County	546
Douglas County	71
Fayette County	62
Forsyth County	44
Fulton County	649
Gwinnett County	353
Henry County	59
Newton County	42
Paulding County	42
Rockdale County	54
Spalding County	54
Walton County	39
Atlantic City, NJ MSA	319
Atlantic County	224
Cape May County	95
Augusta, GA-SC MSA	397
Columbia County, GA	66
McDuffie County, GA	20
Richmond County, GA	190
Aiken County, SC	121
Aurora-Elgin, IL PMSA	357
Kane County	317
Kendall County	39
Austin, TX MSA	782
Hays County	66
Travis County	576
Williamson County	140
Bakersfield, CA MSA	543
Kern County	543
Baltimore, MD MSA	2,382
Anne Arundel County	427
Baltimore County	692
Carroll County	123
Harford County	182
Howard County	187
Queen Anne's County	34
Baltimore city	736
Bangor, ME MSA	89
Penobscot County (pt.)	86
Waldo County (pt.)	3
Baton Rouge, LA MSA	528
Ascension Parish	58
East Baton Rouge Parish	380
Livingston Parish	71
West Baton Rouge Parish	19
Battle Creek, MI MSA	136
Calhoun County	136
Beaumont-Port Arthur, TX MSA	361
Hardin County	41
Jefferson County	239
Orange County	81
Beaver County, PA PMSA	186
Beaver County	186
Bellingham, WA MSA	128
Whatcom County	128
Benton Harbor, MI MSA	161
Berrien County	161
Bergen-Passaic, NJ PMSA	1,278
Bergen County	825
Passaic County	453
Billings, MT MSA	113
Yellowstone County	113
Biloxi-Gulfport, MS MSA	197
Hancock County	32
Harrison County	165
Binghamton, NY MSA	264
Broome County	212
Tioga County	52
Birmingham, AL MSA	908
Blount County	39
Jefferson County	652
St. Clair County	50

Shelby County	99
Walker County	68
Bismarck, ND MSA	**84**
Burleigh County	60
Morton County	24
Bloomington, IN MSA	**109**
Monroe County	109
Bloomington-Normal, IL MSA	**129**
McLean County	129
Boise City, ID MSA	**206**
Ada County	206
Boston, MA PMSA	**2,871**
Bristol County (pt.)	41
Essex County (pt.)	122
Middlesex County (pt.)	1,132
Norfolk County (pt.)	605
Plymouth County (pt.)	237
Suffolk County	664
Worcester County (pt.)	71
Boston-Lawrence-Salem, MA-NH CMSA	4,172
Boston, MA PMSA	2,871
Brockton, MA PMSA	189
Lawrence-Haverhill, MA-NH PMSA	394
Lowell, MA-NH-PMSA	273
Nashua, NH PMSA	181
Salem-Gloucester, MA PMSA	264
Boulder-Longmont, CO PMSA	**225**
Boulder County	225
Bradenton, FL MSA	**212**
Manatee County	212
Brazoria, TX PMSA	**192**
Brazoria County	192
Bremerton, WA MSA	**190**
Kitsap County	190
Bridgeport-Milford, CT PMSA	**444**
Fairfield County (pt.)	335
New Haven County (pt.)	109
Bristol, CT PMSA	**79**
Hartford County (pt.)	68
Litchfield County (pt.)	12

Brockton, MA PMSA	**189**
Bristol County (pt.)	20
Norfolk County (pt.)	5
Plymouth County (pt.)	165
Brownsville-Harlingen, TX MSA	**260**
Cameron County	260
Bryan-College Station, TX MSA	**122**
Brazos County	122
Buffalo, NY PMSA	**969**
Erie County	969
Buffalo-Niagara Falls, NY CMSA	**1,189**
Buffalo, NY PMSA	969
Niagara Falls, NY PMSA	221
Burlington, NC MSA	**108**
Alamance County	108
Burlington, VT MSA	**131**
Chittenden County (pt.)	125
Franklin County (pt.)	4
Grand Isle County (pt.)	3
Canton, OH MSA	**394**
Carroll County	27
Stark County	368
Casper, WY MSA	**61**
Natrona County	61
Cedar Rapids, IA MSA	**169**
Linn County	169
Champaign-Urbana-Rantoul, IL MSA	**173**
Champaign County	173
Charleston, SC MSA	**507**
Berkeley County	129
Charleston County	295
Dorchester County	83
Charleston, WV MSA	**250**
Kanawha County	208
Putnam County	43
Charlotte-Gastonia-Rock Hill, NC-SC MSA	**1,162**
Cabarrus County, NC	99
Gaston County, NC	175

Lincoln County, NC	50
Mecklenburg County, NC	511
Rowan County, NC	111
Union County, NC	84
York County, SC	131
Charlottesville, VA MSA	131
Albemarle County	68
Fluvanna County	12
Greene County	10
Charlottesville city	40
Chattanooga, TN-GA MSA	433
Hamilton County, TN	286
Marion County, TN	25
Sequatchie County, TN	9
Catoosa County, GA	42
Dade County, GA	13
Walker County, GA	58
Cheyenne, WY MSA	73
Laramie County	73
Chicago, IL PMSA	6,070
Cook County	5,105
Du Page County	782
McHenry County	183
Chicago-Gary-Lake County (IL), IL-IN-WI CMSA	8,066
Aurora-Elgin, IL PMSA	357
Chicago, IL PMSA	6,070
Gary-Hammond, IN PMSA	605
Joliet, IL PMSA	390
Kenosha, WI PMSA	128
Lake County, IL PMSA	516
Chico, CA MSA	182
Butte County	182
Cincinnati, OH-KY-IN PMSA	1,453
Clermont County, OH	150
Hamilton County, OH	866
Warren County, OH	114
Boone County, KY	58
Campbell County, KY	84
Kenton County, KY	142
Dearborn County, IN	39
Cincinnati-Hamilton, OH-KY-IN CMSA	1,744
Cincinnati, OH-KY-IN PMSA	1,453
Hamilton-Middletown, OH PMSA	291

Clarksville-Hopkinsville, TN-KY MSA	169
Montgomery County, TN	100
Christian County, KY	69
Cleveland, OH PMSA	1,831
Cuyahoga County	1,412
Geauga County	81
Lake County	215
Medina County	122
Cleveland-Akron-Lorain, OH CMSA	2,760
Akron, OH PMSA	658
Cleveland, OH PMSA	1,831
Lorain-Elyria, OH PMSA	271
Colorado Springs, CO MSA	397
El Paso County	397
Columbia, MO MSA	112
Boone County	112
Columbia, SC MSA	453
Lexington County	168
Richland County	286
Columbus, GA-AL MSA	243
Chattahoochee County, GA	17
Muscogee County, GA	179
Russell County, AL	47
Columbus, OH MSA	1,377
Delaware County	67
Fairfield County	103
Franklin County	961
Licking County	128
Madison County	37
Pickaway County	48
Union County	32
Corpus Christi, TX MSA	350
Nueces County	291
San Patricio County	59
Cumberland, MD-WV MSA	102
Allegany County, MD	75
Mineral County, WV	27
Dallas, TX PMSA	2,553
Collin County	264
Dallas County	1,853
Denton County	274

Ellis County	85	Warren County	36
Kaufman County	52		
Rockwall County	26	**Detroit, MI PMSA**	**4,382**
		Lapeer County	75
Dallas-Fort Worth, TX CMSA	**3,885**	Livingston County	116
Dallas, TX PMSA	2,553	Macomb County	717
Fort Worth-Arlington, TX PMSA	1,332	Monroe County	134
		Oakland County	1,084
Danbury, CT PMSA	**188**	St. Clair County	146
Fairfield County (pt.)	163	Wayne County	2,112
Litchfield County (pt.)	25		
		Detroit-Ann Arbor, MI CMSA	**4,665**
Danville, VA MSA	**109**	Ann Arbor, MI PMSA	283
Pittsylvania County	56	Detroit, MI PMSA	4,382
Danville city	53		
		Dothan, AL MSA	**131**
Davenport-Rock Island-Moline,		Dale County	50
IA-IL MSA	**351**	Houston County	81
Scott County, IA	151		
Henry County, IL	51	**Dubuque, IA MSA**	**86**
Rock Island County, IL	149	Dubuque County	86
Dayton-Springfield, OH MSA	**951**	**Duluth, MN-WI MSA**	**240**
Clark County	148	St. Louis County, MN	198
Greene County	137	Douglas County, WI	42
Miami County	93		
Montgomery County	574	**Eau Claire, WI MSA**	**138**
		Chippewa County	52
Daytona Beach, FL MSA	**371**	Eau Claire County	85
Volusia County	371		
		El Paso, TX MSA	**592**
Decatur, AL MSA	**132**	El Paso County	592
Lawrence County	32		
Morgan County	100	**Elkhart-Goshen, IN MSA**	**156**
		Elkhart County	156
Decatur, IL MSA	**117**		
Macon County	117	**Elmira, NY MSA**	**95**
		Chemung County	95
Denver, CO PMSA	**1,623**		
Adams County	265	**Enid, OK MSA**	**57**
Arapahoe County	392	Garfield County	57
Denver County	468		
Douglas County	60	**Erie, PA MSA**	**276**
Jefferson County	438	Erie County	276
Denver-Boulder, CO CMSA	**1,848**	**Eugene-Springfield, OR MSA**	**283**
Boulder-Longmont, CO PMSA	225	Lane County	283
Denver, CO PMSA	1,623		
		Evansville, IN-KY MSA	**279**
Des Moines, IA MSA	**393**	Posey County, IN	26
Dallas County	30	Vanderburgh County, IN	165
Polk County	327	Warrick County, IN	45

Henderson County, KY	43		
		Fort Wayne, IN MSA	364
Fall River, MA-RI PMSA	157	Allen County	301
Bristol County, MA (pt.)	140	De Kalb County	35
Newport County, RI (pt.)	18	Whitley County	28
Fargo-Moorhead, ND-MN MSA	153	**Fort Worth-Arlington, TX PMSA**	1,332
Cass County, ND	103	Johnson County	97
Clay County, MN	50	Parker County	65
		Tarrant County	1,170
Fayetteville, NC MSA	275		
Cumberland County	275	**Fresno, CA MSA**	667
		Fresno County	667
Fayetteville-Springdale, AR MSA	113		
Washington County	113	**Gadsden, AL MSA**	100
		Etowah County	100
Fitchburg-Leominster, MA MSA	103		
Middlesex County (pt.)	3	**Gainesville, FL MSA**	204
Worcester County (pt.)	100	Alachua County	182
		Bradford County	23
Flint, MI MSA	430		
Genesee County	430	**Galveston-Texas City, TX PMSA**	217
		Galveston County	217
Florence, AL MSA	131		
Colbert County	52	**Gary-Hammond, IN PMSA**	605
Lauderdale County	80	Lake County	476
		Porter County	129
Florence, SC MSA	114		
Florence County	114	**Glens Falls, NY MSA**	119
		Warren County	59
Fort Collins-Loveland, CO MSA	186	Washington County	59
Larimer County	186		
		Grand Forks, ND MSA	71
Fort Lauderdale-Hollywood-Pompano		Grand Forks County	71
Beach, FL PMSA	1,255		
Broward County	1,255	**Grand Rapids, MI MSA**	688
		Kent County	501
Fort Myers-Cape Coral, FL MSA	335	Ottawa County	188
Lee County	335		
		Great Falls, MT MSA	78
Fort Pierce, FL MSA	251	Cascade County	78
Martin County	101		
St. Lucie County	150		
		Greeley, CO MSA	132
Fort Smith, AR-OK MSA	176	Weld County	132
Crawford County, AR	42		
Sebastian County, AR	100	**Green Bay, WI MSA**	195
Sequoyah County, OK	34	Brown County	195
Fort Walton Beach, FL MSA	144	**Greensboro—Winston-Salem—High Point,**	
Okaloosa County	144	**NC MSA**	942
		Davidson County	127

Davie County	28	Harris County	2,818
Forsyth County	266	Liberty County	53
Guilford County	347	Montgomery County	182
Randolph County	107	Waller County	23
Stokes County	37		
Yadkin County	30	**Houston-Galveston-Brazoria, TX CMSA**	**3,711**
		Brazoria, TX PMSA	192
Greenville-Spartanburg, SC MSA	**641**	Galveston-Texas City, TX PMSA	217
Greenville County	320	Houston, TX PMSA	3,302
Pickens County	94		
Spartanburg County	227	**Huntington-Ashland, WV-KY-OH MSA**	**313**
		Cabell County, WV	97
Hagerstown, MD MSA	**121**	Wayne County, WV	42
Washington County	121	Boyd County, KY	51
		Carter County, KY	24
Hamilton-Middletown, OH PMSA	**291**	Greenup County, KY	37
Butler County	291	Lawrence County, OH	62
Harrisburg-Lebanon-Carlisle, PA MSA	**588**	**Huntsville, AL MSA**	**239**
Cumberland County	195	Madison County	239
Dauphin County	238		
Lebanon County	114		
Perry County	41	**Indianapolis, IN MSA**	**1,250**
		Boone County	38
Hartford, CT PMSA	**768**	Hamilton County	109
Hartford County (pt.)	634	Hancock County	46
Litchfield County (pt.)	9	Hendricks County	76
Middlesex County (pt.)	7	Johnson County	88
New London County (pt.)	11	Marion County	797
Tolland County (pt.)	107	Morgan County	56
		Shelby County	40
Hartford-New Britain-Middletown,			
CT CMSA	**1,086**	**Iowa City, IA MSA**	**96**
Bristol, CT PMSA	79	Johnson County	96
Hartford, CT PMSA	768		
Middletown, CT PMSA	90	**Jackson, MI MSA**	**150**
New Britain, CT PMSA	148	Jackson County	150
Hickory-Morganton, NC MSA	**222**	**Jackson, MS MSA**	**395**
Alexander County	28	Hinds County	254
Burke County	76	Madison County	54
Catawba County	118	Rankin County	87
Honolulu, HI MSA	**836**	**Jackson, TN MSA**	**78**
Honolulu County	836	Madison County	78
Houma-Thibodaux, LA MSA	**183**	**Jacksonville, FL MSA**	**907**
Lafourche Parish	86	Clay County	106
Terrebonne Parish	97	Duval County	673
		Nassau County	44
Houston, TX PMSA	**3,302**	St. Johns County	84
Fort Bend County	225		

Jacksonville, NC MSA	150
Onslow County	150
Jamestown-Dunkirk, NY MSA	142
Chautauqua County	142
Janesville-Beloit, WI MSA	140
Rock County	140
Jersey City, NJ PMSA	553
Hudson County	553
Johnson City-Kingsport-Bristol,	
TN-VA MSA	436
Carter County, TN	52
Hawkins County, TN	45
Sullivan County, TN	144
Unicoi County, TN	17
Washington County, TN	92
Scott County, VA	23
Washington County, VA	46
Bristol city, VA	18
Johnstown, PA MSA	241
Cambria County	163
Somerset County	78
Joliet, IL PMSA	390
Grundy County	32
Will County	357
Joplin, MO MSA	135
Jasper County	90
Newton County	44
Kalamazoo, MI MSA	223
Kalamazoo County	223
Kankakee, IL MSA	96
Kankakee County	96
Kansas City, MO-KS MSA	1,566
Cass County, MO	64
Clay County, MO	153
Jackson County, MO	633
Lafayette County, MO	31
Platte County, MO	58
Ray County, MO	22
Johnson County, KS	355
Leavenworth County, KS	64
Miami County, KS	23
Wyandotte County, KS	162

Kenosha, WI PMSA	128
Kenosha County	128
Killeen-Temple, TX MSA	255
Bell County	191
Coryell County	64
Knoxville, TN MSA	605
Anderson County	68
Blount County	86
Grainger County	17
Jefferson County	33
Knox County	336
Sevier County	51
Union County	14
Kokomo, IN MSA	97
Howard County	81
Tipton County	16
La Crosse, WI MSA	98
La Crosse County	98
Lafayette, LA MSA	209
Lafayette Parish	165
St. Martin Parish	44
Lafayette-West Lafayette, IN MSA	131
Tippecanoe County	131
Lake Charles, LA MSA	168
Calcasieu Parish	168
Lake County, IL PMSA	516
Lake County	516
Lakeland-Winter Haven, FL MSA	405
Polk County	405
Lancaster, PA MSA	423
Lancaster County	423
Lansing-East Lansing, MI MSA	433
Clinton County	58
Eaton County	93
Ingham County	282
Laredo, TX MSA	133
Webb County	133

Las Cruces, NM MSA	136
Dona Ana County	136
Las Vegas, NV MSA	741
Clark County	741
Lawrence, KS MSA	82
Douglas County	82
Lawrence-Haverhill, MA-NH PMSA	394
Essex County, MA (pt.)	284
Rockingham County, NH (pt.)	110
Lawton, OK MSA	111
Comanche County	111
Lewiston-Auburn, ME MSA	88
Androscoggin County (pt.)	88
Lexington-Fayette, KY MSA	348
Bourbon County	19
Clark County	29
Fayette County	225
Jessamine County	31
Scott County	24
Woodford County	20
Lima, OH MSA	154
Allen County	110
Auglaize County	45
Lincoln, NE MSA	214
Lancaster County	214
Little Rock-North Little Rock, AR MSA	513
Faulkner County	60
Lonoke County	39
Pulaski County	350
Saline County	64
Longview-Marshall, TX MSA	162
Gregg County	105
Harrison County	57
Lorain-Elyria, OH PMSA	271
Lorain County	271
Los Angeles-Anaheim-Riverside, CA CMSA	14,532
Anaheim-Santa Ana, CA PMSA	2,411
Los Angeles-Long Beach, CA PMSA	8,863
Oxnard-Ventura, CA PMSA	669
Riverside-San Bernardino, CA PMSA	2,589

Los Angeles-Long Beach, CA PMSA	8,863
Los Angeles County	8,863
Louisville, KY-IN MSA	953
Bullitt County, KY	48
Jefferson County, KY	665
Oldham County, KY	33
Shelby County, KY	25
Clark County, IN	88
Floyd County, IN	64
Harrison County, IN	30
Lowell, MA-NH PMSA	273
Middlesex County, MA (pt.)	264
Hillsborough County, NH (pt.)	9
Lubbock, TX MSA	223
Lubbock County	223
Lynchburg, VA MSA	142
Amherst County	29
Campbell County	48
Lynchburg city	66
Macon-Warner Robins, GA MSA	281
Bibb County	150
Houston County	89
Jones County	21
Peach County	21
Madison, WI MSA	367
Dane County	367
Manchester, NH MSA	148
Hillsborough County (pt.)	127
Merrimack County (pt.)	13
Rockingham County (pt.)	8
Mansfield, OH MSA	126
Richland County	126
McAllen-Edinburg-Mission, TX MSA	384
Hidalgo County	384
Medford, OR MSA	146
Jackson County	146
Melbourne-Titusville-Palm Bay, FL MSA	399
Brevard County	399
Memphis, TN-AR-MS MSA	982

Shelby County, TN	826
Tipton County, TN	38
Crittenden County, AR	50
De Soto County, MS	68
Merced, CA MSA	**178**
Merced County	178
Miami-Fort Lauderdale, FL CMSA	**3,193**
Fort Lauderdale-Hollywood-	
Pompano Beach, FL PMSA	1,255
Miami-Hialeah, FL PMSA	1,937
Miami-Hialeah, FL PMSA	**1,937**
Dade County	1,937
Middlesex-Somerset-Hunterdon, NJ PMSA	**1,020**
Hunterdon County	108
Middlesex County	672
Somerset County	240
Middletown, CT PMSA	**90**
Middlesex County (pt.)	90
Midland, TX MSA	**107**
Midland County	107
Milwaukee, WI PMSA	**1,432**
Milwaukee County	959
Ozaukee County	73
Washington County	95
Waukesha County	305
Milwaukee-Racine, WI CMSA	**1,607**
Milwaukee, WI PMSA	1,432
Racine, WI PMSA	175
Minneapolis-St. Paul, MN-WI MSA	**2,464**
Anoka County, MN	244
Carver County, MN	48
Chisago County, MN	31
Dakota County, MN	275
Hennepin County, MN	1,032
Isanti County, MN	26
Ramsey County, MN	486
Scott County,MN	58
Washington County, MN	146
Wright County, MN	69
St. Croix County, WI	50
Mobile, AL MSA	**477**
Baldwin County	98

Mobile County	379
Modesto, CA MSA	**371**
Stanislaus County	371
Monmouth-Ocean, NJ PMSA	**986**
Monmouth County	553
Ocean County	433
Monroe, LA MSA	**142**
Ouachita Parish	142
Montgomery, AL MSA	**293**
Autauga County	34
Elmore County	49
Montgomery County	209
Muncie, IN MSA	**120**
Delaware County	120
Muskegon, MI MSA	**159**
Muskegon County	159
Naples, FL MSA	**152**
Collier County	152
Nashua, NH PMSA	**181**
Hillsborough County (pt.)	161
Rockingham County (pt.)	20
Nashville, TN MSA	**985**
Cheatham County	27
Davidson County	511
Dickson County	35
Robertson County	41
Rutherford County	119
Sumner County	103
Williamson County	81
Wilson County	68
Nassau-Suffolk, NY PMSA	**2,609**
Nassau County	1,287
Suffolk County	1,322
New Bedford, MA MSA	**176**
Bristol County (pt.)	161
Plymouth County (pt.)	14
New Britain, CT PMSA	**148**
Hartford County (pt.)	148

New Haven-Meriden, CT MSA	530
Middlesex County (pt.)	18
New Haven County (pt.)	513
New London-Norwich, CT-RI MSA	267
New London County, CT (pt.)	234
Windham County, CT (pt.)	4
Washington County, RI (pt.)	28
New Orleans, LA MSA	1,239
Jefferson Parish	448
Orleans Parish	497
St. Bernard Parish	67
St. Charles Parish	42
St. John the Baptist Parish	40
St. Tammany Parish	145
New York, NY PMSA	8,547
Bronx County	1,204
Kings County	2,301
New York County	1,488
Putnam County	84
Queens County	1,952
Richmond County	379
Rockland County	265
Westchester County	875
New York-Northern New Jersey-	
Long Island, NY-NJ-CT CMSA	18,087
Bergen-Passaic, NJ PMSA	1,278
Bridgeport-Milford, CT PMSA	444
Danbury, CT PMSA	188
Jersey City, NJ PMSA	553
Middlesex-Somerset-Hunterdon, NJ PMSA	1,020
Monmouth-Ocean, NJ PMSA	986
Nassau-Suffolk, NY PMSA	2,609
New York, NY PMSA	8,547
Newark, NJ PMSA	1,824
Norwalk, CT PMSA	127
Orange County, NY PMSA	308
Stamford, CT PMSA	203
Newark, NJ PMSA	1,824
Essex County	778
Morris County	421
Sussex County	131
Union County	494
Niagara Falls, NY PMSA	221
Niagara County	221
Norfolk-Virginia Beach-Newport News,	

VA MSA	1,396
Gloucester County	30
James City County	35
York County	42
Chesapeake city	152
Hampton city	134
Newport News city	170
Norfolk city	261
Poquoson city	11
Portsmouth city	104
Suffolk city	52
Virginia Beach city	393
Williamsburg city	12
Norwalk, CT PMSA	127
Fairfield County (pt.)	127
Oakland, CA PMSA	2,083
Alameda County	1,279
Contra Costa County	804
Ocala, FL MSA	195
Marion County	195
Odessa, TX MSA	119
Ector County	119
Oklahoma City, OK MSA	959
Canadian County	74
Cleveland County	174
Logan County	29
McClain County	23
Oklahoma County	600
Pottawatomie County	59
Olympia, WA MSA	161
Thurston County	161
Omaha, NE-IA MSA	618
Douglas County, NE	416
Sarpy County, NE	103
Washington County, NE	17
Pottawattamie County, IA	83
Orange County, NY PMSA	308
Orange County	308
Orlando, FL MSA	1,073
Orange County	677
Osceola County	108
Seminole County	288

Maricopa County	2,122

Owensboro, KY MSA	**87**
Daviess County	87

Pine Bluff, AR MSA	**85**
Jefferson County	85

Oxnard-Ventura, CA PMSA	**669**
Ventura County	669

Pittsburgh, PA PMSA	**2,057**
Allegheny County	1,336
Fayette County	145
Washington County	205
Westmoreland County	370

Panama City, FL MSA	**127**
Bay County	127

Pittsburgh-Beaver Valley, PA CMSA	**2,243**
Beaver County, PA PMSA	186
Pittsburgh, PA PMSA	2,057

Parkersburg-Marietta, WV-OH MSA	**149**
Wood County, WV	87
Washington County, OH	62

Pittsfield, MA MSA	**79**
Berkshire County (pt.)	79

Pascagoula, MS MSA	**115**
Jackson County	115

Portland, ME MSA	**215**
Cumberland County (pt.)	197
York County (pt.)	18

Pawtucket-Woonsocket-Attleboro,	
RI-MA PMSA	**329**
Providence County, RI (pt.)	227
Bristol County, MA (pt.)	85
Norfolk County, MA (pt.)	7
Worcester County, MA (pt.)	10

Portland, OR PMSA	**1,240**
Clackamas County	279
Multnomah County	584
Washington County	312
Yamhill County	66

Pensacola, FL MSA	**344**
Escambia County	263
Santa Rosa County	82

Portland-Vancouver, OR-WA CMSA	**1,478**
Portland, OR PMSA	1,240
Vancouver, WA PMSA	238

Peoria, IL MSA	**339**
Peoria County	183
Tazewell County	124
Woodford County	33

Portsmouth-Dover-Rochester, NH-ME MSA	**224**
Rockingham County, NH (pt.)	77
Strafford County, NH (pt.)	98
York County, ME (pt.)	49

Philadelphia, PA-NJ-PMSA	**4,857**
Bucks County, PA	541
Chester County, PA	376
Delaware County, PA	548
Montgomery County, PA	678
Philadelphia County, PA	1,586
Burlington County, NJ	395
Camden County, NJ	503
Gloucester County, NJ	230

Poughkeepsie, NY MSA	**259**
Dutchess County	259

Providence, RI PMSA	**655**
Bristol County	49
Kent County (pt.)	158
Newport County (pt.)	5
Providence County (pt.)	369
Washington County (pt.)	74

Philadelphia-Wilmington-Trenton,	
PA-NJ-DE-MD CMSA	**5,899**
Philadelphia, PA-NJ PMSA	4,857
Trenton, NJ PMSA	326
Vineland-Millville-Bridgeton, NJ PMSA	138
Wilmington, DE-NJ-MD PMSA	579

Providence-Pawtucket-Fall River,	
RI-MA CMSA	**1,142**
Fall River, MA-RI PMSA	157
Pawtucket-Woonsocket-Attleboro,	

Phoenix, AZ MSA	**2,122**

RI-MA PMSA	329
Providence, RI PMSA	655
Provo-Orem, UT MSA	**264**
Utah County	264
Pueblo, CO MSA	**123**
Pueblo County	123
Racine, WI PMSA	**175**
Racine County	175
Raleigh-Durham, NC MSA	**735**
Durham County	182
Franklin County	36
Orange County	94
Wake County	423
Rapid City, SD MSA	**81**
Pennington County	81
Reading, PA MSA	**337**
Berks County	337
Redding, CA MSA	**147**
Shasta County	147
Reno, NV MSA	**255**
Washoe County	255
Richland-Kennewick-Pasco, WA MSA	**150**
Benton County	113
Franklin County	37
Richmond-Petersburg, VA MSA	**866**
Charles City County	6
Chesterfield County	209
Dinwiddie County	21
Goochland County	14
Hanover County	63
Henrico County	218
New Kent County	10
Powhatan County	15
Prince George County	27
Colonial Heights city	16
Hopewell city	23
Petersburg city	38
Richmond city	203
Riverside-San Bernardino, CA PMSA	**2,589**
Riverside County	1,170
San Bernardino County	1,418

Roanoke, VA MSA	**224**
Botetourt County	25
Roanoke County	79
Roanoke city	96
Salem city	24
Rochester, MN MSA	**106**
Olmsted County	106
Rochester, NY MSA	**1,002**
Livingston County	62
Monroe County	714
Ontario County	95
Orleans County	42
Wayne County	89
Rockford, IL MSA	**284**
Boone County	31
Winnebago County	253
Sacramento, CA MSA	**1,481**
El Dorado County	126
Placer County	173
Sacramento County	1,041
Yolo County	141
Saginaw-Bay City-Midland, MI MSA	**399**
Bay County	112
Midland County	76
Saginaw County	212
St. Cloud, MN MSA	**191**
Benton County	30
Sherburne County	42
Stearns County	119
St. Joseph, MO MSA	**83**
Buchanan County	83
St. Louis, MO-IL MSA	**2,444**
Franklin County, MO	81
Jefferson County, MO	171
St. Charles County, MO	213
St. Louis County, MO	994
St. Louis city, MO	397
Clinton County, IL	34
Jersey County, IL	21
Madison County, IL	249
Monroe County, IL	22
St. Clair County, IL	263

Salem, OR MSA	278
Marion County	228
Polk County	50
Salem-Gloucester, MA PMSA	264
Essex County (pt.)	264
Salinas-Seaside-Monterey, CA MSA	356
Monterey County	356
Salt Lake City-Ogden, UT MSA	1,072
Davis County	188
Salt Lake County	726
Weber County	158
San Angelo, TX MSA	98
Tom Green County	98
San Antonio, TX MSA	1,302
Bexar County	1,185
Comal County	52
Guadalupe County	65
San Diego, CA MSA	2,498
San Diego County	2,498
San Francisco, CA PMSA	1,604
Marin County	230
San Francisco County	724
San Mateo County	650
San Francisco-Oakland-San Jose, CA CMSA	6,253
Oakland, CA PMSA	2,083
San Francisco, CA PMSA	1,604
San Jose, CA PMSA	1,498
Santa Cruz, CA PMSA	230
Santa Rosa-Petaluma, CA PMSA	388
Vallejo-Fairfield-Napa, CA PMSA	451
San Jose, CA PMSA	1,498
Santa Clara County	1,498
Santa Barbara-Santa Maria-Lompoc, CA MSA	370
Santa Barbara County	370
Santa Cruz, CA PMSA	230
Santa Cruz County	230
Santa Fe, NM MSA	117
Los Alamos County	18
Santa Fe County	99
Santa Rosa-Petaluma, CA PMSA	388
Sonoma County	388
Sarasota, FL MSA	278
Sarasota County	278
Savannah, GA MSA	243
Chatham County	217
Effingham County	26
Scranton—Wilkes-Barre, PA MSA	734
Columbia County	63
Lackawanna County	219
Luzerne County	328
Monroe County	96
Wyoming County	28
Seattle, WA PMSA	1,973
King County	1,507
Snohomish County	466
Seattle-Tacoma, WA CMSA	2,559
Seattle, WA PMSA	1,973
Tacoma, WA PMSA	586
Sharon, PA MSA	121
Mercer County	121
Sheboygan, WI MSA	104
Sheboygan County	104
Sherman-Denison, TX MSA	95
Grayson County	95
Shreveport, LA MSA	334
Bossier Parish	86
Caddo Parish	248
Sioux City, IA-NE MSA	115
Woodbury County, IA	98
Dakota County, NE	17
Sioux Falls, SD MSA	124
Minnehaha County	124
South Bend-Mishawaka, IN MSA	247
St. Joseph County	247
Spokane, WA MSA	361
Spokane County	361

Springfield, IL MSA	190
Menard County	11
Sangamon County	178
Springfield, MA MSA	530
Hampden County (pt.)	445
Hampshire County (pt.)	84
Springfield, MO MSA	241
Christian County	33
Greene County	208
Stamford, CT PMSA	203
Fairfield County (pt.)	203
State College, PA MSA	124
Centre County	124
Steubenville-Weirton, OH-WV MSA	143
Jefferson County, OH	80
Brooke County, WV	27
Hancock County, WV	35
Stockton, CA MSA	481
San Joaquin County	481
Syracuse, NY MSA	660
Madison County	69
Onondaga County	469
Oswego County	122
Tacoma, WA PMSA	586
Pierce County	586
Tallahassee, FL MSA	234
Gadsden County	41
Leon County	192
Tampa-St. Petersburg-Clearwater, FL MSA	2,068
Hernando County	101
Hillsborough County	834
Pasco County	281
Pinellas County	852
Terre Haute, IN MSA	131
Clay County	25
Vigo County	106
Texarkana, TX-Texarkana, AR MSA	120
Bowie County, TX	82
Miller County, AR	38

Toledo, OH MSA	614
Fulton County	38
Lucas County	462
Wood County	113
Topeka, KS MSA	161
Shawnee County	161
Trenton, NJ PMSA	326
Mercer County	326
Tucson, AZ MSA	667
Pima County	667
Tulsa, OK MSA	709
Creek County	61
Osage County	42
Rogers County	55
Tulsa County	503
Wagoner County	48
Tuscaloosa, AL MSA	151
Tuscaloosa County	151
Tyler, TX MSA	151
Smith County	151
Utica-Rome, NY MSA	317
Herkimer County	66
Oneida County	251
Vallejo-Fairfield-Napa, CA PMSA	451
Napa County	111
Solano County	340
Vancouver, WA PMSA	238
Clark County	238
Victoria, TX MSA	74
Victoria County	74
Vineland-Millville-Bridgeton, NJ PMSA	138
Cumberland County	138
Visalia-Tulare-Porterville, CA MSA	312
Tulare County	312
Waco, TX MSA	189
McLennan County	189
Washington, DC-MD-VA MSA	3,924

District of Columbia	607
Calvert County, MD	51
Charles County, MD	101
Frederick County, MD	150
Montgomery County, MD	757
Prince George's County, MD	729
Arlington County, VA	171
Fairfax County, VA	819
Loudoun County, VA	86
Prince William County, VA	216
Stafford County, VA	61
Alexandria city, VA	111
Fairfax city, VA	20
Falls Church city, VA	10
Manassas city, VA	28
Manassas Park city, VA	7
Waterbury, CT MSA	**222**
Litchfield County (pt.)	39
New Haven County (pt.)	183
Waterloo-Cedar Falls, IA MSA	**147**
Black Hawk County	124
Bremer County	23
Wausau, WI MSA	**115**
Marathon County	115
West Palm Beach-Boca Raton-	
Delray Beach, FL MSA	**864**
Palm Beach County	864
Wheeling, WV-OH MSA	**159**
Marshall County, WV	37
Ohio County, WV	51
Belmont County, OH	71
Wichita, KS MSA	**485**
Butler County	51
Harvey County	31
Sedgwick County	404
Wichita Falls, TX MSA	**122**
Wichita County	122
Williamsport, PA MSA	**119**
Lycoming County	119
Wilmington, DE-NJ-MD PMSA	**579**
New Castle County, DE	442
Salem County, NJ	65
Cecil County, MD	71

Wilmington, NC MSA	**120**
New Hanover County	120
Worcester, MA MSA	**437**
Worcester County (pt.)	437
Yakima, WA MSA	**189**
Yakima County	189
York, PA MSA	**418**
Adams County	78
York County	340
Youngstown-Warren, OH MSA	**493**
Mahoning County	265
Trumbull County	228
Yuba City, CA MSA	**123**
Sutter County	64
Yuba County	58
Yuma, AZ MSA	**107**
Yuma County	107

Appendix C

CENSUS '90

OFFICIAL 1990 U.S. CENSUS FORM

Thank you for taking time to complete and return this census questionnaire. It's important to you, your community, and the Nation.

The law requires answers but guarantees privacy.

By law (Title 13, U.S. Code), you're required to answer the census questions to the best of your knowledge. However, the same law guarantees that your census form remains confidential. For 72 years--or until the year 2062--only Census Bureau employees can see your form. No one else--no other government body, no police department, no court system or welfare agency--is permitted to see this confidential information under any circumstances.

How to get started--and get help.

Start by listing on the next page the names of all the people who live in your home. Please answer all questions with a black lead pencil. You'll find detailed instructions for answering the census in the enclosed guide. If you need additional help, call the toll-free telephone number to the left, near your address.

Please answer and return your form promptly.

Complete your form and return it by April 1, 1990 in the postage-paid envelope provided. Avoid the inconvenience of having a census taker visit your home.

Again, thank you for answering the 1990 Census. Remember: Return the completed form by April 1, 1990.

Para personas de habla hispana --
(For Spanish-speaking persons)

Si usted desea un cuestionario del censo en español, llame sin cargo alguno al siguiente número: 1-800-XXX-XXXX
(o sea 1-800-XXX-XXXX)

U.S. Department of Commerce
BUREAU OF THE CENSUS

FORM **D-2**

OMB No. 0607-0628
Approval Expires 07/31/91

FACSIMILES OF 1990 CENSUS SAMPLE QUESTIONNAIRE PAGES – Con.

Page 1

The 1990 census must count every person at his or her "usual residence." This means the place where the person lives and sleeps most of the time.

1a. **List on the numbered lines below the name of each person living here on Sunday, April 1, including all persons staying here who have no other home. If EVERYONE at this address is staying here temporarily and usually lives somewhere else, follow the instructions given in question 1b below.**

Include

- Everyone who usually lives here such as family members, housemates and roommates, foster children, roomers, boarders, and live-in employees
- Persons who are temporarily away on a business trip, on vacation, or in a general hospital
- College students who stay here while attending college
- Persons in the Armed Forces who live here
- Newborn babies still in the hospital
- Children in boarding schools below the college level
- Persons who stay here most of the week while working even if they have a home somewhere else
- Persons with no other home who are staying here on April 1

Do NOT include

- Persons who usually live somewhere else

- Persons who are away in an institution such as a prison, mental hospital, or a nursing home
- College students who live somewhere else while attending college
- Persons in the Armed Forces who live somewhere else

- Persons who stay somewhere else most of the week while working

Print last name, first name, and middle initial for each person. Begin on line 1 with the household member (or one of the household members) in whose name this house or apartment is owned, being bought, or rented. If there is no such person, start on line 1 with any adult household member.

	LAST	FIRST	INITIAL		LAST	FIRST	INITIAL
1				7			
2				8			
3				9			
4				10			
5				11			
6				12			

1b. **If EVERYONE is staying here only temporarily and usually lives somewhere else, list the name of each person on the numbered lines above, fill this circle** ⟶ ○ **and print their usual address below. DO NOT PRINT THE ADDRESS LISTED ON THE FRONT COVER.**

House number	Street or road/Rural route and box number	Apartment number
City	State	ZIP Code
County or foreign country	Names of nearest intersecting streets or roads	

NOW PLEASE OPEN THE FLAP TO PAGE 2 AND ANSWER ALL QUESTIONS FOR THE FIRST 7 PEOPLE LISTED. USE A BLACK LEAD PENCIL ONLY.

FACSIMILES OF 1990 CENSUS SAMPLE QUESTIONNAIRE PAGES – Con.

Page 2   *PLEASE ALSO ANSWER HOUSING QUESTIONS ON PAGE 3* ⟶

	PERSON 1	PERSON 2
Please fill one column ➡ for each person listed in Question 1a on page 1.	Last name First name Middle initial	Last name First name Middle init

2. How is this person related to PERSON 1?

Fill ONE circle for each person.

If **Other relative** of person in column 1, fill circle and print exact relationship, such as mother-in-law, grandparent, son-in-law, niece, cousin, and so on.

PERSON 1:
START in this column with the household member (or one of the members) in whose name the home is owned, being bought, or rented.

If there is no such person, start in this column with any adult household member.

■

PERSON 2:
If a RELATIVE of Person 1:
○ Husband/wife   ○ Brother/sister
○ Natural-born   ○ Father/mother
    or adopted   ○ Grandchild
    son/daughter   ○ Other relative ⌐
○ Stepson/
    stepdaughter

If NOT RELATED to Person 1:
○ Roomer, boarder,   ○ Unmarried
    or foster child   partner
○ Housemate, ■   ○ Other
    roommate   nonrelative

3. Sex
Fill ONE circle for each person.

Person 1: ○ Male   ○ Female
Person 2: ○ Male   ○ Female

4. Race
Fill ONE circle for the race that the person considers himself/herself to be.

   If **Indian (Amer.)**, print the name of the enrolled or principal tribe. ⟶

If **Other Asian or Pacific Islander (API)**, print one group, for example: Hmong, Fijian, Laotian, Thai, Tongan, Pakistani, Cambodian, and so on. ⟶

If **Other race**, print race. ⟶

Person 1:
○ White
○ Black or Negro
○ Indian (Amer.) (Print the name of the enrolled or principal tribe.) ⌐

○ Eskimo
○ Aleut
Asian or Pacific Islander (API)
○ Chinese   ○ Japanese
○ Filipino ■   ○ Asian Indian
○ Hawaiian   ○ Samoan
○ Korean   ○ Guamanian
○ Vietnamese   ○ Other API ⌐

○ Other race (Print race) ⌐

Person 2:
○ White
○ Black or Negro
○ Indian (Amer.) (Print the name of the enrolled or principal tribe.) ⌐

○ Eskimo
○ Aleut
Asian or Pacific Islander (API)
○ Chinese   ○ Japanese
○ Filipino ■   ○ Asian Indian
○ Hawaiian   ○ Samoan
○ Korean   ○ Guamanian
○ Vietnamese   ○ Other API ⌐

○ Other race (Print race) ⌐

5. Age and year of birth

a. Print each person's age at last birthday. Fill in the matching circle below each box.

b. Print each person's year of birth and fill the matching circle below each box.

Person 1:
a. Age

0	○	0	○	0	○
1	○	1	○	1	○
		2	○	2	○
		3	○	3	○
		4	○	4	○
		5	○	5	○
		6	○	6	○
		7	○	7	○
		8	○	8	○
		9	○	9	○

b. Year of birth
1 ● 8 ○ 0 ○ 0 ○
9 ○ 1 ○ 1 ○
2 ○ 2 ○
3 ○ 3 ○
■ 4 ○ 4 ○
5 ○ 5 ○
6 ○ 6 ○
7 ○ 7 ○
8 ○ 8 ○
9 ○ 9 ○

Person 2:
a. Age
0 ○ 0 ○ 0 ○
1 ○ 1 ○ 1 ○
2 ○ 2 ○
3 ○ 3 ○
4 ○ 4 ○
5 ○ 5 ○
6 ○ 6 ○
7 ○ 7 ○
8 ○ 8 ○
9 ○ 9 ○

b. Year of birth
1 ● 8 ○ 0 ○ 0 ○
9 ○ 1 ○ 1 ○
2 ○ 2 ○
3 ○ 3 ○
■ 4 ○ 4 ○
5 ○ 5 ○
6 ○ 6 ○
7 ○ 7 ○
8 ○ 8 ○
9 ○ 9 ○

6. Marital status
Fill ONE circle for each person.

Person 1:
○ Now married   ○ Separated
○ Widowed   ○ Never married
○ Divorced

Person 2:
○ Now married   ○ Separated
○ Widowed   ○ Never married
○ Divorced

7. Is this person of Spanish/Hispanic origin?
Fill ONE circle for each person.

If **Yes, other Spanish/Hispanic**, print one group. ⟶

Person 1:
○ No (not Spanish/Hispanic)
○ Yes, Mexican, Mexican-Am., Chicano
○ Yes, Puerto Rican ■
○ Yes, Cuban
○ Yes, other Spanish/Hispanic
(Print one group, for example: Argentinean, Colombian, Dominican, Nicaraguan, Salvadoran, Spaniard, and so on.) ⌐

Person 2:
○ No (not Spanish/Hispanic)
○ Yes, Mexican, Mexican-Am., Chicano
○ Yes, Puerto Rican
○ Yes, Cuban
○ Yes, other Spanish/Hispanic
(Print one group, for example: Argentinean, Colombian, Dominican, Nicaraguan, Salvadoran, Spaniard, and so on.) ⌐

FOR CENSUS USE ⟶

Person 1: ○   ○ □
Person 2: ○   ○

FACSIMILES OF 1990 CENSUS SAMPLE QUESTIONNAIRE PAGES – Con.

PERSON 7

Last name

First name   Middle initial

If a RELATIVE of Person 1:
- ○ Husband/wife
- ○ Natural-born or adopted son/daughter
- ○ Stepson/ stepdaughter
- ○ Brother/sister
- ○ Father/mother
- ○ Grandchild
- ○ Other relative ⌐

If NOT RELATED to Person 1:
- ○ Roomer, boarder, or foster child
- ○ Housemate, roommate ■
- ○ Unmarried partner
- ○ Other nonrelative

- ○ Male
- ○ Female

- ○ White
- ○ Black or Negro
- ○ Indian (Amer.) (Print the name of the enrolled or principal tribe.) ⌐

- ○ Eskimo
- ○ Aleut

Asian or Pacific Islander (API)
- ○ Chinese
- ○ Filipino ■
- ○ Hawaiian
- ○ Korean
- ○ Vietnamese
- ○ Japanese
- ○ Asian Indian
- ○ Samoan
- ○ Guamanian
- ○ Other API ⌐

- ○ Other race (Print race) ⌐

a. Age

b. Year of birth

1

a. Age			b. Year of birth	
0 0 0 0 0			1 ● 8 0 0 0 0 0	
1 ○ 1 0 1 0			9 0 1 0 1 0	
2 0 2 0			2 0 2 0	
3 0 3 0			3 0 3 0	
4 0 4 0 ■			4 0 4 0	
5 0 5 0			5 0 5 0	
6 0 6 0			6 0 6 0	
7 0 7 0			7 0 7 0	
8 0 8 0			8 0 8 0	
9 0 9 0			9 0 9 0	

- ○ Now married
- ○ Widowed
- ○ Divorced
- ○ Separated
- ○ Never married

- ○ No (not Spanish/Hispanic)
- ○ Yes, Mexican, Mexican-Am., Chicano
- ○ Yes, Puerto Rican ■
- ○ Yes, Cuban
- ○ Yes, other Spanish/Hispanic (Print one group, for example: Argentinean, Colombian, Dominican, Nicaraguan, Salvadoran, Spaniard, and so on.) ⌐

○

○

NOW PLEASE ANSWER QUESTIONS H1a – H26 FOR THIS HOUSEHOLD

H1a. Did you leave anyone out of your list of persons for Question 1a on page 1 because you were not sure if the person should be listed — for example, someone temporarily away on a business trip or vacation, a newborn baby still in the hospital, or a person who stays here once in a while and has no other home?
- ○ Yes, please print the name(s) and reason(s). ⌐
- ○ No

---

b. Did you include anyone in your list of persons for Question 1a on page 1 even though you were not sure that the person should be listed — for example, a visitor who is staying here temporarily or a person who usually lives somewhere else?
- ○ Yes, please print the name(s) and reason(s). ⌐
- ○ No

H2. Which best describes this building? Include all apartments, flats, etc., even if vacant.
- ○ A mobile home or trailer
- ○ A one-family house detached from any other house
- ○ A one-family house attached to one or more houses
- ○ A building with 2 apartments
- ○ A building with 3 or 4 apartments
- ○ A building with 5 to 9 apartments
- ○ A building with 10 to 19 apartments
- ○ A building with 20 to 49 apartments
- ○ A building with 50 or more apartments
- ○ Other

H3. How many rooms do you have in this house or apartment? Do NOT count bathrooms, porches, balconies, foyers, halls, or half-rooms.
- ○ 1 room ■
- ○ 2 rooms
- ○ 3 rooms
- ○ 4 rooms
- ○ 5 rooms
- ○ 6 rooms
- ○ 7 rooms
- ○ 8 rooms
- ○ 9 or more rooms

H4. Is this house or apartment —
- ○ Owned by you or someone in this household with a mortgage or loan?
- ○ Owned by you or someone in this household free and clear (without a mortgage)?
- ○ Rented for cash rent?
- ○ Occupied without payment of cash rent?

If this is a ONE-FAMILY HOUSE —

H5a. Is this house on ten or more acres?
- ○ Yes
- ○ No

b. Is there a business (such as a store or barber shop) or a medical office on this property?
- ○ Yes
- ○ No

Answer only if you or someone in this household OWNS OR IS BUYING this house or apartment —

H6. What is the value of this property; that is, how much do you think this house and lot or condominium unit would sell for if it were for sale?

- ○ Less than $10,000
- ○ $10,000 to $14,999
- ○ $15,000 to $19,999
- ○ $20,000 to $24,999
- ○ $25,000 to $29,999
- ○ $30,000 to $34,999
- ○ $35,000 to $39,999
- ○ $40,000 to $44,999
- ○ $45,000 to $49,999
- ○ $50,000 to $54,999
- ○ $55,000 to $59,999
- ○ $60,000 to $64,999
- ○ $65,000 to $69,999
- ○ $70,000 to $74,999
- ○ $75,000 to $79,999
- ○ $80,000 to $89,999
- ○ $90,000 to $99,999
- ○ $100,000 to $124,999
- ○ $125,000 to $149,999
- ○ $150,000 to $174,999
- ○ $175,000 to $199,999
- ○ $200,000 to $249,999
- ○ $250,000 to $299,999
- ○ $300,000 to $399,999
- ○ $400,000 to $499,999
- ○ $500,000 or more

Answer only if you PAY RENT for this house or apartment —

H7a. What is the monthly rent?

- ○ Less than $80
- ○ $80 to $99
- ○ $100 to $124
- ○ $125 to $149
- ○ $150 to $174
- ○ $175 to $199
- ○ $200 to $224 ■
- ○ $225 to $249
- ○ $250 to $274
- ○ $275 to $299
- ○ $300 to $324
- ○ $325 to $349
- ○ $350 to $374
- ○ $375 to $399
- ○ $400 to $424
- ○ $425 to $449
- ○ $450 to $474
- ○ $475 to $499
- ○ $500 to $524
- ○ $525 to $549
- ○ $550 to $599
- ○ $600 to $649
- ○ $650 to $699
- ○ $700 to $749
- ○ $750 to $999
- ○ $1,000 or more

b. Does the monthly rent include any meals?
- ○ Yes
- ○ No

FOR CENSUS USE

A. Total persons

B. Type of unit

Occupied	Vacant
○ First form	○ Regular
○ Cont'n	○ Usual home elsewhere

C1. Vacancy status
- ○ For rent
- ○ For sale only
- ○ Rented or sold, not occupied
- ○ For seas/ rec/occ
- ○ For migrant workers
- ○ Other vacant

C2. Is this unit boarded up?
- ○ Yes
- ○ No

D. Months vacant
- ○ Less than 1
- ○ 1 up to 2
- ○ 2 up to 6
- ○ 6 up to 12
- ○ 12 up to 24
- ○ 24 or more

E. Complete after
- ○ LR ○ TC ○ QA   JIC 1
- ○ P/F ○ RE ○ I/T ○
- ○ MV ○ ED ○ EN ■

- ○ P0 ○ P3 ○ P6
- ○ P1 ○ P4 ○ IA   JIC 2
- ○ P2 ○ P5 ○ SM ○

F. Cov.
- ○ 1b ○ 1a ○ 7 ○ H1

G. DO

ID ■

FACSIMILES OF 1990 CENSUS SAMPLE QUESTIONNAIRE PAGES – Con.

    PLEASE ALSO ANSWER THESE

H8. When did the person listed in column 1 on page 2 move into this house or apartment?

- ○ 1989 or 1990
- ○ 1985 to 1988
- ○ 1980 to 1984
- ○ 1970 to 1979
- ○ 1960 to 1969
- ○ 1959 or earlier

H9. How many bedrooms do you have; that is, how many bedrooms would you list if this house or apartment were on the market for sale or rent?

- ○ No bedroom
- ○ 1 bedroom
- ○ 2 bedrooms
- ○ 3 bedrooms
- ○ 4 bedrooms
- ○ 5 or more bedrooms

H10. Do you have COMPLETE plumbing facilities in this house or apartment; that is, 1) hot and cold piped water, 2) a flush toilet, and 3) a bathtub or shower?

- ○ Yes, have all three facilities
- ○ No

H11. Do you have COMPLETE kitchen facilities; that is, 1) a sink with piped water, 2) a range or cookstove, and 3) a refrigerator?

- ○ Yes
- ○ No

H12. Do you have a telephone in this house or apartment?

- ○ Yes
- ○ No

H13. How many automobiles, vans, and trucks of one-ton capacity or less are kept at home for use by members of your household?

- ○ None
- ○ 1
- ○ 2
- ○ 3
- ○ 4
- ○ 5
- ○ 6
- ○ 7 or more

H14. Which FUEL is used MOST for heating this house or apartment?

- ○ Gas: from underground pipes serving the neighborhood
- ○ Gas: bottled, tank, or LP
- ○ Electricity
- ○ Fuel oil, kerosene, etc.
- ○ Coal or coke
- ○ Wood
- ○ Solar energy
- ○ Other fuel
- ○ No fuel used

H15. Do you get water from —

- ○ A public system such as a city water department, or private company?
- ○ An individual drilled well?
- ○ An individual dug well?
- ○ Some other source such as a spring, creek, river, cistern, etc.?

H16. Is this building connected to a public sewer?

- ○ Yes, connected to public sewer
- ○ No, connected to septic tank or cesspool
- ○ No, use other means

H17. About when was this building first built?

- ○ 1989 or 1990
- ○ 1985 to 1988
- ○ 1980 to 1984
- ○ 1970 to 1979
- ○ 1960 to 1969
- ○ 1950 to 1959
- ○ 1940 to 1949
- ○ 1939 or earlier
- ○ Don't know

H18. Is this house or apartment part of a condominium?

- ○ Yes
- ○ No

If you live in an apartment building, skip to H20.

H19a. Is this house on less than 1 acre?

- ○ Yes — *Skip to H20*
- ○ No

b. In 1989, what were the actual sales of all agricultural products from this property?

- ○ None
- ○ $1 to $999
- ○ $1,000 to $2,499
- ○ $2,500 to $4,999
- ○ $5,000 to $9,999
- ○ $10,000 or more

H20. What are the yearly costs of utilities and fuels for this house or apartment? If you have lived here less than 1 year, estimate the yearly cost.

a. Electricity

$ _____ .00
Yearly cost — Dollars

OR

- ○ Included in rent or in condominium fee
- ○ No charge or electricity not used

b. Gas

$ _____ .00
Yearly cost — Dollars

OR

- ○ Included in rent or in condominium fee
- ○ No charge or gas not used

c. Water

$ _____ .00
Yearly cost — Dollars

OR

- ○ Included in rent or in condominium fee
- ○ No charge

d. Oil, coal, kerosene, wood, etc.

$ _____ .00
Yearly cost — Dollars

OR

- ○ Included in rent or in condominium fee
- ○ No charge or these fuels not used

FACSIMILES OF 1990 CENSUS SAMPLE QUESTIONNAIRE PAGES – Con.

QUESTIONS FOR YOUR HOUSEHOLD   Page 5

INSTRUCTION:

Answer questions H21 TO H26, if this is a one-family house, a condominium, or a mobile home that someone in this household OWNS OR IS BUYING; otherwise, go to page 6.

H21. What were the real estate taxes on THIS property last year?

$ _____ .00
Yearly amount — Dollars

OR

○ None

H22. What was the annual payment for fire, hazard, and flood insurance on THIS property?

$ _____ .00
Yearly amount — Dollars

OR

○ None

H23a. Do you have a mortgage, deed of trust, contract to purchase, or similar debt on THIS property?

Yes, mortgage, deed of trust, or similar debt
Yes, contract to purchase
} Go to H23b

No — *Skip to H24a*

b. How much is your regular monthly mortgage payment on THIS property? Include payment only on first mortgage or contract to purchase.

$ _____ .00
Monthly amount — Dollars

OR

○ No regular payment required — *Skip to H24a*

c. Does your regular monthly mortgage payment include payments for real estate taxes on THIS property?

○ Yes, taxes included in payment
○ No, taxes paid separately or taxes not required

d. Does your regular monthly mortgage payment include payments for fire, hazard, or flood insurance on THIS property?

○ Yes, insurance included in payment
○ No, insurance paid separately or no insurance

H24a. Do you have a second or junior mortgage or a home equity loan on THIS property?

Yes
No — *Skip to H25*

b. How much is your regular monthly payment on all second or junior mortgages and all home equity loans?

$ _____ .00
Monthly amount — Dollars

OR

No regular payment required

Answer ONLY if this is a CONDOMINIUM —

H25. What is the monthly condominium fee?

$ _____ .00
Monthly amount — Dollars

Answer ONLY if this is a MOBILE HOME —

H26. What was the total cost for personal property taxes, site rent, registration fees, and license fees on this mobile home and its site last year? Exclude real estate taxes.

$ _____ .00
Yearly amount — Dollars

Please turn to page 6. →

FACSIMILES OF 1990 CENSUS SAMPLE QUESTIONNAIRE PAGES – Con.

PERSON 1

Last name   First name   Middle initial

8. In what U.S. State or foreign country was this person born?

(Name of State or foreign country; or Puerto Rico, Guam, etc.)

9. Is this person a CITIZEN of the United States?

○ Yes, born in the United States — *Skip to 11*
○ Yes, born in Puerto Rico, Guam, the U.S. Virgin Islands, or Northern Marianas
○ Yes, born abroad of American parent or parents
○ Yes, U.S. citizen by naturalization
○ No, not a citizen of the United States

10. When did this person come to the United States to stay?

○ 1987 to 1990   ○ 1970 to 1974
○ 1985 or 1986   ○ 1965 to 1969
○ 1982 to 1984   ○ 1960 to 1964
○ 1980 or 1981   ○ 1950 to 1959
○ 1975 to 1979   ○ Before 1950

11. At any time since February 1, 1990, has this person attended regular school or college?
Include only nursery school, kindergarten, elementary school, and schooling which leads to a high school diploma or a college degree.

○ No, has not attended since February 1
○ Yes, public school, public college
○ Yes, private school, private college

12. How much school has this person COMPLETED?
Fill ONE circle for the highest level COMPLETED or degree RECEIVED. If currently enrolled, mark the level of previous grade attended or highest degree received.

○ No school completed
○ Nursery school
○ Kindergarten
○ 1st, 2nd, 3rd, or 4th grade
○ 5th, 6th, 7th, or 8th grade
○ 9th grade
○ 10th grade
○ 11th grade
○ 12th grade, NO DIPLOMA
○ HIGH SCHOOL GRADUATE - high school DIPLOMA or the equivalent (For example: GED)
○ Some college but no degree
○ Associate degree in college - Occupational program
○ Associate degree in college - Academic program
○ Bachelor's degree (For example: BA, AB, BS)
○ Master's degree (For example: MA, MS, MEng, MEd, MSW, MBA)
○ Professional school degree (For example: MD, DDS, DVM, LLB, JD)
○ Doctorate degree (For example: PhD, EdD)

13. What is this person's ancestry or ethnic origin?
(See instruction guide for further information.)

(For example: German, Italian, Afro-Amer., Croatian, Cape Verdean, Dominican, Ecuadoran, Haitian, Cajun, French Canadian, Jamaican, Korean, Lebanese, Mexican, Nigerian, Irish, Polish, Slovak, Taiwanese, Thai, Ukrainian, etc.)

14a. Did this person live in this house or apartment 5 years ago (on April 1, 1985)?

○ Born after April 1, 1985 — *Go to questions for the next person*
○ Yes — *Skip to 15a*
○ No

b. Where did this person live 5 years ago (on April 1, 1985)?

(1) Name of U.S. State or foreign country

(If outside U.S., print answer above and skip to 15a.)

(2) Name of county in the U.S.

(3) Name of city or town in the U.S.

(4) Did this person live inside the city or town limits?

○ Yes
○ No, lived outside the city/town limits

15a. Does this person speak a language other than English at home?

○ Yes   ○ No — *Skip to 16*

b. What is this language?

(For example: Chinese, Italian, Spanish, Vietnamese)

c. How well does this person speak English?

○ Very well   ○ Not well
○ Well   ○ Not at all

16. When was this person born?

○ Born before April 1, 1975 — *Go to 17a*
○ Born April 1, 1975 or later — *Go to questions for the next person*

17a. Has this person ever been on active-duty military service in the Armed Forces of the United States or ever been in the United States military Reserves or the National Guard? If service was in Reserves or National Guard only, see instruction guide.

○ Yes, now on active duty
○ Yes, on active duty in past, but not now
○ Yes, service in Reserves or National Guard only — *Skip to 18*
○ No — *Skip to 18*

b. Was active-duty military service during —
Fill a circle for each period in which this person served.

○ September 1980 or later
○ May 1975 to August 1980
○ Vietnam era (August 1964—April 1975)
○ February 1955—July 1964
○ Korean conflict (June 1950—January 1955)
○ World War II (September 1940—July 1947)
○ World War I (April 1917—November 1918)
○ Any other time

c. In total, how many years of active-duty military service has this person had?

☐ Years

18. Does this person have a physical, mental, or other health condition that has lasted for 6 or more months and which —

a. Limits the kind or amount of work this person can do at a job?

○ Yes   ○ No

b. Prevents this person from working at a job?

○ Yes   ○ No

19. Because of a health condition that has lasted for 6 or more months, does this person have any difficulty —

a. Going outside the home alone, for example, to shop or visit a doctor's office?

○ Yes   ○ No

b. Taking care of his or her own personal needs, such as bathing, dressing, or getting around inside the home?

○ Yes   ○ No

If this person is a female —
20. How many babies has she ever had, not counting stillbirths? Do not count her stepchildren or children she has adopted.

None 1 2 3 4 5 6 7 8 9 10 11 12 or more
○ ○ ○ ○ ○ ○ ○ ○ ○ ○ ○ ○ ○

21a. Did this person work at any time LAST WEEK?

○ Yes — Fill this circle if this person worked full time or part time. (Count part-time work such as delivering papers, or helping without pay in a family business or farm. Also count active duty in the Armed Forces.)

○ No — Fill this circle if this person did not work, or did only own housework, school work, or volunteer work. — *Skip to 25*

b. How many hours did this person work LAST WEEK (at all jobs)? Subtract any time off; add overtime or extra hours worked.

☐ Hours

22. At what location did this person work LAST WEEK?
If this person worked at more than one location, print where he or she worked most last week.

a. Address (Number and street)

(If the exact address is not known, give a description of the location such as the building name or the nearest street or intersection.)

b. Name of city, town, or post office

c. Is the work location inside the limits of that city or town?

○ Yes   ○ No, outside the city/town limits

d. County

e. State   **f. ZIP Code**

FACSIMILES OF 1990 CENSUS SAMPLE QUESTIONNAIRE PAGES – Con.

FOR PERSON 1 ON PAGE 2 Page 7

23a. How did this person usually get to work LAST WEEK? If this person usually used more than one method of transportation during the trip, fill the circle of the one used for most of the distance.

- ○ Car, truck, or van
- ○ Bus or trolley bus
- ○ Streetcar or trolley car
- ○ Subway or elevated
- ○ Railroad
- ○ Ferryboat
- ○ Taxicab
- ○ Motorcycle
- ○ Bicycle
- ○ Walked
- ○ Worked at home — *Skip to 28*
- ○ Other method

If "car, truck, or van" is marked in 23a, go to 23b. Otherwise, skip to 24a.

b. How many people, including this person, usually rode to work in the car, truck, or van LAST WEEK?

- ○ Drove alone
- ○ 2 people
- ○ 3 people
- ○ 4 people
- ○ 5 people
- ○ 6 people
- ○ 7 to 9 people
- ○ 10 or more people

24a. What time did this person usually leave home to go to work LAST WEEK?

[   ] ○ a.m. ○ p.m.

b. How many minutes did it usually take this person to get from home to work LAST WEEK?

[   ] Minutes — *Skip to 28*

25. Was this person TEMPORARILY absent or on layoff from a job or business LAST WEEK?

- ○ Yes, on layoff
- ○ Yes, on vacation, temporary illness, labor dispute, etc.
- ○ No

26a. Has this person been looking for work during the last 4 weeks?

- ○ Yes
- ○ No — *Skip to 27*

b. Could this person have taken a job LAST WEEK if one had been offered?

- ○ No, already has a job
- ○ No, temporarily ill
- ○ No, other reasons (in school, etc.)
- ○ Yes, could have taken a job

27. When did this person last work, even for a few days?

- ○ 1990
- ○ 1989
- ○ 1988
- ○ 1985 to 1987
} *Go to 28*
- ○ 1980 to 1984
- ○ 1979 or earlier
- ○ Never worked
} *Skip to 32*

28-30. CURRENT OR MOST RECENT JOB ACTIVITY. Describe clearly this person's chief job activity or business last week. If this person had more than one job, describe the one at which this person worked the most hours. If this person had no job or business last week, give information for his/her last job or business since 1985.

28. Industry or Employer

a. For whom did this person work? If now on active duty in the Armed Forces, fill this circle ──────→ ○ and print the branch of the Armed Forces.

[   ]

(Name of company, business, or other employer)

b. What kind of business or industry was this? Describe the activity at location where employed.

[   ]

(For example: hospital, newspaper publishing, mail order house, auto engine manufacturing, retail bakery)

c. Is this mainly — Fill ONE circle

- ○ Manufacturing
- ○ Wholesale trade
- ○ Retail trade
- ○ Other (agriculture, construction, service, government, etc.)

29. Occupation

a. What kind of work was this person doing?

[   ]

(For example: registered nurse, personnel manager, supervisor of order department, gasoline engine assembler, cake icer)

b. What were this person's most important activities or duties?

[   ]

(For example: patient care, directing hiring policies, supervising order clerks, assembling engines, icing cakes)

30. Was this person — Fill ONE circle

- ○ Employee of a PRIVATE FOR PROFIT company or business or of an individual, for wages, salary, or commissions
- ○ Employee of a PRIVATE NOT-FOR-PROFIT, tax-exempt, or charitable organization
- ○ Local GOVERNMENT employee (city, county, etc.)
- ○ State GOVERNMENT employee
- ○ Federal GOVERNMENT employee
- ○ SELF-EMPLOYED in own NOT INCORPORATED business, professional practice, or farm
- ○ SELF-EMPLOYED in own INCORPORATED business, professional practice, or farm
- ○ Working WITHOUT PAY in family business or farm

31a. Last year (1989), did this person work, even for a few days, at a paid job or in a business or farm?

- ○ Yes
- ○ No — *Skip to 32*

b. How many weeks did this person work in 1989? Count paid vacation, paid sick leave, and military service.

[   ] Weeks

c. During the weeks WORKED in 1989, how many hours did this person usually work each week?

[   ] Hours

32. INCOME IN 1989 —
Fill the "Yes" circle below for each income source received during 1989. Otherwise, fill the "No" circle. If "Yes," enter the total amount received during 1989.
For income received jointly, see instruction guide.
If exact amount is not known, please give best estimate.
If net income was a loss, write "Loss" above the dollar amount.

a. Wages, salary, commissions, bonuses, or tips from all jobs — Report amount before deductions for taxes, bonds, dues, or other items.

- ○ Yes ──→ $ [   ].00
- ○ No

Annual amount — Dollars

b. Self-employment income from own nonfarm business, including proprietorship and partnership — Report NET income after business expenses.

- ○ Yes ──→ $ [   ].00
- ○ No

Annual amount — Dollars

c. Farm self-employment income — Report NET income after operating expenses. Include earnings as a tenant farmer or sharecropper.

- ○ Yes ──→ $ [   ].00
- ○ No

Annual amount — Dollars

d. Interest, dividends, net rental income or royalty income, or income from estates and trusts — Report even small amounts credited to an account.

- ○ Yes ──→ $ [   ].00
- ○ No

Annual amount — Dollars

e. Social Security or Railroad Retirement

- ○ Yes ──→ $ [   ].00
- ○ No

Annual amount — Dollars

f. Supplemental Security Income (SSI), Aid to Families with Dependent Children (AFDC), or other public assistance or public welfare payments.

- ○ Yes ──→ $ [   ].00
- ○ No

Annual amount — Dollars

g. Retirement, survivor, or disability pensions — Do NOT include Social Security.

- ○ Yes ──→ $ [   ].00
- ○ No

Annual amount — Dollars

h. Any other sources of income received regularly such as Veterans' (VA) payments, unemployment compensation, child support, or alimony — Do NOT include lump-sum payments such as money from an inheritance or the sale of a home.

- ○ Yes ──→ $ [   ].00
- ○ No

Annual amount — Dollars

33. What was this person's total income in 1989? Add entries in questions 32a through 32h; subtract any losses. If total amount was a loss, write "Loss" above amount.

- ○ None   OR $ [   ].00

Annual amount — Dollars

Please turn the page and answer questions for Person 2 listed on page 1. If this is the last person listed in question 1a on page 1, go to the back of the form.

FACSIMILES OF 1990 CENSUS SAMPLE QUESTIONNAIRE PAGES – Con.

Page 20

Please make sure you have . . .

1. **FILLED this form completely.**

2. **ANSWERED Question 1a** on page 1.

3. **ANSWERED Questions 2 through 7** for each person you listed in Question 1a.

4. **ANSWERED Questions H1a through H26** on pages 3, 4, and 5.

5. **ANSWERED the questions on pages 6 through 19** for each person you listed in Question 1a.

Also . . .

6. **PRINT here the name** of a household member who filled the form, the date the form was completed, and the telephone number at which a person in this household can be called.

Name			Date
Telephone number ⟶	Area code	Number	○ Day ○ Night

Then . . .

7. **FOLD the form the way it was sent to you.**

8. **MAIL it back by April 1**, or as close to that date as possible, in the envelope provided; no stamp is needed. When you insert your completed questionnaire, please make sure that the U.S. Census Office can be seen through the window on the front of the envelope.

NOTE — If you have listed more than 7 persons in Question 1a, please make sure that you have filled the form for the first 7 people. Then mail back this form. A census taker will call to obtain the information for the other people.

Thank you very much.

Appendix D

List of Data Tables, STF 1 and STF 3

PART ONE: SUMMARY TAPE FILE 1A
(Note: Table structure is identical for all subfiles except STF 1B)

Table Number	Title (Matrices) and Universe Measured	Number of data cells
P1.	Persons (1) Universe: Persons	1
P2.	Families (1) Universe: Families	1
P3.	Households (1) Universe: Households	1
P4.	Urban and Rural (4) Universe: Persons	4
P5.	Sex (2) Universe: Persons	2
P6.	Race (5) Universe: Persons	5
P7.	Race (25) Universe: Persons	25
P8.	Persons of Hispanic Origin (1) Universe: Persons of Hispanic origin	1
P9.	Hispanic Origin (5) Universe: Persons	5
P10.	Hispanic Origin (2) by Race (5) Universe: Persons	10
P11.	Age (31) Universe: Persons	31
P12.	Race (5) by Sex (2) by Age (31) Universe: Persons	310
P13.	Sex (2) by Age (31) Universe: Persons of Hispanic origin	62
P14.	Sex (2) by Marital Status (5) Universe: Persons 15 years and over	10
P15.	Household Type and Relationship (13) Universe: Persons	13
P16.	Household Size and Household Type (10) Universe: Households	10
P17.	Persons in Families (1) Universe: Persons in families	1
P17A.	Persons per Family (1) Universe: Families	1
P18.	Age of Household Members (2) by Household Type (5) Universe: Households	10
P19.	Race of Householder (5) by Household Type (8) Universe: Households	40
P20.	Household Type (8) Universe: Households with householder of Hispanic origin	8
P21.	Household Type and Relationship (9) Universe: Persons under 18 years	9

P22.	Relationship and Age (37) Universe: Persons under 18 years	37
P23.	Household Type and Relationship (12) Universe: Persons 65 years and over	12
P24.	Age of Household Members (2) by Household Size and Household Type (3) Universe: Households	6
P25.	Age of Household Members (2) by Household Size and Household Type (3) Universe: Households	6
P26.	Household Type (2) Universe: Households	2
P27.	Household Type and Household Size (13) Universe: Households	13
P28.	Group Quarters (10) Universe: Persons in group quarters	10
P29.	Persons Substituted (3) Universe: Persons	3
P30.	Imputation of Population Items (2) Universe: Persons not substituted	2
P31.	Imputation of Relationship (2) Universe: Persons not substituted	2
P32.	Imputation of Sex (2) Universe: Persons not substituted	2
P33.	Imputation of Age (2) Universe: Persons not substituted	2
P34.	Imputation of Race (2) Universe: Persons not substituted	2
P35.	Imputation of Hispanic Origin (2) Universe: Persons not substituted	2
P36.	Imputation of Marital Status (3) Universe: Persons 15 years and over	3
H1.	Housing Units (1) Universe: Housing units	1
H2.	Occupancy Status (2) Universe: Housing units	2

H3.	Tenure (2) Universe: Occupied housing units	2
H4.	Urban and Rural (4) Universe: Housing units	4
H5.	Vacancy Status (6) Universe: Vacant housing units	6
H6.	Boarded-up Status (2) Universe: Vacant housing units	2
H7.	Usual Home Elsewhere (2) Universe: Vacant housing units	2
H8.	Race of Householder (5) Universe: Occupied housing units	5
H9.	Tenure (2) by Race of Householder (5) Universe: Occupied housing units	10
H10.	Hispanic Origin of Householder (2) by Race of Householder (5) Universe: Occupied housing units	10
H11.	Tenure (2) by Race of Householder (5) Universe: Occupied housing units with householder of Hispanic origin	10
H12.	Tenure (2) by Age of Householder (7) Universe: Occupied housing units	14
H13.	Rooms (9) Universe: Housing units	9
H14.	Aggregate Rooms (1) Universe: Housing units	1
H15.	Aggregate Rooms (1) by Tenure (2) Universe: Occupied housing units	2
H16.	Aggregate Rooms (1) by Vacancy Status (6) Universe: Vacant housing units	6
H17.	Persons in Unit (7) Universe: Occupied housing units	7
H17A.	Persons per Occupied Housing Unit (1) Universe: Occupied housing units	1
H18.	Tenure (2) by Persons in Unit (7) Universe: Occupied housing units	14

H18A. Persons per Occupied Housing Unit by Tenure (2) 2
Universe: Occupied housing units

H19. Aggregate Persons (1) 1
Universe: Persons in occupied housing units

H20. Aggregate Persons (1) by Tenure (2) 2
Universe: Persons in occupied housing units

H21. Persons per Room (5) 5
Universe: Occupied housing units

H22. Tenure (2) by Persons per Room (5) 10
Universe: Occupied housing units

H23. Value (20) 20
Universe: Specified owner-occupied housing units

H23A. Lower Value Quartile (1) 1
Universe: Specified owner-occupied housing units

H23B. Median Value (1) 1
Universe: Specified owner-occupied housing units

H23C. Upper Value Quartile (1) 1
Universe: Specified owner-occupied housing units

H24. Aggregate Value (1) 1
Universe: Specified owner-occupied housing units

H25. Race of Householder (5) 5
Universe: Specified owner-occupied housing units

H26. Aggregate Value (1) by Race of Householder (5) 5
Universe: Specified owner-occupied housing units

H27. Hispanic Origin of Householder (2) 2
Universe: Specified owner-occupied housing units

H28. Aggregate Value (1) by Hispanic Origin of Householder (2) 2
Universe: Specified owner-occupied housing units

H29. Aggregate Value (1) by Units in Structure (6) 6
Universe: Owner-occupied housing units

H30. Vacancy Status (3) 3
Universe: Vacant housing units

H31. Aggregate Price Asked (1) 1
Universe: Specified vacant-for-sale-only housing units

H32. Contract Rent (17) 17
Universe: Specified renter-occupied housing units

H32A. Lower Contract Rent Quartile (1) 1
Universe: Specified renter-occupied housing units paying cash rent

H32B. Median Contract Rent (1) 1
Universe: Specified renter-occupied housing units paying cash rent

H32C. Upper Contract Rent Quartile (1) 1
Universe: Specified renter-occupied housing units paying cash rent

H33. Aggregate Contract Rent (1) 1
Universe: Specified renter-occupied housing units paying cash rent

H34. Race of Householder (5) 5
Universe: Specified renter-occupied housing units paying cash rent

H35. Aggregate Contract Rent (1) by Race of Householder(5) 5
Universe: Specified renter-occupied housing units paying cash rent

H36. Hispanic Origin of Householder (2) 2
Universe: Specified renter-occupied housing units paying cash rent

H37. Aggregate Contract Rent (1) by Hispanic Origin of Householder (2) 2
Universe: Specified renter-occupied housing units paying cash rent

H38. Aggregate Rent Asked (1) 1
Universe: Specified vacant-for-rent housing units

H39. Age of Householder (2) by Meals Included in Rent (3) 6
Universe: Specified renter-occupied housing units

H40. Vacancy Status (3) by Duration of Vacancy (3) 9
Universe: Vacant housing units

H41. Units in Structure (10) 10
Universe: Housing units

H42.	Units in Structure (10) Universe: Vacant housing units	10
H43.	Tenure (2) by Units in Structure (10) Universe: Occupied housing units	20
H44.	Aggregate Persons (1) by Tenure (2) by Units in Structure (10) Universe: Persons in occupied housing units	20
H45.	Housing Units Substituted (2) Universe: Housing units	2
H46.	Imputation of Housing Items (2) Universe: Housing units not substituted	2
H47.	Imputation of Vacancy Status (3) Universe: Vacant housing units	3
H48.	Imputation of Duration of Vacancy (3) Universe: Vacant housing units	3
H49.	Imputation of Units in Structure (2) Universe: Housing units not substituted	2
H50.	Imputation of Rooms (2) Universe: Housing units not substituted	2
H51.	Imputation of Tenure (3) Universe: Occupied housing units	3
H52.	Imputation of Value (3) Universe: Specified owner-occupied housing units	3
H53.	Imputation of Price Asked (3) Universe: Specified vacant-for-sale-only housing units	3
H54.	Imputation of Contract Rent (4) Universe: Specified renter-occupied housing units	4
H55.	Imputation of Meals Included in Rent (4) Universe: Specified renter-occupied housing units	4

PART TWO: SUMMARYTAPE FILE 3A
(Note: Table structure is identical for all STF 3 subfiles)

Table Number	Title (Matrices) and Universe Measured	Number of data cells
P1.	PERSONS (1) Universe: Persons	1
P2.	UNWEIGHTED SAMPLE COUNT OF PERSONS (1) Universe: Persons	1
P3	100-PERCENT COUNT OF PERSONS (1) Universe: Persons	1
P3A.	PERCENT OF PERSONS IN SAMPLE (1) Universe: Persons	1
P4.	FAMILIES (1) Universe: Families	1
P5.	HOUSEHOLDS (1) Universe: Households	1
P6.	URBAN AND RURAL (4) Universe: Persons	4
P7.	SEX (2) Universe: Persons	2
P8.	RACE (5) Universe: Persons	5
P9.	RACE (25) Universe: Persons	25
P10.	PERSONS OF HISPANIC ORIGIN (1) Universe: Persons of Hispanic origin	1
P11.	HISPANIC ORIGIN (16) Universe: Persons	16
P12.	HISPANIC ORIGIN (2) BY RACE (5) Universe: Persons	10
P13.	AGE (31) Universe: Persons	31
P14A.	RACE (1) BY SEX (1) BY AGE (31) Universe: White males	31

P35.   ANCESTRY (37)   37
Universe: Persons

P36.   YEAR OF ENTRY (10)   10
Universe: Foreign-born persons

P37.   AGE (2) BY CITIZENSHIP (3)   6
Universe: Persons

P38.   MARITAL STATUS (2) BY AGE (4)   8
Universe: Females 15 years and over

P39.   AGGREGATE NUMBER OF CHILDREN
EVER BORN (1) BY MARITAL
STATUS (2) BY AGE (4)   8
Universe: Females 15 years and over

P40.   GROUP QUARTERS (10)   10
Universe: Persons in group quarters

P41.   GROUP QUARTERS (2) BY AGE (3)   6
Universe: Persons in group quarters

P42.   PLACE OF BIRTH (9)   9
Universe: Persons

P43.   RESIDENCE IN 1985: STATE AND
COUNTY LEVEL (10)   10
Universe: Persons 5 years and over

P44.   RESIDENCE IN 1985: MSA/PMSA
LEVEL (12)   12
Universe: Persons 5 years and over

P45.   PLACE OF WORK: STATE AND COUNTY
LEVEL (3)   3
Universe: Workers 16 years and over

P46.   PLACE OF WORK: PLACE LEVEL (3)   3
Universe: Workers 16 years and over

P47.   PLACE OF WORK: MSA/PMSA
LEVEL (8)   8
Universe: Workers 16 years and over

P48.   PLACE OF WORK: MINOR CIVIL
DIVISION LEVEL (3)   3
Universe: Workers 16 years and over

P49.   MEANS OF TRANSPORTATION TO
WORK (13)   13
Universe: Workers 16 years and over

P50.   TRAVEL TIME TO WORK (13)   13

Universe: Workers 16 years and over

P51.   AGGREGATE TRAVEL TIME TO
WORK (IN MINUTES) (1)   1
Universe: Workers 16 years and over who did not
work at home

P52.   TIME LEAVING HOME TO GO TO
WORK (15)   15
Universe: Workers 16 years and over

P53.   PRIVATE VEHICLE OCCUPANCY (8)   8
Universe: Workers 16 years and over

P54.   SCHOOL ENROLLMENT AND TYPE OF
SCHOOL (7)   7
Universe: Persons 3 years and over

P55.   RACE (5) BY SCHOOL ENROLL-
MENT (4)   20
Universe: Persons 3 years and over

P56.   SCHOOL ENROLLMENT (4)   4
Universe: Persons of Hispanic origin 3 years and
over

P57.   EDUCATIONAL ATTAINMENT (7)   7
Universe: Persons 25 years and over

P58.   RACE (5) BY EDUCATIONAL ATTAIN-
MENT (7)   35
Universe: Persons 25 years and over

P59.   EDUCATIONAL ATTAINMENT (7)   7
Universe: Persons of Hispanic origin 25 years and
over

P60.   EDUCATIONAL ATTAINMENT (7)   7
Universe: Persons 18 years and over

P61.   SCHOOL ENROLLMENT, EDUCATIONAL
ATTAINMENT, AND EMPLOYMENT
STATUS (13)   13
Universe: Persons 16 to 19 years

P62.   RACE (5) BY SCHOOL ENROLLMENT,
EDUCATIONAL ATTAINMENT, AND
EMPLOYMENT STATUS (13)   65
Universe: Persons 16 to 19 years

P63.   SCHOOL ENROLLMENT, EDUCATIONAL
ATTAINMENT, AND EMPLOYMENT
STATUS (13)   13
Universe: Persons of Hispanic origin 16 to 19 years

Universe: White households

P87B. RACE OF HOUSEHOLDER (1) BY AGE OF HOUSEHOLDER (7) BY HOUSEHOLD INCOME IN 1989 (9)   63
Universe: Black households

P87C. RACE OF HOUSEHOLDER (1) BY AGE OF HOUSEHOLDER (7) BY HOUSEHOLD INCOME IN 1989 (9)   63
Universe: American Indian, Eskimo, or Aleut households

P87D. RACE OF HOUSEHOLDER (1) BY AGE OF HOUSEHOLDER (7) BY HOUSEHOLD INCOME IN 1989 (9)   63
Universe: Asian and Pacific Islander households

P87E. RACE OF HOUSEHOLDER (1) BY AGE OF HOUSEHOLDER (7) BY HOUSEHOLD INCOME IN 1989 (9)   63
Universe: Other race households

P88. AGE OF HOUSEHOLDER (7) BY HOUSE-HOLD INCOME IN 1989 (9)   63
Universe: Households with householder of Hispanic origin

P89. EARNINGS IN 1989 (2)   2
Universe: Households

P90. WAGE OR SALARY INCOME IN 1989 (2)   2
Universe: Households

P91. NONFARM SELF-EMPLOYMENT INCOME IN 1989 (2)   2
Universe: Households

P92. FARM SELF-EMPLOYMENT INCOME IN 1989 (2)   2
Universe: Households

P93. INTEREST, DIVIDEND, OR NET RENTAL INCOME IN 1989 (2)   2
Universe: Households

P94. SOCIAL SECURITY INCOME IN 1989 (2)   2
Universe: Households

P95. PUBLIC ASSISTANCE INCOME IN 1989 (2)   2
Universe: Households

P96. RETIREMENT INCOME IN 1989 (2)   2
Universe: Households

P97. OTHER TYPE OF INCOME IN 1989 (2)   2
Universe: Households

P98. AGGREGATE WAGE OR SALARY INCOME IN 1989 (1)   1
Universe: Households

P99. AGGREGATE NONFARM SELF-EMPLOY-MENT INCOME IN 1989 (1)   1
Universe: Households

P100. AGGREGATE FARM SELF-EMPLOYMENT INCOME IN 1989 (1)   1
Universe: Households

P101. AGGREGATE INTEREST, DIVIDEND, OR NET RENTAL INCOME IN 1989 (1)   1
Universe: Households

P102. AGGREGATE SOCIAL SECURITY INCOME IN 1989 (1)   1
Universe: Households

P103. AGGREGATE PUBLIC ASSISTANCE INCOME IN 1989 (1)   1
Universe: Households

P104. AGGREGATE RETIREMENT INCOME IN 1989 (1)   1
Universe: Households

P105. AGGREGATE OTHER TYPE OF INCOME IN 1989 (1)   1
Universe: Households

P106. AGGREGATE PERSONS IN HOUSEHOLDS (1) BY PUBLIC ASSISTANCE INCOME IN 1989 (2) BY AGE (3)   6
Universe: Persons in households

P107. FAMILY INCOME IN 1989 (25)   25
Universe: Families

P107A. MEDIAN FAMILY INCOME IN 1989 (1)   1
Universe: Families

P108. AGGREGATE FAMILY INCOME IN 1989 (1) BY FAMILY INCOME

P125.   POVERTY STATUS IN 1989 (2) BY FAMILY TYPE AND PRESENCE AND AGE OF CHILDREN (12)   24
Universe: Families with householder of Hispanic origin

P126.   POVERTY STATUS IN 1989 (2) BY FAMILY TYPE AND AGE (9)   18
Universe: Related children under 18 years

P127.   POVERTY STATUS IN 1989 (2) BY AGE OF HOUSEHOLDER (3) BY HOUSEHOLD TYPE (5)   30
Universe: Households

P128.   IMPUTATION OF POPULATION ITEMS (3)   3
Universe: Persons

P129.   IMPUTATION OF RELATIONSHIP (2)   2
Universe: Persons in households

P130.   IMPUTATION OF SEX (3)   3
Universe: Persons

P131.   IMPUTATION OF AGE (3)   3
Universe: Persons

P132.   IMPUTATION OF RACE (3)   3
Universe: Persons

P133.   IMPUTATION OF MARITAL STATUS (3)   3
Universe: Persons 15 years and over

P134.   IMPUTATION OF HISPANIC ORIGIN (3)   3
Universe: Persons

P135.   IMPUTATION OF GROUP QUARTERS (2) 2
Universe: Persons in group quarters

P136.   IMPUTATION OF PLACE OF BIRTH (3)   3
Universe: Persons

P137.   IMPUTATION OF CITIZENSHIP (3)   3
Universe: Persons

P138.   IMPUTATION OF YEAR OF ENTRY (3)   3
Universe: Foreign-born persons

P139.   IMPUTATION OF SCHOOL ENROLLMENT (3)   3
Universe: Persons 3 years and over

P140.   IMPUTATION OF EDUCATIONAL ATTAINMENT (3)   3
Universe: Persons 18 years and over

P141.   IMPUTATION OF EDUCATIONAL ATTAINMENT (3)   3
Universe: Persons 25 years and over

P142.   IMPUTATION OF ANCESTRY (3)   3
Universe: Persons

P143.   IMPUTATION OF MOBILITY STATUS (3) 3
Universe: Persons 5 years and over

P144.   IMPUTATION OF RESIDENCE IN 1985 (5) 5
Universe: Persons 5 years and over

P145.   IMPUTATION OF LANGUAGE STATUS (3) 3
Universe: Persons 5 years and over

P146.   IMPUTATION OF LANGUAGE SPOKEN AT HOME (4)   4
Universe: Persons 5 years and over

P147.   IMPUTATION OF ABILITY TO SPEAK ENGLISH (4)   4
Universe: Persons 5 years and over

P148.   IMPUTATION OF VETERAN STATUS (2) 2
Universe: Persons 16 years and over

P149.   IMPUTATION OF PERIOD OF MILITARY SERVICE (3)   3
Universe: Civilian veterans 16 years and over

P150.   IMPUTATION OF WORK DISABILITY STATUS (3)   3
Universe: Civilian noninstitutionalized persons 16 years and over

P151.   IMPUTATION OF MOBILITY LIMITATION STATUS (3)   3
Universe: Civilian noninstitutionalized persons 16 years and over

P152.   IMPUTATION OF SELF-CARE LIMITATION STATUS (3)   3
Universe: Civilian noninstitutionalized persons 16 years and over

P153.   IMPUTATION OF CHILDREN EVER BORN (3)   3
Universe: Females 15 years and over

HOUSEHOLDER (5)   10
Universe: Occupied housing units

H12.   TENURE (2) BY RACE OF HOUSE-
       HOLDER (5)   10
       Universe: Occupied housing units with
       householder of Hispanic origin

H13.   TENURE (2) BY AGE OF HOUSE-
       HOLDER (7)   14
       Universe: Occupied housing units

H14.   AGGREGATE PERSONS (1) BY
       TENURE (2) BY RACE OF
       HOUSEHOLDER (5)   10
       Universe: Persons in occupied housing units

H15.   AGGREGATE PERSONS (1) BY
       TENURE (2)   2
       Universe: Persons in occupied housing units with
       householder of Hispanic origin

H16.   ROOMS (9)   9
       Universe: Housing units

H17.   AGGREGATE ROOMS (1)   1
       Universe: Housing units

H18.   TENURE (2) BY PERSONS IN UNIT (7) 14
       Universe: Occupied housing units

H19.   AGGREGATE PERSONS (1) BY
       TENURE (2)   2
       Universe: Persons in occupied housing units

H20.   UNITS IN STRUCTURE (10)   10
       Universe: Housing units

H21.   UNITS IN STRUCTURE (10)   10
       Universe: Vacant housing units

H22.   TENURE (2) BY UNITS IN
       STRUCTURE (10)   20
       Universe: Occupied housing units

H23.   SOURCE OF WATER (4)   4
       Universe: Housing units

H24.   SEWAGE DISPOSAL (3)   3
       Universe: Housing units

H25.   YEAR STRUCTURE BUILT (8)   8
       Universe: Housing units

H25A. MEDIAN YEAR STRUCTURE BUILT (1)   1
       Universe: Housing units

H26.   YEAR STRUCTURE BUILT (8)   8
       Universe: Vacant housing units

H27.   TENURE (2) BY YEAR STRUCTURE
       BUILT (8)   16
       Universe: Occupied housing units

H28.   YEAR HOUSEHOLDER MOVED INTO
       UNIT (6)   6
       Universe: Occupied housing units

H29.   TENURE (2) BY YEAR HOUSEHOLDER
       MOVED INTO UNIT (6)   12
       Universe: Occupied housing units

H30.   HOUSE HEATING FUEL (9)   9
       Universe: Occupied housing units

H31.   BEDROOMS (6)   6
       Universe: Housing units

H32.   BEDROOMS (6)   6
       Universe: Vacant housing units

H33.   TENURE (2) BY BEDROOMS (6)   12
       Universe: Occupied housing units

H34.   BEDROOMS (4) BY GROSS RENT (7)   28
       Universe: Specified renter-occupied housing units

H35.   TENURE (2) BY TELEPHONE IN HOUSING
       UNIT (2)   4
       Universe: Occupied housing units

H36.   AGE OF HOUSEHOLDER (4) BY TELEPHONE
       IN HOUSING UNIT (2)   8
       Universe: Occupied housing units

H37.   TENURE (2) BY VEHICLES AVAILABLE (6) 12
       Universe: Occupied housing units

H38.   AGGREGATE VEHICLES AVAILABLE (1) BY
       TENURE (2)   2
       Universe: Occupied housing units

H39.   RACE OF HOUSEHOLDER (5) BY VEHICLES
       AVAILABLE (2)   10
       Universe: Occupied housing units

H40. VEHICLES AVAILABLE (2) 2
Universe: Occupied housing units with householder of Hispanic origin

H41. AGE OF HOUSEHOLDER (2) BY VEHICLES AVAILABLE (2) 4
Universe: Occupied housing units

H42. KITCHEN FACILITIES (2) 2
Universe: Housing units

H43. GROSS RENT (17) 17
Universe: Specified renter-occupied housing units

H43A. MEDIAN GROSS RENT (1) 1
Universe: Specified renter-occupied housing units paying cash rent

H44. AGGREGATE GROSS RENT (1) 1
Universe: Specified renter-occupied housing units paying cash rent

H45. RACE OF HOUSEHOLDER (5) BY GROSS RENT (7) 35
Universe: Specified renter-occupied housing units

H46. HISPANIC ORIGIN (2) BY GROSS RENT (7) 14
Universe: Specified renter-occupied housing units

H47. MEALS INCLUDED IN RENT (2) 2
Universe: Specified renter-occupied housing units paying cash rent

H48. AGGREGATE GROSS RENT (1) BY MEALS INCLUDED IN RENT (2) 2
Universe: Specified renter-occupied housing units paying cash rent

H49. INCLUSION OF UTILITIES IN RENT (2) 2
Universe: Specified renter-occupied housing units

H50. HOUSEHOLD INCOME IN 1989 (5) BY GROSS RENT AS A PERCENTAGE OF HOUSEHOLD INCOME IN 1989 (6) 30
Universe: Specified renter-occupied housing units

H50A. MEDIAN GROSS RENT AS A PERCENTAGE OF HOUSEHOLD INCOME IN 1989 (1) 1
Universe: Specified renter-occupied housing units paying cash rent

H51. AGE OF HOUSEHOLDER (2) BY GROSS RENT AS A PERCENTAGE OF HOUSEHOLD INCOME IN 1989 (6) 12
Universe: Specified renter-occupied housing units

H52. MORTGAGE STATUS AND SELECTED MONTHLY OWNER COSTS (21) 21
Universe: Specified owner-occupied housing units

H52A. MEDIAN SELECTED MONTHLY OWNER COSTS AND MORTGAGE STATUS (2) 2
Universe: Specified owner-occupied housing units

H53. AGGREGATE SELECTED MONTHLY OWNER COSTS (1) BY MORTGAGE STATUS (2) 2
Universe: Specified owner-occupied housing units

H54. RACE OF HOUSEHOLDER (5) BY MORTGAGE STATUS AND SELECTED MONTHLY OWNER COSTS (11) 55
Universe: Specified owner-occupied housing units

H55. MORTGAGE STATUS AND SELECTED MONTHLY OWNER COSTS (11) 11
Universe: Specified owner-occupied housing units with householder of Hispanic origin

H56. AGGREGATE SELECTED MONTHLY OWNER COSTS (1) BY MORTGAGE STATUS (2) 2
Universe: Owner-occupied mobile homes or trailers

H57. AGGREGATE SELECTED MONTHLY OWNER COSTS (1) BY MORTGAGE STATUS (2) 2
Universe: Owner-occupied condominium housing units

H58. MORTGAGE STATUS (2) BY SELECTED MONTHLY OWNER COSTS AS A PERCENTAGE OF HOUSEHOLD INCOME IN 1989 (6) 12
Universe: Specified owner-occupied housing units

H58A. MEDIAN SELECTED MONTHLY OWNER COSTS AS A PERCENTAGE OF HOUSEHOLD INCOME IN 1989 AND MORTGAGE STATUS (2) 2
Universe: Specified owner-occupied housing units

H59.   HOUSEHOLD INCOME IN 1989 (5) BY
SELECTED MONTHLY OWNER COSTS
AS A PERCENTAGE OF HOUSEHOLD
INCOME IN 1989 (6)   30
Universe: Specified owner-occupied housing units

H60.   AGE OF HOUSEHOLDER (2) BY SELECTED
MONTHLY OWNER COSTS AS A
PERCENTAGE OF HOUSEHOLD INCOME
IN 1989 (6)   12
Universe: Specified owner-occupied housing units

H61.   VALUE (20)   20
Universe: Specified owner-occupied housing units

H61A.   MEDIAN VALUE (1)   1
Universe: Specified owner-occupied housing units

H62.   AGGREGATE VALUE (1) BY MORTGAGE
STATUS (2)   2
Universe: Specified owner-occupied housing units

H63.   AGGREGATE HOUSEHOLD INCOME
IN 1989 (1) BY TENURE AND MORTGAGE
STATUS (3)   3
Universe: Occupied housing units

H64.   PLUMBING FACILITIES (2)   2
Universe: Housing units

H65.   PLUMBING FACILITIES (2)   2
Universe: Vacant housing units

H66.   RACE OF HOUSEHOLDER (5) BY PLUMBING
FACILITIES (2)   10
Universe: Occupied housing units

H67.   PLUMBING FACILITIES (2)   2
Universe: Occupied housing units with householder
of Hispanic origin

H68.   AGE OF HOUSEHOLDER (2) BY PLUMBING
FACILITIES (2)   4
Universe: Occupied housing units

H69.   TENURE (2) BY PLUMBING FACILITIES
(2) BY PERSONS
PER ROOM (3)   12
Universe: Occupied housing units

H70.   PLUMBING FACILITIES (2) BY UNITS IN
STRUCTURE (10)   20
Universe: Housing units

H71.   PLUMBING FACILITIES (2) BY PERSONS
PER ROOM (2) BY YEAR STRUCTURE
BUILT (2)   8
Universe: Occupied housing units

H72.   IMPUTATION OF HOUSING ITEMS (2)   2
Universe: Housing units

H73.   IMPUTATION OF CONDOMINIUM
STATUS (2)   2
Universe: Housing units

H74.   IMPUTATION OF PLUMBING
FACILITIES (2)   2
Universe: Housing units

H75.   IMPUTATION OF SOURCE OF WATER
(2)   2
Universe: Housing units

H76.   IMPUTATION OF SEWAGE DISPOSAL
(2)   2
Universe: Housing units

H77.   IMPUTATION OF YEAR STRUCTURE
BUILT (2)   2
Universe: Housing units

H78.   IMPUTATION OF YEAR HOUSEHOLDER
MOVED INTO UNIT (2)   2
Universe: Occupied housing units

H79.   IMPUTATION OF HOUSE HEATING
FUEL (2)   2
Universe: Occupied housing units

H80.   IMPUTATION OF KITCHEN FACILITIES
(2)   2
Universe: Housing units

H81.   IMPUTATION OF BEDROOMS (2)   2
Universe: Housing units

H82.   IMPUTATION OF TELEPHONE IN
HOUSING UNIT (2)   2
Universe: Occupied housing units

H83.   IMPUTATION OF VEHICLES
        AVAILABLE (2)   2
        Universe: Occupied housing units

H84.   IMPUTATION OF MORTGAGE
        STATUS (2)   2
        Universe: Specified owner-occupied housing units

H85.   IMPUTATION OF TENURE (2)   2
        Universe: Occupied housing units

H86.   IMPUTATION OF VACANCY
        STATUS (2)   2
        Universe: Vacant housing units

H87.   IMPUTATION OF ROOMS (2)   2
        Universe: Housing units

H88.   IMPUTATION OF UNITS IN
        STRUCTURE (2)   2
        Universe: Housing units

H89.   IMPUTATION OF VALUE (2)   2
        Universe: Specified owner-occupied housing units

H90.   IMPUTATION OF MEALS INCLUDED IN
        RENT (2)   2
        Universe: Specified renter-occupied housing units
        paying cash rent

H91.   IMPUTATION OF GROSS RENT (2)   2
        Universe: Specified renter-occupied housing units

H92.   IMPUTATION OF MORTGAGE STATUS
        AND SELECTED MONTHLY OWNER
        COSTS (4)   4
        Universe: Specified owner-occupied housing units

Appendix E

For Further Reading

This reading list represents a very selective sampling of the hundreds of books, reports, articles, and news stories published about the 1990 Census. The list is intended to provide additional sources for readers who wish to learn more about major topics discussed in *Understanding the Census*. Most items published by the Bureau are available for free from Customer Services, if they are still in print. Items published by the GPO must be purchased.

Chapter 1. Census Fundamentals

Basic Concepts

Crispell, Diane. *The Insider's Guide to Demographic Know-How*, 3rd edition. (Ithaca, N.Y.: American Demographics Books, 1993).

Dunn, William. *Selling the Story: The Layman's Guide to Collecting and Communicating Demographic Information.* (Ithaca, NY: American Demographics Books, 1992).

Shryock, Henry S., et al. *The Methods and Materials of Demography*, fourth printing (revised). (Washington, D.C.: U.S. Government Printing Office, 1980).

Taeuber, Conrad. "Census." In *International Encyclopedia of Statistics*, edited by William H. Kruskal and Judith M. Tanur. (New York: Free Press, 1978), pp. 41-46.

Census Overview

Anderson, Margo. "Planning the Future in the Context of the Past." *Society* 25 (March/April 1988):39-47.

Morehead, Joe. "Everybody Counts: The Bicentennial Census of These United States." *Serials Librarian* 20 (1991): 37-54.

Riley, David. "The Big Count." *Government Executive* 20 (April 1988): 3-7.

Roberts, Sam. *Who We Are: A Portrait of America Based on the Latest U.S. Census.* (New York: Times Books, 1993).

Robey, Bryant. "Two Hundred Years and Counting: The 1990 Census." *Population Bulletin* 44 (April 1989): 2-38.

U.S. Bureau of the Census. *Census '90 Basics*, Informational Brochure CPH-I-8. (Washington, D.C.: U.S. Government Printing Office, 1993).

U.S. Bureau of the Census. *1990 Census of Population and Housing Guide, Part A.: Text.* (Washington, D.C.: U.S. Government Printing Office, 1992).

History of the Census

Anderson, Margo J. *The American Census: A Social History.* (New Haven, CT: Yale University Press, 1988).

Bohme, Frederick G. and George Dailey. "1990 Census: The 21st Count of 'We the People'." *Social Education* 53 (Nov./Dec. 1989): 421-25.

Bohme, Frederick G. "200 Years of Census Factfinding." *Social Education* 53 (Nov./Dec. 1989): 427-35.

"Congress Orders U.S. Marshals to Take First Decennial Census in August 1790." *The Census and You* 25 (August 1990): 1-4.

Reid-Green, Keith S. "The History of Census Tabulation." *Scientific American* 260 (February 1989): 98-103.

U.S. Bureau of the Census. *History and Organization*, Factfinder for the Nation No. 4, revised edition. (Washington, D.C.: the Bureau, 1988).

Wright, Carroll D. and William C. Hunt. *The History and Growth of the United States Census*. (Washington, D.C.: U.S. Government Printing Office, 1900).

Confidentiality

Bryant, Barbara Everitt and William Dunn. "The Census and Privacy." *American Demographics* 17 (May 1995): 48-54.

Daniels, Roger. "The Bureau of the Census and the Relocation of the Japanese Americans: A Note and a Document." *Amerasia Journal* 9 (Spring/Summer 1982): 101-105.

Okamura, Raymond Y. "The Myth of Census Confidentiality." *Amerasia Journal* 8 (Fall/Winter 1981):111-120.

Chapter 2. Uses of Census Data

General Topics

Gelman, Kenneth. "Life Without the Census." *American Demographics* 17 (October 1995): 38-42.

"How Census Data Are Used." In *Improving Census Accuracy: A Report Prepared by the Congressional Research Service for the Subcommittee on Census and Population,* Committee Print 100-6. (Washington, D.C.: U.S. Government Printing Office, 1987), pp. 15-37.

King, Seth. "Census Data Kept at Kansas 'Bank'." *New York Times* (February 14, 1971): 56.

Myers, Dowell. *Analysis with Local Census Data: Portraits of Change.* (San Diego: Academic Press, 1992).

Paez, Adolfo. "U.S. Census Data Uses." *Government Publications Review* 20 (March/April 1993): 163-182.

"Using Census Data." In *Census '80: Continuing the Factfinder Tradition*, edited by Charles P. Kaplan and Thomas L. Van Valey. (Washington, D.C.: U.S. Government Printing Office, 1980), pp. 361-430.

Legislative Redistricting

Elving, Ronald D. "Redistricting: Drawing Power with a Map." *Editorial Research Reports* (Feb. 15, 1991): 98-108+.

U.S. Bureau of the Census. *P.L. 94-171 Redistricting Data from the Year 2000 Census: The View from the States.* (Washington, D.C.: U.S. Government Printing Office, 1993).

U.S. Bureau of the Census. *Strength in Numbers: Your Guide to 1990 Census Redistricting Data from the U.S. Bureau of the Census.* (Washington, D.C.: the Bureau, 1990).

Government Planning and Regulatory Compliance

U.S. Bureau of the Census. *Federal Legislative Uses of Decennial Census Data*, 1990 Census of Population and Housing Content Determination Report, CDR-14. (Washington, D.C.: U.S. Government Printing Office, 1990).

U.S. General Accounting Office. *Decennial Census: Local Government Uses of Housing Data*, GAO Briefing Report GGD-87-56BR. (Washington, D.C.: U.S. Government Printing Office, 1987).

U.S. General Accounting Office. *Formula Programs: Adjusted Census Data Would Redistribute Small Percent-*

age of Funds to States, GGD-92-12. (Washington, D.C.: U.S. Government Printing Office, 1992).

Business Uses

Baker, Sunny and Kim Baker. *Market Mapping: How to Use Revolutionary New Software to Find, Analyze, and Keep Customers.* (New York: McGraw-Hill, 1993).

Larson, Erik. *The Naked Consumer: How Our Private Lives Become Public Commodities.* (New York: Henry Holt, 1992).

Nichols, Judith E. *By the Numbers: Using Demographics and Psychographics for Business Growth in the '90s.* Chicago: Bonus Books, 1990).

U.S. Bureau of the Census. *Census ABC's: Applications in Business and Community* (Washington, D.C.: the Bureau, 1989).

Genealogy and Age Search

Mueller, Jean West and Wynell Burroughs Schamel. "Little House in the Census : Almanzo and Laura Ingalls Wilder." *Social Education* 53 (November/December 1989): 451-453.

1920 Census Records Opened to the Public." *The Census and You* 27 (March 1992): 1.

U.S. Bureau of the Census. *Age Search Information.* (Washington, D.C.: the Bureau, 1990).

U.S. Bureau of the Census. *Availability of Census Records About Individuals*, Factfinder for the Nation No. 2, revised edition. (Washington, D.C.: the Bureau, 1991).

Chapter 3. Planning the Census

General Topics

Bounpane, Peter A. "Looking Toward 1990: Planning the Next United States Census of Population and Housing." *Government Publications Review* 12 (1985): 111-130.

"The Census Bureau's 1990 Plan." In *Improving Census*

Accuracy: A Report Prepared by the Congressional Research Service for the Subcommittee on Census and Population, U.S. House of Representatives Committee Print 100-6. (Washington, D.C.: U.S. Government Printing Office, 1987): 43-75.

U.S. General Accounting Office. *1990 Census: Overview of Key Issues*, GAO Briefing Report GGD-89-77BR. (Washington, D.C.: U.S. Government Printing Office, 1989).

U.S. National Academy of Sciences, National Research Council. *The Bicentennial Census: New Directions for Methodology in 1990.* (Washington, D.C.: National Academy Press, 1985.)

Specific Procedures and Concerns

Becker, Patricia C. "Issues on 1990 Data Products: Content and Format of Summary Tape Files." *Proceedings of the American Statistical Association, Social Statistics Section.* (Washington, D.C.: the Association, 1986): 245-248.

Bounpane, Peter A. "How Increased Automation Will Improve the 1990 Census of Population and Housing in the United States." *Journal of Official Statistics* 2 (1986): 545-553.

Burt, Catherine and Joan March. "Census '90: How to Train and Manage 500,000 Temps." *Management Review* 79 (April 1990): 40-45.

"1990 Census Tracts: Time to Start Planning." *Data User News* 20 (April 1985): 1+.

"Rehearsal Fine-Tunes Census Procedures for 1990." *The Census and You* 23 (April/May 1988): 4.

"Seven Offices Will Process Over 100 Million '90 Census Questionnaires." *The Census and You 23* (September 1988): 1+.

U.S. Government Accounting Office. *Decennial Census: Issues Related to Questionnaire Development*, GAO Briefing Report GGD-86-74BR. (Washington, D.C.: U.S. Government Printing Office, 1986).

U.S. House of Representatives, Subcommittee on Census and Population. *Improve Census Bureau's Ability to Attract a Qualified Work Force*, Hearing held May 23, 1989, Serial No. 101-6. (Washington, D.C.: U.S. Government Printing Office, 1989).

Whitford, David C. and Carolyn R. Hay. "Address List Development for the 1990 Census." *Proceedings of the American Statistical Association, Social Statistics Section.* (Washington, D.C.: The Association, 1986): 103-108.

Chapter 4. Conducting the 1990 Census

Enumeration

"Enumerators Brave the Elements on S-Night." *The Census and You* 25 (May 1990): 1-2+.

Gallup, George Jr.; and Frank Newport. "Americans Ignorant of Basic Census Facts." *Gallup Poll Monthly* No. 294 (March 1990): 2- 5.

U.S. Bureau of the Census. "Field Enumeration." In *1990 Census of Population and Housing History, Part A.* (Washington, D.C.: U.S. Government Printing Office, 1993), pp. 6-1 to 6-57.

Follow-Up Activities

Bragdon, Peter. "The Census: Low Response Rate to Count Raises Cost for Accuracy." *Congressional Quarterly Weekly Report* 48 (April 21, 1990): 1215

"Census Summer: The Count Continues." *The Census and You* 25 (July 1990): 5-6.

Martz, Larry and Daniel Glick. "Apathy and Foul-Ups Foil the Census." *Newsweek* 115 (April 30, 1990): 23.

U.S. Bureau of the Census. *Programs to Improve Coverage in the 1990 Census*, 1990 Census of Population and Housing Evaluation and Research Reports, No. 3. (Washington, D.C.: U.S. Government Printing Office, 1993).

U.S. House of Representatives, Subcommittee on Census and Population. *Status of Post-Census Local Review Program*, Hearing held September 25, 1990, Serial No. 101-86. (Washington, D.C.: U.S. Government Printing Office, 1990).

Falsified Data

Reardon, Patrick T. "Census Workers Told to Use Incorrect Data." *Chicago Tribune* (July 12, 1990): 1.

Sullivan, Joseph F. "Census Recount Follows Reports of Faked Forms." *New York Times* (October 27, 1990): 27.

Winerip, Michael. "How to Finish a Census Count: Just Make It Up." *New York Times* (October 19, 1990): B-1.

Data Processing

"Deluge Hits Census District Offices." *The Census and You* 25 (May 1990): 3-5.

"Processing Census '90: Full Steam Ahead." *The Census and You* 25 (June 1990): 1-2+.

Rogers, Beth. "Counting Heads." *INFORM* (the Magazine of the Association for Information and Image Management) 4 (July/Aug. 1990): 14+.

Evaluation

Exter, Thomas. "The Survey That Measures the Census." *American Demographics* 12 (November 1990): 12-14.

Gleick, James. "The Census: Why We Can't Count." *New York Times Magazine* (July 15, 1990): 22-26+.

Lewis, Sylvia. "Can You Trust the Census?" *Planning* 57 (January 1991): 14-18.

Mihm, J. Christopher. "The U.S. Decennial Census: An Agenda for Change." *Journal of Government Information* 21 (January/February 1994): 49-58.

Singer, Eleanor; Nancy A. Mathiowetz; and Mick P. Couper. "Impact of Privacy and Confidentiality Concerns on Survey Participation: The Case of the 1990 U.S. Census." *Public Opinion Quarterly* 57 (Winter 1993):465-482.

U.S. Bureau of the Census. *Effectiveness of Quality Assurance*, 1990 Census of Population and Housing Evaluation and Research Report No. 2 (Washington, D.C.: U.S. Government Printing Office, 1993).

U.S. General Accounting Office. *Decennial Census: 1990 Results Show Need for Fundamental Reform*, GAO Report GGD-92-94. (Washington, D.C.: U.S. Government Printing Office, 1992).

U.S. House of Representatives, Subcommittee on Census and Population. *Oversight Hearing to Review the 1990 Census Counts*, Hearing held February 21, 1991, Serial No. 102-2. (Washington, D.C.: U.S. Government Printing Office, 1991).

Chapter 5. Census Terminology and Concepts

General Topics

U.S. Bureau of the Census. *1990 Census of Population and Housing Guide, Part B: Glossary*. (Washington, D.C.: U.S. Government Printing Office, 1993).

Residency Guidelines

Bean, Frank D.; and Rodolfo O. de la Garza. "Illegal Aliens and Census Counts." *Society* 25 (March/April 1988): 48-53.

Braus, Patricia. "What Does 'Hispanic' Mean?" *American Demographics* 15 (June 1993): 46-49+.

Hollmann, Walter P. "Applying Residence Rules to the Military." *Society* 25 (March/April 1988): 54-5.

Idelson, Holly. "The Census: Overseas Military Personnel Counted in Home States." *Congressional Quarterly Weekly Report* 48 (July 21, 1990): 2343.

Martin, Elizabeth, Theresa J. DeMaio, and Pamela C. Campanelli. "Context Effects for Census Measures of Race and Hispanic Origin." *Public Opinion Quarterly* 54 (1990): 551-66.

Mills, Karen. *Americans Overseas in U.S. Censuses*, Technical Paper 62. (Washington, D.C.: U.S. Bureau of the Census, 1993).

Norman, Colin. Who Should Count in the 1990 Census?" *Science* 243 (Feb. 3, 1989):601-602.

Zitter, Meyer. "Enumerating Americans Living Abroad." *Society* 25 (March/April 1988): 56-60.

Race and Ethnicity

Arocha, Zita. "The Business of Counting Hispanics." *Hispanic* 3 (January/February 1990): 24-31.

Farley, Reynolds. "The New Census Question about Ancestry: What Did It Tell Us?" *Demography* 28 (August 1991): 411-29.

Harris, David. "The 1990 Census Count of American Indians: What Do the Numbers Really Mean?" *Social Science Quarterly* 75 (September 1994): 580-593.

Johnson, Robert Alan. "Measurement of Hispanic Ethnicity in the U.S. Census: An Evaluation Based on Latent-Class Analysis." *Journal of the American Statistical Association* 85 (March 1990): 58-65.

Lott, Juanita Tamayo. "Do United States Racial/Ethnic Categories Still Fit?" *Population Today* (January 1993): 6-7.

Petersen, William. "Politics and the Measurement of Ethnicity." In *The Politics of Numbers*, edited by William Alonso and Paul Starr. (New York: Russell Sage Foundation, 1987), pp. 187-234.

Rodriguez, Clara E. "Race, Culture, and Latino 'Otherness' in the 1980 Census." *Social Science Quarterly* 73 (December 1992): 930-37.

Wright, Lawrence. "One Drop of Blood." *New Yorker* 70 (July 25, 1994): 46-55.

Chapter 6. Census Geography

General Topics

Association of Public Data Users and the U.S. Bureau of the Census. *A Guide to State and Local Census Geography*, Informational Brochure CPH-I-18. (Washington, D.C.: U.S. Government Printing Office, 1993).

"Does Your Area Qualify as a Census Designated Place?" *The Census and You* 24 (October 1989): 4-5.

U.S. Bureau of the Census. *Census Geography--Concepts and Products*. Factfinder for the Nation No. 8, revised edition. (Washington, D.C.: the Bureau, 1991).

U.S. Bureau of the Census. *Geographic Areas Reference Manual*. (Washington, D.C.: U.S. Government Printing Office, 1994).

U.S. Bureau of the Census. *Maps and More: Your Guide to Census Bureau Geography*. (Washington, D.C.: the Bureau, 1992).

The TIGER System

Carbaugh, Larry W. and Robert W. Marx. "The TIGER System: A Census Bureau Innovation Serving Data Analysts." *Government Information Quarterly* 7 (1990): 285-306.

Larson, Jan. "TIGER Opens New Mapping Vistas for Businesses." *American Demographics* 12 (June 1990): 16-19.

Marx, Robert W. "The TIGER System: Automating the Geographic Structure of the United States Census." *Government Publications Review* 13 (1986) pp. 181-201.

U.S. Bureau of the Census. *TIGER: The Coast-to-Coast Digital Map Data Base*. (Washington, D.C.: the Bureau, 1990).

U.S. National Institute of Standards and Technology. *Guideline: Codes for Named Populated Places, Primary County Divisions, and Other Locational Entities of the United States, Puerto Rico, and the Outlying Areas*, Federal Information Processing Standards Publication 55-3. (Washington, D.C.: National Technical Information Service, 1994).

Chapter 7. 1990 Census Questionnaire

"1990 Census Questionnaire." *American Demographics* 11 (April 1989): 24-31

Safire, William. "Counting Census Mistakes." *New York Times Magazine* (April 15, 1990): 16.
U.S. Bureau of the Census. *1990 Census of Population*

and Housing Content Determination Reports. (A series of 14 reports) CDR-1 - CDR-14. (Washington, D.C.: the Bureau, 1990).

U.S. Bureau of the Census. *1990 Census Questionnaires and Other Public-Use Forms*, 1990 Census of Population and Housing Reference Report No. 5. (Washington, D.C.: U.S. Government Printing Office, 1993).

U.S. Bureau of the Census. *200 Years of U.S. Census Taking: Population and Housing Questions, 1790-1990*. (Washington, D.C.: U.S. Government Printing Office, 1989).

U.S. General Accounting Office. *Decennial Census: A Comparison of the 1980 and 1990 Census Questionnaire Contents*, GAO Fact Sheet GGD-87-76FS. (Washington, D.C.: U.S. Government Printing Office, 1987).

Chapter 8. CD-ROM Products

Schwartz, Joe. "A Guide to the 1990 Census." *American Demographics* 12 (April 1990): 16-21.

U.S. Bureau of the Census. *Accessing Public Use Microdata Using QuickTab*. (Washington, D.C.: the Bureau, n.d.). Unpublished report from the Data User Services Division.

U.S. Bureau of the Census. *Census, CD-ROM, and You!* (Washington, D.C.: the Bureau, 1993).

U.S. Bureau of the Census. *1990 Census EEO File*, Product Profile No. 3. (Washington, D.C.: the Bureau, 1992).

U.S. Bureau of the Census. *1990 Census of Population and Housing Tabulation and Publication Program*. (Washington, D.C.: the Bureau, 1989).

U.S. Bureau of the Census. *1990 Public Use Microdata Samples (PUMS)*, Product Profile No. 5. (Washington, D.C.: the Bureau, 1993).

U.S. Bureau of the Census. *1992 TIGER/Line Files: Helping You Map Things Out*, Product Profile No. 6. (Washington, D.C.: the Bureau, 1993).

U.S. Bureau of the Census. *Special Tabulation on Aging (STP 14)*, Product Profile No. 9. (Washington, D.C.: the Bureau, 1994).

U.S. Bureau of the Census. *Summary Tape File (STF) 3*, Product Profile 3. (Washington, D.C.: the Bureau, 1992).

Chapter 9. Print and Microform Products

U.S. Bureau of the Census. *Do You Know Which 1990 Report Is Similar to Your Favorite 1980 Report?* Informational Brochure CPH-I-1. (Washington, D.C.: the Bureau, 1990).

U.S. Bureau of the Census. *1990 Census of Population and Housing Tabulation and Publication Program* (Washington, D.C.: the Bureau, 1989).

U.S. Bureau of the Census. *What Do I Need to Map Out 1990 Census Data?* Informational Brochure CPH-I-15. (Washington, D.C.: the Bureau, 1992).

Weintrop, Jane. "Providing Access to the 1990 U.S. Census Maps." *Journal of Government Information* 22 (July/August 1995): 297-309.

Chapter 10. Finding and Using Census Data

Sources of Assistance

Crispell, Diane. "How to Navigate the Census Bureau." *American Demographics* 11 (November 1989): 46-48.

"Discussion Forum: The Census Depository Library Program." *Government Information Quarterly* 8 (1991): 1-10.

"Information Centers Reach Out to New Users." *The Census and You* 28 (August 1993): 5-8.

McClure, Charles R.; and Peter Hernon. *Use of Census Bureau Data in GPO Depository Libraries: Future Issues and Trends.* (Washington, D.C.: U.S. Government Printing Office, 1990).

Redmond, Mary. "State Data Centers: Improving Access to Census Information." *Government Information Quarterly* 3 (August 1986): 291-303.

Rowland, Sandra. *The Role of Intermediaries in the Interpretation and Dissemination of Census Data.* (Washington, D.C.: U.S. Bureau of the Census, 1989).

Stephenson, Elizabeth. "Data Archivists: The Intermediaries the Census Bureau Forgot." *Government Publications Review* 17 (Sept./Oct. 1990): 441-47.

U.S. Bureau of the Census. *Hidden Treasures! Census Bureau Data and Where to Find It.* (Washington, D.C.: the Bureau, 1990).

Census Methodology

Griffin, Richard A., Alfredo Navarro, and Linda Flores-Baez. *Disclosure Avoidance for the 1990 Census.* (Washington, D.C.: U.S. Bureau of the Census, 1990).

"Sampling and Estimation." In *1990 Census of Population and Housing History, Part A.* (Washington, D.C.: U.S. Government Printing Office, 1993), pp. 9-1 to 9-8.

Evaluating Data Quality

Anderson, Margo. "The 1990 Census: How Good Is It?" *Government Publications Review* 19 (March/April 1992): 125-35.

Keane, John C. "Questionable Statistics." *American Demographics* 7 (June 1985): 18-21+.

McKenney, Nampeo R. and Claudette E. Bennett. "Issues Regarding Data on Race and Ethnicity: The Census Bureau Experience." *Public Health Reports* 109 (January/February 1994): 16-25.

Paris, James A. "The Group Quarters Quandary." *American Demographics* 7 (February 1985): 34-37.

U.S. Bureau of the Census. *Content Reinterview Survey: Accuracy of Data for Selected Population and Housing Characteristics as Measured by Reinterview*, 1990 Census of Population and Housing Evaluation and Research Report No. 1. (Washington, D.C.: U.S. Government Printing Office, 1993).

U.S. House of Representatives, Subcommittee on Census and Population. *Improving Census Accuracy: A Report Prepared by the Congressional Research Service*, House Committee Print 100-6. (Washington, D.C.: U.S. Government Printing Office, 1987).

U.S. National Academy of Sciences, National Research Council. *A Census That Mirrors America: Interim Report. A Panel to Evaluate Alternative Census Methods.* (Washington, D.C.: National Academy Press, 1993.

Census Undercount

Fein, David J. "Racial and Ethnic Differences in U.S. Census Omission Rates." *Demography* 27 (May 1990): 285-302.

U.S. Commerce Department. *Census Bureau Releases Preliminary Coverage Estimates from the Post Enumeration Survey and Demographic Analysis*, Commerce Department News Release CB91-131, April 18, 1991. (Washington, D.C.: U.S. Government Printing Office, 1991).

U.S. Commerce Department. *Census Bureau Releases Refined Estimates from Post Enumeration Survey of 1990 Census Coverage*, Commerce Department News Release CB91-221, June 13, 1991. (Washington, D.C.: U.S. Government Printing Office, 1991).

U.S. General Accounting Office. *Components of the 1990 Census Count*, Statement of L. Nye Stevens, Director of Governmental Business Operations Issues before the House Subcommittee on Census and Population, February 21, 1991. GAO Testimony GGD-91-8. (Washington, D.C.: U.S. Government Printing Office, 1991).

U.S. General Accounting Office. *1990 Census: Reported Net Undercount Obscured Magnitude of Error*, GAO Report GGD 91-113. (Washington, D.C.: U.S. Government Printing Office, 1991).

West, Kirsten K. and David J. Fein. "Census Undercount: An Historical and Contemporary Sociological Issue." *Sociological Inquiry* 60 (May 1990): 127-41.

Wolter, Kirk. "Accounting for America's Uncounted and Miscounted" *Science* 253 (July 5, 1991): 12-15.

Counting the Homeless

Haupt, Arthur. "S-Night: Counting the Homeless." *Population Today* 18 (May 1990): 3-4.

Martin, Elizabeth. "Assessment of S-Night Street Enumeration in the 1990 Census." *Evaluation Review: A Journal of Applied Social Research* 16 (August 1992): 418-438.

U.S. General Accounting Office. *Counting the Homeless: Limitations of 1990 Census Results and Methodology*, Statement of L. Nye Stevens, Director of Governmental Business Operations Issues before the House Subcommittee on Census and Population, May 9, 1991. GAO Testimony GGD-91-29. (Washington, D.C.: U.S. Government Printing Office, 1991).

Wright, James and Joel A. Devine. "Counting the Homeless: The Bureau's 'S-Night' in Five U.S. Cities." *Evaluation Review: A Journal of Applied Social Research* 16 (August 1992):355-364.

The Adjustment Controversy

Barringer, Felicity. "Census Revisions Would Widen Political Gains of 3 Big States." *New York Times*. (June 14, 1991): 1

"Down with the Count." *New Republic* 202 (May 21, 1990): 7-8.

"Efforts to Adjust 1990 Census Fail." *CQ Almanac 1991*. (Washington, D.C.: Congressional Quarterly, 1992): 180-83.

Elving, Ronald D. "Refusal to Adjust Undercount Spurs Protest." *Congressional Quarterly Weekly Report* 49 (July 20, 1991): 2006-9.

Freedman, David A. "Adjusting the 1990 Census." *Science* 252 (May 31, 1991): 1233-36.

Hamilton, David P. "Census Adjustment Battle Heats Up." *Science* 248 (March 18, 1990): 807-808.

Skerry, Peter. "The Census Wars." *Public Interest* No. 106 (Winter 1992): 17-31.

Chapter 11. Rules Affecting Metropolitan and Urbanized Areas

Beale, Calvin. "Poughkeepsie's Complaint: Or, Defining Metropolitan Areas." *American Demographics* 6 (January 1984): 29-31+.

Forstall, Richard L.; and Maria E. Gonzalez. "Twenty Questions: What You Should Know About the New Metropolitan Areas." *American Demographics* 6 (April 1984): 22-31+.

"OMB Issues New Metro Area Definitions." *The Census and You* 28 (February 1993): 8-12.

U.S. Bureau of the Census. *Metropolitan Areas and Cities*, 1990 Census Profile No. 3. (Washington, D.C.: U.S. Government Printing Office, 1991).

U.S. Office of Management and Budget, Statistical Policy Office. *Revised Statistical Definitions for Metropolitan Areas, June 30, 1993*, OMB Bulletin 93-17. (Washington, D.C.: National Technical Information Service, 1993).

U.S. Office of Management and Budget, Statistical Policy Office. *Revised Statistical Definitions for Metropolitan Areas, December, 28 1992*, OMB Bulletin 93-05. (Washington, D.C.: National Technical Information Service, 1993).

U.S. Office of the Federal Register. "Office of Management and Budget Revised Standards for Designating Metropolitan Areas in the 1990s; Notice." *Federal Register* 55 (March 30, 1990):12154-12160.

Chapter 12. Congressional Apportionment Explained

Balinski, Michael L. and H. Peyton Young. *Fair Representation: Meeting the Ideal of One Man, One Vote*. (New Haven: Yale University, 1982).

Huckabee, David C. *Apportioning Seats in the House of Representatives: The Method of Equal Proportions*. (Washington, D.C.: Congressional Research Service, U.S. Library of Congress, 1988.)

NCSL Reapportionment Task Force. *Reapportionment Law: The 1990s*. (Denver: National Conference of State Legislatures, 1989).

Thernstrom, Abigail. "Statistics and the Politics of Minority Representation: The Evolution of the Voting Rights Act Since 1965." In *The Politics of Numbers*, edited by William Alonso and Paul Starr. (New York: Russell Sage Foundation, 1987), pp. 303-328.

U.S. Bureau of the Census. *Population Trends and Congressional Apportionment*, 1990 Census Profile No. 1. (Washington, D.C.: U.S. Government Printing Office, 1991).

Chapter 13. Using EXTRACT

Marske, Bob and Paul Zeisset. *Using Census CD-ROMS on Your Microcomputer*, Census Monograph. (Washington, D.C.: U.S. Bureau of the Census, 1991).

U.S. Bureau of the Census. "EXTRACT Technical Documentation," Revised March, 1994. Computer file available on *1992 Economic Census CD-ROM*, Disc 1E. (Washington, D.C.: the Bureau, 1995).

U.S. Bureau of the Census. *Summary Tape File 1: Technical Documentation*. (Washington, D.C.: The Bureau, 1991).

U.S. Bureau of the Census. *Summary Tape File 3: Technical Documentation*. (Washington, D.C.: The Bureau, 1991).

Zeisset, Paul and Bob Marske. *Using EXTRACT with STF 1A (EXTutor 4)*. U.S. Bureau of the Census Monograph. (Washington, D.C.: U.S. Bureau of the Census, 1992).

Chapter 14. Internet Resources and Other Electronic Products

"Because You Asked... More Subject Detail in Summary Tape File 2." *The Census and You* 27 (January 1992): 3-5.

DIALOG Information Services. *Reference Guide to CENDATA on DIALOG.* (Palo Alto, CA: DIALOG, 1993).

Morton, Jackson. "Census on the Internet. *American Demographics* 17 (March 1995): 52-54.

Steinman, Jeff. "You Can Count on the Census Online." *The Internet Connection* 1 (April 1995): 5-6.

U.S. Bureau of the Census. *CENDATA: The Census Bureau Online.* (Washington, D.C.: the Bureau, 1994).

U.S. Bureau of the Census. *Summary Tape File (STF) 4: America's Diversity in Detail,* Product Profile No. 8. (Washington, D.C.: the Bureau, 1994).

Index